Honda CBR1000RR/RA Fireblade
Service and Repair Manual

by Matthew Coombs

Models covered
CBR1000RR Fireblade. 999cc. 2008-on
CBR1000RA Fireblade. 999cc. 2009-on

(5688-320)

© Haynes Publishing 2014

ABCDE
FGHIJ
KLMNO
PQRST

A book in the Haynes Service and Repair Manual Series

All rights reserved. No part of this book may be reproduced or transmitted in any form or by any means, electronic or mechanical, including photocopying, recording or by any information storage or retrieval system, without permission in writing from the copyright holder.

ISBN: 978 0 85733 688 0

Library of Congress Control Number 2013944856

Printed in the USA

Haynes Publishing
Sparkford, Yeovil, Somerset BA22 7JJ, England

Haynes North America, Inc
861 Lawrence Drive, Newbury Park, California 91320, USA

Haynes Publishing Nordiska AB
Box 1504, 751 45 Uppsala, Sweden

Contents

LIVING WITH YOUR HONDA FIREBLADE

Introduction

The Birth of a Dream	Page	0•4
Acknowledgements	Page	0•8
About this manual	Page	0•8
Identification numbers	Page	0•9
Buying spare parts	Page	0•9
Model development	Page	0•10
Bike spec	Page	0•11
Safety first!	Page	0•12

Pre-ride checks

Engine oil level	Page	0•13
Suspension, steering and drive chain	Page	0•13
Brake fluid levels	Page	0•14
Coolant level	Page	0•15
Tyres	Page	0•16
Legal and safety checks	Page	0•16

MAINTENANCE

Routine maintenance and servicing

Specifications	Page	1•2
Lubricants and fluids	Page	1•2
Maintenance schedule	Page	1•3
Component locations	Page	1•4
Maintenance procedures	Page	1•6

Contents

REPAIRS AND OVERHAUL

Engine, transmission and associated systems
Engine, clutch and transmission	Page	2•1
Cooling system	Page	3•1
Engine management system	Page	4•1

Chassis components
Frame and suspension	Page	5•1
Brakes, wheels and final drive	Page	6•1
Bodywork	Page	7•1

Electrical system
Page 8•1

Wiring diagrams
Page 8•30

REFERENCE

Security	Page	REF•2
Lubricants and fluids	Page	REF•5
MOT Test Checks	Page	REF•8
Storage	Page	REF•13
Tools and Workshop Tips	Page	REF•16
Conversion factors	Page	REF•34
Fault Finding	Page	REF•35

Index
Page REF•46

Introduction

The Birth of a Dream

by Julian Ryder

There is no better example of the Japanese post-War industrial miracle than Honda. Like other companies which have become household names, it started with one man's vision. In this case the man was the 40-year old Soichiro Honda who had sold his piston-ring manufacturing business to Toyota in 1945 and was happily spending the proceeds on prolonged parties for his friends. However, the difficulties of getting around in the chaos of post-War Japan irked Honda, so when he came across a job lot of generator engines he realised that here was a way of getting people mobile again at low cost.

A 12 by 18-foot shack in Hamamatsu became his first bike factory, fitting the generator motors into pushbikes. Before long he'd used up all 500 generator motors and started manufacturing his own engine, known as the 'chimney', either because of the elongated cylinder head or the smoky exhaust or perhaps both. The chimney made all of half a horsepower from its 50 cc engine but it was a major success and became the Honda A-type.

Less than two years after he'd set up in Hamamatsu, Soichiro Honda founded the Honda Motor Company in September 1948. By then, the A-type had been developed into the 90 cc B-type engine, which Mr Honda decided deserved its own chassis not a bicycle frame. Honda was about to become Japan's first post-War manufacturer of complete motorcycles. In August 1949 the first prototype was ready. With an output of three horsepower, the 98 cc D-type was still a simple two-stroke but it had a two-speed transmission and most importantly a pressed steel frame with telescopic forks and hard tail rear end. The frame was almost triangular in profile with the top rail going in a straight line from the massively braced steering head to the rear axle. Legend has it that after the D-type's first tests the entire workforce went for a drink to celebrate and try and think of a name for the bike. One man broke one of those silences you get when people are thinking, exclaiming 'This is like a dream!' 'That's it!' shouted Honda, and so the Honda Dream was christened.

Honda C70 and C90 OHV-engined models

'This is like a dream!' 'That's it' shouted Honda

Mr Honda was a brilliant, intuitive engineer and designer but he did not bother himself with the marketing side of his business. With hindsight, it is possible to see that employing Takeo Fujisawa who would both sort out the home market and plan the eventual expansion into overseas markets was a masterstroke. He arrived in October 1949 and in 1950 was made Sales Director. Another vital new name was Kiyoshi Kawashima, who along with Honda himself, designed the company's first four-stroke after Kawashima had told them that the four-stroke opposition to Honda's two-strokes sounded nicer and therefore sold better. The result of that statement was the overhead-valve 148 cc E-type which first ran in July 1951 just two months after the first drawings were made. Kawashima was made a director of the Honda Company at 34 years old.

The E-type was a massive success, over 32,000 were made in 1953 alone, a feat of mass-production that was astounding by the standards of the day given the relative complexity of the machine. But Honda's lifelong pursuit of technical innovation sometimes distracted him from commercial reality. Fujisawa pointed out that they were in danger of ignoring their core business, the motorised bicycles that still formed Japan's main means of transport. In May 1952 the F-type Cub appeared, another two-stroke despite the top men's reservations. You could buy a complete machine or just the motor to attach to your own bicycle. The result was certainly distinctive, a white fuel tank with a circular profile went just below and behind the saddle on the left of the bike, and the motor with its horizontal cylinder and bright red cover just below the rear axle on the same side of the bike. This was the machine that turned Honda into the biggest bike maker in Japan with 70% of the market for bolt-on bicycle motors, the F-type was also the first Honda to be exported. Next came the machine that would turn Honda into the biggest motorcycle manufacturer in the world.

The C100 Super Cub was a typically audacious piece of Honda engineering and marketing. For the first time, but not the last, Honda invented a completely new type of motorcycle, although the term 'scooterette' was coined to describe the new bike which had many of the characteristics of a scooter but the large wheels, and therefore stability, of a motorcycle. The first one was sold in August 1958, fifteen years later over nine-million of them were on the roads of the world. If ever a machine can be said to have brought mobility to the masses it is the Super Cub. If you add in the electric starter that was added for the C102 model of 1961, the design of the Super Cub has remained substantially unchanged ever since, testament to how right Honda got it first time. The Super Cub made Honda the world's biggest manufacturer after just two years of production.

The CB250N Super Dream became a favorite with UK learner riders of the late seventies and early eighties

Honda's export drive started in earnest in 1957 when Britain and Holland got their first bikes, America got just two bikes the next year. By 1962 Honda had half the American market with 65,000 sales. But Soichiro Honda had already travelled abroad to Europe and the USA, making a special

The GL1000 introduced in 1975, was the first in Honda's line of Goldwings

Introduction

Carl Fogarty in action at the Suzuka 8 hour on the RC45

An early CB750 Four

point of going to the Isle of Man TT, then the most important race in the GP calendar. He realised that no matter how advanced his products were, only racing success would convince overseas markets for whom 'Made in Japan' still meant cheap and nasty. It took five years from Soichiro Honda's first visit to the Island before his bikes were ready for the TT. In 1959 the factory entered five riders in the 125. They did not have a massive impact on the event being benevolently regarded as a curiosity, but sixth, seventh and eighth were good enough for the team prize. The bikes were off the pace but they were well engineered and very reliable.

The TT was the only time the West saw the Hondas in '59, but they came back for more the following year with the first of a generation of bikes which shaped the future of motorcycling - the double-overhead-cam four-cylinder 250. It was fast and reliable - it revved to 14,000 rpm - but didn't handle anywhere near as well as the opposition. However, Honda had now signed up non-Japanese riders to lead their challenge. The first win didn't come until 1962 (Aussie Tom Phillis in the Spanish 125 GP) and was followed up with a world-shaking performance at the TT. Twenty-one year old Mike Hailwood won both 125 and 250 cc TTs and Hondas filled the top five positions in both races. Soichiro Honda's master plan was starting to come to fruition, Hailwood and Honda won the 1961 250 cc World Championship. Next year Honda won three titles. The other Japanese factories fought back and inspired Honda to produce some of the most fascinating racers ever seen: the awesome six-cylinder 250, the five-cylinder 125, and the 500 four with which the immortal Hailwood battled Agostini and the MV Agusta.

When Honda pulled out of racing in '67 they had won sixteen rider's titles, eighteen manufacturer's titles, and 137 GPs, including 18 TTs, and introduced the concept of the modern works team to motorcycle racing. Sales success followed racing victory as Soichiro Honda had predicted, but only because the products advanced as rapidly as the racing machinery. The Hondas that came to Britain in the early '60s were incredibly sophisticated. They had overhead cams where the British bikes had pushrods, they had electric starters when the Brits relied on the kickstart, they had 12V electrics when even the biggest British bike used a 6V system. There seemed no end to the technical wizardry. It wasn't that the technology itself was so amazing but just like that first E-Type, it was the fact that Honda could mass-produce it more reliably than the lower-tech competition that was so astonishing.

When in 1968 the first four-cylinder CB750 road bike arrived the world of motorcycling changed for ever, they even had to invent a new word for it, 'Superbike'. Honda raced again with the CB750 at Daytona and won the

World Endurance title with a prototype DOHC version that became the CB900 roadster. There was the six-cylinder CBX, the CX500T – the world's first turbocharged production bike, they invented the full-dress tourer with the GoldWing, and came back to GPs with the revolutionary oval-pistoned NR500 four-stroke, a much-misunderstood bike that was more a rolling experimental laboratory than a racer. Just to show their versatility Honda also came up with the weird CX500 shaft-drive V-twin, a rugged workhorse that powered a new industry, the courier companies that oiled the wheels of commerce in London and other big cities.

It was true, though, that Mr Honda was not keen on two-strokes – early motocross engines had to be explained away to him as lawnmower motors! However, in 1982 Honda raced the NS500, an agile three-cylinder lightweight against the big four-cylinder opposition in 500 GPs. The bike won in its first year and in '83 took the world title for Freddie Spencer. In four-stroke racing the V4 layout took over from the straight four, dominating TT, F1 and Endurance championships with the RVF750, the nearest thing ever built to a Formula 1 car on wheels. And when Superbike arrived Honda were ready with the RC30. On the roads the VFR V4 became an instant classic while the CBR600 invented another new class of bike on its way to becoming a best-seller. The V4 road bikes had problems to start with but the VFR750 sold world-wide over its lifetime while the VFR400 became a massive commercial success and cult bike in Japan. The original RC30 won the first two World Superbike Championships is 1988 and '89, but Honda had to wait until 1997 to win it again with the RC45, the last of the V4 roadsters. In Grands Prix, the NSR500 V4 two-stroke superseded the NS triple and became the benchmark racing machine of the '90s. Mick Doohan secured his place in history by winning five World Championships in consecutive years on it.

In yet another example of Honda inventing a new class of motorcycle, they came up with the astounding CBR900RR FireBlade, a bike with the punch of a 1000 cc motor in a package the size and weight of a 750. It became a cult bike as well as a best seller, and with judicious redesigns continues to give much more recent designs a run for their money.

When it became apparent that the high-tech V4 motor of the RC45 was too expensive to produce, Honda looked to a V-twin engine to power its flagship for the first time. Typically, the VTR1000 FireStorm was a much more rideable machine than its opposition and once accepted by the market formed the basis of the next generation of Superbike racer, the VTR-SP-1.

One of Mr Honda's mottos was that technology would solve the customers' problems, and no company has embraced

The CX500 – Honda's first V-Twin and a favorite choice of dispatch riders

cutting-edge technology more firmly than Honda. In fact Honda often developed new technology, especially in the fields of materials science and metallurgy. The embodiment of that was the NR750, a bike that was misunderstood nearly as much as the original NR500 racer. This limited-edition technological tour-de-force embodied many of Soichiro Honda's ideals. It used the latest techniques and materials in every component, from the oval piston, 32-valve V4 motor to the titanium coating on the windscreen, it was – as Mr Honda would have wanted – the best it could possibly be. A fitting memorial to the man who has shaped the motorcycle industry and motorcyles as we know them today.

Keep on rocking

On the face of it, the new-generation Fireblade first seen in 2008 was a little confusing. It wasn't so much what it had – the usual engine upgrade and styling overhaul – but what it didn't have. The new Blade didn't have the usual slew of electronic

The 2009 CBR1000RR

Introduction

The 2013 CBR1000RA (with C-ABS)

refinements such as variable ignition maps or track-day ready lap timers, it just got on with being a very good super sports bike. That, of course, is what it's always been. Rarely the fastest or most powerful in the flagship class, the Blade has regularly been the top-seller by a distance, the one that holds its value, and the one that comes out on top in the customer-satisfaction surveys.

In short, the Fireblade is just as at home on a track day as it is on the roads. Not something you can say about every 1000cc sports bike. In many ways it has been allowed that flexibility because it has not been a homologation model for a full attack on the World and other Superbike championships. For that you go back to the previous generation of 'Blades, the one that arrived in 2004 with a full complement of MotoGP-inspired design and technology. That was the first Blade that used a full 1000cc capacity and put it in a frame with a Grand Prix style long swinging arm. Then there was the cassette gearbox, obligatory for racing, two-stage fuel-injection and the 'straight-from-Valentino-bike' under-seat exhausts and electronic variable steering damper. With this bike, Honda went trophy hunting in the British and World Superbike Championships with what looked like factory efforts although may have had more to do with testing for the Suzuka 8 Hours.

Given that the 'Blade has been around since 1992, most people are surprised that the bike has only won one World Superbike title. That was in 2007 when James Toseland won for the Dutch Ten Kate team. Ryuichi Kiyonari won the British Championship on a CBR1000RR in both 2006 and '07. Of course, the 'Blade didn't need to be a race winner. At the start of the World Superbike Championship back in 1988 Honda had the RC30 and then the RC45 before the SP-1 and SP-2 took over. While Honda in Japan haven't always been too supportive of Superbike racing, the same cannot be said of Honda Europe and the World Endurance Championship plus the Isle of Man TT and other road races.

In 2010 the Honda TT Legends team was set up to combine both disciplines, for the reason that good TT racers tend to be handy endurance racers as well. The team was the first to use the major innovation of the 2009 model Fireblade, the Combined ABS. Even though Honda said it is not intended for 'the extreme conditions of high-speed track riding', the Legends used it in 24-hour racing. And of course the Fireblade continued to carry the great John McGuinness to the latest of his twenty (and counting) Isle of Man victories.

To win at long-distance or real-roads racing, a motorbike doesn't necessarily have to carry a full-complement of the latest MotoGP technology, in fact it helps if things are kept slightly simpler. And tougher. And the team have to know what they're doing when preparing for the demands placed on the bike and its various subsystems. Components have to last, be easy to replace, and able to survive a lengthy battering on public roads. Not so different from a street bike then.

Interestingly, Honda do intend to keep winning with the 'Blade because rather than spending money on a complete revamp of the bike they brought out an SP version for the 2014 model year as sort of a halfway house between a homologation special and the stock bike. This is a new tactic for Honda and suits the economic realities in the market sector. What's more it means that the standard 'Blade, if any 'double-R" model should ever be called that, will continue to be the usable weapon it's always been.

Acknowledgements

Our thanks are due to Bransons Motorcycles of Yeovil who supplied the machines featured in the illustrations throughout this manual. We would also like to thank NGK Spark Plugs (UK) Ltd for supplying the colour spark plug condition photographs, the Avon Rubber Company for supplying information on tyre fitting and Draper Tools Ltd for some of the workshop tools shown.

Thanks are also due to Julian Ryder who wrote the introduction 'The Birth of a Dream' and to Honda (UK) Ltd. who supplied model photographs.

About this Manual

The aim of this manual is to help you get the best value from your motorcycle. It can do so in several ways. It can help you decide what work must be done, even if you choose to have it done by a dealer; it provides information and procedures for routine maintenance and servicing; and it offers diagnostic and repair procedures to follow when trouble occurs.

We hope you use the manual to tackle the work yourself. For many simpler jobs, doing it yourself may be quicker than arranging an appointment to get the motorcycle into a dealer and making the trips to leave it and pick it up. More importantly, a lot of money can be saved by avoiding the expense the shop must pass on to you to cover its labour and overhead costs. An added benefit is the sense of satisfaction and accomplishment that you feel after doing the job yourself.

References to the left or right side of the motorcycle assume you are sitting on the seat, facing forward.

We take great pride in the accuracy of information given in this manual, but motorcycle manufacturers make alterations and design changes during the production run of a particular motorcycle of which they do not inform us. No liability can be accepted by the authors or publishers for loss, damage or injury caused by any errors in, or omissions from, the information given.

Illegal copying

It is the policy of Haynes Publishing to actively protect its Copyrights and Trade Marks. Legal action will be taken against anyone who unlawfully copies the cover or contents of this Manual. This includes all forms of unauthorised copying including digital, mechanical, and electronic in any form. Authorisation from Haynes Publishing will only be provided expressly and in writing. Illegal copying will also be reported to the appropriate statutory authorities.

Identification numbers 0•9

Frame and engine numbers

The frame serial number is stamped into the right-hand side of the steering head. The engine number is stamped into the upper crankcase half at the front of the engine. Both of these numbers should be recorded and kept in a safe place so they can be given to law enforcement officials in the event of a theft. There is also a colour code label on the top of the rear mudguard, visible after removing the passenger seat, and a VIN plate on the left-hand side of the steering head. The throttle bodies also have an ID number stamped into them.

The frame serial number, engine serial number, and colour code should also be kept in a handy place (such as with your driver's licence) so they are always available when purchasing or ordering parts for your machine.

The procedures in this manual identify models by their code letters and number (e.g. RR-8 for a 2008 model, or RA-B for a 2011 model with C-ABS). The model code or production year is printed on the colour code label.

Model	Year
CBR1000RR-8	2008
CBR1000RR-9/RA-9	2009
CBR1000RR-A/RA-A	2010
CBR1000RR-B/RA-B	2011
CBR1000RR-C/RA-C	2012
CBR1000RR-D/RA-D	2013

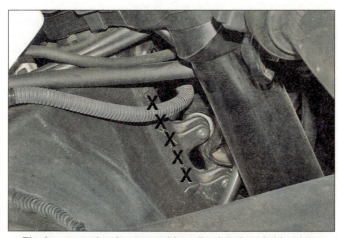

The frame number is stamped into the right-hand side of the steering head

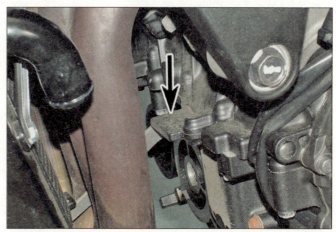

The engine number (arrowed) is on the front of the crankcase

On UK models the VIN plate (arrowed) is riveted to the left-hand side of the steering head

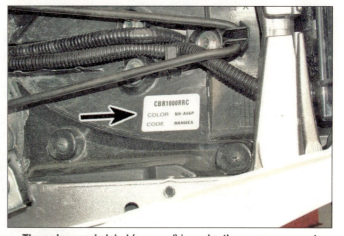

The colour code label (arrowed) is under the passenger seat

Buying spare parts

Once you have found all the identification numbers, record them for reference when buying parts. Since the manufacturers change specifications, parts and vendors (companies that manufacture various components on the machine), providing the ID numbers is the only way to be reasonably sure that you are buying the correct parts.

Whenever possible, take the old part to the dealer so direct comparison with the new component can be made. Along the trail from the manufacturer to the parts shelf, there are numerous places that the part can end up with the wrong number or be listed incorrectly.

The two places to purchase new parts for your motorcycle – the franchised or main dealer and the parts/accessories store – differ in the type of parts they carry. While dealers can obtain every single genuine part for your motorcycle, the accessory store is usually limited to normal high wear items such as chains and sprockets, brake pads, spark plugs and cables, and to tune-up parts and various engine gaskets, etc. Rarely will an accessory outlet have major suspension components, camshafts, transmission gears, or engine cases.

Used parts can be obtained from breakers yards for roughly half the price of new ones, but you can't always be sure of what you're getting. Once again, take your worn part to the breaker for direct comparison, or when ordering by mail order make sure that you can return it if you are not happy.

Whether buying new, used or rebuilt parts, the best course is to deal directly with someone who specialises in your particular make.

Model development

CBR1000RR-8 2008 model

The new CBR1000RR retains the in-line four cylinder liquid-cooled engine configuration of the previous generation model, though the engine itself is new. To achieve design goals the cylinder head was made lighter and more compact with shorter valves, intake valves were made from titanium, and lighter camshafts were fitted. The new separate cylinder block has sleeveless plated bores and lighter pistons to reduce weight, and the cylinder bore is larger and the stroke shorter. Drive to the double overhead camshafts that actuate the four valves per cylinder is by chain from the right-hand end of the crankshaft. The clutch is a wet multi-plate unit with a new slipper mechanism, and is cable operated. The gearbox is 6-speed, though the cassette-type mounting of the previous model is no longer featured. Drive to the rear wheel is by chain and sprockets.

Honda's PGM-DSFI fuel injection system supplies fuel and air to the engine via two injectors per cylinder and 46 mm throttle bodies. Air is drawn in via two air ducts in the fairing. The primary injectors are mounted in the throttle bodies below the throttle valve and operate all the time the engine is running. The secondary injectors mounted in the top of the air filter housing, operate only at high engine speeds and wide throttle openings, and spray fuel into the air entering the throttle bodies above the throttle valves. An electronic engine management system controls both the injection system and the ignition system. The new under-slung exhaust system incorporates Honda's exhaust gas control valve (EGCV).

The engine sits in a new 4-piece die-cast aluminium frame that uses the engine as a stressed member. Front suspension is by fully adjustable oil-damped 43 mm forks with cartridge dampers, which are basically the same units fitted to the previous model. Rear suspension is Honda's Pro-link with a fully adjustable single shock absorber via a three-way rising rate linkage, and mimics the floating design used for the RC211V Moto GP bike by incorporating the upper shock absorber mount in the swingarm as opposed to it being bolted to the frame. The new 'gull-wing' shape swingarm is longer and pivots through the frame.

A new second-generation electronically controlled hydraulic rotary steering damper that is lighter and more compact replaces the unit fitted to the previous model. The damper provides high-speed stability without the loss of low speed balance and control by having a system that provides progressive damping in accordance with information received on vehicle speed and acceleration by the system's control unit, which is integrated with ECM.

The front brake system has two twin-opposed piston radially-mounted monoblock calipers acting on floating discs. The new calipers and discs and the new wheels are all lighter than those on the previous model to reduce unsprung weight. The rear brake system has a single piston sliding caliper acting on a conventional disc.

CBR1000RR-9 and RA-9 2009 models

The RR model remains largely unchanged for 2009.

The RA model was introduced for the 2009 model year. It is basically an RR model with an electronically controlled combined anti-lock braking system, or C-ABS. The C-ABS system provides all the benefits of anti-lock and combined brakes that have been featured on many of Honda's bikes but deliver them in a package designed specifically for a lightweight Supersports bike.

New oval rear turn signals were fitted to all models.

CBR1000RR-A and RA-A 2010 models

A new tail unit holding the licence plate and rear turn signals was fitted, that enables quick and easy removal for track-day riding, and a clear tail light lens was fitted.

CBR1000RR-B and RA-B 2011 models

There were no changes from the RR-A or RA-A (2010) models.

CBR1000RR-C and RA-C 2012 models

There were major changes to the suspension, with new Showa 'big piston' front forks and a new Showa double-tube rear shock absorber. Also new were 12-spoke wheels, a fully LCD instrument unit, and a reshaped fairing. The fuel injection system was remapped to smooth out throttle response, particularly at low openings.

CBR1000RR-D and RA-D 2013 models

There were no changes from the RR-C or RA-C (2012) models.

Bike spec

Dimensions and weights – 2008 to 2011 models
Overall length	2080 mm
Overall width	685 mm
Overall height	1130 mm
Wheelbase	1410 mm
Seat height	820 mm
Ground clearance	130 mm
Weight (wet)	
RR models	199 kg
RA models	210 kg
Maximum weight capacity	
UK and Europe models	180 kg
US models	166 kg

Dimensions and weights – 2012-on models
Overall length	2075 mm
Overall width	685 mm
Overall height	1135 mm
Wheelbase	1410 mm
Seat height	820 mm
Ground clearance	130 mm
Weight (wet)	
RR models	200 kg
RA models	211 kg
Maximum weight capacity	
UK and Europe models	180 kg
US models	166 kg

Engine
Type	Four-stroke in-line four
Capacity	999 cc
Bore	76.0 mm
Stroke	55.1 mm
Compression ratio	12.3 to 1
Cooling system	Liquid cooled
Clutch	Wet multi-plate, cable actuation
Transmission	Six-speed constant mesh
Final drive	Chain and sprockets
Camshafts	DOHC, chain-driven
Fuel system	PGM-DSFI fuel injection, 46 mm throttle bodies
Exhaust system	Four-into-one
Ignition system	Computer-controlled digital transistorised with electronic advance

Chassis
Frame type	Die-cast aluminium, diamond pattern
Rake and Trail	23°18 , 96.3 mm
Fuel tank	
Capacity (including reserve)	17.7 litres
Reserve volume (fuel light on)	approx. 3.5 litres
Front suspension	
Type	43 mm oil-damped cartridge-type upside down telescopic forks
Travel	110 mm
Adjustment	Spring pre-load, rebound and compression damping
Rear suspension	
Type	Single floating shock absorber, rising rate linkage, gull-wing design aluminium swingarm
Travel (at axle)	138 mm
Adjustment	Spring pre-load, rebound and compression damping
Wheels	
2008 to 2011 models	17 inch 3-spoke alloys
2012-on models	17 inch 12-spoke alloys
Tyres	
Front	120/70-ZR17 (58W) Radial
Rear	190/50-ZR17 (73W) Radial
Front brake	Twin 320 mm floating discs with four piston calipers
Rear brake	Single 220 mm disc with single piston sliding caliper

Safety First!

Professional mechanics are trained in safe working procedures. However enthusiastic you may be about getting on with the job at hand, take the time to ensure that your safety is not put at risk. A moment's lack of attention can result in an accident, as can failure to observe simple precautions.

There will always be new ways of having accidents, and the following is not a comprehensive list of all dangers; it is intended rather to make you aware of the risks and to encourage a safe approach to all work you carry out on your bike.

Asbestos

● Certain friction, insulating, sealing and other products - such as brake pads, clutch linings, gaskets, etc. - contain asbestos. Extreme care must be taken to avoid inhalation of dust from such products since it is hazardous to health. If in doubt, assume that they do contain asbestos.

Fire

● Remember at all times that petrol is highly flammable. Never smoke or have any kind of naked flame around, when working on the vehicle. But the risk does not end there - a spark caused by an electrical short-circuit, by two metal surfaces contacting each other, by careless use of tools, or even by static electricity built up in your body under certain conditions, can ignite petrol vapour, which in a confined space is highly explosive. Never use petrol as a cleaning solvent. Use an approved safety solvent.

● Always disconnect the battery earth terminal before working on any part of the fuel or electrical system, and never risk spilling fuel on to a hot engine or exhaust.
● It is recommended that a fire extinguisher of a type suitable for fuel and electrical fires is kept handy in the garage or workplace at all times. Never try to extinguish a fuel or electrical fire with water.

Fumes

● Certain fumes are highly toxic and can quickly cause unconsciousness and even death if inhaled to any extent. Petrol vapour comes into this category, as do the vapours from certain solvents such as trichloro-ethylene. Any draining or pouring of such volatile fluids should be done in a well ventilated area.
● When using cleaning fluids and solvents, read the instructions carefully. Never use materials from unmarked containers - they may give off poisonous vapours.
● Never run the engine of a motor vehicle in an enclosed space such as a garage. Exhaust fumes contain carbon monoxide which is extremely poisonous; if you need to run the engine, always do so in the open air or at least have the rear of the vehicle outside the workplace.

The battery

● Never cause a spark, or allow a naked light near the vehicle's battery. It will normally be giving off a certain amount of hydrogen gas, which is highly explosive.

● Always disconnect the battery ground (earth) terminal before working on the fuel or electrical systems (except where noted).
● If possible, loosen the filler plugs or cover when charging the battery from an external source. Do not charge at an excessive rate or the battery may burst.
● Take care when topping up, cleaning or carrying the battery. The acid electrolyte, evenwhen diluted, is very corrosive and should not be allowed to contact the eyes or skin. Always wear rubber gloves and goggles or a face shield. If you ever need to prepare electrolyte yourself, always add the acid slowly to the water; never add the water to the acid.

Electricity

● When using an electric power tool, inspection light etc., always ensure that the appliance is correctly connected to its plug and that, where necessary, it is properly grounded (earthed). Do not use such appliances in damp conditions and, again, beware of creating a spark or applying excessive heat in the vicinity of fuel or fuel vapour. Also ensure that the appliances meet national safety standards.
● A severe electric shock can result from touching certain parts of the electrical system, such as the spark plug wires (HT leads), when the engine is running or being cranked, particularly if components are damp or the insulation is defective. Where an electronic ignition system is used, the secondary (HT) voltage is much higher and could prove fatal.

Remember...

✘ **Don't** start the engine without first ascertaining that the transmission is in neutral.
✘ **Don't** suddenly remove the pressure cap from a hot cooling system - cover it with a cloth and release the pressure gradually first, or you may get scalded by escaping coolant.
✘ **Don't** attempt to drain oil until you are sure it has cooled sufficiently to avoid scalding you.
✘ **Don't** grasp any part of the engine or exhaust system without first ascertaining that it is cool enough not to burn you.
✘ **Don't** allow brake fluid or antifreeze to contact the machine's paintwork or plastic components.
✘ **Don't** siphon toxic liquids such as fuel, hydraulic fluid or antifreeze by mouth, or allow them to remain on your skin.
✘ **Don't** inhale dust - it may be injurious to health (see Asbestos heading).
✘ **Don't** allow any spilled oil or grease to remain on the floor - wipe it up right away, before someone slips on it.
✘ **Don't** use ill-fitting spanners or other tools which may slip and cause injury.
✘ **Don't** lift a heavy component which may be beyond your capability - get assistance.

✘ **Don't** rush to finish a job or take unverified short cuts.
✘ **Don't** allow children or animals in or around an unattended vehicle.
✘ **Don't** inflate a tyre above the recommended pressure. Apart from overstressing the carcass, in extreme cases the tyre may blow off forcibly.
✔ **Do** ensure that the machine is supported securely at all times. This is especially important when the machine is blocked up to aid wheel or fork removal.
✔ **Do** take care when attempting to loosen a stubborn nut or bolt. It is generally better to pull on a spanner, rather than push, so that if you slip, you fall away from the machine rather than onto it.
✔ **Do** wear eye protection when using power tools such as drill, sander, bench grinder etc.
✔ **Do** use a barrier cream on your hands prior to undertaking dirty jobs - it will protect your skin from infection as well as making the dirt easier to remove afterwards; but make sure your hands aren't left slippery. Note that long-term contact with used engine oil can be a health hazard.
✔ **Do** keep loose clothing (cuffs, ties etc. and long hair) well out of the way of moving mechanical parts.

✔ **Do** remove rings, wristwatch etc., before working on the vehicle - especially the electrical system.
✔ **Do** keep your work area tidy - it is only too easy to fall over articles left lying around.
✔ **Do** exercise caution when compressing springs for removal or installation. Ensure that the tension is applied and released in a controlled manner, using suitable tools which preclude the possibility of the spring escaping violently.
✔ **Do** ensure that any lifting tackle used has a safe working load rating adequate for the job.
✔ **Do** get someone to check periodically that all is well, when working alone on the vehicle.
✔ **Do** carry out work in a logical sequence and check that everything is correctly assembled and tightened afterwards.
✔ **Do** remember that your vehicle's safety affects that of yourself and others. If in doubt on any point, get professional advice.
● If in spite of following these precautions, you are unfortunate enough to injure yourself, seek medical attention as soon as possible.

Pre-ride checks

Note: *The Pre-ride checks outlined in the owner's manual covers those items which should be inspected on a daily basis.*

Engine oil level

Before you start:
✔ Make sure the motorcycle is on level ground.
✔ Start the engine and let it idle for 3 to 5 minutes.
Caution: Do not run the engine in an enclosed space such as a garage or workshop.
✔ Stop the engine and allow the oil level to stabilise for 2 to 3 minutes. Support the motorcycle upright using an auxiliary stand or by having an assistant hold it.

Bike care:
● If you have to add oil frequently, check whether you have any oil leaks from the engine joints, oil seals and gaskets. If not, the engine could be burning oil, in which case there will be white smoke coming out of the exhaust (see *Fault Finding*).

The correct oil:
● Modern, high-revving engines place great demands on their oil. It is very important that the correct oil for your bike is used. Do not use oil designed for use in car engines.
● Always top up with a good quality oil of the specified type and viscosity and do not overfill the engine.
Caution: Do not use chemical additives or oils labelled "ENERGY CONSERVING". Such additives or oils could cause clutch slip.

Oil type	API grade: SG or higher motorcycle oil JASO T 903 grade: MA
Oil viscosity	SAE 10W/30 (or 10W/40)

1 The oil level dipstick (A) and the oil filler cap (B) are in the clutch cover on the right-hand side of the engine.

2 Unscrew the dipstick and wipe the oil off with a clean cloth.

3 Insert the dipstick and seat it on the first thread – do not screw it in.

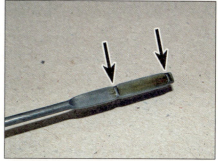

4 Remove the dipstick and check the oil on it, which should be between the upper and lower level lines (arrowed).

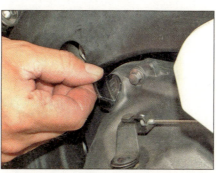

5 If the level is near, on or below the lower line, unscrew the filler cap.

6 Top up the engine with the recommended grade and type of oil to bring the level almost up to the upper line on the dipstick. Do not overfill. Make sure the dipstick and filler cap O-rings are in good condition and correctly seated before refitting them.

Suspension, steering and drive chain

Suspension and Steering:
● Check that the front and rear suspension operates smoothly without binding (see Chapter 1).
● Check that the suspension is adjusted as required (see Chapter 5).
● Check that the steering moves smoothly from lock-to-lock (take into account the effect of the steering damper).

Drive chain:
● Check that the chain isn't too loose or too tight, and adjust it if necessary (see Chapter 1).
● If the chain looks dry, lubricate it (see Chapter 1).

Pre-ride checks

Brake fluid levels

Warning: *Brake hydraulic fluid can harm your eyes and damage painted surfaces, so use extreme caution when handling and pouring it and cover surrounding surfaces with rag. Do not use fluid that has been standing open for some time, as it is hygroscopic (absorbs moisture from the air) which can cause a dangerous loss of braking effectiveness.*

Before you start:
✔ The front brake fluid reservoir is on the right-hand handlebar. The rear brake fluid reservoir is on the right-hand side.
✔ Make sure you have the correct hydraulic fluid. DOT 4 is recommended.
✔ Wrap a rag around the reservoir being worked on to ensure that any spillage does not come into contact with painted surfaces.
✔ When checking the fluid in the front reservoir turn the handlebars so the reservoir is level.
✔ When checking the fluid in the rear reservoir support the motorcycle upright.

Bike care:
● The fluid in the front and rear brake master cylinder reservoirs will drop as the brake pads wear down. If the fluid level is low check the brake pads for wear (see Chapter 1), and replace them with new ones if necessary (see Chapter 6).
● If either fluid reservoir requires repeated topping-up there is a leak somewhere in the system. Check for signs of fluid leakage from the hydraulic hoses and/or brake system components – if found, rectify immediately (see Chapter 6).
● Check the operation of both brakes before taking the machine on the road; if there is evidence of air in the system (spongy feel to lever or pedal), it must be bled (see Chapter 6).

FRONT

1 The front brake fluid level is visible through the window in the reservoir body – it must be between the UPPER and LOWER level lines (arrowed).

2 If the level is on or below the LOWER line, undo the cap clamp screw, then unscrew the cap and remove the diaphragm plate and diaphragm.

3 Top up with new clean DOT 4 hydraulic fluid, until the level is up to the UPPER line on the reservoir. Do not overfill and take care to avoid spills (see **Warning** above).

4 Wipe any moisture off the diaphragm with a tissue.

5 Ensure that the diaphragm is correctly seated before fitting the plate and cap. Secure the cap with the clamp.

Pre-ride checks 0•15

REAR

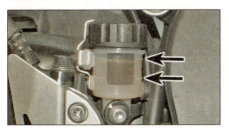

1 The rear brake fluid level is visible through the reservoir body – it must be between the UPPER and LOWER level lines (arrowed).

2 If the level is on or below the LOWER line on RR models, undo the cap clamp screw, then unscrew the cap and remove the diaphragm plate and diaphragm.

3 If the level is on or below the LOWER line on RA models, undo the reservoir screw (arrowed), displace the reservoir, unscrew the cap and remove the diaphragm plate and diaphragm.

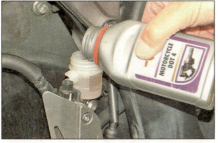

4 Top up with new clean DOT 4 hydraulic fluid, until the level is up to the UPPER line on the reservoir. Do not overfill and avoid spills (see **Warning** on page 0•14).

5 Wipe any moisture off the diaphragm with a tissue.

6 Ensure that the diaphragm is correctly seated before fitting the plate and cap. On RR models secure the cap with the clamp, and on RA models secure the reservoir with its screw.

Coolant level

> ⚠ **Warning: DO NOT remove the radiator pressure cap to add coolant. Topping up is done via the coolant reservoir tank filler. DO NOT leave open containers of coolant about, as it is poisonous.**

Before you start:

✔ The coolant reservoir is located behind the engine and in front of the shock absorber.

✔ Make sure you have a supply of coolant available. Either a bottle of pre-mixed coolant or a prepared mixture of 50% distilled water and 50% silicate-free corrosion inhibited ethylene glycol anti-freeze is neede).

✔ Check the coolant level when the engine is at normal working temperature.

Caution: Do not run the engine in an enclosed space such as a garage or workshop.

✔ Make sure the motorcycle is on level ground. Support it upright using an auxiliary stand or by having an assistant hold it.

Bike care:

● Use only the specified coolant mixture. It is important that anti-freeze is used in the system all year round, and not just in the winter. Do not top the system up using only water, as the system will become too diluted.
● Do not overfill the reservoir tank. If the coolant is significantly above the UPPER level line at any time, the surplus should be siphoned or drained off to prevent the possibility of it being expelled out of the overflow hose.
● If the coolant level falls steadily, check the system for leaks (see Chapter 1). If no leaks are found and the level continues to fall, it is recommended that the machine is taken to a Honda dealer for a pressure test.

1 With the motorcycle vertical, the coolant level should lie between the UPPER and LOWER level lines (arrowed) on the reservoir.

2 If the coolant level is on or below the LOWER line, remove the reservoir filler cap.

3 Top the reservoir up with the recommended coolant mixture to the UPPER level line, using a suitable funnel or piece of hose (as shown) if required. Fit the cap.

Pre-ride checks

Tyres

The correct pressures:
- The tyres must be checked when **cold**, not immediately after riding. The pressure inside the tyre will increase when the tyre is hot. Note that tyre pressure will also change from one day to the next as air temperature changes.
- Use an accurate pressure gauge. Many forecourt gauges are wildly inaccurate. If you buy your own, spend as much as you can justify on a quality gauge.
- Proper air pressure will increase tyre life and provide maximum stability and ride comfort. Incorrect tyre pressures will cause abnormal tread wear and unsafe handling. Low tyre pressures may cause the tyre to slip on the rim or come off.

Front	Rear
36 psi (2.5 Bar)	42 psi (2.9 Bar)

Tyre care:
- Check the tyres carefully for cuts, tears, embedded nails or other sharp objects and excessive wear. Operation of the motorcycle with excessively worn tyres is extremely hazardous, as traction and handling are directly affected.
- Check the condition of the tyre valve and ensure the dust cap is in place.
- Pick out any stones or nails which may have become embedded in the tyre tread. If left, they will eventually penetrate through the casing and cause a puncture.
- If tyre damage is apparent, or unexplained loss of pressure is experienced, seek the advice of a tyre fitting specialist without delay.

Tyre tread depth:
- At the time of writing UK law requires that tread depth must be at least 1 mm over 3/4 of the tread breadth all the way around the tyre, with no bald patches. Many riders, however, consider 2 mm tread depth minimum to be a safer limit. Honda recommend a minimum of 1.5 mm on the front and 2 mm on the rear, but note that German law requires a minimum of 1.6 mm for each tyre.
- Many tyres now incorporate wear indicators in the tread. Identify the location marking on the tyre sidewall to locate the indicator bar and replace the tyre if the tread has worn down to the bar.

1 Remove the dust cap (arrowed) from the valve and do not forget to fit the cap after checking the pressure.

2 Check the tyre pressures when the tyres are **cold**.

3 Measure tread depth at the centre of the tyre using a depth gauge.

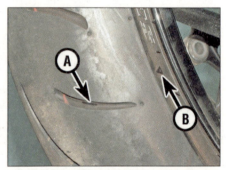

4 Tyre tread wear indicator (A) and its location marking (B) on the edge or sidewall (according to manufacturer).

Legal and safety checks

Lighting and signalling:
- Take a minute to check that the headlight, tail light, brake light, instrument lights and turn signals all work correctly.
- Check that the horn sounds when the button is pressed.
- A working speedometer, graduated in mph, is a statutory requirement in the UK.

Safety:
- Check that the throttle grip rotates smoothly when opened and snaps shut when released, in all steering positions. Also check for the correct amount of freeplay (see Chapter 1).
- Check that the brake lever and pedal, clutch lever and gearchange lever operate smoothly. Lubricate them at the specified intervals or when necessary (see Chapter 1).
- Check that the engine shuts off when the kill switch is operated. Check the starter interlock circuit (see Chapter 1).
- Check that sidestand return springs hold the stand up securely when retracted.

Fuel:
- This may seem obvious, but check that you have enough fuel to complete your journey. If you notice signs of fuel leakage – rectify the cause immediately.
- Ensure you use the correct grade fuel – see Chapter 4 Specifications.

Chapter 1
Routine maintenance and servicing

Contents

	Section number		Section number
Air filter	16	Idle air control valve	see Chapter 4
Battery	21	Headlight aim	9
Brake fluid level check	see *Pre-ride checks*	Nuts and bolts	15
Brake system	2	PAIR system check	8
Clutch	3	Pivot points and cable lubrication	14
Coolant level check	see *Pre-ride checks*	Spark plugs	19
Cooling system check and coolant change	7	Sidestand and starter interlock circuit	10
Drive chain and sprockets	1	Steering head bearings	12
Engine oil and filter change	6	Suspension	11
Engine oil level check	see *Pre-ride checks*	Throttle cables	5
Engine wear assessment	see Chapter 2	Tyre pressure check	see *Pre-ride checks*
EVAP system check (US models)	17	Valve clearances	18
Exhaust gas control valve (EGCV)	20	Wheels, wheel bearings and tyres	13
Fuel system	4		

Degrees of difficulty

| **Easy,** suitable for novice with little experience | **Fairly easy,** suitable for beginner with some experience | **Fairly difficult,** suitable for competent DIY mechanic | **Difficult,** suitable for experienced DIY mechanic | **Very difficult,** suitable for expert DIY or professional |

Servicing specifications

Engine

Cylinder numbering	1 to 4 from left to right
Spark plug type	
NGK	IMR9E-9HES
Denso	VUH27ES
Spark plug electrode gap	0.8 to 0.9 mm
Engine idle speed	1200 ± 100 rpm
Valve clearances (COLD engine)	
Intake valves	0.13 to 0.19 mm
Exhaust valves	0.27 to 0.33 mm

Miscellaneous

Drive chain slack	25 to 35 mm
Throttle cable freeplay	2 to 5 mm at twistgrip flange
Clutch cable freeplay	10 to 20 mm at lever end
Tyre pressures (cold)	see *Pre-ride checks*
Steering head bearing pre-load range (damper detached)	12 to 17 N

Lubricants and fluids

Engine oil	SAE 10W/30 or 10W/40 motorcycle oil. API grade: SG or higher; JASO T 903 grade: MA
Engine oil capacity	
Oil change	2.8 litres
Oil and filter change	3.0 litres
Following engine overhaul – dry engine, new filter	3.7 litres
Coolant type	Pre-mixed coolant, or 50% distilled water, 50% silicate-free corrosion inhibited ethylene glycol anti-freeze
Coolant capacity	
Radiator and engine	3.00 litres
Reservoir	0.34 litre
Brake fluid	DOT 4
Drive chain	Aerosol chain lubricant or SAE 80 or 90 gear oil
Steering head bearings and seals	Urea-based multi-purpose grease with EP2 rating
Swingarm pivot bearings and seal lips	Molybdenum-disulphide grease
Shock absorber bearings and seal lips	Molybdenum-disulphide grease
Suspension linkage bearings and seal lips	Molybdenum-disulphide grease
Sidestand pivot	Molybdenum-disulphide grease
Wheel bearing seal lips	Multi-purpose grease
Wheel axles	Multi-purpose grease
Gearchange lever/rear brake pedal/footrest pivots	Multi-purpose grease
Clutch and brake lever pivot screw	Lithium or molybdenum grease
Throttle twistgrip	Multi-purpose grease
Front brake lever and piston tip	Silicone grease
Cables	Aerosol cable lubricant

Torque settings

Engine oil drain plug	30 Nm
Engine oil filter	26 Nm
Fork clamp bolts (top yoke)	22 Nm
Handlebar clamp bolts	26 Nm
Handlebar end-weight screw	10 Nm
Rear axle nut	113 Nm
Spark plugs	16 Nm
Steering head bearing adjuster nut	37 Nm
Steering stem nut	137 Nm
Timing inspection cap	18 Nm
Water pump drain bolt	12 Nm

Maintenance schedule

Note: *The Pre-ride checks outlined in the owner's manual cover those items that should be inspected before every ride. Also perform the pre-ride inspection at every maintenance interval (in addition to the procedures listed).*

Pre-ride
- [ ] See *'Pre-ride checks'* at the beginning of this manual.

After the initial 600 miles (1000 km)
Note: *This check is usually performed by a Honda dealer after the first 600 miles (1000 km) from new. Thereafter, maintenance is carried out according to the following intervals of the schedule.*

Every 500 miles (800 km)
- [ ] Check, adjust, clean and lubricate the drive chain (Section 1)

Every 4000 miles (6000 km) or 6 months
- [ ] Check the brake pads for wear (Section 2)
- [ ] Check and adjust the clutch cable freeplay (Section 3)

Every 8000 miles (12,000 km) or 12 months
Carry out all the items under the 4000 mile (6000 km) check, plus the following:
- [ ] Check the brake system and brake light switch operation (Section 2)
- [ ] Check the fuel system and hoses (Section 4)
- [ ] Check and adjust the throttle cables (Section 5)
- [ ] Change the engine oil and fit a new filter (Section 6)
- [ ] Check the cooling system (Section 7)
- [ ] Check the pulse secondary air injection (PAIR) system (Section 8)
- [ ] Check the headlight beam aim (Section 9)
- [ ] Check the sidestand and starter interlock circuit (Section 10)
- [ ] Check the front and rear suspension (Section 11)
- [ ] Check and adjust the steering head bearings (Section 12)
- [ ] Check the condition of the wheels, wheel bearings and tyres (Section 13)
- [ ] Lubricate the clutch, gearchange and brake levers, brake pedal, sidestand pivot, and the throttle cables (Section 14)
- [ ] Check the tightness of all nuts, bolts and fasteners (Section 15)

Every 12,000 miles (18,000 km) or 18 months
Carry out all the items under the 4000 mile (6000 km) check, plus the following:
- [ ] Clean the air filter element (Section 16)
- [ ] Check the EVAP (evaporative emission control) system (US models only) (Section 17)

Every 12,000 miles (18,000 km) or two years
Carry out all the items under the 4000 mile (6000 km) check, plus the following:
- [ ] Change the brake fluid (Section 2)

Every 16,000 miles (24,000 km) or two years
Carry out all the items under the 8000 mile (12,000 km) check, plus the following:
- [ ] Check and adjust the valve clearances (Section 18)
- [ ] Check the spark plugs (Section 19)
- [ ] Check the exhaust gas control valve cable (Section 20)

Every 24,000 miles (36,000 km) or two years
Carry out all the items under the 12,000 mile (18,000 km) and 8000 mile (12,000 km) checks, plus the following:
- [ ] Change the coolant (Section 7)

Every 32,000 miles (48,000 km)
Carry out all the items under the 16,000 mile (24,000 km) check, plus the following:
- [ ] Fit new spark plugs (Section 19)

Non-scheduled maintenance
- [ ] Check the battery (Section 21)
- [ ] Change the front fork oil (Section 11)
- [ ] Re-grease the swingarm and suspension linkage bearings (Section 11)
- [ ] Re-grease the steering head bearings (Section 12)

1•4 Component locations

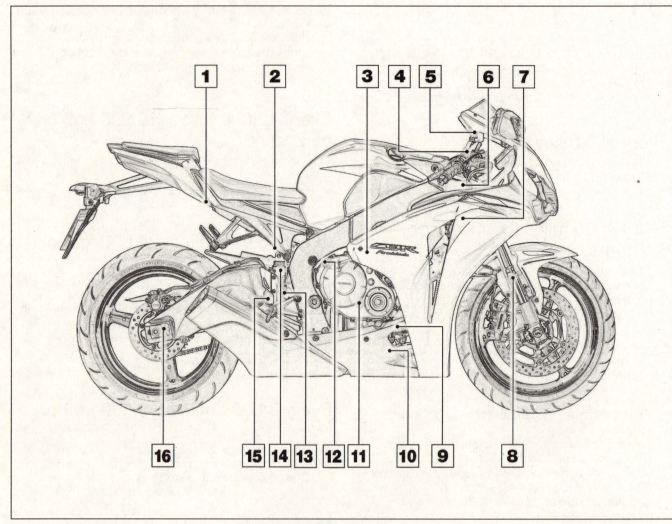

Component locations on the right-hand side

1. EGCV valve
2. Coolant reservoir filler cap
3. Clutch cable adjuster at lower end
4. Throttle cable upper adjuster
5. Front brake fluid reservoir
6. Frame number
7. Radiator pressure cap
8. Fork seals
9. Engine oil filter
10. Engine oil drain plug
11. Engine oil dipstick
12. Engine oil filler cap
13. Rear brake light switch
14. Rear brake fluid reservoir
15. Rear brake pedal height adjuster
16. Drive chain adjuster

Component locations 1•5

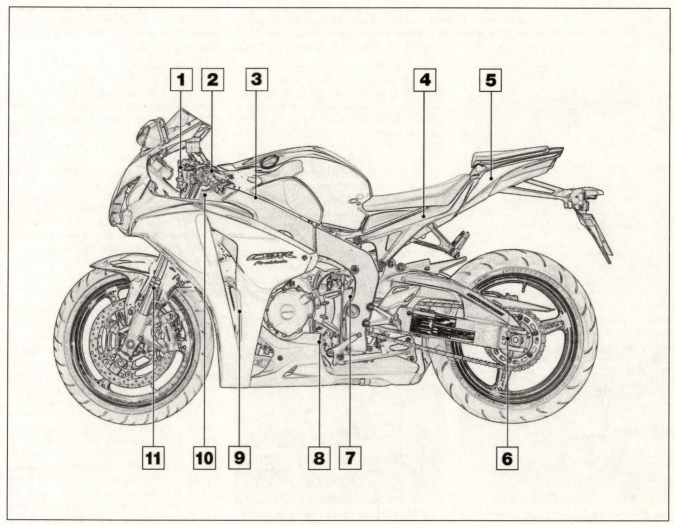

Component locations on left-hand side

1. Clutch cable upper adjuster
2. Steering head bearing adjuster
3. Air filter
4. Battery
5. Colour code lable
6. Drive chain adjuster
7. Coolant reservoir level marks
8. Coolant drain bolt on water pump
9. Engine number
10. VIN plate
11. Fork seals

Routine maintenance and servicing

1 This Chapter is designed to help the home mechanic maintain his/her motorcycle for safety, economy, long life and peak performance.

2 Deciding where to start or plug into the routine maintenance schedule depends on several factors. If your motorcycle has been maintained according to the warranty standards and has just come out of warranty, start routine maintenance as it coincides with the next mileage or calendar interval. If you have owned the machine for some time but have never performed any maintenance on it, start at the nearest interval and include some additional procedures to ensure that nothing important is overlooked. If you have just had a major engine overhaul, then start the maintenance routine from the beginning. If you have a used machine and have no knowledge of its history or maintenance record, combine all the checks into one large service initially and then settle into the specified maintenance schedule.

3 Before beginning any maintenance or repair, the machine should be cleaned thoroughly, especially around the oil filter, drive chain, suspension, wheels, etc. Cleaning will help ensure that dirt does not contaminate the engine and will allow you to detect wear and damage that could otherwise easily go unnoticed. If you use a pressure washer make sure you do not direct the jet at wheel bearing and suspension seals and at the steering head, or at any electrical/ignition components and connectors.

4 Certain maintenance information is sometimes printed on labels attached to the motorcycle. If the information on the labels differs from that included here, use the information on the label.

1 Drive chain and sprockets

Chain slack check

1 A neglected drive chain won't last long and will quickly damage the sprockets. Routine chain adjustment and lubrication isn't difficult and will ensure maximum chain and sprocket life.

2 To check the chain, place the bike on its sidestand and shift the transmission into neutral. Make sure the ignition switch is OFF.

3 Push up on the bottom run of the chain and measure the slack midway between the two sprockets, then compare your measurement to that listed in this Chapter's Specifications **(see illustration)**. As the chain stretches with wear, adjustment will periodically be necessary (see below). Since the chain will rarely wear evenly, roll the bike forward so that another section of chain can be checked (having an assistant to do this makes the task a lot easier); do this several times to check the entire length of chain, and mark the tightest spot.

Caution: Riding the bike with excess slack in the chain could lead to damage.

4 If the chain has been neglected, corrosion and dirt may cause the links to bind and kink, which effectively shortens the chain's length and makes it tight **(see illustration)**. Thoroughly clean and work free any such links, then highlight them with a marker pen or paint. Take the bike for a ride.

5 After the bike has been ridden, repeat the measurement for slack in the highlighted area. If the chain has kinked again and is still tight, replace it with a new one (see Chapter 6). A rusty, kinked or worn chain will damage the sprockets and can damage transmission bearings. If in any doubt as to the condition of a chain, it is far better to install a new one than risk damage to other components and possibly yourself.

6 Check the entire length of the chain for damaged rollers, loose links and pins, and missing O-rings and replace it with a new one if necessary. **Note:** *Never fit a new chain onto old sprockets, and never use the old chain if you fit new sprockets – replace the chain and sprockets as a set.*

Chain slack adjustment

7 Move the bike so that the chain is positioned with the tightest point at the centre of its bottom run, then put it on the sidestand.

8 Slacken the rear axle nut **(see illustration)**.

9 Slacken the locknut on each adjuster bolt **(see illustration)**. Turn the adjuster bolt on each side of the swingarm equally until the amount of freeplay specified at the beginning of the Chapter is obtained at the centre of the bottom run of the chain. Following adjustment, check that the rear edge of each adjustment marker is in the same position in relation to the marks on the swingarm **(see illustration)**. It is important the alignment is the same on each side otherwise the rear wheel will be out of alignment with the front. Always make sure that the front edge of each marker is butted against the end of the adjuster bolt. If there

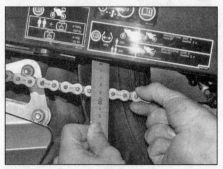

1.3 Push up on the chain and measure the slack

1.4 Neglect has caused the links in this chain to kink

1.8 Slacken the axle nut (arrowed)

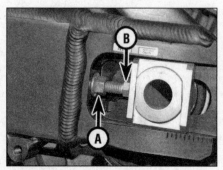

1.9a Slacken each locknut (A) and turn each adjuster bolt (B) by an equal amount...

1.9b ...then check the relative position of the adjustment marker to the alignment marks

Routine maintenance and servicing

1.10 Here the front edge of the marker is in the green zone, so the chain is OK

1.12 Specially shaped chain cleaning brushes are commercially available

1.13 Apply the lubricant to the overlapping sections of the sideplates

is a difference in the positions, adjust one of them so that its position is exactly the same as the other. Check the chain freeplay again and readjust if necessary.

10 Also check the alignment of the front edge of the marker on the left-hand side with the wear decal on the swingarm **(see illustration)**. When the front edge meets the red REPLACE CHAIN zone, the drive chain has stretched excessively and must be replaced with a new one (see Chapter 6).

11 When adjustment is complete, hold the adjuster bolt and tighten locknut on each side **(see illustration 1.9a)**. Push the wheel forwards to make sure each marker is butted against the end of the adjuster bolt and tighten the axle nut to the torque setting specified at the beginning of the Chapter. Recheck the adjustment and alignment as above, then place the machine on an auxiliary stand and spin the wheel to make sure it runs freely.

Chain cleaning and lubrication

12 If required, wash the chain using a dedicated aerosol cleaner, or in paraffin (kerosene) or a suitable non-flammable or high flash-point solvent that will not damage the O-rings, using a soft brush to work any dirt out if necessary **(see illustration)**. Wipe the cleaner off the chain and allow it to dry. If the chain is excessively dirty remove it from the bike and allow it to soak in the paraffin or solvent (see Chapter 6).

Caution: Don't use petrol (gasoline), an unsuitable solvent or other cleaning fluids which might damage the internal sealing properties of the chain. Don't use high-pressure water to clean the chain. The entire process shouldn't take longer than ten minutes, otherwise the O-rings could be damaged.

13 The best time to lubricate the chain is after the motorcycle has been ridden. When the chain is warm, the lubricant will penetrate the joints between the side plates better than when cold. **Note:** *Honda specifies SAE 80 to SAE 90 gear oil or an aerosol chain lube that it is suitable for O-ring or X-ring (sealed) chains; do not use any other chain lubricants – the solvents could damage the chain's sealing rings.* Apply the lubricant to the area where the sideplates overlap – not the middle of the rollers **(see illustration)**.

⚠ **Warning: Take care not to get any lubricant on the tyre or brake components. If any of the lubricant inadvertently contacts them, clean it off thoroughly using a suitable** solvent or dedicated brake cleaner before riding the machine.

Sprocket check

14 Remove the front sprocket cover (see Chapter 6). Check the teeth on the front sprocket and the rear sprocket for wear **(see illustration)**. If the sprocket teeth are worn excessively, renew the chain and both sprockets as a set.

15 With the sprocket cover removed check for wear and damage on the chain slider around the front of the swingarm – if the rubbing surfaces of the slider have worn to the markers **(see illustration)** or there is evidence of damage remove the swingarm and replace the slider with a new one (see Chapter 5).

2 Brake system

Brake pad wear check

1 Each brake pad has wear indicators – on the front calipers there are grooves in the face of the friction material, and on the rear caliper there is a cut-out in the side of the material

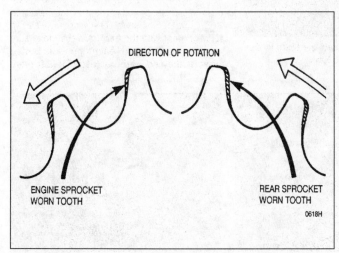

1.14 Check the sprockets in the areas indicated to see if they are worn excessively

1.15 Chain slider wear limit markings

Routine maintenance and servicing

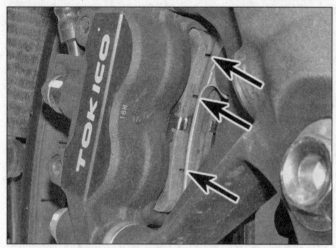

2.1a Front brake pad wear indicator cut-outs (arrowed)

2.1b Rear brake pad wear indicator cut-out (arrowed)

(see illustrations). The wear indicators should be plainly visible by looking from below each front caliper, and from behind the rear caliper, but note that an accumulation of road dirt and brake dust could make them difficult to see.

2 If the pads are worn to the bottom of the grooves or to the beginning of the cut-outs, they must be replaced with new ones (see Chapter 6). **Note:** *Some after-market pads may use different indicators to those on the original equipment.*

3 If the indicators aren't visible, then the amount of friction material remaining should be, and it will be obvious when the pads need replacing. Honda does not specify a minimum thickness for the friction material, but anything less than 1 mm should be considered worn.

4 On the front calipers also check for uneven wear in the brake pads, which is indicative of a sticking or seized piston. If found, the calipers must be overhauled (see Chapter 6).

5 If the pads are dirty or if you are in doubt as to the amount of friction material remaining, remove them for inspection (see Chapter 6).

If the pads have worn to the backing material check the brake discs for scoring (see Chapter 6). From time to time check the thickness of each disc and replace them with new ones if worn below the service limit specified in Chapter 6 and stamped on the disc centre.

Brake system check

6 A routine general check of the brake system will ensure that any problems are discovered and remedied before the rider's safety is jeopardised.

7 Check the brake pads for wear (see above) and make sure the fluid level in the reservoirs is correct (see *Pre-ride checks*).

8 Check the brake lever and pedal pivots for sloppy or rough action, excessive play, bends, and other damage. Replace any damaged parts with new ones (see Chapter 5). Clean and lubricate the lever and pedal pivots if their action is stiff or rough (see Section 14). If the lever or pedal is spongy, bleed the brakes (see Chapter 6).

9 Look for leaks at the hose and pipe connections and check for cracks in the hoses, pipes and unions **(see illustration)**. If a hose shows signs of deterioration it must be replaced with a new one. Make sure all brake hose and pipe fasteners are tight.

10 Also inspect the master cylinders and calipers for any sign of fluid leakage due to failed seals. Leakage from the master cylinders is unlikely, but the caliper pistons can become corroded over a period of time, especially due to road salt over the winter, and this can lead to seal damage. Seal kits are available for the master cylinders and calipers – refer to Chapter 6.

11 Make sure the brake light comes on when the front brake lever or rear pedal is applied. If it fails to operate properly, check the switch (see Chapter 8).

12 Make sure the brake light comes on just before the rear brake takes effect. If adjustment is necessary, hold the switch and turn the adjuster ring on the switch body until the brake light is activated when required **(see illustration)**. The switch is mounted

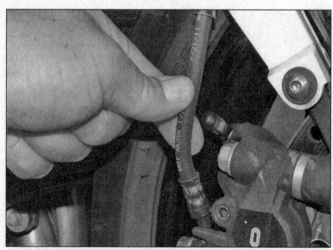

2.9 Check all hoses and unions for cracks and leaks

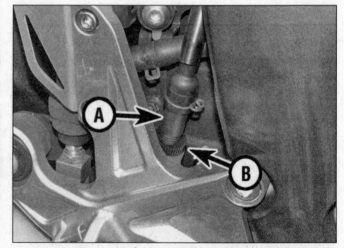

2.12 Hold the rear brake light switch body (A) and turn the adjuster ring (B) as required

Routine maintenance and servicing

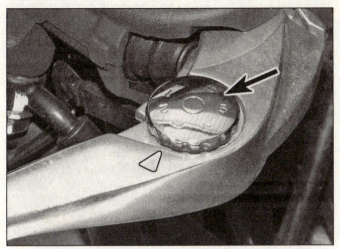

2.13a Front brake lever span adjuster (arrowed)

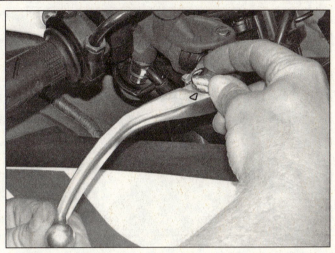

2.13b Push the lever away from the bar and turn the adjuster

behind the rider's right-hand footrest bracket. If the brake light comes on too late or not at all, turn the ring clockwise (when looked at from the top) so the switch threads up out of the bracket. If the brake light comes on too soon or is permanently on, turn the ring anti-clockwise so the switch threads down into the bracket. If the switch doesn't operate the brake light, check it (see Chapter 8).

13 The front brake lever has a span adjuster that alters the distance of the lever from the handlebar **(see illustration)**. Each setting is identified by a number on the adjuster that aligns with the arrow on the lever. Push the lever away from the handlebar and turn the adjuster ring until the setting which best suits the rider is obtained **(see illustration)**. Do not set the adjuster between the defined settings.

14 The height of the rear brake pedal can be adjusted to suit the rider's preference. Slacken the locknut on the bottom of the master cylinder pushrod, then turn the pushrod using a spanner on the hex at the top of the rod until the pedal is at the desired height, but making sure the amount of exposed thread between the top hex and the locknut is no greater than 5.5 mm **(see illustration)**. On completion tighten the locknut. Adjust the rear brake light switch after adjusting the pedal height (see Step 12).

Brake fluid change

Note: *On models with C-ABS (RA models) this is a task for a dealer due to the difficult nature of bleeding the hydraulic system.*

15 The brake fluid should be changed at the prescribed interval or whenever a master cylinder or caliper overhaul is carried out. Refer to Chapter 6 for details. Ensure that all the old fluid is pumped from the hydraulic system and that the level in the fluid reservoirs is checked and the brakes tested before riding the motorcycle.

3 Clutch

1 Check that the clutch lever operates smoothly and easily.
2 If the clutch lever operation is heavy or stiff, lubricate both the cable and the lever (see Section 14). If the cable is still stiff, replace it with a new one.
3 With the cable operating smoothly, check that it is correctly adjusted. Periodic adjustment is necessary to compensate for wear in the clutch plates and stretch of the cable. Check that the amount of freeplay at the clutch lever end is within the specifications listed at the beginning of the Chapter **(see illustration)**.
4 If adjustment is required, this can be done first at the lever end of the cable. Turn the adjuster in or out until the required amount

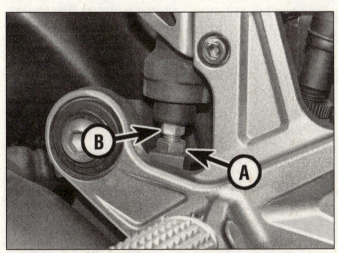

2.14 Slacken the locknut (A) and turn the pushrod using the hex (B) to adjust pedal height

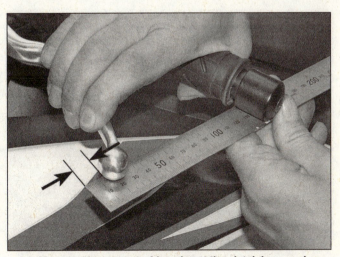

3.3 Measure the amount of freeplay at the clutch lever end as shown

Routine maintenance and servicing

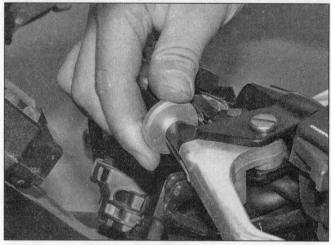

3.4 Turn the adjuster ring as required

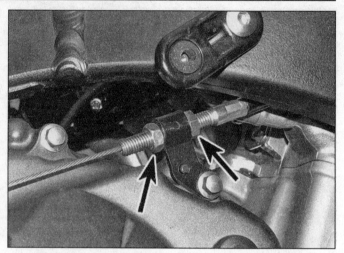

3.8 Slacken and adjust the nuts (arrowed) as described

of freeplay is obtained **(see illustration)**. To reduce freeplay, thread the adjuster out of the bracket. To increase freeplay, thread the adjuster into the lever bracket.

5 Make sure that the slot in the adjuster is not aligned with the slot in the lever bracket – these slots are to allow removal of the cable, and if they are all aligned while the bike is in use the cable could jump out. Also make sure the adjuster is not threaded too far out of the bracket so is only held by a few threads – this will leave it unstable and the threads could be damaged.

6 If all the adjustment has been taken up at the lever, thread the adjuster all the way into the bracket to give the maximum amount of freeplay, then back it out one turn, making sure the slots are offset – this resets the adjuster to its start point.

7 Now set the correct amount of freeplay using the adjuster on the clutch end of cable. The adjuster is set in a bracket on the clutch cover on the right-hand side of the engine – remove the right-hand fairing side panel for access (see Chapter 7).

8 Use the nuts on each end of the threaded section of the cable to adjust freeplay **(see illustration)**. To reduce freeplay, slacken the rear nut and tighten the front nut until the freeplay is as specified, then tighten the rear nut. To increase freeplay, slacken the front nut and tighten the rear nut until the freeplay is as specified, then tighten the front nut. Subsequent adjustments can now be made using the lever adjuster only.

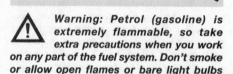

4 Fuel system

⚠ **Warning:** Petrol (gasoline) is extremely flammable, so take extra precautions when you work on any part of the fuel system. Don't smoke or allow open flames or bare light bulbs near the work area, and don't work in a garage where a natural gas-type appliance is present. If you spill any fuel on your skin, rinse it off immediately with soap and water. When you perform any kind of work on the fuel system, wear safety glasses and have a fire extinguisher suitable for a Class B type fire (flammable liquids) on hand.

Check the fuel system hoses, PAIR and EVAP system hoses, and system components

1 Raise the fuel tank (see Chapter 4). Remove the air filter housing jacket, noting how it fits **(see illustration)**.

2 Check the tank, the fuel hoses, the IACV (idle air control valve) hoses, the vacuum hoses, the PAIR (pulse secondary air system) hoses (see Section 8), and, on California models the EVAP (evaporative emission control system) hoses (see Section 17), for signs of leaks, deterioration or damage **(see illustration)**. In particular check that there are no leaks from the fuel hoses or hose unions. Replace any

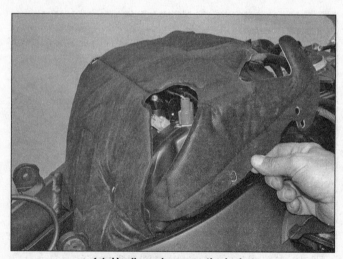

4.1 Unclip and remove the jacket

4.2 Check the fuel system hoses (arrowed)

Routine maintenance and servicing

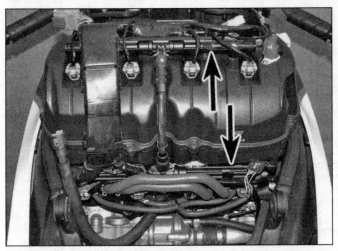

4.4 Check for leakage around each fuel rail (arrowed) and injector

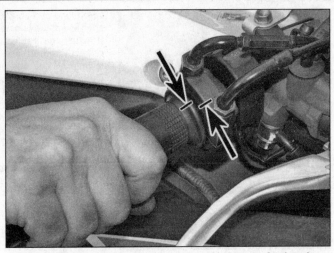

5.2 Throttle cable freeplay is measured in terms of twistgrip rotation

hose that is cracked or deteriorated with a new one (see Chapter 4).

3 Check for signs of leakage around the fuel pump mounting plate on the underside of the tank. If any is evident, check the mounting nuts are tightened to the specified torque setting (see Chapter 4). If the leak persists, remove the pump and fit new seals (see Chapter 4).

4 Inspect the joints between the primary fuel rails, the injectors and the throttle bodies, and the secondary rails, injectors and air filter housing **(see illustration)**. If there are any leaks, remove the fuel rail(s) and fit new seals and O-rings to the injectors (see Chapter 4).

Fuel strainer

5 Fuel strainer cleaning is not a service item. The strainer is integral with the fuel pump, and is not available as a separate component. If fuel starvation is experienced, and all other possibilities have been checked, a blocked strainer could be the cause; in this event a new pump assembly must be installed if it proves impossible to clean the strainer (see Chapter 4).

5 Throttle cables

1 With the engine stopped, make sure the throttle grip rotates smoothly and freely from fully closed to fully open with the front wheel turned at various angles. The grip should return automatically from fully open to fully closed when released. If the throttle sticks, lubricate the cable as described below.

Checking cable freeplay

2 Check for a small amount of freeplay in the cables, measured in terms of the amount of twistgrip rotation before the throttle opens, and compare the amount to that listed in this Chapter's Specifications **(see illustration)**. If it's incorrect, adjust the cables to correct it as follows.

3 Initially adjust freeplay using the adjuster in the throttle opening cable where it leaves the throttle/switch housing on the handlebar. Loosen the locknut and turn the adjuster in or out as required until the specified amount of freeplay is obtained (see this Chapter's Specifications), then retighten the locknut **(see illustration)**.

4 If the adjuster has reached its limit of adjustment, reset it to its start point by turning it fully in, so that freeplay is at a maximum, then remove the air filter housing (see Chapter 4), and adjust the cable at the throttle body end.

5 The adjuster is on the lower cable in the bracket. Slacken the adjuster locknut, then turn the adjuster in or out as required, making sure the lower nut remains captive in the bracket, thereby threading itself along the adjuster as you turn it, until the specified amount of freeplay is obtained, then tighten the locknut **(see illustration)**. Subsequent adjustments can be made at the throttle end when required. If the cable cannot be adjusted as specified, replace it with a new one (see Chapter 4).

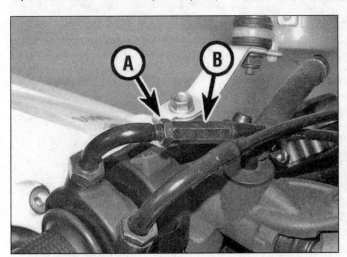

5.3 Slacken the adjuster locknut (A) and turn the adjuster (B) as required

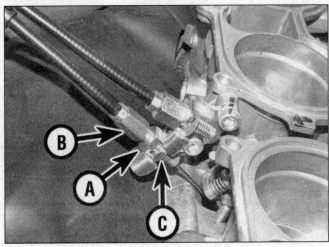

5.5 Throttle cable adjuster locknut (A), adjuster (B) and lower nut (C)

1•12 Routine maintenance and servicing

5.7 Undo the screw to free the end-weight then slide the twistgrip off

Cable and twistgrip lubrication

6 If the throttle sticks, this is probably due to a cable fault. Remove the cables (see Chapter 4) and lubricate them (see Section 14). Check that the inner cables slide freely and easily in the outer cables. If not, replace the cables with new ones.

7 With the cables removed, make sure the throttle twistgrip rotates freely on the handlebar – dirt combined with a lack of lubrication can cause the action to be stiff. If necessary, undo the handlebar end-weight screw, remove the weight and slide the twistgrip off **(see illustration)**. Clean any old grease from the bar and the inside of the tube. Smear some multi-purpose grease onto the bar, then refit the twistgrip. When fitting the end-weight, align the boss with the cut-out on the inner weight inside the handlebar. Clean the threads of the end-weight retaining screw, then apply a suitable non-permanent thread locking compound and tighten it to the torque setting specified at the beginning of the Chapter.

8 Install the cables, making sure they are correctly routed (see Chapter 4). If this fails to improve the operation of the throttle, the cables must be replaced with new ones. Note that in very rare cases the fault could lie in the throttle bodies. Remove the air filter housing and check the action of the throttle pulley and linkage (see Chapter 4).

 Warning: Turn the handlebars all the way through their travel with the engine idling. Idle speed should not change. If it does, the cables may be routed incorrectly. Correct this condition before riding the bike.

6 Engine oil and filter change

Special tool: *A filter removing tool is necessary for this job. Honda can supply one, either as a kit along with the oil filter or separately, or alternatively there are several after-market options.*

 Warning: Be careful when draining the oil, as the exhaust pipes, the engine, and the oil itself can cause severe burns.

1 Consistent routine oil and filter changes are the single most important maintenance procedure you can perform. The oil not only lubricates the internal parts of the engine, transmission and clutch, but it also acts as a coolant, a cleaner, a sealant, and a protector. Because of these demands, the oil takes a terrific amount of abuse and should be replaced often with new oil of the recommended grade and type. The oil filter should be changed with every oil change.

 Saving a little money on the difference in cost between a good oil and a cheap oil won't pay off if the engine is damaged.

2 Before changing the oil, warm up the engine so the oil will drain easily. Make sure the bike is on level ground. The oil drain plug is at the front of the engine. Remove the lower fairing and right-hand fairing side panel (see Chapter 7).

3 Position a large clean drain tray below the engine, so it is under the drain plug and the filter. Unscrew the oil filler cap from the clutch cover to vent the crankcase and to act as a reminder that there is no oil in the engine **(see illustration)**.

4 Unscrew the oil drain plug and allow the oil to flow into the drain tray **(see illustrations)**. Remove the sealing washer from the drain plug – you may have to cut it off. A new washer must be used.

5 Unscrew the filter, preferably using a filter socket (one can be obtained as a kit the new filter from Honda dealers under part No. 15010-MCE-H51, or separately under part No. 07HAA-PJ70101 in Europe or 07AMA-MFJA100 in the US, or otherwise there are commercially available equivalents available from good accessory dealers), or alternatively use filter pliers, or a filter removing strap or a chain-wrench, and tip any residual oil into the drain tray **(see illustrations)**. The

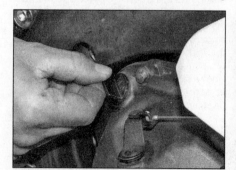

6.3 Unscrew the oil filler cap to act as a vent...

6.4a ...then unscrew the oil drain plug (arrowed)...

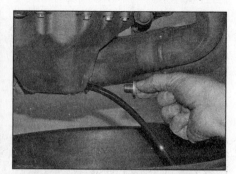

6.4b ...and allow the oil to completely drain

6.5a A filter socket is the best tool to use

6.5b Unscrew the filter...

6.5c ...and allow the oil to drain

Routine maintenance and servicing 1•13

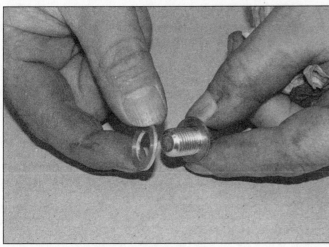

6.6a Fit a new sealing washer...

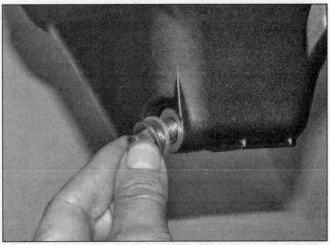

6.6b ...then fit the plug into the sump and tighten to the correct torque

6.8a Smear clean oil onto the seal...

6.8b ...then fit the filter...

6.8c ...and tighten it to the correct torque

filter socket is preferable because it allows a means of tightening the new filter to the correct torque.

6 When the oil has completely drained, fit a new sealing washer onto the drain plug, then fit the plug into the sump and tighten it to the torque setting specified at the beginning of the Chapter **(see illustrations)**. Do not overtighten it as the threads in the sump are easily damaged. Clean any oil off the engine and exhaust.

7 Before fitting the oil filter measure the length of exposed thread on the filter boss to check that it didn't unscrew when removing the filter – there should be 15.4 to 16.4mm of thread exposed.

8 Smear clean engine oil onto the rubber seal on the new filter and thread it onto the engine **(see illustrations)**. Tighten it to the specified torque setting using the filter socket if available **(see illustration)**, or tighten the filter as tight as possible by hand, or by the number of turns specified on the filter itself or its packaging. **Note:** *Do not use a strap or chain filter removing tool to tighten the filter as you will damage it.*

9 Unscrew the dipstick from the clutch cover and wipe it clean **(see illustrations)**. Refer

6.9a Remove the dipstick...

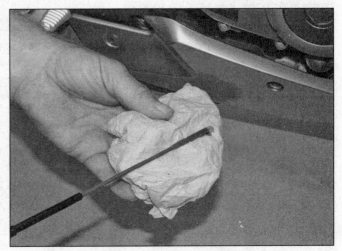

6.9b ...and wipe off all the oil

1•14 Routine maintenance and servicing

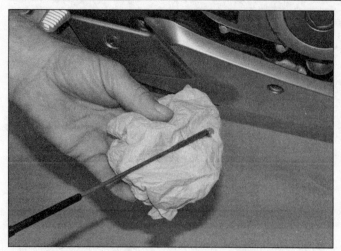
6.9c Add the correct type and amount of oil via the filler hole

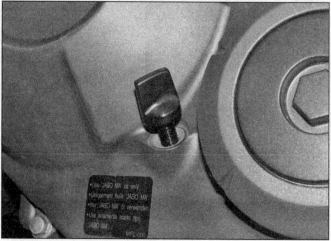
6.9d Check the level with the dipstick resting on its threads

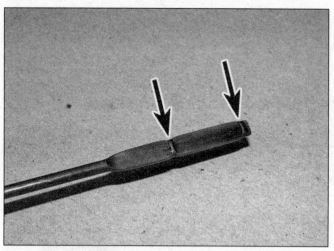
6.9e The level must lie between the lines (arrowed)

6.9f Check the O-rings (arrowed)

to the table below and the Specifications at the beginning of the Chapter and refill the engine to the proper level using the specified type and amount of oil **(see illustration)**. With the motorcycle vertical and the dipstick resting on its threads (i.e. not screwed into the cover), the oil level should lie between the upper and lower level lines **(see illustrations)**. Check the condition of the O-rings on the filler cap and dipstick and replace them with new ones if damaged or worn **(see illustration)**.

Caution: Do not use chemical additives or oils labelled "ENERGY CONSERVING". Such additives or oils could cause clutch slip.

Oil type	API grade: SG or higher motorcycle oil JASO T 903 grade: MA
Oil viscosity	SAE 10W/30 or 10W/40

10 Start the engine and let it run for two or three minutes (make sure that the oil pressure light extinguishes after a few seconds). Shut it off, wait a few minutes, then recheck the oil level. If necessary, add more oil to bring the level close to the upper line, but do not go above it.

11 Check around the drain plug and the oil filter for leaks. A leak around the drain plug probably means a new washer is needed. A leak around the filter probably means it is not tight enough. Install the fairing side panel and lower fairing (see Chapter 7).

Note: It is illegal and anti-social to dump oil down the drain. To find the location of your local oil recycling bank in the UK, call 08708 506 506 or visit www.oilbankline.org.uk

12 The old oil drained from the engine cannot be re-used and should be disposed of properly. Check with your local refuse disposal company, disposal facility or environmental agency to see whether they will accept the used oil for recycling. Don't pour used oil into drains or onto the ground.

HAYNES HiNT *Check the old oil carefully – if it is very metallic coloured, then the engine is experiencing wear from break-in (new engine) or from insufficient lubrication. If there are flakes or chips of metal in the oil, then something is drastically wrong internally and the engine will have to be disassembled for inspection and repair. If there are pieces of fibre-like material in the oil, the clutch is experiencing excessive wear and should be checked.*

Routine maintenance and servicing

7.3 Check all the coolant hoses as described

7.4 Check each hose joint for leakage

7.5 The pump drain hole is on the underside and difficult to see – using a mirror may help spot leakage

7.7 Use a small screwdriver to straighten bent fins

7 Cooling system check and coolant change

Check

Warning: The engine must be cool before beginning this procedure.

1 Remove the lower fairing and fairing side panels (see Chapter 7).
2 Check the coolant level in the reservoir (see *Pre-ride checks*).
3 Check the entire cooling system for evidence of leaks. Examine each rubber coolant hose along its entire length. Look for cracks, abrasions and other damage. Squeeze each hose at various points to see whether they are dried out or hard **(see illustration)**. They should feel firm, yet pliable, and return to their original shape when released. If necessary, replace them with new ones (see Chapter 3).
4 Check for evidence of leaks at each cooling system joint and around the pump on the left-hand side of the engine **(see illustration)**. Tighten the hose clips carefully to prevent future leaks. If the pump is leaking around the cover, check that the bolts are tight. If they are, remove the cover and replace the O-ring with a new one (see Chapter 3). If it is leaking around the crankcase, remove the pump and replace the body O-ring with a new one (see Chapter 3).
5 To prevent leakage of coolant from the cooling system to the lubrication system and vice versa, two seals are fitted on the pump shaft. The coolant seal on the water pump side is of the mechanical type and bears on the rear face of the impeller. The oil seal, mounted behind the mechanical seal, is of the normal feathered lip type. On the underside of the pump housing there is a drain hole **(see illustration)**. If either seal fails, the drain allows the coolant or oil to escape. If on inspection the drain shows signs of leakage, particularly of continuous leakage with the engine running, remove the pump and replace it with a new one (see Chapter 3) – it comes as an assembly and the seals are not available separately. Honda states that a small amount of coolant weeping is normal, so you may have to decide for yourself the difference between a small amount of weeping and continuous leakage – if in doubt seek the advice of your dealer.
6 Check the radiator for leaks and other damage. Leaks leave tell-tale scale deposits or coolant stains on the outside of the core below the leak. If leaks are noted, remove the radiator (see Chapter 3) and have it repaired or replace it with a new one – do not use a liquid leak stopping compound to try to repair leaks.
7 Check the radiator fins for mud, dirt and insects, which will impede the flow of air through the radiator. If the fins are dirty, remove the radiator (see Chapter 3) and clean it using water or low pressure compressed air directed through the fins from the inner side of the radiator. If the fins are bent or distorted, straighten them carefully with a screwdriver **(see illustration)**. If airflow is restricted by

1•16 Routine maintenance and servicing

7.8 Remove the pressure cap as described

7.12 Check the oil cooler (arrowed) for leaks and damage

bent or damaged fins over more than 20% of the radiator's surface area, replace the radiator with a new one.

> **Warning:** *Do not remove the pressure cap when the engine is hot. It is good practice to cover the cap with a heavy cloth and turn the cap slowly anti-clockwise. If you hear a hissing sound (indicating that there is still pressure in the system), wait until it stops, then continue turning the cap until it can be removed.*

8 Remove the pressure cap from the radiator filler neck by turning it anti-clockwise until it reaches the stop. Now press down on the cap and continue turning it until it can be removed **(see illustration)**.

9 Check the condition of the coolant in the system. If it is rust-coloured or if accumulations of scale are visible, drain, flush and refill the system with new coolant (see below). Check the antifreeze content of the coolant with an antifreeze hydrometer – a 50% content should give a reading of 1.084 at 5°C to 1.074 at 25°C, varying accordingly in between. The system must have the correct coolant mixture (see Specifications) – if the coolant is too weak (i.e. too little anti-freeze giving a low reading – anything below 1.07 when cold and 1.06 when hot) there will not be adequate protection against freezing and corrosion, and if it is too strong the ability to cool the engine is reduced. If the hydrometer indicates an incorrect mixture, drain and refill the system (see below).

10 The function of the pressure cap is crucial to the correct running of the cooling system. Check the cap seal for cracks and other damage. If the coolant level consistently drops and/or the bike overheats, and no evidence of leaks can be found, have the cap pressure checked by a Honda dealer, or just fit a new one. If a new cap does not cure the problem have the entire system pressure checked by a dealer.

11 Fit the cap by turning it clockwise until it reaches the first stop then push down on it and continue turning until it can turn no further. Start the engine and let it reach normal operating temperature, then check for leaks again. As the coolant temperature increases, the electric fans (mounted on the back of the radiator) should come on automatically and the temperature should begin to drop. If not, refer to Chapter 3 and check the fans and fan circuit.

12 Check the oil cooler on the front of the engine (next to the oil filter) for any signs of oil leakage between it and the engine **(see illustration)**. If there is leakage check the cooler bolt is tight. If the leakage persists you will have to fit a new O-ring between the cooler and the engine (see Chapter 2). Check that the coolant hoses are secure on the unions, and that there is no evidence of coolant leakage from the body of the cooler. If there is, the cooler is damaged and must be replaced with a new one.

Change the coolant

> **Warning:** *Allow the engine to cool completely before performing this maintenance operation. Also, don't allow anti-freeze to come into contact with your skin or the painted surfaces of the motorcycle. Rinse off spills immediately with plenty of water. Anti-freeze is highly toxic if ingested. Never leave anti-freeze lying around in an open container or in puddles on the floor; children and pets are attracted by its sweet smell and may drink it. Check with local authorities (councils) about disposing of anti-freeze. Many communities have collection centres which will see that anti-freeze is disposed of safely. Anti-freeze is also combustible, so don't store it near open flames.*

Draining

13 Make sure the engine is cold. Support the motorcycle upright on a level surface using an auxiliary stand. Remove the lower fairing and fairing side panels (see Chapter 7).

14 Remove the pressure cap from the filler neck by turning it anti-clockwise until it reaches a stop **(see illustration 7.8)**. Now press down on the cap and continue turning the cap until it can be removed.

15 Position a suitable container beneath the water pump on the left-hand side of the engine. Unscrew the drain bolt and allow the coolant to completely drain from the system **(see illustrations)**. A new sealing washer is needed.

16 Remove the reservoir cap **(see illustration)**. Draw the coolant out of the reservoir using a hand suction tool (such as a kitchen basting implement).

Flushing

17 Flush the system with clean tap water by inserting a hose in the radiator filler neck. Allow the water to run through the system until it is clear and flows out cleanly. If the radiator is extremely corroded, remove it (see Chapter 3) and have it cleaned by a specialist. Also flush the reservoir, then draw the water out as before.

Refilling

18 Fit the drain bolt using a new sealing

7.15a Unscrew the bolt (arrowed)...

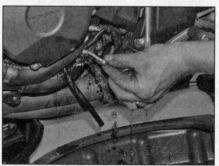

7.15b ...and drain the coolant

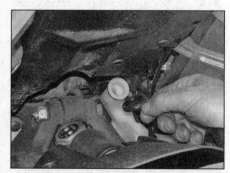

7.16 Remove the cap and draw the coolant out

Routine maintenance and servicing 1•17

7.18 Fit the drain bolt using a new sealing washer

7.19 Fill the system as described

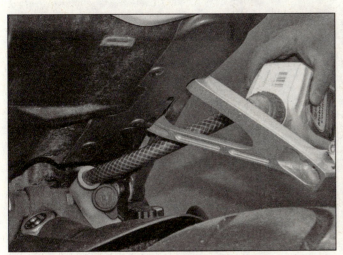

7.21a Fill the reservoir...

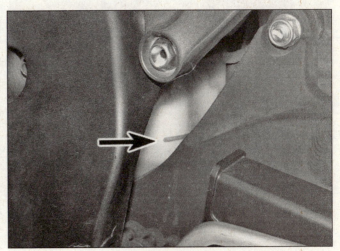

7.21b ...to the UPPER level line (arrowed)

washer and tighten it to the torque setting specified at the beginning of the Chapter **(see illustration)**.

19 Fill the system to the base of the filler neck with the proper coolant mixture (see this Chapter's Specifications) **(see illustration)**. *Note: Pour the coolant in slowly to minimise the amount of air entering the system, and when full carefully waggle the bike from side to side and squeeze the coolant hoses to dislodge any trapped air.* Fill the reservoir to the UPPER level line (see *Pre-ride checks*).

20 Start the engine and allow it to idle for 2 to 3 minutes. Flick the throttle twistgrip part open 3 or 4 times, so that the engine speed rises to approximately 4000 to 5000 rpm, then stop the engine. Any air trapped in the system should bleed back to the filler neck.

21 If necessary, top up the coolant level to the base of the radiator filler neck, then fit the pressure cap. Also top up the coolant reservoir to the UPPER level line – using a suitable funnel or a piece of hose in the bottle neck helps **(see illustrations)**.

22 Start the engine and allow it to reach normal operating temperature, then shut it off. Let the engine cool then remove the pressure cap as described in Step 14. Check that the coolant level is still up to the base of the radiator filler neck. If it's low, add the specified mixture until it reaches the base of the filler neck. Refit the cap.

23 Check the coolant level in the reservoir and top up if necessary.

24 Check the system for leaks. Install the fairing panels (see Chapter 7).

25 Do not dispose of the old coolant by pouring it down the drain. Instead pour it into a heavy plastic container, cap it tightly and take it into an authorised disposal site or service station – see **Warning** at the beginning of this Section.

8 PAIR (Pulse secondary air supply) system

1 To reduce the amount of unburned hydrocarbons released in the exhaust gases, a pulse secondary air supply (PAIR) system is fitted. The system consists of the control valve (mounted above the valve cover on the top of the engine), the reed valves (fitted in the valve cover) and the hoses between the air filter housing, the control valve and the reed valves **(see illustration 8.3d)**. The control valve is actuated electronically by the ECM.

2 Under normal operating conditions, the valve allows filtered air to be drawn through the reed valves and cylinder head passages and into the exhaust ports. The air mixes with the exhaust gases, causing any unburned particles of the fuel in the mixture to be burnt in

1•18 Routine maintenance and servicing

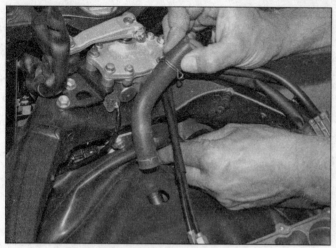

8.3a Remove the crankcase breather hose...

8.3b ...unstick the sides of the heat shield...

8.3c ...and draw it back

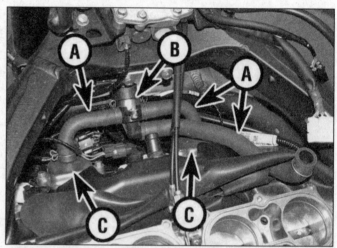

8.3d PAIR hoses (A), control valve (B) and reed valves (C)

the exhaust port/pipes. This process changes a considerable amount of hydrocarbons and carbon monoxide into relatively harmless carbon dioxide and water. The reed valves in the valve cover are fitted to prevent the flow of exhaust gases back up the cylinder head passages and into the air filter housing.

3 The system is not adjustable and requires little more than a visual check of the hoses. To access them remove the fairing side panels (see Chapter 7) and the air filter housing (see Chapter 4). Disconnect the crankcase breather hose, then unstick and displace the rubber heat shield **(see illustrations)**. Check that the hoses are not kinked or pinched, are in good condition and are securely connected at each end **(see illustration)**. Also check the crankcase breather hose. Replace any hoses that are cracked, split or generally deteriorated with new ones.

4 Refer to Chapter 4 for further information on the system and for checks if it is believed to be faulty.

9 Headlight aim

Note: *An improperly adjusted headlight may cause problems for oncoming traffic or provide poor, unsafe illumination of the road ahead. Before adjusting the headlight aim, be sure to consult with local traffic laws and regulations – for UK models refer to MOT Test Checks in the Reference section.*

1 The headlight beam can adjusted both horizontally and vertically. Before making any adjustment, check that the tyre pressures are correct and the suspension is adjusted as required. Make any adjustments to the headlight aim with the machine on level ground, with the fuel tank half full and with an assistant sitting on the seat. If the bike is usually ridden with a passenger on the back, have a second assistant to do this.

2 Vertical adjustment is made by turning the adjuster screw on the bottom inner corner of the relevant beam unit **(see illustration)**. Turn it clockwise to move the beam down, and anti-clockwise to move it up.

3 Horizontal adjustment is made by turning the adjuster screw on the top outer corner of the relevant beam unit **(see illustration 9.2)**. For the main beam (right-hand unit) turn the

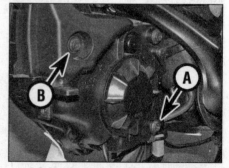

9.2 Vertical adjuster (A), horizontal adjuster (B)

Routine maintenance and servicing 1•19

adjuster clockwise to move the beam to the right, and anti-clockwise to move it to the left. For the dipped beam (left-hand unit) turn the adjuster clockwise to move the beam to the left, and anti-clockwise to move it to the right.

10 Sidestand and starter interlock circuit

1 Check the stand springs for damage and distortion (see illustration). The springs must be capable of retracting the stand fully and holding it retracted when the motorcycle is in use. If a spring is sagged or broken it must be replaced with a new one.
2 Lubricate the stand pivot regularly (see Section 14).
3 Check the stand and its mount for bends and cracks.
4 Check the operation of the starter interlock circuit as follows:
● Make sure the transmission is in neutral, then retract the stand and start the engine. Pull in the clutch lever and select a gear. Keeping the clutch lever pulled in, extend the sidestand. The engine should stop as the sidestand is extended.
● Make sure the engine is in neutral and the sidestand is down, then start the engine. Pull the clutch lever in and select a gear. The engine should cut out.
● Check that when the sidestand is down the engine can only be started if the transmission is in neutral, and when the sidestand is up and the transmission is in gear the engine can only be started if the clutch lever is pulled in.
5 If the circuit does not operate as described, check the sidestand switch, neutral switch (gear position switch), clutch switch and diodes, and the circuit between them (see Chapter 8).

10.1 Check the springs (arrowed) as described

11 Suspension

1 The suspension components must be maintained in top operating condition to ensure rider safety. Loose, worn or damaged suspension parts decrease the motorcycle's stability and control.

Front suspension check

2 While standing alongside the motorcycle, apply the front brake and push on the handlebars to compress the forks several times (see illustration). See if they move up-and-down smoothly without binding. If binding is felt, the forks should be disassembled and inspected (see Chapter 5).
3 Inspect each fork inner tube for scratches, corrosion and pitting in the area of travel through the seals, which will cause premature seal failure (see illustration) – if the damage is excessive, new inner tubes should be fitted (see Chapter 5), or the inner tubes must be re-chromed using hard chrome.
4 Also check the inner tubes for signs of oil leakage. Carefully lever the dust seal out using a flat-bladed screwdriver and inspect the area

11.2 Compress the forks to check their action

around the oil seal. If leakage is evident, the seals must be replaced with new ones (see Chapter 5). If there is evidence of corrosion between the oil seal retaining ring and its groove in the fork tube, spray the area with a penetrative lubricant, otherwise the ring will be difficult to remove if needed. Press the dust seal back into the outer tube on completion.
5 The forks are adjustable for spring pre-load, rebound damping and compression damping and it is essential that both fork legs are adjusted equally. Refer to Chapter 5 and check the settings on each fork if in doubt.
6 Check the tightness of all suspension nuts and bolts to be sure none have worked loose, referring to the torque settings specified at the beginning of Chapter 5.

Rear suspension check

7 Inspect the rear shock absorber for fluid leakage and tightness of its mountings. If leakage is found, the shock must be replaced with a new one (see Chapter 5).
8 With the aid of an assistant to support the bike, compress the rear suspension several times (see illustration). It should move up-and-down freely without binding. If any binding is felt, the worn or faulty component must be identified and checked (see Chapter 5).

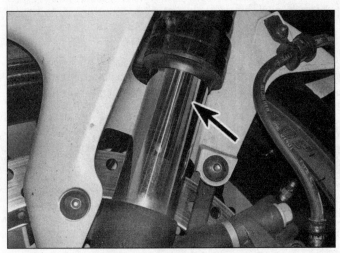

11.3 Check the inner tube (arrowed) for pitting and signs of oil leakage

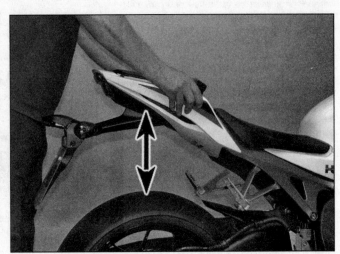

11.8 Compress the rear suspension to check its action

1•20 Routine maintenance and servicing

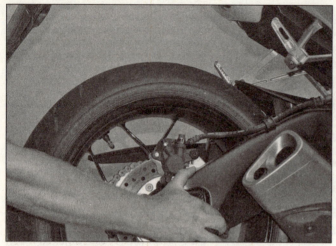

11.9 Checking for play in the swingarm bearings

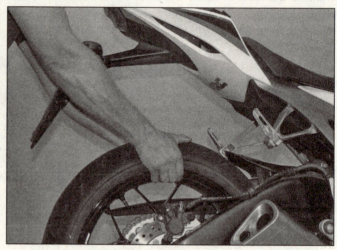

11.10 Checking for play in the rear shock mountings and suspension linkage bearings

The problem could be due to the shock absorber, the suspension linkage components or the swingarm components.

9 Support the bike on an auxiliary stand (but not a paddock stand under the swingarm!) so that the rear wheel is off the ground. Grab the swingarm and rock it from side-to-side – there should be no discernible movement at the rear (see illustration).

10 Next, grasp the top of the rear wheel and pull it upwards – there should be no discernible freeplay before the shock absorber begins to compress (see illustration).

11 If there's a little movement or a slight clicking can be heard, check the tightness of the swingarm pivot, referring to the procedure in Chapter 5, and re-check for movement. Also check the shock absorber mounting bolts/nuts, and the suspension linkage mounting bolts/nuts. If there is still some noise or freeplay after everything has been correctly tightened then there is a worn bearing or bearings in the shock absorber, swingarm or linkage. The worn components must be identified and replaced with new ones (see Chapter 5).

12 You can make a more accurate assessment by isolating the swingarm and shock absorber from the linkage – remove the rear wheel (see Chapter 6) and the bolts securing the linkage to the shock absorber and swingarm (see Chapter 5).

13 Grasp the rear of the swingarm with one hand and place your other hand at the junction of the swingarm and the frame. Try to move the rear of the swingarm from side-to-side. Any wear (play) in the bearings should be felt as movement between the swingarm and the frame at the front. If there is any play, the swingarm will be felt to move forward and backward at the front (not from side-to-side). Next, move the swingarm up and down through its full travel. It should move freely, without any binding or rough spots. If there is any play in the swingarm or if it does not move freely, remove the bearings for inspection (see Chapter 5).

14 With the shock absorber and linkage detached check the bearings and bush in each component for corrosion and wear and failure of the seals, referring to Chapter 5 for details, and clean and re-grease or replace components as required.

Front fork oil change

15 Although there is no set interval for changing the fork oil, the oil will degrade over a period of time and lose its damping qualities. Refer to Chapter 5, Sections 6 and 7 for details of front fork removal, oil draining and refilling. The forks do not need to be completely disassembled to change the oil.

Rear suspension bearing lubrication

16 Although there is no set interval for re-greasing the suspension linkage bearings, over a considerable mileage the seals are likely to fail and the grease in the bearings will be washed out or will harden allowing the ingress of dirt and water.

17 The suspension linkage and the swingarm should be removed periodically and the bearings cleaned and re-greased as necessary (see Chapter 5).

12 Steering head bearings

Freeplay check and adjustment

1 This motorcycle is equipped with caged ball steering head bearings. The bearings can become dented, rough or loose during normal use of the machine and in extreme cases, worn or loose steering head bearings can cause steering wobble – a condition that is potentially dangerous.

Check

2 Remove the lower fairing (see Chapter 7). Remove the steering damper cover and detach the damper arm from the top yoke (see Chapter 5). Raise the front wheel off the ground using an auxiliary stand placed under the engine. Always make sure that the bike is properly supported and secure.

3 Point the front wheel straight-ahead and slowly move the handlebars from lock to lock. Any dents or roughness in the bearing races will be felt and if the bearings are too tight the bars will not move smoothly and freely. Again point the wheel straight-ahead, and tap the front of the wheel to one side. The wheel should 'fall' under its own weight to the limit of its lock, indicating that the bearings are not too tight (take into account the restriction that cables and wiring may have). Check for similar movement to the other side.

4 If available, attach one end of a spring balance (graduated zero to 30 N) around the top of the fork (see illustration). With the steering straight-ahead, pull on the balance

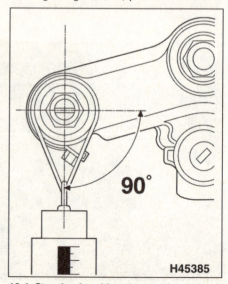

12.4 Steering head bearing pre-load check

Routine maintenance and servicing 1•21

12.5 Checking for play in the steering head bearings

12.7 Fork clamp bolts (arrowed)

and check the reading at which the handlebars start to turn. If the reading is below the minimum value specified in the pre-load range given in the Specifications at the beginning of the Chapter, the steering head is too loose, if the reading is above the maximum value specified the steering head is too tight. If the steering doesn't perform as described, and it's not due to the resistance of cables or hoses, then the bearings should be adjusted as described below.

5 Next, grasp the bottom of the forks and gently pull and push them forward and backward **(see illustration)**. Any looseness or freeplay in the steering head bearings will be felt as front-to-rear movement of the forks. If play is felt, adjust the bearings as described below. If no adjustment is need, refit the damper arm and fairing panels.

Adjustment

Special tool: *Either the Honda special tool (part No. 07HMA-MR70100), equivalent peg spanner, or a suitably sized C-spanner is necessary for this procedure – see Step 11.*

6 As a precaution, remove the fuel tank cover (see Chapter 7) and the complete fairing assembly (see Chapter 5, Section 9. Step 1). Though not actually necessary, this will prevent the possibility of damage should a tool slip. If not already done remove the steering damper cover and detach the damper arm from the top yoke (see Chapter 5).

7 Slacken the fork clamp bolts in the top yoke **(see illustration)**.

8 Unscrew and remove the steering stem nut **(see illustration)**.

9 Gently ease the top yoke up off the forks and position it clear, using a rag to protect other components **(see illustration)**.

10 Bend the lockwasher tabs out of the

> **HAYNES HiNT**
> Stick masking tape around the flats of the steering stem nut to protect its finish.

> **HAYNES HiNT**
> *Make sure you are not mistaking any movement between the bike and stand, or between the stand and the ground, for freeplay in the bearings. Do not pull and push the forks too hard – a gentle movement is all that is needed. Freeplay between the fork tubes due to worn bushes can also be misinterpreted as steering head bearing play – do not confuse the two.*

12.8 Unscrew the steering stem nut...

12.9 ...and gently ease the yoke up off the forks

1•22 Routine maintenance and servicing

12.10a Bend down the tabs securing the locknut...

12.10b ...then unscrew the locknut...

12.10c ...and remove the lockwasher

notches in the locknut **(see illustration)**. Unscrew the locknut using your fingers **(see illustration)** – it shouldn't be tight. If it is tight use a C-spanner located in one of the notches **(see illustration 12.11a)**. Remove the lockwasher **(see illustration)**. Inspect the tabs for cracks or signs of fatigue. If there is any sign of damage, discard the lockwasher and use a new one; otherwise the old one can be re-used, but note that Honda recommend using a new one as a matter of course.

11 To turn the adjuster nut you need the Honda service tool (part No. *07HMA-MR70100*), or a suitable peg spanner (which can be made by cutting castellations into a 35 mm socket or a piece of steel tube with a 41 mm ID and 46 mm OD), or a C-spanner, or a suitable drift to locate in one of the notches **(see illustrations)**. Slacken the adjuster nut slightly until pressure is just released. If the Honda tool or a peg spanner is available, tighten the adjuster nut to the torque setting specified at the beginning of the Chapter, then turn the steering from lock-to-lock five times, then reapply the specified torque setting to the nut. If the tool is not available, tighten the adjuster nut using a C-spanner or drift until all freeplay is removed, yet the steering is able to move freely. The object is to set the adjuster nut so that the bearings are under a very light loading, just enough to remove any freeplay, but not so much that the steering is prevented from moving freely from side-to-side. If the torque setting is applied check the physical feel as described as well. If you have a spring balance (see Step 4), set the adjuster nut so that the steering starts to move at around the mid-point of the pre-load range given in the Specifications at the beginning of the Chapter.

Caution: Take great care not to apply excessive pressure because this will cause premature failure of the bearings.

12 If the bearings cannot be correctly adjusted, disassemble the steering head and check the bearings and races (see Chapter 5).
13 With the bearings correctly adjusted, fit the lockwasher, using a new one if the tabs are weakened or cracked, onto the adjuster nut and fit the two short tabs into the slots in the adjuster nut **(see illustration 12.10c)**.
14 Fit the locknut and tighten it finger-tight **(see illustration 12.10b)**. Tighten the locknut further (but no more than 90°) until its notches align with the remaining lockwasher tabs. Secure the locknut by bending up the long lock washer tabs into its notches **(see illustration)**.
15 Fit the top yoke onto the steering stem **(see illustration 12.9)**, locating the lug on the top of each handlebar clamp into its hole in the underside of the yoke **(see illustration)**. Fit the steering stem nut and tighten it to the

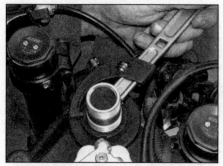

12.11a Adjust the bearings as described using either a C-spanner or a drift...

12.11b ...or the Honda tool or equivalent home-made peg spanner as shown

12.14 Bend the tabs up into the notches in the locknut

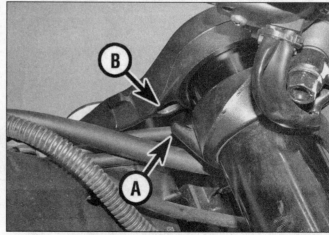

12.15a Make sure the handlebar lug (A) locates in the hole (B)

Routine maintenance and servicing 1•23

12.15b Fit the steering stem nut and tighten to the specified torque

torque setting specified at the beginning of the Chapter **(see illustration)**.
16 Tighten the fork clamp bolts in the top yoke to the specified torque **(see illustration 12.7)**.
17 Check the bearing adjustment as described above and re-adjust if necessary.
18 Attach the steering damper arm and fit the cover (see Chapter 5). Install the fairing and the fuel tank cover (see Chapter 7).

Lubrication

19 Although there is no set interval for re-greasing the steering head bearings, over a considerable time the grease in the bearings will be dispersed or will harden allowing the ingress of dirt and water.
20 Refer to Chapter 5, Section 10 for details of this operation.

13 Wheels, wheel bearings and tyres

Wheels

1 Cast wheels are virtually maintenance free, but they should be kept clean and checked periodically for cracks and other damage. Also check the wheel runout and alignment (see Chapter 6). Never attempt to repair damaged cast wheels; they must be renewed if damaged. Check that the wheel balance weights are fixed firmly to the wheel rim. If you suspect that a weight has fallen off, have the wheel rebalanced by a motorcycle tyre specialist.

Wheel bearings

2 Wheel bearings will wear over a considerable mileage and should be checked periodically to avoid handling problems.
3 Support the motorcycle upright using an auxiliary stand so that the wheel being examined is off the ground. Check for any play in the bearings by pushing and pulling the wheel against the hub **(see illustration)**. Also rotate the wheel and check that it turns smoothly and without any grating noises.
4 If any play is detected in the hub, or if the wheel does not rotate smoothly (and this is not due to brake or chain drag), the wheel should be removed and the bearings inspected for wear or damage (see Chapter 6).

Tyres

5 Check the tyre condition and tread depth thoroughly – see *Pre-ride checks*.
6 Check the valve rubber for signs of damage or deterioration and have it replaced if necessary by a tyre specialist.
7 Make sure the valve stem cap is in place and tight **(see illustration)**. Check the valve for signs of damage.
8 If tyre deflation occurs and it is not due to a slow puncture the valve core may be loose or it could be leaking past the seal – remove the cap and make sure the core is tight. Some valve caps double as a tool for the valve core – these caps are available in bike and automotive accessory dealers. Alternatively special tools are available, or a tool can be made quite easily by cutting a slot into the threaded end of a bolt using a hacksaw – the bolt must fit inside the valve housing and the slot must be deep enough to locate around the flat sides of the core and grip it. If the core leaks when tight fit a new one. A smear of spit or soapy water across the top of the valve will indicate if it is leaking – the leak will show as bubbles.

14 Pivot points and cable lubrication

Pivot points

1 Since the controls, cables and various other components of a motorcycle are exposed to the elements, they should be checked and lubricated periodically to ensure safe and trouble-free operation.
2 The footrest pivots, clutch and brake lever pivots, brake pedal and gearchange lever pivots and linkage and sidestand pivot should be lubricated frequently. In order for the lubricant to be applied where it will do the most good, the component should be disassembled (see Chapter 5). The lubricant recommended by Honda for each application is listed at the beginning of the Chapter.
3 If an aerosol lubricant is used, it can be applied to the pivot joint gaps and will usually work its way into the areas where friction occurs, so less disassembly of the component is needed. If however, the area is dirty or the pivot is stiff to operate it is preferable to dismantle it and clean off all corrosion, dirt and old lubricant first.
4 If motor oil or light grease is being used, apply it sparingly as it may attract dirt (which could cause the controls to bind or wear at an accelerated rate). **Note:** *One of the best lubricants for the control lever pivots is a dry-film lubricant (available from many sources by different names).*

Cables

Special tool: *A cable lubricating adapter is necessary for this procedure* **(see illustration 14.5c)**.

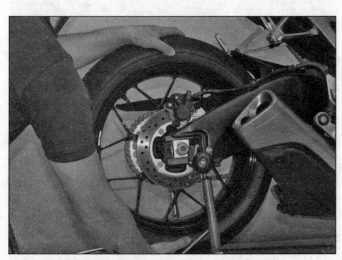

13.3 Checking for play in the wheel bearings

13.7 Check each valve as described and make sure a cap is fitted

1•24 Routine maintenance and servicing

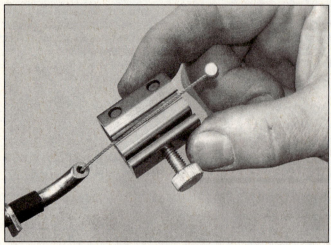

14.5a Fit the cable into the adapter...

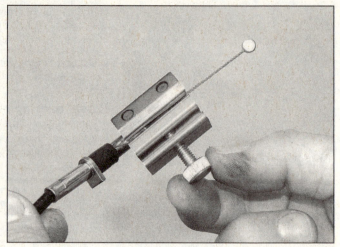

14.5b ...and tighten the screw to seal it in...

5 To lubricate the cables, disconnect the relevant cable at its upper end, then lubricate it with a pressure adapter and aerosol lubricant **(see illustrations)**. See Chapter 4 for throttle cable removal procedures, and Chapter 2 for the clutch cable.

15 Nuts and bolts

1 Since vibration of the machine tends to loosen fasteners, all nuts, bolts, screws, etc. should be periodically checked for proper tightness.
2 Pay particular attention to the following, referring to the relevant Chapter:
   Spark plugs
   Engine oil drain plug
   Lever and pedal bolts

Footrest and sidestand bolts
Engine mounting bolts
Shock absorber and suspension linkage bolts; swingarm pivot bolt nut
Handlebar clamp bolts
Front fork clamp bolts (top and bottom yoke)
Steering stem nut
Steering damper bolts
Front axle bolt and axle clamp bolts
Rear axle nut
Front sprocket bolt and rear sprocket nuts
Brake caliper and master cylinder mounting bolts
Brake hose banjo bolts and caliper bleed valves
Brake disc bolts
Exhaust system bolts/nuts

3 If a torque wrench is available, use it along with the torque settings given at the beginning of this and other Chapters.

16 Air filter

Caution: *If the machine is continually ridden in wet or dusty conditions, the filter should be replaced more frequently.*
1 Raise the fuel tank (see Chapter 4). Remove the air filter housing jacket, noting how it fits **(see illustration 4.1)**.
2 Disconnect the ignition switch and handlebar switch wiring connectors, and where fitted the immobiliser wiring connector **(see illustration)**.
3 Undo the ECM retainer screws and displace the retainer and the ECM and lay it on some rag – do not disconnect or strain the wiring **(see illustrations)**. On 2012-on models displace the lap timer relay **(see illustration)**.

14.5c ...then apply the lubricant using the nozzle provided inserted in the hole in the adapter

16.2 Disconnect the various wiring connectors (arrowed)

Routine maintenance and servicing 1•25

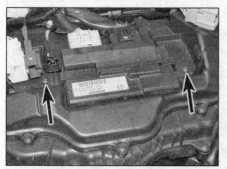
16.3a Undo the screws...

16.3b ...and displace the retainer...

16.3c ...and the ECM

16.3d Lap relay (arrowed) – 2012-on models

16.5a Undo the screws...

16.5b ...and remove the filter element

16.6a Remove any debris from the folds

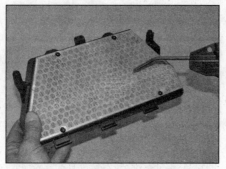
16.6b Direct the air in the opposite direction of normal flow

16.7 Make sure the tabs along the rear edge locate correctly

4 Undo the air filter cover screws and remove the cover.
5 Undo the filter element screws and remove the element from the housing, noting how it fits **(see illustrations)**.
6 Clean the filter by tapping it on a hard surface to dislodge any dirt from the folds, then check for anything stuck between them **(see illustration)**. Use compressed air to blow through it, directing the air in the opposite way to normal flow, i.e. from the throttle body intake duct side **(see illustration)**. Do not use any solvents or cleaning agents on the element. If the element is excessively dirty or is damaged replace it with a new one.
7 Fit the filter element into the housing, making sure it locates correctly and is properly seated, and secure it with its screws **(see illustration)**.
8 Fit the housing cover, the ECM and its retainer, and where fitted the lap relay. Connect the wiring connectors. Install the fuel tank (see Chapter 4).

17 EVAP (Evaporative emission control) system check (US models)

1 Raise the fuel tank (see Chapter 4). Visually inspect all the system hoses between the fuel tank, the purge control solenoid valve, and the canister for kinks and splits and any other damage or deterioration. Make sure that the hoses are securely connected with a clamp on each end. Replace any hoses that are damaged or deteriorated.
2 Check the EVAP canister and the valve for cracks or other damage.
3 See Chapter 4 for further information and tests on the system. Note that there is an emission control system information label under the passenger seat.

18 Valve clearances

Special tool: *A set of feeler gauges is necessary for this job **(see illustration 18.7)**.*
1 The engine must be completely cool for this maintenance procedure, so let the bike stand overnight before beginning.
2 Remove the spark plugs (see Section 19). Remove the valve cover (see Chapter 2). Either retract and lock the cam chain tensioner, or remove the tensioner if the tool is not available (see Chapter 2).
3 Make a chart or sketch of all valve positions so that a note of each clearance can be made against the relevant valve. The cylinders are

1•26 Routine maintenance and servicing

18.4 Remove the timing inspection cap

18.6a Turn the crankshaft clockwise using the bolt...

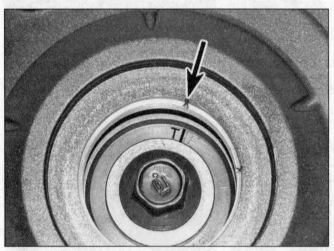
18.6b ...until the line next to the T mark aligns with the notch (arrowed)...

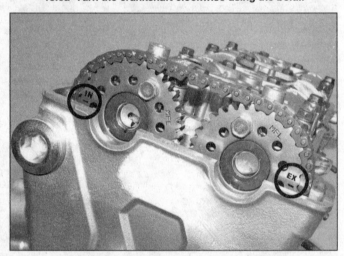
18.6c ...and the camshaft sprocket marks (circled) are as shown

numbered 1 to 4 from left to right. The intake valves are on the back of the cylinder head and the exhaust valves are on the front.

4 Unscrew the timing inspection cap from the clutch cover (see illustration). Check the condition of its O-ring and obtain a new one if necessary.

5 To check the valve clearances the crankshaft must be turned so that the valve being checked is closed. The crankshaft can be turned using a suitable spanner or a socket on the timing rotor bolt and turning it in a clockwise direction only (see illustration 18.6a).

6 Turn the crankshaft clockwise until the line next to the T mark on the timing rotor aligns with the static timing mark, which is a notch in the inspection hole rim, and the IN and EX marks on the intake and exhaust camshaft sprockets respectively are facing away from each other and are flush with the cylinder head top surface (see illustrations). Use a mirror if the marks are difficult to see with the engine in the frame, or use the punch mark on the inner face of the intake camshaft sprocket instead of the IN mark on the outer face (see illustration). If the marks are facing towards each other or if the punch mark is to the front, turn the crankshaft clockwise one full turn (360°) until the line next to the T mark again aligns with the static timing mark. The sprocket marks will now be as required.

7 With the engine in this position, check the clearances on the Nos. 1 and 3 cylinder intake valves, remembering there are two valves per cylinder. Insert a feeler gauge of the same thickness as the correct valve clearance (see Specifications) between the camshaft lobe and the follower of each valve and check that it is a firm sliding fit – you should feel a slight drag when the you pull the gauge out (see illustration). If not, use the feeler gauges to obtain the exact clearance. Record the measured clearance on the chart.

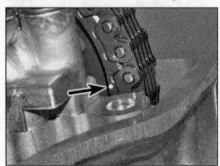
18.6d The punch mark (arrowed) on the inner face of the intake sprocket is easier to see

18.7 Insert the feeler gauge between the base of the cam lobe and the top of the follower as shown

Routine maintenance and servicing

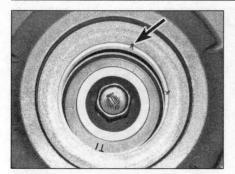

18.8 Turn the crankshaft 180° so the marks are aligned as shown

18.13a Carefully lift out the follower using a magnet, a lapping tool or grips...

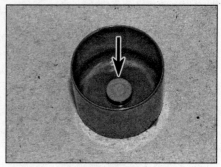

18.13b ...and retrieve the shim (arrowed) from inside it...

8 Now turn the crankshaft 180° clockwise until the line next to the T mark on the timing rotor is diametrically opposite the static timing mark **(see illustration)**. With the engine in this position, check the clearances on the Nos. 2 and 4 cylinder exhaust valves using the method described in Step 7.

9 Now turn the crankshaft 180° clockwise until the line next to the T mark aligns with the static timing mark again **(see illustration 18.6b)**. With the engine in this position, check the clearances on the Nos. 2 and 4 cylinder intake valves using the method described in Step 7.

10 Now turn the crankshaft 180° clockwise until the line next to the T mark on the timing rotor is once again diametrically opposite the static timing mark **(see illustration 18.8)**. With the engine in this position, check the clearances on the Nos. 1 and 3 cylinder exhaust valves using the method described in Step 7.

11 When all clearances have been measured and charted, identify whether the clearance on any valve falls outside the specified range. If any do, the shim must be replaced with one of a thickness that will restore the correct clearance.

12 Shim replacement requires removal of the camshafts (see Chapter 2). Place rags over the spark plug holes and the cam chain tunnel to prevent a shim from dropping into the engine on removal. Work on one valve at a time to prevent the possibility of mixing up the followers, which must be returned to their original location. If you want to remove more than one shim and follower at a time, store them in a marked container or bag, denoting which cylinder and which valve the shim and follower are from, so that they do not get mixed up.

13 With the camshaft removed, remove the cam follower of the valve in question using a magnet or the suction created by a valve lapping tool, or long nosed pliers can be used with care **(see illustration)**. Retrieve the shim from inside the follower or pick it out of the top of the valve spring retainer using either a magnet, a screwdriver with a dab of grease on it (the shim will stick to the grease), or a very small screwdriver and a pair of pliers **(see illustrations)**. Do not allow the shim to fall into the engine.

14 Measure and record the thickness of the shim using a micrometer **(see illustrations)**.

15 Calculate the required replacement shim by using the formula a = (b − c) + d, where a is the required shim size, b is the measured valve clearance, c is the specified valve clearance, and d is the existing shim thickness. For example:

The measured clearance of an exhaust valve is 0.35 mm, so b = 0.35
The specified clearance range for an exhaust valve is 0.27 to 0.33 mm, the mid-point being 0.30 mm, so c = 0.30
The thickness of the existing shim is 2.00 mm, so d = 2.0
Therefore, the required replacement shim a = 0.35 − 0.30 + 2.0, so a = 2.05 mm.

Note: *If the required replacement shim is greater than 2.800 mm (the largest available), the valve is probably not seating correctly due to a build-up of carbon deposits and should be checked and cleaned or resurfaced as required (see Chapter 2).*

16 Shims are available in 0.025 mm increments from 1.200 mm to 2.800 mm. Obtain the replacement shim, then lubricate it with molybdenum disulphide oil (a 50/50 mixture of molybdenum disulphide grease and engine oil) and fit it into the recess in the top of the valve spring retainer with the size mark facing up **(see illustration)**.

17 Check that the shim is correctly seated, then lubricate the follower with molybdenum disulphide oil and fit it onto the valve, making sure it fits squarely in its bore **(see**

18.13c ...or from the top of the valve

18.14a The shim size is marked on one face...

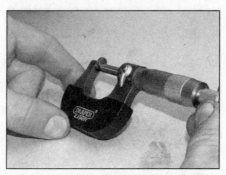

18.14b ...but check the thickness of the shim using a micrometer

18.16 Make sure the shim seats in its recess

1•28 Routine maintenance and servicing

illustration). Repeat the process for any other valves until the clearances are correct, then install the camshafts (see Chapter 2).

18 Rotate the crankshaft clockwise several turns to seat the new shim(s), then check the clearances again. Release the cam chain tensioner, or refit it if it was removed, then install the valve cover (see Chapter 2).

19 Install all disturbed components in a reverse of the removal sequence. Fit the timing inspection cap using a new O-ring if required, and smear the O-ring with oil and the cap threads with grease **(see illustration)**. Tighten the cap to the torque setting specified at the beginning of the Chapter.

18.17 Fit the follower onto the valve

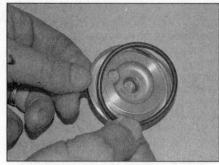
18.19 Use a new O-ring if necessary

19 Spark plugs

Check and adjustment

Special tool: *A wire gauge is necessary for this job (see illustration 19.8b). Do not use a blade-type gauge.*

Note 1: *The spark plug caps are integral with the ignition coils. To avoid damaging the wiring, always disconnect the wiring connectors before removing the coils. Do not attempt to lever the coils off the plugs or pull them off with pliers. Do not drop the coils.*

Note 2: *All models are equipped with plugs that have an iridium coated centre electrode. The plugs must be treated differently to conventional plugs. Do not substitute them with conventional plugs.*

1 Remove the fairing side panels (see Chapter 7).

2 Remove the air filter housing (see Chapter 4). Disconnect the crankcase breather hose, then unstick and displace the rubber heat shield **(see illustrations 8.3a, b and c)**.

3 Clean the area around each ignition coil to prevent any dirt falling into the spark plug channels.

4 Check that the cylinder location is marked on each coil's wiring sleeve, then disconnect the coil wiring connectors **(see illustration)**. Pull the coil off each spark plug **(see illustration)**.

5 If compressed air is available clean around the base of each spark plug to prevent any dirt falling into the combustion chamber.

6 Using the tool provided in the bike's toolkit or the equivalent 16 mm spark plug socket, unscrew and remove the plugs from the cylinder head **(see illustrations)**. Lay each plug out in relation to its cylinder; if any plug shows up a problem it will then be easy to identify the troublesome cylinder.

7 Check the condition of the electrodes, referring to the spark plug reading chart at the end of this manual if signs of contamination are evident. Note that contaminated iridium plugs should not be cleaned – discard them and fit new ones.

8 Examine the pointed iridium-tipped centre electrode; if the tip has rounded off, the plug is worn **(see illustration)**. Measure the gap between the two electrodes with a wire type gauge only **(see illustration)** – do not use blade type feeler gauges because the iridium tip might be damaged. The gap should be as given in the Specifications at the beginning of this chapter – if the electrodes have worn and the gap is wider than it should be, or for some reason the gap is narrower than it should be (if the plug has been dropped for instance) a new plug must be installed. Do not bend the outer electrode to adjust the gap.

19.4a Disconnect the coil wiring connector...

19.4b ...then pull the coil up off the plug

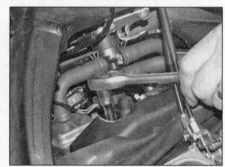
19.6a Unscrew the plug...

19.6b ...and lift it out with the tool

19.8a If the centre electrode has rounded off the plug is worn

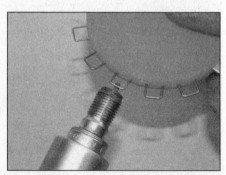
19.8b Using a wire type gauge to measure the spark plug electrode gap

Routine maintenance and servicing

9 Check the threads, the washer and the ceramic insulator body for cracks and other damage.
10 Fit the plug into the end of the tool, then use the tool to insert the plug (see illustration 19.6b). Since the cylinder head is made of aluminium, which is soft and easily damaged, thread the plugs as far as possible into the head turning the tool by hand. Once the plugs are finger-tight, the job can be finished with a spanner on the tool supplied or a socket drive (see illustration 19.6a). If a torque wrench can be applied, tighten the spark plugs to the torque setting specified at the beginning of the Chapter. Otherwise, if new plugs are being used, tighten them by 1/2 a turn after the washer has seated, and if the old plugs are being reused, tighten them by 1/8 to 1/4 turn after they have seated, or tighten them according to the instructions on the box. Do not over-tighten them.
11 Fit the coils, making sure they seat correctly onto the plugs (see illustration 19.4b). Reconnect the coil wiring connectors, making sure they are securely connected to the correct cylinder – each wiring sleeve should be marked with its cylinder number (see illustration 19.4a). Install all other removed components.

 As the plugs are quite recessed, slip a short length of hose over the end of the plug to use as a tool to thread it into place. The hose will grip the plug well enough to turn it, but will start to slip if the plug begins to cross-thread in the hole – this will prevent damaged threads.

 HAYNES HiNT Stripped plug threads in the cylinder head can be repaired with a Heli-Coil insert – see 'Tools and Workshop Tips' in the Reference section.

Renewal

12 At the prescribed interval, whatever the condition of the existing spark plugs, remove the plugs as described above and install new ones.

20 Exhaust gas control valve (EGCV)

Operational checks

1 Refer to Chapter 4, Section 5 and clear any fault codes from the ECM.
2 Start the engine. Stop the engine and check the position of the exhaust control valve in the upper port in the end of the silencer (see illustration) – the valve should be fully closed, in which case it is functioning correctly. If it not fully closed the cable must be adjusted (see below).
3 Remove the seat (see Chapter 7). On RA models displace the fuse/relay box (see illustration). Locate the engine management system data link connector (DLC), which is a red blanked single-sided 4-pin connector. Remove any tape from the connector, then remove the blanking cap (see illustration). Either fit the Honda SCS service connector (Part No. 070PZ-ZY30100, available from

20.2 Check the position of the valve (arrowed)

20.3a Displace the fuse/relay box

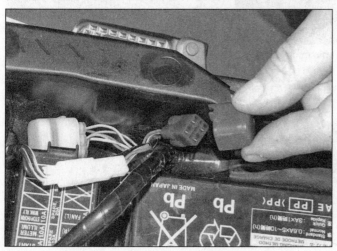
20.3b Locate the connector and remove the cap...

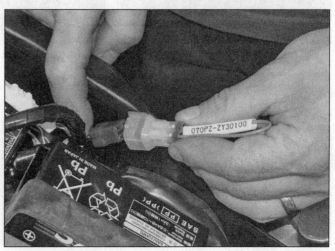
20.3c ...and fit the tool or bridge the terminals as described

Routine maintenance and servicing

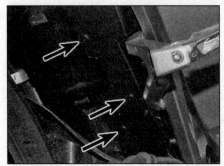

20.5a On RR models release the trim clips (arrowed)...

20.5b ...and remove the cover

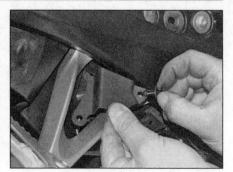

20.5c On RA models remove the brake pipe cover...

your dealer), or bridge the brown and green wire terminals of the connector with a piece of insulated electrical wire with bared ends **(see illustration)**.

4 Turn the ignition switch on and set the kill switch to run. The exhaust control valve should open fully, in which case it is functioning correctly.

Cable check and adjustment

5 Remove the exhaust control valve servo cover **(see illustrations)**.
6 Turn the servo pulley clockwise and disconnect the cable **(see illustrations)**. Pull lightly on the cable end and measure the amount of exposed inner cable as shown **(see illustration)** – there should be 46 to 49 mm. If not, remove the silencer (see Chapter 4), then slacken the cable adjuster locknut and turn the cable until the amount of exposed cable is 49 to 52 mm **(see illustration)**. Install the silencer (see Chapter 4). Connect the cable to the pulley then turn the pulley anti-clockwise and position it as shown **(see illustration)**.
7 Fit the servo cover.

20.5d ...then release the clips (arrowed) and remove the cover

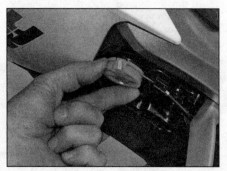

20.6a Turn the pulley...

21 Battery

1 All models covered in this manual are fitted with a sealed MF (maintenance free) battery. **Note:** *Do not attempt to remove the battery caps to check the electrolyte level or battery specific gravity. Removal will damage the caps, resulting in electrolyte leakage and battery damage.* All that should be done is to check that the terminals are clean and tight and that the casing is not damaged or leaking. See Chapter 8 for further details.
2 If the machine is not in regular use, disconnect the battery and give it a refresher charge every month to six weeks (see Chapter 8).

20.6b ...free the outer cable...

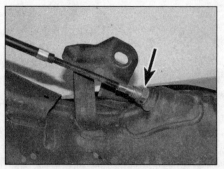

20.6c ...and detach the inner cable

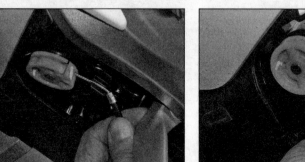

20.6d Measure the amount of exposed inner cable

20.6e Slacken the locknut (arrowed) and adjust the cable

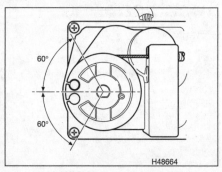

20.6f EGCV valve pulley position

Chapter 2
Engine, clutch and transmission

Contents

	Section number
Alternator	see Chapter 8
Balancer shaft	30
Cam chain tensioner	8
Cam chain, tensioner blades and front guide	10
Camshafts and followers	9
Clutch	14
Clutch cable	15
Clutch check	see Chapter 1
Component access	2
Connecting rod and main bearing information	21
Connecting rods and bearings	23
Crankcase separation and reassembly	19
Crankcases	20
Crankshaft and main bearings	22
Crankshaft position sensor	see Chapter 4
Cylinder block	26
Cylinder head and valve overhaul	12
Cylinder head removal and installation	11
Engine overhaul general information	5
Engine removal and installation	4
Engine wear assessment	3
Gearchange mechanism	16

	Section number
General information	1
Idle speed	see Chapter 4
Neutral switch	see Chapter 8
Oil and filter change	see Chapter 1
Oil cooler	6
Oil level check	see Pre-ride checks
Oil pressure switch	see Chapter 8
Oil pump and pressure relief valve	18
Oil sump and strainer	17
Piston rings	25
Pistons	24
Running-in procedure	31
Selector drum and forks	29
Spark plugs	see Chapter 1
Starter clutch and gears	13
Starter motor	see Chapter 8
Transmission shaft overhaul	28
Transmission shaft removal and installation	27
Valve clearance check and adjustment	see Chapter 1
Valve cover	7
Water pump	see Chapter 3

Degrees of difficulty

Easy, suitable for novice with little experience	Fairly easy, suitable for beginner with some experience	Fairly difficult, suitable for competent DIY mechanic	Difficult, suitable for experienced DIY mechanic	Very difficult, suitable for expert DIY or professional

Specifications

General

Type	Four-stroke in-line four
Capacity	999 cc
Bore	76.0 mm
Stroke	55.1 mm
Compression ratio	12.3 to 1
Cylinder numbering	1 to 4 from left to right
Firing order	1-2-4-3
Cooling system	Liquid cooled
Lubrication	Wet sump, trochoid pump
Clutch	Wet multi-plate
Transmission	Six-speed constant mesh
Final drive	Chain

Camshafts and followers

Intake cam lobe height
   Standard... 37.34 to 37.58 mm
   Service limit (min).................................. 37.32 mm
Exhaust cam lobe height
   Standard... 36.58 to 36.82 mm
   Service limit (min).................................. 36.56 mm
Oil clearance
   Standard... 0.020 to 0.062 mm
   Service limit (max)................................. 0.10 mm
Runout (max)... 0.05 mm
Cam follower diameter
   Standard... 25.978 to 25.993 mm
   Service limit (min).................................. 25.97 mm
Cam follower bore diameter
   Standard... 26.010 to 26.026 mm
   Service limit (max)................................. 26.04 mm

Cylinder head

Warpage (max).. 0.10 mm

Valves, guides and springs

Valve clearances....................................... see Chapter 1
Stem diameter
   Intake valve
     Standard... 4.475 to 4.490 mm
     Service limit (min).............................. 4.465 mm
   Exhaust valve
     Standard... 3.965 to 3.980 mm
     Service limit (min).............................. 3.955 mm
Guide bore diameter
   Intake valve
     Standard... 4.500 to 4.512 mm
     Service limit (max)............................. 4.540 mm
   Exhaust valve
     Standard... 4.000 to 4.012 mm
     Service limit (max)............................. 4.040 mm
Stem-to-guide clearance
   Intake valve
     Standard... 0.010 to 0.037 mm
     Service limit (max)............................. 0.075 mm
   Exhaust valve
     Standard... 0.020 to 0.047 mm
     Service limit (max)............................. 0.085 mm
Seat width (in the head) – intake and exhaust valves
   Standard... 0.90 to 1.10 mm
   Service limit (max)................................. 1.50 mm
Valve guide height above cylinder head
   Intake valve... 15.1 to 15.4 mm
   Exhaust valve....................................... 15.7 to 16.0 mm
Valve spring free length
   Intake – inner spring
     Standard... 35.25 mm
     Service limit (min).............................. 34.5 mm
   Intake – outer spring
     Standard... 38.93 mm
     Service limit (min).............................. 38.2 mm
   Exhaust
     Standard... 39.68 mm
     Service limit (min).............................. 38.9 mm

Starter clutch

Starter driven gear hub OD
   Standard... 45.657 to 45.673 mm
   Service limit (min).................................. 45.642 mm

Clutch

Friction plates...	9
Friction plate thickness	
Type A	
Standard..	3.72 to 3.88 mm
Service limit (min)...................................	3.6 mm
Type B and C	
Standard..	3.22 to 3.38 mm
Service limit (min)...................................	3.1 mm
Plain plates...	8
Plain plate warpage (max)................................	0.3 mm
Diaphragm spring free height	
Standard..	5.7 mm
Service limit (min).....................................	4.7 mm
Clutch guide OD	
2008 models	
No marking	
Standard..	35.004 to 35.012 mm
Service limit (min)...............................	34.994 mm
With marking	
Standard..	34.996 to 35.004 mm
Service limit (min)...............................	34.986 mm
2009-on models	
Two code marks	
Standard..	35.007 to 35.012 mm
Service limit (min)...............................	35.004 mm
Three code marks	
Standard..	35.001 to 35.007 mm
Service limit (min)...............................	34.998 mm
Four code marks	
Standard..	34.996 to 35.001 mm
Service limit (min)...............................	34.993 mm
Clutch guide ID (all models, all types)	
Standard..	27.993 to 28.003 mm
Service limit (max)....................................	28.012 mm
Primary driven gear ID	
2008 models	
Type A – white mark	
Standard..	41.008 to 41.016 mm
Service limit (max)..............................	41.026 mm
Type B – black mark	
Standard..	41.000 to 41.008 mm
Service limit (max)..............................	41.018 mm
2009-on models	
Type A – blue mark	
Standard..	41.011 to 41.016 mm
Service limit (max)..............................	41.019 mm
Type B – yellow mark	
Standard..	41.005 to 41.011 mm
Service limit (max)..............................	41.014 mm
Type C – green mark	
Standard..	41.000 to 41.005 mm
Service limit (max)..............................	41.008 mm
Input shaft OD at clutch guide	
Standard..	27.980 to 27.990 mm
Service limit (min).....................................	27.960 mm

Oil pump

Oil pressure (at oil pressure switch, with engine warm).............	86 psi (6 Bar) @ 6000 rpm, oil @ 80°C
Inner rotor tip-to-outer rotor clearance	
Standard..	0.15 mm
Service limit (max)....................................	0.20 mm
Outer rotor-to-body clearance	
Standard..	0.15 to 0.21 mm
Service limit (max)....................................	0.35 mm
Rotor end-float	
Standard..	0.04 to 0.09 mm
Service limit (max)....................................	0.17 mm

Oil pump (continued)

Oil pump drive sprocket ID
   Standard.. 35.025 to 35.145 mm
   Service limit (max) .... 35.155 mm
Oil pump drive sprocket guide ID
   Standard.. 28.000 to 28.021 mm
   Service limit (max) .... 28.030 mm
Oil pump drive sprocket guide OD
   Standard.. 34.975 to 34.991 mm
   Service limit (min) .... 34.965 mm
Input shaft OD at sprocket guide
   Standard.. 27.980 to 27.990 mm
   Service limit (min) .... 27.960 mm

Cylinders

Bore
   Standard.. 76.000 to 76.015 mm
   Service limit (max) .... 76.025 mm
Warpage (max) .... 0.10 mm
Ovality (out-of-round) (max) .... 0.10 mm
Taper (max)... 0.10 mm
Cylinder compression....................................... 174 psi (12.2 Bar) @ 210 rpm

Pistons

Piston diameter (measured 5 mm up from skirt, at 90° to piston pin axis)
   Standard.. 75.965 to 75.985 mm
   Service limit (min) .... 75.895 mm
Piston-to-bore clearance
   Standard.. 0.015 to 0.050 mm
   Service limit (max) .... 0.10 mm
Piston pin diameter
   Standard.. 16.994 to 17.000 mm
   Service limit (min) .... 16.98 mm
Piston pin bore diameter in piston
   Standard.. 17.002 to 17.008 mm
   Service limit (max) .... 17.030 mm
Piston pin-to-piston pin bore clearance
   Standard.. 0.02 to 0.014 mm
   Service limit (max) .... 0.04 mm

Piston rings

Ring end gap (installed)
   Top ring
      Standard... 0.22 to 0.32 mm
      Service limit (max)..................................... 0.52 mm
   Second ring
      Standard... 0.40 to 0.55 mm
      Service limit (max)..................................... 0.74 mm
   Oil ring side-rail
      Standard... 0.20 to 0.70 mm
      Service limit (max)..................................... 1.0 mm
Ring-to-groove clearance
   Top ring
      Standard... 0.04 to 0.08 mm
      Service limit (max)..................................... 0.12 mm
   Second ring
      Standard... 0.015 to 0.050 mm
      Service limit (max)..................................... 0.075 mm

Crankshaft and bearings

Main bearing oil clearance
   Standard.. 0.019 to 0.037 mm
   Service limit (max) .... 0.05 mm
Runout (max) .... 0.05 mm

	Standard	Service limit (max)
Connecting rods		
Small-end internal diameter	17.030 to 17.042 mm	17.048 mm
Small-end-to-piston pin clearance	0.030 to 0.048 mm	0.07 mm
Big-end side clearance	0.15 to 0.30 mm	0.35 mm
Big-end oil clearance	0.030 to 0.052 mm	0.06 mm

Transmission

Gear ratios (no. of teeth)
- Primary reduction .... 1.717 to 1 (79/46)
- Final reduction .... 2.625 to 1 (42/16)
- 1st gear .... 2.285 to 1 (32/14)
- 2nd gear .... 1.777 to 1 (32/18)
- 3rd gear .... 1.500 to 1 (33/22)
- 4th gear .... 1.333 to 1 (32/24)
- 5th gear .... 1.214 to 1 (34/28)
- 6th gear .... 1.137 to 1 (29/24)

Input shaft 5th and 6th gears ID
- Standard .... 31.000 to 31.025 mm
- Service limit (max) .... 31.04 mm

Input shaft 5th gear bush OD
- Standard .... 30.955 to 30.980 mm
- Service limit (min) .... 30.935 mm

Input shaft 6th gear bush OD
- Standard .... 30.950 to 30.975 mm
- Service limit (min) .... 30.930 mm

Input shaft 5th gear gear-to-bush clearance
- Standard .... 0.020 to 0.070 mm
- Service limit (max) .... 0.10 mm

Input shaft 6th gear gear-to-bush clearance
- Standard .... 0.025 to 0.075 mm
- Service limit (max) .... 0.11 mm

Input shaft 5th gear bush ID
- Standard .... 27.985 to 28.006 mm
- Service limit (max) .... 28.016 mm

Input shaft OD at 5th gear bush point
- Standard .... 27.967 to 27.980 mm
- Service limit (min) .... 27.957 mm

Input shaft-to-bush clearance at 5th gear bush point
- Standard .... 0.005 to 0.039 mm
- Service limit (max) .... 0.06 mm

Output shaft 1st gear ID
- Standard .... 28.000 to 28.021 mm
- Service limit (max) .... 28.04 mm

Output shaft 2nd, 3rd and 4th gears ID
- Standard .... 33.000 to 33.025 mm
- Service limit (max) .... 33.04 mm

Output shaft 2nd gear bush OD
- Standard .... 32.955 to 32.980 mm
- Service limit (min) .... 32.935 mm

Output shaft 3rd and 4th gears bush OD
- Standard .... 32.950 to 32.975 mm
- Service limit (min) .... 32.93 mm

Output shaft 2nd gear gear-to-bush clearance
- Standard .... 0.020 to 0.070 mm
- Service limit (max) .... 0.10 mm

Output shaft 3rd and 4th gears gear-to-bush clearance
- Standard .... 0.025 to 0.075 mm
- Service limit (max) .... 0.11 mm

Output shaft 2nd gear bush ID
- Standard .... 29.985 to 30.006 mm
- Service limit (max) .... 30.021 mm

Output shaft OD at 2nd gear bush point
- Standard .... 29.967 to 29.980 mm
- Service limit (min) .... 29.96 mm

Output shaft-to-bushing clearance at 2nd gear bush point
- Standard .... 0.005 to 0.039 mm
- Service limit (max) .... 0.06 mm

Selector drum and forks
Selector fork end thickness
    Standard... 5.93 to 6.00 mm
    Service limit (min).................................. 5.90 mm
Selector fork bore ID
    Standard... 14.000 to 14.018 mm
    Service limit (max).................................. 14.03 mm
Selector fork shaft OD
    Standard... 13.957 to 13.968 mm
    Service limit (min).................................. 13.95 mm

Torque settings
Cam chain tensioner blades and guide
    Lower tensioner blade pivot bolt..................... 10 Nm
    Upper tensioner blade pivot bolt..................... 74 Nm
    Front guide blade pivot bolt......................... 12 Nm
Camshaft holder bolts.................................... 12 Nm
Camshaft sprocket bolts.................................. 20 Nm
Camshaft position (CMP) sensor rotor bolts............... 12 Nm
Clutch nut... 128 Nm
Connecting rod bolts
    New bolts
        Torque setting................................... 27.5 Nm
        Angle setting.................................... +90°
    Old bolts (for oil clearance check only)
        Torque setting................................... 21.6 Nm
        Angle setting.................................... +90°
Crankcase bolts
    Lower crankcase 9 mm crankshaft journal bolts
        Torque setting................................... 20 Nm (see Section 19)
        Angle setting.................................... +150°
    Lower crankcase 10 mm bolt.......................... 39 Nm
    Lower crankcase 8 mm bolts.......................... 24 Nm
    Lower crankcase 7 mm bolts.......................... 18 Nm
    Upper crankcase 7 mm bolts.......................... 18 Nm
Crankcase oil pipe bolts................................. 12 Nm
Cylinder head 9 mm nuts
    Torque setting...................................... 25 Nm
    Angle setting....................................... 135°
Cylinder head stud bolts................................. 20 Nm
Engine mountings
    Lower rear mounting bolt nut........................ 84 Nm
    Upper rear mounting bolt nut........................ 64 Nm
    Adjuster.. 10 Nm
    Adjuster bolt locknut *(see text)*
        Actual... 54 Nm
        Indicated (with special tool).................... 49 Nm
    Front mounting bolts................................ 64 Nm
Gearchange mechanism retainer plate bolt................. 12 Nm
Oil cooler bolt.. 59 Nm
Oil pipe bolts... 12 Nm
Oil pump body bolts...................................... 12 Nm
Oil pump drive chain guide bolt.......................... 12 Nm
Oil pump driven sprocket bolt............................ 15 Nm
Selector drum bearing retainer bolts..................... 12 Nm
Selector drum cam bolt................................... 23 Nm
Starter clutch bolt...................................... 93 Nm
Stopper arm bolt... 12 Nm
Throttle body duct bolts................................. 12 Nm
Timing inspection cap.................................... 18 Nm
Transmission input shaft bearing/fork shaft retainer plate bolts....... 12 Nm
Valve cover bolts.. 10 Nm

Engine, clutch and transmission

1 General information

The engine/transmission unit is a liquid-cooled in-line four cylinder. The sixteen valves are operated by double overhead camshafts that are chain driven off the right-hand end of the crankshaft. The engine/transmission is a unit assembly constructed from aluminium alloy. The crankcase divides horizontally.

The crankcase incorporates a wet sump, pressure-fed lubrication system with a dual rotor trochoidal oil pump that is chain-driven off the back of the clutch. The system has an oil strainer in the pick-up, a pressure relief valve in the pump, an oil filter, an oil cooler, and an oil pressure switch in the main gallery.

The alternator is on the left-hand end of the crankshaft. The water pump is on the left-hand side of the engine, and its driveshaft is keyed to the oil pump drive shaft. The ignition timing triggers are on the outside of the alternator rotor and the crankshaft position (timing) sensor is mounted in the alternator cover.

Power from the crankshaft is routed to the transmission via the clutch. The clutch is of the wet, multi-plate type and is gear-driven off the crankshaft. The clutch is operated by cable. The transmission is a six-speed constant-mesh unit. Final drive to the rear wheel is by chain and sprockets.

2 Component access

Operations possible with the engine in the frame

The components and assemblies listed below can be removed without having to remove the engine/transmission assembly from the frame. If however, a number of areas require attention at the same time, removal of the engine is recommended.

Valve cover
Cam chain tensioner and blades
Camshafts and cam chain
Clutch
Gearchange mechanism
Alternator
Oil filter and oil cooler
Oil sump, oil pump, oil strainer and pressure relief valve
Starter motor
Starter clutch
Water pump

Operations requiring engine removal

It is necessary to remove the engine/transmission assembly from the frame to gain access to the following components.

Cylinder head
Cylinder block
Pistons and piston rings
Connecting rods and bearings
Crankshaft and bearings
Transmission shafts
Selector drum and forks

3 Engine wear assessment

1 Poor engine performance may be caused by leaking valves, incorrect valve clearances, a leaking head gasket, or worn pistons, piston rings or cylinders. A cylinder compression check will highlight these conditions and can also indicate the presence of excessive carbon deposits in the cylinder head, and a leakdown test (for which special equipment is needed – consult a Honda dealer) will pinpoint the actual cause(s) of the problem.

Cylinder compression check

Special tool: *A compression gauge is needed. You will have to use one with a threaded hose and 10 mm thread adaptor to fit the spark plug holes (use either the Honda gauge and adapter (pt. No. 07RMJ-MY50100) or an aftermarket version). Depending on the outcome of the initial test, a squirt-type oil can may also be needed.*

2 Start by making sure the valve clearances are correctly set (see Chapter 1). Also make sure the battery is well charged.
3 Run the engine until it is at normal operating temperature.
4 Remove the coils and spark plugs (see Chapter 1).
5 Reconnect the ignition switch and handlebar switch wiring connectors, and where fitted the immobiliser wiring connector.
6 Make sure the gauge hose/adapter threads are the same as the spark plug **(see illustration)**. Fit the gauge into the No. 1 cylinder spark plug hole.
7 With the ignition switch ON, the kill switch set to RUN, and the throttle held fully open, turn the engine over on the starter motor until the gauge reading has built up and stabilised **(see illustration)**.
8 Compare the reading on the gauge to the cylinder compression figure specified at the beginning of the Chapter. Repeat for the remaining cylinders.
9 If a reading is low, it could be due to a worn cylinder bore, piston or rings, failure of the head gasket, or worn valve seats. To determine which is the cause, pour a small quantity of engine oil into the spark plug hole to seal the rings, then repeat the compression test. If the figures are noticeably higher the cause is a worn cylinder, piston or rings. If there is no change the cause is a leaking head gasket or worn valve seats.
10 If the unlikely event that the reading is high there could be a build-up of carbon deposits in the combustion chamber. Remove the cylinder head and scrape all deposits off the pistons and the cylinder head (see Section 11).

Leak-down (cylinder leakage) test

11 A leak down or 'cylinder leakage' test is similar to a compression test in that it tells you

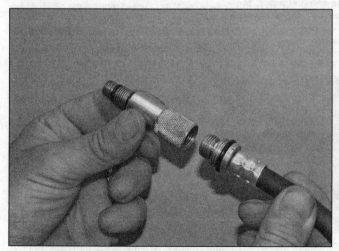

3.6 Fit a 10mm thread dia. adapter onto the gauge hose

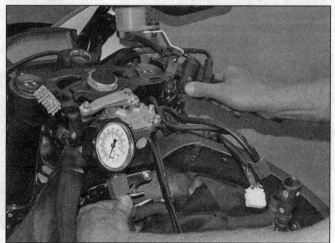

3.7 Checking cylinder compression

2•8 Engine, clutch and transmission

how well a cylinder is sealing, but it does so by testing how much pressure is lost through leakage, as opposed to how much pressure is created through compression. Many professionals prefer a leak test to a compression test as it more accurately pin-points the cause of the problem before any disassembly is done, as it is easy to tell where the leakage is occurring. Generally however the required equipment is more expensive than for a compression test and a source of compressed air is essential. If you think a test is needed take the bike to a suitably equipped dealer or workshop. If you decide to purchase your own equipment follow the manufacturer's instructions.

12 A leakage test can also be used in conjunction with a compression test to diagnose other kinds of problems, such as a faulty valve train component, incorrect valve timing, faulty ignition or fuel delivery problems.

Engine oil pressure check

Special tool: *An oil pressure gauge is required to perform this test.*

13 An oil pressure check can provide useful information about the condition of the engine's lubrication system, and can also be used as an indicator of excessive wear in the engine if no specific faults with the lubrication or pressure warning system are found..

14 The oil pressure warning light should come on when the ignition switch is turned ON and extinguish a few seconds after the engine is started. If the oil pressure light stays on, or comes on whilst the engine is running, low oil pressure is indicated – stop the engine immediately and carry out an oil level check (see *Pre-ride checks*). If the oil level is correct, remove the sump and check the oil pick-up strainer for a blockage (Section 17). Also check the drained oil for sludge, which reduces its ability to flow. Note that it is possible that the cause of the light staying on or coming on while the engine is running is an electrical fault, so make sure the oil pressure switch, warning light and circuit are all functioning correctly (see Chapter 8). If all appears good an oil pressure check must be carried out.

15 To check the oil pressure, a suitable gauge and adapter (which screws into the main oil gallery in place of the oil pressure switch) will be needed. Honda can provide a gauge and adapter (part Nos. 07506-3000001 and 07406-0030000) for this purpose, or one can be obtained commercially. You will also need some rags to catch and mop up any residual oil that gets lost in between removing the oil pressure switch and installing the gauge – place the bike on its sidestand so that the oil gathers at the other end of the gallery to reduce spillage.

16 Remove the lower fairing (see Chapter 7). Check the oil level (see *Pre-ride checks*).

17 Remove the oil pressure switch (see Chapter 8). Screw the gauge adapter in its place **(see illustration)**. Connect the oil pressure gauge to the adapter.

18 Warm the engine up to normal operating temperature, then briefly increase the engine speed to 6000 rpm whilst watching the gauge reading. The oil pressure should be similar to that given in the Specifications at the start of this Chapter.

19 If the pressure is significantly lower than the standard, or there is no pressure at all, and the pick-up strainer is clean, either the pressure relief valve is stuck open, the oil pump or its drive mechanism is faulty, the oil filter is blocked, or there is other engine damage causing an internal oil leak. Also make sure the correct grade oil is being used. Begin diagnosis by checking the oil filter (Chapter 1), strainer and relief valve (see Section 17), then the oil pump (Section 18). If those items check out okay, chances are the bearing oil clearances are excessive and the engine needs to be overhauled.

20 If the pressure is too high, either an oil passage is clogged, the relief valve is stuck closed or the wrong grade of oil is being used.

21 If the pressure is as it should be, and if not already done, then check the oil pressure switch, warning light and circuit (see Chapter 8).

22 Stop the engine and let it cool, then remove the gauge and adapter and install the oil pressure switch (see Chapter 8).

⚠ **Warning: Be careful when removing the pressure gauge adapter as the exhaust pipes, the engine and the oil itself can cause severe burns.**

23 Check the oil level (see *Pre-ride checks*).
24 Install the lower fairing (see Chapter 7).

4 Engine removal and installation

Caution: *The engine is very heavy. Engine removal and installation should be carried out with the aid of at least one assistant; personal injury or damage could occur if the engine falls or is dropped.*

Note 1: *A peg spanner is required to slacken and tighten the adjuster bolt locknut on the upper rear engine mounting bolt. If the Honda service tool (Part no. 07VMA-MBB0101) or an aftermarket peg spanner is not available, one will to fabricated out of a piece of steel tubing or an old 19 mm socket.*

Note 2: *If you are removing the engine for an overhaul it is best to remove the alternator, clutch, water pump, sump, oil strainer and oil pump, and to loosen the starter clutch bolt, with the engine still in the frame – refer to the relevant Sections in this Chapter, and to Chapter 3 for the water pump and Chapter 8 for the alternator.*

Removal

1 Support the bike upright using an auxiliary stand or stands that will not interfere with engine removal – a rear paddock stand is ideal. Make sure the bike is on level ground, and tie the front brake on. Work can be made easier by raising the machine to a suitable working height on an hydraulic ramp or a suitable platform. Make sure the motorcycle is secure and will not topple over (also see *Tools and Workshop Tips* in the Reference section).

2 Remove the lower fairing and fairing side panels (see Chapter 7).

3 If the engine is dirty, particularly around its mountings, wash it thoroughly. This will make work much easier and rule out the possibility of caked on lumps of dirt falling into some vital component.

4 Drain the engine oil and the coolant (see Chapter 1). If required remove the oil filter (see Chapter 1).

5 Disconnect the negative (–ve) lead from the battery (see Chapter 8).

6 Remove the radiator along with its hoses, noting their routing (see Chapter 3). Detach and remove any coolant hoses not already removed as required depending on what work is to be carried out, noting their positions and routing.

7 Remove the exhaust system (see Chapter 4).

8 On RA models remove the C-ABS front valve unit and front power unit (see Chapter 6).

9 On RR models remove the radiator bracket **(see illustration)**.

10 Remove the fuel tank, the air filter housing and the throttle bodies (see Chapter 4). Plug the engine intake manifolds with clean rag.

11 Disconnect the crankcase breather hose,

3.17 Select the correct adapter and fit it onto the gauge hose

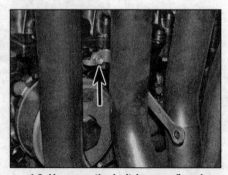

4.9 Unscrew the bolt (arrowed) and remove the bracket

Engine, clutch and transmission 2•9

4.11a Remove the crankcase breather hose...

4.11b ...unstick the sides of the heat shield...

4.11c ...and remove it

then unstick and remove the rubber heat shield **(see illustrations)**.

12 Disconnect the ignition coil and camshaft position (CMP) sensor wiring connectors **(see illustration)**. Remove the PAIR control valve along with the hoses (see Chapter 4).

13 Pull the rubber boot off the oil pressure switch, then undo the screw and detach the wiring connector **(see illustration)**. Release the wiring from its clamps.

14 Unscrew the bolt securing the clutch cable bracket to the clutch cover **(see illustration 14.2a)**. Displace the bracket, noting how it locates, and free the cable end from the release arm **(see illustration 14.2b)**. Position the cable clear of the engine.

15 Disconnect the alternator wiring connector, from the regulator/rectifier on RR models, and at the 3-pin wiring connector (3 yellow wires) on RA models **(see illustrations)**.

16 On US models disconnect the wiring connector and hoses from the EVAP system purge control solenoid valve.

17 Disconnect the crankshaft position (CKP) sensor (red 2-pin) wiring connector **(see illustration)**. Disconnect the speed sensor (black or blue 3-pin) wiring connector **(see illustration)**. Disconnect the sidestand switch (black 2-pin) wiring connector **(see illustration)**. Release the wiring from the engine as required and position it clear, noting its routing.

18 Remove the front sprocket (see Chapter

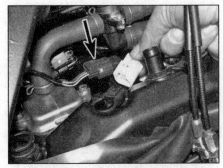
4.12 Disconnect the wiring connector from each coil and from the CMP sensor (arrowed)

4.13 Undo the screw (arrowed) and detach the wiring connector

4.15a Alternator wiring connector (arrowed) – RR models

4.15b Alternator wiring connector (arrowed) – RA models

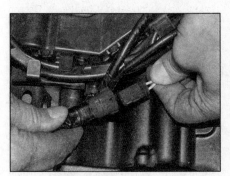
4.17a Disconnect the CKP sensor connector...

4.17b ...the speed sensor connector...

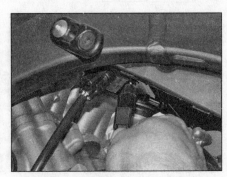
4.17c ...and the sidestand switch connector

2•10 Engine, clutch and transmission

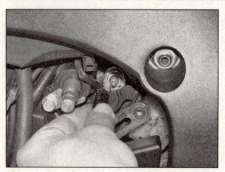

4.19a Pull the connector off the switch on 2008 to 2011 models

4.19b Disconnect the wiring connector on 2012-on models

4.20 Detach the leads (arrowed)

6). Slip the drive chain off the end of the output shaft and let it rest against the front of the swingarm.

19 On 2008 to 2011 models pull the wiring connector off the neutral switch **(see illustration)**. On 2012-on models disconnect the gear position switch (black 8-pin) wiring connector **(see illustration)**.

20 If required, remove the starter motor (see Chapter 8). If not unscrew the terminal nut and the rear mounting bolt and detach the leads **(see illustration)**.

21 Position an hydraulic or mechanical jack under the engine with a block of wood between the jack head and sump. Make sure the jack is centrally positioned so the engine will not topple in any direction when the last mounting bolt is removed. Raise the jack to take the weight of the engine, but make sure it is not lifting the bike and taking the weight of that as well. The idea is to support the engine so that there is no pressure on any of the mounting bolts once they have been slackened, so they can be easily withdrawn.

22 Unscrew the engine front mounting bolt on the right-hand side and remove the spacer on RR models or the C-ABS power unit bracket on RA models **(see illustration)**.

23 Unscrew the front mounting bolt on the left-hand side **(see illustration)**.

24 Counter-hold the right-hand end of the upper rear engine mounting bolt and unscrew the nut on the left-hand end **(see illustration)**.

25 Slacken the upper rear mounting adjuster locknut using a suitable peg spanner **(see illustration)**. The locknut can remain loose on the adjuster, or remove it if required **(see illustration)**. Turn the bolt head anti-clockwise using a hex bit to thread the adjuster back into the frame as far as it will go **(see illustration 4.36)**.

26 Counter-hold the right-hand end of the lower rear engine mounting bolt, unscrew the nut on the left-hand end and remove the washer **(see illustration)**.

27 Check that the engine is properly supported by the jack. Check that all wiring, cables and hoses are free and clear.

28 Hold the engine steady, then withdraw the upper and lower rear mounting bolts from

4.22 Unscrew the front right bolt and remove the spacer or bracket

4.23 Unscrew the front left bolt

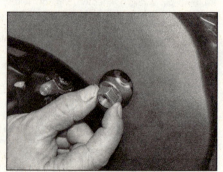

4.24 Unscrew the nut

4.25a Use a suitable peg spanner (here a 20mm aftermarket tool)...

4.25b ...to unscrew the locknut

4.26 Unscrew the nut

Engine, clutch and transmission 2•11

4.28a Withdraw the rear bolts...

4.28b ...and remove the engine

the right-hand side **(see illustration)**. The engine can now be removed from the frame (see *Caution* above). Lower the jack, and with the aid of assistants remove the jack from under the engine and remove the engine **(see illustration)**.

29 If required withdraw the lower rear mounting bolt collar and thread the adjuster out of the frame **(see illustrations)**.

Installation

30 If removed thread the adjuster into the inner side of the upper rear mounting on the right-hand side as far as it will go **(see illustration 4.29b)**. Fit the collar into the lower rear mount from the outside **(see illustration 4.29a)**.

31 Manoeuvre the engine into position under the frame and lift it onto the jack **(see illustration 4.28b)**. Raise the engine to align all the mounting bolt holes, making sure that all cables and wiring are correctly routed and do not get trapped. Note that it may be necessary to adjust the jack as some of the bolts are installed and tightened to realign the other bolt holes.

32 Slide the upper and lower rear mounting bolts through from the right-hand side **(see illustration 4.28a)**. Fit the washer and thread the nut onto the left-hand end of the lower bolt, leaving it loose **(see illustration 4.26)**.

33 Fit the head of the upper rear mounting bolt into the adjuster so they lock together **(see illustration)**. Thread the nut onto the left-hand end of the bolt, leaving it loose **(see illustration 4.24)**.

34 Thread the front mounting bolts in finger-tight, on the right-hand side not forgetting the spacer on RR models or the C-ABS power unit bracket on RA models **(see illustrations 4.23 and 4.22)**.

35 Turn the adjuster on the upper rear engine mount in by turning the mounting bolt using a hex key until the flange just contacts the engine. If removed, thread the locknut loosely onto the adjuster **(see illustration 4.25)**. Now tighten the adjuster to the torque setting specified at the beginning of the Chapter **(see illustration)**.

36 Tighten the locknut to the specified torque setting using the Honda special tool or the peg spanner (see *Note* above). If you do not have the Honda special tool, which allows the bolt head and adjuster to be counter-held while tightening the locknut, it is advisable to make a reference mark between them and the frame to make sure they do not turn as the locknut is being tightened **(see illustration)**. If you have the special tool, tighten the locknut

4.29a Withdraw the collar...

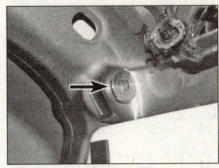
4.29b ...and remove the adjuster (arrowed) if required

4.33 Seat the flats on the head of the bolt between the tabs on the adjuster

4.35 Tighten the adjuster to the specified torque by turning the bolt head

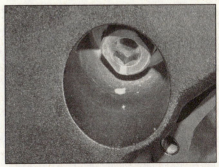
4.36 Make reference marks so you can check the bolt head/adjuster does not turn

2•12 Engine, clutch and transmission

to the 'indicated' torque setting, which allows for the extra leverage provided by the offset. If you are using a fabricated peg spanner tighten the locknut to the 'actual' specified torque setting.

37 Counter-hold the head of the lower rear bolt and tighten the nut on its left-hand end to the specified torque setting.

38 Counter-hold the head of the upper rear bolt and tighten the nut on its left-hand end to the specified torque setting.

39 On RA models push the stopper on the C-ABS power unit bracket against the engine.

40 Tighten the front bolt on each side to the specified torque.

41 The remainder of the installation procedure is the reverse of removal, noting the following points:
- On RA models refer to Chapter 6 for installation of the C-ABS valve unit and to fill and bleed the system.
- Use new gaskets on the exhaust pipe connections.
- Make sure all wires, cables and hoses are correctly routed and connected, and secured by any clips or ties.
- Refill the engine with oil and coolant (see Chapter 1).
- Adjust the throttle and clutch cable freeplay.
- Adjust the drive chain (see Chapter 1).
- Start the engine and check that there are no oil or coolant leaks.

5 Engine overhaul general information

1 Before beginning the engine overhaul, read through the related procedures to familiarise yourself with the scope and requirements of the job. Overhauling an engine is not all that difficult, but it is time consuming. Check on the availability of parts and make sure that any necessary special tools are obtained in advance.

2 Most work can be done with a decent set of typical workshop hand tools, although a number of precision measuring tools are required for inspecting parts to determine if they are worn.

3 To ensure maximum life and minimum trouble from a rebuilt engine, everything must be assembled with care in a spotlessly clean environment.

Disassembly

4 Before disassembling the engine, thoroughly clean and degrease its external surfaces. This will prevent contamination of the engine internals, and will also make the job a lot easier and cleaner. A high flash-point solvent, such as paraffin (kerosene) can be used, or better still, a proprietary engine degreaser such as Gunk. Use old paintbrushes and toothbrushes to work the solvent into the various recesses of the casings. Take care to exclude solvent or water from the electrical components and intake and exhaust ports.

 Warning: The use of petrol (gasoline) as a cleaning agent should be avoided because of the risk of fire.

5 When clean and dry, position the engine on the workbench, leaving suitable clear area for working. Gather a selection of small containers, plastic bags and some labels so that parts can be grouped together in an easily identifiable manner. Also get some paper and a pen so that notes can be taken. You will also need a supply of clean rag, which should be as absorbent as possible.

6 Before commencing work, read through the appropriate section so that some idea of the necessary procedure can be gained. When removing components note that great force is seldom required, unless specified (checking the specified torque setting of the particular bolt being removed will indicate how tight it is, and therefore how much force should be needed). In many cases, a component's reluctance to be removed is indicative of an incorrect approach or removal method – if in any doubt, re-check with the text.

7 When disassembling the engine, keep 'mated' parts that have been in contact with each other during engine operation together (i.e. pistons with their piston rings and connecting rods, valves with their followers, shims and other components, etc). These 'mated' parts must be reinstalled together and in their original location.

8 A complete engine/transmission disassembly should be done in the following general order with reference to the appropriate Sections.

Remove the valve cover
Remove the camshafts
Remove the cylinder head
Remove the starter motor (see Chapter 8)
Remove the starter clutch
Remove the cam chain and blades
Remove the clutch
Remove the gearchange mechanism
Remove the alternator (see Chapter 8)
Remove the oil sump
Remove the oil pump
Separate the crankcase halves
Remove the transmission shafts/selector drum and forks
Remove the crankshaft
Remove the connecting rods and pistons
Remove the cylinder block
Remove the balancer shaft

Reassembly

9 Reassembly is accomplished by reversing the general disassembly sequence.

6 Oil cooler

Removal

1 The cooler is located on the front of the engine next to the oil filter. Remove the lower fairing and fairing side panels (see Chapter 7).

2 Drain the engine oil and coolant (see Chapter 1).

3 The cooler can be removed with the exhaust system in place using a spanner on the bolt rather than a socket, but if you want to tighten the bolt to the correct torque using a torque wrench on installation you need to remove the exhaust system (see Chapter 4).

4 Slacken the clamp securing each hose to the cooler and detach the hoses **(see illustration)**.

5 Unscrew the bolt with its sealing washer and remove the cooler **(see illustration)**. Remove the sealing washer **(see illustration 6.7b)** – a new one must be used. Remove the O-ring from the back of the cooler **(see illustration 6.7a)** – a new one must be used.

6 Check the cooler body for cracks and dents and any evidence of coolant leakage and replace it with a new one if necessary. Also check the hoses for splits, cracks, hardening and deterioration and fit new ones if required.

Installation

7 Installation is the reverse of removal, noting the following:
- Ensure the mating surfaces of the crankcase and the cooler are clean and dry.
- Use a new O-ring on the cooler body and

6.4 Slacken the clamps (arrowed) and detach the hoses

6.5 Unscrew the bolt and remove the cooler

Engine, clutch and transmission 2•13

6.7a Fit a new O-ring into the groove

6.7b Use a new sealing washer

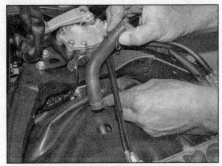
7.2a Remove the crankcase breather hose...

smear it with clean engine oil. Make sure it seats in its groove **(see illustration 6.7a)**.
- On 2008 to 2011 models seat the tabs on the cooler body on each side of the lug on the crankcase.
- On 2012-on models align the arrows on the cooler body with each side of the lug on the crankcase, and make sure they remain aligned while tightening the bolt **(see illustration 6.5)**.
- Use a new sealing washer and smear it with oil, and tighten the bolt to the torque setting specified at the beginning of the Chapter **(see illustration 6.7b)**.
- Make sure the coolant hoses are pressed fully onto their unions and are secured by the clamps **(see illustration 6.4)**.
- Fill the engine with oil to the correct level (see Chapter 1).
- Refill the cooling system (see Chapter 1).

7 Valve cover

Removal

1 Remove radiator (see Chapter 3).
2 Remove the air filter housing (see Chapter 4). Disconnect the crankcase breather hose, then unstick and remove the rubber heat shield **(see illustrations)**.
3 Unscrew the bolt securing the clutch cable bracket to the clutch cover **(see illustration 14.2a)**. Displace the bracket, noting how it locates, and free the cable end from the release arm **(see illustration 14.2b)**.
4 Disconnect the ignition coil and camshaft position (CMP) sensor wiring connectors

(see illustration 4.12). Remove the coils **(see illustration)**.
5 Remove the PAIR control valve along with the hoses (see Chapter 4).
6 Unscrew the four valve cover bolts, lift the cover off the cylinder head and remove it from the front **(see illustrations)**. If it is stuck, do not try to lever it off with a screwdriver. Tap it gently around the sides with a rubber hammer or block of wood to dislodge it. Note the rubber washers for the bolts and remove them if they are loose **(see illustration 7.13a)**.
7 The rubber gasket is normally glued into the groove in the cover, and is best left there if it is re-usable. If the gasket is in any way damaged, deformed or deteriorated, remove it **(see illustration 7.12a)**.
8 Note the four dowels that link the PAIR system air passages between the valve cover and cylinder head and remove them

7.2b ...unstick the sides of the heat shield...

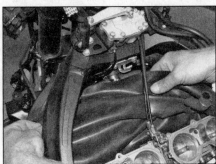
7.2c ...and pull it back

7.4 Remove the coils

7.6a Valve cover bolts (arrowed)

7.6b Lift the cover, moving the clutch cable aside...

7.6c ...and manoeuvre the cover out the front

2•14 Engine, clutch and transmission

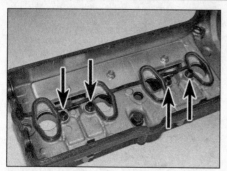

7.8 Remove the dowels (arrowed) if loose

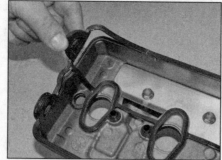

7.12a Make sure the gasket locates in the groove and over the dowels

7.12b Apply sealant to the cutouts in the cylinder head

7.13a Make sure the UP marks on the washers face up

7.13b Install the bolts and tighten them to the specified torque

for safekeeping if they are loose (which is unlikely), taking care not to drop them if they are not in the valve cover **(see illustration)**.

9 If required, remove the PAIR system reed valves (see Chapter 4).

Installation

10 If removed, install the PAIR system reed valves (see Chapter 4).

11 If removed, fit the PAIR system dowels into the valve cover **(see illustration 7.8)**.

12 Examine the valve cover gasket for signs of damage or deterioration and fit a new one if necessary. If a new one is used, clean all traces of the old glue from the groove in the cover and clean it and the cylinder head mating surface with solvent. Fit the new gasket into the perimeter groove and around the plug bores and over the dowels, using a suitable glue, sealant or grease to hold it in place **(see illustration)**. Also apply a suitable sealant to the cut-outs in the cylinder head **(see illustration)**.

13 If removed, fit the rubber washers into the cover, using new ones if required, and making sure the UP marks face up **(see illustration)**. Position the valve cover on the cylinder head, making sure the gasket stays in place **(see illustration 7.6c and b)**. Fit the cover bolts and tighten them to the torque setting specified at the beginning of the Chapter **(see illustration)**.

14 Install the remaining components in the reverse order of removal.

8 Cam chain tensioner

Removal

1 Remove the fairing side panels (see Chapter 7). Remove the fuel tank (see Chapter 4).

2 Unscrew the tensioner cap bolt and remove the sealing washer **(see illustration)**.

3 If the Honda tensioner holding tool (Part no. 070MG-0010100 in the UK or 07AMG-MFJA100 in the US) is available, undo the grub screw and remove the end piece from it. Fit the tool onto the end of the tensioner and turn it clockwise until the plunger is fully retracted, then refit the end piece and tighten the grub screw to lock the tensioner **(see illustration)**. Unscrew the tensioner mounting bolts, then withdraw the tensioner from the engine **(see illustration 8.2)**.

4 If the holding tool is not available, first

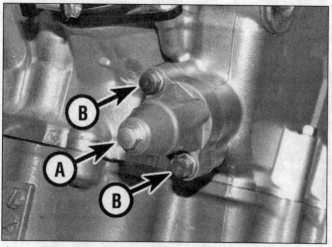

8.2 Tensioner cap bolt (A) and mounting bolts (B)

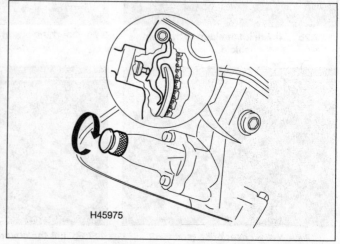

8.3 Using the Honda tool to retract the tensioner plunger

Engine, clutch and transmission 2•15

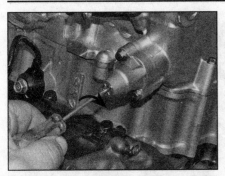

8.4a Insert the screwdriver and retract the plunger...

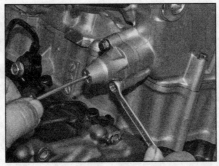

8.4b ...then unscrew the mounting bolts

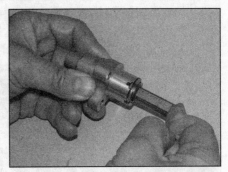

8.6 The plunger must not move in when pushed

slacken the tensioner mounting bolts slightly **(see illustration 8.2)**. Insert a small flat-bladed screwdriver in the end of the tensioner so that it engages the slotted plunger and turn it clockwise until the plunger is fully retracted **(see illustration)**. Hold it in this position while unscrewing the tensioner mounting bolts **(see illustration)**. Remove the bolts, then withdraw the tensioner from the engine and release the screwdriver **(see illustration 8.9b)** – the plunger will spring back out once the screwdriver is removed, but can be easily reset on installation.

5 Discard the gasket and sealing washer – new ones must be used on installation. Do not attempt to dismantle the tensioner.

Inspection

6 Check that the plunger cannot be pushed into the body **(see illustration)** – if it can, fit a new tensioner. Check that the plunger moves smoothly when wound into the tensioner and springs back out freely when released **(see illustration 8.9a)**.

Installation

7 Make sure the tensioner and cylinder block surfaces are clean and dry. Fit a new gasket onto the tensioner body **(see illustration)**.
8 If the Honda holding tool is being used and has been removed, fit it onto the end of the tensioner as before and turn it clockwise until the plunger is fully retracted and held **(see illustration 8.3)**. Fit the tensioner with its mounting bolts and tighten them **(see illustration 8.9b)**. Remove the tool, then fit the tensioner cap bolt with a new sealing washer and tighten it **(see illustration 8.2)**.
9 If the tool is not available, insert a small flat-bladed screwdriver in the end of the tensioner so that it engages the slotted plunger and turn it clockwise until the plunger is fully retracted **(see illustration)**. Hold it in this position, then fit the tensioner with its mounting bolts and tighten them **(see illustration)**. Release and remove the screwdriver. Fit the tensioner cap bolt with a new sealing washer and tighten it **(see illustration)**.
10 If the engine is rotated with the tensioner removed, such as when checking the valve clearances, always remove the valve cover and check the valve timing afterwards just in case the untensioned cam chain has moved on its sprockets.
11 Install the fuel tank and fairing side panels (see Chapters 4 and 7).

9 Camshafts and followers

Note: *Place clean rags over the spark plug holes and the cam chain tunnel to prevent any component from dropping into the engine.*

Removal

1 Remove the spark plugs (see Chapter 1). Remove the valve cover (see Section 7).
2 Unscrew the timing inspection cap from the clutch cover **(see illustration)**. Check the condition of its O-ring and obtain a new one if necessary.
3 The crankshaft must be turned so that the

8.7 Fit a new gasket

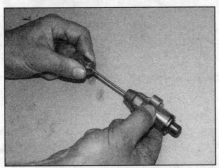

8.9a Insert the screwdriver and retract the plunger...

8.9b ...then install the tensioner

8.9c Use a new sealing washer on the cap bolt

9.2 Remove the timing inspection cap

2•16 Engine, clutch and transmission

9.3a Turn the engine clockwise using the bolt...

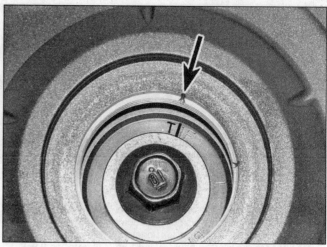

9.3b ...until the line next to the T mark aligns with the notch (arrowed)...

9.3c ...and the camshaft sprocket marks (circled) are as shown...

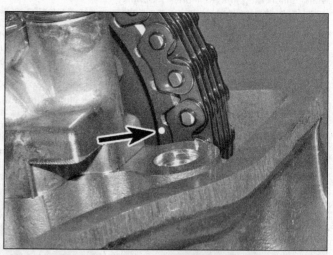

9.3d ...the punch mark (arrowed) on the inner face of the intake sprocket is easier to see

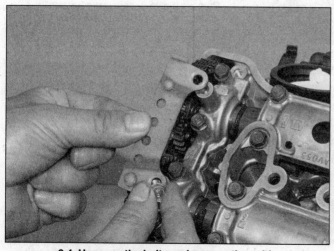

9.4 Unscrew the bolts and remove the guide

9.5a Make some alignment marks (circled) on the end of each camshaft

Engine, clutch and transmission 2•17

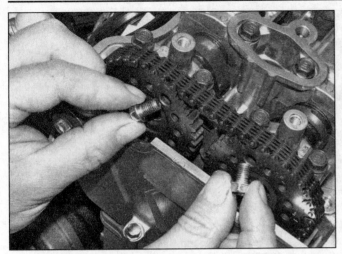

9.5b Unscrew the sprocket bolts as described...

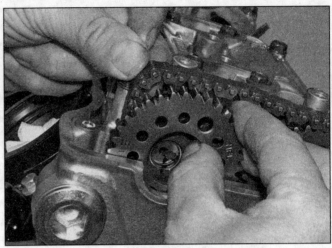

9.5c ...and remove the sprockets

No. 1 piston is at TDC (top dead centre) on its compression stroke. Turn the crankshaft in a clockwise direction only using a suitable spanner or socket on the starter clutch bolt until the line next to the T mark on the timing rotor aligns with the static timing mark, which is a notch in the inspection hole rim, and the IN and EX marks on the outer faces of the intake and exhaust camshaft sprockets respectively are facing away from each other and are flush with the cylinder head top surface **(see illustrations)**. Use a mirror if the marks are difficult to see with the engine in the frame, or use the punch mark on the inner face of the intake camshaft sprocket instead of the IN mark on the outer face **(see illustration)**. If the marks are facing towards each other or if the punch mark is to the front, turn the crankshaft clockwise one full turn (360°) until the line next to the T mark again aligns with the static timing mark. The sprocket marks will now be as required.

4 Either remove the cam chain tensioner (see Section 8), or if you have the tensioner holding tool as described in Section 8, Step 3, retract and lock the tensioner plunger. Unscrew the bolts securing the top cam chain guide and remove it **(see illustration)**.

5 The camshaft sprockets are identical and are therefore interchangeable, and must be removed from the camshafts, so mark them according to the camshaft they fit on. Also make alignment marks on each camshaft parallel with the cylinder head top surface so that they are easy to align correctly first go on installation **(see illustration)**. Now turn the crankshaft clockwise one full turn (360°) until the line next to the T mark again aligns with the static timing mark. Unscrew the exposed sprocket bolts **(see illustration)**. Turn the crankshaft clockwise one full turn (360°) until the line next to the T mark again aligns with the static timing mark, thereby returning the No. 1 piston to TDC on its compression stroke. Unscrew the remaining sprocket bolts, take the sprockets off the camshafts and disengage them from the chain, then lay the chain across the ends of the camshafts **(see illustration)**.

6 There are three camshaft holders, each bridging both camshafts **(see illustration)**. Of the two larger holders, the one on the right-hand end is marked R and the one on the left-hand end L, and these letters are at the back **(see illustration)**. Note the numbers marked on the holders, adjacent to each bolt. These numbers denote the **tightening** sequence for the holder bolts.

7 Unscrew the camshaft holder bolts, slackening them evenly and a very little at a time in a **reverse** of the tightening sequence marked on the holders. Remove the bolts, noting which fits where as there are different lengths, and lift off the holders, noting how

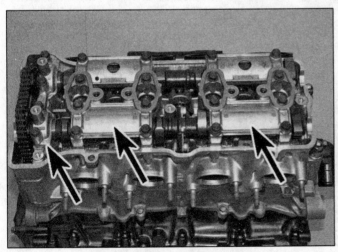

9.6a Camshaft holders (arrowed)

9.6b Note the ID letter and the bolt numbers on each holder

2•18 Engine, clutch and transmission

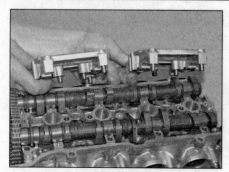

9.7a Unscrew the bolts as described and remove the holders

9.7b Remove the sealing rings and discard them

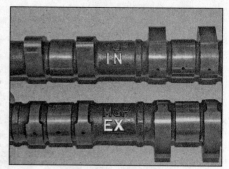

9.8 Note the identification mark on each camshaft

they fit **(see illustration)**. Note the sealing washers fitted with the eight bolts around the spark plug bores **(see illustration 9.29b)**. Remove the sealing rings from their grooves around the spark plug holes on the underside of the holders, noting how they also locate around the PAIR system air passage dowels **(see illustration)**. Discard them as new ones must be used. Note the positions of the locating dowels – do not remove any of the dowels unless they are loose and liable to drop out.

Caution: Make sure the holders lift up squarely and evenly and do not stick on a dowel or distort from some of the bolts being slackened more than the others as they or a camshaft could easily break.

8 Hold the cam chain up and carefully lift each camshaft off the head **(see illustrations 9.28 and 9.27)**. Secure the chain using wire or a rod of some sort to prevent it from dropping down the tunnel. The camshafts are marked for identification – the intake camshaft is marked IN and the exhaust camshaft is marked EX **(see illustration)**. If the marks aren't clear make your own as the camshafts must be installed in their original location.

9 While the camshafts are out do not rotate the crankshaft unless you are holding the chain taut, otherwise it could bind between the crankshaft and case, which could damage these components. Place rag over the spark plug holes and the cam chain tunnel to prevent anything from dropping into the engine.

10 If the followers and shims are being removed from the cylinder head, obtain a container which is divided into sixteen compartments, and label each compartment with the location of a valve, i.e. intake or exhaust camshaft, left or right valve. If a container is not available, use labelled plastic bags (egg cartons also do very well!). Remove the cam follower of the valve in question using a magnet or the suction created by a valve lapping tool, or long nosed pliers can be used with care **(see illustration)**. Remove the shim from inside the follower or pick it out of the top of the valve spring retainer using either a magnet, a screwdriver with a dab of grease on it (the shim will stick to the grease), or a very small screwdriver and a pair of pliers **(see illustrations)**. Do not allow the shim to fall into the engine.

11 Note the alignment and fitting of the camshaft position (CMP) sensor rotor on the exhaust camshaft and remove it if required – it is secured by two bolts **(see illustration)**.

Inspection

12 Inspect the bearing surfaces of the camshaft holders and cylinder head and the corresponding journals on the camshafts **(see illustration)**. Look for score marks, deep scratches and evidence of spalling (a pitted appearance). Check the oil passages for clogging.

13 Check the camshaft lobes for heat discoloration (blue appearance), score marks, chipped areas, flat spots and spalling. Measure the height of each lobe with a

9.10a Carefully lift out the follower using a lapping tool, grips or a magnet...

9.10b ...and retrieve the shim from inside it...

9.10c ...or from the top of the valve

9.11 CMP sensor rotor bolts (arrowed)

9.12 Check all related bearing surfaces

Engine, clutch and transmission 2•19

9.13 Measure the height of the camshaft lobes with a micrometer

9.22a Measure the external diameter of each follower...

9.22b ...and the internal diameter of each bore

micrometer **(see illustration)** and compare the results to the minimum height listed in this Chapter's Specifications. If damage is noted or wear is excessive, the camshaft must be replaced with a new one.

14 Check the amount of camshaft runout by supporting each end on V-blocks, and measuring any runout using a dial gauge. If the runout exceeds the specified limit the camshaft must be replaced with a new one.

> **HAYNES HiNT** *Refer to Tools and Workshop Tips in the Reference section for details of how to read a micrometer and dial gauge.*

15 Next, check the camshaft journal oil clearances. In order to negate the probability of the camshafts rotating (due to the fact that some of the lobes will be depressing their valves) as the holder bolts are tightened down, which will disturb the Plastigauge and lead to a false measurement, the cylinder head should be removed and the valves removed from it (see Sections 11 and 12). Clean the camshafts and the bearing surfaces in the cylinder head and camshaft holder with a clean lint-free cloth, then lay each camshaft in its correct location in the head (see Step 8).

16 Cut some strips of Plastigauge and lay one piece on each journal, parallel with the camshaft centreline. Make sure the camshaft holder dowels are installed. If the valves are installed, fit the holders and tighten the bolts as described in Step 29. If the valves have been removed, fit the holders as described in Step 29 and tighten the bolts evenly and a little at a time in a criss-cross sequence to the specified torque setting, making sure the holders are pulled down squarely onto the dowels. While doing this, don't let the camshafts rotate, or the Plastigauge will be disturbed and you will have to start again.

17 Now unscrew the camshaft holder bolts as described in Step 7 (valves installed) or evenly and a little at a time in a criss-cross sequence (valves removed), and lift off the holder.

18 To determine the oil clearance, compare the crushed Plastigauge (at its widest point) on each journal to the scale printed on the Plastigauge container. Compare the results to this Chapter's Specifications. If the oil clearance is greater than specified, replace the camshaft with a new one and recheck the clearance. If the clearance is still too great, also replace the cylinder head and holder with new ones.

> **HAYNES HiNT** *Before replacing the camshafts, cylinder head or holders because of damage, check with motorcycle cylinder head specialists to see whether worn components can be renewed. Due to the cost of new components it is recommended that all options be explored before condemning them as trash!*

19 Except in cases of oil starvation, the cam chain should wear very little. If the chain has stretched excessively, which makes it difficult to maintain proper tension, or if it is stiff or the links are binding or kinking, replace it with a new one. Refer to Section 10 for replacement.

20 Check the sprockets for wear, cracks and other damage, and replace them with new ones if necessary. If the sprockets are worn, the cam chain is also worn, and so probably is the sprocket on the crankshaft. If severe wear is apparent, the entire engine should be disassembled for inspection.

21 Inspect the cam chain guides and tensioner blade (see Section 10).

22 Inspect the outer surface of each cam follower for evidence of scoring or other damage. If a follower is in poor condition, it is probable that the bore in the cylinder head in which it works is also damaged. Check for clearance between each follower and its bore. Measure the outer diameter of each follower and the inner diameter of its bore and compare the results to the Specifications **(see illustrations)**. If any follower is worn beyond its service limit replace it with a new one. If any bore is worn beyond its limit, is seriously out-of-round or tapered, replace the cylinder head with a new one.

Installation

23 If removed, fit the CMP sensor rotor onto the exhaust camshaft with the LEFT SIDE mark facing the left-hand end of the camshaft **(see illustration 9.11)**. Clean the threads of the bolts, apply a suitable non-permanent thread locking compound and tighten them to the torque setting specified at the beginning of the Chapter.

24 If removed, lubricate each shim and its follower with molybdenum disulphide oil (a 50/50 mixture of molybdenum disulphide grease and engine oil). Fit each shim into its recess in the top of the valve spring retainer with the size mark facing up, making sure it is correctly seated **(see illustration)**. **Note:** *It is most important that the shims and followers are returned to their original valves otherwise the valve clearances will be inaccurate.* Fit each follower, making sure it slides squarely in its bore **(see illustration)**.

9.24a Fit each shim into its recess...

9.24b ...then fit the follower onto the valve

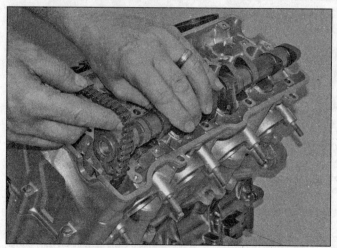
9.27 Seat the exhaust camshaft...

9.28 ...then seat the intake camshaft, aligning them as described

9.29a Fit the longer bolts where the dowels are positioned

9.29b Fit new sealing washers with the spark plug bore bolts

25 Make sure the bearing surfaces on the camshafts and in the cylinder head are clean, then apply molybdenum disulphide oil (a 50/50 mixture of molybdenum disulphide grease and engine oil) to each of them. Also apply it to the camshaft journals and lobes. Make sure that none gets on the mating surfaces between the holder and the head, or in the bolt holes.

26 Check that the line next to the T mark on the timing rotor aligns with the notch in the inspection hole rim **(see illustration 9.3b)**.

27 Lift the cam chain and lay the exhaust camshaft (marked EX) onto the head with the No. 1 cylinder lobes facing forwards **(see illustration)**.

28 Lift the cam chain and lay the intake camshaft (marked IN) onto the head with the No. 1 cylinder lobes facing backwards **(see illustration)**. Now turn each shaft so the alignment marks you made on the end on removal are parallel with the head **(see illustration 9.5a)**.

29 Make sure the bearing surfaces in the camshaft holders are clean. Make sure the camshaft holder bolt dowels and PAIR system air passage dowels are installed. Fit new sealing rings into the grooves around the spark plug holes on the underside of the main holders, making sure they also locate around the PAIR system air passage dowels **(see illustration 9.7b)**. Apply molybdenum disulphide oil (a 50/50 mixture of molybdenum disulphide grease and engine oil) to the bearing surfaces. Lay the holders in the head making sure they are correctly positioned (see Step 6) **(see illustration 9.7a)**. Apply clean engine oil to the threads and under the heads of all the camshaft holder bolts. Fit the bolts, fitting the six longer bolts where the dowels are fitted, and not forgetting new sealing washers with the eight bolts around the spark plug bores, and tighten them finger-tight **(see illustrations)**. First gradually and evenly tighten the bolts until the holders contact the head, making sure they are drawn down squarely and the dowels all locate. Now tighten all the bolts evenly and a little at a time in the correct sequence (i.e. 1 to 20), and to the torque setting specified at the beginning of the Chapter. Check that the marks you made on the ends of the camshafts are parallel with the cylinder head top surface – no provision is made for turning the camshafts so if they are not correctly aligned you will have to turn them as required after fitting the sprocket and engaging the chain by turning the crankshaft, then you have to remove the sprocket again and realign the crankshaft.

Caution: Whilst tightening the bolts, make sure the holders are being pulled evenly and squarely down and are not binding on the dowels or tilting to one side – if they do, adjust the relevant bolts until the holders are again square to the head. A holder or camshaft is likely to break if they are not tightened down evenly and squarely.

30 Clean the threads of the camshaft sprocket bolts. Lift the cam chain off the exhaust camshaft and fit the sprocket with the EX mark facing out and forward and level with the cylinder head top mating surface

Engine, clutch and transmission

9.30a Fit the sprocket onto the exhaust camshaft...

9.30b ...and secure it with one bolt...

9.30c ...then fit the intake sprocket

9.31 Apply threadlock to the sprocket bolts

and aligned with the marks you made on the end of the camshaft, and fit the cam chain around the sprocket, pulling up on the chain to remove all slack in the front run between the crankshaft and the camshaft **(see illustration)**. Check that the exposed bolt holes are aligned, then fit the bolt and tighten it finger-tight **(see illustration)**. Now fit the intake camshaft sprocket with the IN mark on the sprocket facing back and level with the cylinder head top mating surface and aligned with the marks you made on the end of the camshaft, and fit the cam chain around the sprocket, pulling on it to remove all slack from between the two camshaft sprockets **(see illustration)**. Any slack in the chain must lie in the rear run of the chain between the intake camshaft and the crankshaft so that it is later taken up by the tensioner. Check that the exposed bolt holes are aligned, then fit the bolt and tighten it finger-tight. At this point check that all the timing marks are still in **exact** alignment as described in Step 3 **(see illustrations 9.3b and c)**. Note that it is easy to be slightly out (one tooth on the sprocket) without the marks appearing drastically out of alignment. If the marks are out, you will have to work out what is misaligned with what then make the necessary adjustment(s) to the relative position(s) of the camshaft(s) and/or crankshaft by turning the crankshaft with the chain engaged with the camshaft(s) to align the camshaft then disengaged to realign the crankshaft.

31 With everything correctly aligned, remove the two fitted sprocket bolts, apply a suitable non-permanent thread locking compound, refit them and tighten them to the torque setting specified at the beginning of the Chapter while counter-holding the crankshaft. Now turn the crankshaft clockwise one full turn (360°) until the line next to the T mark again aligns with the static timing mark. Apply thread locking compound to the remaining sprocket bolts and tighten them to the specified torque **(see illustration)**. Turn the crankshaft clockwise one full turn (360°) until the line next to the T mark again aligns with the static timing mark, thereby returning the No. 1 piston to TDC on its compression stroke. Check again that all the timing marks align correctly (see Step 3) **(see illustrations 9.3a, b and c)**.

Caution: If the marks are not aligned exactly as described, the valve timing will be incorrect and the valves may strike the pistons, causing extensive damage to the engine.

32 If the tensioner tool was used to retract and hold the tensioner plunger, remove it to release the plunger. If the tensioner was removed, install it (see Section 8). Turn the engine clockwise through two full turns and check again that all the timing marks align correctly (see Step 3) **(see illustrations 9.3a, b and c)**.

33 Fit the cam chain top guide and tighten its bolts **(see illustration 9.4)**.

34 Check the valve clearances and adjust them if necessary (see Chapter 1).

35 Fit the timing inspection cap using a new O-ring if required, and smear the O-ring with oil and the cap threads with grease (see

2•22 Engine, clutch and transmission

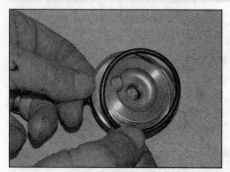

9.35 Fit the cap O-ring and smear it and the threads with grease

illustration). Tighten the cap to the torque setting specified at the beginning of the Chapter.

36 Install the valve cover (see Section 7). Install the spark plugs (see Chapter 1).

10 Cam chain, tensioner blades and front guide

Removal

1 Remove the camshafts – this procedure involves removing the top guide (see Section 9).
2 Remove the starter clutch (see Section 13).
3 Unscrew the lower tensioner blade pivot bolt and draw the blade out of the engine **(see illustrations)**. Remove the collar from the inner side of the blade pivot **(see illustration)**.
4 Unscrew the front guide blade pivot bolt with its washer and draw the blade out of the top of the engine **(see illustrations)**. Remove the collar from the inner side of the blade pivot **(see illustration)**.
5 Draw the cam chain off the crankshaft sprocket and out of the engine **(see illustration)**. If required, slide the sprocket off the end of the crankshaft, noting the offset wide splines that mean it can only be installed in one position **(see illustration)**.
6 Unscrew the upper tensioner blade pivot bolt and draw the blade out of the top of the engine **(see illustration)**. Discard the sealing washer and fit a new one on installation.

Inspection

Cam chain

7 Check the chain for binding, kinks and any obvious damage and replace it with a new one if necessary. Check the camshaft and crankshaft sprocket teeth for wear and replace the cam chain, camshaft sprockets and crankshaft with a new set if necessary.

Tensioner and guide blades

8 Check the sliding surface and edges of

10.3a Unscrew the pivot bolt...

10.3b ...and draw the blade out the bottom

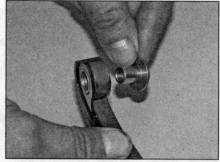

10.3c Note the collar in the back of the pivot

10.4a Unscrew the pivot bolt...

10.4b ...and draw the blade out the top

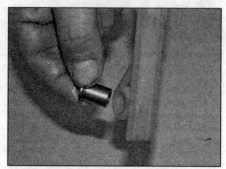

10.4c Note the collar in the back of the pivot

10.5a Remove the cam chain...

10.5b ...then slide the sprocket off the shaft

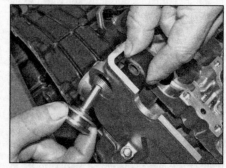

10.6 Unscrew the bolt and remove the upper tensioner blade

Engine, clutch and transmission 2•23

10.9 Make sure the lower blade sits in front of the upper blade

the blades for excessive wear, deep grooves, cracking and other obvious damage, and replace them with new ones if necessary.

Installation

9 Installation of the sprocket, chain and blades is the reverse of removal. Make sure the top of the lower tensioner blade sits to the front of the upper tensioner blade **(see illustration)**. Use a new sealing washer on the upper tensioner blade bolt **(see illustration 10.6)**. Do not omit the collars that fit in the lower tensioner blade and front guide blade pivots **(see illustration 10.4c and 10.3c)**. Clean the threads of the lower tensioner blade and front guide blade bolts and apply a suitable non-permanent thread locking compound, and tighten all bolts to the torque settings specified at the beginning of the Chapter.

11 Cylinder head removal and installation

Removal

1 Remove the engine from the frame (see Section 4).
2 Remove the thermostat housing (see Chapter 3). Either release the knock sensor connector from the bracket, or unscrew the bolt and displace the bracket **(see illustration)**.
3 Remove the camshafts, followers and shims (see Section 9). If not already done (i.e. if the holding tool was used when removing the camshafts) remove the cam chain tensioner (see Section 8).
4 The cylinder head is secured by two 6 mm bolts and ten 9 mm nuts with washers. First unscrew and remove the 6 mm bolts **(see illustration)**. Now unscrew and remove the 9 mm nuts and washers, slackening them evenly and a little at a time in a criss-cross pattern working from the outside to the middle until they are all loose **(see illustration)**.
5 Hold the cam chain up and pull the head up off the block, then pass the cam chain down through the tunnel **(see illustration)**. Do not let the chain fall into the crankcase – secure it with a piece of wire or metal bar to prevent it from doing so. If the head is stuck, tap around the joint faces with a soft-faced mallet. Do not attempt to free the head by inserting a screwdriver between the head and block

mating surfaces – you'll damage them.
6 Remove the gasket and discard it – a new one must be used. If they are loose, remove the dowels from the cylinder block or the underside of the head **(see illustration 11.12)**.
7 If required remove the throttle body ducts from the head – they come as two pairs, each secured by three bolts. Remove the O-rings – new ones must be used.
8 Check the head gasket and the mating surfaces on the cylinder head and block for signs of leakage, which could indicate warpage. Refer to Section 12 and check the cylinder head gasket surface for warpage.
9 Clean all traces of old gasket material from the head and block. If a scraper is used, take care not to scratch or gouge the soft aluminium. Be careful not to let any of the gasket material fall into the crankcase, the cylinder bores or the oil and coolant passages.

Installation

10 If removed fit the throttle body ducts using new O-rings and tighten the bolts to the torque setting specified at the beginning of the Chapter.
11 Ensure both cylinder head and block mating surfaces are clean. If removed, fit the dowels **(see illustration 11.12)**.
12 Lay the new head gasket over the cam chain and blades and onto the block, locating it over the dowels and making sure all the holes are correctly aligned **(see illustration)**. Never re-use the old gasket.

11.2 Either release the connector or unscrew the bolt (arrowed)

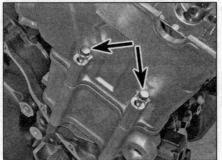

11.4a Cylinder head 6 mm bolts (arrowed)

11.4b Unscrew the nuts and remove the washers...

11.4c ...the nuts (arrowed) on the left-hand end are domed

11.5 Carefully lift the head up off the block

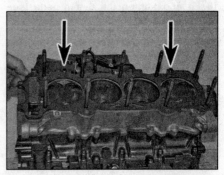

11.12 Fit the dowels (arrowed) then lay the new gasket on the block

2•24 Engine, clutch and transmission

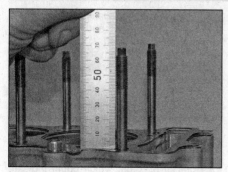

11.13 Measure the height of each stud

13 Measure the height of each stud bolt head above the upper surface of the cylinder head gasket (see illustration) – the two studs on the left-hand end must be 71.5 to 73.5 mm, the three centre studs along the front and the four studs along the back 68.0 to 70.0 mm, and the front stud on the right 73.5 to 75.5 mm. If any are higher than they should be tighten them down to the correct height using the hex on the top.

14 Carefully fit the cylinder head onto the block, making sure it locates correctly onto the dowels and that if not removed the upper tensioner blade sits to the rear of the lower blade (see illustration 11.5). Feed the cam chain up through the tunnel as you fit the head, then secure it in place with a piece of wire to prevent it from falling back down.

15 Apply some engine oil to the stud threads and both sides of the washers. Fit the washers and nuts (domed nuts on the left-hand end) and tighten them all finger-tight (see illustrations 11.4b and c). Tighten the nuts evenly and a little at a time in a criss-cross pattern working from the middle to the outside to the torque setting specified at the beginning of the Chapter. Go round all the bolts again in the same sequence to the same torque. Now tighten each nut in the same sequence through 135° using a degree disc (see illustration 19.17c). Next loosen the nuts evenly and a little at a time in a criss-cross pattern working from the outside to the middle until they are all loose, and remove them. Tighten each stud bolt to the specified torque setting using the hex on the top. Refit each nut and repeat the tightening procedure as described first to the torque setting and then through 135°.

16 Fit and tighten the 6 mm bolts (see illustration 11.4a).

17 Install the remaining components in a reverse of their removal sequence, referring to the relevant Sections or Chapters (see Steps 3 to 1).

12 Cylinder head and valve overhaul

1 Because of the complex nature of this job and the special tools and equipment required, most owners leave servicing of the valves, valve seats and valve guides to a professional.

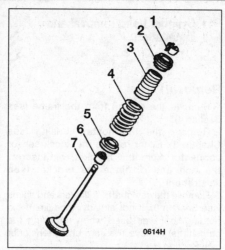

12.5 Valve components (intake valve with two springs shown)

1 Collets
2 Spring retainer
3 Inner valve spring (intake only)
4 Outer valve spring
5 Spring seat
6 Valve stem oil seal
7 Valve

However, you can make an initial assessment of whether the valves are seating correctly, and therefore sealing, by pouring a small amount of solvent into each of the valve ports. If the solvent leaks past any valve into the combustion chamber area the valve is not seating correctly and sealing.

2 With the correct tools (a valve spring compressor is essential – make sure it is suitable for motorcycle work), you can also remove the valves and associated components from the cylinder head, clean them and check them for wear to assess the extent of the work needed, and, unless seat cutting or guide replacement is required, reassemble them in the head.

3 A dealer service department or specialist can replace the guides and re-cut the valve seats. Make sure that anyone working on the valves knows that the intake valves are made of titanium and have a thin oxide coating that will be damaged if they are ground in (lapped) – it is ok to grind in (lap) the exhaust valves after re-cutting their seats.

4 After the valve service has been performed,

12.6a Compressing the valve springs using a valve spring compressor

> There is a quick way of removing valve components that avoids having to use a spring compressor: select a socket that seats on the valve retainer and give it a sharp tap with a soft hammer – this compresses the spring without moving the valve itself and unseats the collets. Note that a valve spring compressor has to be used when refitting the valve assembly.

be sure to clean the head thoroughly before installation to remove any metal particles or abrasive grit that may still be present from the valve service operations. Use compressed air, if available, to blow out all the holes and passages.

Disassembly

5 Before proceeding, arrange to label and store the valves along with their related components in such a way that they can be returned to their original locations without getting mixed up (see illustration). Each intake valve has two springs, and each exhaust valve has one. Either use the same container as the cam followers and shims are stored in (see Section 9), or obtain a separate container and label each compartment accordingly. Alternatively, labelled plastic bags will do just as well.

6 Compress the valve spring(s) on the first valve with a spring compressor, making sure it is correctly located onto each end of the valve assembly (see illustration). On the top of the valve the adaptor needs to be about the same size as the spring retainer – if it is too big it will contact the follower bore and mark it, and if it is too small it will be difficult to remove and install the collets (see illustration). On

12.6b Make sure the compressor locates correctly both on the top of the spring retainer...

Engine, clutch and transmission 2•25

12.6c ...and on the bottom of the valve

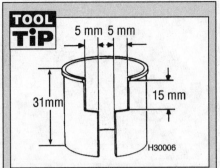

Protect the follower bore in the cylinder head from scratches by the valve spring compressor using either the Honda tool (Part No. 07HMG-MR70002) or by fabricating a shield from an old 35 mm film canister. Cut the canister to the dimensions shown.

12.7a Remove the collets...

the underside of the head make sure the plate on the compressor only contacts the valve and not the soft aluminium of the head (see illustration) – if the plate is too big for the valve, use a spacer between them. Do not compress the springs more than is necessary to release the collets.

7 Remove the collets, using a magnet or a screwdriver with a dab of grease on it (see illustration). Carefully release the valve spring compressor and remove the spring retainer, noting which way up it fits, the spring(s) and the valve (see illustrations) – each intake valve has two springs, each exhaust valve one spring. If the valve binds in the guide and won't pull through, push it back into the head and deburr the area around the collet groove with a very fine file or whetstone (see illustration).

8 Pull the valve stem seal off the top of the valve guide with pliers and discard it (the old seals should never be re-used), then remove the spring seat noting which way up, it fits – using a magnet is the easiest way to remove the seat from the head (see illustrations).

9 Repeat the procedure for the remaining valves. Remember to keep the parts for each valve together so they can be reinstalled in the same location.

10 Clean the cylinder head with solvent and dry it thoroughly. Compressed air will speed the drying process and ensure that all holes and recessed areas are clean. **Note:** *Do not use a wire brush mounted in a drill motor to clean the combustion chambers as the head material is soft and may be scratched or eroded away by the wire brush.*

11 Clean all of the valve springs, collets, retainers and spring seats with solvent and dry them thoroughly. Do the parts from one valve at a time so that no mixing of parts between valves occurs.

12 Scrape off any deposits that may have formed on the valve, then use a motorised wire brush to remove deposits from the valve heads and stems. Again, make sure the valves do not get mixed up.

Inspection

13 Inspect the head very carefully for cracks and other damage. If cracks are found, a new head is required. Check the camshaft bearing surfaces for wear and evidence of seizure.

12.7b ...the spring retainer...

12.7c ...the spring(s)...

12.7d ...and the valve

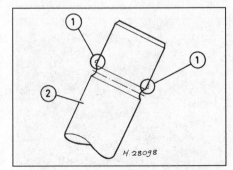

12.7e If the valve stem (2) won't pull through the guide, deburr the area (1) above the collet groove

12.8a Pull the seal off the valve stem...

12.8b ...then remove the spring seat

2•26 Engine, clutch and transmission

12.15 Measure the valve seat width

12.16a Measure the valve stem diameter with a micrometer

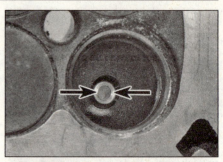

12.16b Measure the valve guide with a small bore gauge, then measure the bore gauge with a micrometer

Check the camshafts and holders for wear as well (see Section 9).

14 Using a precision straight-edge and a feeler gauge set to the warpage limit listed in the specifications at the beginning of the Chapter, check the head gasket mating surface for warpage. Refer to *Tools and Workshop Tips* in the Reference section for details of how to use the straight-edge. If the head is warped beyond the limit specified at the beginning of this Chapter, consult a Honda dealer or take it to a specialist repair shop for an opinion, though be prepared to have to buy a new one.

15 Examine the valve seats in the combustion chamber. If they are pitted, cracked or burned, the head will require work beyond the scope of the home mechanic. Measure the valve seat width and compare it to this Chapter's Specifications **(see illustration)**. If it exceeds the service limit, or if it varies around its circumference, overhaul is required.

12.19 Measure the free length of the valve spring(s) and check them for bend

16 Working on one valve and guide at a time, measure the valve stem diameter **(see illustration)**. Clean the valve's guide using a guide reamer to remove any carbon build-up – insert the reamer from the underside of the head and turn it clockwise only. Now measure the inside diameter of the guide (at both ends and in the centre of the guide) with a small bore gauge, then measure the gauge with a micrometer **(see illustration)**. Measure the guide at the ends and at the centre to determine if they are worn in a bell-mouth pattern (more wear at the ends). Subtract the stem diameter from the valve guide diameter to obtain the valve stem-to-guide clearance. If the stem-to-guide clearance is greater than listed in this Chapter's Specifications, replace whichever component is beyond its specification limits with a new one. If the valve guide is within specifications, but is worn unevenly, it should be replaced with a new one. Repeat for the other valves.

17 Carefully inspect each valve face, stem and collet groove area for cracks, pits and burned spots.

18 Rotate the valve and check for any obvious indication that it is bent, in which case it must be replaced with a new one. Check the end of the stem for pitting and excessive wear. The presence of any of the above conditions indicates the need for valve servicing.

19 Check the end of each valve spring for wear and pitting. Measure the spring free lengths and compare them to the specifications **(see illustration)**. If any spring is shorter than specified it has sagged and must be replaced with a new one. Also place the spring upright on a flat surface and check it for bend by placing a ruler against it, or alternatively lay it against a setsquare. If the bend in any spring is excessive, it must be replaced with a new one.

20 Check the spring seats, retainers and collets for obvious wear and cracks. Any questionable parts should not be re-used, as extensive damage will occur in the event of failure during engine operation.

21 If the inspection indicates that no overhaul work is required, the valve components can be reinstalled in the head.

Reassembly

22 Working on one valve at a time, lay the spring seat in place in the cylinder head with its shouldered side facing up **(see illustration)**. As it is easy to cock the seat on the top of the valve guide, and then tricky to get it to sit properly, fit it using a rod (such as a screwdriver) as a guide for it to slide down.

23 Fit a new valve stem seal onto the guide, using finger pressure, a stem seal fitting tool or an appropriate size deep socket, to push the seal squarely onto the end of the valve guide until it is felt to clip into place **(see illustration)**. Make sure the seal does not get cocked sideways as it could be damaged – using a rod as a guide as for the seat helps.

24 Coat the valve stem with molybdenum disulphide oil (a 50/50 mixture of molybdenum disulphide grease and engine oil), then slide it into its guide, rotating it slowly to avoid damaging the seal **(see illustration)**. Check that the valve moves up-and-down freely in the guide.

12.22 Fit the spring seat using a rod to guide it if necessary

12.23 Fit a new valve stem seal and press it squarely into place

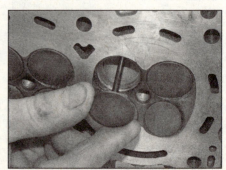

12.24 Lubricate the stem and slide the valve into its correct location

Engine, clutch and transmission 2•27

12.25a Fit the spring(s)...

12.25b ...then fit the spring retainer

12.26 Locate each collet in its groove in the top of the valve stem

25 Next, fit the spring(s), with the closer-wound coils facing down into the cylinder head **(see illustrations)**. Note that the intake valve outer springs are colour-coded yellow and the exhaust valve springs are coded grey so they cannot be mixed up. Fit the spring retainer with its shouldered side facing down so that it fits into the top of the spring(s) **(see illustration)**.

26 Apply a small amount of grease to the collets to help hold them in place. Compress the valve spring(s) with a spring compressor, making sure it is correctly located onto each end of the valve assembly (see Step 6) **(see illustrations 12.6a, b and c)**. Do not compress the spring(s) any more than is necessary to slip the collets into place. Locate each collet in turn into the groove in the valve stem using a screwdriver with a dab of grease on it **(see illustration)**. Carefully release the compressor, making sure the collets seat and lock in the retaining groove.

27 Repeat the procedure for the remaining valves. Remember to keep the parts for each valve together and separate from the other valves so they can be reinstalled in the same location.

28 Support the cylinder head on blocks so the valves can't contact the work surface, then tap the end of each valve stem lightly to seat the collets in their grooves **(see illustration)**.

29 After the cylinder head and camshafts have been installed, check the valve clearances and adjust as required (see Chapter 1).

13 Starter clutch and gears

Check

1 The operation of the starter clutch can be checked while it is in situ. Remove the starter motor (see Chapter 8). Check that the reduction gear is able to rotate freely clockwise as you look at it via the starter motor aperture, but locks when rotated anti-clockwise **(see illustration)**. If not, the starter clutch is faulty and should be removed for inspection.

Removal

2 Remove the clutch cover (see Section 14, Steps 1 to 3).

3 To prevent the crankshaft from turning while unscrewing the starter clutch bolt hold the starter clutch using a clutch holding tool as shown **(see illustration)**. Unscrew the bolt and remove the washer. Remove the idle gear shaft and gear, along with the washers if not already removed **(see illustration)**.

4 Slide the starter clutch off the shaft, noting the offset wide splines that mean it can only be installed in one position **(see illustration)**. Remove the thrust washer **(see illustration)**.

12.28 Seat the collets as described

13.1 Check the gear turns as described

13.3a Use a holding tool on the driven gear while unscrewing the bolt

13.3b Remove the idle gear and shaft

13.4a Slide the starter clutch off...

13.4b ...and remove the thrust washer

2•28 Engine, clutch and transmission

13.5 Remove the reduction gear

13.6 Check the operation of the clutch as described

13.7a Withdraw the driven gear...

5 If you need to remove the reduction gear first remove the clutch (see Section 14). Remove the reduction gear **(see illustration)**.

Inspection

6 With the starter clutch face down on a workbench, check that the starter driven gear rotates freely clockwise and locks against the rotor anti-clockwise **(see illustration)**. If it doesn't, the starter clutch should be dismantled for further investigation.

7 Withdraw the starter driven gear from the starter clutch **(see illustration)**. If the gear appears stuck, rotate it clockwise as you withdraw it to free it from the starter clutch. Remove the needle bearing **(see illustration)**.

8 Check the condition of the sprags inside the clutch body – if they are damaged, marked or flattened at any point, the sprag assembly must be replaced with a new one **(see illustration)**. To remove the sprag assembly release the retaining circlip that holds it and push it from the housing using a small screwdriver through the holes **(see illustrations)**. Install the new assembly in a reverse sequence – there should be a paint mark on the sprag assembly which must face out of the housing – and squeeze the assembly circlips, one on the top and one on the bottom, in to get them past the retaining circlip groove **(see illustrations)**. Secure the sprag assembly with the retaining circlip. Apply clean engine oil to the sprags.

9 Check the external surface on the driven gear hub **(see illustration 13.8a)**. Measure the outside diameter of the hub and check that it has not worn beyond the service limit specified. Check the needle roller bearing and the bearing surfaces on the starter driven gear hub and the starter clutch housing boss. If the bearing surfaces show signs of excessive wear or the bearing itself is worn or damaged, they should be replaced with new ones.

10 Check the teeth of the reduction and idle gears and the corresponding teeth of the starter driven gear and starter motor drive shaft. Replace the gears and/or starter motor if worn or chipped teeth are discovered on related gears. Also check the idle gear shaft for damage, and check that the gear is not a loose fit on it. Check the reduction gear shaft ends and the bores they run in for wear.

Installation

11 Lubricate the needle roller bearing with clean engine oil and fit it over the starter clutch boss **(see illustration 13.7b)**. Lubricate the outside of the starter driven gear hub with clean engine oil, then fit the gear into the clutch, rotating it clockwise as you do so to

13.7b ...and remove the bearing

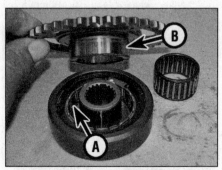

13.8a Check the sprags (A) and the surface of the hub (B)

13.8b Remove the circlip...

13.8c ...and push the sprag assembly out

13.8d Fit the assembly with the paint mark (arrowed) facing out...

13.8e ...and squeeze the assembly circlips in to get them past the groove

Engine, clutch and transmission 2•29

spread the sprags and allow the hub to enter **(see illustration 13.7a)**.
12 If removed, lubricate the reduction gear shaft ends with clean engine oil then locate the inner end of the shaft in its bore in the crankcase, engaging it with the starter motor shaft teeth if installed **(see illustration 13.5)**. Install the clutch (see Section 14).
13 Slide the inner thrust washer onto the crankshaft and against the cam chain sprocket **(see illustration 13.4b)**. Align the wide splines on the starter clutch with those on the crankshaft and slide the starter clutch on with the driven gear on the inside **(see illustration 13.4a)**.
14 Apply clean oil to the threads and under the head of the starter clutch bolt. Fit the bolt with its washer and tighten it finger-tight **(see illustration)**. Wedge a thick piece of rag material or a piece of aluminium (DO NOT use steel) between the primary drive and driven gears at the bottom as shown **(see illustration)** – if using aluminium hold it in place with pliers so it can't drop into the sump. With the gears locked tighten the bolt to the torque setting specified at the beginning of the Chapter.
15 Lubricate the idle gear shaft with clean engine oil and fit it into the gear. Locate the idle gear between the reduction gear and the driven gear and slide the shaft into its bore in the crankcase **(see illustration 13.3b)**.
16 Install the clutch cover (see Section 14, Steps 39 to 42).

14 Clutch

Note: *The clutch nut must be discarded and a new one used on installation – it is best to obtain the new nut in advance.*

Removal

1 Remove the lower fairing and the right-hand fairing side panel (see Chapter 7). Drain the engine oil and remove the dipstick (see Chapter 1).
2 Unscrew the bolt securing the clutch cable bracket to the clutch cover **(see illustration)**. Displace the bracket, noting how it locates, and free the cable end from the release arm **(see illustration)**.
3 Unscrew the clutch cover bolts evenly in a criss-cross pattern, noting the one with the sealing washer and the two securing the wiring guides **(see illustration)**. Remove the cover, turning the release lever arm back (anti-clockwise) as you do to disengage the shaft from the pull-rod. Note that there is a thrust washer and a wave washer on the end of the idle gear shaft which may come away with the cover and could therefore drop from it – if they stay on the end of the shaft remove them for safekeeping **(see illustration)**. Be prepared to catch any residual oil. Remove the four dowels from either the cover or the crankcase if they are loose. Do not turn the engine with the clutch cover removed or the reduction gear could be damaged.
4 Remove the idle gear shaft and gear **(see illustration 13.3b)**.

13.14a Fit the lubricated bolt with its washer

13.14b Fit the wedge between the gears at the bottom (arrow) while tightening the bolt

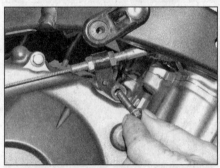

14.2a Unscrew the bolt and detach the bracket...

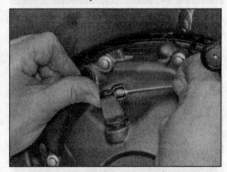

14.2b ...then detach the cable end

14.3a Unscrew the bolts (arrowed) and remove the cover

14.3b Remove the thrust washer and wave washer (arrowed) if required

2•30 Engine, clutch and transmission

14.5a Release the circlip...

14.5b ...and remove the seat...

14.5c ...the pressure plate and the pull-rod (arrowed)

14.6a Unstake the nut

14.6b Slacken the clamp (arrowed) and detach the hose

5 Release the diaphragm spring circlip and remove the seating ring **(see illustrations)**. Remove the lifter plate **(see illustration)**. Remove the pull-rod from either the back of the lifter plate or the end of the shaft.

6 The clutch nut is staked against the input shaft. Unstake the nut using a hammer and punch – take care not to damage the threads on the end of the shaft **(see illustration)**. To remove the clutch nut, the input shaft must be locked. The Honda service tool (Pt. No. 070MB-MFL0100 in the UK or 070MB-MFLA100 in the US) can be used to stop the clutch centre from turning whilst the nut is slackened. Alternatively you can use a commercially available clutch holding tool to hold the rear sprocket (it will not fit on the clutch itself) – to do this drain the cooling system (see Chapter 1), then detach the top hose from the pump; remove the front sprocket (see Chapter 6), move the drive chain off the end of the shaft and slide the sprocket back on, then fit the tool onto the sprocket as shown **(see illustrations)**. Using either of the above methods unscrew the nut and remove the washer **(see illustration)**. Discard the nut – a new one must be used on installation.

7 Remove the spring holder and outer spring seat, the diaphragm springs and the inner spring seat **(see illustrations)**.

8 Fit three M6 x 35 mm bolts into the holes

14.6c Clutch holding tool on the front sprocket

14.6d Unscrew the nut and remove the washer

14.7a Remove the spring holder and its seat...

14.7b ...the springs...

14.7c ...and their seat

Engine, clutch and transmission 2•31

14.8 Fit three bolts into the three holes

14.9 Remove the clutch plate assembly

14.11a Ease the bearing and guide out from the middle of the housing...

in the pressure plate and tighten them lightly **(see illustration)**.

9 Remove the complete clutch plate assembly **(see illustration)**. The assembly is arranged in one of two ways, as shown **(see illustration 14.28 or 14.29)** – 2008 models with the original components have the anti-judder assembly on the outer side against the pressure plate, while all later models, and any 2008 models that have been fitted with the updated arrangement, have the anti-judder assembly on the inner side against the clutch centre, with the clutch friction plates arranged accordingly. Note which way round your clutch is assembled and keep all components in order by keeping the M6 x 35 mm bolts in place, unless new plates are being fitted in which case remove the bolts. If new plates are being fitted on 2008 models still with the original arrangement, you can upgrade to the later arrangement, noting you will need to obtain a new anti-judder spring and spring seat – ask the advice of your dealer.

10 Remove the thrust washer from the shaft **(see illustration 14.33)**.

11 Ease out the clutch guide and needle bearing from between the clutch housing and the input shaft – this can be done using pliers on the raised tab and by sliding the housing on the shaft to help push them along if necessary **(see illustration)**. Remove the clutch housing **(see illustration)**. Note how the holes in the

14.11b ...then remove the housing

back of the housing engage with the pins on the oil pump drive sprocket.

12 If required, draw the guide out from between the oil pump drive sprocket and the shaft, then disengage the chain from the driven sprocket on the pump and remove the drive sprocket and chain **(see illustration)**.

13 If required unscrew the chain guide bolt and remove the guide, noting how it locates over the pin, and note the collar fitted into the inner side of the guide **(see illustration)**.

Inspection

14 After an extended period of service the clutch friction plates will wear and promote clutch slip. Measure the thickness of each friction plate using a Vernier caliper, noting

14.12 Draw the guide out then remove the sprocket and chain

that the plate with the narrower ID that fits over the anti-judder assembly is the Type A thicker one **(see illustration)**. If any plate has worn to or beyond the service limits given in the Specifications at the beginning of the Chapter, or if any of the plates smell burnt or are glazed, replace all the friction plates with a new set.

15 The plain plates should not show any signs of excess heating (bluing). Check for warpage using a flat surface and feeler gauges **(see illustration)**. If any plate exceeds the maximum permissible amount of warpage, or shows signs of bluing, replace all the plain plates with a new set.

16 Measure the free height of each diaphragm spring using a Vernier caliper

14.13 Chain guide bolt (arrowed)

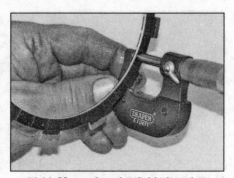
14.14 Measuring clutch friction plate thickness

14.15 Check the plain plates for warpage

2•32 Engine, clutch and transmission

14.16 Measure the free height of each clutch spring and check them for distortion

14.17a Check the friction plate tabs and housing slots...

14.17b ...and the plain plate teeth and pressure plate slots as described

(see illustration). Also check the spring for distortion. If either spring is below the minimum free height specified or is distorted, replace both the springs with a new set. Also check the anti-judder spring and spring seat for damage or distortion and replace them with new ones if necessary.

17 Inspect the friction plates and the clutch housing for burrs and indentations on the edges of the protruding tabs on the plates and/or the slots in the housing **(see illustration)**. Similarly check for wear between the inner teeth of the plain plates and the slots in the clutch pressure plate **(see illustration)**. Wear of this nature will cause clutch drag and slow disengagement during gear changes as the plates will snag when the pressure plate is lifted. With care a small amount of wear can be corrected by dressing with a fine file, but if this is excessive the worn components should be renewed.

18 Check the cam surfaces on the pressure plate and clutch centre of wear and damage, and make sure the rivets are tight **(see illustration)**.

19 Inspect the needle roller bearing and the bearing surfaces on the clutch guide and in the clutch housing **(see illustration)**. If there are any signs of wear, pitting or other damage the affected parts must be replaced with new ones. A new bearing must be selected according to marks on the primary driven gear and clutch guide. On 2008 models the primary driven gear will be marked white or black, and the guide will either be marked or not on its outer (grooved) rim, and on 2009-on models the primary driven gear will be marked blue, yellow or green, and the guide will have two, three or four marks on its outer (grooved) rim **(see illustrations)**. Refer to the table below for your model to select the correct bearing.

20 Using a Vernier caliper, measure the internal and external diameter of the clutch guide, the internal diameter of the clutch housing and the external diameter of the input shaft where the guide sits. Compare the measurements to the specifications at the beginning of the Chapter according to model and the code marks on the outer (grooved) rim of the guide, and replace any part that is worn beyond its service limit with a new one. Similarly check and measure the internal and external diameter of the oil pump drive sprocket guide, the internal diameter of the sprocket and the external diameter of the input shaft where the guide sits.

21 Check the lifter plate and its bearing and

14.18 Check the cam surfaces and rivets

2008 models

	Guide without mark	Guide with mark
Primary driven gear marked white	Bearing B	Bearing A
Primary driven gear marked black	Bearing C	Bearing B

2009-on models

	Guide with two marks	Guide with three marks	Guide with four marks
Primary driven gear marked blue	Bearing B	Bearing A	
Primary driven gear marked yellow	Bearing C	Bearing B	Bearing A
Primary driven gear marked green		Bearing C	Bearing B

14.19a Check the bearing and the bearing surfaces in the housing and on the guide

14.19b Primary driven gear colour marking (arrowed)

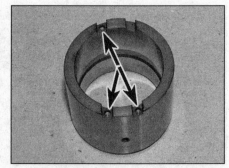

14.19c Clutch guide marks (arrowed)

Engine, clutch and transmission 2•33

14.21 Check the lifter plate and its bearing

14.22a Withdraw the shaft...

14.22b ...and remove the spring (arrowed)

14.22c Remove the seal

14.22d Check the bearings (arrowed)

14.22e The inner end of the spring locates in the slot in the end of the shaft

the pull-rod for signs of wear or damage and roughness **(see illustration)**. Check that the bearing outer race is a good fit in the centre of the lifter, and that the inner race rotates freely without any rough spots. Check the pull-rod end and the corresponding cut-out in the release lever shaft for signs of wear or damage. Replace any parts necessary with new ones.

22 Check the release mechanism in the clutch cover for a smooth action. If the action is stiff or rough, withdraw the shaft and remove the spring, noting how its ends locate **(see illustrations)**. Check the oil seal in the top of the cover – it can be removed by levering it out with a seal hook or screwdriver **(see illustration)**. Clean and check the two needle bearings in the cover **(see illustration)**. Press the new seal in. Lubricate the bearings with oil and the seal lips with grease before installing the shaft. Make sure the return spring ends locate correctly **(see illustration)**.

23 Check the teeth of the primary driven gear on the back of the clutch housing and the corresponding teeth of the primary drive gear on the crankshaft. Replace the clutch housing and/or crankshaft with a new one if worn or chipped teeth are discovered. Also check the oil pump drive sprocket holes and the corresponding pins on the sprocket.

Installation

24 Remove all traces of old sealant from the crankcase and clutch cover surfaces. Note that if removed the starter reduction gear must be installed now as it cannot be fitted once the clutch is in place – see Section 13, Step 12.

25 If removed, clean the threads of the oil pump drive chain guide bolt and apply a suitable non-permanent thread locking compound. Make sure the collar is fitted into the guide, then fit the guide, locating the hole over the pin **(see illustration 14.13)**.

26 Smear the inside and outside of the oil pump drive sprocket guide and the inside of the sprocket with molybdenum disulphide oil (a 50/50 mixture of molybdenum disulphide grease and engine oil). Slide drive sprocket and chain onto the shaft, making sure the pins face out, and slip the chain around the driven sprocket **(see illustration)**. Slide the guide onto the input shaft with the grooved side outwards and fit it between the sprocket and the shaft **(see illustration)**.

27 If the clutch plate assembly has been

14.26a Slide the drive sprocket and chain onto the shaft and around the driven sprocket...

14.26b ...then fit the guide

2•34 Engine, clutch and transmission

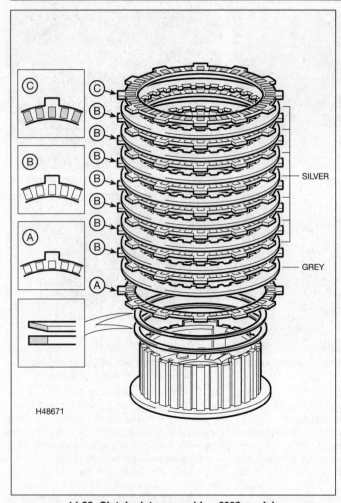

14.28 Clutch plate assembly – 2008 models

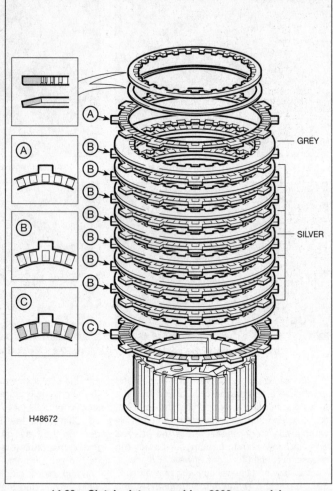

14.29a Clutch plate assembly – 2009-on models

disturbed (i.e. the M6 x 35 mm bolts fitted on removal have been removed and the plates disassembled), follow Steps 28 to 31. If the assembly has not been disturbed go straight to Step 32.

28 On 2008 models with the original plates being refitted, coat each clutch plate with engine oil prior to installation, then build up the plates on the pressure plate as follows **(see illustration)**: fit the anti-judder spring seat into the clutch centre, then fit the spring so that its outer edge is raised off the seat and facing outwards. Fit the Type A friction plate (with black coloured tab end and the larger internal diameter), over the spring and spring seat, then fit the grey plain plate, then alternate Type B friction plates (with blue coloured tab end, and offsetting the tabs with those of the Type A plate) and silver plain plates until all except the Type C plate (with green coloured tab end) are installed, then fit that.

29 On 2008 models with the updated plates being fitted and on 2009-on models, coat each clutch plate with engine oil prior to installation, then build up the plates on the pressure plate as follows **(see illustration)**: fit the Type C friction plate (with green coloured tab end), then fit a silver plain plate, then alternate Type B friction plates (with blue coloured tab end, and offsetting the tabs with those of the Type C plate) and silver plain plates until all are fitted, then fit the grey plain plate **(see illustrations)**. Fit the anti-judder spring so that its inner edge

14.29b Fit the green-tabbed (arrowed) friction plate...

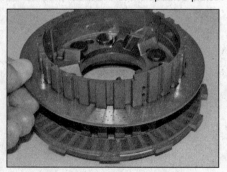

14.29c ...then a silver plain plate...

14.29d ...then a blue-tabbed friction plate and so on...

14.29e ...with the grey plain plate going on last

14.29f Fit the anti-judder spring...

14.29g ...with its inner edge raised off the plain plate...

is raised and the outer edge seats on the grey plain plate, then fit the spring seat with the chamfered side of the teeth facing down onto the spring **(see illustrations)**. Finally fit the Type A plate (with the larger internal diameter) around the anti-judder components **(see illustration)**.

30 Fit the clutch centre, seating the cam with the punch mark adjacent to that with the punch mark on the pressure plate, and check it is correctly seated **(see illustrations)**. Carefully turn the assembly over and loosely fit three M6x35 bolts into the holes to keep it together **(see illustration)**. Align the eight inner friction plate tabs with each other, and offset the outer plate tabs between them.

31 Fit the clutch plate assembly into the clutch housing, aligning the inner plate tabs with the deep slots in the housing and seating the outer plate tabs in the shallow slots **(see illustration)**.

14.29h ...then fit the spring seat with the chamfered side facing down

Tighten the M6x35 bolts to keep everything correctly aligned **(see illustration)**. Remove the clutch pack from the housing **(see illustration)**.

14.29i Fit the friction plate with the larger internal diameter around the anti-judder assembly

32 Smear the inside and outside of the clutch guide, the inside of the clutch housing and the needle bearing with molybdenum disulphide

14.30a Align the cams with the punch marks...

14.30b ...then fit the centre onto the pressure plate

14.30c Turn the assembly over and fit the bolts

14.31a Fit the plate pack into the clutch housing, aligning the tabs as necessary...

14.31b ...then tighten the bolts...

14.31c ...and lift the aligned pack out

14.32a Position the housing over the shaft and engage the primary gears and drive pins...

14.32b ...then slide the bearing...

14.32c ...and the guide in

14.33 Fit the thrust washer

oil (a 50/50 mixture of molybdenum disulphide grease and engine oil) (see illustration 14.19a). Position the clutch housing, making sure the primary drive and driven gear teeth engage and the pins on the oil pump drive sprocket locate in the holes in the rear of the housing – turn the driven sprocket with your finger while pressing on the housing until the pins are felt to locate and the housing moves in a bit further, then double-check by making sure the sprocket can't turn independently of the housing (see illustration). Hold the housing and slide the needle bearing and clutch guide, grooved side outwards, onto the shaft and into the centre of the housing (see illustrations).

33 Slide the thrust washer onto the shaft (see illustration).

34 Fit the clutch plate assembly into the clutch housing, aligning the inner plate tabs with the deep slots in the housing and seating the outer plate tabs in the shallow slots (see illustration 14.9) – it may be necessary to turn the input shaft slightly if its splines do not align exactly with those in the clutch centre. Remove the M6x35 bolts (see illustration 14.8).

35 Fit the inner spring seat with its outer edge raised off the pressure plate (see illustration 14.7c). Fit the diaphragm springs with their inner edges raised off (see illustration 14.7b). Fit the outer spring seat onto the spring holder with its outer edge facing onto the holder flange, then fit the holder into the springs (see illustration 14.7a).

36 Smear the new clutch nut threads and seat with oil, then fit the washer and thread the nut onto the input shaft (see illustration 14.6d). Using the method employed on removal to lock the shaft (see Step 6), tighten the nut to the torque setting specified at the beginning of the Chapter. Stake the collar of the nut into the indent on the end of the shaft (see illustration).

37 Lubricate the bearing in the lifter plate (see illustration 14.21). Fit the pull-rod into the shaft (see illustration). Fit the lifter plate onto the clutch, then fit the seating ring and the circlip, seating it in its groove (see illustration 14.5c, b and a) – make sure the circlip can turn in its groove, indicating it is correctly located.

38 Lubricate the idle gear shaft with molybdenum disulphide oil and fit it into the gear. Locate the idle gear between the reduction gear and the driven gear and slide the shaft into its bore in the crankcase (see illustration 13.3b).

39 Fit the wave washer and the thrust washer onto the end of the idle gear shaft (see illustration 14.3b). Lubricate the reduction and idle gear shaft outer ends with molybdenum disulphide oil.

40 Apply a smear of a suitable sealant (such as Three Bond 1207B or equivalent RTV sealant – ask your dealer) to the entire mating surface on the clutch cover (see illustration). Also apply the sealant 10 to 15 mm either side

14.36 Stake the nut against the detent in the shaft end

14.37 Fit the rod into the shaft

14.40a Apply sealant to the cover...

Engine, clutch and transmission 2•37

14.40b ...and crankcase joints (A). Make sure the dowels (B) are fitted

14.40c Fit the cover...

14.40d ...making sure the release mechanism engages

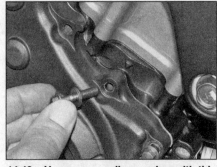

14.40e Use a new sealing washer with this bolt

15.1 Turn the adjuster in

of the crankcase joints on the mating surface with the clutch cover. Fit the four dowels into the crankcase if removed **(see illustration)**. Fit the cover, pulling the release lever arm back (anti-clockwise) as you do then moving it forward so that it engages behind the pull-rod end as you push the cover home on the dowels and shaft ends **(see illustration)**. Fit the bolts (except the clutch cable bracket bolt) finger-tight, not forgetting the wiring guides, and using a new sealing washer on the one bolt, then tighten them evenly and a little at a time in a criss-cross pattern **(see illustration)**.

41 Engage the clutch cable end in the release lever arm, then locate the bracket on the cover and tighten the bolt **(see illustrations 14.2b and a)**.
42 Fill the engine with the correct amount of oil (see Chapter 1). Install the fairing panel (See Chapter 7).

15 Clutch cable

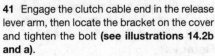

1 Thread the adjuster at the handlebar end of the cable fully in **(see illustration)**. This provides freeplay in the cable and re-sets the adjuster to the beginning of its span.
2 Remove the lower fairing and the right-hand fairing side panel (see Chapter 7).
3 Slacken the nuts on the threaded section of the cable in the bracket on the clutch cover, then thread the rear nut off so it is loose on the inner cable and thread the front nut as far up as it will go **(see illustrations)**. Slide the cable into the bracket to get some freeplay and free the cable end from the release lever, noting

15.3a Slacken the nuts (arrowed)...

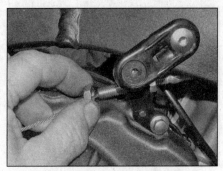

15.3b ...thread the rear nut off...

15.3c ...and the front nut up

2•38 Engine, clutch and transmission

15.3d Free the cable end...

15.3e ...then draw the cable out

15.4a Align the slot(s) and free the cable from the adjuster...

15.4b ...and from the lever

16.2a Note the alignment of the punch mark (arrowed) with the slit in the clamp...

16.2b ...then unscrew the bolt and slide the arm off

how it fits **(see illustration)**. Draw the threaded section of the cable out of the bracket and slip the inner cable out **(see illustration)**.

4 Align the slot in the adjuster at the handlebar end of the cable with that in the lever bracket, then pull the outer cable end from the socket in the adjuster and release the inner cable from the lever **(see illustrations)**. Remove the cable from the machine, noting its routing.

 Before removing the cable from the bike, tape the lower end of the new cable to the upper end of the old cable. Slowly pull the lower end of the old cable out, guiding the new cable down into position. Using this method will ensure the cable is routed correctly.

5 Installation is the reverse of removal. Apply grease to the cable ends. Make sure the cable is correctly routed. Adjust the amount of clutch lever freeplay (see Chapter 1).

16 Gearchange mechanism

Note: *If the gearchange shaft oil seal is leaking it can be removed and a new one fitted without having to remove the shaft itself – see Step 9.*

Removal

1 Make sure the transmission is in neutral. Remove the clutch (see Section 14) – there is no need to remove the oil pump sprocket(s) and chain. Block the holes into the sump with clean rag to prevent anything falling in.
2 Remove the left-hand fairing side panel (see Chapter 7). Note how the slit in the gearchange linkage arm aligns with the punch mark on the shaft, then unscrew pinch bolt and slide the arm off **(see illustrations)**.

3 Wrap a single layer of thin insulating tape around the gearchange shaft splines to protect the oil seal lips as the shaft is removed.
4 Unscrew the gearchange mechanism retainer plate bolt and remove the plate **(see illustration)**. Note how the gearchange shaft centralising spring ends fit on each side of the locating pin in the casing, and how the pawls on the selector arm locate onto the pins on the end of the selector drum cam. Grasp the end of the shaft and withdraw the shaft/ arm assembly **(see illustration)**. Retrieve the washer from the crankcase if it didn't come with the shaft.
5 If required, note how the stopper arm spring ends locate and how the roller on the arm locates in the neutral detent on the selector drum cam, then unscrew the stopper arm bolt and remove the arm, the washer and the spring, noting how they fit **(see illustration)**.

16.4a Unscrew the bolt (arrowed) and remove the plate

16.4b Withdraw the shaft/arm assembly, noting how it fits

16.5 Note how the spring ends locate, and how the roller sits in the neutral detent, then unscrew the bolt (arrowed) and remove the arm

Engine, clutch and transmission 2•39

16.6a Check the selector arm pawls and the pins...

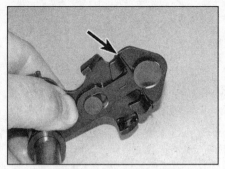

16.6b ...and check the action of the arm and its spring (arrowed)

16.6c Check the stopper arm roller and cam as described

16.7a Check the springs (arrowed)

16.7b Make sure the pin (arrowed) is tight

16.9a Unscrew the bolt (arrowed) and remove the plate...

Inspection

6 Check the selector arm for cracks, distortion and wear of its pawls, and check for any corresponding wear on the pins of the selector drum cam (see illustration). Check the arm moves up smoothly and freely and returns under pressure of its spring (see illustration). Also check the stopper arm roller and the detents in the selector drum cam for any wear or damage, and make sure the roller turns freely (see illustration). Replace any components that are worn or damaged with new ones. If required, refer to the illustrations in Section 29 and remove the selector drum cam by unscrewing the bolt in its centre. Note the locating pin in the end of the drum and remove it for safekeeping if required. On installation, locate the pin in the wider cut-out in the back of the cam. Clean the threads of the cam bolt and apply a suitable non-permanent thread locking compound, and tighten it to the torque setting specified at the beginning of the Chapter.

7 Inspect the shaft centralising spring and the stopper arm return spring for fatigue, wear or damage (see illustration). If any is found, they must be replaced with new ones. To replace the shaft spring, slide the inner washer off the shaft, then remove the circlip and slide the outer washer and the spring off the shaft, noting how its ends locate. Fit the new spring, locating the ends on each side of the tab, and the outer washer and secure them with the circlip, making sure it locates in its groove. Slide the inner washer against the circlip. Also check that the centralising spring locating pin in the crankcase is securely tightened (see illustration). If it is loose, remove it, clean the threads and apply a non-permanent thread locking compound, then tighten it.

8 Check the gearchange shaft is straight and look for damage to the splines. If the shaft is bent you can attempt to straighten it, but if the splines are damaged the shaft must be replaced with a new one.

9 Check the condition of the shaft oil seal in the left-hand side of the crankcase – on RA models remove the engine trim cover to see it (see Chapter 7). If it is damaged, deteriorated or shows signs of leakage it must be replaced with a new one – unscrew the seal retainer plate bolt and remove the plate (see illustration). Lever out the old seal with a seal hook or screwdriver (see illustration). If the shaft has been removed, check the condition of the needle bearing, and replace that with a new one as well if necessary – refer to *Tools and Workshop Tips* in the Reference Section. Smear the lip of the new seal with grease, and fit it with the marked side facing out (see illustration). Press the seal squarely into place using your fingers, a seal driver or suitable socket (see illustration).

16.9b ...then lever out the seal

16.9c Fit the seal...

16.9d ...and press it into its housing

2•40 Engine, clutch and transmission

16.10a Sit the spring on its post

16.10b Assemble the stopper arm components as shown...

16.10c ...then fit the arm as described and tighten the bolt

16.11 Make sure everything is correctly positioned then fit the retainer plate

Fit the retainer plate and tighten its bolt. On RA models install the engine trim cover (see Chapter 7).

Installation

10 If removed, clean the threads of the stopper arm bolt and apply a suitable non-permanent thread locking compound. Fit the spring onto its post as shown **(see illustration)**. Fit the bolt through the stopper arm so the hole in the arm seats around the shoulder, then fit the washer **(see illustration)**. Fit the arm and turn the bolt a few threads, then seat the cut-out in the arm against the return spring and continue to tighten the bolt, making sure the arm remains seated over the shoulder on the bolt, and locating the roller onto the neutral detent on the selector drum as the bolt tightens **(see illustrations)**. Tighten the bolt to the torque setting specified at the beginning of the Chapter. Check that the arm and spring ends are correctly positioned **(see illustration 16.5)**.

11 Check that the shaft centralising spring is properly positioned and slide the washer onto the shaft if removed **(see illustration 16.7a)**. Apply some grease to the lips of the gearchange shaft oil seal in the left-hand side of the crankcase. Slide the shaft into place and push it all the way through the case until the splined end comes out the other side **(see illustration 16.4b)**. Locate the selector arm pawls onto the pins on the selector drum and the centralising spring ends onto each side of the locating pin in the crankcase **(see illustration)**. Clean the threads of the retainer plate bolt and apply a suitable non-permanent thread locking compound, then fit the plate and tighten the bolt to the specified torque **(see illustration 16.4a)**.

12 Remove the rag that was blocking the sump, then install the clutch (see Section 14).

13 Remove the insulating tape from around the gearchange shaft splines. Slide the gearchange linkage arm onto the shaft, aligning its slit with the punch mark on the shaft **(see illustrations 16.2b and a)**. Fit the pinch bolt and tighten it.

17 Oil sump and strainer

Removal

1 Remove the fairing side panels (see Chapter 7). Drain the engine oil (see Chapter 1).
2 While the oil is draining, remove the exhaust downpipe assembly (see Chapter 4).
3 Slacken the sump bolts evenly in a criss-cross sequence to prevent distortion, then remove the bolts, and remove the sump **(see illustrations)**.
4 Pull the strainer out, noting how it locates

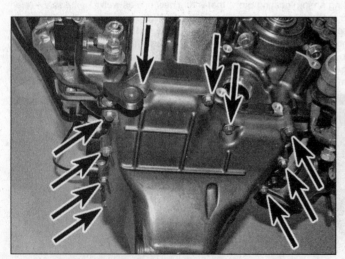
17.3a Unscrew the bolts (arrowed) all the way around...

17.3b ...and remove the sump

Engine, clutch and transmission

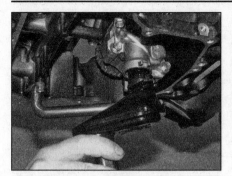

17.4a Remove the strainer, noting how the tab locates in the groove

17.4b Remove the seal

17.6 Clean the mesh (arrowed)

(see illustration). Remove the rubber seal and discard it – a new one must be used **(see illustration)**.

Inspection

5 Remove all traces of sealant from the sump and crankcase mating surfaces, and clean the inside of the sump with solvent. Blow the sump dry with compressed air if available.

6 Clean the oil strainer in solvent and remove any debris caught in the mesh **(see illustration)**. If the strainer gauze is damaged, replace the strainer with a new one.

Installation

7 Fit a new rubber seal smeared with clean oil into the strainer orifice in the oil pump **(see illustration)**. Do not fit it onto the strainer as it will distort when the strainer is fitted. Fit the strainer, locating the tab between the lugs **(see illustration)**.

8 Clean the mating surfaces of the sump and crankcase with solvent. Apply a suitable sealant (such as Three Bond 1207B or equivalent RTV sealant – ask your dealer) to the sump mating surface **(see illustration)**. Position the sump onto the crankcase and fit the bolts finger-tight **(see illustration)**. Tighten the bolts evenly and a little at a time in a criss-cross pattern.

9 Install the exhaust system, but do not yet fit the fairing panels.

10 Fill the engine with the correct type and quantity of oil as described in Chapter 1. Start the engine and check that there are no leaks around the sump.

11 Install the fairing panels (see Chapter 7).

18 Oil pump and pressure relief valve

Removal

1 Remove the sump and oil strainer (Section 17).

2 Unscrew the oil pipe bolts and remove the pipe **(see illustration)**. Remove the sealing rings – new ones must be used.

3 Lock the oil pump driven sprocket to prevent it from turning and unscrew the bolt **(see illustration)**. Remove the driven sprocket **(see illustration 18.19)**.

17.7a Lubricate the rubber seal and fit it into the crankcase

17.7b Locate the tab (arrowed) between the lugs

17.8a Apply the sealant...

17.8b ...then install the sump

18.2 Oil pipe bolts (arrowed)

18.3 Lock the sprocket and unscrew its bolt

2•42 Engine, clutch and transmission

18.4 Unscrew the bolts (arrowed) and remove the pump

18.5a Unscrew the bolts...

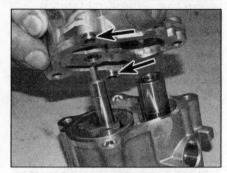

18.5b ...and remove the cover, noting the dowels (arrowed)

18.5c Withdraw the shaft and remove the washer and drive pin from it

18.5d Remove the rotors

18.9 Measure the inner rotor tip-to-outer rotor clearance

4 Unscrew the pump mounting bolts and remove the pump, noting how it fits **(see illustration)**. Remove the dowels from either the crankcase or the pump if they are loose (see illustration 18.18).

Inspection

5 Unscrew the pump body bolts and draw the cover off the shaft **(see illustrations)**. Remove the dowels from the cover or body if loose. Withdraw the shaft from the pump and remove the thrust washer and drive pin **(see illustration)**. Remove the inner and outer rotors, marking which way round the outer rotor fits **(see illustrations)**.

6 To remove the pressure relief valve, pull it out of its socket in the pump – it is a push-fit **(see illustration 18.14)**. Discard the O-ring as a new one must be used.

7 Clean all the components, including the oil pipe, in solvent.

8 Inspect the pump body and rotors for scoring and wear. If any damage, scoring or uneven or excessive wear is evident, replace the pump with a new one (individual components are not available).

9 Fit the inner and outer rotors into the pump body, then insert the shaft and fit the drive pin in the cut-outs in the inner rotor **(see illustrations 18.5d and 18.15a)**. Align the rotors as shown and measure the clearance between the inner rotor tip and the outer rotor at the point shown with a feeler gauge, and compare it to the service limit listed in the specifications at the beginning of the Chapter **(see illustration)**. If the clearance measured is greater than the maximum listed, replace the pump with a new one.

10 Measure the clearance between the outer rotor and the pump body with a feeler gauge and compare it to the maximum clearance listed in the specifications at the beginning of the Chapter **(see illustration)**. If the clearance measured is greater than the maximum listed, replace the pump with a new one.

11 Lay a straight-edge across the rotors and the pump body and, using a feeler gauge, measure the rotor end-float (the gap between the rotors and the straight-edge) **(see illustration)**. If the clearance measured is greater than the maximum listed, replace the pump with a new one.

12 Check the pump drive chain and drive and driven sprockets for wear or damage, and replace them with a new set if necessary.

13 Push the relief valve plunger into the valve body and check that it moves smoothly and freely against spring pressure **(see illustration)**. If not, remove the circlip,

18.10 Measure the outer rotor-to-body clearance

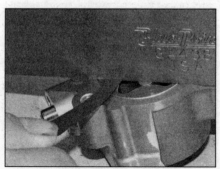

18.11 Measure rotor end-float

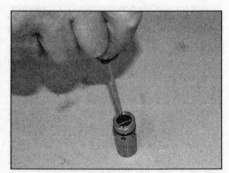

18.13a Push the plunger into the body and check that it moves smoothly

Engine, clutch and transmission 2•43

18.13b A circlip (arrowed) secures the washer, spring and plunger

18.14 Fit a new O-ring (arrowed) and push the relief valve into its socket

18.15a Fit the drive pin...

noting that it is under spring pressure, then remove the washer, spring and plunger **(see illustration)**. Clean all components in solvent, then check the plunger and the valve body for evidence of scoring, wear and any other damage. If any is found, replace the relief valve with a new one – individual components are not available. Otherwise, coat the plunger with oil and fit it closed end first back into the valve and recheck the movement. If it is good, install the spring and washer and secure them with the circlip.

14 Fit a new O-ring onto the relief valve and smear it with clean oil, then push the valve into its socket in the sump **(see illustration)**.

15 Make sure all the pump components are clean, then lubricate them with new engine oil. Fit the outer rotor into the pump body the same way as noted on removal, then fit the inner rotor into the outer rotor with the cut-outs in the inner rotor facing out **(see illustration 18.5d)**. Slide the driveshaft through the inner rotor and pump body, making sure the end with the driven sprocket bolt hole is on the outer side and the tabbed end is on the inner side **(see illustration 18.5c)**. Slide the drive pin into its hole in the driveshaft and locate it into the cut-outs in the inner rotor, then slide the thrust washer onto the shaft so it covers the drive pin **(see illustrations)**. Fit the dowels if removed **(see illustration 18.5b)**. Slide the cover onto the pump. Fit the bolts and tighten them to the torque setting specified at the beginning of the Chapter **(see illustration 18.5a)**.

16 Rotate the pump shaft by hand and check it turns the rotors smoothly and freely.

18.15b ...seat it in the cut-outs then fit the washer

Installation

17 Pour some clean engine oil into the pump and rotate the shaft to prime the pump.
18 Fit the locating dowels into the pump if removed **(see illustration)**. Fit the pump, making sure the dowels locate squarely, and tighten the mounting bolts **(see illustration 18.4)**.
19 Clean the threads of the pump driven sprocket bolt and apply a suitable non-permanent thread locking compound. Engage the sprocket with the chain, making sure the OUT mark faces out, then locate the sprocket on the shaft and fit the bolt with its washer **(see illustration)**. Lock the sprocket and tighten the bolt to the torque setting specified at the beginning of the chapter **(see illustration 18.3)**.
20 Clean the threads of the oil pipe bolts. Fit a new sealing ring smeared with oil onto each

18.18 Make sure the dowels (arrowed) seat correctly

end of the pipe **(see illustration)**. Locate the pipe in the pump and crankcase, then apply a suitable non-permanent thread locking compound to the bolts and tighten them to the specified torque setting **(see illustration)**.
21 Install the oil strainer and sump (Section 17).

19 Crankcase separation and reassembly

Note: *The 9 mm crankshaft journal bolts in the lower crankcase are of the stretch type, which can only be used in a running engine once, though they can be used when performing the oil clearance check detailed in Section 22 to prevent having to buy two sets of new bolts. The new bolts come pre-coated with an oil additive that must not be cleaned off.*

18.19 Engage and locate the sprocket and fit the bolt

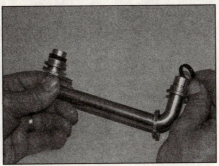

18.20a Fit new sealing rings onto the pipe...

18.20b ...and seat it in its holes

2•44 Engine, clutch and transmission

19.3a Upper crankcase bolts (arrowed)

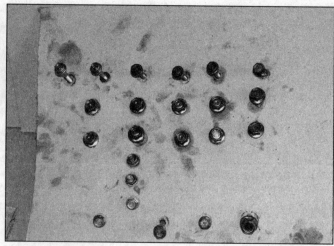

19.3b Cardboard template for storing the lower crankcase bolts

Separation

1 To access the pistons, connecting rods, crankshaft, bearings, balancer shaft, transmission shafts and selector drum and forks, the crankcase must be split into its two halves. To do this, remove the engine from the frame (see Section 4).

2 Before the crankcases can be separated the following components must be removed:

Valve cover (Section 7)
Camshafts (Section 9) – see Note
Cylinder head (Section 11) – see Note
Alternator (Chapter 8)
Starter clutch (Section 13)
Cam chain and blades (Section 10) – see Note
Clutch, oil pump drive chain and sprockets (Section 14)
Water pump and hoses (Chapter 3)
Gearchange mechanism (Section 16) – see Note
Oil cooler (Section 6)
Starter motor (Chapter 8) – see Note
Oil sump and strainer (Section 17)
Oil pump and pressure relief valve (Section 18)
Knock sensor (if required – Chapter 4)
Speed sensor, neutral switch/gear position switch and oil pressure switch (if required – Chapter 8)

Note: *If the crankcases are being separated to inspect the crankshaft without removing it, the camshafts and cylinder head can remain in situ. To remove the crankshaft without removing the connecting rods and pistons, the camshafts must be removed but the head can stay. However, if removal of the connecting rod assemblies is intended, full disassembly of the top-end is necessary. To inspect or remove the transmission shafts and selector drum and forks, the camshafts and cylinder head can remain in situ. The gearchange mechanism can remain in situ unless the transmission and selector drum and forks are being removed.*

3 Unscrew and remove the three 7 mm upper crankcase bolts (see illustration). **Note:** *As each crankcase bolt is removed, store it in its relative position in a cardboard template of the crankcase halves (see illustration). This will ensure all bolts and washers are installed in the correct location on reassembly.*

4 Turn the engine upside down and support it as required using wooden blocks – do not allow the engine to rest on the studs.

5 Unscrew the one 10 mm bolt, the three 8 mm bolts and the ten 7 mm bolts (noting the one with a sealing washer) in the lower crankcase evenly, a little at a time and in a criss-cross sequence until they are finger-tight, then remove them and store them in the template (see illustrations).

6 Now unscrew the ten 9 mm crankshaft journal bolts evenly, a little at a time and in a reverse of the tightening sequence shown, i.e. starting from the outside and working to the centre, until they are finger-tight, then remove them (see illustration 19.17b).

7 Carefully lift the lower crankcase half off the upper half, using a soft-faced hammer to

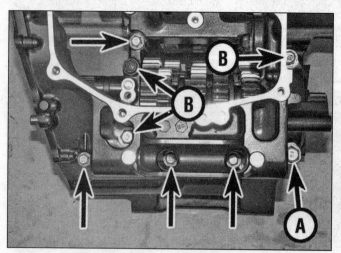

19.5a Undo the lower crankcase 10 mm bolt (A), 8 mm bolts (B) and 7 mm bolts (arrowed) around the back...

19.5b ...and the 7 mm bolts (arrowed) across the front

Engine, clutch and transmission 2•45

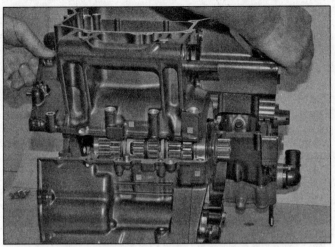

19.7 Carefully separate the crankcase halves

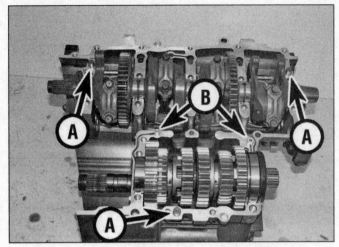

19.8 Remove the dowels (A) and the oil jets (B) if loose

tap around the joint to initially separate the halves if necessary **(see illustration)**. **Note:** *If the halves do not separate easily, make sure all fasteners have been removed. Do not try to separate the halves by levering against the crankcase mating surfaces as they are easily scored and will leak oil in the future if damaged.* The balancer shaft will come away with the lower crankcase half, leaving the crankshaft, transmission shafts and selector drum and forks in the upper crankcase half.

8 Remove the three locating dowels from the crankcase if they are loose (they could be in either crankcase half), and the two oil jets, noting how and where they fit **(see illustration)**. There is also an oil orifice that should be a tight fit, but check to see if it is loose and remove it if required **(see illustration 19.13c)**.

9 Refer to Sections 20 to 30 for the removal and installation of the components housed within the crankcases.

Reassembly

10 Remove all traces of sealant from the crankcase mating surfaces.

11 Ensure that all components and their bearings are in place in the upper and lower crankcase halves. If the transmission shafts have not been removed, check the condition of the oil seal on the left-hand end of the output shaft and replace it with a new one if it is damaged or deteriorated – it is advisable to fit a new one as a matter of course **(see illustration 27.11)**.

12 Generously lubricate the crankshaft and transmission shafts, particularly around the bearings, with clean engine oil, then use a rag soaked in high flash-point solvent to wipe over the mating surfaces of both crankcase halves to remove all traces of oil.

13 If removed, fit the three locating dowels in the upper crankcase half **(see illustration 19.8)**. Also fit the two oil jets, making sure each is the correct way up **(see illustrations)**. Fit the oil orifice if removed, and check it is correctly seated if not **(see illustration)**. Thread the starter clutch bolt with its washer into the end of the crankshaft and use this to turn the crankshaft to position the white paint mark on the balancer drive gear roughly as shown **(see illustrations)**.

14 Apply a small amount of suitable sealant (Three-Bond 1207B or equivalent RTV sealant

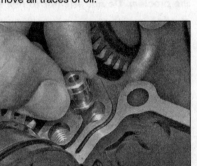

19.13a Make sure each jet...

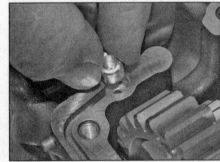

19.13b ...is the correct way up

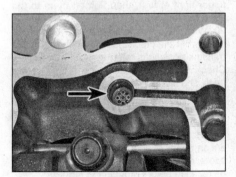

19.13c Oil orifice (arrowed)

19.13d Fit the starter clutch bolt and use it to turn the crankshaft...

19.13e ...so the paint mark (arrowed) is as shown

2•46 Engine, clutch and transmission

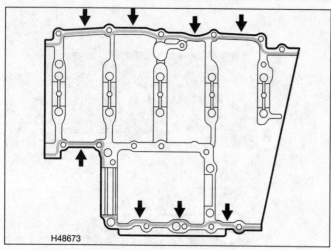

19.14 Apply sealant to the shaded area shown

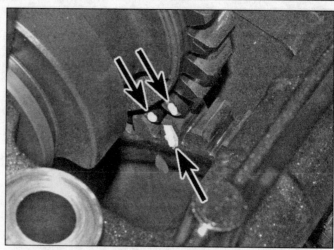

19.15 Make sure the balancer drive and driven gear alignment marks (arrowed) are as shown

– ask your dealer) to the outer mating surface of the lower crankcase half as shown (see illustration).

Caution: Apply the sealant only to the shaded areas. Do not apply an excessive amount as it will ooze out when the case halves are assembled and may obstruct oil passages. Do not apply the sealant close to any of the bearing shells or surfaces, or oil passages.

15 Check again that all components are in position, particularly that the bearing shells are still correctly located in the lower crankcase half. Carefully fit the lower crankcase half down onto the upper crankcase half (see illustration 19.7), turning the balancer shaft and crankshaft as required (see illustration 19.13d) so the index marks on the driven gear sit on either side of the white paint mark on the drive gear, and making sure the dowels locate correctly (see illustration).

16 Check that the lower crankcase half is correctly seated all round.

Caution: The crankcase halves should fit together without being forced. If the casings are not correctly seated, remove the lower crankcase half and investigate the problem. Do not attempt to pull them together using the crankcase bolts as the casing will crack and be ruined.

17 Fit the ten NEW 9 mm crankshaft journal bolts – there are two different lengths, with two longer ones, so make sure all are correctly positioned as shown (see illustration). Secure all bolts finger-tight at first, then tighten them evenly, in the numerical sequence shown and in three stages, first to 10 Nm, then to 15 Nm, then to 20 Nm (see illustration). Now, using a degree disc, tighten each bolt in turn and in one go by a further 150°, again following the numerical sequence (see illustration).

18 Clean the threads of the remaining lower crankcase bolts and insert them in their original locations (see illustrations 19.5a and b) – fit a new sealing washer with the 7 mm bolt in the rear corner (see illustration). Secure all bolts finger-tight at first, then tighten the 10 mm bolt to its specified torque. Now tighten the 8 mm bolts evenly and a little at a time in a criss-cross sequence starting in the middle and working outwards to the specified torque setting. Finally tighten the 7 mm bolts in the same way to the specified torque setting.

19 Turn the engine over. Clean the threads of the three 7 mm upper crankcase bolts and insert them in their original locations (see illustration 19.3a). Secure the bolts finger-tight at first, then tighten them to the specified torque.

20 With all crankcase fasteners tightened, check that the crankshaft, balancer shaft and transmission shafts rotate smoothly and easily. Check that the transmission shafts rotate freely and independently in neutral, then rotate the selector drum by hand and select each gear in turn whilst rotating the input shaft. Check that all gears can be selected and that the shafts rotate freely in every gear. If there are any signs of undue stiffness, tight or rough spots, or of any other problem, the fault must be rectified before proceeding further.

21 Install all other removed assemblies in a reverse of the sequence given in Step 2.

19.17a Fit the longer bolts as shown

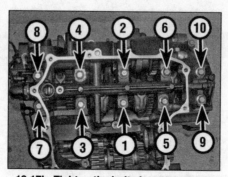

19.17b Tighten the bolts in sequence to the specified torque setting...

19.17c ...and through the specified angle

19.18 Use a new sealing washer with this bolt

Engine, clutch and transmission 2•47

20.2a Right-hand oil pipe bolt (arrowed)

20.2b Left-hand oil pipe bolt (arrowed)

20.2c Withdraw the front pipes...

20.2d ...and the transmission shaft pipe

20.8a Fit a new O-ring onto each pipe

20.8b Seat the tab in the cut-out

20 Crankcases

1 After the crankcases have been separated, remove the crankshaft, balancer shaft, connecting rods and pistons, cylinder block, transmission shafts and selector drum and forks, plus the knock sensor, speed sensor, neutral switch/gear position switch (according to model) and oil pressure switch if not already removed. If there are any other components or assemblies that have not been removed as part of your disassembly procedure, for example the starter motor or the coolant inlet union, remove these as well, referring to the relevant Chapter. Also remove the transmission input shaft bearing in the crankcase if required, but note that if you do a new one must be fitted – see Section 27.

2 Unscrew the bolt securing each front oil jet pipe (one on each side of the upper crankcase), then draw the pipes out (see illustrations). Pull the transmission oil jet pipe out (see illustration). Remove the O-ring from each pipe (see illustration 20.8a) – new ones must be used.

3 Clean the crankcases and all oil passages, including the oil jets and oil jet pipes, with new solvent and dry them with compressed air, blowing it through the passages, jets and pipes.

4 Remove all traces of old gasket sealant from the mating surfaces. Clean up minor damage to the surfaces with a fine sharpening stone or grindstone.

Caution: Be very careful not to nick or gouge the crankcase mating surfaces or oil leaks will result. Check both crankcase halves very carefully for cracks and other damage.

5 Small cracks or holes in aluminium castings can be repaired with an epoxy resin adhesive as a temporary measure. Permanent repairs can be made professionally by argon-arc welding, and only a specialist in this process is in a position to advise on the economy or practical aspect of such a repair. Alternatively if the damage is minor, one of the low temperature aluminium fusion welding kits could be used to make the repair. If any damage is found that can't be repaired, replace the crankcase halves as a set.

6 Damaged threads can be economically reclaimed using a diamond section wire insert, for example of the Heli-Coil type (though there are other makes), which are easily fitted after drilling and re-tapping the affected thread.

7 Sheared studs or screws can usually be removed with extractors, which consist of a tapered, left-hand thread screw of very hard steel. These are inserted into a pre-drilled hole in the stud, and usually succeed in dislodging the most stubborn stud or screw. If a stud has sheared above its bore line, it can be removed using a conventional stud extractor which avoids the need for drilling.

 Refer to Tools and Workshop Tips for details of installing a thread insert and using screw extractors.

8 Fit a new O-ring smeared with oil onto each oil jet pipe (see illustration). Insert the pipes (see illustrations 20.2c and d) – the end plate on the front pipe for the left-hand side has straight sides and the one for the right has a figure-of-eight shape (see illustration 20.2b and a). Clean the threads of the bolts and apply a non-permanent thread locking compound, and tighten them to the torque setting specified at the beginning of the Chapter. Make sure the tab on the head of the transmission pipe locates in the cut-out (see illustration).

9 Install all other components and assemblies, referring to the relevant Sections of this and the other Chapters, before reassembling the crankcase halves.

21 Connecting rod and main bearing information

1 Even though new main and connecting rod bearings are generally fitted during engine overhaul, the old bearings should be retained for close examination as they may reveal valuable information about the condition of the engine.

2 Bearing failure occurs mainly because of lack of lubrication, the presence of dirt or other foreign particles, overloading the engine and/or corrosion. Regardless of the cause of bearing failure, it must be corrected before the engine is reassembled to prevent it from happening again.

2•48 Engine, clutch and transmission

3 When examining the bearings, lay them out on a clean surface in the same general position as their location on the crankshaft journals. This will enable you to match any noted bearing problems with the corresponding crankshaft journal.

4 Dirt and other foreign particles get into the engine in a variety of ways. They may be left in the engine during assembly or they may pass through filters or breathers, then get into the oil and from there into the bearings. Metal chips from machining operations and normal engine wear are often present. Abrasives are sometimes left in engine components after reconditioning operations, especially when parts are not thoroughly cleaned using the proper cleaning methods. Whatever the source, foreign objects often end up imbedded in the soft bearing material and are easily recognised. Large particles will not imbed in the bearing and will score or gouge the bearing and journal. The best prevention for this cause of bearing failure is to clean all parts thoroughly and keep everything spotlessly clean during engine reassembly. Regular oil and filter changes are also recommended.

5 Lack of lubrication or lubrication breakdown has a number of interrelated causes. Excessive heat (which thins the oil), overloading (which squeezes the oil from the bearing face) and oil leakage or throw off (from excessive bearing clearances, worn oil pump or high engine speeds) all contribute to lubrication breakdown. Blocked oil passages will starve a bearing of lubrication and destroy it. When lack of lubrication is the cause of bearing failure, the bearing material is wiped or extruded from the steel backing of the bearing. Temperatures may increase to the point where the steel backing and the journal turn blue from overheating.

 Refer to Tools and Workshop Tips for bearing fault finding.

6 Riding habits can have a definite effect on bearing life. Full throttle low speed operation, or labouring the engine, puts very high loads on bearings, which tend to squeeze out the oil film. These loads cause the bearings to flex, which produces fine cracks in the bearing face (fatigue failure). Eventually the bearing material will loosen in pieces and tear away from the steel backing. Short trip riding leads to corrosion of bearings, as insufficient engine heat is produced to drive off the condensed water and corrosive gases produced. These products collect in the engine oil, forming acid and sludge. As the oil is carried to the engine bearings, the acid attacks and corrodes the bearing material.

7 Incorrect bearing installation during engine assembly will lead to bearing failure as well. Tight fitting bearings which leave insufficient bearing oil clearances result in oil starvation. Dirt or foreign particles trapped behind a bearing shell result in high spots on the bearing which lead to failure.

8 To avoid bearing problems, clean all parts thoroughly before reassembly, double check all bearing clearance measurements and lubricate the new bearings with clean engine oil during installation.

22 Crankshaft and main bearings

Note: *The connecting rod bolts can only be used in a running engine once, though they can be used to do a big-end oil clearance check to prevent having to buy two sets of new bolts.*

Removal

1 Remove the engine from the frame (see Section 4) and separate the crankcase halves (see Section 19).

2 Using paint or a felt marker pen, mark the relevant cylinder identity on the front face of each connecting rod and cap to ensure that they are fitted correctly on reassembly **(see illustration)**. Note that the number already across the rod and cap indicates rod size grade **(see illustration 23.21b)**.

3 Unscrew the connecting rod cap bolts **(see illustration)**. Separate the caps from the crankpin, noting the locating pins **(see illustration 22.26)**. If the cap is difficult to remove partially thread the bolts back into the rods then tap them on the top to push the rod off the cap **(see illustration)**. Push the rods and pistons up to the tops of the bores so that the bottom ends are clear of the crankshaft, taking care to keep the rods clear of the cylinder liners – it is best to protect the liners with some rag **(see illustration)**. *Note: If no work is to be carried out on the piston/connecting rod assemblies there is no need to remove them from the bores. If you do remove them, refer to Section 23.*

4 Lift the crankshaft out of the upper crankcase half, bringing the cam chain with it if it hasn't been removed, and taking care not to dislodge the main bearing shells **(see illustration)**. Wrap some rag around each connecting rod to protect the cylinder walls.

5 Remove the main bearing shells from the

22.2 Mark the relevant cylinder number on each connecting rod and cap

22.3a Unscrew the bolts (arrowed) and remove the connecting rod caps

22.3b If the cap is difficult to remove dislodge the rod from it

22.3c Push each rod off its crankpin

22.4 Lift the crankshaft out of the crankcase

crankcase halves **(see illustration)**. Keep the shells in order. If required remove the oil jet pipes (See Section 20, Step 2).

Inspection

6 Clean the crankshaft with solvent, squirting it under pressure through all the oil passages. Also clean through the oil jet pipes, removing them if required (Section 20, Steps 2 and 3). If available, blow the crank dry with compressed air, and blow through the oil passages and pipes. Check the primary drive gear and balancer drive gear for wear or damage **(see illustration)**. If any of the gear teeth are excessively worn, chipped or broken, the crankshaft must be replaced with a new one. If wear or damage is found, also inspect the primary driven gear on the back of the clutch housing (see Section 14) and the driven gear on the balancer shaft (see Section 30).

7 Refer to Section 21 and examine the main bearing shells. If they are scored, badly scuffed or appear to have been seized, new bearings must be installed. Always replace the main bearings as a set. If they are badly damaged, check the corresponding crankshaft journals. Evidence of extreme heat, such as discoloration, indicates that lubrication failure has occurred. Be sure to thoroughly check the oil pump and pressure relief valve as well as all oil holes and passages before reassembling the engine.

8 Give the crankshaft journals a close visual examination, paying particular attention where damaged bearings have been discovered. If the journals are scored or pitted in any way a new crankshaft will be required. Note that undersizes are not available, precluding the option of regrinding the crankshaft.

9 Place the crankshaft on V-blocks and check the runout at the centre main bearing journal using a dial gauge. Compare the reading to the maximum specified at the beginning of the Chapter. If the runout exceeds the limit, the crankshaft must be replaced with a new one.

Oil clearance check

10 Whether new bearing shells are being fitted or the original ones are being re-used, the main bearing oil clearance should be checked before the engine is reassembled. Main bearing oil clearance is measured with a product known as Plastigauge.

11 Clean both sides of the bearing shells, the bearing housings in both crankcase halves, and the journals on the crankshaft.

12 Press the bearing shells into their cut-outs, ensuring that the tab on each shell engages in the notch in the crankcase **(see illustration 22.5)**. Make sure the bearings are fitted in the correct locations and take care not to touch any shell's bearing surface with your fingers.

13 Ensure the shells and crankshaft are clean and dry. Lay the crankshaft in position in the upper crankcase **(see illustration 22.4)**. Fit the three crankcase dowels if removed **(see illustration 19.8)**.

14 Cut five lengths of the appropriate size Plastigauge (they should be slightly shorter

22.5 Remove the main bearing shells from their housings

than the width of the crankshaft journals). Place a strand of Plastigauge on each (cleaned) journal, avoiding the oil hole. Make sure the crankshaft is not rotated.

15 Carefully fit the lower crankcase half onto the upper half **(see illustration 19.7)**. Check that the lower half is correctly seated. **Note:** *Do not tighten the crankcase bolts if the casing is not correctly seated.* Fit the original ten 9 mm crankshaft journal bolts and tighten them as described in Section 19, Step 17.

16 Slacken each bolt evenly and a little at a time in a reverse of the tightening sequence, i.e. starting from the outside and working to the centre, until they are all finger-tight, then remove the bolts. Carefully lift off the lower crankcase half, making sure the Plastigauge is not disturbed.

17 Compare the width of the crushed Plastigauge on each crankshaft journal to the scale printed on the Plastigauge envelope to obtain the main bearing oil clearance. Compare the reading to the specifications at the beginning of the Chapter.

18 On completion carefully scrape away all traces of the Plastigauge material from the crankshaft journal and bearing shells; use a fingernail or other object which is unlikely to score them.

19 If the oil clearance falls into the specified range, no bearing shell replacement is required (provided they are in good condition). If the clearance is beyond the service limit, refer to the marks on the case and the marks on the crankshaft and select new bearing shells (see Steps 21 and 22). Fit the new shells and

22.21a Main bearing journal size numbers

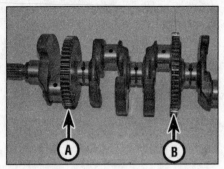

22.6 Primary drive gear (A), balancer drive gear (B)

check the oil clearance once again (the new shells may bring the bearing clearance within the specified range). Always replace all of the shells at the same time.

20 If the clearance is still greater than the service limit listed in this Chapter's Specifications (even with replacement shells), the crankshaft journals are worn and the crankshaft should be replaced with a new one.

Main bearing shell selection

21 Replacement bearing shells for the main bearings are supplied on a selected fit basis. Code letters and numbers stamped on the crankshaft and crankcase are used to identify the correct replacement bearings. The crankshaft main bearing journal size numbers are stamped on the outside of the left-hand crankshaft web and will be either 1, 2 or 3 **(see illustration)**. The first letter, after the L, is for the left-hand journal, and the numbers correspond consecutively for each journal. The corresponding main bearing housing size letters are stamped into the left-hand side of the upper crankcase half and will be either A, B or C **(see illustration)**. The left-hand letter corresponds to the left-hand journal, and the letters correspond consecutively from left to right.

22 A range of bearing shells is available. To select the correct bearing for a particular journal, use the table below and cross-refer the main bearing journal size number (stamped on the crank web) with the main bearing housing size letter (stamped on the crankcase) to determine the colour code of the bearing required. For example, if the journal code is 3,

22.21b Main bearing housing size letters

2•50 Engine, clutch and transmission

22.22 Bearing shell colour code (arrowed)

22.26 Fit the cap, locating the pins in the holes

22.27a Lubricate and fit the new bolts...

and the housing code is A, then the bearing required is yellow. The colour is marked on the side of the shell (see illustration).

Main bearing journal code	Main bearing housing code		
	A	B	C
1	Red	Pink	Yellow
2	Pink	Yellow	Green
3	Yellow	Green	Brown

Installation

23 Clean both sides of the bearing shells, the bearing housings in both crankcase halves, and the journals on the crankshaft. If new shells are being fitted, ensure that all traces of the protective grease are cleaned off using paraffin (kerosene). Wipe the shells, crankcase halves and journals dry with a lint-free cloth. Make sure all the oil passages and holes are clear, and blow them through with compressed air if available and not already done. If removed install the oil jet pipes (Section 20, Step 8).

24 Press the bearing shells into their locations. Make sure the tab on each shell engages in the notch in the casing (see illustration 22.5). Make sure the bearings are fitted in the correct locations and take care not to touch any shell's bearing surface with your fingers. Lubricate the bearing surface of each shell with molybdenum disulphide oil (a 50/50 mixture of molybdenum disulphide grease and clean engine oil).

25 Remove the rag from around the connecting rods. Lower the crankshaft into position in the upper crankcase, making sure all bearings remain in place (see illustration 22.4).

26 Lubricate the crankpins with molybdenum disulphide oil (a 50/50 mixture of molybdenum disulphide grease and clean engine oil). Carefully pull the connecting rods onto the crankpins, taking care not to mark the cylinders (see illustration 22.3c). Fit the caps onto the rods, locating the pins in the holes (see illustration). Make sure each cap is fitted the correct way around so the previously made markings align, and that the rod is facing the right way (see Step 2 and Section 23).

27 Apply some clean oil to the threads and under the heads of the NEW connecting rod bolts, then fit them and tighten them finger-tight (see illustration). Tighten both bolts alternately in three stages, first to 9 Nm, then to 18 Nm, then to 27.5 Nm (see illustration). Now, using a degree disc, tighten each bolt in turn by a further 90° (see illustration). You are recommended to have an assistant to hold the crankshaft down in the crankcase while tightening the bolts as it could jump out.

28 Carefully turn the crankshaft to check the connecting rod is not tight – if there are any signs of roughness or tightness, try tapping the bottom of the connecting rod cap as this may relieve tightness, but if in doubt remove the rod and recheck the bearing clearance.

29 Install the other connecting rods in the same way. Check to make sure that all components have been returned to their original locations using the marks made on disassembly.

30 Reassemble the crankcase halves (see Section 19).

23 Connecting rods and bearings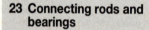

Note: *The connecting rod bolts can only be used in a running engine once, though they can be used to do the oil clearance check to prevent having to buy two sets of new bolts.*

Removal

1 Remove the engine from the frame (see Section 4) and separate the crankcase halves (see Section 19). Remove the transmission shafts (see Section 27).

2 Before removing the rods from the crankshaft, measure the big-end side clearance (the gap between the connecting

23.2 Measure the side clearance using a feeler gauge

22.27b ...and tighten them as described first to the specified torque and then through the specified angle

rod big-end and the crankshaft web) with a feeler gauge (see illustration). If the clearance is greater than the service limit listed in this Chapter's Specifications, replace the rods with new ones. If the clearance is still excessive, replace the crankshaft with a new one.

3 Using paint or a felt marker pen, mark the relevant cylinder identity on the front face of each connecting rod and cap to ensure that they are fitted correctly on reassembly (see illustration 22.2).

4 Remove the crankshaft (see Section 22, Steps 3 and 4). Wrap some rag around each connecting rod to protect the cylinder walls.

5 Turn the crankcase on its side. Push each piston/connecting rod assembly up its bore and remove it from the top making sure the connecting rod does not mark the cylinder walls (see illustration).

23.5 Push the piston and connecting rod assembly up and withdraw it from the top of the cylinder

Engine, clutch and transmission 2•51

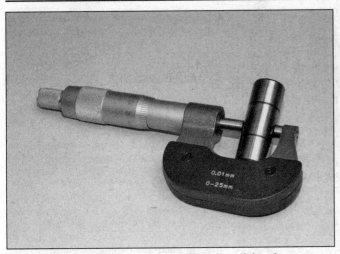
23.9a Measure the external diameter of the pin...

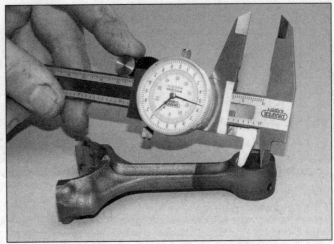
23.9b ...and the internal diameter of the connecting rod small-end

HAYNES HiNT *To ease removal of the pistons, carefully remove any ridge of carbon built up on the top of each cylinder bore using a scraper, Stanley knife blade or scouring cloth. If there is a pronounced wear ridge, remove it using a ridge reamer.*

Caution: *Do not try to remove the piston/connecting rod from the bottom of the cylinder bore. The piston will not pass the crankcase main bearing webs. If the piston is pulled right to the bottom of the bore the oil control ring will expand and lock the piston in position. If this happens it is likely the ring will break.*

6 Keep the rod, cap, bolts (if they are to be used for an oil clearance check), and the bearing shells (if they are to be re-used) together in their correct positions to ensure correct installation – fit the caps back onto the rods and finger-tighten the bolts to make sure.

7 Remove the pistons from the connecting rods if required (see Section 24), but note that if you are doing a big-end oil clearance check they must be on the rods to prevent them rotating on the crankpin and dislodging the Plastigauge.

Inspection

8 Check the connecting rods for cracks and other obvious damage.

9 Apply clean engine oil to the piston pin, slide it into the connecting rod small-end and check for any freeplay between the two. Measure the pin external diameter in its centre and the small-end bore diameter, then calculate the difference to obtain the small-end-to-piston pin clearance **(see illustrations)**. Compare the result to the specifications at the beginning of the Chapter. If the clearance is greater than specified, replace the components that are worn beyond their specified limits with new ones.

10 Refer to Section 21 and examine the connecting rod bearing shells. If they are scored, badly scuffed, corroded, or appear to have seized, new shells must be installed. Remove them using a small screwdriver as a lever in the notch, or by pushing their centres out to the side then lifting them out **(see illustration)**. Always replace the shells in the connecting rods as a set. If they are badly damaged, check the corresponding crankpin. Evidence of extreme heat, such as discoloration, indicates that lubrication failure has occurred. Be sure to thoroughly check the oil pump and pressure relief valve as well as all oil holes and passages before reassembling the engine.

11 Have the rods checked for twist and bend by a Honda dealer if you are in doubt about their straightness.

Oil clearance check

12 Whether new bearing shells are being fitted or the original ones are being re-used, the connecting rod bearing oil clearance should be checked prior to reassembly. Check the clearance on one rod at a time.

13 Clean both sides of the bearing shells, the bearing housings in both the connecting rod and cap, and the crankpin journals.

14 Press the bearing shells into their housings, making sure the tab on each shell engages the notch in the connecting rod/cap **(see illustration 23.10)**. Make sure the bearings are fitted in the correct location and take care not to touch any shell's bearing surface with your fingers. Refer to Step 25 and fit the rod and piston into its correct cylinder, making sure it is the correct way round. Lay the crankshaft in the upper crankcase half, then pull the connecting rod onto the crankpin **(see illustrations 22.4 and 22.3c)**.

15 Cut a length of the appropriate size Plastigauge (it should be slightly shorter than the width of the crankpin). Place a strand of Plastigauge on the crankpin journal, making sure it is not over the oil hole. Fit the cap onto the rod **(see illustration 22.26)**. Make sure the cap is fitted the correct way around so the previously made markings align. Apply some clean oil to the threads and under the heads of the connecting rod bolts **(see illustration 22.27a)**. Secure the bolts finger-tight at first. Tighten both bolts alternately in three stages, first to 7 Nm, then to 14 Nm, then to 21.6 Nm, all the time ensuring that the crankshaft does not rotate. Now, using a degree disc, tighten each bolt in turn and in one go by a further 90° **(see illustration 22.27b)**. It is highly advisable to have an assistant to hold the crankshaft down in the crankcase while tightening the bolts as it could dislodge.

16 Slacken the bolts and remove the connecting rod cap. Compare the width of the crushed Plastigauge on the crankpin to the scale printed on the Plastigauge envelope to obtain the connecting rod bearing oil clearance. Compare the reading to the specifications at the beginning of the Chapter.

17 On completion carefully scrape away all traces of the Plastigauge material from the crankpin and bearing shells using a fingernail or other soft object which is unlikely to score the shells.

18 If the clearance is within the range listed in this Chapter's Specifications and the bearings are in perfect condition, they can be re-used.

23.10 Remove the big-end shells

2•52 Engine, clutch and transmission

23.21a Crankpin journal size letters

23.21b Connecting rod size number

Crankpin journal code	Connecting rod code		
	1	2	3
A	Yellow	Green	Brown
B	Green	Brown	Black
C	Brown	Black	Blue

If the clearance is beyond the service limit, replace the bearing shells with new ones (see Steps 21 and 22). Check the oil clearance once again (the new shells may be thick enough to bring bearing clearance within the specified range). Always replace all of the shells at the same time.

19 If the clearance is still greater than the service limit listed in this Chapter's Specifications, the crankpin is worn and the crankshaft should be replaced with a new one.

20 Repeat the oil clearance check for the other connecting rods.

Bearing shell selection

21 Replacement bearing shells for the big-end bearings are supplied on a selected fit basis. Code letters and numbers stamped on the crankshaft and connecting rod are used to identify the correct replacement bearings. The crankpin journal size letters are stamped on the outside of the left-hand crankshaft web, and will be either A, B or C **(see illustration)**. The first letter after the L is for the No. 1 cylinder connecting rod (left-hand journal), and the letters correspond consecutively for each cylinder. The connecting rod size code number is marked across the flat face of the connecting rod and cap and will be either 1, 2 or 3 **(see illustration)**.

22 A range of bearing shells is available. To select the correct bearing shell colour code for a particular big-end, use the table below and cross-refer the crankpin journal size letter (stamped on the web) with the connecting rod size number (stamped on the rod). For example, if the crankpin size is B, and the connecting rod size is 1, then the bearing required is green. The colour is marked on the side of the shell **(see illustration 22.22)**.

Installation

23 Fit the pistons onto the connecting rods (see Section 24).

24 Clean both sides of the bearing shells, the bearing housings in both cap and rod, and the crankpin journals. If new shells are being fitted, ensure that all traces of any protective grease are cleaned off using paraffin (kerosene). Wipe the shells, cap and rod dry with a clean lint free cloth. Fit the bearing shells in the connecting rods and caps, making sure the tab on each shell engages the notch **(see illustration 23.10)**. Lubricate the shells with molybdenum disulphide oil (a 50/50 mixture of molybdenum disulphide grease and clean engine oil).

25 Lubricate the pistons, rings and cylinder bores with clean engine oil. The piston/rod assembly must be fitted with the IN mark on the underside of the piston crown and the connecting rod bearing shell notch on the intake side **(see illustration 24.2)**. Wrap some rag round the bottom of each connecting rod. Insert the piston/connecting rod assembly into the top of its bore, taking care not to allow the connecting rod to mark the bore **(see illustration 23.5)**. Carefully compress and feed each piston ring into the bore until the piston crown is flush with the top of the bore **(see illustration)**. If available, a piston ring compressor makes installation a lot easier – fit the compressor around the piston and over the rings and tighten it to compress the rings, then locate the assembly on the top of the bore and tap the top of the piston using a wooden or plastic tool (such as the handle end of a hammer) until the piston is completely in the bore **(see illustrations)** – make sure the bottom of the connecting rod does not come up against the oil pipe in the crankcase as you tap the piston in.

26 Install the crankshaft (see Section 22).

27 Reassemble the crankcase halves (see Section 19).

23.25a Carefully compress and feed each ring in

23.25b Fit the compressor over the piston and rings...

23.25c ...then compress the rings by tightening the bands on the compressor

23.25d Fit the rod into the bore and rest the compressor on the crankcase...

23.25e ...then tap the top of the piston with a wooden or soft-faced tool so that it enters

Engine, clutch and transmission 2•53

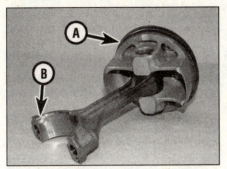

24.2 Note the IN mark (A) on the piston on the same side as the bearing shell notch (B)

24.3a Prise out the circlip using a suitable tool in the notch...

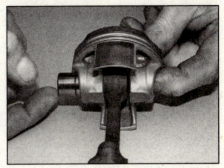

24.3b ...then push out the pin and separate the piston from the rod

24 Pistons

Removal

1 Remove the connecting rods (see Section 23).

2 Before removing the piston from the connecting rod, use a felt marker pen to write the cylinder identity on the skirt of each piston. The underside of the piston crown is marked IN and this mark faces the intake side of the cylinder, the same way as the bearing shell notch in the big-end of the connecting rod **(see illustration)**.

3 Carefully prise out the circlip on one side of the piston using needle-nose pliers or a small flat-bladed screwdriver inserted into the notch **(see illustration)**. Push the piston pin out from the other side to free the piston from the connecting rod **(see illustration)**. If required remove the other circlip. New circlips must be used. When the piston has been removed, slide its pin back into its bore so that related parts do not get mixed up.

> **HAYNES HiNT**
> *If a piston pin is a tight fit in the piston bosses, soak a rag in boiling water then wring it out and wrap it around the piston – this will expand the alloy piston sufficiently to release its grip on the pin. If the piston pin is particularly stubborn, extract it using a drawbolt tool, but be careful to protect the piston's working surfaces.*

4 Using your thumbs or a piston ring removal and installation tool, carefully remove the rings from the pistons **(see illustrations 25.10, 25.9b, 25.7c, b and a)**. Do not nick or gouge the pistons in the process. Carefully note which way up each ring fits and in which groove as they must be installed in their original positions if being re-used. The upper surface of the top ring should be marked with the letter R at one end, and the second (middle) ring marked RNE. The top and middle rings can also be identified by the fact that the top ring is narrower in width than the second (middle) ring, and their cross-section profiles are different.

5 Scrape all traces of carbon from the tops of the pistons. A hand-held wire brush or a piece of fine emery cloth can be used once most of the deposits have been scraped away. Do not use a wire brush mounted in a drill motor to remove deposits from the pistons – the piston material is soft and will be eroded away by the wire brush.

6 Use a piston ring groove cleaning tool to remove any carbon deposits from the ring grooves. If a tool is not available, a piece broken off an old ring will do the job. Be very careful to remove only the carbon deposits. Do not remove any metal and do not nick or gouge the sides of the ring grooves.

7 Once the deposits have been removed, clean the pistons with solvent and dry them thoroughly. If the identification mark previously made on the piston is cleaned off, be sure to re-mark it with the correct identity. Make sure the oil return holes below the oil ring groove are clear.

Inspection

8 Carefully inspect each piston for cracks around the skirt, at the pin bosses and at the ring lands. Normal piston wear appears as even, vertical wear on the thrust surfaces of the piston. If the skirt is scored or scuffed, the engine may have been suffering from overheating and/or abnormal combustion, which caused excessively high operating temperatures. Also check that the circlip grooves are not damaged.

9 Burned areas around the edge of the piston crown, indicate that pre-ignition or knocking under load have occurred. If you find evidence of any problems the cause must be corrected or the damage will occur again (see *Fault Finding* in the *Reference* section).

10 Measure the piston ring-to-groove clearance by laying each piston ring in its groove and slipping a feeler gauge in beside it **(see illustration)**. Make sure you have the correct ring for the groove (see Step 4). Check the clearance at three or four locations around the groove. If the clearance is greater than specified, replace both the piston and rings as a set. If new rings are being used, measure the clearance using the new rings. If the clearance is greater than that specified, the piston is worn and must be replaced with a new one.

11 Check the piston-to-bore clearance by measuring the bore (see Section 26), then measure the piston 5 mm up from the bottom of the skirt and at 90° to the piston pin axis **(see illustration)**. Make sure each piston is matched to its correct cylinder. Refer to the Specifications at the beginning of the Chapter and subtract the piston diameter from the bore diameter to obtain the clearance. If it is greater than the specified figure, the piston must be replaced with a new one (assuming the bore itself is within limits).

24.10 Measure the piston ring-to-groove clearance with a feeler gauge

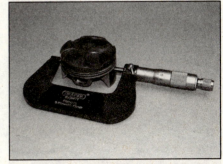

24.11 Measure the piston diameter with a micrometer at the specified distance from the bottom of the skirt

2•54 Engine, clutch and transmission

24.12a Measure the external diameter of the pin...

24.12b ...and the internal diameter of the bore in the piston

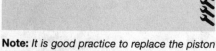

25 Piston rings

Note: *It is good practice to replace the piston rings with new ones when an engine is being overhauled.*

Removal

1 See Section 24, Steps 1 to 4.

Inspection

2 Whether re-using the old rings or fitting new ones, check the installed end gaps with the rings installed in the bore, as follows. Lay out each piston with its ring set and keep them together so the rings will be matched with the same piston and bore during the measurement procedure and engine assembly.

3 Insert the top ring into the top of the bore and square it up with the bore walls by pushing it in with the top of the piston **(see illustration)**. The ring should be at least 20 mm below the top edge of the bore, so it is within its area of travel in the bore. Slip a feeler gauge between the ends of the ring and compare the measurement to the specifications at the beginning of the Chapter **(see illustration)**.

4 If the gap is larger or smaller than specified, double check to make sure that you have the correct rings before proceeding; excess end gap is not critical unless it exceeds the service limit.

5 If the service limit is exceeded with new rings, check the bore for wear (see Section 26). If the gap is too small, the ring ends may come in contact with each other during engine operation, which can cause serious damage.

6 Repeat the procedure for the second (middle) ring and the oil control ring side-rails, but not the expander ring. Remember to keep the rings, pistons and bores matched up.

Installation

7 Fit the oil control ring (lowest on the piston) first. It is composed of three separate components, namely the expander and the upper and lower side-rails. Slip the expander into the groove, making sure the ends don't overlap **(see illustration)**. Next fit the lower

24.16a Slide the pin through the piston and rod...

24.16b ...and secure it with new circlips

12 Apply clean engine oil to the piston pin, insert it into the piston and check for any freeplay between the two. Measure the pin external diameter near each end **(see illustration)**, and the pin bore in each side of the piston **(see illustration)**. Calculate the difference to obtain the piston pin-to-piston pin bore clearance. Compare the result to the specifications at the beginning of the Chapter. If the clearance is greater than specified, replace the components that are worn beyond their specified limits. If not already done (see Section 23), repeat the measurements between the pin and the connecting rod small-end.

Installation

13 Inspect and install the piston rings (see Section 25).

14 Lubricate the piston pin, the piston pin bore and the connecting rod small-end bore with molybdenum disulphide oil (a 50/50 mixture of molybdenum disulphide grease and clean engine oil).

15 When fitting the pistons onto the connecting rods make sure the IN mark on the underside of the piston crown faces the same way as the bearing shell notch in the big-end **(see illustration 24.2)**.

16 If both circlips were removed fit one **new** circlip into one side of the piston (do not re-use old circlips). Line up the piston on its correct connecting rod, and insert the piston pin from the other side **(see illustration)**. Secure the pin with another **new** circlip **(see illustration)**. When fitting the circlips, compress them only just enough to fit them in the piston, and make sure they are properly seated in their grooves with their open end away from the removal notch.

17 Install the connecting rods (see Section 23) and reassemble the crankcase halves (see Section 19).

25.3a Set the ring square in its bore using the piston...

25.3b ...and measure the end gap using a feeler gauge

25.7a Fit the oil ring expander in its groove...

Engine, clutch and transmission 2•55

25.7b ...then fit the lower side rail...

25.7c ...and the upper side rail on each side of it

25.9a Note the marking on each ring and make sure it faces up

25.9b Install the middle ring...

25.10 ...and the top ring as described

11 Once the rings are correctly installed, check they move freely without snagging and stagger their end gaps as shown **(see illustration)**.

26 Cylinder block

Removal

Note: *The bores are specially coated and so great care must be taken not to scratch or gouge them. If there is no need to remove the piston/connecting rod assemblies from the cylinder block they can be left in their bores.*

1 Separate the crankcase halves (Section 19), and remove the crankshaft (Section 22), the transmission input shaft (Section 27), and if required (see **Note**) the connecting rods and pistons (Section 23). If required remove the coolant inlet union (see Chapter 3).
2 Unscrew the two bolts securing the block to the crankcase **(see illustration)**.
3 Carefully lift the block up off the crankcase **(see illustration)**: If it is stuck, tap around the joint faces with a soft-faced mallet. Do not attempt to free the block by inserting a screwdriver between the block and crankcase mating surfaces – you'll damage them.
4 Remove the gasket and discard it – a new one must be used. If they are loose, remove the dowels from the block or the crankcase **(see illustration 26.12)**.
5 Clean all traces of old gasket material from the block and crankcase. If a scraper is used,

side-rail **(see illustration)**. Do not use a piston ring installation tool on the side-rails as they may be damaged. Instead, place one end of the side-rail into the groove between the expander and the ring land. Hold it firmly in place and slide a finger around the piston while pushing the rail into the groove. Next, fit the upper side-rail in the same manner **(see illustration)**. Check that the ends of the expander have not overlapped.
8 After the three oil ring components have been installed, check to make sure that both the upper and lower side-rails can be turned smoothly in the ring groove.
9 Fit the second (middle) ring next – it should be marked with the letters RNE at one end, and it can also be identified by its cross-section profile **(see illustration)**. Fit the ring into the middle groove in the piston with the identification letters facing up **(see illustration)**. Do not expand the ring any more than is necessary to slide it into place. To avoid breaking the ring, use a piston ring installation tool.
10 Finally, fit the top ring, marked with the letter R, which must face up, in the same manner into the top groove in the piston **(see illustration)**.

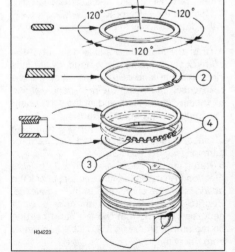
25.11 Piston ring installation details – stagger the ring end gaps as shown
1 Top ring
2 Second (middle) ring
3 Oil ring expander
4 Oil ring side rails

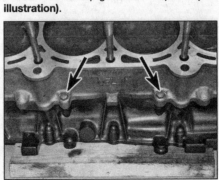
26.2 Unscrew the bolts (arrowed)

26.3 Removing the block

2•56 Engine, clutch and transmission

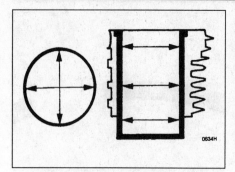

26.9a Measure the cylinder bore in the directions shown...

26.9b ...using a telescoping gauge, then measure the gauge with a micrometer

26.12 Fit the dowels (arrowed) then lay the new gasket on the crankcase

take care not to scratch or gouge the soft aluminium. Be careful not to let any of the gasket material fall into the oil passages.

Inspection

6 Check the cylinder walls carefully for scratches and score marks.
7 Check the gasket and the mating surfaces on the block and crankcase for signs of leakage, which could indicate warpage.
8 Using a precision straight-edge and a feeler gauge set to the warpage limit listed in the specifications at the beginning of the Chapter, check the block upper surface for warpage. Refer to *Tools and Workshop Tips* in the Reference section for details of how to use the straight-edge. If warpage is excessive the crankcases must be replaced with new ones.
9 Using telescoping gauges and a micrometer (see *Tools and Workshop Tips*), check the dimensions of each cylinder to assess the amount of wear, taper and ovality. Measure near the top (but below the level of the top piston ring at TDC), centre and bottom (but above the level of the oil ring at BDC) of the bore, both parallel to and across the crankshaft axis **(see illustrations)**. Compare the results to the specifications at the beginning of the Chapter. If the cylinders are worn, oval or tapered beyond the service limit the block must be replaced with a new one.
10 If the precision measuring tools are not available, take the block to a Honda dealer or specialist motorcycle repair shop for assessment and advice.

Installation

11 Ensure both cylinder block and crankcase mating surfaces are clean. If removed, fit the dowels **(see illustration 26.12)**.
12 Lay the new base gasket over the studs and onto the crankcase, locating it over the dowels and making sure all the holes are correctly aligned **(see illustration)**. Never re-use the old gasket.
13 Carefully fit the cylinder block onto the crankcase, making sure it locates correctly onto the dowels **(see illustration 26.3)**.
14 Fit and tighten the bolts **(see illustration 26.2)**.
15 Install the remaining components in a reverse of their removal sequence (see Step 1).

27 Transmission shaft removal and installation

Removal

1 Remove the engine from the frame (see Section 4) and separate the crankcase halves (see Section 19).
2 Lift the output shaft out of the casing, noting how it engages with the input shaft and its selector forks **(see illustration)**. If the shaft is stuck, use a soft-faced hammer and gently tap on the ends. Remove the oil seal and discard it as a new one must be used **(see illustration 27.11)**.
3 Remove the selector forks (see Section 29) – the drum can stay in place, but remove it as well if required.
4 Draw the input shaft a little way out of the crankcase until the right-hand bearing is clear (the left-hand bearing should stay in the crankcase), then slide the right-hand bearing off the end of the shaft and lift the shaft out of the crankcase **(see illustrations)**.
5 The transmission shafts can be disassembled and inspected for wear or damage (see Section 28).
6 Referring to *Tools and Workshop Tips* (Section 5) in the Reference Section, check the bearings on the shafts and in the crankcase. Replace the bearings with new ones if necessary, noting that the left-hand bearing on the output shaft is not available separately from the shaft.
7 Pull the transmission oil jet pipe out **(see illustration 20.2d)**. Remove the O-ring **(see illustration 20.8a)** – a new one must be used.

Installation

8 Clean the oil jet pipe with new solvent and dry it with compressed air, blowing it through

27.2 Lift out the output shaft

27.4a Draw the input shaft and bearing out...

27.4b ...then slide the bearing off...

27.4c ...and remove the input shaft

Engine, clutch and transmission 2•57

the jets and pipe. Fit a new O-ring smeared with oil onto the pipe **(see illustration 20.8a)**. Insert the pipe **(see illustration 20.2d)** – make sure the tab on the head of the pipe locates in the cut-out **(see illustration 20.8b)**.

9 Make sure the thrust washer is on the left-hand end of the input shaft **(see illustration 28.20b)**. Position the shaft in the crankcase then fit the right-hand bearing onto the outer end of the shaft with its marked side facing out **(see illustration 27.4c and b)**. Slide the shaft in locating the inner end in the left-hand bearing and pressing the right-hand bearing into the crankcase **(see illustration)**.

10 Install the selector drum (if removed) and the selector forks (see Section 29).

11 Lubricate the left-hand end of the output shaft with clean oil and slide the new oil seal on **(see illustration)**. Smear the seal outer lip with oil.

12 Lower the output shaft into position in the upper crankcase **(see illustration 27.2)**, making sure the selector forks locate in their pinion grooves, the left-hand bearing locating ring, oil seal lip and pin all seat correctly in the grooves and cut-out, and the right-hand bearing pin sits in its cut-out **(see illustrations)**.

Caution: If the ring retainer or dowel do not locate correctly, the crankcase halves will not seat properly.

13 Position the gears in the neutral position and check the shafts are free to rotate easily and independently (i.e. the input shaft can turn whilst the output shaft is held stationary) before proceeding further. Also check that each gear can be selected by turning the input shaft with one hand and the selector drum with the other.

14 Reassemble the crankcase halves (see Section 19).

28 Transmission shaft overhaul

1 Remove the transmission shafts from the crankcase (see Section 27). Always disassemble the transmission shafts separately to avoid mixing up the components.

> **HAYNES HINT** *When disassembling the transmission shafts, place the parts on a long rod or thread a wire through them to keep them in order and facing the proper direction.*

Input shaft

Disassembly

2 Mark the outer face of the 2nd gear pinion on the left-hand end of the shaft so it can re-fitted the same way round. Slide the thrust washer and the pinion off the shaft **(see illustration and 28.20b and a)**.

27.9 Seat the inner end of the input shaft in its bearing

27.11 Lubricate the end of the output shaft and fit the oil seal

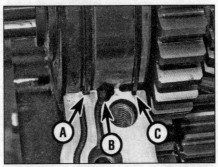

27.12a Make sure the oil seal lip (A), pin (B) and locating ring (C)...

27.12b ...and the locating pin (arrowed) locate correctly

3 Slide the tabbed lockwasher off the shaft, then turn the slotted splined washer to offset the splines and slide it off the shaft **(see illustrations 28.19c, b and a)**. Slide the 6th gear pinion and its splined bush off the shaft, followed by the splined washer **(see illustrations 28.18c, b and a)**.

4 Remove the circlip, then slide the combined

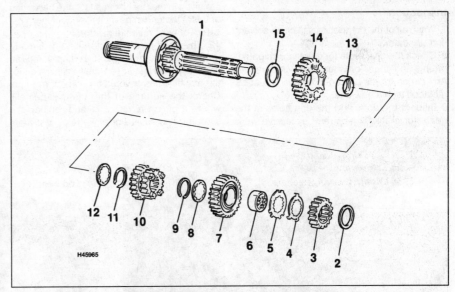

28.2 Transmission input shaft components

1 Input shaft and bearing	9 Circlip
2 Thrust washer	10 Combined 3rd/4th gear pinion
3 2nd gear pinion	11 Circlip
4 Tabbed lockwasher	12 Splined washer
5 Slotted splined washer	13 5th gear pinion bush
6 6th gear pinion splined bush	14 5th gear pinion
7 6th gear pinion	15 Thrust washer
8 Splined washer	

2•58 Engine, clutch and transmission

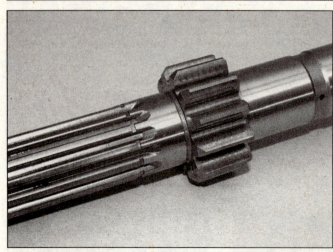

28.5 1st gear pinion (arrowed) is part of the input shaft

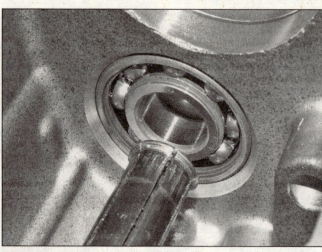

28.6a Locate the knife-end behind the inner race and expand it...

3rd/4th gear pinion off the shaft **(see illustrations 28.17b and a)**.

5 Remove the circlip, then slide the splined washer, the 5th gear pinion and its bush, and the thrust washer off the shaft **(see illustrations 28.16e, d, c, b and a)**. The 1st gear pinion is integral with the shaft **(see illustration)**.

6 If required, remove the left-hand bearing from the crankcase – you will need an expanding puller to lock behind the bearing inner race and a slide-hammer attachment to jar the bearing out **(see illustrations)**. Heat around the bearing housing first using a hot air gun to make removal easier

Inspection

7 Wash all of the components in clean solvent and dry them off.

8 Check the gear teeth for cracking, chipping, pitting and other obvious wear or damage. Any pinion that is damaged as such must be replaced with a new one.

9 Inspect the dogs and the dog holes in the gears for cracks, chips, and excessive wear especially in the form of rounded edges. Make sure mating gears engage properly. Replace the paired gears as a set if necessary.

10 Check for signs of scoring or bluing on the pinions, bushes and shaft. This could be caused by overheating due to inadequate lubrication. Check that all the oil holes and passages are clear. Replace any damaged pinions or bushes.

11 Check that each pinion moves freely on the shaft or its bush but without undue freeplay. Check that each bush moves freely on the shaft but without undue freeplay. If the necessary equipment is available the individual components for which dimensions are given in the Specifications at the beginning of this Chapter can be measured to assess the extent of wear **(see illustration)**.

12 The shaft is unlikely to sustain damage unless the engine has seized, placing an unusually high loading on the transmission, or the machine has covered a very high mileage. Check the surface of the shaft, especially where a pinion turns on it, and replace the shaft if it has scored or picked up, or if there are any cracks. Damage of any kind can only be cured by replacement.

13 Check the washers and circlips and replace any that are bent or appear weakened or worn. Use new ones if in any doubt. Note that it is good practice to renew all circlips when overhauling gearshafts.

Reassembly

14 During reassembly, apply molybdenum disulphide oil (a 50/50 mixture of molybdenum disulphide grease and clean engine oil) to the mating surfaces of the shaft, pinions and bushes. When fitting the circlips, do not expand their ends any further than is necessary. Fit the stamped circlips and washers so that their chamfered side faces away from the thrust side.

15 If removed, fit the ball bearing into the crankcase with its marked side facing out of the housing, referring to *Tools and Workshop Tips* in the Reference Section **(see illustration)**. Put the new bearing in the freezer for a while, and when it is cold heat the bearing housing with a hot air gun. Fit the bearing and tap it squarely

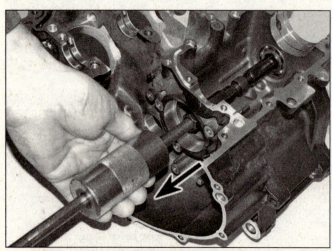

28.6b ...then use the slide-hammer to jar the bearing out

28.11 Measure the dimensions of the related components as listed in the Specifications

Engine, clutch and transmission 2•59

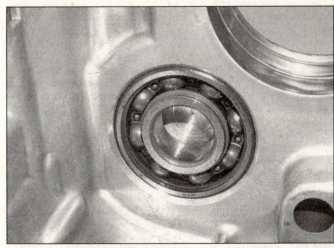
28.15 Fit the bearing into the crankcase

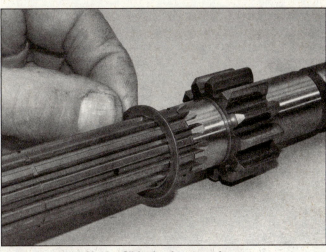
28.16a Slide the thrust washer...

in using a socket or bearing driver that bears on the outer race until it seats.

16 Slide the thrust washer onto the left-hand end of the shaft, followed by the 5th gear pinion bush **(see illustrations)**. Fit the 5th gear pinion onto the bush with its dogs facing away from the integral 1st gear **(see illustration)**. Slide the splined washer onto the shaft, then fit the circlip, making sure that it locates correctly in the groove in the shaft **(see illustrations)**.

17 Slide the combined 3rd/4th gear pinion onto the shaft with the larger 4th gear pinion facing the 5th gear pinion **(see illustration)**. Fit the circlip, making sure it is locates correctly in its groove in the shaft **(see illustrations)**.

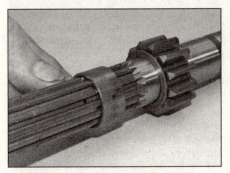
28.16b ...the 5th gear pinion bush...

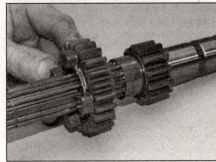
28.16c ...the 5th gear pinion...

28.16d ...and the splined washer onto the shaft...

28.16e ...and secure them with the circlip...

28.16f ...making sure it locates properly in its groove

28.17a Slide the combined 3rd/4th gear pinion onto the shaft...

28.17b ...and secure it with the circlip...

28.17c ...making sure it locates properly in its groove

2•60 Engine, clutch and transmission

28.18a Slide the splined washer...

28.18b ...the 6th gear pinion splined bush...

28.18c ...and the 6th gear pinion onto the shaft

28.19a Slide on the slotted splined washer...

28.19b ...and locate it as shown...

28.19c ...then slide on the tabbed lockwasher and locate its tabs in the slots

28.20a Slide on the 2nd gear pinion...

18 Slide the splined washer onto the shaft, followed by the 6th gear pinion splined bush, aligning the oil hole in the bush with the hole in the shaft (**see illustrations**). Slide the 6th gear pinion onto the bush, making sure its dogs face the 3rd/4th gear pinion (**see illustration**).

19 Slide the slotted splined washer onto the shaft and locate it in its groove, then turn it in the groove so that the splines on the washer align with the splines on the shaft and secure the washer in the groove (**see illustrations**). Slide the tabbed lockwasher onto the shaft, locating the tabs in the slots in the outer rim of the splined washer (**see illustration**).

20 Slide the 2nd gear pinion onto the end of the shaft with the mark made on removal facing out (**see illustration**). Fit the thrust washer (**see illustration**).

21 Check that all components have been correctly installed (**see illustration**).

Output shaft

Disassembly

22 Slide the bearing off the right-hand end

28.20b ...and the thrust washer

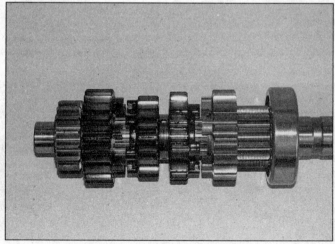

28.21 The assembled input shaft

Engine, clutch and transmission 2•61

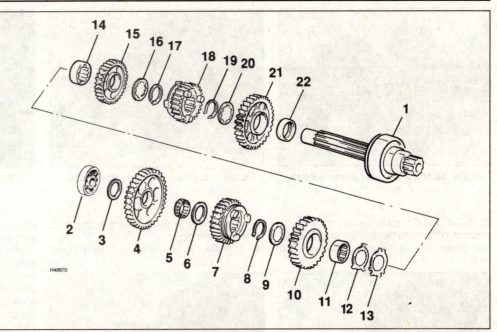

1 Output shaft and bearing
2 Bearing
3 Thrust washer
4 1st gear pinion
5 Needle roller bearing
6 Thrust washer
7 5th gear pinion
8 Circlip
9 Splined washer
10 4th gear pinion
11 4th gear pinion splined bush
12 Tabbed lockwasher
13 Slotted splined washer
14 3rd gear pinion splined bush
15 3rd gear pinion
16 Splined washer
17 Circlip
18 6th gear pinion
19 Circlip
20 Splined washer
21 2nd gear pinion
22 2nd gear pinion bush

28.22 Transmission output shaft components

of the shaft **(see illustration and illustration 28.37d)**.

23 Slide the thrust washer off the shaft, followed by the 1st gear pinion and its needle roller bearing, the thrust washer and the 5th gear pinion **(see illustrations 28.37c, b and a, and 28.36b and a)**.

24 Remove the circlip, then slide the splined washer, the 4th gear pinion and its splined bush off the shaft **(see illustrations 28.35d, c, b and a)**.

25 Slide the tabbed lockwasher off the shaft, then turn the slotted splined washer to offset the splines and slide it off the shaft **(see illustrations 28.34c, b and a)**.

26 Slide the 3rd gear pinion and its splined bush, followed by the splined washer, off the shaft **(see illustrations 28.33c, b and a)**.

27 Remove the circlip, then slide the 6th gear pinion off the shaft **(see illustrations 28.32b and a)**.

28 Remove the circlip, then slide the splined washer, the 2nd gear pinion and its bush off the shaft **(see illustrations 28.31d, c, b and a)**.

Inspection
29 Refer to Steps 7 to 13 above.

Reassembly
30 During reassembly, apply engine oil to the mating surfaces of the shaft, pinions and bushes. When fitting the circlips, do not expand the ends any further than is necessary. Fit the stamped circlips and washers so that their chamfered side faces away from the thrust side.

31 Slide the 2nd gear pinion bush onto the shaft, then slide the 2nd gear pinion onto the bush with its dog holes facing away from the bearing, followed by the splined washer **(see illustrations)**. Fit the circlip, making sure it is locates correctly in its groove in the shaft **(see illustrations)**.

28.31a Slide the 2nd gear pinion bush...

28.31b ...the 2nd gear pinion...

28.31c ...and the splined washer onto the shaft...

28.31d ...and secure them with the circlip...

28.31e ...making sure it locates in the groove

28.32a Slide the 6th gear pinion onto the shaft...

28.32b ...and secure it with the circlip...

28.32c ...making sure it locates in the groove

32 Slide the 6th gear pinion on with its selector fork groove facing away from the 2nd gear pinion, then fit the circlip, making sure it is locates correctly in its groove in the shaft **(see illustrations)**.

33 Slide the splined washer and the 3rd gear pinion splined bush onto the shaft, making sure the oil hole in the bush aligns with the hole in the shaft, then slide the 3rd gear pinion onto its bush with its dog holes facing the 6th gear pinion **(see illustrations)**.

34 Slide the slotted splined washer onto the shaft and locate it in its groove, then turn it in the groove so that the splines on the washer align with the splines on the shaft and secure the washer in the groove **(see illustrations)**. Slide the lockwasher onto the shaft, locating the tabs on the lockwasher in the slots in the outer rim of the splined washer **(see illustration)**.

35 Slide the 4th gear pinion splined bush onto the shaft, making sure the oil hole in the bush aligns with the hole in the shaft **(see illustration)**. Slide the 4th gear pinion onto its bush with its dog holes face away from the 3rd gear pinion **(see illustration)**. Slide the

28.33a Slide the splined washer...

28.33b ...the 3rd gear pinion splined bush...

28.33c ...and the 3rd gear pinion onto the shaft

28.34a Slide the slotted splined washer onto the shaft...

28.34b ...and locate it as shown

28.34c Slide the lockwasher onto the shaft and engage it with the slotted washer

28.35a Slide the 4th gear pinion splined bush...

28.35b ...the 4th gear pinion...

Engine, clutch and transmission 2•63

28.35c ...and the splined washer onto the shaft...

28.35d ...and secure them with the circlip...

28.35e ...making sure it locates in the groove

28.36a Slide the 5th gear pinion...

28.36b ...and the thrust washer onto the shaft

28.37a Slide the needle bearing...

splined washer on, then fit the circlip, making sure it is locates correctly in its groove in the shaft **(see illustrations)**.

36 Slide the 5th gear pinion onto the shaft with its selector fork groove facing the 4th gear pinion, followed by the thrust washer **(see illustrations)**.

37 Slide the 1st gear pinion needle roller bearing onto the shaft, then slide the 1st gear pinion onto the bearing with its dog holes facing the 5th gear pinion **(see illustrations)**. Fit the thrust washer, then fit the bearing onto the end of the shaft **(see illustrations)**.

38 Check that all components have been correctly installed **(see illustration)**.

28.37b ...the 1st gear pinion...

28.37c ...and the thrust washer onto the shaft...

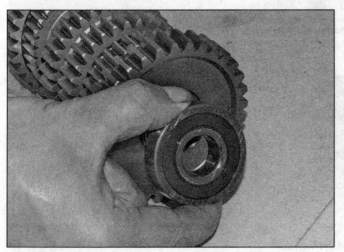
28.37d ...then fit the bearing onto the end of the shaft

28.38 The assembled output shaft

2•64 Engine, clutch and transmission

29.3 Unscrew the bolts (arrowed) and remove the plate

29.4 Note the identification markings on the forks

29.6a Unscrew the bolts...

29 Selector drum and forks

Removal

1 The selector drum and forks are located in the upper crankcase half. Remove the engine (see Section 4) and separate the crankcase halves (see Section 19).

2 Remove the transmission output shaft (see Section 27). If not already done, remove the gearchange mechanism (see Section 16).

3 Unscrew the transmission input shaft bearing/fork shaft retainer plate bolts and remove the plate, noting how it fits (see illustration).

4 Before removing the selector forks, note that each fork carries an identification letter or letters (see illustration). The right-hand fork has RL facing the right-hand (clutch) side of the engine, the centre fork has C facing the right-hand (clutch side), and the left-hand fork has RL facing the left-hand (alternator) side. The RL forks fit into the output shaft and the C fork fits into the input shaft.

5 Support the selector forks and withdraw the shaft from the casing, then remove the forks (see illustrations 29.14d, c, b and a). Slide the forks back onto the shaft to keep them in the correct order.

6 Unscrew and remove the selector drum bearing retainer bolts (see illustration). Withdraw the selector drum from the right-hand side of the engine (see illustration).

Inspection

7 Inspect the selector forks for any signs of wear or damage, especially around the fork ends where they engage with the groove in the pinion. Check that each fork fits correctly in its pinion groove. Check closely to see if the forks are bent. If the forks are in any way damaged they must be replaced with new ones.

8 Measure the thickness of the fork ends and compare the readings to the specifications (see illustration). Replace the forks with new ones if they are worn beyond their specifications.

9 Check that the forks fit correctly on their shaft (see illustration). They should move freely with a light fit but no appreciable freeplay. Measure the diameter of the fork shaft and the internal diameter of the fork bores (see illustrations). Replace the forks and/or shaft with new ones if they are worn beyond their specifications. Check that the fork shaft holes in the casing are neither worn nor damaged.

10 Check the selector fork shaft is straight by rolling it along a flat surface. A bent rod will cause difficulty in selecting gears and make the gearchange action heavy. Replace the shaft with a new one if it is bent.

11 Inspect the selector drum grooves and selector fork guide pins for signs of wear or

29.6b ...and withdraw the selector drum

29.8 Measure the fork end thickness

29.9a Check the fit of each fork on the shaft...

29.9b ...then measure the fork shaft OD...

29.9c ...and the fork bore ID

Engine, clutch and transmission 2•65

29.11 Check the guide pins and their grooves in the drum

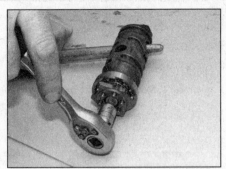

29.12a Counter-hold the drum as shown and unscrew the bolt

29.12b Remove the old bearing and fit a new one. Note the locating pin (arrowed)

29.12c Locate the cut-out (arrowed) over the pin

29.12d Apply a threadlock to the bolt

29.13 Position the drum so the neutral detent (arrowed) is aligned as shown

damage **(see illustration)**. If either component shows signs of wear or damage the fork(s) and drum must be replaced with new ones.

29.14a Slide the shaft in and through the right-hand fork with RL facing the clutch side...

29.14b ...then fit the centre fork with C also facing the clutch side...

12 Check that the selector drum bearing rotates freely and has no sign of freeplay between it and the casing. To fit a new bearing, remove the selector drum cam by unscrewing the bolt in its centre – pass a rod through the drum to counter-hold it **(see illustration)**. Note the locating pin in the end of the drum and remove it for safekeeping if required. Remove the old bearing and fit a new one (see *Tools and Workshop Tips* in the Reference Section if necessary) **(see illustration)**. Fit the selector drum cam, locating the pin in the wider cut-out in the back of the cam **(see illustration)**. Clean the threads of the cam bolt and apply a suitable non-permanent thread locking compound, and tighten it to the torque setting specified at the beginning of the Chapter **(see illustration)**.

Installation

13 Slide the selector drum into position in the crankcase **(see illustration 29.6b)**. Make sure the drum end locates into its bore in the casing. Clean the threads of the drum retainer bolts, then apply a suitable non-permanent thread locking compound. Fit the bolts and tighten them to the torque setting specified at the beginning of the Chapter **(see illustration 29.6a)**. Align the drum so that the neutral detent in the cam plate is positioned as shown **(see illustration)**.

14 Lubricate the selector fork shaft with clean engine oil and slide it into the crankcase, locating each fork in the correct order and way round (see Step 4), fitting each fork's guide pin in its groove in the selector drum, and fitting the centre fork ends in its pinion groove in the input shaft **(see illustrations)**.

15 Clean the threads of the input shaft

29.14c ...and slide the shaft through...

29.14d ...then fit the left-hand fork with RL facing the alternator side, and seat the shaft in its bore in the crankcase

bearing/fork shaft retainer plate bolts and apply a suitable thread locking compound. Fit the plate with the OUTSIDE mark facing out, and tighten the bolts to the torque setting specified at the beginning of the Chapter **(see illustration 29.3)**.

16 Install the transmission output shaft, then reassemble the crankcase halves and the rest of the engine.

30 Balancer shaft

Removal

1 Separate the crankcase halves (see Section 19) – the balancer shaft is in the lower half.
2 If you intend to separate the shaft holder from the shaft (there is no need unless you are fitting new parts), make an alignment mark across the holder and shaft – this will give a good indication as to the starting point for resetting the backlash adjustment when the crankcases are reassembled **(see illustration)**.
3 Unscrew the shaft retainer bolt and the holder mounting bolt **(see illustration)**. Support the balancer gear/weight assembly, then withdraw the shaft and remove the gear/weight **(see illustration)** – you may need to either rotate the shaft as you withdraw it or lift the gear/weight assembly to ease removal against the offset of the shaft.
4 Remove the O-ring from the shaft – a new one must be used **(see illustration 30.11)**.

If required slacken the holder pinch bolt and slide the holder off the shaft.

Inspection

5 Inspect the gear teeth for signs of wear or damage, and replace the gear with a new one if necessary. If damage is found, check the drive gear teeth on the crankshaft. The gear/weight can be disassembled if required – all components are available individually.
6 Remove the washer from each end of the gear/weight, noting which fits where **(see illustrations 30.10d and c)**. Slide the shaft back into the gear/weight and check that it runs freely and smoothly in the bearings. If there is any evidence of wear on the shaft, or it is a sloppy fit in the bearings, and the bearings are good, replace the shaft with a new one. If the bearings do not run smoothly and freely, or if there is any wear or damage evident, replace them with new ones. Note that all components are matched by size and should be replaced either as a set, or by matching them using the coded markings (see Steps 8 and 9). Withdraw the shaft and the bearings. Clean them with solvent.
7 Separate the weight from the gear **(see illustration 30.10b)**. Check the condition of the rubber dampers in the gear for damage, deformation and deterioration, and replace them with new ones if necessary **(see illustration 30.10a)**.

Bearing selection

8 Replacement bearings for the balancer are supplied on a selected fit basis according to the internal diameter (ID) of the end it runs in. Code letters stamped on the weight web are used to identify the correct replacement bearings, which are colour coded. The balancer gear/weight size code letters (the right-hand one for the gear end and the left-hand one for the weight end) will be either an A, a B or a C **(see illustration)**.
9 Measure the internal diameter of each end of the balancer and check it according to its letter against the specifications given in the table below to check the weight bearing surface has not worn. If it has worn beyond its specification replace the balancer with a new one and select new bearings according to the numbers on the new one. If the balancer has not worn select new bearings according to the letters. For example, if the gear end size is B, then the bearing required for the gear end of the shaft is white. The colour is marked on the bearing.

Balancer gear/weight ID codes	Bearing colour
A – 26.996 to 27.000 mm	Blue
B – 26.991 to 26.996 mm	White
C – 26.987 to 26.991 mm	Green

Installation

10 Smear the dampers with grease, then fit them onto the gear **(see illustration)**. Fit the gear onto the balancer, aligning the notch in the inner rim with the line on the balancer, and making sure the dampers locate correctly **(see illustration)**. Lubricate the bearings with clean

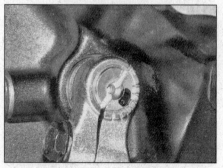

30.2 Make an alignment mark between the shaft and the holder if required

30.3a Unscrew the retainer bolt (A) and holder mounting bolt (B)

30.3b Withdraw the shaft and lift the balancer out

30.8 Balancer gear and weight size code letters (arrowed)

30.10a Fit the dampers onto the gear...

30.10b ...then fit the gear onto the balancer, aligning the marks (arrowed)

Engine, clutch and transmission 2•67

30.10c Fit the bearing and the shouldered washer into the gear end...

30.10d ...then fit the bearing and the dished washer into the weight end

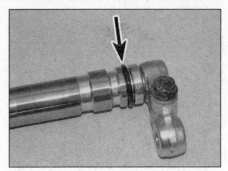
30.11 Fit a new O-ring (arrowed) into the outer groove

oil and slide them into the balancer, making sure they are correctly located according to the codes (see Steps 8 and 9), and fit the shouldered washer onto the gear end and the dished washer onto the weight end **(see illustrations)**.

11 Fit a new O-ring onto the balancer shaft and smear it with clean oil **(see illustration)**. If removed fit the holder onto the end of the shaft, aligning the marks made on removal, and tighten the pinch bolt **(see illustration 30.2)**.

12 Position the balancer gear/weight assembly in the crankcase with the weight facing the left-hand end, then slide the shaft in with the O-ring on the outer end **(see illustration 30.3b)**. Fit and tighten the holder mounting bolt. Fit the retaining bolt with a new washer and tighten it **(see illustration)**.

13 Reassemble the crankcase halves (see Section 19). Finish rebuilding the engine and install it (see Section 4).

14 Carry out the static backlash adjustment procedure (see below).

15 Carry out the dynamic backlash adjustment procedure (see below).

Backlash adjustment

Note: *A backlash adjustment is provided so that the gears mesh at their optimum point for quiet running with minimal wear. If the amount of backlash is too great, the shafts will clatter. If the gears are running tight, they will whine, and wear very quickly. At the optimum point the gears will run very quietly – it is easy to tell the difference with the engine running. Adjustment is possible due to the offset which allows eccentric movement of the balancer gear in relation to its drive gear when the shaft is turned. The static adjustment procedure allows the backlash to be set up in roughly the optimum position, but the dynamic procedure should always be carried out as well to fine tune the setting.*

Static adjustment

Note: *This procedure must be carried out when the engine is cold.*

16 Slacken the balancer shaft holder pinch bolt **(see illustration)**.

17 Turn the shaft slightly clockwise using a screwdriver in the slotted end, then turn it anti-clockwise until resistance is felt – at this point backlash between the gears has been eliminated. Now turn the shaft clockwise so the slot moves 2.5 to 3 graduations as marked on the holder, then temporarily tighten the pinch bolt.

18 Now carry out the dynamic adjustment procedure (see below).

Dynamic adjustment

Note: *This procedure must be carried out when the engine is warm.*

19 Remove the lower fairing (see Chapter 7). Start the engine and allow it to warm up, then let it idle.

20 Slacken the balancer shaft holder pinch bolt **(see illustration 30.16)**.

21 Turn the shaft slightly one way then the other to find the point at which the gears run at their quietest. Too far one way and the gears will whine (no backlash), too far the other and they will clatter (excessive backlash). Rev the engine and check that there is no unwanted noise at varying speeds.

22 On completion, tighten the pinch bolt. Install the lower fairing (see Chapter 7).

31 Running-in procedure

1 Make sure the engine oil and coolant levels are correct (see *Pre-ride checks*). Make sure there is fuel in the tank.

2 Turn the engine kill switch to the RUN position and shift the gearbox into neutral. Turn the ignition ON.

3 Start the engine and allow it to run with

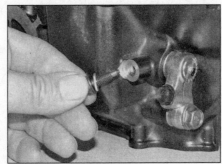
30.12 Fit a new sealing washer onto the retaining bolt

no throttle applied until it reaches operating temperature.

 Warning: *If the oil pressure warning light doesn't go off, or it comes on while the engine is running, stop the engine immediately.*

4 If the oil pressure warning light does not go out, stop the engine immediately and try to find the cause – refer to Section 3. If an engine is run without oil pressure, even for a short period of time, severe damage will occur.

5 Check carefully for oil and coolant leaks and make sure the transmission and controls, especially the brakes, function properly before road testing the machine.

6 Treat the machine gently for the first few miles to make sure oil has circulated throughout the engine and any new parts installed have started to seat.

7 Even greater care is necessary if new pistons/rings or a new crankcase/bores have been fitted, and the bike will have to be run in as when new. This means greater use of the transmission and a restraining hand on the throttle until at least 300 miles (500 km) have been covered. There's no point in keeping to any set speed limit – the main idea is to keep from labouring the engine and to gradually increase performance up to the 300 miles (500 km) mark. Experience is the best guide, since it's easy to tell when an engine is running freely.

8 Upon completion of the road test, and after the engine has cooled down completely, recheck the valve clearances (see Chapter 1) and check the engine oil and coolant levels (see *Pre-ride checks*).

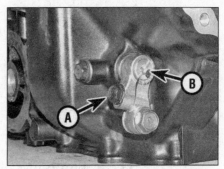
30.16 Slacken the pinch bolt (A) and turn the shaft (B) using a screwdriver

Notes

Chapter 3
Cooling system

Contents

	Section number
Coolant change	see Chapter 1
Coolant hoses, pipes and unions	8
Coolant level check	see Pre-ride checks
Coolant reservoir	7
Cooling fans and relay	2
Cooling system checks	see Chapter 1

	Section number
General information	1
Radiator	5
Temperature display and ECT sensor	3
Thermostat housing and thermostat	4
Water pump	6

Degrees of difficulty

Easy, suitable for novice with little experience   Fairly easy, suitable for beginner with some experience   Fairly difficult, suitable for competent DIY mechanic Difficult, suitable for experienced DIY mechanic   Very difficult, suitable for expert DIY or professional

Specifications

Coolant
Mixture type and capacity	see Chapter 1

ECT sensor
Resistance @ 50°C	6.8 to 7.4 K-ohms
Resistance @ 80°C	2.1 to 2.7 K-ohms

Thermostat
Opening temperature	80 to 84°C
Fully open	95°C
Valve lift	8 mm (min)

Radiator
Cap valve opening pressure	16 to 20 psi (1.1 to 1.4 Bar)

Torque settings
Right-hand cooling fan assembly	
Fan blade nut	2.7 Nm
Fan bracket bolts	8.4 Nm
Fan motor nuts	5.2 Nm
Left-hand cooling fan assembly	
Fan blade nut	1 Nm
Fan bracket bolts	8.4 Nm
Fan motor screws	2.7 Nm
ECT sensor	23 Nm
Thermostat cover bolts	12 Nm
Water pump bolts	12 Nm

1 General information

The cooling system uses a water/anti-freeze coolant to carry away excess heat from the engine and maintain as constant a temperature as possible. The cylinders are surrounded by a water jacket from which the heated coolant is circulated by thermo-syphonic action in conjunction with a water pump, which is driven by the oil pump. The hot coolant passes upwards to the thermostat and through to the radiator. The coolant then flows across the core of the radiator, then to the water pump and back to the engine where the cycle is repeated.

A thermostat is fitted in the system to prevent the coolant flowing through the radiator when the engine is cold, therefore accelerating the speed at which the engine reaches normal operating temperature. The ECT (engine coolant temperature) sensor mounted in the thermostat housing transmits information to the temperature gauge and to the instrument panel, and to the ECM (engine control module). Two cooling fans fitted to the back of the radiator aid cooling in extreme conditions by drawing extra air through. The fan motors are controlled by a relay that receives a signal from the ECM that in turn receives information from the ECT sensor.

The complete cooling system is partially sealed and pressurised, the pressure being controlled by a valve contained in the spring-loaded radiator cap. By pressurising the coolant the boiling point is raised, preventing premature boiling in adverse conditions. The overflow pipe from the system is connected to a reservoir into which excess coolant is expelled under pressure. The discharged coolant automatically returns to the radiator by the vacuum created when the engine cools.

⚠ **Warning:** *Do not remove the pressure cap from the radiator when the engine is hot. Scalding hot coolant and steam may be blown out under pressure, which could cause serious injury. When the engine has cooled, place a thick rag, like a towel, over the pressure cap; slowly rotate the cap anti-clockwise to the first stop. This procedure allows any residual pressure to escape. When the steam has stopped escaping, press down on the cap while turning it anti-clockwise and remove it.*

Caution: *Do not allow anti-freeze to come in contact with your skin or painted surfaces of the motorcycle. Rinse off any spills immediately with plenty of water. Anti-freeze is highly toxic if ingested. Never leave anti-freeze lying around in an open container or in puddles on the floor; children and pets are attracted by its sweet smell and may drink it. Check with the local authorities about disposing of used anti-freeze. Many communities will have collection centres which will see that anti-freeze is disposed of safely.*

Caution: *At all times use the specified type of anti-freeze, and always mix it with distilled water in the correct proportion. The anti-freeze contains corrosion inhibitors which are essential to avoid damage to the cooling system. A lack of these inhibitors could lead to a build-up of corrosion which would block the coolant passages, resulting in overheating and severe engine damage. Distilled water must be used as opposed to tap water to avoid a build-up of scale which would also block the passages.*

2 Cooling fans and relay

1 The cooling fans are on the back of the radiator, one on each side. The fans are independently controlled, with the right-hand one coming on at 102.6°C and the left-hand one coming on at 106.2°C. Each fan has its own fuse and relay. If the engine is overheating and a cooling fan isn't coming on, check the relevant cooling fan fuse (see Chapter 8). If the fuse is good, check the relevant relay as described below. If neither fan comes on check the ECT sensor.

Cooling fans

Check

2 To test a cooling fan motor, remove the relevant fairing side panel (see Chapter 7). Disconnect the fan wiring connector (see illustration). Using a 12 volt battery and two jumper wires with suitable connectors, connect the battery positive (+) lead to the black/blue (2008 to 2011 models) or blue (2012-on models) wire terminal on the fan side of the wiring connector, and the battery negative (–) lead to the black wire terminal on the connector. Once connected the fan should operate. If it does not, and the connector and wiring between it and the motor is good, then the fan motor is faulty.

Replacement

⚠ **Warning:** *The engine must be completely cool before carrying out this procedure.*

3 Remove the radiator (see Section 5).
4 Unscrew the bolts securing the fan bracket to the radiator and remove the fan assembly (see illustration).
5 To disassemble the fan free the wiring connector from its holder. Unscrew the fan blade nut and remove the blade (see illustration). Undo the three nuts on the front of the fan motor or the three screws on the back (depending on which fan you are working on) and separate the motor from its bracket (see illustration).
6 Installation is the reverse of removal. Tighten the fan motor nuts or screws to the relevant torque setting specified at the beginning of the Chapter. Clean the threads of the motor shaft. Align the flats on the motor shaft with those in the bore in the fan blade. Apply a suitable non-permanent thread locking compound to the fan blade nut and tighten it to the relevant

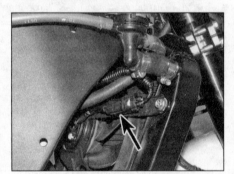

2.2 Fan wiring connector (arrowed) – right-hand radiator

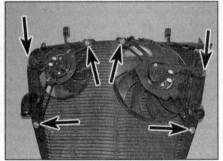

2.4 Fan bracket bolts (arrowed)

2.5a Fan blade nut (arrowed)

2.5b Fan motor screws (arrowed) – left-hand fan

Cooling system 3•3

specified torque. Tighten the bracket bolts to the specified torque.
7 Install the radiator (see Section 5).

Cooling fan relays
Check
8 Remove the relay (see Steps 13 and 14).
9 Set a multimeter to the ohms x 1 scale and connect it across the relay's A and B terminals **(see illustration)**. There should be no continuity (infinite resistance). Using a fully-charged 12 volt battery and two insulated jumper wires, connect the positive (+) terminal of the battery to the C terminal on the relay, and the negative (–) terminal to the D terminal on the relay. At this point the relay should be heard to click and the multimeter read 0 ohms (continuity). If this is the case the relay is proved good. If the relay does not click when battery voltage is applied and still indicates no continuity (infinite resistance) across its terminals, it is faulty and must be replaced with a new one.
10 If the relay is good, check for battery voltage at the blue or blue/red (according to the relay being tested) wire terminal in the relay socket with the ignition switch ON. If there is no voltage, check the wiring between the relay, the fusebox and the ignition switch for continuity, referring to the relevant wiring diagram at the end of Chapter 8. Next check for voltage at the black/white wire terminal, and if there is none check the wire to the engine stop relay for continuity, then check the relay (see Chapter 4, Section 8). If voltage is present, check that there is continuity to the fan wiring connector in the black/blue or black/red (according to relay) wire with the ignition switch OFF. If there is no continuity, check the wiring between the relay and the fan wiring connector, then to the fan and back to the connector. Next check for continuity to earth in the green wire in the loom side of the connector. If all is good check the grey/blue or grey/black wire between the relay and the ECM (engine control module). There should be continuity in all wires.
11 If the fan is on the whole time, refer to Steps 13 and 14 and remove the relay – the fan should stop. If it does, the relay is defective and must be replaced with a new one.
12 If the fan works but is suspected of cutting

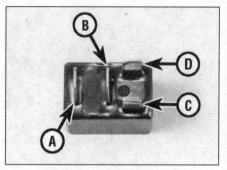

2.9 Fan relay test terminal ID

in at the wrong temperature, check the ECT sensor (see Section 3).

Replacement
13 Remove the rider's seat (see Chapter 7).
14 Open the relay box lid, then pull the relevant relay out **(see illustration)**.
15 Installation is the reverse of removal.

3 Temperature display and ECT sensor

Temperature and warning display
Check
1 The circuit consists of the ECT (engine coolant temperature) sensor mounted in the thermostat housing and the digital display and warning light in the instrument cluster. When the ignition is first switched on all the segments in the LCD display and the warning light should come on temporarily – this serves as an indication that the display is functioning correctly (if not, refer to Chapter 8).
2 Under normal operating conditions, when the coolant temperature is below 34°C the display will show '- -'. When the temperature is between 35°C and 121°C the display will show the actual temperature. Should the temperature reach 122°C the display will start to flash, and the temperature warning symbol will come on. If this occurs stop the engine and check the coolant level in the reservoir (see *Pre-ride checks*). If the temperature goes

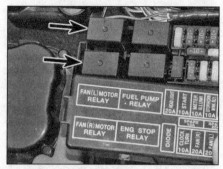

2.14 The location of the relays (arrowed) is marked on the box lid

above 132°C the display will continue to flash that temperature.
3 If the display is not working at all, check the instrument cluster power input (see Chapter 8). If the power lines are good, then either the printed circuit board (PCB) or the LCD display unit could be faulty.
4 If the display as a whole works but the coolant function doesn't or is thought to be inaccurate, check the sensor (see below). If the sensor is good, displace and support the fairing, leaving the wiring connected (see Chapter 7) and check the wiring between the sensor and the instrument cluster connector for continuity. If the wiring is good the display is faulty.

Replacement
5 The temperature display is part of the LCD unit in the instrument cluster PCB. No individual components are available for the instrument cluster PCB. If it is faulty, replace it with a new one (see Chapter 8).

ECT sensor
Check
6 Raise the fuel tank (see Chapter 4). Remove the air filter housing jacket, noting how it fits **(see illustration)**. The sensor is mounted in the thermostat housing **(see illustration 3.8)**. First make sure the connector is secure on the sensor and all wires are intact.
7 The resistance of the sensor changes with changes in temperature – see the Specifications at the beginning of the chapter. While in theory it is possible to bench test the sensor at those temperatures, in practice the test is difficult to set up and perform.
8 However you can test the resistance of the sensor in the bike with the engine cold, warm and hot. Raise the fuel tank (see Chapter 4). Remove the air filter housing jacket, noting how it fits **(see illustration 3.6)**. Disconnect the ECT sensor wiring connector **(see illustration)**. Connect the positive probe of a multimeter set to read resistance to the grey/red wire terminal on the sensor and the negative probe to the body of the sensor, and check that the resistance decreases as the sensor gets warmer – see the values specified at 50°C and 80°C in the Specifications. If the sensor fails it is most likely to give a zero,

3.6 Unclip and remove the jacket

3.8 ECT sensor wiring connector (arrowed)

constant value, or infinite resistance reading at all temperatures.

Replacement

 Warning: The engine must be completely cool before carrying out this procedure.

9 Remove the thermostat housing (see Section 4).
10 Unscrew and remove the sensor **(see illustration)**.
11 Fit a new sealing washer onto the sensor. Fit the sensor and tighten it to the torque setting specified at the beginning of the Chapter.
12 Install the thermostat housing (see Section 4).

4 Thermostat housing and thermostat

1 The thermostat is automatic in operation and should give many years service without requiring attention. In the event of a failure, the valve will probably jam open, in which case the engine will take much longer than normal to warm up. Conversely, if the valve jams shut, the coolant will be unable to circulate and the engine will overheat. Neither condition is acceptable, and the fault must be investigated promptly.

Thermostat housing

Removal

 Warning: The engine must be completely cool before carrying out this procedure.

3.10 ECT sensor (arrowed)

2 The thermostat housing is on the back of the engine in the middle. Drain the cooling system (see Chapter 1). Remove the fuel tank, and for best access remove the throttle bodies (see Chapter 4). If you don't remove the throttle bodies remove the air filter housing jacket, noting how it fits **(see illustration 3.6)**.
3 Disconnect the ECT sensor wiring connector **(see illustration 3.8)**.
4 Slacken the clamps securing the hoses to the housing and detach them, noting which fits where **(see illustration)** – if the large bore hose is difficult to detach do so after displacing the housing.
5 Unscrew the thermostat housing bolts and remove the housing **(see illustration)**. Remove the O-ring **(see illustration 4.6)** – a new one must be used.

Installation

6 Fit the housing using a new O-ring and tighten the bolts **(see illustrations)**.

7 Connect the ECT sensor wiring **(see illustration 3.8)**.
8 Connect the hoses and tighten the clamps **(see illustration 4.4)**.
9 Fill the cooling system (see Chapter 1).

Thermostat

Removal

 Warning: The engine must be completely cool before carrying out this procedure.

10 Remove the thermostat housing.
11 Unscrew the thermostat cover bolts and detach it from the housing **(see illustration)**.
12 Withdraw the thermostat, noting how it fits **(see illustration)**.

Check

13 Examine the thermostat visually before carrying out the test. If it remains in the open position at room temperature, it should be replaced with a new one. Also check the condition of the seal.
14 Suspend the thermostat by a piece of wire in a container of cold water. Place a thermometer capable of reading temperatures up to 110°C in the water so that the bulb is close to the thermostat **(see illustration)**. Heat the water, noting the temperature when the thermostat opens, and compare the result with the specifications given at the beginning of the Chapter. Also check the amount the valve opens after it has been heated for a few minutes and compare the measurement to the specifications. If the readings obtained differ from those given, the thermostat is faulty and must be replaced with a new one.

4.4 Slacken the clamps (arrowed) and detach the hoses

4.5 Thermostat housing bolts (arrowed)

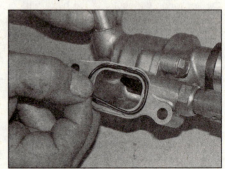

4.6 Fit a new O-ring into the groove

4.11 Unscrew the bolts (arrowed) and detach the cover...

4.12 ...then withdraw the thermostat from the housing

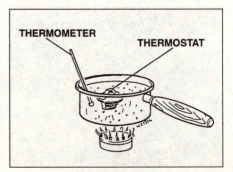

4.14 Thermostat test set-up

Cooling system 3•5

15 In the event of thermostat failure, if the thermostat is permanently closed, as an emergency measure only it can be removed and the machine used without it (this is better than leaving it in as the engine will overheat). If it is permanently open you are better to leave it in. In both cases take care when starting the engine from cold as it will take much longer than usual to warm up. Ensure that a new unit is installed as soon as possible.

Installation

16 Check the seal for signs of damage or deterioration and fit a new one if necessary **(see illustration)**. Fit the thermostat into the housing with the bleed hole at the top, aligning it with the raised mark **(see illustration 4.12)**.
17 Fit the cover and tighten the bolts to the torque setting specified at the beginning of the Chapter **(see illustration)**.
18 Install the thermostat housing.

4.16 Fit a new seal if necessary

4.17 Fit the cover and tighten the bolts

5 Radiator

Note: *If the radiator is being removed as part of the engine removal procedure, detach the hoses from their unions on the engine rather than on the radiator and remove the radiator with the hoses attached to it. Note the routing of the hoses.*

Removal

⚠️ **Warning: The engine must be completely cool before carrying out this procedure.**

1 Remove the fairing side panels (see Chapter 7). Drain the cooling system (see Chapter 1).
2 Disconnect the fan wiring connectors **(see illustration 2.2)**.
3 Release the trim clip and displace the guard on the left-hand end **(see illustration)**.
4 Slacken the clamps securing the hoses to the radiator and detach the hoses **(see illustrations)**.
5 Unscrew the upper and lower mounting bolts **(see illustration)**. Ease the radiator to the right to free the mounting lug from its grommet, then remove the radiator, taking care not to catch the fins on the bracket **(see illustration)**. Note the arrangement of the collars and rubber grommets in the radiator mounts. Replace the grommets with new ones if they are damaged, deformed or deteriorated **(see illustration 5.7)**.
6 If necessary, remove the cooling fans from the radiator (see Section 2). Check the radiator for signs of damage and clear any dirt or debris that might obstruct air flow and inhibit cooling. If the radiator fins are badly damaged or broken the radiator must be replaced with a new one.

Installation

7 Installation is the reverse of removal, noting the following.
- Make sure the coolant hoses and their clamps are in good condition (see Chapter 1).
- Make sure the rubber grommets are in place with the collars fitted in them **(see illustration)**.
- Push the hoses fully onto their unions and tighten the clamps.
- Make sure that the fan wiring is connected **(see illustration 2.2)**.
- On completion refill the cooling system as described in Chapter 1.

5.3 Release the trim clip and displace the guard

5.4a Slacken the clamps (arrowed), and detach the hoses from the right-hand side...

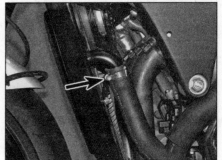
5.4b ...and the left-hand side

5.5a Unscrew the bolts (arrowed)

5.5b Release the radiator from the peg (arrowed) and remove it

5.7 Note the collars and check the condition of the grommets

3•6 Cooling system

6.4 Slacken the clamps (arrowed) and detach the hoses

6.5a Unscrew the bolts (arrowed)...

6.5b ...and withdraw the pump

Pressure cap check

8 If problems such as overheating or loss of coolant occur, check the entire system as described in Chapter 1. The radiator cap opening pressure should be checked by a Honda dealer with the special tester required to do the job. If the cap is defective, replace it with a new one.

6 Water pump

Check

1 Refer to Chapter 1, Section 7.

Removal

2 Drain the coolant (see Chapter 1).

3 Remove the front sprocket cover (see Chapter 6).
4 Slacken the clamps securing the coolant hoses to the pump and detach the hoses, noting which fits where (see illustration).
5 Unscrew the three pump mounting bolts, then draw the pump from the crankcase, noting how it fits (see illustrations). It may be necessary to lever it out to overcome the O-ring on the pump body. Remove the O-ring from the rear of the body – a new one must be used (see illustration 6.9).
6 To remove the cover unscrew the remaining bolt (see illustrations) – if the cover is stuck lever it off using a small screwdriver in the leverage point provided (see illustration). Remove the O-ring – a new one must be used (see illustration 6.8). Do not attempt to remove the impeller and seals – the pump comes as an assembly and no internal components are available.

7 Wiggle the water pump impeller back-and-forth and in-and-out (see illustration). If there is excessive movement, replace the pump with a new one. Also check for corrosion or a build-up of scale in the pump body and clean or replace the pump as necessary.

Installation

8 If the cover was removed smear the new O-ring with grease and fit it into its groove (see illustration). Fit the cover onto the pump (see illustration 6.6b). Fit the bolt with the different head into the upper rear hole and tighten it lightly (see illustration 6.6a).
9 Apply a smear of engine oil to the new pump body O-ring and fit it onto the body (see illustration). Slide the pump into the crankcase, aligning the slot in the shaft end with the tab on the oil pump shaft (see illustration 6.5b). Make sure the bolt holes

6.6a Unscrew the bolt...

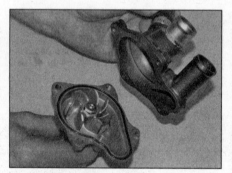

6.6b ...and remove the cover...

6.6c ...using a screwdriver in the lever point if necessary

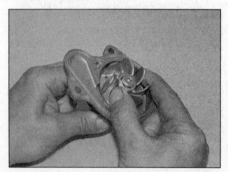

6.7 Check the pump impeller as described

6.8 Fit the new O-ring into its groove

6.9 Fit a new O-ring (arrowed) onto the body up against the flange

Cooling system 3•7

6.10 Connect and secure the hoses

7.1 Disconnect the hose (arrowed)

7.3 Release the trim clips (arrowed) and remove the reservoir

are aligned. Fit the three mounting bolts and tighten all four bolts to the torque setting specified at the beginning of the Chapter (see illustration 6.5a).
10 Fit the coolant hoses onto the pump and secure them with their clamps (see illustration).
11 Refill the cooling system (see Chapter 1). Install the front sprocket cover (see Chapter 6).

7 Coolant reservoir

Removal

1 The coolant reservoir is located behind the engine. Raise the fuel tank (see Chapter 4). Disconnect the feed hose at the joint (see illustration).
2 Remove the swingarm (see Chapter 5).
3 Release the trim clips (see Chapter 7) and manoeuvre the reservoir out, noting the routing of the hoses (see illustration). Remove the cap and drain the reservoir. Remove the hoses if required.

Installation

4 Installation is the reverse of removal. On completion refill the reservoir to the UPPER level line with the specified coolant mixture (see Chapter 1).

8 Coolant hoses, pipes and unions

Removal

1 Before removing a hose or pipe, drain the coolant (see Chapter 1).
2 Use a screwdriver to slacken the larger-bore hose clamps, then slide them clear. The smaller-bore hoses are secured by spring clamps that can be expanded by squeezing their ears together with pliers.
Caution: The radiator unions are fragile. Do not use excessive force when attempting to remove the hoses.
3 If a hose proves stubborn, release it by rotating it on its union before working it off. If all else fails, cut the hose with a sharp knife. Whilst this means replacing the hose with a new one, it is preferable to buying a new radiator.
4 The inlet union to the cylinder block can be removed by unscrewing its bolts (see illustration). If the union is removed, the O-ring must be replaced with a new one. The outlet from the cylinder head goes into the thermostat housing, which is covered in Section 4.

Installation

5 Slide the clamps onto the hose and then work the hose on to its union as far as the spigot where present (see illustration).

> **HAYNES HiNT**: If the hose is difficult to push on its union, soften it by soaking it in very hot water, or alternatively a little soapy water on the union can be used as a lubricant.

6 Rotate the hose on its unions to settle it in position before sliding the clamps into place and tightening them securely.
7 If the inlet union to the cylinder block has been removed, fit a new O-ring into the groove, using a dab of grease to hold it in place if necessary. Fit the union and tighten the mounting bolts.
8 Refill the cooling system with fresh coolant (see Chapter 1).

8.4 Inlet union bolts (arrowed)

8.5 Push the hose on up to the spigot (arrowed)

Notes

Chapter 4
Engine management system

Contents

	Section number		Section number
Air filter	see Chapter 1	Fuel system hoses	18
Air filter housing and air intake system	3	Fuel tank	2
Catalytic converter	21	General information and precautions	1
Clutch switch	see Chapter 8	Idle air control valve	11
Engine control module (ECM)	7	Ignition coils	23
Engine stop relay	8	Ignition switch	see Chapter 8
Evaporative emission control (EVAP) system	20	Ignition system check	22
Exhaust gas control valve (EGCV)	17	Ignition timing	24
Exhaust system	16	Immobiliser system	25
Fuel gauge and sensor	14	Neutral/gear position switch	see Chapter 8
Fuel injection system description	4	Pulse secondary air (PAIR) system	19
Fuel injection system fault diagnosis	5	Sidestand switch	see Chapter 8
Fuel injection system sensors	6	Spark plugs	see Chapter 1
Fuel pressure check	12	Steering damper (HESD)	see Chapter 5
Fuel pump	13	Throttle bodies	9
Fuel pump relay	8	Throttle cable check and adjustment	see Chapter 1
Fuel rails and injectors	10	Throttle cables	15
Fuel system check	see Chapter 1		

Degrees of difficulty

| Easy, suitable for novice with little experience | Fairly easy, suitable for beginner with some experience | Fairly difficult, suitable for competent DIY mechanic | Difficult, suitable for experienced DIY mechanic | Very difficult, suitable for expert DIY or professional |

Specifications

General information
Cylinder numbering	1 to 4 from left to right
Firing order	1-2-4-3
Spark plugs	See Chapter 1

Fuel
Grade	Unleaded. Minimum 95 RON (Research Octane Number) for Europe. Minimum pump octane number 91 for the US
Fuel tank capacity (including reserve)	17.7 litres
Reserve volume	approx. 3.5 litres

Fuel injection system
Engine idle speed	1200 ± 100 rpm
Fuel pressure at idle speed	50 psi (3.5 Bar)
Minimum fuel flow rate	167 cc every 10 seconds

Fuel injection system test data
Note: *All values given are only accurate at 20°C (68°F)*

Crankshaft position (CKP) sensor	
Resistance	approx. 460 ohms
Minimum peak voltage output	0.7 volts
Engine coolant temperature (ECT) sensor resistance	2.3 to 2.6 K-ohms
Fuel injector resistance	11 to 13 ohms
Idle air control valve resistance	99 to 121 ohms
Intake air duct control valve resistance	28 to 32 ohms
Intake air temperature (IAT) sensor resistance	1 to 4 K-ohms @ 20 to 30°C
Oxygen sensor heater resistance	5 to 20 ohms

Exhaust gas control valve (EGCV)
Servo static resistance . . . . 3.5 to 6.5 K-ohms
Servo variable resistance . . . . 0 to 5 K-ohms

Emission control systems
PAIR system control valve resistance . . . . 23 to 27 ohms
EVAP system control valve resistance . . . . 30 to 34 ohms

Ignition system
Timing . . . . 3.3° BTDC (F mark) at idle
Coil primary winding resistance . . . . 1.6 to 1.8 ohms
Coil secondary winding resistance. . . . . 8 K-ohms
Initial voltage (see text). . . . . Battery voltage (approximately 12 volts)

Torque settings
Engine coolant temperature (ECT) sensor . . . . 23 Nm
Exhaust downpipe nuts . . . . 12 Nm
Exhaust silencer clamp bolt . . . . 17 Nm
Footrest bracket-to-frame bolts . . . . 37 Nm
Fuel pump mounting plate nuts . . . . 12 Nm
Fuel rail bolts . . . . 5.1 Nm
Fuel tank front mounting bolts . . . . 10 Nm
Knock sensor bolt . . . . 22 Nm
Oxygen sensor . . . . 24.5 Nm
PAIR system reed valve cover bolts . . . . 12 Nm
Throttle body adapter bolts . . . . 12 Nm
Timing inspection cap . . . . 18 Nm

1 General information and precautions

General information

Fuel system

The fuel supply system consists of the fuel tank, an integrated fuel pump, pressure regulator, filter and level sensor, the fuel hoses, fuel rails, injectors, throttle bodies, and control cables. The fuel pump is switched on and off with the engine via the fuel pump relay. The injection system, known as PGM-DSFI, supplies fuel and air to the engine via 46 mm throttle bodies. There are two injectors per cylinder. The primary injectors are mounted in the throttle bodies below the throttle valve and operate all the time the engine is running. The secondary injectors are mounted in the top of the air filter housing, operate only at engine speeds above 5000 rpm and throttle openings of more than 10°, and spray fuel into the air entering the throttle bodies above the throttle valves. The injectors are operated by the Engine Control Module (ECM) using the information obtained from the various sensors it monitors (refer to Section 4 for more information on the operation of the fuel injection system).

Idle speed is controlled electronically by the idle air control valve (IACV), which supplies more air for cold start and warm-up with the throttle closed, based on information supplied to the ECM from the system temperature sensors.

The exhaust system is a four-into-one, and incorporates an exhaust gas control valve (EGCV) that regulates the flow of gases according to throttle opening and engine speed for optimum performance. The system also has a closed-loop catalytic converter with an oxygen sensor supplying information to the ECM.

All models have a low fuel warning light incorporated in the instrument cluster LCD, actuated by a level sensor that is part of the fuel pump inside the fuel tank. The warning light comes on when there is approximately 3.5 litres of fuel left.

Ignition system

The transistorised electronic ignition system is combined with the fuel injection system, both being controlled by the ECM (engine control module). The ignition system comprises a rotor, crankshaft position sensor (CKP sensor), engine control module (ECM) and ignition coils.

The ignition triggers are on the alternator rotor, which is on the left-hand end of the crankshaft, and generate a signal in the CKP sensor as the crankshaft rotates. The CKP sensor sends that signal to the ECM which, in conjunction with information received from the throttle position sensor, camshaft position sensor, engine coolant temperature sensor and knock sensor, calculates the ignition timing and supplies the ignition coils with the power necessary to produce a spark at the plugs. There is no provision for adjusting the ignition timing.

The system uses four HT coils, one for each cylinder. The coils are of the plug top type known as 'stick coils', with the coil windings being incorporated in the spark plug cap. This eliminates the need for HT leads and saves space.

The system incorporates a safety interlock circuit that cuts the ignition if the sidestand is extended whilst the engine is running and in gear, or if a gear is selected whilst the engine is running and the sidestand is down. It also prevents the engine from being started if the sidestand is down and the engine is in gear. The engine can be started with the sidestand up when it is in gear as long as the clutch lever is pulled in.

Models sold in certain markets are fitted with an immobiliser system (HISS – Honda Ignition Security System) that will not allow the engine to be started unless the correct key is used. The immobiliser system has its own fault diagnosis function.

Note: *Individual engine management system components can be checked but not repaired. If system troubles occur, and the faulty component can be isolated, the only cure for the problem in most cases is to replace the part with a new one. Keep in mind that most electronic parts, once purchased, cannot be returned. To avoid unnecessary expense, make very sure the faulty component has been positively identified before buying a new part.*

Precautions

Warning: *Petrol (gasoline) is extremely flammable, so take extra precautions when you work on any part of the fuel system. Always remove the battery (see Chapter 8). Don't smoke or allow open flames or bare light bulbs near the work area, and don't work in a garage where a natural gas-type appliance is present. If you spill any fuel on your skin, rinse it off immediately with soap and water. When you perform any kind of work on the fuel system, wear safety glasses and have a fire extinguisher suitable for a class B type fire (flammable liquids) on hand.*

Engine management system 4•3

With the fuel injection system, some residual pressure will remain in the fuel feed hoses and fuel rail assemblies after the motorcycle has been used. Before disconnecting any fuel hose, ensure the ignition is switched OFF then release fuel system pressure (see Section 2). It is vital that no dirt or debris is allowed to enter the fuel tank or the fuel rail assembly whilst the fuel hoses are disconnected. Any foreign matter in the fuel system components could result in injector damage or malfunction. Ensure the ignition is switched OFF before disconnecting or reconnecting any fuel injection system wiring connector. If a connector is disconnected or reconnected with the ignition switched ON, the engine control module (ECM) may be damaged.

Always perform service procedures in a well-ventilated area to prevent a build-up of fumes.

Never work in a building containing a gas appliance with a pilot light, or any other form of naked flame. Ensure that there are no naked light bulbs or any sources of flame or sparks nearby.

Do not smoke (or allow anyone else to smoke) while in the vicinity of petrol (gasoline) or of components containing it. Remember the possible presence of vapor from these sources and move well clear before smoking.

Check all electrical equipment belonging to the house, garage or workshop where work is being undertaken (see the *Safety first!* section of this manual). Remember that certain electrical appliances such as drills, cutters etc, create sparks in the normal course of operation and must not be used near petrol (gasoline) or any component containing it.

Again, remember the possible presence of fumes before using electrical equipment.

Always mop up any spilt fuel and safely dispose of the rag used.

Any stored fuel that is drained off during servicing work must be kept in sealed containers that are suitable for holding petrol (gasoline), and clearly marked as such; the containers themselves should be kept in a safe place. Note that this last point applies equally to the fuel tank if it is removed from the machine; also remember to keep its filler cap closed at all times.

Read the *Safety first!* section of this manual carefully before starting work.

2 Fuel tank

Warning: *Refer to the precautions given in Section 1 before starting work.*

Raise

1 Make sure the fuel cap is secure. Remove the fuel tank cover (see Chapter 7).
2 On RR models draw the fuel tank overflow hose up from the left-hand side of the lower fairing, noting its routing **(see illustration)**. On US models disconnect the fuel tank breather hose at the hose joint.
3 On RA models remove the left-hand fairing side panel and engine trim cover (see Chapter 7). Disconnect the fuel tank overflow hose at the hose joint **(see illustration)**.

4 Unscrew the front mounting bolt on each side, noting the washers **(see illustration)**. Get a suitable piece of wood (such as a piece of 2 x 1 inch, about 14 inches long). Lift the tank and fit the wood between it and the frame to support it in the raised position **(see illustration)**. Note the sleeves in the grommets **(see illustration 2.13)**.

Lower

5 Remove the prop and pivot the tank down onto the frame, making sure the hoses and wiring do not get squashed or kinked. Fit the front mounting bolts with their washers and tighten to the torque setting specified at the beginning of the Chapter. Connect or locate the breather and overflow hoses as required according to model.

Removal

Note: *Removing the tank may involve a small amount of unavoidable fuel spillage, which is obviously dangerous. Refer to the precautions given in Section 1 before starting work, and have plenty of rag to hand. Try to time the removal procedure with a near empty tank, which makes it much easier to lift. Once the tank has been removed, rest it on some soft rag to prevent damaging the paintwork or hose unions.*

6 Raise the tank as described above.
7 To improve access to the fuel hose connector release the overflow hose guide from the bracket **(see illustration)**.
8 Disconnect the fuel pump and level sensor wiring connectors **(see illustration)**. Free the wiring from the clamp.

2.2 Draw the hose up so it is free

2.3 Disconnect the hose at the joint (arrowed)

2.4a Unscrew the bolt on each side

2.4b Tank in raised position with wood support

2.7 Release the hose guide

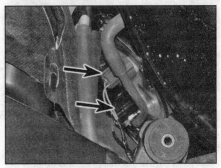

2.8 Disconnect the wiring connectors (arrowed)

2.11a Remove the cover

2.11b Press and hold the retainer tabs and pull the hose connector off

2.12a Unscrew the bolt (arrowed) on each side...

2.12b ...then carefully lift the tank away

9 To eliminate any residual pressure in the fuel system start the engine and let it idle until it stops. Turn the ignition OFF.
10 Disconnect the battery negative (–) lead (see Chapter 8).
11 Remove the fuel hose connector cover (see illustration). Clean any dirt from the connector. Place a wad of rag for catching any residual fuel in the hose under the connector. Press the retainer tabs in then pull the connector off the pipe union (see illustration). Remove the retainer – note that Honda specify to replace it with a new one whenever the fuel hose is disconnected. Seal the union and the connector with a piece from a plastic bag or the finger from a latex glove, secured with an elastic band, to prevent dirt getting in.
12 Note the routing of the overflow/breather hose – it is removed with the tank. Remove the support and lower the tank. Unscrew the rear mounting bolt on each side, noting the washers (see illustration). Carefully lift the tank off the frame and remove it (see illustration).
13 Remove the sleeves from the front mounting grommets and the collars from the rear if required (see illustration). Check all the tank rubbers and hoses for signs of damage or deterioration and replace them with new ones if necessary.

Installation

14 Fit the mounting rubbers into their mounts if removed, and fit the sleeves into the front rubbers and collars into the rear (see illustration 2.13).
15 Depending on how the tank has been stood and how full it is there is the possibility of fuel having made its way into the breather pipe which could spurt out of the hose when the tank is moved – be prepared with some rag for this. Once the tank is upright the pipe will fill itself with air.
16 Position the tank on the frame and insert the rear bolts (see illustrations 2.12b and a). Tighten the bolts. Raise and support the tank as before (see illustration 2.4b).
17 Fit a new retainer into the connector, aligning the tabs with the holes (see illustration). Fit the connector onto the pipe and push it until both retainer tabs click into place, then try to pull the connector off to make sure it has locked (see illustration). Fit the connector cover (see illustration 2.11a.).
18 Connect the fuel pump and level sensor wiring connectors and secure the wiring its clamp (see illustration 2.8). Fit the overflow hose guide into the bracket (see illustration 2.7). Route the overflow/breather hose(s) down as required according to model (see illustration 2.2 or 2.3). Make sure all the hoses and wiring are securely connected.
19 Connect the battery (see Chapter 8). Make sure the kill switch is set to RUN, then turn the ignition ON to allow the fuel pump to pressurise the system, then turn it off. Repeat a couple of times and each time check for leaks at the hose connector. Fit the connector cover.
20 Lower the tank as described above.

Repair

21 All repairs to the fuel tank should be carried out by a professional who has experience in this critical and potentially dangerous work. Even after cleaning and flushing of the fuel system, explosive fumes can remain and ignite during repair of the tank.
22 If the fuel tank is removed from the bike, it should not be placed in an area where sparks or open flames could ignite the fumes coming out of the tank. Be especially careful inside garages where a natural gas-type appliance is located, because the pilot light could cause an explosion.

2.13 Remove the sleeves and collars and make sure the rubbers are in good condition

2.17a Fit a new retainer into the connector...

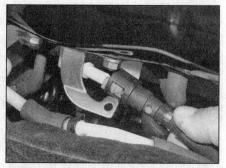

2.17b ...then push the connector onto the union

Engine management system

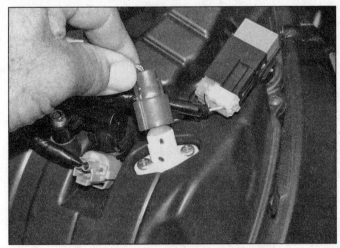

3.4a Disconnect the IAT sensor connector...

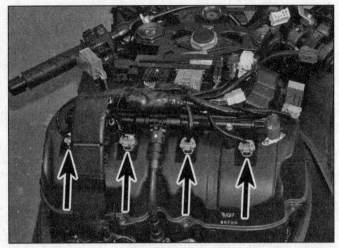

3.4b ...and each injector connector (arrowed)

3 Air filter housing and air intake system

Air filter housing

Removal

1 Disconnect the battery negative (–) lead (see Chapter 8).
2 Remove the fuel tank (see Section 2).
3 Remove the air filter (see Chapter 1).
4 Disconnect the IAT sensor wiring connector **(see illustration)**. Disconnect the secondary fuel injector wiring connectors **(see illustration)**. If required remove the secondary fuel rail and injector assembly (Section 10).
5 Displace the wire loom cover, then fold the loom back off the housing **(see illustration)**.
6 Clean any dirt from the fuel hose connector on the secondary fuel rail. Place a wad of rag for catching any residual fuel in the hose under the connector. Pull the rubber restrictor out of the connector retainer, noting how it seats **(see illustration)**. Press the retainer tabs in and pull the connector off the fuel rail union **(see illustration)**. Remove the retainer – note that Honda specify to replace it with a new one whenever the fuel hose is disconnected **(see illustration)**. Also check the condition of the restrictor and replace it with a new one if necessary. Seal the union and the connector with a piece off a plastic bag or the finger from a latex glove to prevent dirt getting in.
7 Undo the screws securing the upper

3.5 Displace the cover and fold it back

3.6a Pull the restrictor out of the retainer...

3.6b ...then press and hold the retainer tabs and pull the hose connector off

3.6c Remove the retainer from the union

4•6 Engine management system

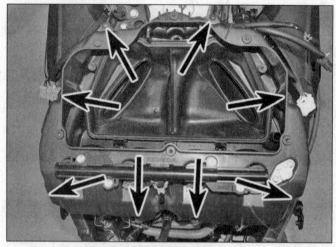

3.7a Undo the screws (arrowed)...

3.7b ...and remove the upper section

3.8a Disconnect the MAP sensor wiring...

3.8b ...and hose

section of the filter housing and remove it **(see illustrations)**.

8 Disconnect the MAP sensor wiring connector and vacuum hose **(see illustrations)**.

9 Undo the air funnel/filter housing mounting screws and remove the funnels, noting which fits where **(see illustration)**.

10 Lift the lower housing up off the throttle bodies, disconnect the crankcase breather hose on the front and the PAIR system supply hose on the right-hand side, and remove the housing, noting how it engages with the air

3.9 Undo the screws (arrowed) and lift the funnels out of the housing

3.10a Lift the housing and disconnect the crankcase breather hose...

Engine management system 4•7

3.10b ...and the PAIR hose

3.11a Make sure each duct end is seated inside the rubber intake on the housing

3.11b The taller funnels fit in the middle

intake ducts **(see illustrations)**. Cover the throttle bodies with a clean rag.

Installation

11 Installation is the reverse of removal, noting the following:
- Check the condition of the seals on the underside of the housing, and make sure they are in their grooves.
- Make sure the crankcase breather, PAIR system and MAP sensor hoses are in good condition. Connect the PAIR hose first, then the crankcase hose, pushing them fully onto their unions and securing them with their clamps where fitted, before seating the housing on the throttle bodies **(see illustrations 3.10b and a)**.
- Make sure the intake rubbers seat around the ends of the air ducts correctly as they can easily ruck up **(see illustration 3.11a)**.
- Fit the air intake funnels so the taller funnels are above the middle (Nos. 2 and 3) throttle bodies **(see illustration 3.11b)**.
- Make sure the MAP sensor, secondary injector and IAT sensor wiring connectors are securely connected **(see illustrations 3.8a and 3.4b and a)**.
- To connect the fuel hose, if removed fit the rubber restrictor onto the union between the two ribs. Fit a new retainer into the

3.11c Fit a new retainer into the connector...

connector, aligning the tabs with the holes **(see illustration 3.11c)**.
- Fit the connector onto the union and push it until both retainer tabs click into place, then try to pull the connector off to make sure it has locked **(see illustration 3.11d)**. Fit the rubber restrictor into the retainer, so the tabs cannot be pushed in **(see illustration 3.11e)**.

Air intake system

12 The system consists of a flap in each air intake duct that affects the flow of air to the air filter housing. The flap is actuated by a diaphragm valve that responds to a vacuum taken from the throttle bodies, with the vacuum

3.11d ...then push the connector onto the union

passing through a control valve actuated electronically by the ECM. If it is not functioning, first make sure the vacuum hoses between the throttle bodies, control valves, diaphragm valves, one-way valve and vacuum chamber are in good condition, not split or cracked, and are securely fitted on their union at each end – see below for access to the various components. Replace hoses with new ones as required.

Air ducts

13 There is a duct on each side – remove the relevant fairing side panel (see Chapter 7).
14 On 2008 to 2011 models remove the inner panel from the fairing side panel **(see illustration)**

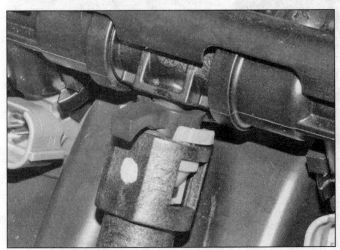
3.11e Seat the restrictor in the retainer as shown

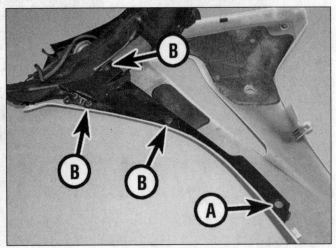
3.14 Undo the screw (A) and release the trim clips (B) and remove the inner panel

4•8 Engine management system

3.15a Disconnect the wiring and the hose (arrowed)

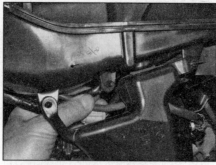

3.15b Displace the connector and release the wiring

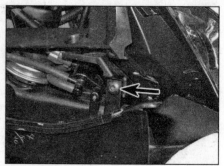

3.15c Undo the screw (arrowed)...

– refer to Chapter 7 for details on trim clips if required. Release the trim clips and undo the screws securing the air duct and its cover and remove them from the panel.

15 On 2012-on models disconnect the wiring connector and vacuum hose from the control valve **(see illustration)**. Release the wiring and hoses from the duct. When removing the left-hand duct release the wiring clip and connector from the resonator chamber **(see illustration)**. Undo the screw, release the duct from the headlight and frame and remove it **(see illustrations)**. If required remove the cover **(see illustration)**.

16 If required release the trim clips and detach the resonator chamber from the duct **(see illustration)**.

17 Installation is the reverse of removal. Make sure the air duct seats inside the end of the intake rubber on the air filter housing correctly as it can easily ruck the rubber up – if in doubt remove the air filter for a visual check **(see illustration 3.11a)**. Make sure the vacuum hose is securely connected at each end.

Diaphragm valves

18 Remove the air duct.

19 Twist the valve anticlockwise to release it, then lift it out of the duct and detach the rod from the flap **(see illustrations)**. Make sure the intake flap opens and closes. Check that the rod moves in and out of the diaphragm valve. If not replace the valve with a new one.

20 Check the diaphragm valve by applying a 250 mmHg vacuum to its union to check the rod moves and holds its position – if not the diaphragm may be split.

Control valve

21 Remove the air duct.

22 Displace the valve and detach the vacuum hoses, noting which fits where **(see illustrations)**.

23 Check the operation of the control valve by blowing through the union A; no air should

3.15d ...release and remove the duct

3.15e Undo the screws (arrowed) and remove the cover

3.16 Resonator chamber trim clips (arrowed) – 2012 model shown

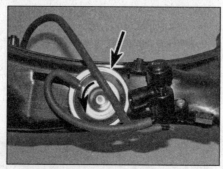

3.19a Twist the valve (arrowed) anti-clockwise...

3.19b ...and detach the rod (arrowed)

3.22a On 2008 to 2011 models displace the valve from its holder

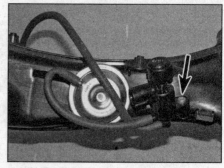

3.22b On 2012-on models undo the screw (arrowed) securing the valve

Engine management system 4•9

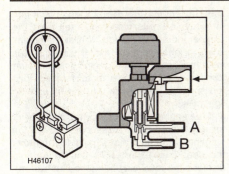

3.23 Control valve test

flow through the valve and out of union B **(see illustration)**. Now connect battery voltage (12 volts – + to white wire terminal, – to yellow) across the valve terminals and repeat the check; air should now flow freely through the valve if it is functioning correctly.

24 Check the resistance of the control valve windings by connecting an ohmmeter to its terminals and compare the reading obtained to that given in the Specifications. Replace the valve with a new one if faulty.

25 Installation is the reverse of removal. Make sure the vacuum hoses are securely connected at each end.

One-way valve and vacuum chamber

26 To access the one-way valve release the trim clips securing the front air duct cover and remove the cover **(see illustration)**. Detach the vacuum hoses, noting which fits where **(see illustration)**. Check the operation of the valve by blowing through the union A; air should flow through the valve and out of unions B and C. Now blow through union B; no air should flow through the valve and out of unions C and A.

27 To access the vacuum chamber remove the fairing (see Chapter 7). Remove the chamber, noting how it locates, and detach the hose if required **(see illustration)**. To remove the holder undo the two screws then release the wiring connector and clip **(see illustration)**.

4 Fuel injection system description

1 All models are equipped with Honda's programmed fuel injection (PGM-DSFI) system. It is controlled by a management system with an engine control module (ECM) that operates both the injection and ignition systems.

2 The engine control module (ECM) monitors signals from the following sensors.
- Throttle position (TP) sensor – informs the ECM of the throttle position, and the rate of throttle opening or closing.
- Engine coolant temperature (ECT) sensor – informs the ECM of engine temperature. It also actuates the temperature display (see Chapter 3).
- Manifold absolute pressure (MAP) sensor – informs the ECM of the engine load by monitoring the pressure in the throttle body intake tracts.

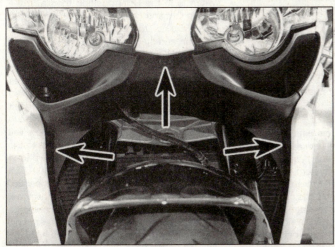

3.26a Front air duct cover trim clips (arrowed) – 2008 to 2011 model shown

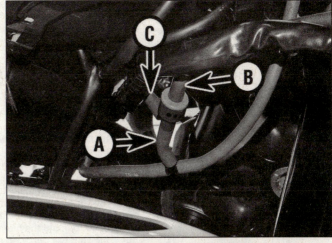

3.26b One-way valve union identification

3.27a Release the chamber from its holder

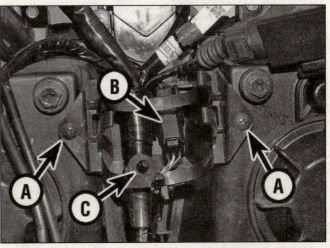

3.27b Undo the screws (A) and release the connector (B) and clip (C)

4•10 Engine management system

- **Intake air temperature (IAT) sensor** – informs the ECM of the temperature of the air entering the throttle body.
- **Camshaft position (CMP) sensor** – informs the ECM of engine speed and camshaft position.
- **Crankshaft position (CKP) sensor** – informs the ECM of engine speed and crankshaft position.
- **Speed sensor** – informs the ECM of the road speed of the motorcycle (see Chapter 8).
- **Oxygen sensor** – informs the ECM of the oxygen content of the exhaust gases.
- **Knock sensor** – detects and informs the ECM of detonation in each cylinder pair.
- **Lean angle sensor** – cuts the ignition and fuel pump if the bike falls over.

3 All the information from the sensors is analysed by the ECM, and from that it determines the appropriate ignition and fuelling requirements of the engine. The ECM controls each fuel injector by varying its pulse width – the length of time the injector is held open – to provide more or less fuel, as appropriate for cold starting, warm up, idle, cruising, and acceleration. Due to the layout of the engine, the fuelling needs for each cylinder are slightly different and the ECM is programmed to compensate for this; the injection system is fully sequential, with each injector receiving its own signal from the ECM.

4 Cold starting, warm up and idle speeds are controlled by an automatic idle control system.

5.3a Displace the fuse/relay box

An idle air control valve (IACV), actuated by the ECM, allows additional air to bypass the throttle valves when the throttle is closed, and this increases the engine idle speed.

5 If there is an abnormality in any of the readings obtained from any sensor, the ECM enters its back-up mode. In this event, the ECM ignores the abnormal sensor signal, and assumes a pre-programmed value that will allow the engine to continue running (albeit at reduced efficiency). If the ECM enters this back-up mode, or when any faults occur, the fuel injection system (FI) warning light in the instrument cluster will come on, and the relevant fault code will be stored in the ECM memory. The fault can be identified using the fault codes, which can be accessed using the self-diagnosis function (see Section 5). However if there are certain faults detected in the injectors or the camshaft position or crankshaft position sensors, the back-up mode becomes ineffective and the ECM will not allow the engine to run at all.

6 The HISS (Honda Ignition Security System) immobiliser system will not allow the engine to be started unless the correct key is used. A fault in this system should not be confused with a fuel injection system fault. The immobiliser system has its own warning light and fault diagnosis function (see Section 25).

5 Fuel injection system fault diagnosis

1 If the fuel injection system (FI) warning light on the instrument cluster illuminates when the motorcycle is running, a fault has occurred in the fuel injection/ignition system. The engine control module (ECM) will store the relevant fault code in its memory and this code can be read as follows using the self-diagnostic mode of the ECM. While the engine is running above 5000 rpm and the motorcycle is being ridden, the light will come on and stay on. When the motorcycle is on its sidestand and the engine is idling, the light will flash, the pattern of the flashes indicating the code for the fault the ECM has identified.

2 If the engine can be started, place the motorcycle on its sidestand then start the engine and allow it to idle. Whilst the engine is idling, observe the FI warning light on the instrument cluster. If the engine does not start turn it over on the starter motor for more than ten seconds and check that the FI warning light blinks.

3 If the engine cannot be started, or to check for any stored fault codes even though the warning lights have not illuminated, remove the seat (see Chapter 7). On RA models displace the fuse/relay box **(see illustration)**. Locate the engine management system data link connector (DLC), which is a red blanked single-sided 4-pin connector **(see illustration)**. Remove any tape from the connector, then remove the blanking cap. Either fit the Honda SCS service connector (Part No. 070PZ-ZY30100, available from your dealer), or bridge the brown and green wire terminals of the connector with a piece of insulated electrical wire with bared ends **(see illustration)**. With the terminals connected, make sure the kill switch is in the RUN position then turn the ignition ON and observe the FI warning light. If there are no stored fault codes, the light will come on and stay on. If there are stored fault codes, the light will flash.

4 The fuel injection system warning light uses long (1.3 second) and short (0.5 second) flashes to give out the fault code. A long flash is used to indicate the first digit of a double digit fault code (i.e. 10 and above). If a single digit fault code is being displayed (i.e. 0 – 9), there will be a number of short flashes equivalent to the code being displayed. For example, two long (1.3 sec) flashes followed by five short (0.5 sec) flashes indicate the fault code number 25. If there is more than one fault code, there will be a gap before the other codes are revealed (the codes will be revealed in order, starting with the lowest and finishing with the highest). Once all codes have been revealed, the ECM will continuously run through the code(s) stored in its memory, revealing each one in turn with a short gap between them. The fault codes are shown in the table.

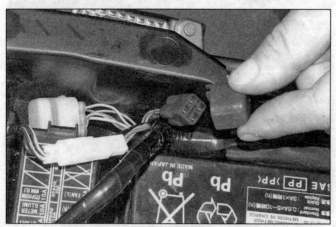

5.3b Locate the connector and remove the cap...

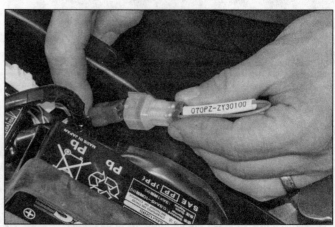

5.3c ...and fit the tool or bridge the terminals as described

Engine management system 4•11

Fault code	Symptoms	Possible causes	Reference
0 – no code; warning light off	Engine does not start	Blown FI 20A fuse or BANK ANGLE/START 10A fuse	Chapter 8
		Faulty power supply to or from ECM	Section 7
		Faulty engine stop relay or wiring	Section 8
		Faulty engine stop switch or wiring	Chapter 8
		Faulty ignition switch	Chapter 8
		Faulty lean angle (bank angle) sensor or wiring	Section 6
		Faulty ECM	Section 7
0 – no code; warning light off	Engine runs normally	Open or short circuit in FI warning light wiring	Chapter 8
		Faulty ECM	Section 7
0 – no code; warning light constantly on	Engine runs normally	Short circuit in data link connector or wiring	Chapter 8
		Faulty ECM	Section 7
1	Engine runs normally	Faulty manifold absolute pressure (MAP) sensor or wiring	Section 6
2	Engine runs normally	Faulty manifold absolute pressure (MAP) sensor or vacuum hose disconnected/broken	Section 6
7	Engine difficult to start at low temperatures	Faulty engine coolant temperature (ECT) sensor or wiring	Section 6
8	Poor throttle response	Faulty throttle position (TP) sensor or wiring	Section 6
9	Engine runs normally	Faulty intake air temperature (IAT) sensor or wiring	Section 6
11	Engine operates normally	Faulty speed sensor or wiring	Section 6
12	Engine does not start	Faulty No. 1 primary injector or wiring	Section 10
13	Engine does not start	Faulty No. 2 primary injector or wiring	Section 10
14	Engine does not start	Faulty No. 3 primary injector or wiring	Section 10
15	Engine does not start	Faulty No. 4 primary injector or wiring	Section 10
16	Engine does not start	Faulty No. 1 secondary injector or wiring	Section 10
17	Engine does not start	Faulty No. 2 secondary injector or wiring	Section 10
18	Engine does not start	Faulty camshaft position (CMP) sensor or wiring	Section 6
19	Engine does not start	Faulty crankshaft position (CKP) sensor or wiring	Section 6
21	Engine operates normally	Faulty oxygen sensor or wiring	Section 6
23	Engine operates normally	Faulty oxygen sensor heating element	Section 6
25	Engine operates normally	Faulty knock sensor or wiring	Section 6
29	Engine stalls, hard to start, rough idle	Faulty idle air control valve	Section 11
34	Engine operates normally	Faulty potentiometer in exhaust gas control valve (EGCV) servo	Section 17
35	Engine operates normally	Faulty exhaust gas control valve (EGCV) servo	Section 17
48	Engine does not start	Faulty No. 3 secondary injector or wiring	Section 10
49	Engine does not start	Faulty No. 4 secondary injector or wiring	Section 10
51	Engine starts normally Steering damper inoperative	Faulty electronic steering damper (HESD) solenoid or wiring	Chapter 5
56	Engine operates normally	Faulty knock sensor integrated circuit	Section 6

Once all the codes have been revealed, switch off the ignition and (where necessary) remove the auxiliary wire from the data link connector. Identify the fault using the table above, then refer below for checking procedures.

5 Once the fault has been identified and corrected, it will be necessary to reset the system by removing the fault code from the ECM memory. To do this, ensure the ignition is switched OFF, then bridge the brown and green wire terminals of the data link connector (DLC) (see Step 3). Make sure the kill switch is in the RUN position, then turn the ignition switch ON. Disconnect the auxiliary wire or tool from the DLC. When the wire is disconnected the warning light should come on for about five seconds, during which time the auxiliary wire or tool must be reconnected. The light should start to flash when it is reconnected, indicating that all fault codes have been erased. Turn off the ignition then remove the auxiliary wire or tool. Check the FI warning light (in some cases it may be necessary to repeat the erasing procedure more than once).

6 If a fault appears, use the diagnostic function and fault code system described above to work out which component is faulty. First ensure that the relevant system wiring connectors are securely connected and free of corrosion – poor connections are the cause of the majority of problems. Also check the wiring itself for any obvious faults or breaks, and use a continuity tester to check the wiring between the component, its connectors and the ECM, referring to the wiring diagrams at the end of Chapter 8. Next refer to the relevant Section in this Chapter or to other Chapters as required as given in the table above to see if there are any other specific checks that can be made on that particular component or its circuit using home equipment. If this fails to reveal the cause of the problem, the motorcycle should be taken to a Honda dealer for testing. They will have the special tools that should locate the fault quickly and simply.

7 Also ensure that the fault is not due to poor maintenance – i.e. check that the air filter element is clean, that the spark plugs are in good condition, that the valve clearances are correctly adjusted, the cylinder compression pressures are correct, and the ignition timing is correct (refer to Chapters 1 and 2, and to Section 24). Where relevant it is also worth removing the sensor(s) in question and checking that the sensing head is clean and not obstructed by anything. Where there is a vacuum hose to a sensor, make sure it is securely connected at both ends and has no cracks or splits.

6 Fuel injection system sensors

Caution: *Ensure the ignition is switched OFF before disconnecting/reconnecting any fuel injection system wiring connector. If a connector is disconnected/reconnected with the ignition switched ON the engine control module (ECM) could be damaged.*

Manifold absolute pressure (MAP) sensor

Check

1 The MAP sensor is mounted on the underside of the air filter housing at the back. Raise the fuel tank (see Section 2). Remove the air filter housing jacket, noting how it fits **(see illustration)**. Make sure that the vacuum hoses to the sensor are securely fixed at both ends, and have no cracks or splits **(see illustration)**.

2 Disconnect the wiring connector from the sensor **(see illustration 3.8a)**.

3 Connect the positive (+) lead of a voltmeter to the yellow/red wire terminal in the wiring connector, and connect the negative (–) lead to the grey/black wire terminal. Turn the ignition switch ON and set the kill switch to RUN and check that a voltage of 4.75 to 5.25 volts is present. Turn the ignition OFF. If there is no voltage, check for continuity in the wires to the ECM. If there is no continuity locate the break and repair it. If the wiring is good, the ECM could be faulty.

4 If the voltage was good, check there is continuity in the light green/yellow wire to the ECM, and no continuity to earth. If the wiring is good, the MAP sensor is faulty.

5 The MAP sensor itself can only be tested by a Honda dealer.

Removal and installation

6 Raise the fuel tank (see Section 2). Remove the air filter housing jacket, noting how it fits **(see illustration 6.1a)**.

7 Disconnect the wiring connector from the sensor, then detach the hose **(see illustrations 3.8a and b)**. Undo the screw and remove the sensor **(see illustration)**. If you don't have the correct tools to engage the screwhead remove the air filter housing (see Section 3).

8 Installation is the reverse of removal.

6.1a Unclip and remove the jacket

6.1b Check the sensor hoses (arrowed)

Engine coolant temperature (ECT) sensor

Note: *The sensor also operates the coolant temperature display – refer to Chapter 3 to check this aspect of its function.*

Check

9 The ECT sensor is mounted in the thermostat housing. Raise the fuel tank (see Section 2). Remove the air filter housing jacket, noting how it fits **(see illustration 6.1a)**.

10 Disconnect the wiring connector from the sensor **(see illustration)**. With the engine cold, connect an ohmmeter between the blue/yellow and grey/black wire terminals on the sensor and measure its resistance. Compare the reading obtained to that given in the Specifications, noting that the specified value is valid at 20°C (68°F); the sensor resistance will increase at lower temperatures and decrease at higher temperatures. If the resistance reading differs greatly from that specified, the sensor is probably faulty.

11 Connect the positive (+) lead of a voltmeter to the blue/yellow wire terminal in the wiring connector, and connect the negative (–) lead to the grey/black wire terminal. Turn the ignition switch ON and set the kill switch to RUN and check that a voltage of 4.75 to 5.25 volts is present. Turn the ignition OFF. If there is no voltage, check for continuity in the wires to the ECM. If there is no continuity locate the break and repair it. If the wiring is good, the ECM could be faulty.

Removal and installation

 Warning: *The engine must be completely cool before carrying out this procedure.*

12 See Chapter 3, Section 3.

Throttle position (TP) sensor

Check

13 The sensor is on the right-hand end of the throttle body assembly. Remove the air filter housing (Section 3). Disconnect the wiring connector from the sensor **(see illustration)**.

14 Connect the positive (+) lead of a voltmeter to the yellow/red wire terminal in the wiring connector, and connect the negative (–) lead to the grey/black wire terminal. Turn the ignition switch ON and set the kill switch to RUN and check that a voltage of 4.75 to 5.25 volts is present. Turn the ignition OFF. If there is no voltage, check for continuity in the wires to the ECM. If there is no continuity locate the break and repair it. If the wiring is good, the ECM could be faulty. If there is voltage, check for continuity to the ECM in the blue/yellow wire.

15 If all the wiring is good have the sensor output voltage checked by a Honda dealer. If that is good, then the ECM is faulty.

Removal and installation

16 The throttle sensor is an integral part of the throttle body assembly and is not available separately. If the sensor is faulty, a complete new throttle body assembly will have to be

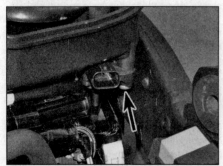

6.7 MAP sensor screw (arrowed)

6.10 ECT sensor wiring connector (arrowed)

6.13 TP sensor wiring connector (arrowed)

Engine management system 4•13

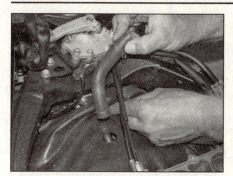
6.30a Remove the crankcase breather hose...

6.30b ...unstick the sides of the heat shield...

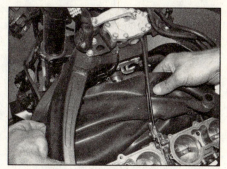
6.30c ...and draw it back

installed, though it is worth checking with your Honda parts specialist whether anything can be done to avoid this.

Intake air temperature (IAT) sensor

Check

17 The sensor is mounted in the top of the air filter housing. Raise the fuel tank (see Section 2). Remove the air filter housing jacket, noting how it fits (see illustration 6.1a). Disconnect the wiring connector from the sensor (see illustration 3.4a).
18 With the sensor cold, connect an ohmmeter to the sensor terminals and measure its resistance. Compare the reading obtained to that given in the Specifications noting that the specified value is only valid between 20 to 30°C (68 to 86°F) – the sensor resistance will increase at lower temperatures and decrease at higher temperatures. If the resistance reading differs greatly from that specified, the sensor is probably faulty.
19 Connect the positive (+) lead of a voltmeter to the grey/blue wire terminal in the wiring connector, and connect the negative (–) lead to the grey/black wire terminal. Turn the ignition switch ON and set the kill switch to RUN and check that a voltage of 4.75 to 5.25 volts is present. Turn the ignition OFF. If there is no voltage, check for continuity in the wires to the ECM. If there is no continuity locate the break and repair it.
20 If all the wiring is good have the sensor output voltage checked by a Honda dealer. If that is good, then the ECM is faulty.

Removal and installation

21 The sensor is mounted in the top of the air filter housing. Raise the fuel tank (see Section 2). Remove the air filter housing jacket, noting how it fits (see illustration 6.1a). Disconnect the wiring connector from the sensor (see illustration 3.4a).
22 Undo the screws and remove the sensor. Check the condition of the O-ring – if necessary replace it with a new one.
23 Installation is the reverse of removal.

Speed sensor

24 See Chapter 8, Section 16.

Camshaft position (CMP) sensor

Check

25 Remove the air filter housing (see Section 3). Disconnect the crankcase breather hose, then unstick and displace the rubber heat shield (see illustrations 6.30a, b and c).
26 Disconnect the wiring connector from the sensor (see illustration 6.31).
27 Connect the positive (+) lead of a voltmeter to the grey wire terminal in the wiring connector, and connect the negative (–) lead to earth. Turn the ignition switch ON and set the kill switch to RUN and check that a voltage of 4.75 to 5.25 volts is present. Turn the ignition OFF. If there is no voltage, check for continuity in the wire to the ECM. If there is no continuity locate the break and repair it.
28 Connect the positive (+) lead of a voltmeter to the yellow/red wire terminal in the wiring connector, and connect the negative (–) lead to the grey/black wire terminal. Turn the ignition switch ON and set the kill switch to RUN and check that a voltage of 4.75 to 5.25 volts is present. Turn the ignition OFF. If there is no voltage, check for continuity in the wires to the ECM. If there is no continuity locate the break and repair it.
29 If the voltage is good the sensor is faulty.

Removal and installation

30 Remove the air filter housing (see Section 3). Disconnect the crankcase breather hose, then unstick and displace the rubber heat shield (see illustrations).
31 Disconnect the wiring connector from the sensor (see illustration).
32 Unscrew the bolt and draw the sensor out of the head (see illustration). Remove the O-ring – a new one must be used.
33 On installation, fit a new O-ring smeared with oil into the groove in the sensor. Fit the sensor and tighten the bolt.
34 Connect the wiring connector. Fit the heat shield and install the air filter housing.

Crankshaft position (CKP) sensor

Check

35 Raise the fuel tank (see Section 2). Disconnect the sensor wiring connector (see illustration).
36 Using an ohmmeter check for continuity

6.31 CMP sensor wiring connector (arrowed)

6.32 CMP sensor bolt (arrowed)

6.35 CKP sensor wiring connector (arrowed)

first between the yellow wire terminal on the sensor side of the connector and earth (ground), and then between the white/yellow wire terminal and earth. If there is continuity in either case the CKP sensor is faulty. Measure the resistance of the sensor by connecting the meter, set to the ohms x 100 scale, to the terminals and compare the reading to that specified at the beginning of the chapter. If the value obtained differs greatly or is zero or infinity the sensor is faulty.

37 Connect the positive (+) lead of a voltmeter and peak voltage adapter arrangement* to the yellow terminal on the sensor side of the connector and the negative (–) lead to the white/yellow terminal of the connector. Turn the engine over on the starter motor and note the voltage reading obtained. If this reading is below the specified minimum, the CKP sensor is faulty. *Note: *Honda specify their own peak voltage adapter (Pt. No. 07HGJ-0020100 in the UK or MTP07-0286 in the US) with an aftermarket digital multimeter having an impedance of 10 M-ohm/DCV minimum for this test.*

38 If the sensor functions correctly check both wires for continuity from the loom side of the connector to the ECM. If the wiring is good the ECM could be faulty.

Removal and installation

39 The CKP sensor is integrated with the alternator stator. Refer to Chapter 8 and replace the stator assembly with a new one.

Oxygen sensor

40 The sensor is in the left-hand side of the silencer (see illustration 6.47a) – it is not fitted on 2008 to 2011 US models.

Check

41 To access the wiring connector, on RR models remove the left-hand fairing side panel (see Chapter 7), and on RA models raise the fuel tank (see Section 2). Trace the wiring from the sensor and disconnect the connector (see illustration).

42 Apart from wiring and connector checks, the operation of the oxygen sensor itself cannot be checked – if the sensor circuit is good (have this checked by a dealer for confirmation) and the sensor is thought to be faulty, replace it with a new one.

43 To check the sensor heater connect an ohmmeter between the white wire terminals on the sensor side of the connector and check that the resistance is between 5 and 20 ohms. Also check that there is no continuity to earth (ground) in each white wire. If the resistance is not as specified or if there is continuity to earth, replace the sensor with a new one.

44 Check for battery voltage between the black/white (+) wire terminal in the loom side of the connector and earth with the ignition ON. If there is no voltage, check the black/white wire for continuity to the engine stop relay, then check the relay.

45 If there is voltage check for continuity between the connector and the ECM in the grey/black, black/red and white wires. If all the wiring is good the ECM could be faulty.

Removal and installation

Note: *The oxygen sensor is delicate and will not work if dropped or knocked, or if any cleaning materials are used on it. Ensure the exhaust system is cold before proceeding. To tighten the sensor to the correct torque setting either a special socket to accommodate the sensor wiring (you can get one from Honda, part No. 07LAA-PT50101, or source a commercially available equivalent), or a crows foot socket, is required (see illustration 6.47b).*

46 To access the wiring connector, on RR models remove the left-hand fairing side panel (see Chapter 7), and on RA models raise the fuel tank (see Section 2). Trace the wiring from the sensor and disconnect the connector (see illustration 6.41). Feed the wiring down to the sensor, releasing any ties and guides, noting its routing (see illustrations) – either cut the cable-ties securing the wiring to the guide on the frame, or slide a 6 mm spanner or socket over the top of the guide to push the prongs in and release the clip, as required (see illustration).

47 Unscrew and remove the oxygen sensor (see illustrations).

48 Installation is the reverse of removal. Tighten the sensor to the torque setting specified at the beginning of the Chapter.

6.41 Oxygen sensor wiring connector (arrowed) – RR model

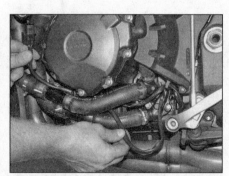

6.46a Note the routing of the wire...

6.46b ...release it from the guides on the sprocket cover...

6.46c ...and cut the ties (arrowed) or release the guide from the frame using a ring spanner

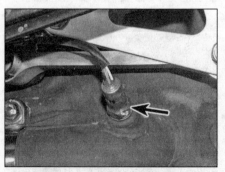

6.47a Oxygen sensor (arrowed)

6.47b This is a purpose built socket that fits over the wiring

Engine management system 4•15

Knock sensor

Check

49 The sensor is mounted on the back of the engine below the thermostat housing. Raise the fuel tank (Section 2). Disconnect the sensor wiring connector **(see illustration)**.

50 Connect the positive (+) lead of a voltmeter to the yellow/red terminal of the sensor wiring connector, then connect the negative (–) lead to a good earth. Turn the ignition switch ON and set the kill switch to RUN and check that a voltage of 4.75 to 5.25 volts is present. If it isn't, there is a break in the yellow/red wire or a fault in the ECM. If there is voltage, check for continuity to the ECM in the blue wire and the orange wire.

51 Next check for continuity between the yellow/red and blue terminals in the sensor side of the connector – if there is none the sensor is faulty. Also check for continuity to earth in the blue wire terminal – if there is, the sensor is faulty.

52 If all the wiring is good the ECM could be faulty.

Removal and installation

53 Remove the thermostat housing (see Chapter 3).

54 If you haven't removed the throttle bodies, disconnect the sensor wiring connector **(see illustration 6.49)**. Release the connector from the bracket **(see illustration)**.

55 Unscrew the bolt and remove the sensor **(see illustration)**.

56 Installation is the reverse of removal. Tighten the bolt to the torque setting specified at the beginning of the Chapter.

Lean angle (bank angle) sensor

Check

57 The lean angle sensor is mounted in the fairing. Position the motorcycle on an auxiliary stand so that the motorcycle is level. Remove the rider's seat (see Chapter 7). Open the fuse/relay box lid **(see illustration)**. Displace the fairing, disconnecting the instrument cluster wiring connector but leaving the front loom wiring connected (see Chapter 7).

58 Hold the fairing horizontal and switch the ignition ON and set the kill switch to RUN; the engine stop relay in the fuse/relay box should click, indicating the power supply is closed (on). Slowly tilt the fairing to the left whilst listening to the engine stop relay; once the sensor reaches an angle of approximately 60° the relay should be heard to click, indicating the power supply is open (off). Switch the ignition OFF and return the fairing to the horizontal, then switch the ignition back ON again (engine stop relay should click again) and tilt the fairing to the right. The engine stop relay should be heard to click again once the sensor reaches an angle of around 60°.

59 If the relay does not click as described, remove the intake air system vacuum chamber and its holder (see Section 3). Disconnect the sensor wiring connector **(see illustration)**. With the ignition switch ON and the kill switch set to run, connect the positive (+) lead of a voltmeter to the white/yellow wire terminal of the lean angle sensor connector and the negative (-) lead to the green wire terminal and check that battery voltage (approximately 12 volts) is present. If not check the BANK ANGLE fuse on 2008 to 2011 models or the START fuse on 2012-on models (see Chapter 8). If that is good check the white/yellow wire from the fuse to the connector for continuity, then check the green wire for continuity to earth.

60 Next check for battery voltage at the red/blue wire, and if there is none check the wire between the sensor and the relay, and if that is good check the relay. If all is good, it is likely the sensor is faulty.

Removal and installation

61 Remove the fairing (see Chapter 7). Remove the intake air system vacuum chamber and its holder (see Section 3). Release and disconnect the sensor wiring connector **(see illustration 6.59)**.

62 On 2008 to 2011 models undo the screws and remove the sensor.

63 On 2012-on models remove the headlight from the fairing (see Chapter 8). Undo the nuts and remove the sensor **(see illustration)**.

64 Installation is the reverse of removal. Make sure the sensor is fitted with its UP mark facing upwards.

6.49 Knock sensor wiring connector (arrowed)

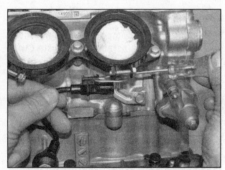

6.54 Use a small screwdriver to release the clip

6.55 Knock sensor bolt (arrowed)

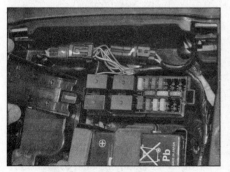

6.57 Open the fuse/relay box

6.59 Lean angle sensor wiring connector (arrowed)

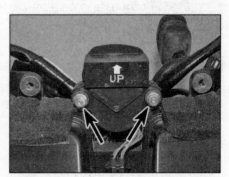

6.63 Lean angle sensor nuts (arrowed)

4•16 Engine management system

7.3 Disconnect the various wiring connectors (arrowed)

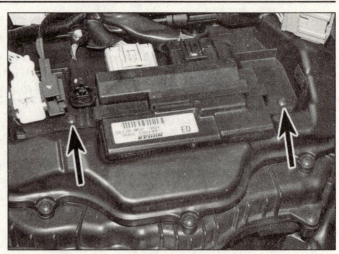

7.4a Undo the screws...

7.4b ...and displace the retainer

7.5 Disconnect the ECM wiring

(See Chapter 8). Remove the air filter housing jacket, noting how it fits **(see illustration 6.1a)**.
3 Disconnect the ignition switch and handlebar switch wiring connectors, and where fitted the immobiliser wiring connector **(see illustration)**.
4 Undo the ECM retainer screws and displace the retainer **(see illustrations)**.
5 Lift the ECM and disconnect the wiring connectors **(see illustration)**.
6 Installation is the reverse of removal.

8 Engine stop relay and fuel pump relay

7 Engine control module (ECM)

Check

1 The engine control module (ECM) itself cannot be checked, but a process of elimination of other possible faulty components can point to it being faulty. First check the FI system fuse (see Chapter 8). Next disconnect the ECM wiring connectors (see below) and check for loose or broken terminal pins in the connectors or ECM sockets. Check for continuity in each wire to/from the ECM and to its related component or connector, or to earth (ground) as appropriate; start with the wires to/from the engine stop relay, fuel pump relay and lean angle sensor, and the green and green/pink wires to earth (ground). If any wire does not show continuity check the connectors and terminals in the circuit before assuming there is a break in the wire. Alternatively take the bike to a dealer who will plug in their diagnostic tester.

Removal and installation

2 Raise the fuel tank (see Chapter 7). Disconnect the battery negative (–) terminal

Check

1 Remove the relay (see below).
2 Set a multimeter to the ohms x 1 scale and connect it across the relay's A and B terminals **(see illustration)**. There should be no continuity (infinite resistance). Using a fully-charged 12 volt battery and two insulated jumper wires, connect the positive (+) terminal of the battery to the C terminal on the relay, and the negative (–) terminal to the D terminal on the relay. At this point the relay should be heard to click and the multimeter read 0 ohms (continuity). If this is the case the relay is proved good. If the relay does not click when battery voltage is applied and still indicates no continuity (infinite resistance) across its terminals, it is faulty and must be replaced with a new one.
3 If the relay is good refer to the wiring diagrams at the end of Chapter 8 and check the wiring and connectors in the circuit to and from the relay.

Removal and installation

4 Remove the rider's seat (see Chapter 7).
5 Open the fuse/relay box lid, then pull the relay out **(see illustration)**.
6 Installation is the reverse of removal.

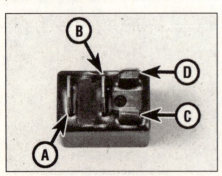

8.2 Relay test terminal ID

8.5 The location of the relays (arrowed) is marked on the box lid

Engine management system 4•17

9.2a Fan wiring connector (arrowed)

9.2b Oil pressure switch connector (arrowed)

9.2c TP sensor sub-loom connector (arrowed)

9 Throttle bodies

 Warning: *Refer to the precautions given in Section 1 before starting work.*

Removal

1 Remove the fairing side panels (see Chapter 7). Remove the air filter housing (see Section 3).
2 Disconnect the right-hand cooling fan wiring connector (see illustration). Disconnect the oil pressure switch wiring connector (see illustration). Disconnect the knock sensor wiring connector (see illustration 6.49). Disconnect the ECT sensor wiring connector (see illustration 6.10). Disconnect the IACV wiring connector (see illustration 11.3a). Disconnect the TP sensor wiring at the loom connector (see illustration). Release the wiring clip from the fuel rail (see illustration). Disconnect the primary injector wiring connectors (see illustration).
3 Disconnect the air intake system vacuum hose (see illustration). On US models, disconnect the EVAP system solenoid valve vacuum hose from the five-way hose joint on the throttle body assembly.
4 Fully slacken the throttle body clamps using a long screwdriver, noting their orientation (see illustrations). Ease the throttle body assembly up off the cylinder head and rest it on some rag – do not use the fuel rail as a handle for removal (see illustration).

9.2d Release the clip (arrowed)

9.2e Primary injector connectors (arrowed)

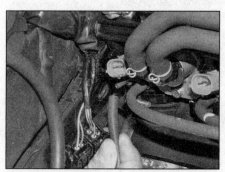
9.3 Disconnect the vacuum hose

9.4a Slacken the left-hand clamp screw...

9.4b ...the right-hand screw...

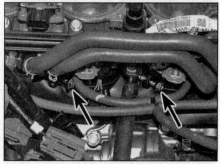
9.4c ...and the centre screws (arrowed)...

9.4d ...then lift the throttle bodies out of the ducts

4•18 Engine management system

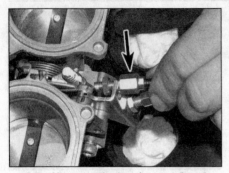

9.5a Unscrew the hex (arrowed) and release the cable from the bracket...

9.5b ...and detach the end from the pulley

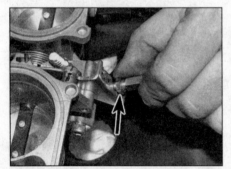

9.5c Unscrew the locknut (arrowed) and release the cable from the bracket...

9.5d ...and detach the end from the pulley

5 Free the upper throttle cable from the bracket by unscrewing the hex until the captive nut is free, then detach the cable end from the pulley **(see illustrations)**. Free the lower throttle cable by slackening the locknut and threading it up the cable until the captive nut is free, then detach the cable end from the pulley **(see illustrations)**.

Caution: Do not snap the throttle cam/ valves from fully open to fully closed once the cables have been disconnected because this can lead to engine idle speed problems.

6 Plug the engine intake ducts with clean rag **(see illustration)**. If required disconnect the crankcase breather hose, then unstick and remove the rubber heat shield **(see illustrations 6.30a, b and c)**. If required remove the throttle body adapters from the head – they come as two pairs, each secured by three bolts. Remove the O-rings – new ones must be used.

7 If required remove the primary fuel rail and injectors (Section 10).

Caution: The throttle body assembly must be treated as a sealed unit. With the exception of the idle air control valve (IACV) screws, NEVER loosen any of the green-painted nuts/bolts/screws on the assembly as these are pre-set at the factory to ensure correct synchronisation of the throttle valves.

Caution: NEVER use a solvent-based cleaner to clean the throttle body components. The throttle bores are covered with a molybdenum coating which could be removed by the cleaner.

Installation

8 If removed fit the throttle body adapters using new O-rings and tighten the bolts to the torque setting specified at the beginning of the Chapter. If removed fit and secure the rubber heat shield and connect the crankcase breather hose **(see illustration)**. Remove the tape/plugs from the intakes **(see illustration 9.6)**. Make sure the throttle body clamps are correctly orientated **(see illustrations 9.4b and c)**. Lubricate the inside of the adapters with a light smear of engine oil to aid installation **(see illustration)**.

9 If removed install the primary fuel rail and injectors (Section 10).

10 Connect the throttle cable ends to the pulley and feed the inner cables into their track, then fit the outer cables into the bracket on the throttle body – the throttle opening cable is the lower of the two **(see illustrations 9.5d, c, b and a)**. Thread the lower cable locknut down so the cable is secure and the captive nut is held in the bracket. Tighten the upper cable hex fully making sure the nut is held in the bracket.

11 Ease the throttle body assembly onto the adapters and push them down until they are fully engaged – do not use the fuel rail as a handle **(see illustration 9.4d)**. Tighten the clamps so that the gap between the ends is 6 to 8 mm **(see illustrations 9.4c, b and a)**.

12 Connect the air intake system vacuum hose **(see illustration 9.3)**. On US models, connect the EVAP system solenoid valve vacuum hose to the five-way hose joint on the throttle body assembly.

13 Refer to Step 2 and connect the injector, TP sensor, IACV, ECT sensor, knock sensor, oil pressure switch and cooling fan wiring connectors, making sure they are all secure. Fit the wiring clip onto the fuel rail.

14 Install the air filter housing and the fairing side panels.

10 Fuel rails and injectors

Caution: Ensure the ignition is switched OFF before disconnecting/reconnecting any fuel injection system wiring connector. If a connector is disconnected/reconnected with the ignition switched ON the engine control module (ECM) could be damaged.

9.6 Plug the ducts

9.8a Fit the heat shield

9.8b A smear of oil in each duct helps

Engine management system 4•19

10.3a Disconnect the wiring

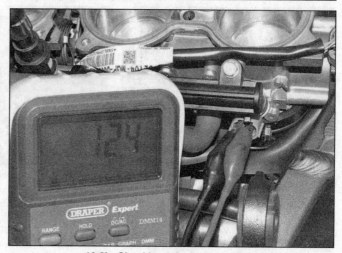

10.3b Checking injector resistance

10.8a Unscrew the bolts (arrowed)...

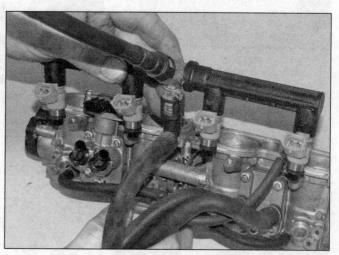

10.8b ...and remove the fuel rail and injectors

 Warning: *Refer to the precautions given in Section 1 before starting work.*

Check

1 Raise the fuel tank (see Section 2). Remove the air filter housing jacket, noting how it fits **(see illustration 6.1a)**.

2 If the engine runs, start it and allow it to idle. Check the operation of each primary injector in the throttle bodies using a stethoscope or sounding rod; an injector will emit a 'clicking' noise when functioning. If any injector is silent, either the injector or its wiring harness is faulty. Check the secondary injectors in the top of the air filter housing in the same way, but note that the throttle must be open more than 10° and the engine must be running at over 5000 rpm before these injectors are active.

3 If the engine does not run, disconnect the wiring connector from the injector in question **(see illustration)**. Connect an ohmmeter between the terminals of each injector in turn and measure the resistance **(see illustration)**. Compare the reading for each injector to that given in the Specifications.

4 Check for battery voltage at the black/white wire terminal in the wiring connector with the ignition ON and the kill switch set to RUN. If there is no voltage, check the wiring between the injector and the engine stop relay, then check the relay. Check for continuity in the other wire to the ECM connector.

5 Check that there is no continuity to earth in either wire in the connector.

Removal

Primary rail and injectors

6 Remove the air filter housing (see Section 3). If required, remove the throttle bodies (see Section 9) – this is not essential, but will provide better access.

7 If the throttle bodies are *in situ* disconnect the wiring connector from each injector **(see illustration 9.2e)**.

8 Unscrew the fuel rail bolts **(see illustration)**. Carefully lift off the fuel rail assembly and injectors **(see illustration)**. Remove the seals from the injectors, or from the injector seats in the throttle bodies **(see illustration)**. New seals must be used.

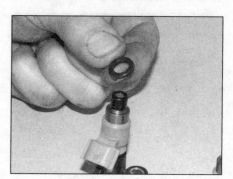

10.8c Remove the seals

4•20 Engine management system

10.9a Ease the injector out...

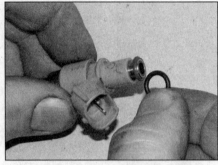

10.9b ...and remove its O-ring

9 If required pull the injectors out of the fuel rail **(see illustration)**. Remove the O-rings **(see illustration)** – new ones must be used.
10 If required pull each fuel rail off the centre joint piece **(see illustration)**. Remove the

O-rings **(see illustration)** – new ones must be used.
11 If required detach the fuel hoses from the joint piece as described in Section 3, Step 6.

Secondary rail and injectors

12 Raise or remove the fuel tank (see Section 2). Remove the air filter housing jacket, noting how it fits **(see illustration 6.1a)**.
13 If the fuel tank is not being removed disconnect the brown wiring connector from the fuel pump **(see illustration 2.8)**. Eliminate any residual pressure in the fuel system by starting the engine and letting it idle until it stops. Turn the ignition OFF.
14 Disconnect the battery negative (–) lead (see Chapter 8).
15 Refer to Section 7 and displace the ECM **(see illustrations 7.3, 7.4a and b and 7.5)** – there is no need to disconnect the wiring from it.
16 Disconnect the intake air temperature (IAT) sensor wiring connector and the secondary injector wiring connectors **(see illustrations 3.4a and b)**.
17 Displace the wire loom cover, then fold the loom back off the housing **(see illustration 3.5)**.
18 Detach the fuel hose from the rail as described in Section 3, Step 6.
19 Unscrew the fuel rail bolts and remove the bracket **(see illustrations)**. Carefully lift off the fuel rail assembly and injectors **(see illustration)**. Remove the seals from the injectors, or from the injector seats in the air filter housing **(see illustration)**. New seals must be used.
20 If required, remove the injector retainers then pull the injectors out of the fuel rail **(see illustration)**. Remove the O-rings **(see illustration)** – new ones must be used.

10.10a Detach the rail...

10.10b ...and remove its O-ring

10.19a Unscrew the bolts (arrowed)...

10.19b ...and remove the bracket...

10.19c ...then lift off the fuel rail and injectors

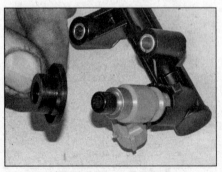

10.19d Remove the seals

10.20a Ease the injector out...

10.20b ...and remove its O-ring

Engine management system 4•21

21 If required pull each fuel rail off the centre joint piece **(see illustration 10.10a)**. Remove the O-rings **(see illustration 10.10b)** – new ones must be used.

Installation

Note: *The primary injectors have green bodies and the secondary injectors have grey bodies.*

22 Refer to Section 3, Step 11 for connection of the fuel hoses to the primary fuel rail.
23 If the fuel rails have been separated from the joint piece, fit a new O-ring lubricated with clean engine oil into the groove in the end of each rail **(see illustration 10.10b)**. Push each rail onto the joint, making sure the O-ring stays in place **(see illustration 10.10a)**.
24 If the injectors have been removed from their rail, fit a new O-ring lubricated with clean engine oil into the groove in the top of each injector **(see illustration 10.9b or 10.20b)**.
25 Align the injector connector and ease the injector into place, taking care not to dislodge the O-ring **(see illustration 10.9a or 10.20a)**.
26 Fit the retainer onto each secondary injector.
27 Fit a new seal onto each injector nozzle **(see illustration 10.8c or 10.19d)**.
28 Fit the fuel rail assembly, making sure each injector enters its seat and the seals stay in place and locate correctly **(see illustration 10.8b or 10.19c)**. On the primary fuel rail fit the bolts and tighten them to the torque setting specified at the beginning of the Chapter **(see illustration 10.8a)**. On the secondary fuel rail fit the bracket and the bolts and tighten them **(see illustrations 10.19b and a)**.

29 Refer to Section 3, Step 11 for connection of the fuel hoses to the primary fuel rail.
30 Reconnect the injector wiring connectors **(see illustration 9.2e or 3.4b)**.
31 Install the remaining components in reverse order of removal. Run the engine and check that the fuel system is working correctly and there is no leakage before taking the bike out on the road.

11 Idle air control valve

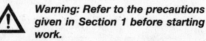

⚠ **Warning:** *Refer to the precautions given in Section 1 before starting work.*

Check

1 Idle speed is controlled automatically by a valve that adjusts a flow of air that bypasses the throttle valves in the throttle bodies. The valve is actuated by the ECM and adjusts according to information received from sensors on engine and air temperature and throttle position. When the ignition is switched ON the valve self-checks by turning through its range of movement, and should emit a beep. If there is a fault, a fault code should be indicated by the FI warning light in the instrument cluster (see Section 5).
2 If the engine idle speed is not as specified at the beginning of the Chapter, and there is no fault indicated, check the throttle cable freeplay, spark plugs, air filter and the valve clearances (see Chapter 1).

3 Next raise the fuel tank (see Section 2). Remove the air filter housing jacket, noting how it fits **(see illustration 6.1a)**. Inspect the intake adapters that the throttle bodies sit in for anything loose or cracked that could cause an air leak, causing a weak mixture. Make sure the idle air distribution hoses are in good condition and are securely connected at each end **(see illustration)**. The air hose unions on the left-hand end have an O-ring, which if deteriorated could cause an air leak – if necessary remove the air filter housing (Section 3), and for best access the throttle body assembly (Section 9), then remove the unions and replace the O-rings with new ones **(see illustrations)**.
4 If a fault code is given, raise the fuel tank (see Section 2). Disconnect the control valve wiring connector **(see illustration 11.3a)**. Check the connector wires and terminals are secure and clean. Connect an ohmmeter between the black/yellow and black/orange wire terminals on the sensor and measure the resistance. Repeat the check between the black/red and black/blue wire terminals. Compare the readings obtained to that given in the Specifications. If the resistance readings are not as specified, the sensor is probably faulty.
5 If necessary remove the valve (see below), then reconnect the wiring, turn the ignition ON and check the valve moves and beeps.
6 If all is good check each wire between the connector and the ECM for continuity.
7 If all is good the ECM could be faulty.

Removal

8 Remove the air filter housing (see Section 3).
9 Disconnect the control valve wiring connector **(see illustration 11.3a)**.
10 Clean the area around the valve to prevent any dirt entering the air passages.
11 Undo the control valve screws and remove the plate, then draw the valve out **(see illustrations)**. Remove the O-ring **(see illustration 11.12a)** – a new one must be used. Check the action of the valve by turning it.

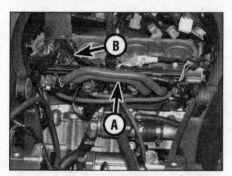

11.3a Check the hoses (A). IACV wiring connector (B)

11.3b Detach the hoses, remove the unions...

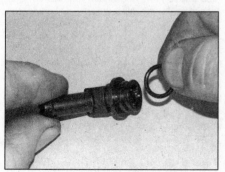

11.3c ...and fit new O-rings

11.11a Undo the screws (arrowed) and remove the plate...

11.11b ...and the valve

4•22 Engine management system

11.12a Fit a new O-ring

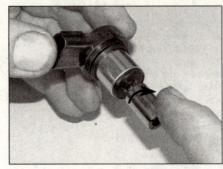

11.12b Turn the valve until it seats

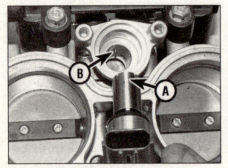

11.12c Align the groove (A) with the pin (B)

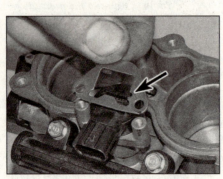

11.12d Fit the plate with the cut-out (arrowed) to the right

Installation

12 Fit a new O-ring onto the valve and smear it with clean oil **(see illustration)**. Turn the valve clockwise until lightly seated **(see illustration)**. Align the groove in the valve with the pin in its housing – turn the valve if required, then insert the valve **(see illustration)**. Fit the plate, seating the cut-out over the lug, and tighten the screws **(see illustration)**.

13 Reconnect the wiring. Turn the ignition ON and check the valve moves and beeps.
14 Install the air filter housing (see Section 3).

12 Fuel pressure check

⚠ **Warning:** *Refer to the precautions given in Section 1 before starting work.*

Note: *A pressure gauge along with some adapters and hoses that are compatible with the quick-release fittings of the bike's fuel hose are required for this check. Honda can supply the various parts required, but it may be cheaper to get a dealer to perform the check, especially as hopefully you will not need the equipment more than once.*

1 Raise the tank as described in Section 2. Disconnect the brown wiring connector from the fuel pump **(see illustration 2.8)**. Start the engine and let it idle until it stops. Turn the ignition OFF. This process relieves fuel pressure in the system.

2 Disconnect the battery negative (-) lead (see Chapter 8). Disconnect the fuel hose from the secondary fuel rail as described in Section 3, Step 6.

3 Connect the fuel pressure gauge assembly between the fuel hose and the secondary fuel rail **(see illustration)**. Reconnect the fuel pump wiring and reconnect the battery negative lead.

4 Start the engine and allow it to idle. Note the pressure present in the fuel system by reading the gauge, then turn the engine off. Compare the reading obtained to that given in the Specifications.

5 If the fuel pressure is higher than specified, the pressure regulator in the fuel pump or the pump itself is faulty and must be replaced with a new one (see Section 13).

6 If the fuel pressure is lower than specified, first check for a leak, which should be obvious from the smell of fuel. If there are no leaks check for a pinched or blocked tank breather hose or fuel hose. Next remove the pump (see Section 13), and check the strainer for a blockage (though this is unlikely). Otherwise the fuel filter is clogged or the pressure regulator is faulty, both of which are integral components of the pump assembly, or the pump itself is faulty – in these cases the pump must be replaced with a new one.

7 Relieve the fuel pressure as before (Step 1). Disconnect the battery negative (–) lead again. Remove the pressure gauge assembly, being prepared to catch any residual fuel, then reconnect the fuel hose (Section 3, Step 11). Lower the tank.

8 Reconnect the battery negative lead (see Chapter 8). Start the engine and check that there is no sign of fuel leakage.

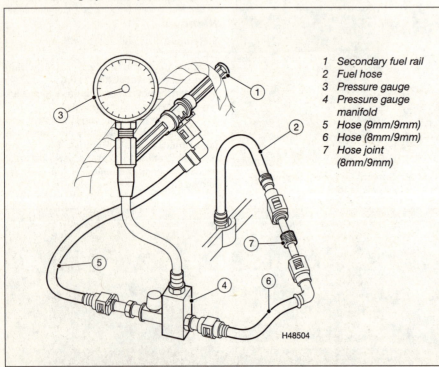

1 Secondary fuel rail
2 Fuel hose
3 Pressure gauge
4 Pressure gauge manifold
5 Hose (9mm/9mm)
6 Hose (8mm/9mm)
7 Hose joint (8mm/9mm)

12.3 Fuel pressure test set-up using Honda tools

Engine management system 4•23

13 Fuel pump

⚠ **Warning:** Refer to the precautions given in Section 1 before starting work.

Check

1 The fuel pump is located inside the fuel tank. The pump should run for a few seconds when the ignition is switched ON to pressurise the fuel system, and then cuts out until the engine is started. Check that it does this. If the pump does not run, first check the FI fuse, and the lean angle sensor fuse on 2008 to 2011 models or the start fuse on 2012-on models (see Chapter 8). If they are in good condition proceed as follows.
2 Raise the fuel tank (see Section 2).
3 Ensure the ignition is switched OFF then disconnect the brown wiring connector from the fuel pump **(see illustration 2.8)**. Connect the positive (+) lead of a voltmeter to the brown wire terminal on the loom side of the connector and the negative (–) lead to the green wire terminal. Switch the ignition ON whilst noting the reading obtained on the meter.
4 If battery voltage is present for a few seconds, the fuel pump circuit is operating correctly and the fuel pump itself is faulty and must be replaced with a new one.
5 If no reading is obtained, refer to Section 2 in Chapter 8 and the wiring diagrams at the end of it, and check the fuel pump circuit wiring for continuity and make sure all the connectors are free from corrosion and are securely connected. Repair/replace the wiring as necessary and clean the connectors using electrical contact cleaner. If this fails to reveal the fault, check the following components.
- Engine kill switch (see Chapter 8, Section 19).
- Fuel pump relay (see Section 8).
- Engine stop relay (see Section 8).
- Lean angle sensor (see Section 6).
- Engine control module (ECM) (see Section 7).

Removal

6 Remove the fuel tank (see Section 2). Drain or siphon as much fuel as possible from the

13.7 Remove the drain/breather hose arrangement – 2012 UK models shown

13.8b ...and the outer seal...

tank. Make sure the fuel cap is secure, then place the tank upside down on plenty of rag.
7 Disconnect and release the drain and breather hoses as required **(see illustration)**.
8 Unscrew the fuel pump mounting plate nuts and remove the mounting plate and outer seal **(see illustrations)**. Carefully lift the pump assembly out of the tank **(see illustration)**. Remove the inner seal **(see illustration 13.11)** – new seals must be used on installation. The pump comes as a complete assembly and, apart from the mounting hardware and seals, no individual components are available.
9 Check the strainer in the base of the pump housing for signs of dirt and clean it if necessary.

Installation

10 Make sure all wires and connectors are secure **(see illustration)**.

13.8a Unscrew the nuts, remove the plate...

13.8c ...and carefully withdraw the pump assembly, noting its orientation

11 Ensure the mounting plate and tank surfaces are clean and dry, then fit the new inner seal onto the pump **(see illustration)**.
12 Carefully manoeuvre the pump into the tank, aligning it so the fuel hose union is at the front **(see illustration 13.8c)**.
13 Fit the new outer seal **(see illustration 13.8b)**. Fit the mounting plate with the hose guide to the front and seat the cut-outs around the pegs **(see illustration 13.8a)**. Fit the nuts and tighten them finger-tight at first, and then evenly and a little at a time in the numerical sequence shown to the torque setting specified at the beginning of the Chapter **(see illustration)**.
14 Connect and secure the hoses as required **(see illustration 13.7)**.
15 Install the fuel tank (see Section 2).

13.10 Fuel pump internal wiring connector (arrowed)

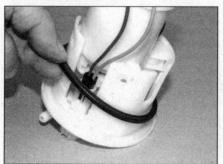
13.11 Fit a new inner seal

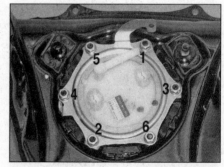
13.13 Fuel pump nut tightening sequence

4•24 Engine management system

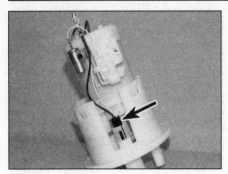

14.4 Fuel level sensor internal wiring connector (arrowed)

14 Fuel gauge and sensor

Check

1 The circuit consists of the sensor, which is an integral part of the fuel pump assembly in the fuel tank, and the low fuel warning LED and reserve fuel consumption display, which are part of the instrument cluster printed circuit board. The LED should come on for a few seconds when the ignition is switched on, then go out if there is more than 3.5 litres of fuel. When the amount of fuel reaches 3.5 litres the LED should come on, and the amount of fuel used thereafter (either in litres or gallons) is displayed in the lower segment of the instrument cluster. This display will flash at an increasing rate the more fuel is used
2 If the fuel warning light is permanently on irrespective of the amount of fuel in the tank, raise the fuel tank (see Section 2), and disconnect the black wiring connector from the fuel pump (see illustration 2.8). Turn the ignition ON. If the warning light is now off replace the fuel pump assembly with a new one. If it is still on, displace and support the fairing, disconnecting the instrument cluster wiring connector but leaving the front loom wiring connected (see Chapter 7). Check the brown/black wire between the fuel pump connector and the instrument cluster connector for continuity. If there is continuity, the instrument cluster PCB is faulty; if there isn't check the wiring and connectors for a break or dirty contact.
3 If the fuel warning light is permanently off irrespective of the amount of fuel in the tank, first check the instrument cluster (see Chapter 8). If it is good, raise the fuel tank (see Section 2), and disconnect the black wiring connector from the fuel pump (see illustration 2.8). Using a piece of wire jump across the brown/black and green wire terminals in the loom side of the connector. Turn the ignition ON. If the warning light is now on replace the fuel pump assembly with a new one. If it is still off, displace and support the fairing, disconnecting the instrument cluster wiring connector but leaving the front loom wiring connected (see Chapter 7). Check the brown/black wire between the fuel pump connector and the instrument cluster connector for continuity. If there is continuity, the instrument cluster PCB is faulty; if there isn't check the wiring and connectors for a break or dirty contact.
4 If no faults are found, remove the pump (see Section 13) and check the internal wiring connectors (see illustration).

Removal and installation

5 If the warning light is faulty refer to Chapter 8 for replacement of the instrument cluster PCB.
6 If the sensor is faulty replace the fuel pump assembly with a new one (see Section 13) – the sensor is not available separately.

15 Throttle cables

Warning: Refer to the precautions given in Section 1 before proceeding.

Removal

1 Remove the air filter housing (see Section 3). Mark each cable according to its location.
2 Refer to Section 9, displace the throttle bodies and detach the cables – it is not possible to detach and fit the lower cable with the throttle bodies in place. Withdraw the cables from the frame noting their correct routing.
3 Unscrew the cable elbow nuts at the throttle pulley housing, then remove the housing screws and separate the halves (see illustrations). Detach the throttle closing cable end from the pulley, then remove the cable from the housing (see illustration). Detach the throttle opening cable end from the pulley, then thread the housing off the throttle opening cable elbow and withdraw the cable (see illustrations). Mark each cable to ensure it is connected correctly on installation.

15.3a Unscrew the nuts (arrowed)...

15.3b ...then remove the housing screws (arrowed) and separate the halves

15.3c Detach the lower cable end...

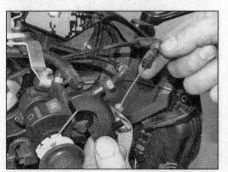

15.3d ...and draw it out the housing

15.3e Detach the upper cable end...

15.3f ...then thread the housing off

Engine management system 4•25

Installation

4 Fit the throttle opening cable elbow into the upper socket of the throttle pulley housing and thread the housing onto it without it becoming tight on the bottom of the threads (see illustration 15.3f) – the elbow must stay loose so that it aligns itself – then thread the nut onto the elbow, again not so that it is tight. Lubricate the cable end with multi-purpose grease and fit it into the pulley (see illustration 15.3e). Fit the closing cable into the lower socket and tighten the nut finger-tight (see illustration 15.3d). Lubricate the cable end with multi-purpose grease and fit it into the pulley (see illustration 15.3c). Assemble the housing onto the handlebar, making sure the pin locates in the hole, then fit the screws and tighten them, upper screw first (see illustration).
5 Feed the cables through to the throttle bodies, making sure they are correctly routed. The cables must not interfere with any other component and should not be kinked or bent sharply. Position the cable elbows as shown and tighten both nuts on the housing (see illustration 15.3a).
6 Refer to Section 9 to connect the cables and install the throttle bodies.
7 Operate the throttle to check that it opens and closes freely.
8 Check and adjust the throttle cable freeplay (see Chapter 1). Turn the handlebars back-and-forth to make sure the cable doesn't cause the steering to bind.
9 Install the air filter housing (see Section 3).
10 Start the engine and check that the idle speed does not rise as the handlebars are turned. If it does, the throttle cables are routed incorrectly. Correct the problem before riding the motorcycle.

16 Exhaust system

 Warning: If the engine has been running the exhaust system will be very hot. Allow the system to cool before carrying out any work.

Note: *Refer to the information in Section 21 regarding the catalytic converter.*

Silencer

Removal

1 Remove the left-hand fairing side panel (see Chapter 7). On RA models raise the fuel tank (see Section 2).

 Exhaust system clamp bolts tend to become corroded and seized. It is advisable to spray them with WD40 or a similar product before attempting to slacken them.

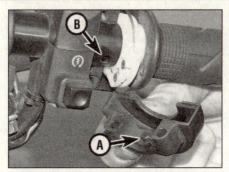

15.4 Locate the pin (A) in the hole (B)

2 Refer to Section 6, Step 46, disconnect the oxygen sensor wiring connector (not fitted on 2008 to 2011 US models) and feed the wiring down to the sensor.
3 Remove the exhaust control valve servo cover (see illustrations 17.2a and b or 17.2c and d). Turn the servo pulley clockwise and disconnect the cable (see illustrations 17.2e, f and g).
4 Slacken the silencer clamp bolt (see illustration 16.6a). Place a support under the back of the silencer.
5 Unscrew the silencer mounting bolt, noting the washer (see illustration).
6 Ease the silencer back off the downpipe assembly and manoeuvre it out, bringing the cable with it and noting its routing (see illustrations).
7 If required remove heat guard, the side cover and the end cap – a gasket is fitted with the end cap on 2008 models, which will need replacing with a new one.
8 Remove the EGCV cable if required (see Section 17).
9 Remove the oxygen sensor if required (see Section 6).
10 Check the condition of the downpipe-to-silencer sealing ring and replace it with a new one if it is damaged or deformed or no longer sealing correctly (see illustration) – note that Honda specify to always use a new one. If fitting a new sealing ring, slide the clamp back and expand the tangs on the end of the pipe slightly to make it easier to fit.
11 Check the condition of the bolts, washers,

16.6a Clamp bolt (arrowed). Draw the silencer off the downpipe...

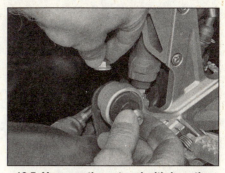

16.5 Unscrew the nut and withdraw the bolt

collars and rubbers and replace them with new ones if necessary.

Installation

12 Installation is the reverse of removal, noting the following:

- Replace any damaged, deformed or deteriorated mounting rubbers with new ones. Make sure the collars are fitted in the rubbers.
- Use a new sealing ring between the downpipe assembly and the silencer if necessary – see Step 10.
- Replace any rusted or deformed screws and bolts with new ones. Apply a smear of copper grease to all screws and bolts to prevent them from seizing up.
- Ease the silencer onto the downpipe, feeding the cable up as you do, and support it as before, then fit the silencer mounting bolt and washer loosely, then tighten the silencer clamp bolt to the specified torque, then tighten the silencer bolt. Fit the cable into its guide (see illustration 16.6b).
- Connect the EGCV cable to the servo pulley then turn the pulley anti-clockwise and position it as shown (see illustrations 17.11).
- Connect the oxygen sensor wiring connector. Make sure the wiring is correctly routed and secured (see Section 6, Step 46).
- Run the engine and check the system for leaks. Check the operation of the EGCV, and adjust the cable if required (see Chapter 1). Fit the servo cover.

16.6b ...and draw the cable out, noting its routing through the guide (arrowed)

4•26 Engine management system

16.10 Check the sealing ring (arrowed)

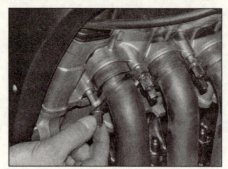

16.15 Unscrew the nuts...

16.16 ...and the bolt...

16.17 ...and remove the downpipe assembly

16.18 Remove the old sealing rings and discard them

- Apply a smear of copper grease to all studs and the bolt to prevent them from seizing up.
- Locate the downpipes in the cylinder head and loosely fit the mounting bolt and washer. Tighten the downpipe nuts first, tightening them to the torque setting specified at the beginning of the Chapter, then tighten the downpipe bolt.
- Install the radiator and the refill the cooling system (see Chapter 3). Install the silencer.

Downpipe assembly

Removal

13 Remove the radiator (see Chapter 3).
14 Remove the silencer (see above).
15 Unscrew the nuts securing the header pipes to the cylinder head (see illustration).
16 Unscrew the downpipe mounting bolt (see illustration).
17 Draw the flanges off the studs and manoeuvre the downpipe assembly off the head and remove it (see illustration).
18 Remove the sealing ring from each port in the cylinder head and discard them as new ones must be used (see illustration).
19 Refer to Step 10 and check the downpipe-to-silencer sealing ring.
20 Check the condition of the nuts, bolt, washer, collar and rubber and replace them with new ones if necessary (see illustration).

Installation

21 Installation is the reverse of removal, noting the following:
- Check the condition of the mounting rubber and replace it with a new one if necessary. Make sure the collar is fitted in the rubber (see illustration 16.20). Clean the bolt threads, or fit a new bolt if necessary.
- Check that the amount of protrusion of each stud from the cylinder head port (with the gasket removed) is 37 to 38 mm when measured as shown (see illustration 16.21a).
- Use a new sealing ring in each cylinder head port, and dab them with grease to stick them in place (see illustration 16.21b).
- Use a new sealing ring between the downpipe assembly and the silencer if necessary – see Step 10.

17 Exhaust gas control valve (EGCV)

1 The system controls the flow of gases through the silencer using two butterfly valves, one is the control valve and is actuated electronically by the ECM, switching at a pre-determined engine speed, and connected by cable to a servo motor, the other is a sprung bypass valve to the rear chamber, reacting only to internal pressure in the front chamber and opening accordingly at engine speeds over 7000 rpm. Refer to Chapter 1 to check the control valve cable adjustment. If the control valve system malfunctions the fault could be in either the servo motor, the valve in the exhaust, the cable that links them, or in the wiring from the ECM to the servo. It is not possible to check or service the bypass valve.

16.20 Check the mounting components for damage and excess corrosion

16.21a Measure stud protrusion as shown

16.21b Use a new sealing ring in each port

Engine management system 4•27

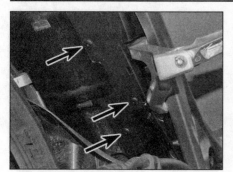
17.2a On RR models release the trim clips (arrowed)...

17.2b ...and remove the cover

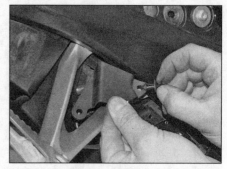
17.2c On RA models remove the brake pipe cover...

Servo motor

Check

2 Remove the servo cover **(see illustrations)**. Turn the servo pulley clockwise and disconnect the cable **(see illustrations)**.

3 On RR models remove the rider's seat (see Chapter 7). On RA models remove the battery (see Chapter 8), then lift the fuse/relay box off its clip and move it aside **(see illustration)**. On all models disconnect the servo motor wiring connector **(see illustrations)**.

4 Using a fully charged 12V battery and some jumper leads, connect the positive (+) terminal of the battery to the red wire terminal in the servo side of the connector, and the negative (–) terminal to the blue wire terminal – the servo should operate. Disconnect the battery immediately after the test. If the servo does not operate, replace it with a new one.

Caution: Disconnect the battery immediately after the test to prevent possible damage to the servo motor.

5 If the servo now operates, yet did not beforehand, check for voltage at the loom side of the wiring connector using a voltmeter – connect the positive (+) probe of the meter to the red wire terminal on the loom side of the connector, and the negative (–) terminal to the blue wire terminal. With the ignition ON there should be battery voltage. If not, check the connector for loose or corroded terminals, then check the wiring between the loom side of the connector and the ECM for continuity, referring to the *Wiring Diagrams* in Chapter 8.

17.2d ...then release the clips (arrowed) and remove the cover

17.2f ...free the outer cable...

If the wiring is good, the ECM could be faulty.
6 Using an ohmmeter or multimeter set to the K-ohms scale check the static resistance between the yellow/red and green wire

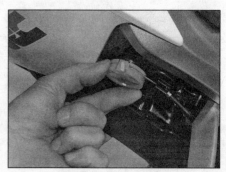
17.2e Turn the pulley...

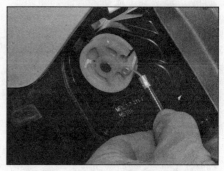
17.2g ...and detach the inner cable

terminals in the servo connector. Compare the reading to that specified at the beginning of the Chapter. Now check the variable resistance between the brown and green wire terminals in

17.3a Displace the fuse/relay box

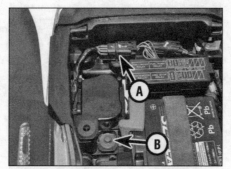
17.3b EGCV wiring connector (A) and mounting bolt (B) – RR models

17.3c EGCV black 6-pin wiring connector (arrowed) hidden next to C-ABS unit – RA models

17.9 On RA models mounting nut (arrowed) is on underside

17.11 Position the pulley as shown

the servo's connector while turning the servo pulley by hand. Compare the reading range to that specified at the beginning of the Chapter. If the readings from either test are not within the range specified, replace the servo with a new one. If the readings are good check the yellow/red, light green/black and grey/black wires between the loom side of the connector and the ECM for continuity, referring to the *Wiring Diagrams* in Chapter 8. If the wiring is good, the ECM could be faulty.

Removal

7 Remove the servo cover (see illustrations 17.2a and b or 17.2c and d). Turn the servo pulley clockwise and disconnect the cable (see illustrations 17.2e, f and g).
8 On RR models remove the rider's seat (see Chapter 7). On RA models remove the battery (see Chapter 8), then lift the fuse/relay box off its clip and move it aside (see illustration 17.3a). Disconnect the servo motor wiring connector (see illustration 17.3b or c).
9 Unscrew the bolt (RR models – see illustration 17.3b) or nut (RA models – see illustration), noting the collar, and remove the servo from the underside, noting the routing of the wiring. On RA models release the servo wiring clamp.
10 Check the condition of the rubber grommets and replace them with new ones if necessary.

Installation

11 Installation is the reverse of removal, noting the following:
● Replace damaged, deformed or deteriorated mounting rubbers with new ones. Make sure the collar is fitted in the mounting bolt/nut rubber. Seat the un-collared rubber over the mounting post.
● Smear some grease onto the cable end. Connect the cable to the servo pulley then turn the pulley anti-clockwise and position it as shown (see illustration).
● Run the engine and check the system for leaks. Check the operation of the EGCV, and adjust the cable if required (see Chapter 1). Fit the servo cover.

Exhaust valves

Control valve check

12 See Section 20 in Chapter 1.

Removal and Installation

13 The control valve and bypass valve are both integral parts of the silencer.

Cable renewal

14 Remove the silencer (see Section 16). Remove the end cap from the silencer, noting the washers with the screws (see illustration). On 2008 models there is a gasket between the cap and the silencer, which may need replacing with a new one.
15 Slacken the cable locknut at the silencer end and free the inner cable end from the valve (see illustration). Thread the cable out.
16 Smear some copper grease onto the cable end, then fit the cable into the silencer and attach it to the control valve.
17 Fit the end cap, using a new gasket if necessary on 2008 models. Install the silencer (see Section 16).
18 Smear some grease onto the cable end. Connect the cable to the servo pulley then turn the pulley anti-clockwise and position it as shown (see illustration 17.11).
19 Check the operation of the EGCV, and adjust the cable (see Chapter 1). Fit the servo cover.

18 Fuel system hoses

1 The fuel delivery, vacuum, IACV and PAIR system hoses should be replaced with new ones at the first sign of deterioration. On US models, also replace the EVAP system hoses.
2 Refer to the relevant Sections of this Chapter for further details and illustrations. Raise or remove the fuel tank as required, and if required remove the air filter housing (see Sections 2 and 3).
3 Note the routing of each hose and how it is secured – it is advisable to photograph the hose positions and routing before removing them to ensure they are correctly installed. Make sure each new hose is fully pushed onto its union. Use new clamps if necessary where fitted.
4 The fuel supply hose runs from the fuel tank to the lower union on the primary fuel rail, then from the upper union to the secondary fuel rail. Details of how to remove and install the hoses are covered in Sections 2 and 3.
5 Run the engine and check that the fuel system is working correctly before taking the machine out on the road.

19 Pulse secondary air (PAIR) system

General information

1 To reduce the amount of unburned hydrocarbons released in the exhaust gases, a pulse secondary air (PAIR) system is fitted. The system consists of the control valve (mounted above the engine valve cover), the reed valves (fitted in the engine valve cover) and the hoses linking them. The control valve is actuated electronically by the ECM.
2 Under normal operating conditions the valve is open allowing filtered air to be drawn through the reed valves and cylinder head passages and into the exhaust ports. The air mixes with the exhaust gases, causing any unburned particles of the fuel in the mixture to be burnt in the exhaust port/pipes. This process changes a considerable amount of hydrocarbons and carbon monoxide into relatively harmless carbon dioxide and water. Reed valves fitted in the valve cover prevent the flow of exhaust gases back up the cylinder head passages and into the air filter housing.

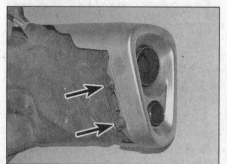

17.14 Undo the screws (arrowed) and remove the cap

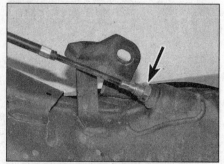

17.15 EGCV cable locknut (arrowed)

Engine management system 4•29

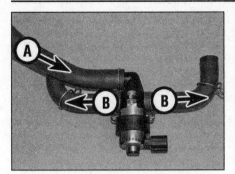

19.5a When blowing into hose (A) air should flow out of hoses (B)

19.5b Connect battery voltage to the terminals (arrowed)

19.10 Detach the hoses...

Testing

3 Start the engine and warm it up normal temperature. Stop the engine. Remove the fairing side panels (see Chapter 7).

4 Refer to Chapter 1, Section 16 and remove the air filter. Check that the PAIR air intake port in the right-hand side of the housing is clean – the presence or carbon deposits indicates a faulty system. Start the engine again and open the throttle slightly, and check the air is being sucked into the port. If not, stop the engine, then perform the following checks.

5 Remove the air filter housing (Section 3). Disconnect the crankcase breather hose, then unstick and displace the rubber heat shield **(see illustrations 6.30a, b and c)**. Disconnect the control valve wiring connector **(see illustration 19.11)**. Clean the end of the air filter housing hose. Manually check the operation of the system by blowing through the hose – air should flow through the control valve and reed valves **(see illustration)**. Apply battery voltage (12 volts) across the control valve terminals and repeat the check **(see illustration)** – no air should flow through the control valve. Disconnect the battery. If the valve does not behave as described check its resistance (Step 7).

6 Now suck on the air filter hose union; you should not be able to suck air back up the hose, indicating the reed valves are closing and sealing correctly. If you can suck air through, first identify which reed valve is faulty by blocking one hose, then the other. Having identified the faulty valve remove it for cleaning, then test it again. Replace the valve with a new one if necessary.

19.11 ...disconnect the wiring connector...

7 Check the resistance of the control valve solenoid by connecting an ohmmeter between its connector terminals and compare the reading obtained to that given in the Specifications. Replace the valve with a new one if faulty.

Component renewal

Control valve

8 Remove the fairing side panels (see Chapter 7).

9 Remove the air filter housing (Section 3). Disconnect the crankcase breather hose, then unstick and displace the rubber heat shield **(see illustrations 6.30a, b and c)**.

10 Detach the hoses from the reed valve housings **(see illustration)**.

11 Disconnect the control valve wiring connector **(see illustration)**.

12 Release the wiring holder from the back

19.12 ...and pull the wiring holder out of the rubber sleeve

of the valve and remove the valve with the hoses, then detach them if required **(see illustration)**.

13 Installation is the reverse of removal.

Reed valves

14 Remove the fairing side panels (see Chapter 7).

15 Remove the air filter housing (Section 3). Disconnect the crankcase breather hose, then unstick and displace the rubber heat shield **(see illustrations 6.30a, b and c)**.

16 Release the clamp and detach the air hose from the reed valve cover **(see illustration 19.10)**. Unscrew the bolts and remove the cover **(see illustration)**. Remove the reed valve and the baseplate, noting which way around they fit **(see illustration)**.

17 Gently push the reed off its seat from the underside to check it is not stuck **(see illustration)**. Release it and make sure

19.16a Remove the cover...

19.16b ...and lift the reed valve and its baseplate out

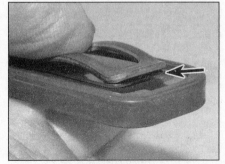

19.17a Check the reed (arrowed) is not stuck to its seat

4•30 Engine management system

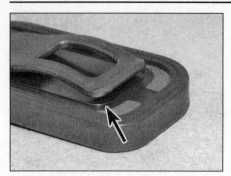

19.17b Make sure there is no gap between the reed (arrowed) and its seat

there is no gap between it and its seat **(see illustration)**. Check the condition of the rubber around the valve. Replace the valve with a new one if necessary.

18 Installation is the reverse of removal. Make sure the reed valve components and housings are clean and free of carbon deposits, and that the baseplates and valves seat correctly. Clean the threads of the cover bolts and apply fresh threadlock, and tighten the bolts to the torque setting specified at the beginning of the Chapter.

20 Evaporative emission control (EVAP) system

Note: *This system is fitted to US models only.*

General information

1 The evaporative emission control system (EVAP) is fitted to minimise the escape of fuel vapour into the atmosphere. The fuel tank is sealed and a charcoal canister collects the fuel vapours generated when the motorcycle is parked and stores them until they can be cleared from the canister, via the control valve, into the throttle body intake tracts to be burned by the engine during normal combustion. The purge control valve for the fuel tank vapour is opened and closed by the ECM.
2 The valve should be tested if there is a problem starting the engine when it is hot.

Testing
Purge control valve

3 Remove the valve (see below).
4 Check the operation of the control valve by blowing through the inlet (canister hose) union – air should not flow through the valve and out the outlet hose union. Connect battery voltage (12 volts) across the valve terminals, connecting the positive lead to the black/white wire terminal, and repeat the check – air should flow through the valve if it is functioning correctly.
5 If an ohmmeter is available, check the resistance of the control valve windings and compare the reading obtained to that given in the Specifications. Replace the valve with a new one if the reading differs.
6 If the valve behaves as described, check for battery voltage using a multimeter across the terminals on the loom side of the valve wiring connector with the ignition ON – connect the positive lead to the black/white wire terminal. If no voltage is present check the wiring.

Charcoal canister

7 No testing of the canister is possible, if it is thought to be faulty a new one must be installed.

Component renewal
Purge control valve

8 The valve is mounted behind the starter motor. Raise the fuel tank (see Section 2).
9 Disconnect the wiring connector and hoses from the valve, noting which fits where.
10 Unscrew the bolts and remove the valve. If required unscrew the bolts and remove the bracket – note the collars in the grommets.
11 Installation is the reverse of removal. Make sure the grommets are in good condition.

Charcoal canister

12 The canister is mounted behind the engine. Remove the silencer (see Section 16). Remove the shock absorber lower mounting bolt and pivot the bottom of the shock back (see Chapter 5).
13 Disconnect the hoses, noting which fits where.
14 Unscrew the canister mounting bolts, noting the washers, and remove the canister. Note the collars in the grommets.
15 Installation is the reverse of removal. Make sure the grommets are in good condition.

21 Catalytic converter

General information

1 A catalytic converter is incorporated in the silencer to minimise the level of exhaust pollutants released into the atmosphere.
2 The catalytic converter consists of a canister containing a fine mesh impregnated with a catalyst material, over which the hot exhaust gases pass. The catalyst speeds up the oxidation of harmful carbon monoxide, unburned hydrocarbons and soot, effectively reducing the quantity of harmful products released into the atmosphere via the exhaust gases.
3 On all except US models from 2008 to 2011 the catalytic converter is of the closed-loop type with exhaust gas oxygen content information being fed back to the ECM by the oxygen sensor.
4 The oxygen sensor (where fitted) contains a heating element that is controlled by the ECM. When the engine is cold, the ECM switches on the heating element, which warms the exhaust gases as they pass over the sensor. This brings the catalytic converter quickly up to its normal operating temperature and decreases the level of exhaust pollutants emitted whilst the engine warms up. Once the engine is sufficiently warmed up, the ECM switches off the heating element.
5 Refer to Section 16 for exhaust system removal and installation, and Section 6 for oxygen sensor removal and installation information.

Precautions

6 The catalytic converter is a reliable and simple device which needs no maintenance in itself, but there are some facts of which an owner should be aware if the converter is to function properly for its full service life.
● DO NOT use leaded or lead replacement petrol (gasoline) – the additives will coat the precious metals, reducing their converting efficiency and will eventually destroy the catalytic converter.
● Always keep the ignition and fuel systems well-maintained in accordance with the manufacturer's schedule – if the fuel/air mixture is suspected of being incorrect have it checked on an exhaust gas analyser.
● If the engine develops a misfire, do not ride the bike at all (or at least as little as possible) until the fault is cured.
● DO NOT use fuel or engine oil additives – these may contain substances harmful to the catalytic converter.
● DO NOT continue to use the bike if the engine burns oil to the extent of leaving a visible trail of blue smoke.
● Remember that the catalytic converter and oxygen sensor are FRAGILE – do not strike them with tools during servicing work.

22 Ignition system check

⚠ **Warning:** *The energy levels in electronic systems can be very high. On no account should the ignition be switched on whilst the plugs or coils are being held. Shocks from the HT circuit can be most unpleasant.*

1 As no means of adjustment is available, any failure of the system can be traced to failure of a system component or a simple wiring fault. Of the two possibilities, the latter is by far the most likely. The first step in checking the ignition system is to see whether there is a spark at the plug. If the engine does not run at all test each plug in turn, starting with the No. 1 (left-hand) plug, and work across the engine. If the engine runs but not on all cylinders, first identify the non-firing cylinder by seeing which exhaust downpipe is cold.
2 Make sure the ignition is switched off. Refer to Chapter 1 and remove the spark plug being tested. Reconnect the wiring connector to the removed coil. Disconnect the wiring connector from the other three coils. Fit the spark plug into the removed coil, then hold the coil so the plug threads are pressed against the cylinder head to earth it – do not hold the plug against the valve cover. If it is difficult to contact the cylinder head use a length of fairly thick insulated wire with crocodile clips at each end to link the plug threads to the cylinder head, or some other known good earth point.

Engine management system 4•31

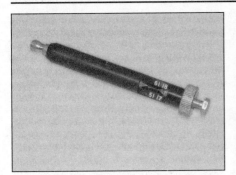

22.4 Ignition spark gap testing tool

23.5a Disconnect the wiring connector...

23.5b ...and pull the coil off the spark plug

⚠ **Warning: Cover the open spark plug hole with rag to prevent atomised fuel being pumped out of the hole and igniting. Make sure the plug being tested is earthed otherwise the ECM could be damaged.**

3 Having observed the above precautions, check that the kill switch is in the RUN position and the transmission is in neutral, then turn the ignition switch ON and turn the engine over on the starter motor. If the system is in good condition a regular, fat blue spark should be evident at the plug electrodes. If the spark appears thin or yellowish, or is non-existent, further investigation is necessary. Turn the ignition OFF and repeat the check for each coil. Note that ideally the test should be carried out with either a new spark plug or one that is known to be good; if there is doubt about a plug's condition, renew it.

4 The ignition system must be able to produce a spark that is capable of jumping at least a 6 mm gap. Simple ignition spark gap testing tools are commercially available **(see illustration)** – follow the manufacturer's instructions.

5 If the test results are good the entire ignition system can be considered good. If the spark appears thin or yellowish, or is non-existent, further investigation is necessary.

6 Ignition faults can be divided into two categories, namely those where the ignition system has failed completely, and those that are due to a partial failure. The likely faults are listed below, starting with the most probable source of failure. Work through the list systematically, referring to the subsequent sections for full details of the necessary checks and tests. **Note:** *Before checking the following items ensure that the battery is fully charged and that the FI system fuses are in good condition.*

- Loose, corroded or damaged wiring connections, broken or shorted wiring between any of the component parts of the ignition system (see Chapter 8).
- Faulty coil connection, faulty spark plug, dirty, worn or corroded plug electrodes.
- Faulty neutral/gear position, clutch or sidestand switch (see Chapter 8).
- Faulty ignition coil(s) (Section 23).
- Faulty ignition switch or engine kill switch (see Chapter 8).
- Faulty crankshaft position (CKP) sensor

(Section 6) or damaged trigger on alternator rotor (Chapter 8).
- Faulty throttle position sensor (Section 6).
- Faulty lean angle sensor (Section 6).
- Faulty engine stop relay (Section 8).
- Faulty ECM (Section 7).

7 If the above checks don't reveal the cause of the problem, have the ignition system tested by a Honda dealer.

23 Ignition coils

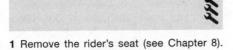

1 Remove the rider's seat (see Chapter 8). Disconnect the battery negative (–) lead.
2 Remove the fairing side panels (see Chapter 7).
3 Remove the air filter housing (see Section 3). Disconnect the crankcase breather hose, then unstick and displace the rubber heat shield **(see illustrations 6.30a, b and c)**.
4 Check the coils visually for loose or damaged connectors and terminals, cracks and other damage. Clean the area around each ignition coil to prevent any dirt falling into the spark plug channels.
5 Check that the cylinder location is marked on each coil's wiring sleeve, then disconnect the wiring connector from the coil being tested **(see illustration)**. Pull the coil off the spark plug **(see illustration)**.
6 To check the condition of the primary windings, set a multimeter to the ohms x 1 scale. Connect one meter probe to one terminal in the coil socket and the other probe to the other terminal and measure the resistance **(see illustration)**. If the reading obtained is not within the range given in the Specifications, it is likely that the coil is defective.
7 To check the resistance of the secondary windings, set the meter to the K-ohm scale. Connect one meter probe to one of the terminals in the coil socket, and the other to the spark plug contact, using a thick piece of wire or a nail as an extension if your probe is not long enough **(see illustration)**. If the reading obtained is not within the range given in the Specifications, it is likely that the coil is defective.
8 To confirm a coil is defective have it peak voltage tested by a Honda dealer.
9 To check the initial voltage supply to the coil, fit the coil(s) onto the plug(s) and connect all wiring connectors so far disconnected to access the coils, with the exception of the fuel pump connector. Disconnect the connector from the coil being tested and connect the positive (+) lead of a voltmeter to the black/white wire terminal in the coil wiring connector, and connect the negative (–) lead to a suitable earth (ground) point.
10 Check that the kill switch is in the RUN position and the transmission is in neutral, then turn the ignition switch ON. Note the voltage reading on the meter. Turn the ignition switch off and disconnect the meter.
11 If the initial voltage reading is not as specified then a fault is present somewhere else in the ignition system circuit (see Section 22).
12 If the initial voltage reading is as specified and the plug does not spark (when tested using a

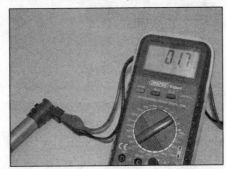

23.6 To test the coil primary resistance, connect the multimeter leads between the connector socket terminals

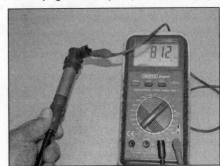

23.7 To test the coil secondary resistance, connect the multimeter leads between one terminal and the spark plug socket

new plug as in Section 22), then the coil is faulty and must be replaced with a new one; the coil is a sealed unit and cannot therefore be repaired.

24 Ignition timing

General information

1 Since no provision exists for adjusting the ignition timing and since no component is subject to mechanical wear, there is no need for regular checks; only if investigating a fault such as a loss of power or a misfire should the ignition timing be checked.
2 The ignition timing is checked dynamically (engine running) using a stroboscopic lamp. The inexpensive neon lamps should be adequate in theory, but in practice may produce a pulse of such low intensity that the timing mark remains indistinct. If possible, one of the more precise xenon tube lamps should be used. Whatever type is used make sure it is one that connects between the plug and the plug socket in the coil, and not one that clips onto the HT lead, as there are no HT leads on this machine.

Check

3 Warm the engine up to normal operating temperature then stop it.
4 Unscrew the timing inspection cap from the clutch cover **(see illustration)**. Check the condition of its O-ring and obtain a new one if necessary.
5 The dynamic timing mark on the rotor that indicates the firing point at idle speed for the No. 1 cylinder is the line next to the F mark **(see illustration)**. The static timing mark with which this should align is the notch in the inspection hole rim.

 The timing marks can be highlighted with white paint to make them more visible under the stroboscope light.

6 Connect the timing light between the No. 1 cylinder coil and plug.
7 Start the engine and aim the light at the static timing mark.
8 With the machine idling, the line next to the F should align with the static timing mark (see Step 5). Now increase engine speed – the dynamic timing mark should move anti-clockwise in relation to the static mark. This confirms the ignition is advancing.
9 As already stated, there is no means of adjustment of the ignition timing. If the ignition timing is incorrect, or suspected of being incorrect, one of the ignition system components is at fault, and the system must be tested as described in the preceding Sections of this Chapter.
10 When the check is complete, fit the timing inspection cap having smeared its O-ring with oil and the cap threads with grease **(see illustration)**. Tighten the cap to the torque setting specified at the beginning of the Chapter.

25 Immobiliser system

General information

1 An immobiliser system (known as HISS – Honda Ignition Security System) is fitted either as standard or as an option (depending on market) as an anti-theft device. The system will only allow the machine to be started if the correct registered key is used to turn the ignition ON. The system consists of a transponder which is part of the ignition key, a receiver which is fitted around the ignition switch, and the ECM.
2 When the ignition is switched ON, the ECM sends power through the receiver to the transponder. The transponder sends a coded signal back through the receiver to the ECM. If the signal sent by the transponder matches the signal stored in the ECM memory, the HISS immobiliser indicator light in the instrument cluster comes on for two seconds, then goes out, and the ECM allows the engine to be started. If the key code signal is not recognised, or if there is a fault in the system, the indicator light stays on. If the light stays on, refer to the fault diagnosis and troubleshooting Sections below. Likewise if the light does not come on at all.
3 The ECM can store the codes for up to four registered keys. They keys should be kept separately (i.e. not on the same key-ring) as the proximity of another key to the one being used in the switch can lead to the signal from it being jammed, and the bike will not start. The key has a built in transponder which can be damaged if the key is dropped or knocked, gets too hot, is too close to a magnetic object, or is submerged in water for too long. If all the keys are lost, the ECM must be replaced with a new one, so always make sure you have at least one spare key. If a new key is obtained, it must be registered into the system before the bike can be started with the key.

Key registration procedure

Note: *The following procedures refer to the Honda special tools (Part Nos. 07XMZ-MBW0101 and 070MZ-MEC0100), which are wiring loom adapters to connect a battery into the loom side of the crankshaft position (CKP) sensor wiring connector.*

With the old ignition switch

4 Obtain a new key from a Honda dealer, and have it cut to match the original key.
5 Raise the fuel tank (see Section 2). Disconnect the CKP sensor wiring connector **(see illustration 6.35)**. Connect the special tools (see **Note** above) together at the connector, then connect the wiring connector end to the loom side of the CKP sensor connector, and connect the red clip of the tool to the battery positive (+) terminal and the green clip to the battery negative (–) terminal.
6 Turn the ignition switch ON using your original key. The immobiliser indicator light should come on and stay on – if it starts to flash after ten seconds, then there is a fault in the system, which will have gone into fault diagnosis, and the pattern of the flashes it emits should be matched with the fault code (see below). Now disconnect the red clip from the battery positive terminal and leave it disconnected for at least two seconds, then reconnect it. The indicator should now come on for two seconds, then begin to flash repeatedly four times. This indicates that the system is in registration mode. At this point the registrations of all keys except the one in the switch will have been cancelled, so if you have another spare apart from the new one you want to register, this will also have to be registered.
7 Turn the ignition OFF and remove the original key, placing it well away from the receiver.
8 Insert the new key into the switch and turn

24.4 Unscrew the timing inspection cap

24.5 F mark and static timing mark aligned

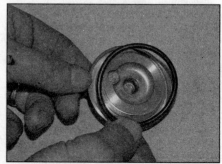

24.10 Fit the O-ring to the cap

Engine management system 4•33

it ON. The indicator should now come on for two seconds, then begin to flash repeatedly four times. This indicates that the system has registered the new key. If the indicator starts to flash after ten seconds, then there is a fault in the system, which will have gone into fault diagnosis, and the pattern of the flashes it emits should be matched with the fault code (see below). Turn the ignition OFF and remove the key.

9 To register any other spare keys that will have been cancelled, repeat Step 8. Up to four keys can be registered.

10 On completion turn the ignition OFF, then remove the special tool and reconnect the crankshaft position (CKP) sensor wiring connector. Now turn the ignition ON using any of the registered keys to return the system to normal mode.

11 Check that all registered keys can start the motorcycle.

With a new ignition switch

12 Obtain a new switch and two (or more) new keys.

13 Remove the faulty switch (see Chapter 8), but retain the HISS receiver to fit with the new switch.

14 Raise the fuel tank (see Section 2). Disconnect the CKP sensor wiring connector **(see illustration 6.35)**. Connect the special tools (see **Note** above) together at the connector, then connect the wiring connector end to the loom side of the CKP sensor connector, and connect the red clip of the tool to the battery positive (+) terminal and the green clip to the battery negative (–) terminal.

15 Place one of the original registered keys for the faulty switch next to the receiver.

16 Connect the new ignition switch to its connector in the wiring loom, but keep it away from the receiver. Turn the new switch ON with one of the new keys. The immobiliser indicator light should come on and stay on, which means the ECM recognises the old key that is next to the receiver – if it starts to flash after ten seconds, then there is a fault in the system, which will have gone into fault diagnosis, and the pattern of the flashes it emits should be matched with the fault code (see below). Now disconnect the red clip from the battery positive terminal and leave it disconnected for at least two seconds, then reconnect it. The indicator should now come on for two seconds, then begin to flash repeatedly four times. This indicates that the system is in registration mode. At this point the registrations of all keys except the one near the receiver will have been cancelled.

17 Turn the ignition OFF and remove the new key.

18 Install the new ignition switch, then fit the receiver onto it (see Chapter 8).

19 Insert the new key into the switch and turn it ON. The indicator should now come on for two seconds, then begin to flash repeatedly four times. This indicates that the system has registered the new key. If the indicator starts to flash after ten seconds, then there is a fault in the system, which will have gone into fault diagnosis, and the pattern of the flashes it emits should be matched with the fault code (see below). Turn the ignition OFF and disconnect the red clip of the special tool from the battery positive terminal.

20 Turn the ignition ON using the newly registered key. The indicator light should come on for two seconds, then go off.

21 Turn the ignition OFF and reconnect the red clip to the battery positive terminal.

22 Turn the ignition ON using the newly registered key. The indicator light should come on and stay on. Now disconnect the red clip from the battery positive terminal and leave it disconnected for at least two seconds, then reconnect it. The indicator should now come on for two seconds, then begin to flash repeatedly four times. This indicates that the system is in registration mode. At this point the registrations of all old keys (for the faulty switch) are cancelled.

23 Turn the ignition OFF and remove the key, placing it well away from the receiver.

24 Insert the second new unregistered key and turn the ignition ON. The indicator should now come on for two seconds, then begin to flash repeatedly four times. This indicates that the system has registered the second new key. Turn the ignition OFF and remove the key.

25 To register any other new spare keys, repeat Step 24. Up to four keys can be registered.

26 On completion turn the ignition OFF, then remove the special tool and reconnect the CKP sensor wiring connector. Now turn the ignition ON using any of the registered keys to return the system to normal mode.

27 Check that all newly registered keys can start the motorcycle.

With a new ECM

28 Obtain a new ECM along with two new keys. Install the new ECM (see Section 7). Have the keys cut to match the original key for your ignition switch.

29 Insert a new key into the switch and turn it ON. The indicator should now come on for two seconds, then begin to flash repeatedly four times. This indicates that the system has registered the new key. If the indicator stays on for ten seconds then starts to flash, then there is a fault in the system, which will have gone into fault diagnosis, and the pattern of the flashes it emits should be matched with the fault code (see below).

30 Turn the ignition OFF and remove the key.

31 Insert the second new key and turn the ignition ON. The indicator should now come on for two seconds, then begin to flash repeatedly four times. This indicates that the system has registered the second new key.

32 Turn the ignition OFF and remove the key.

33 The new ECM will only register two new keys at this stage. If you have a third key to register, refer to Steps 4 to 10 to register it, noting that you will need the special tool mentioned therein.

34 Check that both newly registered keys can start the motorcycle.

Fault diagnosis

35 There are two fault diagnosis modes, one for faults that occur during normal use, and one for a fault that occurs when registering a new key. Make sure you refer to the correct table below when matching the fault code pattern.

36 If the indicator light has come on and stayed on during normal use, raise the fuel tank (see Section 2). Disconnect the CKP sensor wiring connector **(see illustration 6.35)**. Connect the special tools (see **Note** above) together at the connector, then connect the wiring connector end to the loom side of the CKP sensor connector, and connect the red clip of the tool to the battery positive (+) terminal and the green clip to the battery negative (–) terminal.

37 Turn the ignition switch ON. The indicator light will come on for ten seconds, then start to flash. This means it has entered diagnostic mode, and the pattern of the flashes indicates the fault that has occurred. The pattern repeats continuously. Match the pattern with the fault codes below, making sure you refer to the relevant table. If the indicator stays on after ten seconds and does not flash, then there is no fault logged in the system.

If fault is indicated during normal use		
Flash pattern	Fault	Solution
Two short, one long, one short	Faulty ECM	Install new ECM
Two short, two long	Faulty receiver or wiring	Follow Troubleshooting procedure below
One long, three short	Signal jammed by other key	Place other key well away from receiver
One long, two short, one long	Signal jammed by other key	Place other key well away from receiver

If fault is indicated during key registration		
Flash pattern	Fault	Solution
One short, one long, one short, one long	Key already registered	Use a new or cancelled key
Two short, two long	Faulty receiver or wiring	Follow Troubleshooting procedure below
One short, one long, two short	Key already registered on old ECM	Use a new key

4•34 Engine management system

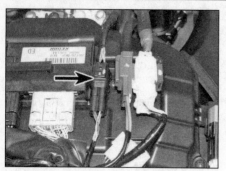

25.48 HISS wiring connector (arrowed)

25.52a Release the cover...

25.52b ...then undo the screws (arrowed)

Troubleshooting procedure

Indicator light does not come on when ignition switched ON

38 Check the turn signal/clock fuse (see Chapter 8).

39 If the fuse is good, make sure the engine is in neutral then turn the ignition ON and check whether the neutral light has come on.

40 If the light has not come on, displace and support the fairing, leaving the wiring connected (see Chapter 7). Pull back the rubber boot on the instrument cluster wiring connector. Using a voltmeter, connect the positive (+) probe to the red/green wire terminal (connector still connected) and the negative (−) probe to the green/black wire terminal in the connector. With the ignition ON there should be battery voltage. If voltage is present, the instrument cluster is faulty (see Chapter 8). If there is no voltage, check for continuity in the wiring, referring to the wiring diagrams at the end of Chapter 8. The green/black wire goes to earth (ground).

41 If the light has come on, refer to Section 7 to access the ECM and disconnect the ECM grey wiring connector. Using a voltmeter, connect the positive (+) probe to the white/red wire terminal on the loom side of the ECM connector and the negative (−) probe to earth (ground). Turn the ignition ON – there should be battery voltage.

42 If there was no voltage, using a voltmeter, connect the positive (+) probe to the white/red wire terminal in the instrument cluster connector and the negative (−) probe to earth. Turn the ignition ON – there should be no voltage for two seconds, then there should be battery voltage. If there is no voltage after two seconds, check for continuity in the white/red wire, and also in the green/black wire to earth, referring to the wiring diagrams at the end of Chapter 8. If voltage is present, the instrument cluster is faulty (see Chapter 8).

43 If there is voltage in Step 41, using a voltmeter, connect the positive (+) probe to the black/white (ECM) wire terminal on the loom side of the ECM black connector and the negative (−) probe to earth (ground). Turn the ignition ON – there should be battery voltage. If there is no voltage, check for continuity in the black/white wire, and if that is good check the FI fuse (Chapter 8) and the engine stop relay and its wiring (Section 8). If voltage is present, check for continuity to earth (ground) in the green and green/pink wires. If the wiring is good, check the ECM connector for loose, damaged or corroded terminals. If the connector is good, then the ECM could be faulty, and should be checked by a Honda dealer.

Indicator light stays on when ignition switched ON

44 Check that none of the other registered keys are close to the receiver. If they are, remove them and try the ignition again.

45 Turn the ignition ON with a spare key and check the indicator light, which should come on for two seconds, then go out. If it does, the first key is faulty. If it doesn't, perform the fault diagnosis procedure described above. If a fault code is displayed, use the appropriate table to determine the fault and the solution.

46 If no fault code is displayed, or the system does not go into fault diagnosis mode, refer to Section 7 to access the ECM and disconnect the ECM grey wiring connector. Using a voltmeter, connect the positive (+) probe to the white/red wire terminal on the loom side of the connector and the negative (−) probe to earth (ground). Turn the ignition ON – there should be battery voltage. If there is no voltage, check for continuity in the white/red wire between the ECM and the instrument connector.

47 If there is voltage, check for continuity in the yellow and white/yellow wires between the ECM and the crankshaft position (CKP) sensor, referring to the wiring diagrams at the end of Chapter 8. If there is no continuity, trace the fault and repair or replace the wiring as necessary. If there is continuity, the ECM could be faulty and should be taken to a Honda dealer for assessment.

Fault code indicated by flash pattern

48 If the 'two short, two long' flash pattern has been indicated during the fault diagnosis procedure, raise the fuel tank (see Section 2). Remove the air filter housing jacket, noting how it fits **(see illustration 6.1a)**. Disconnect the receiver wiring connector **(see illustration)**. Using a voltmeter, connect the positive (+) probe to the yellow/red wire terminal on the loom side of the receiver connector and the negative (−) probe to earth (ground). Turn the ignition ON – there should be approximately 5 volts present. If there is no voltage, check for continuity in the yellow/red wire between the ECM and the receiver, and repair or replace the wiring if there is no continuity.

49 If there is 5 volts present, check for continuity to earth (ground) in the grey/black wire on the loom side of the connector, and repair or replace the wiring if there is no continuity.

50 If the wiring is good, using a voltmeter, connect the positive (+) probe to the pink wire terminal on the loom side of the receiver connector and the negative (−) probe to earth (ground). Turn the ignition ON – there should be approximately 5 volts present. If there is, the receiver is faulty.

51 If there is no voltage, check for continuity in the blue/orange and pink wires between the ECM and the receiver, and repair or replace the wiring if there is no continuity between the connectors, or if there is continuity in either to earth (ground). If the wiring is good, the receiver is faulty.

Replacement

52 To replace the receiver, raise the fuel tank (see Section 2). Remove the air filter housing jacket, noting how it fits **(see illustration 6.1a)**. Disconnect the receiver wiring connector **(see illustration 25.48)**. Feed the wiring back to the receiver, freeing it from any ties and noting its routing. Displace the cover, then undo the screws and remove the receiver, turning the handlebars as required for best access **(see illustrations)**. If you can't easily access the screws, displace the top yoke (refer to Chapter 1, Section 12, following the relevant Steps).

53 To replace the ECM see Section 7.

Chapter 5
Frame and suspension

Contents

	Section number		Section number
Footrests, brake pedal and gearchange lever	3	Sidestand	4
Fork oil change	7	Sidestand lubrication	see Chapter 1
Fork overhaul	8	Sidestand switch	see Chapter 8
Fork removal and installation	6	Steering damper (HESD)	11
Frame inspection and repair	2	Steering head bearing check and adjustment	see Chapter 1
General information	1	Steering head bearings	10
Handlebar switches	see Chapter 8	Steering stem	9
Handlebars and levers	5	Suspension adjustment	14
Rear shock absorber	12	Suspension check	see Chapter 1
Rear suspension linkage	13	Swingarm	15

Degrees of difficulty

Easy, suitable for novice with little experience	**Fairly easy,** suitable for beginner with some experience	**Fairly difficult,** suitable for competent DIY mechanic	**Difficult,** suitable for experienced DIY mechanic	**Very difficult,** suitable for expert DIY or professional

Specifications

Front forks

Fork oil type .... Honda SS-47 suspension fluid or equivalent 10W fork oil
Fork oil capacity
   2008 to 2011 models .... 517 ± 2.5 cc
   2012-on models .... 515 ± 2.5 cc
Fork oil level*
   2008 to 2011 models .... 93 mm
   2012-on models .... 84 mm
Fork spring free length
   2008 to 2011 models
     Standard .... 234.0 mm
     Service limit (min) .... 229.3 mm
   2012-on models
     Standard .... 229.5 mm
     Service limit (min) .... 224.9 mm
Fork tube runout limit .... 0.2 mm

*Oil level is measured from the top of the tube with the leg fully compressed. On 2008 to 2011 models the fork spring should be removed and on 2012-on models the spring should be installed.

5•2 Frame and suspension

Steering head bearings
Bearing pre-load (steering damper detached – see text) . . . . 12 to 17 N

Steering damper
Solenoid valve resistance . . . . 10 to 15 ohms

Torque settings
Chain slider bolts	9 Nm
Chainguard bolts	12 Nm
Fork damper cartridge bolt (2008 to 2011 models)	34 Nm
Fork rod guide (2012-on models)	90 Nm
Fork top bolt	
2008 to 2011 models	34 Nm
2012-on models	35 Nm
Fork yoke clamp bolts	
Top yoke bolts	22 Nm
Bottom yoke bolts	27 Nm
Front brake master cylinder clamp bolts	12 Nm
Gearchange lever pivot bolt	22 Nm
Handlebar clamp bolts	26 Nm
Handlebar end-weight screws	10 Nm
Lever pivot screw	1 Nm
Lever pivot screw nut	6 Nm
Passenger footrest bracket bolts	27 Nm
Rear brake master cylinder bolt nuts	10 Nm
Rider's footrest bracket bolts	37 Nm
Shock absorber bolts/nuts	44 Nm
Sidestand pivot bolt	10 Nm
Sidestand pivot bolt nut	29 Nm
Steering damper linkage arm nuts	12 Nm
Steering damper mounting bolts	10 Nm
Steering head bearing adjuster nut	37 Nm
Steering stem nut	137 Nm
Suspension linkage bolt nuts	44 Nm
Swingarm pivot bolt nut	
RR models and 2009 RA models (with washer)	113 Nm
2010-on RA models (no washer)	124 Nm

1 General information

All models have a die-cast diamond pattern aluminium frame that uses the engine as a stressed member.

Front suspension is by Honda's HMAS (Honda Multi-Action System) 43 mm oil-damped upside-down telescopic forks with a cartridge damper. The forks are adjustable for spring pre-load and both rebound and compression damping on all models. Models from 2012-on use Showa 'Big Piston' forks.

At the rear, a gull-wing design aluminium swingarm acts on an HMAS single shock absorber via a three-way linkage, and using a floating design that incorporates the upper shock absorber mount in the swingarm as opposed to it being bolted to the frame. The swingarm pivots through the frame. The Showa shock absorber is adjustable for spring pre-load and both rebound and compression damping.

2 Frame inspection and repair

1 The frame should not require attention unless accident damage has occurred. In most cases, fitting a new frame is the only satisfactory remedy for such damage. A few frame specialists have the jigs and other equipment necessary for straightening frames to the required standard of accuracy, but even then there is no simple way of assessing to what extent the frame may have been over stressed.
2 After a high mileage, the frame should be examined closely for signs of cracking or splitting at the welded joints. Loose engine mounting bolts can cause ovaling or fracturing of the mounting points. Minor damage can often be repaired by specialised welding, depending on the extent and nature of the damage.
3 Remember that a frame that is out of alignment will cause handling problems. If, as the result of an accident, misalignment is suspected, it will be necessary to strip the machine completely so the frame can be thoroughly checked.

3 Footrests, brake pedal and gearchange lever

Footrests

1 Remove the split pin and washer from the bottom of the footrest pivot pin, then withdraw the pivot pin and remove the footrest (see illustration). On the rider's footrests, note the

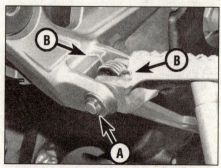

3.1a Split pin and washer (A), return spring ends (B) – rider's footrests

Frame and suspension 5•3

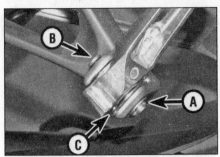

3.1b Split pin and washer (A), pivot pin (B), detent plate, ball and spring (C) – passenger footrests

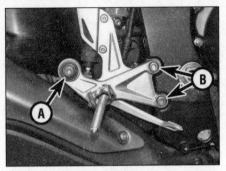

3.3a Unscrew the nut and bolt (A) and the bolts (B)

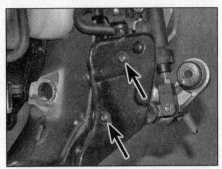

3.3b Guard plate screws (arrowed)

fitting of the return spring. On the passenger footrests, note the fitting of the detent plate, ball and spring, and take care not to let the ball and spring ping away when removing the footrest (see illustration).

2 Installation is the reverse of removal. Apply a small amount of copper-based grease to the pivot pin.

Brake pedal

Removal

3 Place a support under the rear of the silencer. Unscrew the silencer and footrest bracket mounting bolts and displace the bracket so that you can access the back (see illustrations). Undo the guard plate screws and remove the plate (see illustration).

4 Unhook the brake light switch spring and the pedal return spring (see illustration). Release the EGCV cable from its guide on the reservoir bracket.

5 Undo the nuts on the master cylinder mounting bolts then withdraw the bolts, noting the collar with the upper bolt, and remove the heel plate (see illustration).

6 Release the circlip securing the brake pedal, then remove the thrust washer (see illustration). Slide the pedal off its pivot. Remove the wave washer from the pivot.

7 Remove the split pin from the clevis pin securing the brake pedal to the master cylinder pushrod, then withdraw the clevis pin and detach the pushrod from the pedal (see illustration 3.6).

Installation

8 Installation is the reverse of removal, noting the following:
● Use a new split pin on the master cylinder pushrod clevis pin (see illustration 3.6).
● Clean any old grease off the pedal and pivot, then apply fresh grease.

● Slide the wave washer onto the pivot, then slide the pedal on, then the thrust washer. Make sure the circlip locates correctly in the groove, and use a new one if the old one deformed when removed (see illustration 3.6).
● Make sure the heel plate and reservoir bracket are correctly secured by the master cylinder bolts and the EGCV cable is in its guide, and do not forget the collar with the upper bolt (see illustration 3.5). Tighten the master cylinder bolt nuts to the torque setting specified at the beginning of the Chapter.
● Make sure the springs are correctly located (see illustration 3.4).
● Tighten the rider's footrest bracket bolts to the torque setting specified at the beginning of the Chapter.
● Check the operation of the rear brake light switch (see Chapter 1).

Gearchange lever and linkage

Removal

9 Counter-hold the gearchange lever linkage rod using a spanner on its flats and slacken the locknuts (see illustration). Unscrew the rod and separate it from the lever and the arm – the rod is reverse-threaded on one end and so will simultaneously unscrew from both lever and arm when turned in the one direction. Note how far the rod is threaded onto the lever and arm as this determines the height of the lever relative to the footrest.

10 Unscrew the gearchange lever pivot bolt and remove the lever, noting the wave washer and thrust washer (see illustration).

3.4 Unhook the springs (arrowed)

3.5 Unscrew the nuts (arrowed) and displace the master cylinder

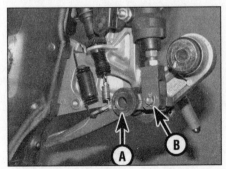

3.6 Brake pedal circlip (A) and clevis pin (B)

3.9 Hold the rod and slacken the locknuts (arrowed)

3.10 Unscrew the bolt (arrowed) and remove the lever

5•4 Frame and suspension

3.11a Note the alignment of the arm on the shaft...

3.11b ...then unscrew the pinch bolt and slide the arm off

4.3 Unhook the springs (arrowed)

11 Note the alignment of the punch mark on the gearchange shaft with the slit in the linkage arm **(see illustration)**. Unscrew the linkage arm bolt and slide the arm off the shaft **(see illustration)**.

Installation

12 Installation is the reverse of removal, noting the following:
- Align the slit in the linkage arm clamp with the mark on the shaft.
- Apply grease to the pivot section on the lever bolt.
- Slide the wave washer onto the pivot section, then the lever, then the thrust washer. Tighten the bolt to the torque setting specified at the beginning of the Chapter.
- Adjust the gear lever height as required by screwing the linkage rod in or out of the lever and arm. Tighten the locknuts securely.

4 Sidestand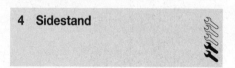

Removal

1 Remove the lower fairing (see Chapter 7).
2 Support the bike using an auxiliary stand.
3 Carefully unhook and remove the stand springs **(see illustration)**.
4 Unscrew the sidestand switch bolt and displace the switch, noting how it locates **(see illustration)** – there is no need to disconnect

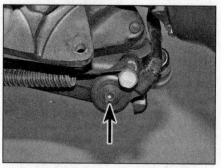

4.4 Sidestand switch bolt (arrowed)

its wiring connector or remove it completely, just let it hang from its wiring.
5 Unscrew the nut from the pivot bolt **(see illustration)**. Unscrew the pivot bolt and remove the stand.

Installation

6 Apply grease to the pivot bolt shank and tighten the bolt to the torque setting specified at the beginning of the Chapter. Fit the nut finger-tight, then counter-hold the bolt and tighten the nut to the specified torque.
7 Fit the sidestand switch **(see illustration 4.4)**.
8 Reconnect the springs and check that they hold the stand securely up when not in use – an accident is almost certain to occur if the stand extends while the machine is in motion **(see illustration 4.3)**.
9 Check the operation of the stand and switch (see Chapter 1).

4.5 Sidestand pivot nut (arrowed)

5 Handlebars and levers

1 As a precaution, remove the fuel tank cover and the fairing (see Chapter 7). Though not actually necessary, this will prevent the possibility of damage should a tool slip.

Right handlebar removal

2 Disconnect the wires from the brake light switch **(see illustration)**. Unscrew the two master cylinder assembly clamp bolts and position the assembly clear of the handlebar, making sure no strain is placed on the hydraulic hose **(see illustration)**. Keep the master cylinder reservoir upright to prevent possible fluid leakage.
3 Undo the handlebar switch housing screws and separate the halves **(see illustration)**.

5.2a Disconnect the wiring connectors (arrowed)

5.2b Master cylinder clamp bolts (arrowed)

5.3 Switch housing screws (arrowed)

Frame and suspension

5.4 Throttle pulley housing screws (arrowed)

5.5 Remove the handlebar end-weight

5.7 Slacken the clamp bolts (arrowed)

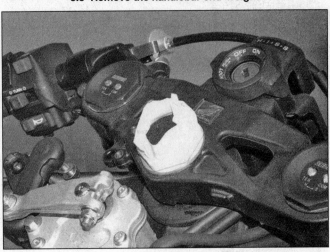
5.8a Wrap some tape around the nut...

4 Undo the throttle pulley housing screws and detach the rear of the housing **(see illustration)**.

5 Undo the handlebar end-weight screw and remove the weight **(see illus-tration)**.

6 Remove the steering damper cover and detach the steering damper arm from the top yoke (see Section 11).

7 Slacken the fork clamp bolts in the top yoke **(see illustration)**.

8 Wrap a layer of masking tape around the steering stem nut, then unscrew it **(see illustrations)**. Ease the yoke up and off the forks and lay it aside on some rag **(see illustration)**.

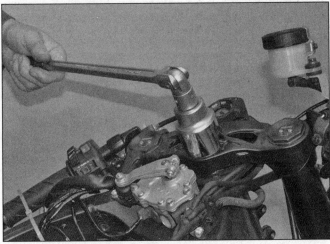
5.8b ...then unscrew it...

5.8c ...and ease the yoke up and off the forks

5•6 Frame and suspension

5.9a Handlebar clamp bolts (arrowed)

5.9b Unscrew the brake hose guide bolt

5.9c Ease the handlebar up and off the fork. Handlebar stopper ring (arrowed)

5.10a Disconnect the wiring connectors (arrowed)

5.10b Slacken the bolt (arrowed)

9 Slacken the handlebar clamp bolt **(see illustration)**. Release the brake hose guide from the bottom yoke **(see illustration)**. Ease the handlebar up and off the fork and slide the throttle twistgrip off **(see illustration)**. Note the handlebar stopper ring in the groove in the fork.

Left handlebar removal

10 Disconnect the wires from the clutch switch **(see illustration)**. Slacken the clutch lever bracket bolt **(see illustration)**.
11 Undo the handlebar switch housing screws and separate the halves **(see illustration)**.
12 Refer to Steps 6, 7 and 8 and displace the top yoke.

13 Undo the handlebar end-weight retaining screw, then remove the weight from the end of the handlebar and prise off the grip **(see illustration 5.5)**.
14 Slacken the handlebar clamp bolt **(see illustration 5.9a)**. Ease the handlebar up and off the fork and slide the clutch lever assembly off **(see illustration)**. Note the handlebar stopper ring in the groove in the fork.

Handlebar weights

15 If a new handlebar is being installed, you need to remove the inner weight from the old bar so it can be used in the new one – to do this, fit the end-weight and tighten its screw.

Squirt some lubricant (such as WD40) into the inner weight retainer tab hole, then press down on the tab using a screwdriver and twist and pull the end-weight, drawing the inner weight assembly out **(see illustration)**. Remove the end-weight and discard the retainer as a new one should be used. Check the condition of the rubbers on the inner weight and fit new ones if they are damaged, deformed or deteriorated.

5.11 Switch housing screws (arrowed)

5.14 Ease the handlebar up and off the fork. Handlebar stopper ring (arrowed)

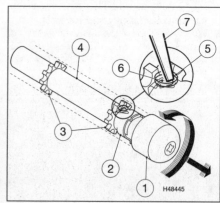

5.15 Removing the handlebar inner weight

1 End-weight
2 Retainer
3 Rubbers
4 Inner weight
5 Hole in handlebar
6 Retainer tab
7 Screwdriver

Frame and suspension

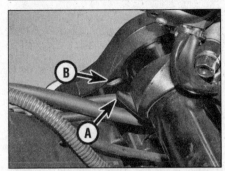

5.16a Locate the lug (A) in the hole (B) to align the handlebar

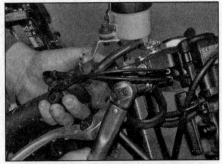

5.16b Hold the handlebar up against the yoke when tightening the clamp bolt

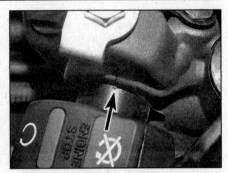

5.16c Align the clamp mating surfaces with the punch mark (arrowed)

Handlebar installation

16 Installation is the reverse of removal, noting the following.
- Make sure the handlebar stopper ring is in its groove in the fork (see illustration 5.9c and 5.14).
- Smear some grease onto the right handlebar and slide the throttle twistgrip and cable housing assembly on before fitting the handlebar onto the fork.
- Slide the clutch lever bracket onto the left handlebar before fitting the handlebar onto the fork.
- When fitting the handlebar onto the fork, slide it down onto the ring so the ring seats just up inside the bottom. Do not tighten the handlebar clamp bolts until the top yoke has been fitted.
- When fitting the top yoke onto the forks, locate the lug on the top of each handlebar clamp in its hole in the underside of the yoke, so that the handlebars are set in the correct position (see illustration 5.16a). Tighten the steering stem nut first, then the top yoke clamp bolts, then the handlebar clamp bolts, tightening them all to the torque settings specified at the beginning of the Chapter, and lifting the handlebar so its top surface seats against the underside of the yoke (see illustration 5.16b).
- When installing the handlebar inner weights, locate the tab on the retainer in the hole in the handlebar (see illustration 5.15).
- When installing the handlebar end-weights, align the boss with the cut-out on the inner weight inside the handlebar (see illustration 5.5). Clean the threads of the

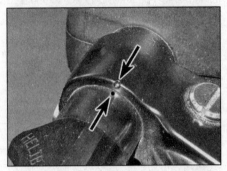

5.16d Align the punch marks (arrowed)

end-weight retaining screws and apply a suitable non-permanent thread locking compound. Tighten them to the specified torque setting. If new grips are being fitted, secure them using Honda Bond A or Pro Honda Handgrip Cement (according to market) or suitable equivalent adhesive, and rotate the grip as you fit it to spread the glue evenly.
- Make sure the front brake master cylinder clamp is installed with the UP mark facing up (see illustration 5.2b), and with the clamp mating surfaces aligned with the punch mark on the top of the handlebar (see illustration 5.16c). Tighten the master cylinder clamp bolts to the specified torque setting, tightening the top bolt first.
- Align the punch mark on the clutch lever bracket with the punch mark on the top of the handlebar (see illustration 5.16d).
- Make sure the pin in the bottom half of

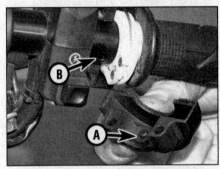

5.16e Locate the pin (A) in the hole (B)

each switch housing locates in its hole in the handlebar. Tighten the front screw first, then the rear, and do not overtighten them.
- Make sure the pin in the rear half of the throttle cable housing locates in its hole in the handlebar (see illustration 5.16e). Tighten the upper screw first, then the lower.
- Reconnect the front brake light switch and clutch switch wiring connectors (see illustrations 5.2a and 5.10a).

Levers

17 To remove the front brake lever, undo the lever pivot screw locknut, then undo the pivot screw and remove the lever (see illustration).
18 To remove the clutch lever turn the cable adjuster into the bracket to provide freeplay in the cable (see illustration). Undo the lever pivot screw locknut, then undo the pivot screw and remove the lever, detaching the cable nipple as you do (see illustration).

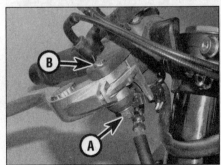

5.17 Front brake lever locknut (A) and pivot screw (B)

5.18a Turn the adjuster in

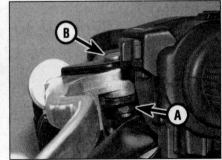

5.18b Clutch lever locknut (A) and pivot screw (B)

5•8 Frame and suspension

19 Installation is the reverse of removal. Apply silicone grease to the contact area between the front brake master cylinder pushrod tip and the brake lever. Apply lithium or molybdenum grease to the pivot screw shafts and the contact areas between the lever and its bracket. Tighten the pivot screw lightly (to the torque setting specified at the beginning of the Chapter if the correct tools are available), then hold it and tighten the locknut to the specified torque. Apply a spray lubricant such as WD40, or a dry-film Teflon lubricant to the brake lever span adjuster mechanism. Adjust clutch cable freeplay (see Chapter 1).

6 Fork removal and installation

Caution: *Although not strictly necessary, before removing the forks it is recommended that the fairing and fairing panels are removed (see Chapter 7). This will prevent accidental damage to the paintwork.*

Removal

1 Remove the fairing side panels (see Chapter 7). On RA models remove the wheel sensor (see Chapter 6).
2 If the fork oil is being changed, or if the fork is to be disassembled, adjust spring pre-load and damping to their minimum settings, noting the number of turns made so it can be reset the same (see Section 14).
3 Remove the front wheel (see Chapter 6). Tie the front brake calipers and hoses back so that they are out of the way.
4 Remove the front mudguard (see Chapter 7).
5 Note the routing of all cables, hoses and wiring around the forks.
6 Working on one fork at a time, slacken the fork clamp bolt in the top yoke and the handlebar clamp bolt **(see illustrations 5.7 and 5.9a)**. If the fork is to be disassembled, or if the fork oil is being changed, slacken the fork top bolt now **(see illustration)** – wrapping some masking tape round the hex helps preserve the finish, but on 2012-on models the depth of the hex on the bolt is minimal and it is possible that a normal socket (which will usually have a chamfered lead in) will slip off, so it is best to obtain the special socket from Honda (part No. 07SMA-GBC0100), which is plastic and is squared edged, thereby preserving the finish and also giving good grip.
7 Hold the fork, then slacken the clamp bolts in the bottom yoke, and remove the fork by twisting it and pulling it downwards, guiding the handlebar off as you do **(see illustrations)**. Note the handlebar stopper ring in the groove in the fork and remove it if required **(see illustration)**. Keep the right-hand handlebar positioned so the brake fluid reservoir stays upright.

> **HAYNES HiNT** *If the fork legs are seized in the yokes, spray the area with penetrating oil and allow time for it to soak in before trying again.*

Installation

8 Remove all traces of dirt and corrosion from the fork tube and in the yokes. If removed fit the handlebar stopper ring into its groove **(see illustration 6.7c)**. Slide the fork up through the bottom yoke and the handlebar clamp and into the top yoke, making sure all cables, hoses and wiring are routed on the correct side of the fork **(see illustration)**. Locate the lug on the top of the handlebar clamp in its hole in the underside of the yoke **(see illustration 5.16a)**.
9 Make sure the fork is set so the joint between the outer tube and the top bolt is flush with the upper surface of the top yoke, and on 2012-on models so the damping adjusters in the top bolt are set in line across the top yoke **(see illustration)**. Tighten the fork clamp bolts in the bottom yoke to the torque setting specified at the beginning of the Chapter **(see illustration 6.7a)**.
10 If the fork has been dismantled or if the fork oil was changed, tighten the fork top bolt to the specified torque setting.
11 Tighten the fork clamp bolt in the top yoke to the specified torque setting **(see illustration 5.7)**. Lift the handlebar so its top surface seats against the underside of the yoke, then tighten its clamp bolt to the specified torque **(see illustration 5.16b)**.
12 Install the front mudguard (see Chapter 7) and the front wheel (see Chapter 6).
13 Reset the spring pre-load and damping adjusters as noted or required (see Section 14). On RA models install the wheel sensor

6.6 Fork top bolt (arrowed) – this shows the special socket for 2012-on models

6.7a Slacken the clamp bolts (arrowed)...

6.7b ...then draw the fork down and out of the yokes guiding the handlebar off the top

6.7c Remove the stopper ring if required

6.8 Make sure all cables, hoses and wiring are correctly routed

6.9 Set the tube/top bolt joint flush with the yoke, and with the adjusters as shown on 2012-on models

Frame and suspension 5•9

7.3 Thread the top bolt out of the tube

7.4a Spacer holding tool and slotted washer – home-made equivalent to the Honda tools

7.4b Fit the holding tool onto the spacer, adjusting the rod lengths as required then tightening the locknuts. This also shows how the slotted washer must be fitted next

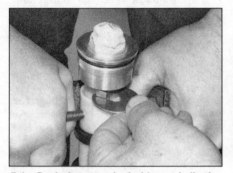

7.4c Push down on the holder and slip the washer under the nut

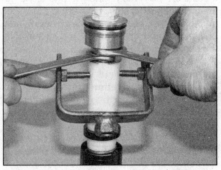

7.5a Hold the locknut and loosen the top bolt...

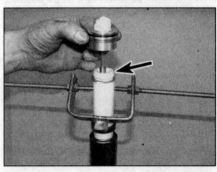

7.5b ...then unscrew the top bolt and draw the adjuster rod out, and remove the seat (arrowed)

(see Chapter 6). Install the fairing side panels (see Chapter 7).

14 Check the operation of the front forks and brakes before taking the machine out on the road.

7 Fork oil change

2008 to 2011 models

Special tool: *A holding tool and stopper plate are required for this procedure – see Step 4 for details.*

1 After a high mileage the fork oil will deteriorate and its damping and lubrication qualities will be impaired. Always change the oil in both fork legs.
2 Remove the fork – make sure you adjust the pre-load and damping to its minimum (see Section 14), and loosen the top bolt while the leg is still clamped in the bottom yoke (see Section 6).
3 Unscrew the fork top bolt from the top of the outer tube **(see illustration)**. The bolt will remain on the damper rod, held by the locknut on its top. Slide the outer tube down gently until it seats on the bottom.
4 Next you need either the Honda service tools (spacer holder Pt. No. 070MF-MBZC110 and stopper plate Pt. No. 070MF-MBZC130 in Europe, or fork spring compressor Pt. No. 07AMC-MFJA100 and stopper plate Pt. No. 07AMB-KZ3A100 in the US), or an equivalent home-made set-up as shown **(see illustration)**. Fit the holder onto the fork spacer as shown **(see illustration)**. Now with the aid of an assistant, pull up on the fork top bolt and the spacer seat just below it, then press down on the spacer using the holding tool to compress the spring and expose the locknut on the damper rod, and insert the stopper plate or slotted washer under the locknut and on top of the spacer, keeping the spacer seat above it **(see illustration)**. Carefully release the pressure on the spacer and allow the plate or slotted washer to rest against the underside of the locknut under spring pressure.
5 Counter-hold the locknut using one spanner and loosen the top bolt assembly using another spanner on the flats just above the locknut, then thread the top bolt off and draw the damping adjuster rod out **(see illustrations)**. **Note:** *The top bolt should not be disassembled.* Remove the spacer seat.
6 Push down on the spacer and remove the plate or slotted washer, then carefully allow the spring to relax **(see illustration)**. Remove the spacer. Withdraw the spring from the tube, noting which way up it fits **(see illustration)**.
7 Invert the fork leg over a suitable container and pump the fork and damper rod several

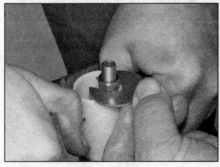

7.6a Remove the slotted washer and the spacer...

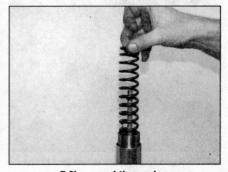

7.6b ...and the spring

5•10 Frame and suspension

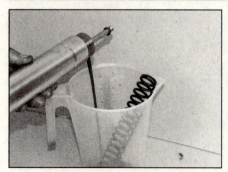

7.7 Drain the oil as described

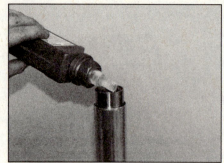

7.8a Add the oil slowly to prevent air bubbles

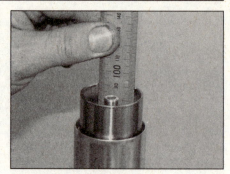

7.8b Measure the distance from the top of the tube to the oil

times to expel as much fork oil as possible **(see illustration)**. Support the fork upside down in the container for a while to allow as much oil as possible to drain, then pump the fork and rod again. If the fork oil contains metal particles inspect the fork bushes for wear (see Section 8). Wipe any excess oil off the spring and spacer.

8 Stand the fork upright and slide the outer tube down gently until it seats on the bottom. Slowly pour in the specified quantity of the specified grade of fork oil **(see illustration)**. Draw the outer tube up about 25 cm, then cover the top with your hand and slowly push it down. Remove your hand and draw it up, and repeat two or three times. Now pump the damper rod slowly at least ten times – this distributes the oil and expels all air from the damper. Slide the outer tube down gently until it seats on the bottom, and leave to stand for five minutes. After this, measure the oil level from the top of the tube **(see illustration)**. Add or subtract oil until it is at the level specified at the beginning of this Chapter.

9 Check the amount of thread exposed above the damper rod locknut – there should be 10.9 mm **(see illustration)**. Pull the damper rod out as far as possible, then fit the spring with the tapered end at the top **(see illustration 7.6b)**. Fit a piece of thin wire around the rod under the locknut to help keep it extended **(see illustration)**. Fit the spacer, sliding it down over the wire **(see illustration)**.

10 Keeping the damper rod extended push down on the spacer to compress the spring (see Step 4), then insert the stopper plate or slotted washer under the locknut **(see illustration)**. Remove the wire.

11 Fit the spacer seat **(see illustration)**. Insert the damping adjuster rod and thread the top bolt onto the damper rod and down to the locknut, making sure the nut does not move **(see illustration 7.5b)**. Counter-hold the locknut and tighten the top bolt assembly securely against it using a spanner on the flats as before **(see illustration 7.5a)**. Press down on the spacer to compress the spring and remove the plate or slotted washer, then carefully release the spring pressure **(see illustration 7.4c)**. Remove the holding tool.

12 If the top bolt O-ring is damaged or deteriorated fit a new one **(see illustration)**. Smear some fork oil onto the O-ring. Extend the outer tube and thread the top bolt into it, making sure it does not cross-thread, and tighten it as much as possible holding the inner tube by hand. **Note:** *Tighten the top bolt*

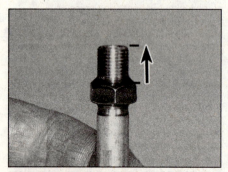

7.9a Set the locknut 10.9 mm from the top

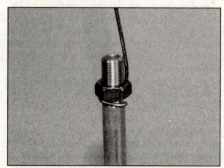

7.9b Tie some wire under the locknut...

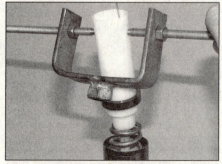

7.9c ...then fit the spacer

7.10 Push the spacer down and fit the washer under the nut

7.11 Fit the seat

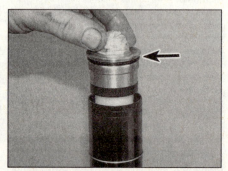

7.12 Check and lubricate the O-ring (arrowed), then thread the top bolt into the tube

Frame and suspension 5•11

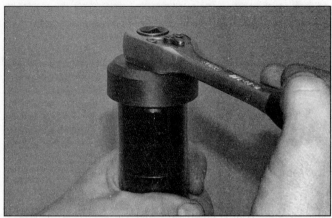
7.16 Unscrew the top bolt

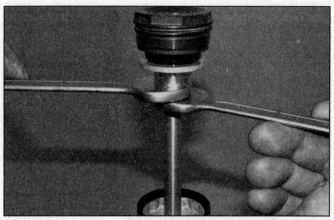
7.17a Hold the locknut and loosen the top bolt...

7.17b ...then unscrew the top bolt...

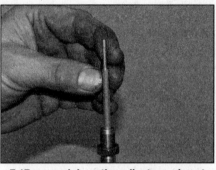
7.17c ...and draw the adjuster rods out

7.18a Home-made tool for unscrewing the rod guide

to the specified torque setting when the fork has been installed in the bike and is held in the bottom yoke, but before the top yoke clamp bolt is tightened.
13 Install the fork (see Section 6). Set the spring pre-load and damping adjusters as noted or required (see Section 14).

2012-on models

Special tool: *A special tool is required for this procedure – see Step 18 for details.*
14 After a high mileage the fork oil will deteriorate and its damping and lubrication qualities will be impaired. Always change the oil in both fork legs.
15 Remove the fork – make sure you adjust the pre-load and damping to its minimum (see Section 14), and loosen the top bolt while the leg is still clamped in the bottom yoke (see Section 6).
16 Unscrew the fork top bolt from the top of the outer tube **(see illustration)**. The bolt will remain on the damper rod, held by the locknut on its top. Slide the outer tube down gently until it seats on the bottom.
17 Counter-hold the locknut using one spanner and loosen the top bolt assembly using another spanner on the flats just above the locknut, then thread the top bolt off **(see illustrations)**. Draw the damping adjuster rods out **(see illustration)**. *Note: The top bolt should not be disassembled.*
18 Next you need either the Honda service tool (Pt. No. 070MB-MGP0100 in Europe and 070MB-MGPA100 in the US), or an equivalent home-made set-up as shown **(see illustration)**, to fit into the bi-hex in the top of the rod guide in the top of the inner tube – the tool shown comprises two 35 mm nuts with circular flanges braised (or welded) onto each end of a piece of steel tube with an OD of 42 mm and 150 mm long, but you could use a single deep 35 mm nut to fit into the rod guide and either a very deep 35 mm socket to fit onto it if available (which will allow a torque wrench to be used on installation), or if you don't have a torque wrench then use a ring spanner on the nut. Place the bottom of the fork in a vice with pieces of wood to protect it as shown, then unscrew and remove the rod guide and damper assembly **(see illustrations)**.

7.18b Secure the bottom of the fork in a vice...

7.18c ...then unscrew the guide...

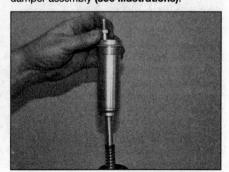
7.18d ...and remove the damper assembly

5•12 Frame and suspension

7.19a Drain the oil...

7.19b ...and remove the upper collar...

7.19c ...and the spring...

7.21a If removed, fit the lower collar

7.21b Fit the spring...

7.21c ...and the upper collar

7.22a Add the oil...

19 Get a suitable container to hold the oil, then tip the fork over it, drain the oil and remove the upper collar and the spring **(see illustrations)**.

20 Support the fork upside down in the container for a while to allow as much oil as possible to drain. If the fork oil contains metal particles inspect the fork bushes for wear (see Section 8). Wipe any excess oil off the spring and collar. Note that there is lower collar that may come out when you tip out the oil, though it didn't on the fork shown.

21 If the lower collar came out fit it with the rounded end at the bottom **(see illustration)**. Fit the spring and the upper collar **(see illustrations)**.

22 Stand the fork upright and slide the inner tube down gently until it seats on the bottom. Slowly pour in most of the specified quantity of the specified grade of fork oil, until it is up to the level of the holes in the inner tube **(see illustrations)**. Draw the outer tube up about 25 cm, then cover the top with your hand and slowly push it down **(see illustration)**. Remove your hand and draw it up, and repeat eight to ten times – this distributes the oil and expels all air.

23 Place the bottom of the fork in a vice with pieces of wood to protect it as before **(see illustration 7.18b)**. Fit the damper assembly and rod guide into the top of the fork, then

7.22b ...up to the holes (arrowed)...

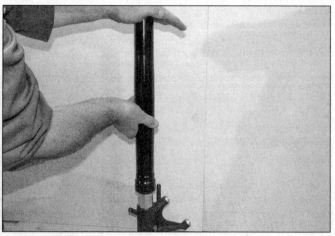

7.22c ...then bleed the fork of air as described

Frame and suspension 5•13

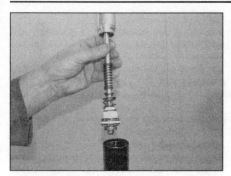

7.23a Fit the damper assembly into the fork...

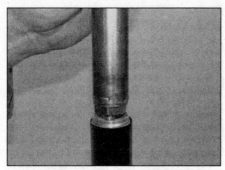

7.23b ...then thread the rod guide in...

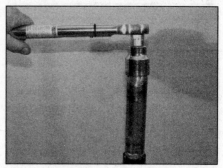

7.23c ...and tighten to the specified torque

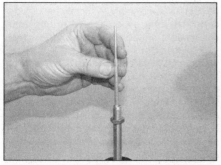

7.24 Fit the adjuster rods into the damper rod

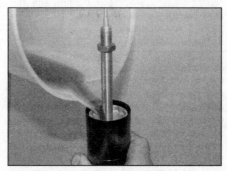

7.25 Add the remaining oil

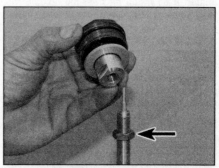

7.26a Thread the locknut (arrowed) all the way down, then thread the top bolt on until seated

thread the rod guide into the inner tube and tighten it to the torque setting specified at the beginning of the Chapter using the tool used in Step 18 **(see illustrations)**.

24 Fit the damping adjuster rods into the damper rod **(see illustration)**.

25 Tip the remaining fork oil into the rod guide **(see illustration)**.

26 Thread the damper rod locknut down to the bottom of its threads, then thread the top bolt onto the damper rod until it seats **(see illustration)**. Thread the locknut up against the top bolt, then counter-hold the top bolt using a spanner on the flats as before and tighten the locknut securely against it **(see illustrations)**.

27 Hold the fork cap and pump the outer tube up and down several times, then slide it fully down **(see illustration)**. Measure the oil level

7.26b Thread the nut up against the top bolt...

from the top of the tube **(see illustration)**. Add or subtract oil until it is at the level specified at the beginning of this Chapter.

28 If the top bolt O-ring is damaged or

7.26c ...then hold the top bolt and tighten the locknut against it

deteriorated fit a new one **(see illustration)**. Smear some fork oil onto the O-ring. Extend the outer tube and thread the top bolt into it, making sure it does not cross-thread, and

7.27a Hold the cap and pump the tube...

7.27b ...then measure the oil level

7.28a Check and lubricate the O-ring (arrowed)...

5•14 Frame and suspension

7.28b ...then thread the top bolt into the tube

8.2a Remove the axle clamp bolts

8.2b Slacken the damper cartridge bolt

tighten it as much as possible holding the inner tube by hand **(see illustration)**. **Note:** *Tighten the top bolt to the specified torque setting when the fork has been installed in the bike and is held in the bottom yoke, but before the top yoke clamp bolt is tightened.*

29 Install the fork (see Section 6). Set the spring pre-load and damping adjusters as noted or required (see Section 14).

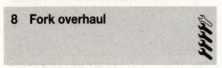

8 Fork overhaul

Disassembly

1 Remove the fork – make sure you adjust the pre-load and damping to its minimum (see Section 14), and loosen the top bolt while the leg is still clamped in the bottom yoke (see Section 6). Always dismantle the fork legs separately to avoid interchanging parts and thus causing an accelerated rate of wear. Store all components in separate, clearly marked containers.

2 On 2008 to 2011 models lay the fork flat on the bench with the caliper mounting lugs to the left. Remove the wheel axle clamp bolts **(see illustration)**. Hold the fork down and slacken the damper cartridge bolt in the base of the fork **(see illustration)**. If the damper cartridge rotates inside the fork whilst attempting to unscrew the bolt, compress the fork so that the spring exerts pressure on the cartridge body whilst the bolt is unscrewed. Alternatively, if available use an air wrench.

3 Refer to Section 7, Steps 3 to 7 (2008 to 2011 models) or 16 to 20 (2012-on models) and drain the oil form the fork.

4 On 2008 to 2011 models remove the damper cartridge bolt and its sealing washer from the bottom of the fork **(see illustration)**.

Discard the sealing washer as a new one must be used on reassembly. Withdraw the damper cartridge from inside the fork tube **(see illustration)**. Pump the damper a few times over the oil drain tray to expel any residual oil.

5 Carefully prise out the dust seal from the bottom of the outer tube **(see illustration)**.

6 Carefully prise out the oil seal retaining clip, taking care not to scratch the surface of the inner tube **(see illustration)**.

7 To separate the inner and outer tubes it is necessary to displace the bottom bush and oil seal from the bottom of the outer tube. The top bush on the inner tube will not pass through the bottom bush, and this can be used to good effect. Grasp the inner tube in one hand and the outer tube in the other and compress them slightly, then pull them apart so that the top bush strikes the bottom bush **(see illustration)**. Repeat this operation until the bottom bush and seal are tapped out **(see illustration)**.

8.4a Remove the bolt...

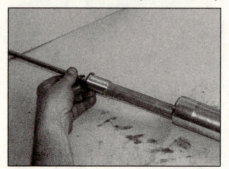

8.4b ...then withdraw the damper cartridge

8.5 Prise out the dust seal using a flat-bladed screwdriver

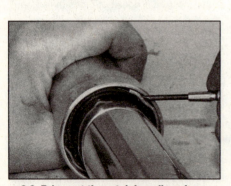

8.6 Prise out the retaining clip using a flat-bladed screwdriver

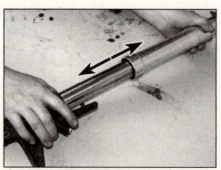

8.7a To separate the tubes pull them apart firmly several times...

8.7b ...the slide-hammer effect will displace the oil seal, washer and top bush

Frame and suspension 5•15

8.8 Tip the lower collar out

8.9a Carefully lever the ends apart to expand it over the top bush

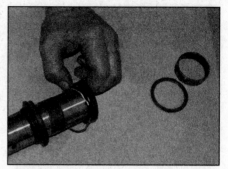

8.9b Slide the remaining components off

8 On 2012-on models, if the lower collar did not come out when draining the oil tip it out of the inner tube now **(see illustration)**.

9 To remove the bottom bush carefully lever its ends apart using a screwdriver and slide it over the top bush **(see illustration)**. Slide the oil seal washer, the oil seal, the retaining ring and the dust seal over the top bush and off the inner tube, noting which way up they fit **(see illustration)**. Discard the oil seal and the dust seal as new ones must be used. Note that Honda specify to use a new top bush if it is removed from its recess – if required remove it by levering its ends apart until it clears its recess **(see illustration)**.

8.9c Only remove the top bush if you are replacing it with a new one

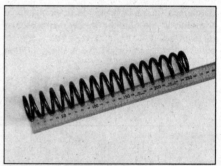

8.13 Measure the free length of the spring

Inspection

10 Clean all parts in solvent and blow them dry with compressed air, if available.

11 Check the fork inner tube for score marks, dents, pitting, scratches, flaking of its surface and excessive or abnormal wear. Fit a new tube if any are found. Check the inner tube for runout using V-blocks and a dial gauge. If the amount of runout exceeds the service limit specified, a new tube should be fitted.

 Warning: If the inner tube is bent or exceeds the runout limit, it should not be straightened; replace it with a new one.

12 Check the fork outer tube for cracks. Check the fork seal seat and housing for nicks, gouges and scratches. If damage is evident, leaks will occur. Also check the oil seal washer for damage or distortion and fit a new one if necessary.

13 Check the spring for cracks and other damage. Measure the spring free length and compare the measurement to the specifications at the beginning of the Chapter **(see illustration)**. If it is defective or sagged below the service limit, replace the springs in both forks with new ones. Never renew only one spring.

14 Examine the working surfaces of the two bushes (i.e. the inner surface of the bottom bush and the outer surface of the top bush) **(see illustration)**; if the grey Teflon outer surface has been worn away to reveal the copper inner surface over more than 75% of the surface area, or if the bushes are scored or badly scuffed, they must be replaced with new ones. Note that it is a good idea to replace the bushes with new ones as a matter of course as part of a fork overhaul.

15 On 2008 to 2011 models check the damper cartridge and rod, and the oil lock valve fitted on it, for damage and wear **(see illustration)**. Hold the body of the cartridge and pump the rod in and out. If any wear or

8.14 Check the working surface (arrowed) of each bush for wear

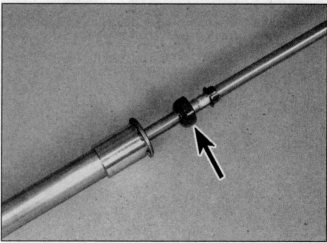

8.15 Check the damper and oil lock valve (arrowed)

5•16 Frame and suspension

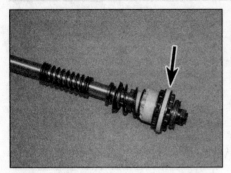

8.16a Check the piston ring (arrowed)...

damage is found, or if the rod does not move smoothly in the damper, a new damper must be installed.

16 On 2012-on models check the condition of the piston ring in the bottom of the damper assembly and replace it with a new one if necessary **(see illustration)**. Check the ring in the top of the rod guide for wear and damage

8.16b ...and the ring (arrowed) in the guide

and replace with a new one if necessary **(see illustration)**. Check all other components on the damper assembly for signs of wear and damage and if necessary fit a complete new assembly – the rings are the only components available separately. Make sure the damping rod and the damping adjuster rods are straight.

Reassembly

17 Wrap some thin insulating tape over the edges of the recess for the top bush in the inner tube, or over the bush itself if not removed, to protect the seal lips **(see illustration)**. Smear some oil over the tape, and also over the oil seal lips. Slide the new dust seal, retaining clip, new oil seal, and oil seal washer onto the inner tube, making sure they are the correct way round **(see illustrations)**. Remove the tape, then lubricate the inner surface of the bottom bush and slide it on, over the top bush if in place **(see illustration)**. If removed fit the new top bush into its recess in the bottom of the inner tube **(see illustration)**. Apply a smear of the specified clean fork oil to the bushes.

18 Slide the inner tube fully into the outer tube **(see illustration)**. Support the fork upside down, and have an assistant hold the inner tube and the components on it up. Slide the bottom bush into the bottom of the outer tube, then squeeze the ends together using two suitable plastic or wooden tools to close the gap to allow the bush the drop in (if you

8.17a Use insulating tape to cover sharp edges...

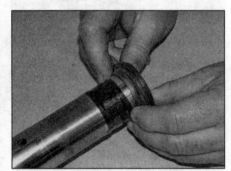

8.17b ...then slide the dust seal...

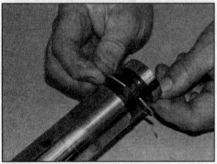

8.17c ...retaining clip...

8.17d ...oil seal...

8.17e ...and oil seal washer on

8.17f Slide the bottom bush on...

8.17g ...then fit the top bush into its recess

8.18a Slide the inner tube into the outer tube

Frame and suspension 5•17

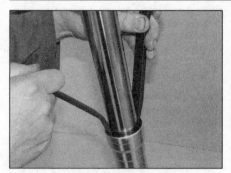

8.18b Slide the top bush down and into the outer tube, squeezing its ends together to fit it

8.19a Use a drift to drive the bush in, with the washer as an interface…

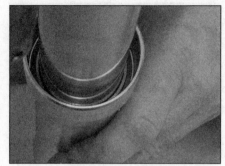

8.19b …until the bush is fully seated

are lucky), or at least to start to go in **(see illustration)**.

19 To get the bush fully in slide the oil seal washer onto it **(see illustration 8.20)**. Using either the special service tool (Pt No. 07YMD-MCF0100 in Europe, and 07NMD-KZ3010A in the US) or a suitable drift, carefully drive the bottom bush fully into its recess until the bush and washer seat – the washer prevents damaging the edges of the bush **(see illustration)**. If using a drift, wrap tape around it to prevent scratching the inner tube. Make sure the bush enters the recess squarely. It is best to make sure that the inner tube is withdrawn as much as possible from the outer tube so that any accidental scratching is confined to the area that does not affect the oil seal. Lift the washer to check the bush is seated fully and squarely in its recess in the slider, then wipe the recess clean.

20 Slide the oil seal washer onto the bush **(see illustration)**.

21 Slide the oil seal down and into the outer tube **(see illustration)**. Push the seal into place, driving it in as in Step 19 if you have the Honda tool, until the retaining clip groove is visible. If you don't have the tool cut the old seal in half and use it as an interface between the drift and the new seal, and then push the seal in or use a piece of wood as a drift **(see illustrations)**. When the old seal is flush with the rim of the fork tube the new seal is seated – remove the pieces of old seal and check the retaining clip groove is visible.

8.20 Fit the washer onto the bush

8.21a Slide the seal down and into the outer tube

8.21b Cut the old seal in half…

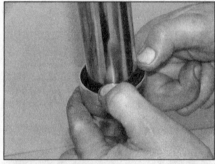

8.21c …and use it push the new seal in…

8.21d …or to protect it if driving it in . . .

8.21e …then use a small screwdriver to retrieve it

8.21f Make sure the retaining clip groove (arrowed) is fully exposed

5•18 Frame and suspension

8.22 Fit the retaining clip in its groove...

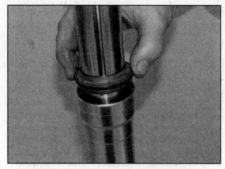
8.23 ...then press the dust seal in

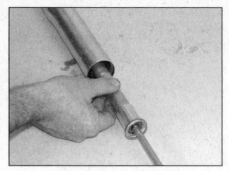
8.24a Insert the damper

8.24b Fit a new sealing washer and apply threadlock...

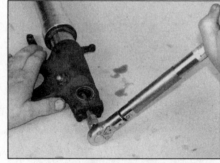
8.24c ...and tighten the bolt to the specified torque

sealing washer onto the cartridge bolt and apply a few drops of a suitable non-permanent thread locking compound **(see illustration)**. Fit the bolt into the bottom of the fork and thread it into the cartridge, tightening it to the torque setting specified at the beginning of the Chapter **(see illustration)**. If the cartridge rotates inside the tube as you tighten the bolt, wait until the fork is fully reassembled and then tighten it (the pressure of the spring on the cartridge will prevent it from turning).

25 Refer to Section 7, Steps 8 to 13 (2008 to 2011 models) or 21 to 29 (2012-on models) and fill the fork with oil and finish reassembly.

22 Fit the retaining clip, making sure it is correctly located in its groove **(see illustration)**.

23 Press the dust seal into the top of the outer tube **(see illustration)**.

24 On 2008 to 2011 models clean the threads of the damper cartridge bolt. Lay the fork flat on the bench with the caliper mounting lugs to the right. Slide the damper cartridge fully into the fork tube **(see illustration)**. Fit a new

26 On 2008 to 2011 models, if the damper rod bolt requires tightening (see Step 24), place the fork upside down on the floor, using a rag to protect it, then have an assistant compress the fork so that maximum spring pressure is placed on the damper cartridge head while tightening the bolt to the specified torque setting. Fit the axle clamp bolts **(see illustration 8.2a)**.

27 Install the fork (see Section 6). Set the spring pre-load and damping adjusters as noted or required (see Section 14).

9.1a Disconnect the wiring...

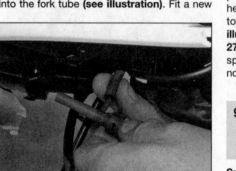
9.1b ...and the vacuum hose

9 Steering stem

Special tool: *Either the Honda special tool (Pt No. 07HMA-MR70100), equivalent peg spanner, or a suitably sized C-spanner is necessary for this procedure – see Step 14.*

Removal

1 Remove the fairing side panels (see Chapter 7). Disconnect the front loom wiring connectors on the left-hand side **(see illustration)**. Detach the hose to the vacuum chamber from the one-way valve **(see illustration)**. Unscrew the two bolts securing the fairing stay to the steering head and remove the complete fairing assembly **(see illustration)**.

2 Remove the steering damper cover and detach the steering damper arm from the top yoke (see Section 11).

3 Unscrew the bolt securing the brake hose

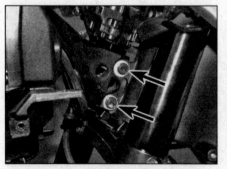
9.1c Unscrew the bolts (arrowed)...

9.1d ...and remove the fairing

Frame and suspension 5•19

9.5a Unclip and remove the jacket

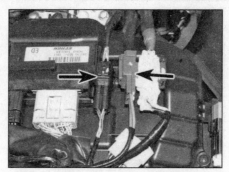
9.5b Ignition switch and HISS receiver wiring connectors (arrowed)

9.6a Unscrew the nut...

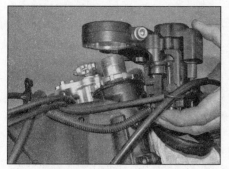
9.6b ...then lift the yoke off

9.9a Unscrew the adjuster nut...

9.9b ...then draw the bottom yoke/steering stem out of the steering head

guide to the bottom yoke and displace it **(see illustration 5.9b)**.
4 Remove the front forks (see Section 6). Tie the handlebars to the frame so they are clear.
5 If the top yoke is being removed from the bike rather than just being displaced, raise the fuel tank (see Chapter 4). Remove the air filter housing jacket, noting how it fits **(see illustration)**. Disconnect the ignition switch, and where fitted the HISS receiver, connector(s) **(see illustration)**. Release the wiring from any clips or ties and feed it through to the yoke, noting its routing.
6 Wrap a layer of masking tape around the steering stem nut, then unscrew it **(see illustration)**. Ease the yoke up and off, and if

not being removed lay it aside on some rag **(see illustration)**.
7 Bend the lockwasher tabs out of the notches in the locknut **(see illustration 9.18b)**. Unscrew the locknut using your fingers **(see illustration 9.18a)** – it shouldn't be tight. If it is tight use a C-spanner located in one of the notches. Remove the lockwasher **(see illustration 9.17)**. Inspect the tabs for cracks or signs of fatigue. If there is any sign of damage, discard the lockwasher and use a new one; otherwise the old one can be re-used, but note that Honda recommend using a new one as a matter of course.
8 If the peg spanner mentioned above is not available, make an alignment mark between

the adjuster nut and the frame – this can serve as a rough guide for the tightness of the adjuster nut on installation. As you unscrew the nut count the number of turns.
9 Support the bottom yoke then unscrew the adjuster nut using either a C-spanner, a peg-spanner or socket, or a drift located in one of the notches **(see illustration)**. Gently lower the bottom yoke and steering stem out of the frame **(see illustration)**. Check the condition of the grease seal and discard it if it is damaged.
10 Remove the grease seal, inner race and bearing from the top of the steering head **(see illustration)**. Remove the bearing from the base of the steering stem **(see illustration)**.

9.10a Remove the grease seal, inner race and upper bearing...

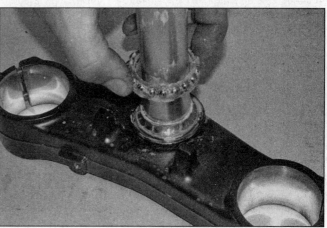
9.10b ...and the lower bearing

5•20 Frame and suspension

9.13a Fit the steering stem into the head...

9.13b ...then seat the upper bearing...

9.13c ...the inner race...

9.13d ...and the grease seal...

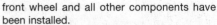
9.13e ...and thread the adjuster nut on

11 Remove all traces of old grease from the bearings and races and check them for wear or damage as described in Section 10. **Note:** *Do not attempt to remove the races from the steering head or the steering stem unless they are to be replaced with new ones.*

Installation

12 Smear a liberal quantity of Urea-based multi-purpose grease with EP2 rating onto the bearing races, and work some grease well into both the upper and lower bearings. Also smear the grease seal lip, using a new seal if necessary. Fit the lower bearing onto the steering stem **(see illustration 9.10b)**.
13 Carefully lift the steering stem/bottom yoke up through the steering head and support it there **(see illustration)**. Fit the upper bearing and its inner race into the top of the steering head **(see illustrations)**. Fit the grease seal **(see illustration)**. Apply some Urea-based multi-purpose EP2 grease to the adjuster nut threads and thread the nut onto the steering stem **(see illustration)**.
14 Using the Honda service tool (Pt. No. 07HMA-MR70100), or a suitable peg spanner, which can be made by cutting castellations into an old 35 mm socket or a piece of steel tube with a 41 mm ID and 46 mm OD **(see illustration)**, tighten the adjuster nut to the torque setting specified at the beginning of the Chapter, then turn the steering from lock-to-lock five times, then reapply the specified torque setting to the nut. Check that the steering stem is able to move smoothly (though it may feel a bit tight, but this is normal as the weight of the forks and wheel is not influencing the feel) from lock-to-lock following adjustment – note that it is best to check and if necessary reset the bearing adjustment as described in Chapter 1 after the forks and front wheel and all other components have been installed.
15 If the correct tools are not available and you are refitting the original parts, tighten the nut the number of turns recorded on removal using a C-spanner until the marks align **(see illustration)**. Turn the steering from lock-to-lock five times, then slacken the nut, and tighten it again until the marks align. Install the forks and wheel, then refer to the procedure in Chapter 1 and check the feel of the bearings as described, and adjust if necessary.
16 If you have not made an alignment mark or are using new parts, tighten the nut using a C-spanner so that bearing play is eliminated, but the steering stem is able to move smoothly (though it may feel a bit tight, but this is normal as the weight of the forks and wheel is not influencing the feel) from lock-to-lock – refer to the procedure in Chapter 1 for details, and set the bearings after the forks and wheel are installed as their leverage and inertia need to be taken into account. Make sure the nut is tight enough to hold the steering stem in the head without any play, then install the forks and wheel, then refer to the procedure in Chapter 1.
Caution: Take great care not to apply excessive pressure because this will cause premature failure of the bearings.
17 With the bearings correctly adjusted, fit the lockwasher, using a new one if the tabs are weakened or cracked, onto the adjuster nut and fit the two short tabs into the notches in the adjuster nut **(see illustration)**.

9.14 Home-made peg spanner

9.15 Tighten the adjuster nut as described

9.17 Fit the lockwasher

Frame and suspension 5•21

9.18a Thread the locknut on and tighten as described

9.18b Bend the lockwasher tabs up into the notches in the nut

10.3 Check the outer races in the top and bottom of the steering head

18 Fit the locknut and tighten it finger-tight **(see illustration)**. Tighten the locknut further (but no more than 90°) until its notches align with the remaining lockwasher tabs, making sure the adjuster nut does not turn as well (though that is unlikely). Secure the locknut in position by bending up the long lock washer tabs into its notches **(see illustration)**.

19 Fit the top yoke onto the steering stem **(see illustration 9.6b)**. Fit the steering stem nut and tighten it finger-tight **(see illustration 9.6a)**. Temporarily install one of the forks to align the top and bottom yokes, and secure it by tightening the bottom yoke clamp bolts only (see Section 6). Now tighten the steering stem nut to the torque setting specified at the beginning of the Chapter.

20 Install the remaining components in a reverse of the removal procedure, referring to the relevant Sections or Chapters, and to the torque settings specified at the beginning of the Chapter.

21 Carry out a final check of the steering head bearing freeplay as described in Chapter 1, and if necessary re-adjust.

10 Steering head bearings

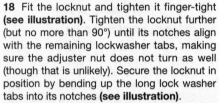

Inspection

1 Remove the steering stem (see Section 9).
2 Remove all traces of old grease from the bearings and races and check them for wear or damage – the outer races are in the top and bottom of the steering head, and the lower bearing inner race is on the bottom of the steering stem.

3 The races should be polished and free from indentations **(see illustration)**. Inspect the bearing balls for signs of wear, damage or discoloration, and examine the ball retainer cage for signs of cracks or splits. If there are any signs of wear on any of the above components both upper and lower bearing assemblies must be renewed as a set. Only remove the outer races in the steering head and the lower bearing inner race on the steering stem if they need to be replaced with new ones – do not re-use them once they have been removed.

Replacement

4 The outer races are an interference fit in the steering head – tap them from position using a suitable drift located in the recesses provided in the steering head that expose the lip of the race **(see illustrations)**. Tap firmly and evenly around each race to ensure that it is driven out squarely. Curve the end of the drift slightly to improve access if necessary.

5 Press the new outer races into the head using a drawbolt arrangement **(see illustration)**, or drive them in using a large diameter tubular drift. Ensure that the drawbolt washer or drift (as applicable) bears only on the outer edge of the race and does not contact the working surface. Alternatively, have the races installed by a Honda dealer equipped with the bearing race installation tools.

> **HAYNES HINT** *Installation of new bearing outer races is made much easier if the races are left overnight in the freezer. This causes them to contract slightly making them a looser fit. Alternatively, use a freeze spray. You can also heat the race seat in the steering stem using a hot air gun.*

6 Only remove the lower bearing inner race from the steering stem if a new one is being fitted. To remove the race, first thread the steering stem nut onto the top then position the yoke on its front for stability – the nut will protect the threads from the transmitted force of the impact of the chisel. Tap under the race using a cold chisel to displace it, and if required use two screwdrivers placed on opposite sides to work it free, using blocks of wood to improve leverage and protect the

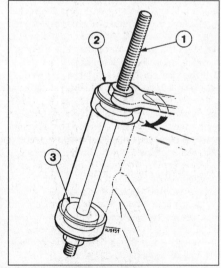

10.5 Drawbolt arrangement for fitting steering stem bearing races

1 Long bolt or threaded bar
2 Thick washer
3 Guide for lower race

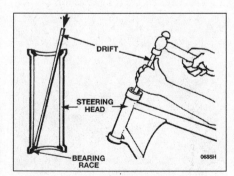

10.4a Drive the bearing races out with a brass drift...

10.4b ...locating it in the cut-outs

5•22 Frame and suspension

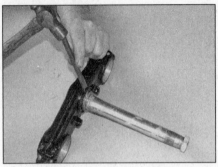

10.6a Dislodge the lower bearing using a cold chisel and/or screwdrivers...

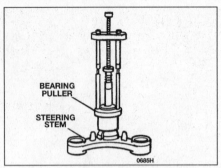

10.6b ...or using a puller if necessary

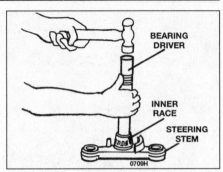

10.8 Drive the new inner race on using a suitable bearing driver or a length of pipe that bears only against the inner rim and not the bearing surface

yoke **(see illustration)**. If the race is firmly in place it will be necessary to use a puller **(see illustration)**. Take the steering stem to a Honda dealer if required.

7 Remove the dust seal from the bottom of the stem and replace it with a new one. Smear the new one with grease then fit it onto the stem.

8 Fit the new lower race onto the steering stem. Drive the new race into position using a length of tubing with an internal diameter slightly larger than the steering stem **(see illustration)** – heating the race and cooling the steering stem will make installation easier, or use an hydraulic press if necessary.

9 Install the steering stem (see Section 9).

11 Steering damper (HESD)

Inspection

1 The Honda Electronic Steering Damper (HESD) has a self-diagnostic feature linked to the fuel injection system – refer to Chapter 4, Section 5, for details on the fault codes relevant to the HESD (11 and 51). If a fault is detected the system operates at its minimum damping capability as a fail-safe.

2 If the damper does not function correctly yet no fault is indicated by the MIL, detach the damper arm from the top yoke (Steps 11 to 13 below), and make sure that a steering problem is not due to worn, un-lubricated or over-tight steering head bearings (see Chapter 1 and if required Sections 9 and 10 of this Chapter).

3 Make sure the linkage arm joints are in good condition. Refit the arm.

4 The amount of damping provided should be at a minimum at standstill, and should increase as vehicle speed increases. If there is no change in the amount of damping as vehicle speed changes, the valve controlling the flow of damping fluid is stuck.

5 The damper has its own individual function test mode, allowing the maximum and minimum damping characteristics to be compared with the vehicle at a standstill. Remove the lower fairing (see Chapter 7). Raise the front wheel off the ground using an auxiliary stand. Always make sure that the bike is properly supported and secure.

6 Check minimum damping characteristics by turning the steering in a smooth and quick lock-to-lock movement.

7 Now set the HESD into its own function test mode by lowering the sidestand and selecting a gear. Open the throttle fully, and with it held open turn the ignition ON. The HESD indicator in the instrument display should start blinking, indicating that it is in function mode – it stays in this mode for ten seconds. Turn the steering as before during this time and compare the damping characteristics. If there is no change between the two tests replace the damper with a new one.

8 If no fault can be found remove the damper and make sure the wiring connector and socket terminals are not corroded or broken and there are no loose connections. Also check for continuity in the wiring from the loom side of the connector to the ECM, referring to the Wiring Diagrams at the end of Chapter 8.

Fault code indicated

9 If the fault code is 11 check the speed sensor (see Chapter 8).

10 If the fault code is 51, remove the damper (see below). Connect the probes of a multimeter or ohmmeter set to the ohms x 1 scale to the terminals of the damper wiring connector and measure the resistance of the solenoid valve. If it is not as specified at the beginning of the Chapter replace the damper with a new one. If the reading is as specified refer to Step 2.

Removal and installation

11 Remove the air filter housing (see Chapter 4).
12 Undo the damper cover screw and remove the cover **(see illustrations)**.
13 Lift the arm cover, then counter-hold the hex, unscrew the nut, lift the arm off the top yoke, retrieving the washer that sits between them as you do **(see illustrations)**.

11.12a Undo the screw (arrowed)...

11.12b ...and remove the cover

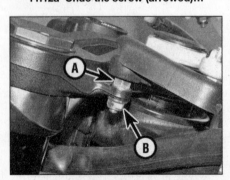

11.13a Counter-hold the hex (A) and unscrew the nut (B)

11.13b Retrieve the washer (arrowed) as you draw the stud out

Frame and suspension 5•23

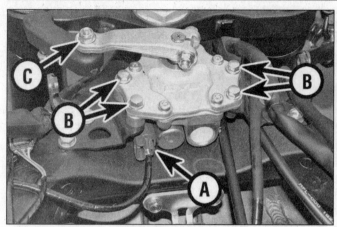

11.14 Damper wiring connector (A), mounting bolts (B) and linkage arm nut (C)

12.2 Method of supporting the bike so the rear wheel is off the ground

14 Disconnect the wiring connector **(see illustration)**. Unscrew the damper mounting bolts and lift the damper off.

15 If required unscrew the nut securing the linkage arm and remove the arm, the washer and the arm cover **(see illustration 11.14)**.

16 Installation is the reverse of removal. Clean the threads of the mounting bolts and apply some fresh threadlock. Tighten the mounting bolts and linkage arm nuts to the torque settings specified at the beginning of the Chapter.

12 Rear shock absorber

⚠ **Warning:** *Do not attempt to disassemble this shock absorber. It is nitrogen-charged under high pressure. Improper disassembly could result in serious injury. No individual components are available for it.*

Removal

Note: *If you are removing the suspension linkage as well, do so first (see Section 13).*

1 Remove the silencer (see Chapter 4).
2 Support the motorcycle so that no weight is transmitted through any part of the rear suspension – in this procedure axle stands were positioned under the frame as shown **(see illustration)**. Tie the front brake lever to the handlebar to ensure the bike can't roll forward. Position a support under the rear wheel or swingarm so that it does not drop when the shock absorber is removed, but also making sure that the weight of the machine is off the rear suspension so that the shock is not compressed.
3 Unscrew the nut and withdraw the bolt securing the linkage plates to the swingarm **(see illustration)**.
4 Unscrew the nut and withdraw the bolt securing the shock absorber to the linkage plates and pivot the linkage down **(see illustration)**.
5 Unscrew the nut on the bolt securing the top of the shock absorber to the swingarm **(see illustration)**. Support the shock from the bottom and withdraw the bolt, then lower the shock absorber and remove it **(see illustration)**.

Inspection

Note: *Refer to Tools and Workshop Tips in the Reference Section for information on bearing removal and installation methods using a suitable driver or socket or a drawbolt. Note that applying some heat to the bearing housing using a hot air gun will ease removal and installation.*

6 Inspect the shock absorber for obvious physical damage and oil leakage, and the coil spring for looseness, cracks or signs of fatigue **(see illustration)**.

12.3 Unscrew the nut and withdraw the linkage plate-to-swingarm bolt

12.4 Unscrew the nut and withdraw the linkage plate-to-shock absorber bolt

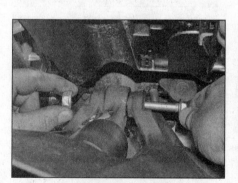

12.5a Unscrew the nut, withdraw the bolt...

12.5b ...and remove the shock absorber

12.6 Check around the rod (arrowed) for signs of oil

5•24 Frame and suspension

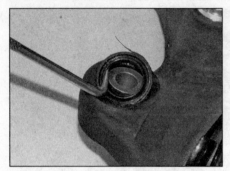

12.7a Lever the seals out

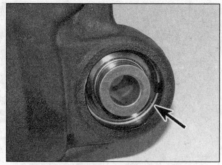

12.7b The bearing is retained by a ring (arrowed)

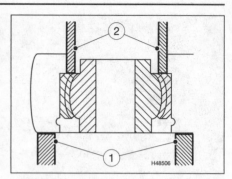

12.7c Support the mount then drive the bearing down

1 Support   2 Driver

7 Inspect the spherical bearing in the top of the shock absorber for wear or damage. If necessary lever out the grease seals, noting which way round they fit **(see illustration)**. Discard the seals as they must be replaced with new ones. Remove the bearing stopper ring **(see illustration)** – you may need to drive the bearing in slightly away from the ring in order to remove it. Support the top mount on a socket larger than the hole and with the stopper ring groove facing down and drive the old bearing out from the top using a socket that fits onto the bearing **(see illustration)**. To fit the new bearing support the mount with the ring groove upwards and drive the new bearing in from the top until it seats. Fit the stopper ring into its groove in the left-hand side **(see illustration 12.7b)**. Tap the bearing up against the stopper ring. Smear the new seals with grease and press them squarely into place with the marked flat side facing in towards the bearing, noting that the seal with the larger diameter goes into the stopper ring side – use a thin-rimmed socket located in the dish of the seal to drive it in if necessary.

8 Withdraw the sleeve from the bottom mount **(see illustration)**. Clean off old grease and dirt. Check the condition of the grease seals and bearing. If required, lever out the grease seals **(see illustration)**. Fit the sleeve back in and check for play between it and the bearing. Refer to *Tools and Workshop Tips* (Section 5) in the Reference section for more information on bearings. If the bearing is worn drive it out of the bore – do not re-use the bearing after removing it **(see illustration)**. The new bearing should be pressed or drawn in, not driven in. When fitting the new bearing make sure it is central in the bore. Lubricate the bearing, sleeve and new seals with molybdenum disulphide grease. Press the new seals squarely into place **(see illustration)**. Fit the sleeve **(see illustration 12.8a)**.

9 With the exception of the pivot components, parts are not available for the shock absorber. If it is worn or damaged, it must be replaced with a new one. Before disposing of an old shock absorber, you should release the nitrogen gas from the reservoir. To do this, point the valve in the end of the reservoir away from you and anyone else and push the blanking plug inwards using a 2 mm pin **(see illustration)**.

 Warning: Be very careful when releasing the gas pressure – it is possible for fine debris particles to be released with it, and as the pressure is high these could damage your eyes if done carelessly. Always wear eye protection and point the valve well away.

Installation

10 Installation is the reverse of removal, noting the following:
- Apply molybdenum disulphide grease to the bearings, seals and sleeves in the shock absorber and linkage plate and arm.
- Install the shock absorber with the reservoir facing back.
- Install the bolts from the right-hand side **(see illustrations 12.5a, 12.4 and 12.3)**.
- Tighten the nuts to the torque setting specified at the beginning of the Chapter.

12.8a Withdraw the sleeve

12.8b Lever the old seal out

12.8c Fit a new bearing if required

12.8d Press the new seals in

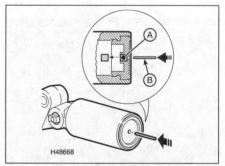

12.9 Shock absorber reservoir gas dispersal

A Blanking plug   B 2 mm pin

Frame and suspension 5•25

13.6 Removing the linkage rod-to-frame bolt

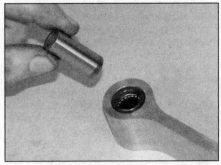

13.7a Withdraw the sleeves from the rod...

13.7b ...and the swingarm

13 Rear suspension linkage

Removal

1 Remove the silencer (see Chapter 4).
2 Support the motorcycle so that no weight is transmitted through any part of the rear suspension – in this procedure axle stands were positioned under the frame as shown **(see illustration 12.2)**. Tie the front brake lever to the handlebar to ensure the bike can't roll forward. Position a support under the rear wheel or swingarm so that it does not drop when the shock absorber is removed, but also making sure that the weight of the machine is off the rear suspension so that the shock is not compressed.
3 Unscrew the nut and withdraw the bolt securing the linkage plates to the swingarm **(see illustration 12.3)**.
4 Unscrew the nut and withdraw the bolt securing the linkage plates to the shock absorber **(see illustration 12.4)**.
5 Unscrew the nut and withdraw the bolt securing the linkage plates to the linkage rod and remove the plates.
6 Unscrew the nut and withdraw bolt securing the linkage rod to the frame and remove the rod **(see illustration)**.

Inspection

7 Withdraw the sleeves from the linkage rod and the linkage plate mount on the swingarm **(see illustrations)**.

8 Thoroughly clean all components, removing all traces of dirt, corrosion and grease.
9 Check the linkage rod and plates and their swingarm mount, looking for obvious signs of wear such as heavy scoring, or for damage such as cracks or distortion. Replace worn or damaged components with new ones as required.
10 Check the condition of the grease seals and bearings. Fit the sleeves back in and check for play between them and the bearings. Refer to *Tools and Workshop Tips* (Section 5) in the Reference section for more information on bearings. Inspect all components closely, looking for corrosion and obvious signs of wear such as heavy scoring, or for damage such as cracks or distortion. Replace worn or damaged components with new ones as required.
11 If required, lever out the grease seals using a seal hook or screwdriver **(see illustration)**. Discard them – new one must be used.
12 Worn bearings can be driven or drawn out of their bores, but note that removal will destroy them; new bearings should be obtained before work commences. The new bearings should be pressed or drawn into their bores rather than driven into position. In the absence of a press, a suitable drawbolt tool can be made up as described in *Tools and Workshop Tips* in the Reference section. When fitting the new bearings make sure they are as central as possible in their bores – in each bore in the rod the gap between the outer end and the rim can be 5.2 to 5.7 mm, and in the swingarm mount 5.5 to 6.0 mm.

13 Lubricate the needle bearings, sleeves and seals with a molybdenum disulphide grease.
14 Press the new seals squarely into place, with the marked flat side facing out **(see illustration)**. Fit the sleeves **(see illustration 13.6a and b)**.

Installation

15 Installation is the reverse of removal, noting the following:
- Apply molybdenum-disulphide grease to the bearings, seals and sleeves.
- Insert the linkage rod-to-frame bolt from the left-hand side and the three linkage plate bolts from the right **(see illustrations 13.6, 12.5a, 12.4 and 12.3)**.
- Tighten the nuts/bolts to the torque setting specified at the beginning of the Chapter.

14 Suspension adjustment

Front forks

1 The front forks are adjustable for spring pre-load and both rebound and compression damping. Always make sure both forks are set equally.

2008 to 2011 models

2 Spring pre-load is adjusted using a spanner on the adjuster flats **(see illustration)** – a spanner should be provided in the toolkit. Turn the adjuster clockwise to increase pre-load and

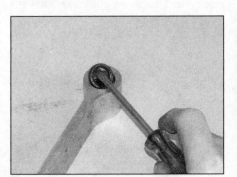

13.11 Lever the seals out

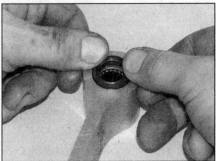

13.14 Press the new seals in

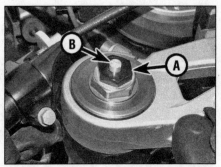

14.2 Spring pre-load adjuster (A); rebound damping adjuster (B)

5•26 Frame and suspension

14.4 Compression damping adjuster (arrowed)

14.5 Spring pre-load adjuster (arrowed)

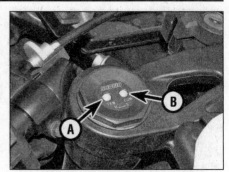

14.6 Rebound damping adjuster (A), compression damping adjuster (B)

anti-clockwise to decrease it. To set the standard position, turn the adjuster fully anti-clockwise until it stops, then turn it clockwise 6 full turns.

3 Rebound damping is adjusted using a screwdriver to turn the adjuster protruding from the pre-load adjuster (see illustration 14.2). Turn it clockwise to increase damping and anti-clockwise to decrease it. To set the standard position, turn the adjuster fully clockwise until it stops, then turn it anti-clockwise 2¼ turns until the punch mark on the adjuster aligns with the reference mark on the directional arrow.

4 Compression damping is adjusted using a screwdriver to turn the adjuster on the bottom of the fork (see illustration). Turn it clockwise to increase damping and anti-clockwise to decrease it. To set the standard position, turn the adjuster fully clockwise until it stops, then turn it anti-clockwise 2 turns on RR models and 2¼ turns on RA models, until the punch mark on the adjuster aligns with the index mark on the housing.

2012-on models

5 Spring pre-load is adjusted using a hex key in the adjuster bolt in the bottom of the fork (see illustration). Turn the adjuster clockwise to increase pre-load and anti-clockwise to decrease it. To set the standard position, turn the adjuster fully anti-clockwise until it stops, then turn it clockwise 7½ full turns.

6 Rebound damping is adjusted using a screwdriver to turn the adjuster marked TEN in the fork top bolt (see illustration). Turn it clockwise to increase damping and anti-clockwise to decrease it. To set the standard position, turn the adjuster fully clockwise until it stops, then turn it anti-clockwise 4¾ turns.

7 Compression damping is adjusted using a screwdriver to turn the adjuster marked COM in the fork top bolt (see illustration 14.6). Turn it clockwise to increase damping and anti-clockwise to decrease it. To set the standard position, turn the adjuster fully clockwise until it stops, then turn it anti-clockwise 5½ turns.

Rear shock absorber

8 The shock absorber is adjustable for spring pre-load and both rebound and compression damping.

2008 to 2011 models

9 Spring pre-load is adjusted using a suitable C-spanner (one is provided in the toolkit) to turn the spring seat on the bottom of the shock absorber (see illustrations). There are ten positions. Position 1 is the lowest setting for light loads, position 4 the standard, and position 10 the highest, for heavy loads. Align the setting required with the adjustment stopper.

10 Rebound damping is adjusted using a screwdriver to turn the adjuster on the bottom of the shock absorber on the left-hand side (see illustration). To increase the damping, turn the adjuster clockwise. To decrease the damping, turn the adjuster anti-clockwise. To set the standard position, turn the adjuster clockwise until it stops, then turn it anti clockwise 2¼ turns.

11 Compression damping is adjusted using a screwdriver to turn the adjuster on the left-hand side of the shock absorber reservoir (see illustration). To increase the damping, turn the adjuster clockwise. To decrease the damping, turn the adjuster anti-clockwise. To set the standard position, turn the adjuster clockwise until it stops, then turn it anti-clockwise 2 turns on 2008 and 2009 RR

14.9a Spring pre-load adjuster (arrowed)

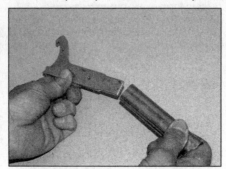

14.9b Use the tools provided...

14.9c ...to turn the adjuster

14.10 Rebound damping adjuster (arrowed)

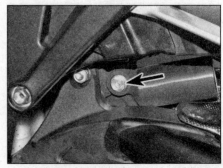

14.11 Compression damping adjuster (arrowed)

Frame and suspension 5•27

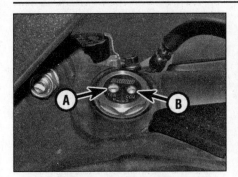

14.13 Rebound damping adjuster (A), compression damping adjuster (B)

15.3a Undo the guide screws (arrowed)...

15.3b ...then tie or support the caliper out of the way

models and 2½ turns on 2010 and 2011 RR models and all RA models.

2012-on models

12 Spring pre-load is adjusted using a suitable C-spanner (one is provided in the toolkit) to turn the spring seat on the bottom of the shock absorber **(see illustrations 14.9a, b and c)**. There are ten positions. Position 1 is the lowest setting for light loads, position 4 the standard, and position 10 the highest, for heavy loads. Align the setting required with the adjustment stopper.

13 Rebound damping is adjusted using a screwdriver to turn the adjuster marked TEN on the top of the shock absorber **(see illustration)**. To increase the damping, turn the adjuster clockwise. To decrease the damping, turn the adjuster anti-clockwise. To set the standard position, turn the adjuster clockwise until it stops, then turn it anti-clockwise 2½ turns.

14 Compression damping is adjusted using a screwdriver to turn the adjuster marked COM on the top of the shock absorber **(see illustration 14.13)**. To increase the damping, turn the adjuster clockwise. To decrease the damping, turn the adjuster anti-clockwise. To set the standard position, turn the adjuster clockwise until it stops, then turn it anti-clockwise 2¾ turns.

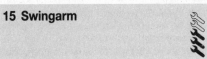

15 Swingarm

Removal

1 Remove the front sprocket (see Chapter 6).
2 Remove the rear wheel (see Chapter 6).
3 Unscrew the brake hose/wheel sensor wiring guide screws on the swingarm **(see illustration)**.

Tie the rear brake caliper up or hook the bracket over the footrest or brake pedal **(see illustration)**. If required undo the remaining screw securing the hugger and remove it **(see illustration)**. If required undo the screws and remove the chainguard **(see illustration)**.
4 Remove the shock absorber (Section 12).
5 On US models disconnect the EVAP system canister hoses.
6 Unscrew the nut on the left-hand end of the pivot bolt and remove the washer, where fitted **(see illustration)**.
7 Withdraw the pivot bolt then manoeuvre the swingarm out of the frame **(see illustration)**.
8 Remove the slider from the swingarm if necessary – note the collars that fit with the slider rear bolts **(see illustration)**. If the slider is badly worn or damaged, it should be replaced with a new one – there are some wear limit arrows on the front **(see illustration)**. Inspect all pivot components for wear or damage.

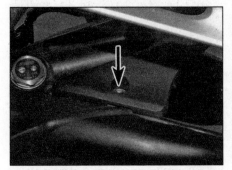

15.3c Rear hugger screw (arrowed)

15.3d Chainguard screws (arrowed)

15.6 Unscrew the nut and remove the washer

15.7 Withdraw the pivot bolt and remove the swingarm

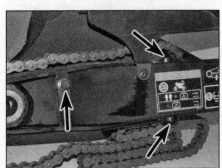

15.8a Chain slider bolts (arrowed)

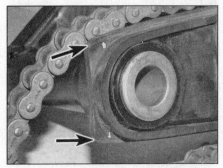

15.8b Wear limit lines (arrowed) are marked by arrows on the slider

15.12a Remove the collars

15.12b Lever the seal out from each side of the swingarm pivot

15.12c Withdraw the spacer

Inspection

9 Thoroughly clean the swingarm, removing all traces of dirt, corrosion and grease.

10 Inspect the swingarm closely, looking for obvious signs of wear such as heavy scoring, and cracks or distortion due to accident damage. Any damaged or worn component must be replaced.

11 Check the swingarm pivot bolt is straight by rolling it on a flat surface such as a piece of plate glass (first wipe off all old grease and remove any corrosion using steel wool). Replace the pivot bolt with a new one if it is bent.

Bearing check and replacement

12 Remove the collar from each pivot **(see illustration)** – mark them L or R according to side with a felt pen to prevent mixing them up. Lever the grease seal out from each side, noting which size fits where **(see illustration)**. New seals must be used, but keep the old ones laid out in order so the new seals can be matched for position. Withdraw the central spacer **(see illustration)**.

13 Refer to *Tools and Workshop Tips* in the Reference section and check the bearings – there is a needle bearing and a caged ball bearing in the right-hand pivot, and a needle bearing in the left-hand pivot. Clean them and inspect them for corrosion, wear and damage. If the bearings do not run smoothly and freely or if there is excessive freeplay between them and the collars, they must be replaced with new ones – refer to the Reference Section for removal and installation methods, noting that Honda specify the need for an hydraulic press. The bearings in the right-hand pivot are held by a circlip **(see illustration)**. The bearings must be replaced with new ones if removed – they cannot be reused.

14 When installing the new bearings, pack them with molybdenum disulphide grease. On the right-hand side press the caged ball bearing in until it seats, then press the needle bearing against it, with its marked end facing out. Press the left-hand needle bearing in with its marked end facing out and so that its outer end is set in to a depth of 6 to 7 mm. Do not forget to fit the circlip into the groove in the right-hand side, using a new one if the old one deformed on removal **(see illustration 15.13)**.

15 Lubricate the spacer, collars, and grease seal lips with molybdenum disulphide grease. Slide the spacer into the swingarm so it sits between the bearings **(see illustration 15.12c)**. Press the new seals into place – the right-hand seal has a larger external diameter **(see illustration)**. Fit the collars **(see illustration 15.12a)**.

Installation

16 If removed, fit the chain slider, making sure its tab locates correctly in the groove in the front of the swingarm. Clean the threads of the bolts and apply a suitable non-permanent thread locking compound, then fit them with the collars on the rear bolts and tighten them to the torque setting specified at the beginning of the Chapter **(see illustration 15.8a)**.

17 If not already done remove the collar from each pivot **(see illustration 15.12a)**. Clean off all old grease, then lubricate the grease seals, bearings, collars and the pivot bolt with molybdenum disulphide grease. Fit the collars.

18 Offer up the swingarm and have an assistant hold it in place. Make sure the drive chain is looped over the front of the swingarm. Slide the pivot bolt through from the right-hand side **(see illustration 15.7)**.

19 Fit the nut, with its washer where fitted, onto the left-hand end of the pivot bolt, then hold the bolt and tighten the nut to the torque setting specified at the beginning of the Chapter for your model **(see illustration 15.6)**.

20 On US models connect the EVAP system canister hoses.

21 Install the shock absorber (see Section 12).

22 Fit the chainguard and hugger if removed. Fit the brake hose guide screws **(see illustration 15.3a)**.

23 Install the rear wheel (see Chapter 6).

24 Install the front sprocket (see Chapter 6).

25 Check and adjust the drive chain slack (see Chapter 1). Check the operation of the rear suspension and brake before taking the machine on the road.

15.13 A circlip (arrowed) secures the right-hand bearings

15.15 Make sure you select the correct seal for each side of the pivot

Chapter 6
Brakes, wheels and final drive

Contents

	Section number
Brake fluid level check	see *Pre-ride checks*
Brake hoses and fittings	10
Brake light switches	see Chapter 8
Brake pad wear check	see Chapter 1
Brake system bleeding and fluid change	11
Brake system check	see Chapter 1
C-ABS components – RA models	14
C-ABS fault diagnosis – RA models	13
C-ABS operation – RA models	12
Drive chain	21
Drive chain check, adjustment, cleaning and lubrication	see Chapter 1
Front brake calipers	3
Front brake discs	4
Front brake master cylinder	5
Front brake pads	2
Front wheel	17

	Section number
General information	1
Rear brake caliper	7
Rear brake disc	8
Rear brake master cylinder	9
Rear brake pads	6
Rear sprocket coupling/rubber dampers	23
Rear wheel	18
Sprockets	22
Tyre pressure, tread depth and condition	see *Pre-ride checks*
Tyres	20
Wheel alignment check	16
Wheel bearing check	see Chapter 1
Wheel bearings	19
Wheel check	see Chapter 1
Wheel inspection and repair	15

Degrees of difficulty

Easy, suitable for novice with little experience	**Fairly easy,** suitable for beginner with some experience	**Fairly difficult,** suitable for competent DIY mechanic	**Difficult,** suitable for experienced DIY mechanic	**Very difficult,** suitable for expert DIY or professional

Specifications

Brake fluid
Brake fluid type .... DOT 4

Front brake master cylinder
Master cylinder bore ID
   Standard .... 17.460 to 17.503 mm
   Service limit .... 17.515 mm
Master cylinder piston OD
   Standard .... 17.321 to 17.367 mm
   Service limit .... 17.321 mm

Front brake calipers
Caliper bore ID
  Upper bore
    Standard.. 32.080 to 32.130 mm
    Service limit .... 32.130 mm
  Lower bore
    Standard.. 30.280 to 30.330 mm
    Service limit .... 30.330 mm
Caliper piston OD
  Upper piston
    Standard.. 31.967 to 32.000 mm
    Service limit .... 31.967 mm
  Lower piston
    Standard.. 30.167 to 30.200 mm
    Service limit .... 30.167 mm

Front brake discs
Disc thickness
  Standard.. 4.5 mm
  Service limit .... 3.5 mm
Disc maximum runout .... 0.2 mm

Rear brake master cylinder
Master cylinder bore ID
  Standard.. 14.000 to 14.043 mm
  Service limit .... 14.043 mm
Master cylinder piston OD
  Standard.. 13.957 to 13.984 mm
  Service limit .... 13.957 mm

Rear brake caliper
Caliper bore ID
  Standard.. 30.230 to 30.280 mm
  Service limit .... 30.280 mm
Caliper piston OD
  Standard.. 30.082 to 30.115 mm
  Service limit .... 30.082 mm

Rear brake disc
Disc thickness
  Standard.. 5.0 mm
  Service limit .... 4.0 mm
Disc maximum runout .... 0.3 mm

C-ABS system
Wheel speed sensor air gap...................................... 0.4 to 1.2 mm

Wheels
Maximum wheel runout (front and rear)
  Axial (side-to-side) .... 2.0 mm
  Radial (out-of-round) .... 2.0 mm
Maximum axle runout (front and rear) .... 0.2 mm

Tyres
Tyre pressures and tread depth .... see Pre-ride checks
Tyre sizes*
  Front .... 120/70-ZR17 (58W) Radial
  Rear .... 190/50-ZR17 (73W) Radial
*Refer to the owners handbook or the tyre information label on the swingarm for approved tyre brands.

Final drive
Drive chain slack and lubricant .... see Chapter 1
Drive chain type and no. of links
  DID DID50VA11-120ZB/116
  RK RK50HFOZ6-120LJFZ/116
Joining link pin projection from side plate (unstaked) .... 1.20 to 1.40 mm
Joining link staked ends diameter .... 5.50 to 5.80 mm
Sprocket sizes (No. of teeth)
  Front (engine) sprocket.. 16
  Rear (wheel) sprocket.. 42

Torque settings

Brake caliper bleed valves	
Front calipers	8 Nm
Front master cylinder	6 Nm
Rear caliper	6 Nm
Brake disc bolts	
Front	20 Nm
Rear	42 Nm
Brake hose banjo bolts	34 Nm
Brake pipe joint bolts	34 Nm
Brake pipe nuts	14 Nm
Front axle bolt	79 Nm
Front axle clamp bolts	22 Nm
Front brake caliper mounting bolts	45 Nm
Front brake master cylinder clamp bolts	12 Nm
Front brake pad retaining pins	15 Nm
Front sprocket bolt	54 Nm
Front wheel pulse ring bolts (C-ABS models)	7 Nm
Rear axle nut	113 Nm
Rear brake pad retaining pin	18 Nm
Rear brake master cylinder mounting bolts/nuts	10 Nm
Rear sprocket nuts	64 Nm
Rear wheel pulse ring bolts (C-ABS models)	7 Nm
Rider's footrest bracket bolts	37 Nm

1 General information

All models covered in this manual are fitted with cast alloy wheels designed for tubeless tyres only. Both front and rear brakes are hydraulically operated disc brakes.

CBR1000RR models have a conventional braking system using two radial calipers with four opposed pistons acting on 320 mm discs at the front, and a single piston sliding caliper acting on a 220 mm disc at the rear.

CBR1000RA models have an electronically controlled combined anti-lock braking system (C-ABS), with two radial calipers with four opposed pistons acting on 320 mm discs at the front, and a single piston sliding caliper acting on a 220 mm disc at the rear. The C-ABS electronically links and controls the front and rear brake systems via a central control unit and a front and rear power unit and valve unit to provide optimum braking power and balance while preventing wheel lock-up under heavy braking.

Caution: Disc brake components rarely require disassembly. Do not disassemble components unless absolutely necessary. If an hydraulic brake hose is loosened or disconnected, the banjo union sealing washers must be replaced with new ones and the system must be bled upon reassembly. Do not use solvents on internal brake components. Solvents will cause the seals to swell and distort. Use only clean DOT 4 brake fluid for cleaning. Use care when working with brake fluid as it can injure your eyes and it will damage painted surfaces and plastic parts.

2 Front brake pads

Note: *Honda recommend using new caliper mounting bolts. This is because the bolts are pre-treated with a locking compound. If they are not available it is possible, however, to clean up the old bolts and reinstall them using a suitable non-permanent thread locking compound that is commercially available.*

Caution: Do not operate the brakes while a caliper is off the disc.

1 Slacken the pad retaining pins **(see illustration)**.

2 Unscrew the caliper mounting bolts and slide the caliper off the disc **(see illustration 2.15)**. Remove the caliper locating dowels if loose.

3 Unscrew and remove the pad pins, then remove the pads from the bottom of the caliper **(see illustrations)**. The pad spring can stay in place unless you are overhauling the caliper – to remove the spring the pistons must be pushed all the way back into their bores to give clearance (see Step 7) **(see illustration 2.11)**.

4 Where fitted and if required remove the shim from the back of each pad, noting how it fits **(see illustration 2.12)** – note that new

2.1 Brake pad pins (A), caliper mounting bolts (B)

2.3a Remove the pad pins...

2.3b ...then remove the pads

6•4 Brakes, wheels and final drive

2.7a Clean off any dirt from around the pistons

2.7b Press the pistons in as described to make clearance for new pads

2.7c This is a commercially available piston pushing tool

pads should come with new shims where applicable.

5 Inspect the surface of each pad for contamination and check that the friction material has not worn to or beyond its service limit (see Chapter 1, Section 2). If any pad is worn, is fouled with oil or grease, or is heavily scored or damaged, fit a complete set of new pads. Also check for even wear across the pad – uneven wear is indicative of a sticking or seized piston (see Steps 7 and 8). **Note:** *It is not possible to degrease the friction material; if the pads are contaminated in any way they must be replaced with new ones.*

6 If the pads are in good condition clean them carefully using a fine wire brush that is completely free of oil and grease to remove all dirt and dust. Using a pointed instrument, clean the grooves and dig out any embedded particles of foreign matter. Spray with a dedicated brake cleaner.

7 Clean around the exposed section of each piston to remove any dirt or debris that could cause the seals to be damaged **(see illustration)**. If new pads are being fitted check the fluid level in the reservoir (see *Pre-ride checks*) – if the level is much above the LOWER level line remove the master cylinder reservoir cap, plate and diaphragm and remove some fluid before pushing the pistons in to create room for the new pads. If new pads are being fitted, push the pistons all the way back into the caliper to create room for them; if the old pads are still serviceable push the pistons in a little way. To push the pistons back use finger pressure or a piece of wood as leverage, or place the old pads back in the caliper and use a metal bar or a screwdriver inserted between them (but take care not to damage the friction surface if the pads are being re-used), or use grips and a piece of wood, with rag or card to protect the caliper body **(see illustration)**. Alternatively obtain a proper piston-pushing tool from a good tool supplier **(see illustration)**. If the pistons are difficult to push back, remove the bleed valve cap, then attach a length of clear hose to the bleed valve and place the open end in a suitable container, then open the valve and try again (see Section 11). Take great care not to draw any air into the system. If in doubt, bleed the brakes afterwards.

8 If any of the pistons appear seized, first block or hold the other pistons using wood or cable-ties, then apply the brake lever and check whether the piston in question moves at all. If it moves out but can't be pushed back in the chances are there is some hidden corrosion stopping it. If it doesn't move at all, or to fully clean and inspect the pistons, disassemble the caliper and overhaul it (see Section 3).

9 Remove all dirt and corrosion from the pad pins and check for wear and damage. If required remove the pad spring and clean it.

10 Check the condition of the brake disc (see Section 4).

11 If the pad spring was removed fit it into the caliper, making sure it locates correctly **(see illustration)**.

12 Where fitted and if removed fit the shim onto the back of each pad, making sure it locates correctly **(see illustration)**. Clean the outer face of each shim so it is shiny.

13 Lightly smear the edges of the backing material where it contacts the caliper body with copper-based grease, making sure that none gets on the friction material. Also smear the pad pins.

14 Fit the pads into the caliper so the friction material on each pad faces the other **(see illustration 2.3b)**. Press them up against the spring to align the holes, then insert the pad pins and tighten them finger-tight **(see illustration 2.3a)**.

15 Make sure the caliper locating dowels are fitted. Slide the caliper onto the disc making sure the pads locate correctly on each side **(see illustration)**. Either fit the new caliper mounting bolts, or clean the threads of the original bolts and apply a suitable non-permanent thread locking compound, then tighten them to the torque setting specified at the beginning of the Chapter.

16 Tighten the pad pins to the torque setting specified at the beginning of this Chapter.

17 Operate the brake lever until the pads contact the disc. Check the level of fluid in each reservoir and top-up if necessary (see *Pre-ride checks*).

18 Check the operation of the brakes before riding the motorcycle.

2.11 Fit the pad spring with the tabbed ends (arrowed) towards the lower end of the caliper

2.12 Make sure the shims are correctly seated

2.15 Slide the caliper onto the disc and fit the bolts

Brakes, wheels and final drive 6•5

3.1 Brake hose guide bolt (arrowed)

3.2a Brake hose banjo bolt (arrowed)

3.2b Seal the banjo using a nut and bolt and the sealing washers

3 Front brake calipers

Warning: Overhaul of the brake calipers must be done in a spotlessly clean work area to avoid contamination and possible failure of the brake hydraulic system components. Do not, under any circumstances, use petroleum-based solvents to clean brake parts. Use clean DOT 4 brake fluid, dedicated brake cleaner or denatured alcohol only, as described. To prevent damage from spilled brake fluid, always cover paintwork when working on the braking system, and have plenty of absorbent rag to hand to catch and wipe off any spilled fluid.

Note 1: If a caliper is in need of an overhaul it is best to drain all old brake fluid from the system, then fill with new fluid after the overhaul (see Section 11). On RA (C-ABS) models, before draining the brake fluid read the information given in that Section regarding the refilling and bleeding of the system.

Removal

Note 2: Honda recommend using new caliper mounting bolts. This is because the bolts are pre-treated with a locking compound. If they are not available it is possible, however, to clean up the old bolts and reinstall them using a suitable non-permanent thread locking compound that is commercially available.

Note 3: If the caliper is being overhauled (usually due to sticking pistons or fluid leaks) read through the entire procedure first and make sure that you have obtained all the new parts required, including some new DOT 4 brake fluid.

Caution: Do not operate the brakes while a caliper is off the disc.

1 If you just want to displace the calipers for front wheel removal displace the brake hose guides and on RA models the wheel sensor wire from the mudguard **(see illustration)**. Unscrew the caliper mounting bolts and slide the caliper off the disc **(see illustration 2.1)**. Tie the calipers and hoses back so that they are out of the way. Remove the caliper locating dowels if loose.

2 If the caliper is being completely removed or overhauled, unscrew the brake hose banjo bolt and detach the banjo union, noting the alignment with the caliper **(see illustration)**. If the brake fluid has not been drained seal the banjo union – one way of doing this is to fit a suitable bolt and nut with the old sealing washers **(see illustration)**. Note that new sealing washers will be required later.

3 If the caliper is being overhauled, refer to Section 2, Steps 1 to 3, and remove the brake pads – this involves removing the caliper from the disc.

Overhaul

4 Clean the exterior of the caliper with denatured alcohol or brake system cleaner. Have some clean rag ready to catch any spilled brake fluid.

5 To remove the pistons you need either a supply of compressed air, or a piston removal tool, or if neither are available a good pair of external circlip removal pliers.

6 Push the pistons in one side of the caliper all the way in (see Section 2, Step 7). Remove the pad spring **(see illustration 2.11)**.

7 If you are using compressed air retain the pistons you pushed in using cable-ties **(see illustration)**. Wedge some rag or a thin piece of wood between the pistons, then gradually and progressively apply the compressed air, starting with a fairly low pressure, to the fluid passage and allow the free pistons to ease out of their bores until they can be removed **(see illustrations)**. Mark each piston and the caliper body to ensure that the pistons can be matched to their original bores on reassembly. Note that two sizes of piston are used in each caliper (see Specifications at the beginning of this Chapter). Now block the empty piston bores with rag and use compressed air to remove the pistons from the other side **(see illustration)**.

3.7a Tie the pistons on one side back...

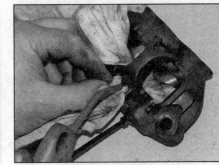
3.7b ...then use compressed air to force the other pistons out...

3.7c ...and remove them

3.7d Block the empty bores with rag and blow the remaining pistons out

6•6 Brakes, wheels and final drive

3.8 Using circlip pliers to extract a piston

3.10a Remove the dust seals...

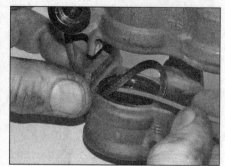

3.10b ...and the piston seals

3.12 Check the surfaces of the pistons and bores – the plating on this piston is lifting off

3.13a Lubricate the new piston seals with brake fluid...

3.13b ...then fit them into the lower grooves

8 If you are using a dedicated tool or the circlip pliers, grip the inner wall then twist and pull the piston out, keeping it square to the bore wall until it is free **(see illustration)**. Do not try to remove a piston by levering it out or by using pliers or other grips that may scratch the outer wall, unless you are prepared to fit a new piston, and possibly a new caliper.

9 If a piston is stuck in its bore due to corrosion the caliper should be replaced with a new one. Do not try to remove a piston by levering it out or by using pliers or other grips.

10 Remove the dust seals and the piston seals from the bores using a plastic tool to avoid scratching the bores **(see illustrations)**. Discard the seals – new ones must be fitted on reassembly.

11 Clean the pistons and bores with clean brake fluid. If compressed air is available, blow it through the fluid passages to ensure they are clear (make sure it is filtered and unlubricated).

Caution: Do not, under any circumstances, use a petroleum-based solvent to clean brake parts.

12 Inspect the caliper bores and pistons for signs of corrosion, nicks and burrs and loss of plating **(see illustration)**. If surface defects are present, the pistons and/or the caliper assembly must be replaced with new ones. If one caliper is in poor condition, the other front caliper and the master cylinder should also be checked.

13 Lubricate the new piston seals with clean brake fluid and fit them into their grooves in the caliper bores **(see illustrations)**. Note that there are two sizes of bore in each caliper and care must therefore be taken to ensure that the correct size seals are fitted to the correct bores (see Specifications). The same applies when fitting the new dust seals and pistons.

14 Lubricate the new dust seals with silicone grease and fit them into their grooves in the caliper bores **(see illustrations)**.

15 Lubricate the pistons with clean brake fluid and fit them, closed-end first, into the caliper bores, taking care not to displace the seals **(see illustrations)**. Using your thumbs, push the pistons all the way in, making sure they enter the bore squarely.

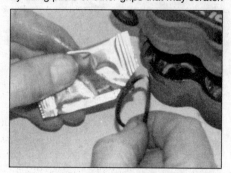

3.14a Lubricate the new dust seals with silicone grease...

3.14b ...then fit them into the upper grooves

3.15a Fit the pistons...

3.15b ...and push them all the way in

Brakes, wheels and final drive 6•7

3.18 Use a new sealing washer on each side of the banjo union

4.2a The minimum thickness is marked on the disc

4.2b Measuring disc thickness using a micrometer

Installation

16 If the caliper was overhauled refer to Section 2 and if not already done clean and check the pads and pad spring. Fit the pad spring and brake pads into the caliper and the caliper onto the disc following the procedure in Section 2, Steps 11 to 18.

17 If the caliper was just displaced make sure the locating dowels are fitted, then slide the caliper onto the disc making sure the pads locate correctly on each side (see illustration 2.15). Either fit the new caliper mounting bolts, or clean the threads of the original bolts and apply fresh thread locking compound, then tighten them to the torque setting specified at the beginning of the Chapter.

18 If detached, connect the brake hose to the caliper, using new sealing washers on each side of the banjo fitting (see illustration). Align the hose as noted on removal (see illustration 3.2a). Tighten the banjo bolt to the specified torque setting.

19 Secure the brake hose/wiring on the front mudguard according to model (see illustration 3.1).

20 Refer to Section 11 and fill and/or bleed the system as required.

21 Operate the brake lever until the pads contact the disc. Check the level of fluid in each reservoir and top-up if necessary (see *Pre-ride checks*).

22 Check that there are no fluid leaks and test the operation of the brakes before riding the motorcycle.

4 Front brake discs

Inspection

1 Inspect the surface of the disc for score marks and other damage. Light scratches are normal after use and won't affect brake operation, but deep grooves and heavy score marks will reduce braking efficiency and accelerate pad wear. If a disc is badly grooved it must be replaced with a new one.

2 The disc must not be allowed to wear down to a thickness less than the service limit listed in this Chapter's Specifications. The minimum thickness is also stamped on the disc (see illustration). Check the thickness of the disc in the middle of the pad contact area using a micrometer (see illustration) – do not measure across the rim of the disc with a ruler. Replace the disc with a new one if necessary.

3 To check if the disc is warped, position the bike on an auxiliary stand with the front wheel raised off the ground. Mount a dial gauge to the fork leg, with the gauge plunger touching the surface of the disc about 10 mm from its outer edge (see illustration). Rotate the wheel and watch the gauge needle, comparing the reading with the limit listed in the Specifications at the beginning of this Chapter. If the runout is greater than the service limit, check the wheel bearings for play (see Chapter 1), and also check the wheel itself for runout before assuming the disc is warped (see Section 15). If the bearings are worn, fit new ones (see Section 19) and repeat this check. If the disc runout is still excessive, remove the disc (Steps 4 and 5) and check for corrosion where it seats on the hub and clean it up if necessary. You can also try moving the disc around the wheel one bolt hole at a time and after each movement rechecking for runout. In most cases a new disc will have to be fitted.

Removal

Note: *Honda recommend using new disc mounting bolts. This is because the bolts are pre-treated with a locking compound. If they are not available it is possible, however, to clean up the old bolts and reinstall them using a suitable non-permanent thread locking compound that is commercially available.*

4 Remove the wheel (see Section 17). On RA models remove the pulse ring from the right-hand side of the wheel (see Section 14).

Caution: *Don't lay the wheel down and allow it to rest on either disc – the disc could become warped. Set the wheel on wood blocks so the wheel rim supports the weight of the wheel.*

5 If you are not replacing the disc with a new one, mark the alignment of the disc to the wheel, so it can be installed in the same position. Unscrew the disc bolts, loosening them evenly and a little at a time in a criss-cross pattern to avoid distorting the disc, then remove the disc (see illustration).

Installation

6 Before installing the disc, make sure there is no dirt or corrosion where the disc seats on the hub. If the disc does not sit flat when it is bolted down, it will appear to be warped when checked or when the front brake is used.

7 Fit the disc on the wheel with its marked side facing out, aligning the previously applied marks (if you're reinstalling the original disc), and making sure the arrow points in the direction of normal rotation, matching the

4.3 Checking disc runout with a dial gauge

4.5 The disc is secured by six bolts

6•8 Brakes, wheels and final drive

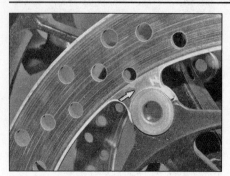

4.7a Note the directional arrow...

4.7b ...and check those on the wheel and tyre as well

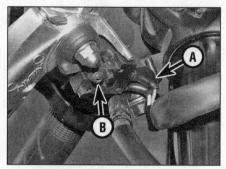

5.1 Disconnect the brake light switch wires (A). Switch mounting screw (B)

arrows on both the wheel and the tyre **(see illustrations)**.

8 Either fit the new bolts, or clean the threads of the original bolts and apply fresh thread locking compound, and tighten them evenly and a little at a time in a criss-cross pattern to the torque setting specified at the beginning of this Chapter. Clean the disc using acetone or brake system cleaner. If new discs have been installed, remove any protective coating from their working surfaces and fit new brake pads.

9 On RA models fit the pulse ring onto the right-hand side of the wheel (see Section 14). Install the front wheel (see Section 17).

10 Operate the brake lever until the pads contact the disc. Check the level of fluid in each reservoir and top-up if necessary (see Pre-ride checks).

11 Check the operation of the brakes before riding the motorcycle.

5 Front brake master cylinder

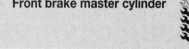

> **Warning:** *Overhaul must be done in a spotlessly clean work area to avoid contamination and possible failure of the brake hydraulic system components. Do not, under any circumstances, use petroleum-based solvents to clean brake parts. Use clean DOT 4 brake fluid, dedicated brake cleaner or denatured alcohol only, as described. To prevent damage from spilled brake fluid, always cover paintwork when working on the braking system, and have plenty of absorbent rag to hand to catch and wipe off any spilled fluid.*

Note: *If the master cylinder is in need of an overhaul it is best to drain all old brake fluid from the system, then fill with new fluid after the overhaul (see Section 11). On RA models, before draining the brake fluid read the information given in that Section regarding the refilling and bleeding of the system.*

Removal

Note: *If the master cylinder is being overhauled (usually due to sticking or poor action, or fluid leaks) read through the entire procedure first and make sure that you have obtained all the new parts required, including some new DOT 4 brake fluid.*

1 Disconnect the brake light switch wiring connectors **(see illustration)**.

2 If the master cylinder is just being displaced unscrew the clamp bolts and remove the clamp, then cover the master cylinder and reservoir in rag and position it clear of the handlebar **(see illustration)**. Make sure no strain is placed on the hydraulic hose. Keep the reservoir upright to prevent air entering the system.

3 If the master cylinder is being overhauled, remove the brake lever (see Chapter 5).

4 If the brake fluid wasn't drained, remove the reservoir cap clamp screw and clamp **(see illustration)**.

5 Unscrew the brake hose banjo bolt and detach the banjo union, noting its alignment with the master cylinder **(see illustration)**. If the brake fluid has not been drained seal the banjo union – one way of doing this is to fit a suitable bolt and nut with the old sealing washers **(see illustration 3.2b)**. Note that new sealing washers will be required later.

6 Unscrew the master cylinder clamp bolts and remove the clamp, then lift the master cylinder away from the handlebar **(see illustration 5.2)**.

7 Remove the reservoir cap, diaphragm plate and the diaphragm. If the brake fluid wasn't drained tip the fluid from the master cylinder and reservoir into a suitable container. Wipe any remaining fluid out of the reservoir with a clean rag.

8 If required, undo the screw securing the brake light switch to the bottom of the master cylinder and remove the switch **(see illustration 5.1)**.

Overhaul

9 If required lift the dust cap from the fluid reservoir hose union, then remove the circlip and detach the union from the master cylinder

5.2 Unscrew the bolts (arrowed)

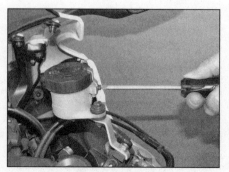

5.4 Remove the clamp

5.5 Brake hose banjo bolt (arrowed)

(see illustration). Remove the O-ring – a new one must be fitted on reassembly. Unscrew the reservoir bracket bolt and remove the reservoir assembly. Inspect the reservoir hose for cracks or splits and replace it with a new one if necessary.

10 Remove the pushrod and the rubber boot from the master cylinder. Depress the piston and use circlip pliers to remove the circlip, then slide out the piston assembly, the spring and the spring guide, noting how they fit. If they are difficult to remove, apply low pressure compressed air to the brake fluid outlet. Lay the parts out in the proper order to prevent confusion during reassembly.

11 Clean the master cylinder and reservoir with clean brake fluid. If compressed air is available, blow it through the fluid galleries to ensure they are clear (make sure the air is filtered and unlubricated).

Caution: Do not, under any circumstances, use a petroleum-based solvent to clean brake parts.

12 Check the master cylinder bore for corrosion, scratches, nicks and score marks. If damage or wear is evident, the master cylinder must be replaced with a new one. If the master cylinder is in poor condition, then the calipers should be checked as well.

13 The dust boot, circlip, piston and its cup and seal, spring, and spring guide are all included in a master cylinder rebuild kit, and all other components are available individually. Use all of the new parts, regardless of the apparent condition of the old ones. Remove the pushrod from the boot as this does not come in the kit.

14 Smear the cup and seal with new brake fluid and if not already in place fit them into their grooves in the piston so their wider ends will fit into the master cylinder first **(see illustration)**.

15 Lubricate the master cylinder bore with new brake fluid.

16 Fit the spring guide into the end of the spring **(see illustration)**. Fit the spring guide and spring into the master cylinder. Lubricate the piston, cup and seal with clean brake fluid and slide it into the master cylinder and up against the spring. Make sure the lips on the cup and seal do not turn inside out. Push the piston in to compress the spring and fit the new circlip, making sure it locates in the groove. Smear the inner end of the pushrod and inside the rubber boot with silicone grease. Fit the boot onto the pushrod so its narrow end lips locate in the groove. Locate the inner end of the pushrod in the end of the piston and carefully push the wide rim of the boot onto its seat in the master cylinder.

17 If removed fit the reservoir assembly and tighten the bracket bolt. Fit a new O-ring smeared with brake fluid onto the fluid reservoir hose union, then press the union into the master cylinder and secure it with the circlip. Fit the dust cap over the circlip. Inspect the reservoir diaphragm and fit a new one if it is damaged or deteriorated.

Installation

18 If removed, fit the brake light switch onto the bottom of the master cylinder, making sure the pin locates in the hole, and tighten the screw **(see illustration 5.1)**.

19 Attach the master cylinder to the handlebar, aligning the clamp joint with the punch mark on the top of the handlebar, then fit the back of the clamp with its UP mark facing up **(see illustration)**. Tighten the upper bolt to the torque setting specified at the beginning of this Chapter, followed by the lower bolt.

20 Connect the brake hose to the master cylinder, using new sealing washers on each side of the banjo fitting **(see illustration 3.18)**. Align the hose as noted on removal **(see illustration 5.5)**. Tighten the banjo bolt to the torque setting specified at the beginning of this Chapter.

21 Install the brake lever (see Chapter 5).

22 Connect the brake light switch wiring **(see illustration 5.1)**.

23 Refer to Section 11 and fill and/or bleed the system as required. Check that there are no fluid leaks and test the operation of the brakes before riding the motorcycle.

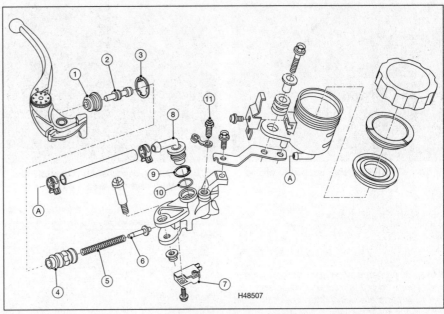

5.9 Front brake master cylinder

1 Rubber boot
2 Pushrod
3 Circlip
4 Piston/seal/cup assembly
5 Spring
6 Spring guide
7 Brake light switch
8 Reservoir union
9 Circlip
10 Reservoir union O-ring
11 Bleed valve

5.14 Make sure the cup and seal are correctly installed

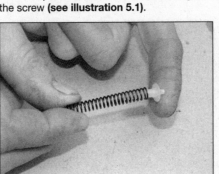

5.16 Fit the guide into the spring

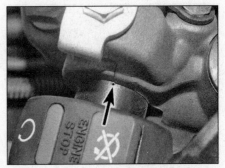

5.19 Align the mating surfaces with the punch mark (arrowed)

6•10 Brakes, wheels and final drive

6.1a On RR models release the clamp

6.1b On RA models undo the screw (arrowed) and displace the reservoir

6.1c Push against the caliper to force the piston in

6 Rear brake pads

Note: *Do not operate either brake with the pads removed or the caliper off the disc.*

1 If new pads are being fitted check the fluid level in the reservoir (see *Pre-ride checks*) – if the fluid level is not near the LOWER level line, on RR models, undo the cap clamp screw and on RA models undo the reservoir screw and displace the reservoir, then on all models unscrew the cap and remove the diaphragm plate and diaphragm and remove some fluid before pushing the piston in to create room for the new pads **(see illustrations)**. Push the caliper against the disc, as far as it will go if new pads are being fitted so the piston is pushed fully back into the caliper **(see illustration)**. If the piston is difficult to push back, remove the bleed valve cap, then attach a length of clear hose to the bleed valve and place the open end in a suitable container, then open the valve and try again (see Section 11). Take great care not to draw any air into the system. If in doubt, bleed the brake afterwards.

2 If the caliper is difficult to push in the chances are there is some hidden corrosion stopping it. If it doesn't move at all, or to fully clean and inspect the pistons, remove the caliper and overhaul it (see Section 7).

3 Unscrew and remove the pad pin, then draw the pads out **(see illustrations)**.

4 Where fitted and if required remove the shim and its inner sheet from the back of each pad, noting how they fit **(see illustration 6.9)** – note that new pads should come with new shims where applicable.

5 Inspect the surface of each pad for contamination and check that the friction material has not worn beyond its service limit (see Chapter 1, Section 2). If either pad is worn, is fouled with oil or grease, or heavily scored or damaged, fit a set of new pads.

Note: *It is not possible to degrease the friction material; if the pads are contaminated in any way they must be replaced with new ones.*

6 If the pads are in good condition clean them carefully using a fine wire brush that is completely free of oil and grease to remove all dirt and dust. Using a pointed instrument, dig out any embedded particles of foreign matter. Spray with a dedicated brake cleaner.

7 Remove all traces of corrosion from the pad pin and check it for wear and damage **(see illustration)**. Check the condition of the stopper ring on the pin and replace it with a new one if it is damaged or deformed.

8 Check the condition of the brake disc (see Section 8).

9 Where fitted and if removed fit the inner sheet and shim onto the back of each pad, making sure they locate correctly and each is on the correct side as they are different **(see illustration)**. Clean the outer face of each shim so it is shiny.

10 Lightly smear the edges of the backing material where it contacts the caliper body with copper-based grease, making sure that none gets on the friction material. Also smear the pad pin, but not the stopper ring.

11 Apply a smear of silicone grease to the stopper ring on the pad pin.

12 Fit the pads into the caliper so the friction material on each pad faces the other **(see illustration 6.3b)**, and seat the pads against the guide on the bracket **(see illustration)**.

6.3a Unscrew the pin (arrowed)...

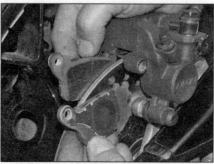

6.3b ...and remove the pads

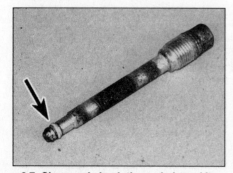

6.7 Clean and check the pad pin and its stopper ring (arrowed)

6.9 Make sure the correct shim is fitted to each pad

6.12a Make sure the inner end (arrowed) locates correctly against the guide...

Brakes, wheels and final drive 6•11

6.12b ...then press the pads up against the spring and insert the pin

7.2 Brake hose banjo bolt (arrowed)

7.5 Slide the caliper and bracket apart

Press them up against the spring to align the holes, then insert the pad pin and tighten it to the torque setting specified at the beginning of this Chapter (see illustration).
13 Operate the brake pedal until the pads contact the disc. Check the level of fluid in each reservoir and top-up if necessary (see Pre-ride checks).
14 Check the operation of the brakes before riding the motorcycle.

7 Rear brake caliper

⚠ **Warning:** Overhaul must be done in a spotlessly clean work area to avoid contamination and possible failure of the brake hydraulic system components. Do not, under any circumstances, use petroleum-based solvents to clean brake parts. Use clean DOT 4 brake fluid, dedicated brake cleaner or denatured alcohol only, as described. To prevent damage from spilled brake fluid, always cover paintwork when working on the braking system.

Note: If the caliper is in need of an overhaul it is best to drain all old brake fluid from the system, then fill with new fluid after the overhaul (see Section 11). On RA models, before draining the brake fluid read the information given in that Section regarding the refilling and bleeding of the system.

Removal

Note 1: If the caliper is being overhauled (usually due to a sticking piston or fluid leak) read through the entire procedure first and make sure that you have obtained all the new parts required, including some new DOT 4 brake fluid.

Note 2: Do not operate either brake while the caliper is off the disc.

1 On RA models displace the wheel sensor (see Section 14).
2 If the caliper is being completely removed or overhauled, unscrew the brake hose banjo bolt and detach the banjo union, noting its alignment with the caliper (see illustration). If the brake fluid has not been drained seal

the banjo union – one way of doing this is to fit a suitable bolt and nut with the old sealing washers (see illustration 3.2b). Note that new sealing washers will be required later.
3 If the caliper is being overhauled remove the brake pads (see Section 6).
4 Remove the rear wheel (see Section 18).
5 Slide the caliper and bracket apart (see illustration).
6 Remove the pad spring from the caliper and the guide from the bracket if required (see illustrations). Clean all old grease off the slider pins and rubber boots. Check the condition of the rubber boots and replace them with new ones if they have split.

Overhaul

7 Clean the exterior of the caliper with denatured alcohol or brake system cleaner. Have some clean rag ready to catch any spilled brake fluid.

7.6a Pad spring (A), slider pin (B) and rubber boot (C)...

7.9a Use compressed air to force the piston out...

8 To remove the piston you need either a supply of compressed air, or a piston removal tool, or if neither are available a good pair of external circlip removal pliers.
9 If you are using compressed air wedge some rag or a piece of wood between the piston and the inner side of the caliper (see illustration). Gradually and progressively apply the compressed air, starting with a fairly low pressure, to the fluid passage and allow the piston to ease out of the bore (see illustration).
10 If you are using a dedicated tool or circlip pliers grip the inner wall, then twist and pull the piston out, keeping it square to the bore wall (see illustration 3.8). Do not try to remove the piston by levering it out or by using pliers or other grips that may scratch the outer wall, unless you are prepared to fit a new piston, and possibly a new caliper.
11 If the piston is stuck in its bore due to corrosion the caliper should be replaced with

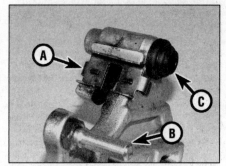
7.6b ...pad guide (A), slider pin (B) and rubber boot (C)

7.9b ...and remove it

6•12 Brakes, wheels and final drive

7.12 Remove the dust seal and piston seal

7.15a Lubricate the new piston seal with brake fluid...

7.15b ...then fit it into the lower groove

7.16 Lubricate the new dust seal with silicone grease and fit it into the upper groove

7.17a Fit the piston...

7.17b ...and push it all the way in

a new one. Do not try to remove the piston by levering it out or by using pliers or other grips.
12 Remove the dust seal and the piston seal from the caliper being careful not to scratch the bore **(see illustrations)**. Discard the seals as new ones must be fitted on reassembly.
13 Clean the piston and bore with clean brake fluid. If compressed air is available, blow it through the fluid passages to ensure they are clear (make sure it is filtered and unlubricated).
Caution: Do not, under any circumstances, use a petroleum-based solvent to clean brake parts.
14 Inspect the caliper bore and piston for signs of corrosion, nicks and burrs and loss of plating **(see illustration 3.12)**. If surface defects are present, the piston and/or the caliper assembly must be replaced with new ones. If the caliper is in poor condition, the master cylinder should also be checked.
15 Lubricate the new piston seal with clean brake fluid and fit it into the inner groove in the caliper bore **(see illustrations)**.
16 Lubricate the new dust seal with silicone grease and fit it into the outer groove in the caliper bore **(see illustration)**.
17 Lubricate the piston with clean brake fluid and fit it, closed-end first, into the caliper bore, taking care not to displace the seals **(see illustration)**. Using your thumbs, push the piston all the way in, making sure it enters the bore squarely **(see illustration)**.

Installation
18 If the pad spring was removed, make sure it is clean then fit it into the caliper, making sure

it locates correctly **(see illustration 7.6a)**. Make sure the pad guide on the bracket is clean and correctly fitted **(see illustration 7.6b)**.
19 Make sure the slider pins are tight. Smear the slider pins and inside the rubber boots with silicone grease.
20 Slide the caliper and bracket together, making sure each boot lip locates correctly in the groove in the pin **(see illustration 7.5)**.
21 Install the wheel (see Section 18).
22 If removed, install the brake pads (see Section 6).
23 If removed, connect the brake hose to the caliper, using new sealing washers on each side of the banjo fitting **(see illustration 3.18)**. Align the fitting as noted on removal **(see illustration 7.2)**. Tighten the banjo bolt to the specified torque setting.
24 On RA models install the wheel sensor (see Section 14).
25 Refer to Section 11 and fill and/or bleed the system as required. Check that there are

8.4 Rear brake disc bolts (arrowed)

no fluid leaks and test the operation of the brakes before riding the motorcycle.

8 Rear brake disc

Inspection
1 Refer to Section 4 of this Chapter, noting that the dial gauge should be attached to the swingarm.

Removal
Note: Honda recommend using new disc mounting bolts. This is because the bolts are pre-treated with a locking compound. It is possible, however, to clean up the old bolts and reinstall them using a suitable non-permanent thread locking compound that is commercially available.
2 Remove the rear wheel (see Section 18).
3 On RA models remove the pulse ring from the wheel (see Section 14).
Caution: Don't lay the wheel down and allow it to rest on the disc or sprocket – they could become warped. Set the wheel on wood blocks so the wheel rim supports the weight of the wheel.
4 If you are not replacing the disc with a new one, mark the relationship of the disc to the wheel so it can be installed in the same position. Unscrew the disc bolts, loosening them evenly and a little at a time in a criss-cross pattern to avoid distorting the disc, then remove the disc **(see illustration)**.

Installation

5 Before installing the disc, make sure there is no dirt or corrosion where the disc seats on the hub. If the disc does not sit flat when it is bolted down, it will appear to be warped when checked or when the rear brake is used.

6 Fit the disc on the wheel with its marked side facing out, aligning the previously applied marks (if you're reinstalling the original disc), and making sure the arrow points in the direction of normal rotation, matching the arrows on both the wheel and the tyre.

7 Either fit the new bolts, or clean the threads of the original bolts and apply fresh thread locking compound. Tighten the bolts evenly and a little at a time in a criss-cross pattern to the torque setting specified at the beginning of this Chapter. Clean the disc using acetone or brake system cleaner. If a new disc has been installed, remove any protective coating from its working surfaces and fit new brake pads.

8 On RA models fit the pulse ring onto the wheel (see Section 14).

9 Install the rear wheel (see Section 18).

10 Operate the brake pedal several times to bring the pads into contact with the disc. Check the operation of the brakes before riding the motorcycle.

9 Rear brake master cylinder

⚠ **Warning:** *Overhaul must be done in a spotlessly clean work area to avoid contamination and possible failure of the brake hydraulic system components. Do not, under any circumstances, use petroleum-based solvents to clean brake parts. Use clean DOT 4 brake fluid, dedicated brake cleaner or denatured alcohol only, as described. To prevent damage from spilled brake fluid, always cover paintwork when working on the braking system.*

Note: *If the master cylinder is in need of an overhaul it is best to drain all old brake fluid from the system, then fill with new fluid after the overhaul (see Section 11). On RA models, before draining the brake fluid read the information given in that Section regarding the refilling and bleeding of the system.*

Removal

Note: *If the master cylinder is being overhauled (usually due to sticking or poor action, or fluid leaks) read through the entire procedure first and make sure that you have obtained all the new parts required, including some new DOT 4 brake fluid.*

1 Unscrew the brake hose banjo bolt and detach the banjo union, noting its alignment with the master cylinder **(see illustration)**. If the brake fluid has not been drained seal the banjo union – one way of doing this is to fit a suitable bolt and nut with the old sealing washers **(see illustration 3.2b)**. Note that new sealing washers will be required later.

2 Remove the rear brake pedal (see Chapter 5, Section 3) – this procedure leaves the master cylinder and reservoir free.

Overhaul

3 If the system wasn't drained, on RR models undo the reservoir cap clamp screw and remove the clamp, then on all models remove the cap, diaphragm plate and diaphragm, and tip the fluid out, retrieving the float.

4 Undo the screw securing the reservoir to its bracket. Release the clip securing the reservoir hose to the union on the master cylinder and detach the hose, being prepared to catch any residual fluid. Check the hose for cracks or splits and replace it with a new one if necessary.

5 If required, release the circlip securing the reservoir hose union and detach the union from the master cylinder. Remove the O-ring – a new one must be used.

9.1 Brake hose banjo bolt (arrowed)

6 Mark the position of the clevis locknut on the pushrod, then loosen the locknut and thread the clevis and locknut off the pushrod.

7 Dislodge the rubber boot from the base of the master cylinder and from around the pushrod, noting how it locates, and remove it **(see illustration)**. Push the pushrod in and, using circlip pliers, remove the circlip from its groove in the master cylinder and remove the pushrod, piston and spring, noting how they fit **(see illustrations)**. Lay the parts out in order as you remove them to prevent confusion during reassembly.

8 Clean the master cylinder with clean brake fluid. If compressed air is available, blow it through the fluid galleries to ensure they are clear (make sure the air is filtered and unlubricated).

Caution: Do not, under any circumstances, use a petroleum-based solvent to clean brake parts.

9 Check the master cylinder bore for corrosion, scratches, nicks and score marks **(see illustration)**. If damage or wear is evident, the master cylinder must be replaced with a new one. If the master cylinder is in poor condition, then the caliper should be checked as well.

10 The dust boot, circlip, piston, seal, cup and spring are all included in the master cylinder rebuild kit. Use all of the new parts, regardless of the apparent condition of the old ones.

11 Fit the circlip and boot onto the pushrod, seating the lower lip of the boot in the groove in the pushrod.

9.7a Remove the rubber boot...

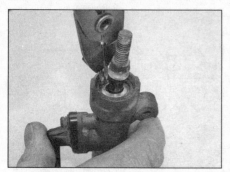

9.7b ...then release the circlip...

9.7c ...and remove the pushrod, piston and spring

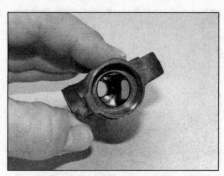

9.9 Check the cylinder for damage and wear

6•14 Brakes, wheels and final drive

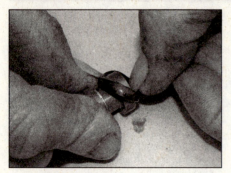
9.12a Fit the seal onto the piston...

9.12b ...as shown

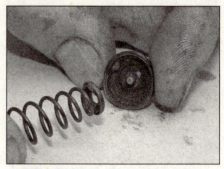
9.12c Fit the cup onto the end of the spring, locating the peg in the hole

12 Smear the cup and seal with new brake fluid. If the seal is not already on the piston, fit it into its groove so the wider end will fit into the master cylinder first **(see illustrations)**. Fit the cup onto the narrow end of the spring, locating the peg in the hole **(see illustration)**.

Lubricate the master cylinder bore with new brake fluid. Fit the new circlip onto the pushrod if not already in place.

13 Fit the spring wide-end first into the master cylinder and push the cup in, making sure its lips do not turn inside out **(see illustration)**.

14 Lubricate the piston with clean brake fluid and slide it into the master cylinder and up against the cup and spring **(see illustration)**. Make sure the lips on the seal do not turn inside out.

15 Smear some silicone grease onto the rounded end of the pushrod and around the lips of the boot. Push the piston in using the pushrod until the washer is beyond the circlip groove, then locate the circlip in the groove **(see illustrations)**. Carefully push the upper lip of the boot into the master cylinder, making sure it is seated correctly, and that the lower lip is still in its groove in pushrod **(see illustrations)**.

16 Thread the locknut and clevis onto the pushrod, setting them as noted on removal – Honda specify the distance between the centre of the clevis pin hole and the lower mounting bolt hole measured parallel to the pushrod should be 74 to 76 mm **(see illustration)**. Hold the clevis and tighten the locknut against it.

9.13 Fit the spring making sure the cup locates correctly in the bore...

9.14 ...then push the piston in

9.15a Position the circlip on the washer...

9.15b ...then depress the pushrod and fit the circlip into the groove

9.15c Fit the new boot...

9.15d ...then press it into the cylinder...

9.15e ...and make sure it is correctly located around the pushrod

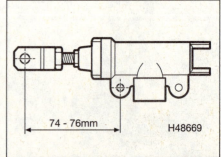
9.16 Set the eye of the clevis the specified distance from the mounting hole

Brakes, wheels and final drive

17 If removed fit a new fluid reservoir hose union O-ring smeared with brake fluid, then press the union into the master cylinder and secure it with a new circlip.
18 Connect the hose to the union on the master cylinder and secure it with the clip. Check that the hose is secured with a clip at the reservoir end as well. If the clips have weakened, use new ones. Fit the reservoir onto its bracket.

Installation

19 Refer to Section 3 in Chapter 5 and follow the procedure for installing the rear brake pedal.
20 Align the brake hose as noted on removal and connect the hose to the master cylinder, using a new sealing washer on each side of the banjo fitting **(see illustration 3.18)**. Tighten the banjo bolt to the torque setting specified at the beginning of this Chapter.
21 Refer to Section 11 and fill and/or bleed the system as required. Check that there are no fluid leaks and test the operation of the brakes before riding the motorcycle.

10 Brake hoses and fittings

Inspection

1 To fully inspect all the brake hoses and pipes on RA models remove the fairing side panels (see Chapter 7).
2 Check brake hose condition regularly (see Chapter 1). Twist and flex the hoses while looking for cracks, bulges and seeping hydraulic fluid. Check extra carefully around the areas where the hoses connect with the banjo fittings, as these are common areas for hose failure.
3 On RA models also check the brake pipes, the hose and pipe joints, the valve units and power units, referring to Section 14 of this Chapter, for signs of fluid leakage and for any dents or cracks in the pipes.
4 Inspect the banjo fittings connected to the brake hoses and on RA models also inspect the pipe joints. If the fittings are rusted, scratched or cracked, fit new ones.

Removal and installation

Note: *On RA models, before draining the brake fluid read the information given in that Section regarding the refilling and bleeding of the system.*
5 Drain all old brake fluid from the system (see Section 11).
6 The brake hoses have banjo fittings on each end. Cover the surrounding area with plenty of rags and unscrew the banjo bolt at each end of the hose, noting the alignment of the fitting with the master cylinder or brake caliper **(see illustrations 3.2a, 5.5, 7.2 and 9.1)**. Free the hose from any clips or guides and remove it, noting its routing. Discard the sealing washers.
Note: *Do not operate the brake lever or pedal while a brake hose is disconnected.*
7 Position the new hose, making sure it isn't twisted or otherwise strained, and ensure that it is correctly routed through any clips or guides and is clear of all moving components.
8 Check that the fittings align correctly, then install the banjo bolts, using new sealing washers on both sides of the fittings **(see illustration 3.18)**. Tighten the banjo bolts to the torque setting specified at the beginning of this Chapter.
9 On RA models the brake pipes are secured by nuts **(see illustration 14.25)**. There are no sealing washers. Unscrew the nuts and detach the pipes. Make sure the pipe is correctly positioned, fitted into any clips, and with any joint blocks secured, before tightening the nuts. If the correct tools are available tighten the nuts to the torque setting specified at the beginning of this Chapter.
10 Refill the system with new DOT 4 brake fluid (see *Pre-ride checks*) and bleed the air from it (see Section 11).
11 Check the operation of the brakes before riding the motorcycle.

11 Brake system bleeding and fluid change

RR models

Bleeding principles

1 Bleeding a brake is the process of removing aerated brake fluid from the master cylinder, the hose(s) and the brake caliper(s). Bleeding is necessary whenever a brake system hydraulic connection is loosened, after a component or hose is replaced with a new one, when a master cylinder or a caliper is overhauled, or when there is a spongy feel to the lever or pedal and it travels all the way to its stop, and where braking force is less than it should be, and it is not due to any mechanical fault in the system (i.e. a sticking piston in the caliper, or a pad that is not moving as it should due to corrosion, for example on the pad pin). Leaks in the system may also allow air to enter, but leaking brake fluid will reveal their presence and warn you of the need for repair.
2 Brake bleeding is considered by some as a bit of a black art – professional technicians sometimes have trouble getting a good firm feel in the brake lever, while a first timer may have no trouble at all. One of the problems is that you are working against natural principles – science dictates that air bubbles in a liquid will rise to the top, but the process entails pumping the brake fluid and any air bubbles it contains down, from the master cylinder at the top to the bleed valve in the caliper at the bottom, so while the fluid is moving down the air bubbles will try to rise. Air bubbles can also get trapped, particularly where there are high points in its path.
3 To bleed the brakes using the conventional method, you will need some new DOT 4 brake fluid, a length of clear flexible hose, a small container partially filled with clean brake fluid, some rags, and a spanner to fit the brake caliper bleed valve. Bleeding kits that include the hose, a one-way valve and a container are available relatively cheaply from a good auto store, and simplify the task.
4 Cover painted components to prevent damage in the event that brake fluid is spilled.
Caution: Brake fluid attacks painted finishes and some plastics – to prevent damage from spilled fluid, always cover paintwork when working on the braking system, and clean up any spills immediately using brake cleaner.

Bleeding the front brake system

5 Remove the reservoir cap clamp, cap, diaphragm plate and diaphragm **(see illustrations)**. Slowly pump the brake lever a few times to dislodge any air bubbles from the holes in the bottom of the reservoir.
6 Pull the dust cap off the master cylinder bleed valve **(see illustration)**. If using a

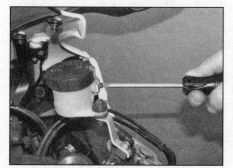

11.5a Undo the clamp screw...

11.5b ...and remove the cap, diaphragm plate and diaphragm

11.6 Master cylinder bleed valve (arrowed)

6•16 Brakes, wheels and final drive

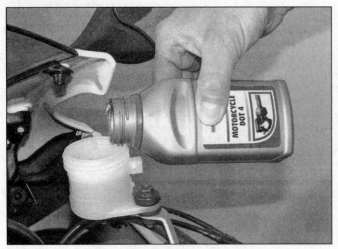
11.7 Keep the reservoir topped up

11.10a Fit the ring spanner over the valve then connect the hose...

11.10b ...and bleed the brake as described

11.13a Undo the clamp screw...

ring spanner (which is preferable to an open-ended one) fit it onto the valve **(see illustration 11.10a)**. Attach one end of the bleed hose to the bleed valve and, if not using a kit, submerge the other end in the clean brake fluid in the container **(see illustration 11.10b)**.

7 Check the fluid level in the reservoir – keep it topped up and do not allow the level to drop below the bottom of the window during the procedure **(see illustration)**.

8 Slowly pump the brake lever three or four times, then hold it in and open the bleed valve a quarter turn. When the valve is opened, brake fluid will flow out of the master cylinder into the clear tubing, and the lever will move toward the handlebar. If there is air in the top of the system there will be air bubbles in the brake fluid coming out of the master cylinder.

9 Tighten the bleed valve, then release the brake lever gradually. Repeat the process until no air bubbles are visible in the brake fluid leaving the master cylinder, and the lever is firm when applied, topping the reservoir up when necessary.

10 Now transfer the equipment to the bleed valve on the right-hand caliper, and repeat the bleeding procedure **(see illustrations)**. When all air has been removed, transfer the equipment to the bleed valve on the left-hand caliper, and repeat the bleeding procedure.

11 When the system has been successfully bled there should be a good and progressively firm feel as the lever is applied, and the lever should not be able to travel all the way back to the handlebar.

12 On completion remove the equipment used and make sure the bleed valve is tight (to the torque setting specified at the beginning of the Chapter if you have a suitable torque wrench), then fit the dust cap. Top-up the reservoir, then fit the diaphragm, diaphragm plate, cap and clamp **(see illustrations 11.5 and a)**. Check for spilled brake fluid and clean up as required. Check that there are no fluid leaks from the system and check the operation of the brake before riding the motorcycle.

Bleeding the rear brake system

13 Undo the cap clamp screw, then unscrew the cap and remove the diaphragm plate and diaphragm **(see illustrations)**. Slowly pump the brake pedal a few times to dislodge any air bubbles from the holes in the bottom of the reservoir.

14 Pull the dust cap off the caliper bleed

11.13b ...and remove the cap, diaphragm plate and diaphragm

Brakes, wheels and final drive 6•17

11.14a Pull the cap off the bleed valve...

11.14b ...then fit the ring spanner and connect the hose

11.15 Keep the reservoir topped up

valve (see illustration). If using a ring spanner (which is preferable to an open-ended one) fit it onto the valve (see illustration). Attach one end of the bleed hose to the bleed valve and, if not using a kit, submerge the other end in the clean brake fluid in the container.

15 Check the fluid level in the reservoir – keep it topped up and do not allow the level to drop below the bottom of the window during the procedure (see illustration).

16 Slowly pump the brake pedal three or four times, then hold it down and open the bleed valve a quarter turn (see illustration). When the valve is opened, brake fluid will flow out, and the pedal will move down. If there is air in the system there will be air bubbles in the brake fluid coming out of the caliper.

17 Tighten the bleed valve, then release the brake pedal gradually. Repeat the process until no air bubbles are visible in the brake fluid leaving the caliper, and the pedal is firm when applied, topping the reservoir up when necessary.

18 When the system has been successfully bled there should be a good and progressively firm feel as the pedal is applied.

19 On completion remove the equipment used and make sure the bleed valve is tight (to the torque setting specified at the beginning of the Chapter if you have a suitable torque wrench), then fit the dust cap. Top-up the reservoir, then fit the diaphragm, diaphragm plate and cover. Secure the cap with the clamp. Check for spilled brake fluid and clean up as required. Check that there are no fluid leaks from the system and check the operation of the brake before riding the motorcycle.

Bleeding problems

20 If it is not possible to produce a firm feel to the lever or pedal, remove the body panels as required (see Chapter 7) and look for any high point in the system in which a pocket of air may become trapped. Displace and move the hose so the bubble can be dislodged – tapping it may help. If necessary displace the master cylinder and/or the caliper(s), and free the brake hose(s) from its guides and move the parts around to dislodge the air and encourage it towards a bleed valve – refer to the relevant Sections as required to displace components.

21 If you are still having trouble the fluid may be full of many tiny air bubbles rather than a few big ones. To remedy this apply some pressure to the system, for the front brake by tying the front brake lever lightly back to the handlebar, and for the rear by tying a weight to the brake pedal – do not apply too much pressure or the cup and seals in the master cylinder and caliper may fail. Let the fluid stabilise for a few hours, after which the tiny bubbles should either have risen to the top in the reservoir, or have formed into one or more big bubbles that can be more easily bled out by repeating the bleeding procedure.

22 If bleeding the system using the conventional tools and methods stated does not give satisfactory results, you can use a vacuum-type brake bleeding tool, such as the Mity-vac shown, following the manufacturer's instructions (see illustration). This type of tool sucks the fluid out by creating a vacuum at the bleed valve. Users may find that air is sucked past the bleed valve threads (air provides less resistance to the vacuum than the brake fluid) where it mixes with the fluid being drawn out. If this is the case the vacuum applied may be too great, or the bleed valve may have been loosened too much. One way to get round this is to remove the bleed valve and thread some PTFE tape around its threads, but note that doing so will be a bit messy, so have some rag to hand. Also make sure the hose from the brake bleeding tool forms an air-tight fit over the bleed valve head, otherwise air will be drawn in from around the valve head.

Fluid change

23 Changing the brake fluid is a similar process to bleeding the brake and requires

11.16 Bleeding the rear brake

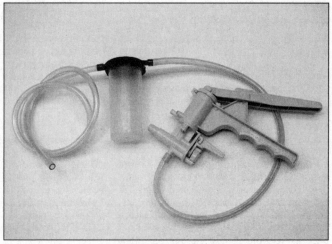
11.22 Vacuum-type brake bleeding tool

the same materials plus a suitable tool (such as a syringe, or alternatively lots of absorbent rag or paper) for siphoning the fluid out of the reservoir.

24 Remove the reservoir cap or cover, diaphragm plate and diaphragm and siphon the old fluid out of the reservoir **(see illustrations 11.5a and b (front) or 11.13a and b (rear))**. Wipe the reservoir clean. Fill the reservoir with new brake fluid **(see illustration 11.7 (front) or 11.15 (rear))**.

25 Connect the brake bleeding hose to the caliper bleed valve (see Step 10 (front) and Step 14 (rear)). Slowly pump the brake lever or pedal three or four times then hold it in and open the bleed valve. When the valve is opened, brake fluid will flow out of the caliper into the clear tubing, and the lever will move toward the handlebar, or the pedal will move down.

26 Tighten the bleed valve, then release the brake lever or pedal gradually. Keep the reservoir topped-up with new fluid at all times or air may enter the system and greatly increase the length of the task. Repeat the process until new fluid can be seen emerging from the caliper bleed valve.

 Old brake fluid is invariably much darker in colour than new fluid, making it easy to see when all old fluid has been expelled from the system.

27 Check the operation of the brakes before riding the motorcycle. If the lever or pedal action is spongy, carry out the bleeding operation as described above.

Draining the system for overhaul

28 Draining the brake fluid is again a similar process to bleeding the brakes. The quickest and easiest way is to use a vacuum-type brake bleeding tool (see Step 22). Otherwise follow the procedure described above for changing the fluid, but quite simply do not put any new fluid into the reservoir – the system fills itself with air instead.

RA (C-ABS) models

29 Refilling and bleeding the combined anti-lock braking system on RA models is extremely complex. Honda state that it must be carried out by a qualified Honda technician.
30 This does not mean to say that you cannot work on the C-ABS system yourself according to the procedures given in this manual, but it does mean that you must take the bike to a Honda dealer afterwards, and before you ride the bike, to perform the procedure.
31 If you are draining the fluid before removing a master cylinder, caliper or valve unit, follow the procedure given in Step 28, but note that in the case of the valve units, and also the power units, there is going to be a certain amount of residual fluid that cannot be drained from all the various passages within the units (due to valves that will remain closed), and in the brake pipes.

12 C-ABS operation – RA models

System operation

1 The C-ABS (combined anti-lock brake system) electronically controls synchronisation of the front and rear brake systems to provide optimum braking distribution and balance, and hence stability, and prevents the wheels from locking up under hard braking or on uneven road surfaces. The front and rear systems are not linked directly as in a conventional combined or linked system. Instead each system has a valve unit and a power unit that are linked hydraulically between its master cylinder and caliper(s). Both the valve and power units are linked electronically to the C-ABS control unit.
2 When the front brake lever or rear brake pedal is applied hydraulic pressure is applied directly to the front or rear brake caliper(s) via the front or rear valve unit. A pressure sensor in the valve unit provides information on the brake pressure being applied.
3 If the amount of applied pressure exceeds a pre-determined level the system goes from standby to operational mode, and a valve in the direct hydraulic link between master cylinder and caliper closes and thereafter the applied pressure is read by a second pressure sensor and a stroke simulator inside a second circuit in the valve unit. This information is passed to the control unit, and then the actual pressure applied to the caliper is controlled electronically via the power unit, that contains a stepper motor acting on a piston in a third hydraulic circuit from the power unit and through the valve unit.
4 At the same time each wheel transmits information about its speed of rotation to the C-ABS control unit. Using this information in conjunction with the information on applied pressure the control unit also computes whether some rear brake is needed even though only the front lever is applied, or vice versa, and if so sends a signal to the power unit of the required system that in turn applies hydraulic pressure via the valve unit of that system to the caliper(s). If the control unit senses that a wheel is about to lock, it releases brake pressure to that wheel momentarily, preventing a lock-up.

System self-diagnosis

5 The C-ABS is self-checking and is activated when the ignition switch is turned on – the ABS indicator light in the instrument cluster will come on and will remain on until road speed increases above 4 mph (6 kmh) at which point, if the system is normal, the light will go off. **Note:** *If the ABS indicator light does not come on when the ignition is turned on, or if it stays on but no fault code is given, refer to Steps 88-on in Section 13.* When the ignition is off and at speeds up to 4 mph (6 kmh) the braking system acts conventionally, i.e. without combined and ABS functions.
6 If the indicator light remains on, or starts flashing while the machine is being ridden, there is a fault in the system and the ABS function will be switched off – the brakes will still function but in conventional mode. If you turn the ignition OFF while the light is flashing, the fault code will not be displayed again if the ignition is switched on again, but will be stored in the system's memory.
7 The indicator light emits long (1.3 second) and short (0.3 second) flashes to give out the fault code. A long flash is used to indicate the first digit of the double digit fault code. For example, two long (1.3 sec) flashes followed by three short (0.3 sec) flashes indicates the fault code 2-3. If there is more than one fault code, there will be a 3.6 sec gap before the next code is revealed (the codes will be revealed in ascending numerical order). Once all codes have been revealed, the display will continuously run through the code(s) stored in its memory, revealing each one in turn with a short gap between them. The fault codes are shown in the table in Section 13.
8 To retrieve any stored fault codes, remove the EGCV servo cover (see Chapter 4) to gain access to the service check connector, which is a red 3-pin connector with two wires **(see illustration)**. Ensure the ignition is switched OFF. Release the connector. Using a short jumper wire, connect between the brown and green wire terminals in the connector. With the terminals connected, turn the ignition ON and observe the ABS warning light. If there are stored fault codes, the light will come on for 2 seconds, then go out for 3.6 seconds, then start to flash the fault code. If the light comes on and stays on without flashing after the 3.6 second gap no fault codes are stored. Do not apply the brake lever or pedal during code retrieval.
9 Turn the ignition switch OFF and remove the jumper wire when the code or codes have been recorded.
10 To check the ABS components see Section 14.
11 Once the fault has been corrected, erase the fault code(s) as follows. Follow Step 8 to

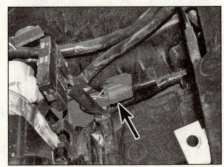

12.8 C-ABS service check connector (arrowed – shown from the top with battery removed)

connect the terminals in the service check connector. Hold the front brake lever on and with the kill switch set to RUN turn the ignition switch on – the ABS light should come on for two seconds, then go out. When the light goes out immediately release the brake lever – the light should come on. When the light comes on immediately re-apply the brake lever – the light should go out. When the light goes out immediately release the brake lever. The code(s) should now be erased, in which case the light will flash twice, then come on and stay on.

12 Turn the ignition switch OFF and remove the jumper wire when the code or codes have been erased. Check that the ABS is operating normally (see Step 5). If necessary, repeat the fault code retrieval and reset procedure.

 The ABS indicator may indicate a fault if tyre sizes other than those specified by Honda are fitted, if the tyre pressures are incorrect, if the machine has been run continuously over bumpy roads, if the front wheel comes off the ground whilst riding (wheelie) or if the machine is on an auxiliary stand with the engine running and the rear wheel turning.

13 C-ABS fault diagnosis – RA models

1 If a fault is indicated in the C-ABS, first check that the battery is fully charged, then check the C-ABS fuses (see Chapter 8).
2 Unless specified otherwise, carry-out all checks with the ignition switch OFF.
3 Refer to Chapter 8, Section 2, for general electrical fault finding procedures and equipment.
4 If after a thorough check, the source of a fault has not been identified, have the C-ABS tested by a Honda dealer.

Note: *Before carrying out any of the checks, follow the procedure in Section 12 to reset the control unit memory, then activate the self-checking procedure. If the fault code is the result of unusual riding or conditions and the ABS is normal, the indicator light will go off. Also make sure that the fault is not due to a loose wiring connector or broken terminal related to the components identified by the fault code, referring to Section 14 for access to the wiring connectors. Otherwise perform the following checks – to perform wiring continuity checks two special probes are required to attach to the terminals in the wiring connectors, available from Honda (Pt No 07ZAJ-RDJA110), or otherwise obtain commercially available equivalents.*

Fault codes	Faulty component or system
1-1	Front wheel speed sensor circuit, front wheel speed sensor, front wheel pulse ring
1-2	Rear wheel speed sensor circuit, rear wheel speed sensor, rear wheel pulse ring
1-3	You've done a wheelie!
1-4	Front wheel speed sensor circuit, front wheel speed sensor, front wheel pulse ring
1-5	Rear wheel speed sensor circuit, rear wheel speed sensor, rear wheel pulse ring
1-6	Front wheel speed sensor circuit, front wheel speed sensor, front wheel pulse ring
1-7	Rear wheel speed sensor circuit, rear wheel speed sensor, rear wheel pulse ring
1-8	Front wheel speed sensor circuit, front wheel speed sensor, front wheel pulse ring
1-9	Rear wheel speed sensor circuit, rear wheel speed sensor, rear wheel pulse ring
2-1	Battery voltage low or zero, blown fuse
2-2	C-ABS control unit
2-3	C-ABS control unit, or high voltage input to control unit
2-5	Pressure sensor input voltage to control unit
3-1	Front master cylinder pressure sensor
3-2	Rear master cylinder pressure sensor
3-3	Front brake caliper pressure sensor
3-4	Rear brake caliper pressure sensor
3-5	Front master cylinder pressure sensor
3-6	Rear master cylinder pressure sensor
3-7	Front brake caliper pressure sensor
3-8	Rear brake caliper pressure sensor
3-9	Front master cylinder pressure sensor
3-10	Rear master cylinder pressure sensor
3-11	Front valve unit or control unit
3-12	Rear valve unit or control unit
4-1	Front valve unit or control unit
4-2	Rear valve unit or control unit
4-3	Front valve unit
4-4	Rear valve unit
4-5	Front valve unit or control unit
4-6	Rear valve unit or control unit
5-1	Front power unit, incomplete bleeding procedure
5-2	Rear power unit, incomplete bleeding procedure
5-3	Front power unit, incomplete bleeding procedure, front caliper piston
5-4	Rear power unit, incomplete bleeding procedure, rear caliper piston
5-5	Front brake continuously applied from 0 to 31 mph (50 km/h)
5-6	Rear brake continuously applied from 0 to 31 mph (50 km/h)
6-1	Front valve unit solenoid
6-2	Front valve unit solenoid
6-3	Front valve unit solenoid
6-4	Rear valve unit solenoid
6-5	Rear valve unit solenoid
6-6	Rear valve unit solenoid
7-1	Front power unit drive circuit
7-2	Rear power unit drive circuit
7-3	Front power unit earth circuit short
7-4	Rear power unit earth circuit short
7-5	Front valve unit solenoid
7-6	Rear valve unit solenoid
8-1 to 8-4	Control unit
9-1 to 9-3	Control unit
10-1 to 10-10	Control unit

6•20 Brakes, wheels and final drive

Fault codes 1-1 and 1-6

5 Measure the air gap between the front wheel speed sensor and the pulse ring with a feeler gauge at several points (by rotating the wheel), then compare the result with the Specification at the beginning of this Chapter **(see illustration)**. The gap is not adjustable – if it is outside the specification, check that the sensor and pulse ring fixings are tight, that the components are not damaged and that there is no dirt or anything else on the sensor tip or between the slots in the pulse ring. If any of the components are damaged they must be replaced with new ones (Section 14).

6 If all appears good refer to Section 14 and disconnect the wheel sensor wiring connector and the C-ABS control unit black 21-pin wiring connector. Check for continuity first in the blue wire between the control unit wiring connector and the loom side of the sensor wiring connector and then in the white wire – there should be continuity in each wire. If not locate and repair the break. Also check that neither wire shows continuity to earth.

7 If there is continuity in the wiring next check for continuity between each terminal in the sensor side of the sensor connector and earth (ground). If there is continuity in either of the wires the sensor is faulty and must be replaced with a new one.

8 If all the checks have failed to identify the fault, replace the wheel sensor with a known good one. Connect all wiring connectors then follow the procedure in Section 12 to reset the control unit memory, then activate the self-checking procedure. If the indicator light is no longer flashing, the original sensor was faulty. If the fault code reappears have the control unit checked by a Honda dealer.

Fault codes 1-2 and 1-7

9 Measure the air gap between the rear wheel speed sensor and the pulse ring with a feeler gauge at several points (by rotating the wheel), then compare the result with the Specification at the beginning of this Chapter **(see illustration)**. The gap is not adjustable – if it is outside the specification, check that the sensor and pulse ring fixings are tight, that the components are not damaged and that there is no dirt or anything else on the sensor tip or between the slots in the pulse ring. If any of the components are damaged they must be replaced with new ones (Section 14).

10 If all appears good refer to Section 14 and disconnect the wheel sensor wiring connector and the C-ABS control unit grey 21-pin wiring connector. Check for continuity first in the blue wire between the control unit wiring connector and the loom side of the sensor wiring connector and then in the white wire – there should be continuity in each wire. If not locate and repair the break. Also check that neither wire shows continuity to earth.

11 If there is continuity in the wiring next check for continuity between each terminal in the sensor side of the sensor connector and earth (ground). If there is continuity in either of the wires the sensor is faulty and must be replaced with a new one.

12 If all the checks have failed to identify the fault, replace the wheel sensor with a known good one. Connect all wiring connectors then follow the procedure in Section 12 to reset the control unit memory, then activate the self-checking procedure. If the indicator light is no longer flashing, the original sensor was faulty. If the fault code reappears have the control unit checked by a Honda dealer.

Fault code 1-4 or 1-5

13 See Steps 5 and 8 for code 1-4, or Steps 9 and 12 for code 1-5.

Fault code 1-8 or 1-9

14 See Steps 6 to 8 for code 1-8, or 10 to 12 for code 1-9.

Fault code 2-1

15 Check the battery voltage and the ABS fuses (see Chapter 8).

16 If all appears good check the wiring between the fusebox and the C-ABS control unit 5-pin connectors.

Fault code 3-1

17 Refer to Section 14 and disconnect the black 21-pin wiring connectors from the control unit and front valve unit.

18 Check for continuity in the black wire between the control unit wiring connector and the valve unit wiring connector – there should be continuity. If not locate and repair the break. Also check that the wire does not show continuity to earth.

19 If all is good erase the fault code (see Section 12). Start the engine and go for a short ride so the C-ABS system performs its self-diagnosis. If the ABS indicator light flashes the same fault code, replace the front valve unit with a new one (Section 14). If the code appears again replace the control unit with a new one.

Fault code 3-2

20 Refer to Section 14 and disconnect the black 21-pin connectors from the control unit and rear valve unit.

21 Check for continuity in the blue wire between the control unit wiring connector and the valve unit wiring connector – there should be continuity. If not locate and repair the break. Also check that the wire does not show continuity to earth.

22 If all is good erase the fault code (see Section 12). Start the engine and go for a short ride so the C-ABS system performs its self-diagnosis. If the ABS indicator light flashes the same fault code, replace the rear valve unit with a new one (Section 14). If the code appears again replace the control unit with a new one.

Fault code 3-3

23 Refer to Section 14 and disconnect the black 21-pin wiring connectors from the control unit and front valve unit.

24 Check for continuity in the red/white wire between the control unit wiring connector and the valve unit wiring connector – there should be continuity. If not locate and repair the break. Also check that the wire does not show continuity to earth.

25 If all is good erase the fault code (see Section 12). Start the engine and go for a short ride so the C-ABS system performs its self-diagnosis. If the ABS indicator light flashes the same fault code, replace the front valve unit with a new one (Section 14). If the code appears again replace the control unit with a new one.

Fault code 3-4

26 Refer to Section 14 and disconnect the black 21-pin connectors from the control unit and rear valve unit.

27 Check for continuity in the white wire between the control unit wiring connector and the valve unit wiring connector – there should be continuity. If not locate and repair the break. Also check that the wire does not show continuity to earth.

28 If all is good erase the fault code (see Section 12). Start the engine and go for a short ride so the C-ABS system performs its self-diagnosis. If the ABS indicator light flashes the same fault code, replace the rear valve unit with a new one (Section 14). If the code appears again replace the control unit with a new one.

Fault code 3-5

29 Refer to Section 14 and disconnect the black 21-pin wiring connectors from the control unit and front valve unit.

13.5 Measuring front wheel speed sensor air gap

13.9 Measuring rear wheel speed sensor air gap

Brakes, wheels and final drive 6•21

30 Check for continuity in the black and brown wires between the control unit wiring connector and the valve unit wiring connector – there should be continuity. If not locate and repair the break. Also check that the wires do not show continuity to earth.
31 If all is good erase the fault code (see Section 12). Start the engine and go for a short ride so the C-ABS system performs its self-diagnosis. If the ABS indicator light flashes the same fault code, replace the front valve unit with a new one (Section 14). If the code appears again replace the control unit with a new one.

Fault code 3-6
32 Refer to Section 14 and disconnect the black 21-pin connectors from the control unit and rear valve unit.
33 Check for continuity in the blue and brown wires between the control unit wiring connector and the valve unit wiring connector – there should be continuity. If not locate and repair the break. Also check that the wires do not show continuity to earth.
34 If all is good erase the fault code (see Section 12). Start the engine and go for a short ride so the C-ABS system performs its self-diagnosis. If the ABS indicator light flashes the same fault code, replace the rear valve unit with a new one (Section 14). If the code appears again replace the control unit with a new one.

Fault code 3-7
35 Refer to Section 14 and disconnect the black 21-pin wiring connectors from the control unit and front valve unit.
36 Check for continuity in the red/white and yellow wires between the control unit wiring connector and the valve unit wiring connector – there should be continuity. If not locate and repair the break. Also check that the wires do not show continuity to earth.
37 If all is good erase the fault code (see Section 12). Start the engine and go for a short ride so the C-ABS system performs its self-diagnosis. If the ABS indicator light flashes the same fault code, replace the front valve unit with a new one (Section 14). If the code appears again replace the control unit with a new one.

Fault code 3-8
38 Refer to Section 14 and disconnect the black 21-pin connectors from the control unit and rear valve unit.
39 Check for continuity in the white and yellow wires between the control unit wiring connector and the valve unit wiring connector – there should be continuity. If not locate and repair the break. Also check that the wires do not show continuity to earth.
40 If all is good erase the fault code (see Section 12). Start the engine and go for a short ride so the C-ABS system performs its self-diagnosis. If the ABS indicator light flashes the same fault code, replace the rear valve unit with a new one (Section 14). If the code appears again replace the control unit with a new one.

Fault code 3-9
41 Refer to Section 14 and disconnect the black 21-pin wiring connectors from the control unit and front valve unit.
42 Check for continuity in the white wire between the control unit wiring connector and the valve unit wiring connector – there should be continuity. If not locate and repair the break. Also check that the wire does not show continuity to earth.
43 If all is good erase the fault code (see Section 12). Start the engine and go for a short ride so the C-ABS system performs its self-diagnosis. If the ABS indicator light flashes the same fault code, replace the front valve unit with a new one (Section 14). If the code appears again replace the control unit with a new one.

Fault code 3-10
44 Refer to Section 14 and disconnect the black 21-pin connectors from the control unit and rear valve unit.
45 Check for continuity in the black wire between the control unit wiring connector and the valve unit wiring connector – there should be continuity. If not locate and repair the break. Also check that the wire does not show continuity to earth.
46 If all is good erase the fault code (see Section 12). Start the engine and go for a short ride so the C-ABS system performs its self-diagnosis. If the ABS indicator light flashes the same fault code, replace the rear valve unit with a new one (Section 14). If the code appears again replace the control unit with a new one.

Fault code 3-11, 4-1 or 4-5
47 Replace the front valve unit with a new one (Section 14).
48 Erase the fault code (see Section 12). Start the engine and go for a short ride so the C-ABS system performs its self-diagnosis. If the ABS indicator light flashes the same fault code, replace the control unit with a new one.

Fault code 3-12, 4-2 or 4-6
49 Replace the rear valve unit with a new one (Section 14).
50 Erase the fault code (see Section 12). Start the engine and go for a short ride so the C-ABS system performs its self-diagnosis. If the ABS indicator light flashes the same fault code, replace the control unit with a new one.

Fault code 4-3
51 Erase the fault code (see Section 12). Start the engine and go for a short ride so the C-ABS system performs its self-diagnosis. If the ABS indicator light flashes the same fault code, replace the front valve unit with a new one (Section 14).

Fault code 4-4
52 Erase the fault code (see Section 12). Start the engine and go for a short ride so the C-ABS system performs its self-diagnosis. If the ABS indicator light flashes the same fault code, replace the rear valve unit with a new one (Section 14).

Fault code 5-1
53 Bleed the system (Section 11).
54 Erase the fault code (see Section 12). Start the engine and go for a short ride so the C-ABS system performs its self-diagnosis. If the ABS indicator light flashes the same fault code, replace the front power unit with a new one (Section 14).
55 Erase the fault code (see Section 12). Start the engine and go for a short ride so the C-ABS system performs its self-diagnosis. If the ABS indicator light flashes the same fault code, replace the front valve unit with a new one (Section 14).

Fault code 5-2
56 Bleed the system (Section 11).
57 Erase the fault code (see Section 12). Start the engine and go for a short ride so the C-ABS system performs its self-diagnosis. If the ABS indicator light flashes the same fault code, replace the rear power unit with a new one (Section 14).
58 Erase the fault code (see Section 12). Start the engine and go for a short ride so the C-ABS system performs its self-diagnosis. If the ABS indicator light flashes the same fault code, replace the rear valve unit with a new one (Section 14).

Fault code 5-3
59 With the ignition off, pump the brake lever and check that the pistons in the front calipers are pushing the pads against the disc. Check for correct installation of the pads, or if the calipers have been overhauled check the pistons are correctly installed and not jammed.
60 Erase the fault code (see Section 12). Start the engine and go for a short ride so the C-ABS system performs its self-diagnosis. If the ABS indicator light flashes the same fault code, bleed the system (Section 11).
61 Erase the fault code (see Section 12). Start the engine and go for a short ride so the C-ABS system performs its self-diagnosis. If the ABS indicator light flashes the same fault code, replace the front power unit with a new one (Section 14).
62 Erase the fault code (see Section 12). Start the engine and go for a short ride so the C-ABS system performs its self-diagnosis. If the ABS indicator light flashes the same fault code, replace the front valve unit with a new one (Section 14).

Fault code 5-4
63 With the ignition off pump the brake pedal and check that the piston in the rear caliper is pushing the pads against the disc. Check

for correct installation of the pads and that the caliper is sliding correctly on its bracket, or if the caliper has been overhauled check the piston is correctly installed and not jammed.
64 Erase the fault code (see Section 12). Start the engine and go for a short ride so the C-ABS system performs its self-diagnosis. If the ABS indicator light flashes the same fault code, bleed the system (Section 11).
65 Erase the fault code (see Section 12). Start the engine and go for a short ride so the C-ABS system performs its self-diagnosis. If the ABS indicator light flashes the same fault code, replace the rear power unit with a new one (Section 14).
66 Erase the fault code (see Section 12). Start the engine and go for a short ride so the C-ABS system performs its self-diagnosis. If the ABS indicator light flashes the same fault code, replace the rear valve unit with a new one (Section 14).

Fault code 5-5
67 Erase the fault code (see Section 12). Start the engine and go for a short ride so the C-ABS system performs its self-diagnosis. Check for a fault code.

Fault code 5-6
68 Erase the fault code (see Section 12). Start the engine and go for a short ride so the C-ABS system performs its self-diagnosis. Check for a fault code.

Fault code 6-1, 6-2, 6-3 or 7-5
69 Refer to Section 14 and disconnect the black 21-pin wiring connectors from the control unit and front valve unit.
70 Check for continuity in the green/pink, black/red, green/orange, black/pink, green/red and black/orange wires between the control unit wiring connector and the valve unit wiring connector – there should be continuity in each wire. If not locate and repair the break. Also check that the wires do not show continuity to earth.
71 If all is good erase the fault code (see Section 12). Start the engine and go for a short ride so the C-ABS system performs its self-diagnosis. If the ABS indicator light flashes the same fault code, replace the front valve unit with a new one (Section 14). If the code appears again replace the control unit with a new one.

Fault code 6-4, 6-5, 6-6 or 7-6
72 Refer to Section 14 and disconnect the black 21-pin connectors from the control unit and rear valve unit.
73 Check for continuity in the light green/white, blue/red, light green/black, blue/pink, light green/red and blue/orange wires between the control unit wiring connector and the valve unit wiring connector – there should be continuity in each wire. If not locate and repair the break. Also check that the wires do not show continuity to earth.
74 If all is good erase the fault code (see Section 12). Start the engine and go for a short ride so the C-ABS system performs its self-diagnosis. If the ABS indicator light flashes the same fault code, replace the rear valve unit with a new one (Section 14). If the code appears again replace the control unit with a new one.

Fault code 7-1
75 Refer to Section 14 and disconnect the black 5-pin wiring connector from the control unit and the black 2-pin wiring connector from the front power unit.
76 Check for continuity in the red and black wires between the control unit wiring connector and the power unit wiring connector – there should be continuity. If not locate and repair the break. Also check that the wires do not show continuity to earth.
77 If all is good erase the fault code (see Section 12). Start the engine and go for a short ride so the C-ABS system performs its self-diagnosis. If the ABS indicator light flashes the same fault code, replace the control unit with a new one (Section 14). If the code appears again replace the front power unit with a new one.

Fault code 7-2
78 Refer to Section 14 and disconnect the grey 5-pin wiring connector from the control unit and the black 2-pin wiring connector from the rear power unit.
79 Check for continuity in the red and black wires between the control unit wiring connector and the power unit wiring connector – there should be continuity. If not locate and repair the break. Also check that the wires do not show continuity to earth.
80 If all is good erase the fault code (see Section 12). Start the engine and go for a short ride so the C-ABS system performs its self-diagnosis. If the ABS indicator light flashes the same fault code, replace the control unit with a new one (Section 14). If the code appears again replace the rear power unit with a new one.

Fault code 7-3
81 Refer to Section 14 and disconnect the black 2-pin wiring connector from the front power unit.
82 Check for continuity to earth in the black wire – there should be no continuity. If there is, locate the short circuit and repair the wire.
83 If the wire is good erase the fault code (see Section 12). Start the engine and go for a short ride so the C-ABS system performs its self-diagnosis. If the ABS indicator light flashes the same fault code, replace the control unit with a new one (Section 14).

Fault code 7-4
84 Refer to Section 14 and disconnect the black 2-pin wiring connector from the rear power unit.
85 Check for continuity to earth in the black wire – there should be no continuity. If there is, locate the short circuit and repair the wire.
86 If the wire is good erase the fault code (see Section 12). Start the engine and go for a short ride so the C-ABS system performs its self-diagnosis. If the ABS indicator light flashes the same fault code, replace the control unit with a new one (Section 14).

Fault code 2-2, 2-3, 2-5, 8-1, 8-2, 8-3, 8-4, 9-1, 9-2, 9-3, all 10- codes
87 Erase the fault code (see Section 12). Start the engine and go for a short ride so the C-ABS system performs its self-diagnosis. If the ABS indicator light flashes the same fault code, replace the control unit with a new one (Section 14).

No ABS indicator light
88 If the ABS indicator light does not come on with the ignition switch, check the instrument cluster power input and earth wires (see Chapter 8).
89 If all is good, refer to Section 14 and disconnect the black 5-pin connector from the control unit. Turn the ignition on – if the light comes on the control unit is faulty.
90 If the light does not come on, check for continuity in the orange/green wire between the control unit wiring connector and the instrument wiring connector – there should be continuity. If not locate and repair the break. Also check that the wire does not show continuity to earth.

ABS indicator light on, no fault code
91 If the ABS indicator light stays on the whole time, check the C-ABS 10A fuse (see Chapter 8). If the fuse has blown, remove it. Refer to Section 14 and disconnect the grey 5-pin wiring connector from the control unit. Check for continuity in the orange/black wire terminal in the connector to earth. If there is continuity, repair the wire. If not replace the blown fuse with a new one. Connect all wiring connectors then follow the procedure in Section 12 to reset the control unit memory, then activate the self-checking procedure. If the fault code is no longer shown there was a temporary fault.
92 If the fuse has not blown, refer to Section 14 and disconnect the grey 5-pin wiring connector from the control unit. Check for battery voltage at the orange/black wire terminal in the connector with the ignition on. If there is no voltage check the wire from the connector to the fusebox for continuity.
93 If there is voltage check for continuity in the green wire terminal in the connector to earth. If there is no continuity, repair the wire.
94 If there is continuity, refer to Chapter 8 and access the instrument cluster wiring connector. Using a suitable probe and jumper wire short the orange/green wire in the instrument cluster wiring connector to earth with the connector still connected and the ignition ON. If the ABS indicator light stays on the instrument cluster PCB is faulty (see Chapter 8).

Brakes, wheels and final drive 6•23

95 If the ABS indicator light goes out repeat the check in the previous step at the 5-pin black wiring connector on the control unit. If the ABS indicator light stays on there is a break in the orange/green wire.

96 If the light goes out short between the orange/green and green wire terminals in the control unit connector using a jumper wire with the ignition on. If the ABS light goes out the control unit is faulty. If the light stays on check the green wire for continuity to earth – if there is none repair the wire.

14 C-ABS components – RA models

Front wheel sensor

1 Remove the left-hand fairing side panel (see Chapter 7). On 2012-on models remove the air duct (see Chapter 4, Section 3). Lift the rubber heat shield and disconnect the orange 2-pin wiring connector **(see illustration)**.
2 Release the sensor wiring clamps and feed the connector down to the sensor, noting its routing. Unscrew the sensor bolts and remove the sensor **(see illustration)**.
3 Make sure the tip of the sensor, its mounting surfaces, and the pulse ring are clean. Fit the sensor and tighten the bolts. Feed the wiring up to the connector, routing and securing it as noted on removal.
4 Check the air gap (see Section 13, Step 5). Install the fairing panel.

Front pulse ring

5 Remove the front wheel (see Section 17).
6 Undo the screws securing the ring and lift it off **(see illustration)**.
7 Ensure there is no dirt or corrosion where the ring seats on the hub – if the ring does not sit flat when it is installed the sensor air gap will be incorrect. Clean the threads of the bolts and apply a non-permanent thread locking compound (or alternatively use new bolts from Honda which come pre-treated) and tighten them to the torque setting specified at the beginning of the Chapter.
8 Install the front wheel (see Section 17). Check the sensor air gap (see Section 13, Step 5).

Rear wheel sensor

9 Remove the fuel tank (see Chapter 4). Disconnect the orange 2-pin wiring connector **(see illustration)**.
10 Release the sensor wiring clamps and feed the connector down to the sensor, noting its routing. Unscrew the sensor bolts and remove the sensor **(see illustration)**.
11 Make sure the tip of the sensor, its mounting surfaces, and the pulse ring are clean. Fit the sensor and tighten the bolts. Feed the wiring up to the connector, routing and securing it as noted on removal.
12 Check the air gap (see Section 13, Step 9). Install the fuel tank (see Chapter 4).

Rear pulse ring

13 Remove the rear wheel (see Section 18).
14 Undo the screws securing the ring and lift it off **(see illustration)**.
15 Ensure there is no dirt or corrosion where the ring seats on the hub – if the ring does not sit flat when it is installed the sensor air gap will be incorrect. Clean the threads of the bolts and apply a non-permanent thread locking compound (or alternatively use new bolts from Honda which come pre-treated) and tighten them to the torque setting specified at the beginning of the Chapter.
16 Install the rear wheel (see Section 18). Check the sensor air gap (see Section 13, Step 9).

C-ABS control unit

17 On 2009 to 2011 models remove the seat cowling (see Chapter 7). Displace the fuse/relay box **(see illustration 14.18a)**. Disconnect the rear sub-loom wiring connectors **(see illustration 14.18b)**. Undo the two screws on the top and the four bolts on the underside, noting the washers, and remove the rear light/turn signal/licence plate assembly, noting the routing of the wiring **(see illustration 14.18e)**. Remove the collars for the bolts fitted on the top of the tray for safekeeping if loose.

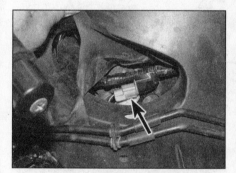

14.1 Lift the shield to access the wiring connector (arrowed)

14.2 Front wheel sensor bolts (arrowed)

14.6 Front wheel pulse ring (arrowed)

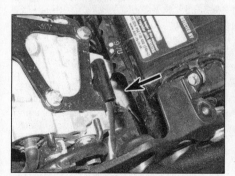

14.9 Rear wheel sensor wiring connector (arrowed)

14.10 Rear wheel sensor bolts (arrowed)

14.14 Rear wheel pulse ring (arrowed)

6•24 Brakes, wheels and final drive

14.18a Lift the box off its clip...

14.18b ...and disconnect the wiring

14.18c Undo the screw (arrowed)

18 On 2012-on models remove the seat cowling (see Chapter 7). Displace the fuse/relay box **(see illustration)**. Disconnect the rear sub-loom wiring connectors **(see illustration)**. Move the wiring aside and undo the screw on the top **(see illustration)** – remove the battery for extra clearance if required (see Chapter 8). Release the trim clip and unscrew the four bolts on the underside, noting the washers, and remove the rear light/turn signal/licence plate assembly, noting the routing of the wiring **(see illustrations)**. Remove the collars for the bolts fitted on the top of the tray for safekeeping if loose.
19 Draw the control unit out and disconnect the wiring connectors **(see illustration)**.
20 Installation is the reverse of removal – make sure the wiring connectors are secure.

Front valve unit

Note: *Before removing the valve unit read the information given in Section 11 regarding the refilling and bleeding of the system.*
21 Raise the fuel tank (see Chapter 4). Remove the left-hand fairing side panel and the engine trim cover (see Chapter 7). Remove the fairing bracket **(see illustration)**.

14.18d Release the trim clip (arrowed) and unscrew the four bolts...

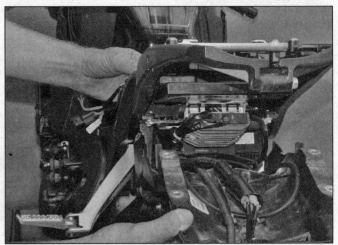

14.18e ...and remove the assembly

14.19 Remove the control unit

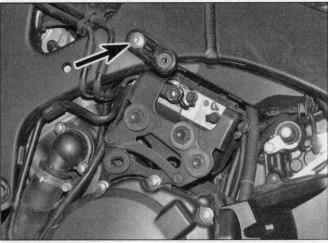

14.21 Undo the screw (arrowed) and remove the bracket

22 Drain the brake fluid from the front brake system (see Section 11).
23 Release the sidestand switch wiring connector, and where fitted the oxygen sensor wiring connector, from the bracket on the top of the unit, and free the wiring clamp. Disconnect the drain hose from the valve unit. Disconnect the valve unit 21-pin wiring connector.
24 Have some clean rag to hand to catch any residual brake fluid when detaching the pipes.
25 Release the front wheel sensor wire from the pipe in front of the radiator, then unscrew the two brake pipe nuts at the joint and detach the pipes **(see illustration)**.
26 Unscrew the outer brake pipe nut on the joint above the coolant hoses at the front of the alternator cover and detach the pipe.
27 Unscrew the valve unit and bracket bolts, remove the outer bracket and draw the unit out, bringing the brake pipes with it **(see illustration)** – take care not to snag the pipes.
28 If required, unscrew the remaining bracket bolts and remove the inner bracket and the cover. Mark the position of each brake pipe, then unscrew the nuts and detach the pipes. If required, note the location colour code mark and alignment of each pipe joint, then unscrew the bolts and remove the joints and sealing washers – new washers must be used.
29 Installation is the reverse of removal, noting the following:
● Use new sealing washers on the brake pipe joints. Make sure they are installed in their correct place according to the colour codes and aligned as noted on removal, and tighten the bolts to the torque setting specified at the beginning of the Chapter.
● Make sure the pipes are correctly connected. Smear the pipe nut threads with clean brake fluid, and tighten them finger-tight only until the unit has been installed and the pipes are correctly aligned, and then tighten the nuts to the specified torque setting, using a torque wrench if the correct tools are available.

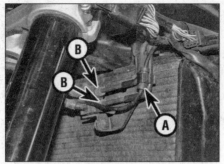

14.25 Release the wire (A), brake pipe nuts (B)

● Make sure the rubber grommets are in good condition and the collars are in place.
● Make sure the wiring connector is secure.
● Transport the bike to a Honda dealer to refill and bleed the brake system.

Front power unit

Note: Before removing the power unit read the information given at the end of Section 11 regarding the refilling and bleeding of the hydraulic system.

30 Remove the radiator (see Chapter 3). Remove the exhaust system (see Chapter 4).
31 Unscrew the power unit bracket bolts and screw and the heat guard bolt and remove the heat guard **(see illustration)**.
32 Have some clean rag to hand to catch any residual brake fluid. Unscrew the inner brake pipe nut on the joint above the coolant hoses at the front of the alternator cover and detach the pipe.
33 Unscrew the inner mounting bolt, displace the power unit and remove the radiator bracket, noting how it locates.
34 Remove the rubber cover and disconnect the 2-pin wiring connector.
35 If required unscrew the bolt on the underside and remove the mounting brackets, noting how they fit. Unscrew the brake pipe nut and detach the pipe. Note the alignment

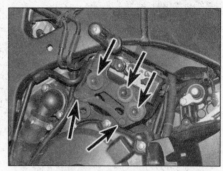

14.27 Unscrew the bolts (arrowed) and remove the bracket, then draw the unit out

of the pipe joint, then unscrew the bolt and remove the joint and sealing washers – new washers must be used.
36 Installation is the reverse of removal, noting the following:
● Use new sealing washers on the brake pipe joint. Make sure it is aligned as noted on removal, and tighten the bolt to the torque setting specified at the beginning of the Chapter.
● Make sure the rubber grommets are in good condition and the collars are in place.
● Smear the pipe nut threads with clean brake fluid, and tighten it to the specified torque setting, using a torque wrench if the correct tools are available.
● Make sure the wiring connector is secure.
● Transport the bike to a Honda dealer to refill and bleed the brake system.

Rear valve unit and power unit

Note: Before removing the valve unit read the information given in Section 11 regarding the refilling and bleeding of the system.

37 Remove the fuel tank (see Chapter 4).
38 Remove the exhaust gas control valve servo motor (see Chapter 4).
39 Drain the brake fluid from the rear brake system (see Section 11).
40 Release the wiring clamp **(see illustration)**.

14.31 Front power unit (arrowed)

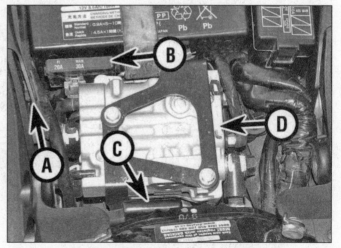

14.40 Wiring clamp (A), main/FI fuse holder (B), connector cover (C), rear valve unit/power unit (D)

6•26 Brakes, wheels and final drive

Displace the main fuse/FI fuse holder from the bracket.

41 Remove the cover and disconnect the valve unit 21-pin wiring connector. Disconnect the power unit 2-pin wiring connector.

42 Disconnect the drain hose from the valve unit.

43 Have some clean rag to hand to catch any residual brake fluid. Unscrew the brake pipe joint bolts on the right-hand side so the unions are loose, but leave the bolts in place.

44 Unscrew the three mounting bolts and draw the valve/power unit assembly out, holding the banjo unions clear. Withdraw the pipe joint bolts and remove the sealing washers – new ones must be used.

45 If required unscrew the power unit bracket bolts and remove the bracket. Unscrew the link pipe nuts and detach the pipe. Unscrew the power unit mounting bolt and remove the power unit. Unscrew the valve unit bracket bolts and remove the brackets. Note the location colour code mark and alignment of the link pipe joint on each unit, then unscrew the bolts and remove the joints and sealing washers – new washers must be used.

46 Installation is the reverse of removal, noting the following:
- Use new sealing washers on the link pipe joints. Make sure the pipe joints are installed in their correct place and aligned as noted on removal, and tighten the bolts to the torque setting specified at the beginning of the Chapter.
- Smear the link pipe nut threads with clean brake fluid, and tighten them to the specified torque setting, using a torque wrench if the correct tools are available.
- Make sure the rubber grommets are in good condition and the collars are in place.

- Use new sealing washers on the brake pipe joints on the right-hand side. Fit the bolts and their new sealing washers loosely in the joints before installing the valve/power unit assembly. Tighten the bolts to the specified torque after tightening the valve/power unit mounting bolts.
- Make sure the wiring connectors are secure.
- Transport the bike to a Honda dealer to refill and bleed the brake system.

15 Wheel inspection and repair

1 In order to carry out a proper inspection of the wheels, support the bike on an auxiliary stand. Clean the wheels thoroughly to remove mud and dirt that may interfere with the inspection procedure or mask defects. Make a general check of the wheels (see Chapter 1) and tyres (see *Pre-ride checks*).

2 Inspect the wheels for cracks, flat spots on the rim and other damage. Look very closely for dents in the area where the tyre bead contacts the rim. Dents in this area may prevent complete sealing of the tyre against the rim, which leads to deflation of the tyre over a period of time. If damage is evident, or if runout in either direction is excessive, the wheel will have to be renewed. Never attempt to repair a damaged alloy wheel.

3 To check axial (side-to-side) runout of the wheel rim attach a dial gauge to the fork or the swingarm and position its tip against the side of the wheel rim. Spin the wheel slowly and check the amount of run-out, comparing it to the specification listed at the beginning of the Chapter **(see illustration)**.

4 In order to accurately check radial (out of round) runout with the dial gauge, remove the wheel from the machine, and the tyre from the wheel. With the axle clamped in a vice and the dial gauge positioned on the top of the rim, the wheel can be rotated to check the runout **(see illustration 15.3)**.

5 An easier, though slightly less accurate, method is to attach a stiff wire pointer to the fork or the swingarm and position the end a fraction of an inch from the wheel rim where the wheel and tyre join. If the wheel is true, the distance from the pointer to the rim will be constant as the wheel is rotated. **Note:** *If wheel runout is excessive, check the wheel bearings very carefully before renewing the wheel.*

16 Wheel alignment check

1 Misalignment of the wheels due to a bent frame or forks can cause strange and possibly serious handling problems. If the frame or forks are at fault, repair by a frame specialist or renewal are the only options. Note that failure to set the drive chain adjustment markers to the same setting on each side can cause poor wheel alignment (see Chapter 1, Section 1).

2 To check wheel alignment you will need an assistant, a length of string or a perfectly straight piece of wood and a ruler. A plumb bob or spirit level for checking that the wheels are vertical will also be required.

3 Support the bike upright on an auxiliary stand. Measure the width of both tyres at their widest points. Subtract the smaller measurement from the larger measurement, then divide the difference by two. The result is the amount of offset that should exist between the front and rear tyres on both sides of the machine.

4 If the string method is used, have your assistant hold one end of it about halfway between the floor and the rear axle, with the string touching the back edge of the rear tyre sidewall.

5 Run the other end of the string forward and pull it tight so that it is roughly parallel to the floor **(see illustration)**. Slowly bring the string into contact with the front edge of the rear tyre sidewall, then turn the front wheel until it is parallel with the string. Measure the distance from the front tyre sidewall to the string.

6 Repeat the procedure on the other side of the motorcycle. The distance from the front tyre sidewall to the string should be equal on both sides.

7 As previously mentioned, a perfectly

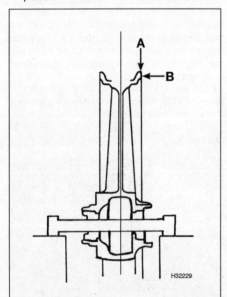

15.3 Check the wheel for radial (out-of-round) runout (A) and axial (side-to-side) runout (B)

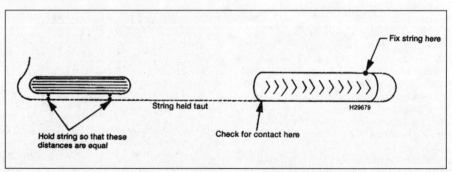

16.5 Wheel alignment check using string

Brakes, wheels and final drive 6•27

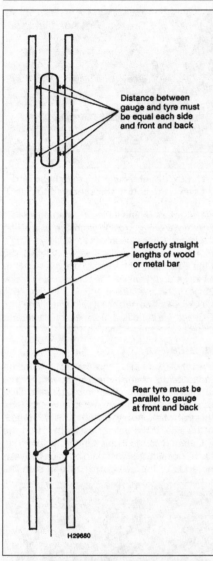

16.7 Wheel alignment check using a straight-edge

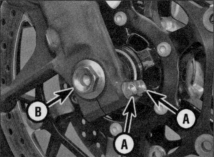

17.4 Slacken the axle clamp bolts (A), then unscrew the axle bolt (B)

17.5 Slacken the axle clamp bolts (arrowed) then withdraw the axle and remove the wheel

straight length of wood or metal bar may be substituted for the string (see illustration).
8 If the distance between the string and tyre is greater on one side, or if the rear wheel appears to be out of alignment, have your machine checked by a Honda dealer or frame specialist.
9 If the front-to-back alignment is correct, the wheels still may be out of alignment vertically.
10 Using a plumb bob or spirit level, check the rear wheel to make sure it is vertical. To do this, hold the string of the plumb bob against the tyre upper sidewall and allow the weight to settle just off the floor. If the string touches both the upper and lower tyre sidewalls and is perfectly straight, the wheel is vertical. If it is not, adjust the stand until it is.
11 Once the rear wheel is vertical, check the front wheel in the same manner. If both wheels are not perfectly vertical, the frame and/or major suspension components are bent.

17 Front wheel

Removal

1 Support the motorcycle on an auxiliary stand so that the front wheel is off the ground. Always make sure the motorcycle is properly supported. If a support is being placed under the engine, remove the lower fairing (see Chapter 7).
2 On RA models displace the wheel sensor (see Section 14).
3 Displace the front brake calipers (see Section 3). Support the calipers with a cable-tie or a bungee cord so that no strain is placed on the hydraulic hoses. There is no need to disconnect the hoses from the calipers. **Note**: *Do not operate the brakes with the calipers removed.*
4 Slacken the axle clamp bolts on the bottom of the right-hand fork, then unscrew the axle bolt from the right-hand end of the axle **(see illustration)**.
5 Slacken the axle clamp bolts on the bottom of the left-hand fork **(see illustration)**. Take the weight of the wheel, then push the axle through from the right-hand side and withdraw it from the left-hand side. Carefully lower the wheel and draw it forwards.
6 Remove the spacer from each side of the wheel **(see illustrations 17.9a and b)**. Clean all old grease off the spacers, axle and seals.

Caution: Don't lay the wheel down and allow it to rest on either disc – the disc could become warped. Set the wheel on wood blocks so the disc doesn't support the weight of the wheel.
7 Clean off all old grease and remove any corrosion from the axle with steel wool. Check the axle is straight by rolling it on a flat surface such as a piece of plate glass; if the equipment is available, place the axle in V-blocks and measure the runout using a dial gauge. If the axle is bent or the runout exceeds the limit specified, replace it with a new one.
8 Check the condition of the grease seals and wheel bearings (see Section 19).

Installation

9 Apply a smear of grease to the inside and outside of the wheel spacers. Fit the shouldered spacer into the right-hand side and the plain spacer into the left **(see illustrations)**. Apply a thin coat of grease to the axle.
10 Manoeuvre the wheel into position between the forks, making sure the directional arrows on the tyre, wheel and brake discs are pointing in the normal direction of rotation **(see illustrations 4.7a and b)**.
11 Lift the wheel into place, making sure the spacers stay in place. Slide the axle in from the left **(see illustration 17.5)**.
12 Fit the axle bolt, counter-hold the axle head and tighten the bolt to the torque setting

17.9a Fit the shouldered spacer...

17.9b ...and the plain spacer

6•28 Brakes, wheels and final drive

specified at the beginning of the Chapter **(see illustrations)**.

13 Tighten the axle clamp bolts on the bottom of the right-hand fork to the specified torque setting **(see illustration 17.4)**.

14 Lower the front wheel to the ground, then install the brake calipers (see Section 3, and the **Note** therein regarding the caliper mounting bolts).

15 Apply the front brake a few times to bring the pads back into contact with the discs, then with the brake applied pump the front forks a few times to settle all components in position. Now tighten the axle clamp bolts on the bottom of the left-hand fork to the specified torque.

16 On RA models install the wheel sensor (see Section 14).

18 Rear wheel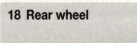

Removal

1 Support the motorcycle on an auxiliary stand or stands so that the rear wheel is off the ground. Always make sure the motorcycle is properly supported.

2 Create some slack in the chain (see Chapter 1, Section 1).

3 Unscrew the axle nut and remove the washer and the right-hand chain adjustment marker **(see illustration)**.

4 Push the wheel forwards and take the weight, then withdraw the axle from the

17.12a Fit the axle bolt

left-hand side, bringing the left-hand chain adjustment marker with it, and lower the wheel to the ground **(see illustration)**. If the axle is difficult to withdraw, drive it out using a soft mallet to prevent damage to the threads.

5 Disengage the chain from the sprocket **(see illustration)**. Draw the wheel back until the brake caliper bracket is clear of its guide on the swingarm, then lift the caliper assembly out from between the swingarm and the wheel and support it clear **(see illustration)**. Remove the wheel. Fit the caliper bracket back onto the swingarm if required, and secure it using a cable-tie.

Caution: Do not lay the wheel down and allow it to rest on the disc or the sprocket – they could become warped. Set the wheel on wood blocks so neither the disc nor the sprocket supports the weight of the wheel. Do not operate the brakes with the wheel removed.

6 Remove the spacer from each side of the wheel **(see illustrations 18.9a and b)**. Clean

17.12b Counter-hold the axle head and tighten the bolt to the specified torque

all old grease off the spacers, axle and seals.

7 Remove any corrosion from the axle using steel wool. Check the axle is straight by rolling it on a flat surface such as a piece of plate glass; if the equipment is available, place the axle in V-blocks and measure the runout using a dial gauge. If the axle is bent or the runout exceeds the limit specified, replace it with a new one.

8 Check the condition of the grease seals and wheel bearings (see Section 19).

Installation

9 Apply a smear of grease to the inside and outside of the wheel spacers. Fit the shouldered spacer into the left-hand side and the plain spacer into the right. **(see illustrations)**. Apply a thin coat of grease to the axle. If the caliper assembly is on the swingarm displace it and support it clear.

10 Manoeuvre the wheel into position between the ends of the swingarm, making sure the

18.3 Unscrew the axle nut and remove the washer and the adjustment marker (arrowed)

18.4 Withdraw the axle and lower the wheel

18.5a Slip the chain off the sprocket

18.5b Draw the wheel back and displace the caliper bracket when clear

18.9a Fit the shouldered spacer...

18.9b ...and the plain spacer

Brakes, wheels and final drive 6•29

18.12a Seat the axle head in the marker as shown

18.12b Make sure the marker is the correct way around

directional arrows on the disc, wheel and tyre are pointing in the normal direction of rotation **(see illustrations 4.7a and b)**, and fit the drive chain around the sprocket **(see illustration 18.5a)**. Slide the brake caliper bracket between the wheel and the swingarm **(see illustration 18.5b)** and locate it in its guide.

11 Slide the left-hand chain adjustment marker onto the axle with the raised sections vertical and facing the axle head.

12 Lift the wheel into position and slide the axle in from the left **(see illustration 18.4)**, making sure the spacers and caliper bracket remain correctly installed. Align the flat edges of the axle head vertically between the raised sections of the adjustment marker **(see illustration)**. Check that everything is correctly aligned. Fit the right-hand adjustment marker onto the end of the axle with its chamfered edges top and bottom **(see illustration)**. Fit the washer and axle nut but leave it loose **(see illustration 18.3)**.

13 Check and adjust the drive chain slack (see Chapter 1). On completion tighten the axle nut to the torque setting specified at the beginning of the Chapter.

14 Operate the brake pedal several times to bring the pads into contact with the disc. Check the operation of the rear brake carefully before riding the bike.

19 Wheel bearings

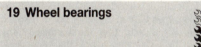

Note: *Always renew the wheel bearings in sets, never individually. Avoid using a high pressure cleaner on the wheel bearing area.*

Front wheel bearings

1 Remove the wheel (see Section 17). Support the wheel rim (not the discs) on wood blocks.

2 Inspect the seals and bearings – check that the bearing inner race turns smoothly and that the outer race is a tight fit in the hub (see *Tools and Workshop Tips* in the Reference Section). **Note:** *Do not remove the bearings unless they are going to be replaced with new ones.*

3 If new bearings are needed it is best to remove the brake discs (see Section 4). Lever out the bearing seal from each side of the hub using a flat-bladed screwdriver or a seal hook **(see illustration)**. Take care not to damage the hub. Discard the seals as new ones must be fitted on reassembly.

4 Move the centre spacer to one side to expose the inner race of the lower bearing, then locate a drift on it and drive the bearing out **(see illustrations)**. If you can't get sufficient purchase, turn the wheel over and remove the bearing using an internal expanding puller with slide-hammer attachment, which can be obtained commercially – select the correct attachment and locate it behind the inner race of the bearing, then tighten the inner bolt to expand and lock the puller **(see illustration)**. Attach the slide-hammer, hold the wheel firmly down and jar the bearing out **(see illustration)**. Having removed the first bearing, remove the spacer that fits between the bearings.

5 Remove the other bearing using a suitable drift (such as a socket on an extension) inserted from the opposite side to the bearing.

6 Thoroughly clean the hub area of the wheel with a suitable solvent and inspect the bearing housing for scoring and wear.

7 Drive the new bearings into the hub using a bearing driver or suitable socket **(see illustration)**.

19.3 Lever out the bearing seals

19.4a Drive the bearing out using a drift...

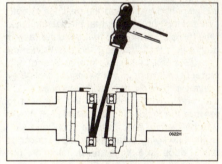
19.4b ...locating it as shown

19.4c Fit the attachment behind the bearing...

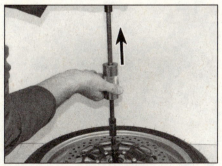
19.4d ...then fit the slide-hammer and jar the bearing out

19.7 Using a socket to drive the bearing in

19.9 Fit the seal, setting it flush with the rim

19.11 Lift the sprocket coupling off the wheel

19.13 Lever out the bearing seal

Fit the right-hand bearing first, with its marked side facing outwards. Make sure that the driver or socket bears only on the outer race and the bearing fits squarely and all the way into its seat.

8 Turn the wheel over and fit the bearing spacer. Fit the second bearing in the same way as the first.

9 Fit the new seals into the hub using finger pressure or a socket on a piece of wood, setting them flush with the rim **(see illustration)**. Smear the seal lips with grease.

10 Install the brake discs if removed (see Section 4). Clean the discs using brake system cleaner, then install the wheel (see Section 17).

Rear wheel bearings

11 Remove the wheel (see Section 18). Support the wheel rim (not the disc or sprocket) on wood blocks. Lift the sprocket coupling out of the hub **(see illustration)**.

12 Inspect the seal and the bearings in both sides of the hub – check that the bearing inner race turns smoothly and that the outer race is a tight fit in the hub (see *Tools and Workshop Tips* (Section 5) in the Reference section). **Note:** *Do not remove the bearings unless they are going to be replaced with new ones.*

13 If new bearings are needed it is best to remove the brake disc (see Section 8). Lever out the bearing seal from the right-hand side of the hub using a flat-bladed screwdriver or a seal hook **(see illustration)**. Take care not to damage the hub. Discard the seal as a new one should be fitted on reassembly.

14 Move the centre spacer to one side to expose the inner race of the lower bearing, then locate a drift on it and drive the bearing out **(see illustrations 19.4a and b)**. If you can't get sufficient purchase, turn the wheel over and remove the bearing using an internal expanding puller with slide-hammer attachment – select the correct attachment and locate it behind the inner race of the bearing, then tighten the inner bolt to expand and lock the puller **(see illustration 19.4c)**. Attach the slide-hammer, hold the wheel firmly down and jar the bearing out **(see illustration 19.4d)**. Having removed the first bearing, remove the spacer that fits between the bearings.

15 Remove the other bearing using a suitable drift (such as a socket on an extension) inserted from the opposite side to the bearing.

16 Thoroughly clean the hub area of the wheel with a suitable solvent and inspect the bearing housing for scoring and wear.

17 Drive the new bearings into the hub using a bearing driver or suitable socket **(see illustration 19.7)**. Fit the right-hand bearing first, with its marked side facing outwards. Make sure that the driver or socket bears only on the outer race and the bearing fits squarely and all the way into its seat.

18 Turn the wheel over and fit the bearing spacer. Fit the second bearing in the same way as the first.

19 Fit the new seal it into the right-hand side of the hub using finger pressure or a socket that seats around the perimeter of the seal **(see illustration 19.9)**. Smear the seal lips with grease.

20 Check the sprocket coupling/rubber dampers (see Section 23). Check the condition of the hub O-ring and clean it or replace it with a new one if necessary **(see illustration)**. Smear the O-ring with oil. Fit the sprocket coupling into the wheel **(see illustration 19.11)**. Clean the brake disc using acetone or brake system cleaner, then install the wheel (see Section 18).

Sprocket coupling bearing

21 Remove the wheel (see Section 18). Lift the sprocket coupling out of the hub **(see illustration 19.11)**.

22 Inspect the seal and bearing – check that the bearing inner race turns smoothly and that the outer race is a tight fit in the coupling (see *Tools and Workshop Tips* in the Reference Section). **Note:** *Do not remove the bearing unless it is being replaced with a new one.*

23 If a new bearing is needed lever out the bearing seal using a flat-bladed screwdriver or a seal hook **(see illustration)**. Take care not to damage the rim of the coupling. Discard the seal – a new one must be fitted.

24 Place the coupling on the work surface, sprocket side up, and drive the spacer out of the bearing using a suitably sized socket **(see illustration)**.

25 Support the coupling on blocks of wood, sprocket side down, and drive the bearing

19.20 Fit a new O-ring if necessary

19.23 Lever out the bearing seal

19.24 Drive the spacer out of the bearings from the outside

Brakes, wheels and final drive 6•31

19.25 Drive the bearings out from the inside

19.28 Drive the bearing and spacer assembly in from the outside

19.29 Press the new seal into the hub

out from the inside using a bearing driver or socket **(see illustration)**.

26 Thoroughly clean the coupling with a suitable solvent and inspect the bearing housing for scoring and wear.

27 Place the new bearing marked side down on a hard flat surface, then drive the spacer fully in until its rim seats on the inner race of the bearing.

28 Drive the bearing and spacer as one squarely into the coupling with the spacer innermost using a driver or suitable socket on the outer race of the bearing until the bearing seats (see *Tools and Workshop Tips*) **(see illustration)**.

29 Press the new seal into the coupling **(see illustration)**. Level the seal with the rim of the coupling with a small block of wood. Smear the seal lip with grease.

30 Check the sprocket coupling/rubber dampers (see Section 23). Check the condition of the hub O-ring and clean it or replace it with a new one if necessary **(see illustration 19.20)**. Smear the O-ring with oil. Fit the sprocket coupling into the wheel. Install the wheel (see Section 18).

20 Tyres

General information

1 The wheels are designed to take tubeless tyres only. Tyre sizes are given in the Specifications at the beginning of this chapter.

2 Refer to the *Pre-ride checks* listed at the beginning of this manual for tyre maintenance.

Fitting new tyres

3 When selecting new tyres, refer to the tyre information in the Owner's Handbook. Ensure that front and rear tyre types are compatible, the correct size and correct speed rating; if necessary seek advice from a Honda dealer or tyre fitting specialist **(see illustration)**.

4 It is recommended that tyres are fitted by a motorcycle tyre specialist rather than attempted in the home workshop. This is particularly relevant in the case of tubeless

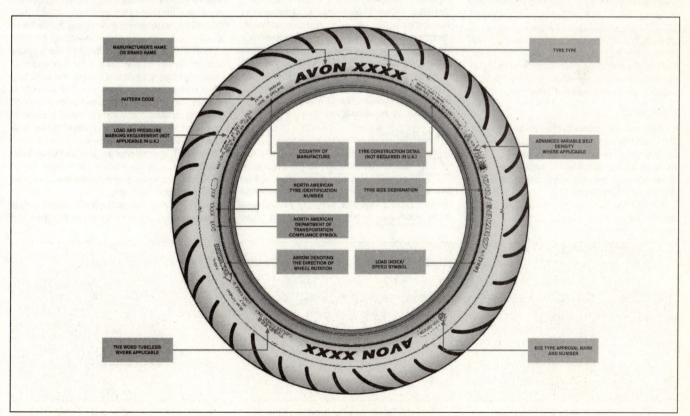

20.3 Common tyre sidewall markings

tyres because the force required to break the seal between the wheel rim and tyre bead is substantial, and is usually beyond the capabilities of an individual working with normal tyre levers. Additionally, the specialist will be able to balance the wheels after tyre fitting.

5 Note that punctured tubeless tyres can in some cases be repaired. External repairs made using a repair kit should only ever be considered as a temporary measure to get you to a dealer for a new tyre, and riding at speed or with any extra load should be avoided. Internal repairs carried out by a motorcycle tyre fitting specialist are better. Make sure a wheel with a repaired tyre is balanced before it is fitted back on the bike. Honda advise that a repaired tyre should not be used at speeds above 50 mph (80 kmh) for the first 24 hours, and not above 80 mph (130 kmh) thereafter, and carrying heavy loads should be avoided.

21 Drive chain

Note: *The original equipment drive chain fitted to these models has a staked-type master (joining) link which can be disassembled using either the Honda service tool, Pt. No. 07HMH-MR10103, or one of several commercially-available drive chain cutting/staking tools (but the cheap ones are best avoided). Such chains can be recognised by the master joining link side plate's identification marks (and usually its different colour), as well as by the staked ends of the link's two pins which look as if they have been deeply centre-punched, instead of peened over as with all the other pins.*

Removal

1 Support the motorcycle on an auxiliary stand so that the rear wheel is off the ground. Locate the joining link in a suitable position to work on by rotating the back wheel **(see illustration)**. Slacken the drive chain as described in Chapter 1.

2 If required, remove the chainguard **(see illustration)**.

21.1 Example of the different pin ends of the joining link

3 Remove the front sprocket cover (see Section 22).

4 Split the chain at the joining link using the chain cutter, following carefully the manufacturer's operating instructions (see also *Tools and Workshop Tips* in the Reference Section). Remove the chain from the bike, noting its routing through the swingarm.

Cleaning

5 Refer to Chapter 1, Section 1, for details of routine cleaning with the chain installed on the sprockets.

6 If the chain is extremely dirty remove it from the motorcycle and soak it in paraffin (kerosene) for approximately five or six minutes, then clean it using a soft brush.

Caution: *Don't use petrol (gasoline), solvent or other cleaning fluids that might damage its internal sealing properties. Don't use high-pressure water. Remove the chain, wipe it off, then blow dry it with compressed air immediately. The entire process shouldn't take longer than ten minutes – if it does, the O-rings in the chain rollers could be damaged.*

Installation

 Warning: *NEVER install a drive chain which uses a clip-type master (split) link. Use ONLY the correct service tools to secure the staked-type of master link – if you do not have access to such tools, have the chain*

21.2 Chainguard screws (arrowed)

replaced by a dealer to be sure of having it securely installed.

7 Route the drive chain around the sprockets and through the swingarm, leaving the two ends mid-way between the sprockets along the bottom run.

8 Referring to *Tools and Workshop Tips* in the Reference Section, install the new joining link from the inside using new O-rings. Fit the new sideplate using new O-rings and with its identification marks facing out, then use the tool to press it into place. Measure the amount that the joining link pins project from the sideplate and check they are within the measurements specified at the beginning of the Chapter **(see illustration)**. Stake the new link using the drive chain cutting/staking tool, following carefully the instructions of both the chain manufacturer and the tool manufacturer. DO NOT re-use old joining link components.

9 After staking, check the joining link and staking for any signs of cracking **(see illustration)**. If there is any evidence of cracking, the joining link, O-rings and sideplate must be replaced. Measure the diameter of the staked ends in two directions and check that it is evenly staked and within the measurements specified at the beginning of the Chapter **(see illustration)**. Check that the link pivots freely.

10 Install the sprocket cover (see Section 22).

11 Install the chainguard if removed.

12 On completion, adjust and lubricate the chain following the procedures described in Chapter 1.

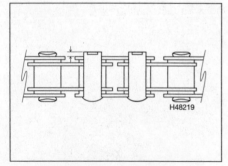

21.8 Measure the joining link pin projection beyond the sideplate

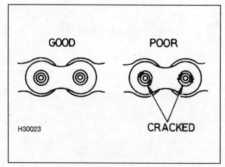

21.9a Check staking for any signs of cracking

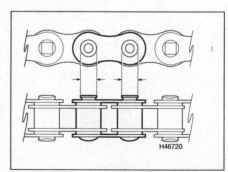

21.9b Check the diameter of the staked pin ends

Brakes, wheels and final drive 6•33

22.1a Note the alignment...

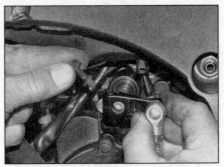

22.1b ...then unscrew the bolt and slide the arm off the shaft

22.3a Release the wire from the guides (arrowed)

22 Sprockets

Front sprocket cover removal and installation

1 On RR models note the alignment of the punch mark on the gearchange shaft with the slit in the linkage arm clamp (see illustration). Unscrew the linkage arm bolt and slide the arm off the shaft (see illustration).

2 On RA models remove the left-hand fairing side panel and the engine trim cover (see Chapter 7).

3 Release the wiring from the guides on the bottom of the cover (see illustration). Unscrew the bolts and remove the cover (see illustrations). Note the guide plate fitted in the cover and remove it if required (see illustration).

4 Clean all old road dirt and grease from the inside of the cover and from the guide plate. Fit the guide plate onto the cover, then fit the cover and tighten its bolts (see illustrations 22.3d, c and b). Feed the wiring into the guides (see illustration 22.3a).

5 On RR models slide the gearchange linkage arm onto the shaft, aligning the punch mark with the slit in the clamp, then

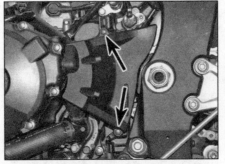

22.3b Unscrew the bolts (arrowed)...

tighten the pinch bolt (see illustrations 22.1b and a).

6 On RA models install the engine trim cover and the left-hand fairing side panel (see Chapter 7).

Sprocket check

7 Check the wear pattern on both sprockets (see illustration). If the sprocket teeth are worn excessively, replace the chain and both sprockets as a set. Whenever the sprockets are inspected, the drive chain should be inspected also (see Chapter 1). Always renew the chain and sprockets as a set – worn sprockets can ruin a new drive chain and *vice versa*.

22.3c ...and remove the cover

8 Adjust and lubricate the chain following the procedures described in Chapter 1.

Sprocket removal and installation

Front sprocket

9 Remove the front sprocket cover (see Steps 1 to 3).

10 Shift the transmission into a high gear and have an assistant apply the rear brake, then unscrew the sprocket bolt and remove the washer (see illustration).

11 Fully slacken the drive chain as described in Chapter 1. If the rear sprocket is being removed as well, remove the rear wheel now to give full slack (see Section 18).

22.3d Remove the guide if required

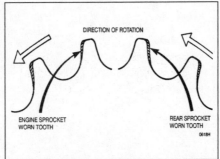

22.7 Check the sprocket teeth for wear in the areas shown

22.10 Unscrew the bolt and remove the washer

6•34 Brakes, wheels and final drive

22.12a Draw the sprocket off the shaft...

22.12b ...and disengage the chain

22.18 Unscrew the nuts (arrowed) and remove the sprocket

12 Slide the chain and sprocket off the shaft and slip the sprocket out of the chain **(see illustrations)**.
13 Engage the new sprocket with the chain, making sure the marked side of the sprocket is facing out, and slide it on the shaft **(see illustrations 22.12b and a)**.
14 If removed, fit the rear sprocket now, and install the wheel (see Section 18). Take up the slack in the chain.
15 Fit the sprocket bolt with its washer **(see illustration 22.10)**. Tighten the bolt to the torque setting specified at the beginning of the Chapter, using the rear brake to prevent the sprocket turning.
16 Fit the sprocket cover (see Steps 4 to 6). Adjust and lubricate the chain following the procedures described in Chapter 1.

Rear sprocket

17 Remove the rear wheel (see Section 18). Support the wheel rim (not the disc) on some blocks of wood with the sprocket side up.
18 Unscrew the nuts and remove the washers, then lift the sprocket off the bolts, noting which way round it fits **(see illustration)**. Check the condition of the bolts and replace them all if any are damaged.
19 Make sure the flats sides of the sprocket bolts are correctly seated on the inner side of the coupling. Fit the sprocket onto the hub with the marked side facing out. Fit the washers. Fit the nuts and tighten them evenly and in a criss-cross sequence to the torque setting specified at the beginning of the Chapter.
20 Install the rear wheel (see Section 18).

23 Rear sprocket coupling/ rubber dampers

1 Remove the rear wheel (see Section 18). Check for play between the sprocket coupling and the wheel hub by turning the sprocket. Any play indicates worn rubber damper segments.
Caution: Do not lay the wheel down on the disc as it could become warped. Lay the wheel on wooden blocks so that the disc is off the ground.
2 Lift the sprocket coupling off the wheel leaving the rubber dampers in position **(see illustration 19.11)**. Check the coupling for cracks or any obvious signs of damage.
3 Lift the rubber damper segments from the wheel and check them for cracks, hardening and general deterioration **(see illustration)**. Replace them with a new set if necessary.
4 Check the condition of the hub O-ring and clean it or replace it with a new one if necessary **(see illustration 19.20)**. Smear the O-ring with oil.
5 Checking and replacement procedures for the sprocket coupling bearing are in Section 19.
6 Installation is the reverse of removal. Align the coupling correctly with the rubber dampers and press it fully into the hub.
7 Install the rear wheel (see Section 18).

23.3 Check the rubber dampers as described

Chapter 7
Bodywork

Contents

	Section number		Section number
Fairing panels	6	Mirrors	4
Front mudguard	7	Seat cowling	3
Fuel tank cover	5	Side covers and seats	2
General information	1		

Degrees of difficulty

Easy, suitable for novice with little experience	**Fairly easy,** suitable for beginner with some experience	**Fairly difficult,** suitable for competent DIY mechanic	**Difficult,** suitable for experienced DIY mechanic	**Very difficult,** suitable for expert DIY or professional

1 General information

This Chapter covers the procedures necessary to remove and install the bodywork.

In the case of damage to the bodywork, it is usually necessary to remove the broken component and replace it with a new (or used) one. The material that the body panels are composed of doesn't lend itself to conventional repair techniques, but there are some companies that specialise in 'plastic welding' and there are a number of bodywork repair kits now available for motorcycles.

When attempting to remove any body panel, first study it closely, noting any fasteners and associated fittings, to be sure of returning everything to its correct place on installation. Refer to the beginning of Section 7 for more information on the types of trim clip used and how to release and refit them. In some cases the aid of an assistant may be useful when removing panels, to help avoid the risk of damage to paintwork. Once the evident fasteners have been removed, try to remove the panel as described but DO NOT FORCE IT – if it will not release the chances are a locating tab is stuck, but first check that all fasteners have been removed before trying again.

When installing a body panel, be sure of returning every fastener to its correct place. Check that all fasteners are in good condition, including the trim clips and damping/rubber mounts; replace any faulty fasteners with new ones before the panel is reassembled. Check also that all mounting brackets are straight and repair them or replace them with new ones if necessary before attempting to install the panel.

Make sure all locating tabs engage correctly with their related panel. Tighten the fasteners securely, but be careful not to overtighten any of them or the panel may break (not always immediately) due to the uneven stress.

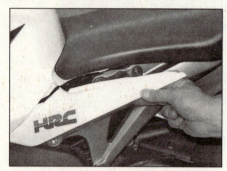
2.1a Pull the rear away…

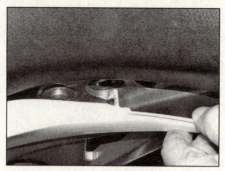
2.1b …to free the peg from the grommet…

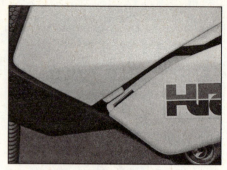
2.1c …then release the tab

2.2a Undo the screw on each side…

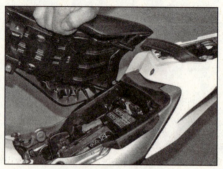
2.2b …and remove the seat

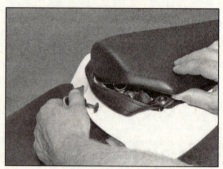
2.3a Unlock and lift the seat

2 Side covers and seats

Removal

Rider's seat

1 Carefully pull each side cover out to free the peg from the grommet, then release the tab at the front and remove the cover **(see illustrations)**.
2 Undo the screw on each side **(see illustration)**. Lift the front of the seat and draw it forwards to disengage the tabs at the back **(see illustration)**.

Passenger seat

3 Insert the ignition key into the seat lock and turn it clockwise to unlock the seat **(see illustration)**. Lift the front of the seat and draw it forward to disengage the tab **(see illustration)**. If required undo the grab-strap screws and remove the strap.

Installation

4 Installation is the reverse of removal. Make sure the tabs on the back of the rider's seat locate correctly **(see illustration 2.2b)**. Make sure the tab at the back of the passenger seat locates correctly, and push down on the front to engage the latch **(see illustration 2.3b)**.

3 Seat cowling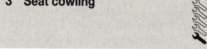

1 Remove both seats (see Section 2).
2 Undo the four screws securing the cowling **(see illustration)**.
3 Draw the cowling to the rear to release the tabs at the front, then carefully pull one side out and up and draw the cowling off the bike

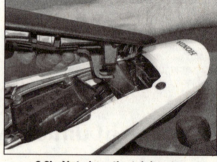
2.3b Note how the tab locates

(see illustrations) – do not worry about the amount the cowling has to flex to be removed as it is designed to do so, but do not flex it more than necessary.
4 Installation is the reverse of removal. Make sure the rubber well-nuts for the screws are in good condition and correctly seated.

3.2 Undo the screws (arrowed)…

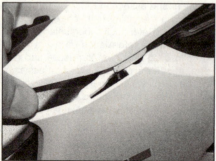
3.3a …release the tabs…

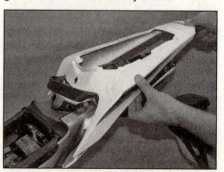
3.3b …and remove the cowling

Bodywork 7•3

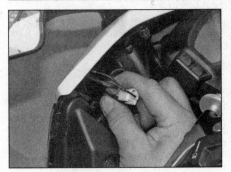
4.1 Disconnect the wiring

4.2a Undo the nuts (arrowed)...

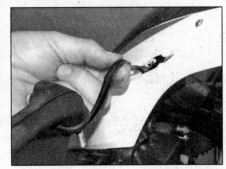
4.2b ...and remove the mirror

4 Mirrors

1 Draw the rubber boot out from behind the instrument panel and disconnect the turn signal and sidelight wiring connectors **(see illustration)**.
2 Undo the two nuts and remove the mirror, taking care not to snag the wiring as you draw it through **(see illustrations)**.
3 Installation is the reverse of removal.

5 Fuel tank cover

1 Remove the rider's seat (see Section 2).
2 Undo the two screws on each side and remove the cover **(see illustrations)**.
3 If required undo the screw securing each side trim panel, then release their tabs and remove them from the cover.
4 Installation is the reverse of removal. Check the condition of the rubber grommet in each mount and replace them with new ones if necessary. Make sure the side trim panel tabs locate correctly. Spray or smear a suitable lubricant over the fuel cap rubber rim to ease installation, and make sure it does not deform when fitting the cover.

6 Fairing panels

Trim clips

1 Three types of plastic trim clip are used, so carefully note which fits where when removing the fairing panels.
2 The first type has a centre pin with a round head. To release the clip push the head of the pin into the body of the clip then draw the clip out of the panel **(see illustrations)**. To install them, push the centre pin back out so its head protrudes from the body, then fit the body into its hole and push the centre pin in so that it is flush with the body **(see illustration)**. The clip should now be locked in place.
3 The second type has a centre pin with an oblong head. To release the clip push the head of the pin into the body of the clip then draw the clip out of the panel **(see illustration)**. To install them, first expand the end tabs

5.2a Undo the screws (arrowed) on each side...

5.2b ...and lift the cover off

6.2a Push the centre pin (arrowed)...

6.2b ...into the body to release the clip

6.2c Push the centre pin out before installing the clip, then push it in when installed to lock it

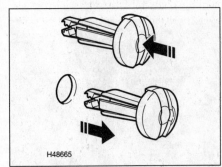
6.3a Push the oblong head into the body of the clip and withdraw it from the panel

7•4 Bodywork

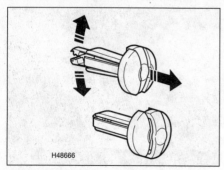

6.3b Ease the inner tabs of the clip apart and pull the oblong head out...

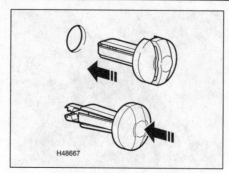

6.3c ...insert the clip in the hole and push the oblong head in to lock it

6.4a Undo the centre screw then pull the clip out

of the pin and push it back out so its head protrudes from the body **(see illustration)**. Fit the body into its hole and push the centre pin in so that it is flush with the body **(see illustration)**. The clip should now be locked in place.

4 The third type has a centre pin with a Phillips screw head. To release the clip unscrew the centre pin using a screwdriver then pull the body of the clip out of the panel **(see illustration)**. To install them, fit the body into its hole then screw the centre pin in so that it is flush with the body **(see illustration)**. You can push the centre pin in instead of screwing it in, but as they are made of plastic the threads easily become worn in which case after a while the centre pin may not unscrew again. If this happens, carefully lever the centre pin out of the body using a small screwdriver and replace the trim clip with a new one.

Lower fairing

2008 to 2011 models

5 When removing the left-hand panel release the hoses from their guide **(see illustration 6.9)**.
6 Place a soft support such as a cushion under the back of the lower fairing. Undo the two screws on each side **(see illustrations)**.
7 Slide the lower fairing rearwards to release the front vertical tabs from the fairing side panels, then draw each side panel out to release the tabs from the lower fairing slots and sides **(see illustrations)**.
8 Installation is the reverse of removal – engage the tab with the slot on the side, then the two horizontal tabs/slots on the underside, then push the lower fairing forwards to engage the front vertical tabs.

2012-on models

9 When removing the left-hand panel release the hoses from their guide **(see illustration)**.

6.4b Fit the clip in the hole then push the centre in to lock it

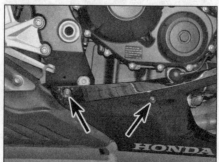

6.6a Lower fairing screws (arrowed) – right-hand side

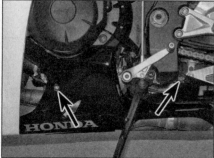

6.6b Lower fairing screws (arrowed) – left-hand side

6.7a Release the front vertical tabs...

6.7b ...and horizontal tabs...

6.7c ...and the side tab (arrowed)

6.9 Release the hoses

Bodywork 7•5

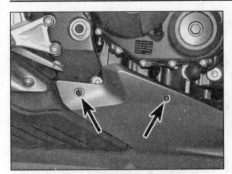
6.10a Lower fairing screws (arrowed) – right-hand side

6.10b Lower fairing screws (arrowed) – left-hand side

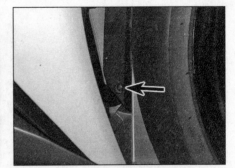
6.11a Undo the screw (arrowed)...

10 Place a soft support such as a cushion under the back of the lower fairing. Undo the two screws on each side (see illustrations).
11 Undo the screw securing the bottom of each inner panel to its fairing side panel, then release the hole from the peg to give it some freedom of movement (see illustrations).
12 Release the tabs on one side by sliding the lower fairing rearwards, then repeat for the other side (see illustration).
13 Installation is the reverse of removal.

Fairing side panels

2008 to 2011 models

14 Remove the lower fairing.
15 Release the trim clips securing the front air duct cover and remove the cover

6.11b ...and release the hole from the peg

6.12 Release the tabs on each side in turn

(see illustrations). Disconnect the relevant vacuum hose from the three-way junction (see illustration).
16 When removing the left-hand panel

release the top trim clip on the inner panel (see illustration).
17 Undo the two screws (see illustrations).
18 Carefully release the tabs from the fairing

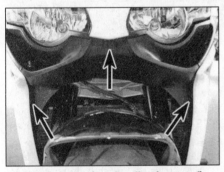
6.15a Release the trim clips (arrowed)...

6.15b ...and remove the cover

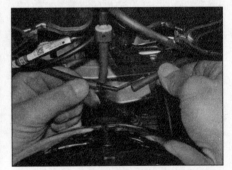
6.15c Disconnect the hose to the side being removed

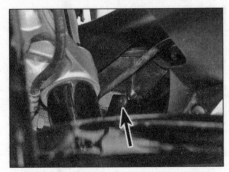
6.16 Release the trim clip (arrowed)

6.17a Undo the screw (arrowed) at the back...

6.17b ...and the screw on the top

7•6 Bodywork

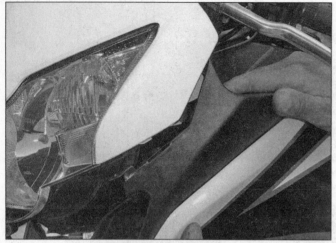

6.18a Release the tabs...

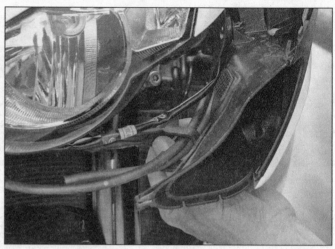

6.18b ...and the Velcro...

6.18c ...and on the left panel the wiring connector

6.19a Release the trim clips...

and the Velcro patch on the air duct, release the hose(s) and wiring from the guide(s) as required according to side, and displace the front loom wiring connector when removing the left-hand panel **(see illustrations)**.

19 When accessible release the trim clips securing the top air duct cover and remove the cover, then disconnect the air intake system control valve wiring connector and remove the fairing side panel **(see illustrations)**.

20 If required remove the air duct (see Chapter 4).

21 Installation is the reverse of removal. Make sure the air duct seats inside the end of the intake rubber on the air filter housing correctly as it can easily ruck the rubber up **(see illustration)** – if in doubt remove the air filter for a visual check.

2012-on models

22 Remove the lower fairing.

23 Release the trim clips securing the front air duct cover and remove the cover **(see illustrations 7.15a and b)**. Disconnect the

6.19b ...remove the cover...

6.19c ...and disconnect the connector

6.21 Make sure the duct locates inside the rubber all around

Bodywork 7•7

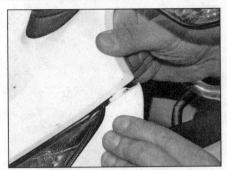

6.26a Release the fairing tab...

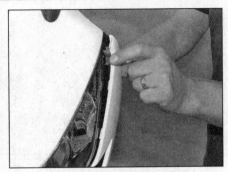

6.26b ...and the headlight tabs..

6.26c ...then lift the cover off the screw tab...

6.26d ...slide the panel forwards to release the tabs from the slots...

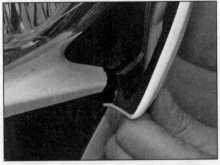

6.26e ...and release the front from the fairing

6.29 Unscrew the bolt and slide the arm off

relevant diaphragm valve vacuum hose from the three-way junction **(see illustration 6.15c)**.
24 Release the top trim clip on the inner panel **(see illustration 6.16)**.
25 Undo the two screws **(see illustrations 6.17a and b)**.
26 Carefully release the top tab from the fairing, then release the tabs from the headlight, lift the air duct cover to release the side panel screw tab and slide the panel forwards to release the tabs from the slots in the air duct cover, then release the front slot from the fairing and remove the panel, noting how the inner panel seats around the air duct **(see illustrations)**.
27 Installation is the reverse of removal. Lift the air duct cover to seat the side panel screw tab between it and the air duct **(see illustration 6.26c)**.

Engine trim cover – RA models

28 Remove the left-hand fairing side panel (see above).

29 Unscrew the gearchange linkage arm pinch bolt and slide the arm off the shaft, noting how the slit in the arm aligns with the punch mark on the shaft **(see illustration)**.
30 Undo the two screws **(see illustration)**. On 2012-on models release the rim of the cover from the hook at the front. Carefully pull the cover away to free the peg from the grommet **(see illustration)**.
31 Installation is the reverse of removal.

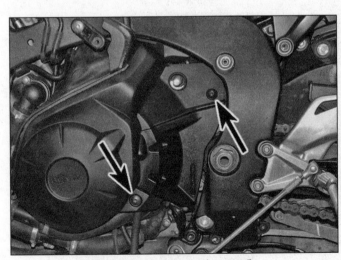

6.30a Undo the screws (arrowed)...

6.30b ...and remove the cover

7•8 Bodywork

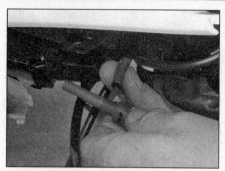

6.34 Disconnect the vacuum hose...

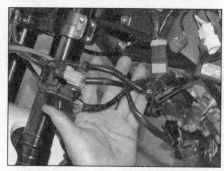

6.35 ...and the front loom connectors

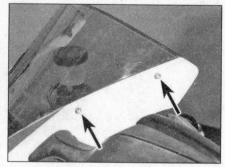

6.37 Undo the screws (arrowed)

Fairing and windshield

32 Remove the fairing side panels (see above).
33 On 2012-on models remove the air ducts (see Chapter 4, Section 3).
34 Disconnect the vacuum hose from the one-way valve **(see illustration)**.
35 Disconnect the front loom wiring connectors **(see illustration)**.
36 Remove the mirrors (see Section 4).
37 Undo the four windshield screws **(see illustration)**.
38 Draw the fairing forwards, noting how the tab on the bottom of the windshield locates in the slot and the pegs locate in the grommets on the stay, then disconnect the instrument wiring connector and the horn wiring connectors and remove the fairing **(see illustrations)**.
39 Thread a windshield screw part-way back into each of the lower well-nuts, then push

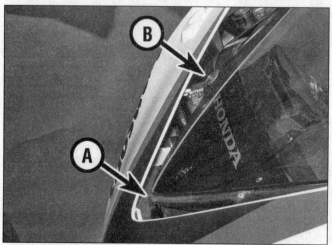

6.38a Draw the fairing slot off the tab (A) at the front of the windshield and the peg on each side from the grommet (B)

6.38b Ease the peg (arrowed) on each side at the back from the grommets...

6.38c ...then disconnect the instrument wiring...

6.38d ...and the horn wiring

Bodywork

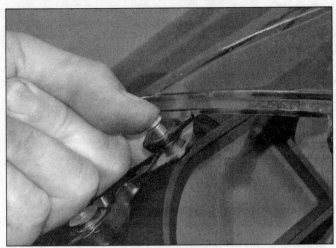

6.39 Fit the screw, push it down and simultaneously lift the windshield

6.40 Lubricate the rubber to help it through the hole

down on the head of the screw to stretch the crease of the well-nut so it can then be drawn out of its hole in the fairing stay by lifting the windshield **(see illustration)**.

40 Installation is the reverse of removal. Make sure the rubber wellnuts are in good condition and replace them with new ones if necessary. Smear some oil onto the body of each lower well-nut to help ease it into its hole in the fairing stay **(see illustration)**.

7 Front mudguard

1 Release the brake hoses from each side of the mudguard, and on RA models release the wheel sensor wiring from the right-hand side **(see illustration)**.

2 Undo the screws on each side, then lift the mudguard up and then draw it forwards, squeezing the sides in to ensure the lug on the right-hand side and the stud on the left do not scratch the fork, and remove it **(see illustration)**. Note the collars in the grommets **(see illustration 7.3)**.

3 Installation is the reverse of removal. Make sure the grommets are in good condition and the collars are fitted **(see illustration)**.

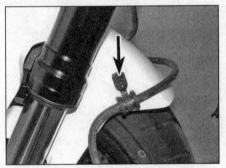

7.1 Release the brake hose guide (arrowed) from each side

7.2 Undo the screws (arrowed) on each side

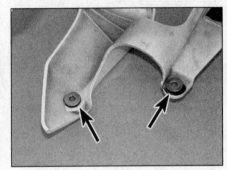

7.3 Check the grommets and collars

Notes

Chapter 8
Electrical system

Contents

	Section number
Alternator	29
Battery charging	4
Battery removal and maintenance	3
Brake light switches	14
Brake/tail light	9
Charging system testing	28
Clutch switch	22
Diode block	23
Electrical system fault finding	2
Fuses	5
General information	1
Handlebar switches	19
Headlights	8
Headlight bulbs and sidelights	7
Horn	24
Ignition switch	18

	Section number
Ignition system components	see Chapter 4
Instrument check and replacement	16
Instrument removal and installation	15
Licence plate light	10
Lighting system check	6
Neutral switch/gear position switch	20
Oil pressure switch	17
Regulator/rectifier	30
Sidestand switch	21
Speed sensor	16
Starter motor overhaul	27
Starter motor removal and installation	26
Starter relay	25
Turn signal assemblies	13
Turn signal bulbs	12
Turn signal circuit check	11

Degrees of difficulty

| **Easy,** suitable for novice with little experience | **Fairly easy,** suitable for beginner with some experience | **Fairly difficult,** suitable for competent DIY mechanic | **Difficult,** suitable for experienced DIY mechanic | **Very difficult,** suitable for expert DIY or professional |

Specifications

Battery
Type
- RR models YTZ7S
- RA models YTZ10S

Capacity
- RR models ..... 12 V, 6.0 Ah
- RA models ..... 12 V, 8.6 Ah

Voltage
- Fully-charged ..... 13.0 to 13.2 V
- Uncharged ..... below 12.4 V

Charging rate   **Normal**   **Quick**
- RR models ..... 0.6 A for 5 to 10 hrs   4.5 A for 1 hr
- RA models ..... 0.9 A for 5 to 10 hrs   4.5 A for 1 hr

Current leakage ..... 2 mA (max)

Charging system
Regulated voltage output ..... 15.5 V max. @ 5000 rpm

Alternator output
- 2008 and 2009 RR models ..... 399 W @ 5000 rpm
- 2010-on RR models ..... 372 W @ 5000 rpm
- 2009 RA models ..... 413 W @ 5000 rpm
- 2010-on RA models ..... 417 W @ 5000 rpm

Alternator stator coil resistance ..... 0.1 to 1.0 ohms

Starter motor
Brush length
- Standard ..... 12.0 mm
- Service limit (min) ..... 6.5 mm

8•2 Electrical system

Fuses
RR models
- Main .... 30 A
- Others .... 20 A x 4, 10 A x 4

RA models
- Main .... 30 A
- C-ABS .... 30 A x 2, 10 A x 1
- Others .... 20 A x 4, 10 A x 4

Bulbs
Headlights
- High beam .... 55 W
- Low beam .... 55 W

Sidelight .... LED
Brake/tail light .... LED
Licence plate light .... 5 W
Turn signal lights .... 21 W x 4 (amber)
Instrument lights .... LED
Turn signal indicator light .... LED
HI beam indicator light .... LED
Neutral indicator light .... LED
Oil pressure light .... LED
Temperature warning light .... LED
PGM-FI malfunction indicator light .... LED
HESD indicator light .... LED
C-ABS indicator light (where fitted) .... LED
Immobiliser indicator light (where fitted) .... LED

Torque settings
Alternator rotor bolt
- 2008 and 2009 models .... 113 Nm
- 2010-on models .... 103 Nm

Alternator stator bolts .... 12 Nm
Ignition switch bolts .... 26 Nm
Neutral switch (2008 to 2011 models) .... 12 Nm
Oil pressure switch .... 12 Nm
Sidestand switch bolt .... 10 Nm

1 General information

All models have a 12 volt electrical system charged by a three-phase alternator with a separate regulator/rectifier.

The regulator maintains the charging system output within the specified range to prevent overcharging, and the rectifier converts the ac (alternating current) output of the alternator to dc (direct current) to power the lights and other components and to charge the battery. The alternator rotor is mounted on the left-hand end of the crankshaft.

The starter motor is mounted on the top of the crankcase behind the cylinders. The starting system includes the motor, the battery, the relay and the various wires and switches. Some of the switches are part of a starter interlock system that prevents the engine from being started if the sidestand is down and the engine is in gear. The engine can be started with the sidestand up when it is in gear as long as the clutch lever is pulled in. The system will also cut the engine should the sidestand extend while the engine is running and in gear – see Chapter 1 for further information and checks on the system.

Note: *Keep in mind that electrical parts, once purchased, often cannot be returned. To avoid unnecessary expense, make very sure the faulty component has been positively identified before buying a replacement part.*

2 Electrical system fault finding

1 A typical electrical circuit consists of an electrical component, the switches, relays, etc, related to that component and the wiring and connectors that link the component to the battery and the frame.

2 Before tackling any troublesome electrical circuit, first study the wiring diagram thoroughly to get a complete picture of what makes up that individual circuit. Trouble spots can often be located by noting if other components related to that circuit are operating properly or not. If several components or circuits fail at one time, chances are the fault lies either in the fuse or in a common earth (ground) connection, as several circuits are often routed through the same fuse and earth (ground) connections **(see illustration)**.

3 Electrical problems often stem from simple causes, such as loose or corroded connections or a blown fuse. Prior to any electrical fault finding, always visually check the condition of the fuse, wires and connections in the problem circuit. Intermittent failures can be especially frustrating, since you can't always duplicate the failure when it's convenient to test. In such situations, a good practice is to clean all connections in the affected circuit, whether or

2.2 Common earth point (arrowed) – raise the fuel tank to check it

Electrical system 8•3

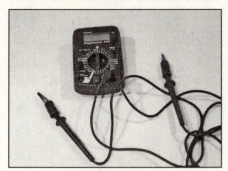
2.4a A digital multimeter can be used for all electrical tests

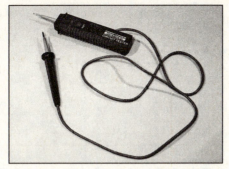
2.4b A battery-powered continuity tester

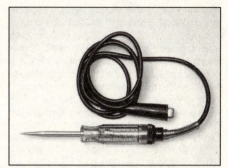
2.4c A simple test light is useful for voltage tests

not they appear to be good – where possible use a dedicated electrical cleaning spray along with sandpaper, wire wool or other abrasive material to remove corrosion, and a dedicated electrical protection spray to prevent further problems. All of the connections and wires should also be wiggled to check for looseness that can cause intermittent failure.

4 If you don't have a multimeter it is highly advisable to obtain one – they are not expensive and will enable a full range of electrical tests to be made **(see illustration)**. Go for a modern digital one with an LCD display, as they are easier to use. A continuity tester and/or test light are useful for certain electrical checks as an alternative, though are limited in their usefulness compared to a multimeter **(see illustrations)**.

Continuity checks

5 The term continuity describes the uninterrupted flow of electricity through an electrical circuit. Continuity can be checked with a multimeter set either to its continuity function (a beep is emitted when continuity is found), or to the resistance (ohms / Ω) function, or with a dedicated continuity tester. Both instruments are powered by an internal battery, therefore the checks are made with the ignition OFF. As a safety precaution, always disconnect the battery negative (-) lead before making continuity checks, particularly if ignition switch checks are being made.

6 If using a multimeter, select the continuity function if it has one, or the resistance (ohms) function. Touch the meter probes together and check that a beep is emitted or the meter reads zero, which indicates continuity. If there is no continuity there will be no beep or the meter will show infinite resistance. After using the meter, always switch it OFF to conserve its battery.

7 A continuity tester can be used in the same way – its light should come on or it should beep to indicate continuity in the switch ON position, but should be off or silent in the OFF position.

8 Note that the polarity of the test probes doesn't matter for continuity checks, although care should be taken to follow specific test procedures if a diode or solid-state component is being checked.

Switch continuity checks

9 If a switch is at fault, trace its wiring to the wiring connectors. Separate the connectors and inspect them for security and condition. A build-up of dirt or corrosion here will most likely be the cause of the problem – clean up and apply a water dispersant such as WD40, or alternatively use a dedicated contact cleaner and protection spray.

10 If using a multimeter, select the continuity function if it has one, or the resistance (ohms) function, and connect its probes to the terminals in the connector **(see illustration)**. Simple ON/OFF type switches, such as brake light switches, only have two wires whereas combination switches, like the handlebar switches, have many wires. Study the wiring diagram to ensure that you are connecting to the correct pair of wires. Continuity should be indicated with the switch ON and no continuity with it OFF.

Wiring continuity checks

11 Many electrical faults are caused by damaged wiring, often due to incorrect routing or chaffing on frame components. Loose, wet or corroded wire connectors can also be the cause of electrical problems.

12 A continuity check can be made on a single length of wire by disconnecting it at each end and connecting the meter or continuity tester probes to each end of the wire **(see illustration)**. Continuity (low or no resistance – 0 ohms) should be indicated if the wire is good. If no continuity (high resistance) is shown, suspect a broken wire.

13 To check for continuity to earth in any earth wire connect one probe of your meter or tester to the earth wire terminal in the connector and the other to the frame, engine, or battery earth (-) terminal. Continuity (low or no resistance – 0 ohms) should be indicated if the wire is good. If no continuity (high resistance) is shown, suspect a broken wire or corroded or loose earth point (see below).

Voltage checks

14 A voltage check can determine whether power is reaching a component. Use a multimeter set to the dc voltage scale, or a test light. The test light is the cheaper component, but the meter has the advantage of being able to give a voltage reading.

15 Connect the meter or test light in parallel, i.e. across the load **(see illustration)**.

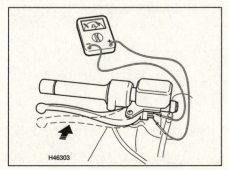
2.10 Continuity should be indicated across switch terminals when lever is operated

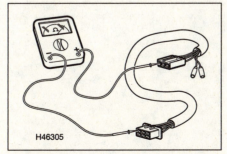
2.12 Wiring continuity check. Connect the meter probes across each end of the same wire

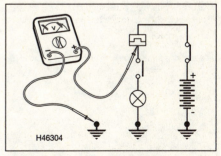
2.15 Voltage check. Connect the meter positive probe to the component and the negative probe to earth

8•4 Electrical system

16 First identify the relevant wiring circuit by referring to the wiring diagram at the end of this manual. If other electrical components share the same power supply (i.e. are fed from the same fuse), take note whether they are working correctly – this is useful information in deciding where to start checking the circuit.

17 If using a meter, check first that the meter leads are plugged into the correct terminals on the meter (red to positive (+), black to negative (-). Set the meter to the dc volts function, where necessary at a range suitable for the battery voltage – 0 to 20 vdc. Connect the meter red probe (+) to the power supply wire and the black probe to a good metal earth (ground) on the bike's frame or directly to the battery negative terminal. Battery voltage should be shown on the meter with the ignition switch, and if necessary any other relevant switch, ON.

18 If using a test light, connect its positive (+) probe to the power supply terminal and its negative (-) probe to a good earth (ground) on the bike's frame. With the switch, and if necessary any other relevant switch, ON, the test light should illuminate.

19 If no voltage is indicated, work back towards the fuse continuing to check for voltage. When you reach a point where there is voltage, you know the problem lies between that point and your last check point.

Earth (ground) checks

20 Earth connections are made either directly to the engine or frame via the mounting of the component, or by a separate wire into the earth circuit of the wiring harness. Alternatively a short earth wire is sometimes run from the component directly to the bike's frame.

21 Corrosion is a common cause of a poor earth connection, as is a loose earth terminal fastener.

22 If total or multiple component failure is experienced, check the security of the main earth lead from the negative (-) terminal of the battery, the earth lead bolted to the engine, and the main earth point(s) on the frame **(see illustrations 2.2a and b)**. If corroded, dismantle the connection and clean all surfaces back to bare metal. Remake the connection and prevent further corrosion from forming by smearing battery terminal grease over the connection.

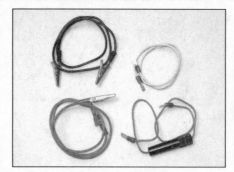

2.23 A selection of insulated jumper wires

23 To check the earth of a component, use an insulated jumper wire to temporarily bypass its earth connection **(see illustration)** – connect one end of the jumper wire to the earth terminal or metal body of the component and the other end to the bike's frame. If the circuit works with the jumper wire installed, the earth circuit is faulty.

24 To check an earth wire first check for corroded or loose connections, then check the wiring for continuity (Step 13) between each connector in the circuit in turn, and then to its earth point, to locate the break.

3 Battery removal and maintenance

Caution: Be extremely careful when handling or working around the battery. The electrolyte is very caustic and an explosive gas (hydrogen) is given off when the battery is charging.

Removal and installation

1 Make sure the ignition is switched OFF.
2 Remove the rider's seat (see Chapter 7).
3 Unscrew the negative (–) terminal bolt first and disconnect the lead from the battery **(see illustration)**. Lift up the red insulating cover to access the positive (+) terminal, then unscrew the bolt and disconnect the lead.
4 Release the retaining strap then lift the battery out **(see illustrations)**.
5 Installation is the reverse of removal. Clean the battery terminals and lead ends with a wire

3.3 Disconnect the negative lead first then disconnect the positive lead (arrowed)

brush, emery paper or steel wool. Reconnect the leads, connecting the positive (+) terminal first.

> **HAYNES HINT** *Battery corrosion can be kept to a minimum by applying a layer of battery terminal grease or petroleum jelly (Vaseline) to the terminals after the leads have been connected. DO NOT use a mineral based grease.*

Inspection and maintenance

6 The battery on all models is of the maintenance free (sealed) type, therefore requiring no regular maintenance. However, the following checks should still be performed.

7 Check the state of charge by measuring the voltage at the battery terminals **(see illustration)**. Connect the voltmeter positive (+) probe to the battery positive (+) terminal, and the negative (–) probe to the battery negative (–) terminal. When fully-charged there should be 13.0 to 13.2 volts present. If the voltage falls below 12.4 volts remove the battery (see above), and recharge it as described below in Section 4.

8 Check the battery terminals and leads are tight and free of corrosion. If corrosion is evident, clean the terminals as described in Step 5, then protect them from further corrosion (see **Haynes Hint**).

9 Keep the battery case clean to prevent current leakage, which can discharge the battery over a period of time (especially when it sits unused). Wash the outside of the case

3.4a Release the strap...

3.4b ...and remove the battery

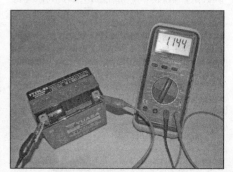

3.7 Checking battery voltage

Electrical system 8•5

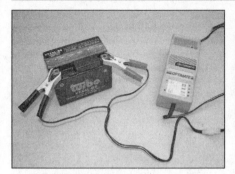

4.2 Battery connected to a charger

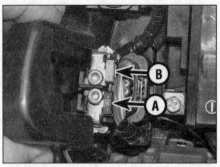

5.2 Remove the relay cover to access the main fuse (A) and FI fuse (B) – RR models

5.3 Main and FI fuse holder (arrowed) – RA models

with a solution of baking soda and water. Rinse the battery thoroughly, then dry it.
10 Look for cracks in the case and replace the battery with a new one if any are found. If acid has been spilled on the frame or battery box, neutralise it with a baking soda and water solution, then dry it thoroughly.
11 If the motorcycle sits unused for long periods of time, disconnect the leads from the battery terminals, negative (–) terminal first. Refer to Section 4 and charge the battery once every month to six weeks.

4 Battery charging

Caution: Be extremely careful when handling or working around the battery. The electrolyte is very caustic and an explosive gas (hydrogen) is given off when the battery is charging.

1 Remove the battery (see Section 3). Connect the charger to the battery, making sure that the positive (+) lead on the charger is connected to the positive (+) terminal on the battery, and the negative (–) lead is connected to the negative (–) terminal.
2 Honda recommend that the battery is charged at the normal rate specified at the beginning of the Chapter. A higher 'quick charge' rate that can be used if absolutely necessary is also specified, but note that exceed this could cause the battery to overheat, buckling the plates and rendering it useless. If a normal domestic charger is used check that after a possible initial peak, the charge rate falls to a safe level **(see illustration)**. If the battery becomes hot during charging **stop**. Further charging will cause damage. Note that there are many bike-specific chargers available from good suppliers that are designed for the maintenance and recovery of motorcycle batteries, in particular catering for the requirements of heavily discharged MF batteries. They are a worthwhile investment, especially if the bike is not used over winter. Follow the manufacturer's instructions.
3 If the recharged battery discharges rapidly when left disconnected it is likely that an internal short caused by physical damage or

sulphation has occurred. A new battery will be required. A sound item will tend to lose its charge at about 1% per day.
4 Install the battery (see Section 3).
5 If the motorcycle sits unused for long periods of time, charge the battery once every month to six weeks and leave it disconnected.

5 Fuses

1 The electrical system as a whole is protected by the main fuse, and individual circuits are protected by other fuses of different ratings.
2 On RR models the main fuse and the FI (fuel injection system) fuses are housed in the starter relay – to access them remove the rider's seat (see Chapter 7), then unclip the relay cover **(see illustration)**.

5.4a Fusebox (arrowed)

5.5a Pull the fuse out

3 On RA models the main fuse and the FI (fuel injection system) fuses are housed in a holder in front of the battery – to access them remove the rider's seat (see Chapter 7), then unclip the fuseholder lid **(see illustration)**.
4 All other fuses are housed in the fuse/relay box, also located under the rider's seat **(see illustration)**. The location, identity and rating of each fuse (and relay) is marked on the box lid. Unclip the lid to access the fuses (and relays) **(see illustration)**. A spare fuse of each rating is provided.
5 The fuses can be removed and checked visually – if you can't pull the fuse out with your fingertips, use a pair of suitable pliers **(see illustration)**. A blown fuse is easily identified by a break in the element **(see illustration)**, but if there is any doubt check the fuse for continuity (see Section 2). Each fuse is clearly marked with its rating and must only be replaced by a fuse of the correct rating. If

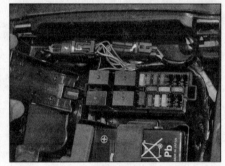

5.4b Unclip the lid to access the fuses and relays

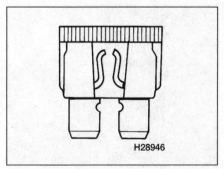

5.5b A blown fuse can be identified by a break in its element a spare fuse is used, always replace it with a new one so that a spare of each rating is carried on the bike at all times.

⚠️ **Warning: Never put in a fuse of a higher rating or bridge the terminals with any other substitute, however temporary it may be. Serious damage may be done to the circuit, or a fire may start.**

6 If the new fuse blows immediately check the wiring circuit very carefully for evidence of a short-circuit. Look for bare wires and chafed, melted or burned insulation.

7 Occasionally a fuse will blow or cause an open-circuit for no obvious reason. Corrosion of the fuse ends and fusebox terminals may occur and cause poor fuse contact. If this happens, remove the corrosion with a wire brush or emery paper, then spray the fuse end and terminals with electrical contact cleaner.

6 Lighting system check

Note: *Refer to electrical system fault finding in Section 2 and to the wiring diagram for your model at the end of this Chapter.*

1 If a light fails first check the bulb (applies to headlight, licence plate light and turn signals), and the bulb terminals in the connector or holder. If none of the lights work, check the battery (see Section 3). Low battery voltage indicates either a faulty battery or a defective charging system. Refer to Section 3 for battery checks and Section 28 for charging system tests. Also, check the fuses (Section 5) – if there is more than one problem at the same time, it is likely to be a fault relating to a multi-function component, such as one of the fuses governing more than one circuit, or the ignition switch. When checking for a blown filament in a bulb, it is advisable to back up a visual check with a continuity test of the filament as it is not always apparent that a bulb has blown.

Headlights

2008 to 2011 models

2 Two single filament bulbs are fitted – one bulb works on LO beam and both bulbs work on HI beam, in conjunction with a HI beam relay. If one headlight beam fails to work, first check the bulb (see Section 7). If both headlight beams fail to work, first check the fuse (see Section 5), and then the bulbs. If they are good, the problem lies in the black/red wire from the fusebox to the starter button and HI beam relay, or in the blue/white wire from the starter button to the dimmer switch, or in the starter button itself. Refer to Section 2 for continuity testing procedures, and also to the wiring diagrams at the end of this Chapter.

3 If the HI beam does not work and the relay is suspected of being faulty, remove the fairing (see Chapter 7). Pull the relay off its socket and test it as follows **(see illustrations)**: set a multimeter to the ohms x 1 scale and connect it across the relay's A and B terminals. There should be no continuity (infinite resistance). Using a fully-charged 12 volt battery and two insulated jumper wires, connect the positive (+) terminal of the battery to the C terminal on the relay, and the negative (–) terminal to the D terminal. At this point the relay should be heard to click and the meter read 0 ohms (continuity). If this is the case the relay is good. If the relay does not click when battery voltage is applied and indicates no continuity (infinite resistance) across its terminals, it is faulty and must be replaced with a new one.

4 If the relay is good, check there is battery voltage at the black/red wire terminal on the relay wiring connector with the ignition ON. If there is no voltage, check the wiring between the relay socket and the fusebox. If voltage is present, check all wires between the relay socket, the headlight connector and the dimmer switch for continuity, and check there is continuity to earth (ground) in the green wires from the relay socket and the headlight connector. Repair or renew the wiring or connectors as necessary.

5 If the LO beam does not work, check for battery voltage at the blue/white wire terminal on the headlight wiring connector with the ignition ON **(see illustration 7.2)**. If voltage is present, check for continuity to earth (ground) in the green wire from the wiring connector. If no voltage is present check the blue/white wire from the connector to the starter button, and then the black/red wire between the button and the fusebox – there should be continuity through the button with it at rest, and no continuity with the button pushed. Repair or renew the wiring or connectors as necessary.

2012-on models

6 Two single filament bulbs are fitted – one bulb works on LO beam and both bulbs work on HI beam, in conjunction with a relay that is controlled by the instrument panel. If one headlight beam fails to work, first check the bulb (see Section 7). If both headlight beams fail to work, first check the fuse (see Section 5), then the bulbs (see Section 7). If all is good so far check the relay (Step 7).

7 To test the relay remove the fairing (see Chapter 7). Pull the relay off its socket and test it as follows **(see illustrations 6.3a and b)**: set a multimeter to the ohms x 1 scale and connect it across the relay's A and B terminals. There should be no continuity (infinite resistance). Using a fully-charged 12 volt battery and two insulated jumper wires, connect the positive (+) terminal of the battery to the C terminal on the relay, and the negative (–) terminal to the D terminal. At this point the relay should be heard to click and the meter read 0 ohms (continuity). If this is the case the relay is good. If the relay does not click when battery voltage is applied and indicates no continuity (infinite resistance) across its terminals, it is faulty and must be replaced with a new one. If the relay is good check for battery voltage at each of the black/red wires in the socket with the ignition ON. If there is no voltage check the wires to the fusebox for continuity.

8 If the relay and its power source are good but the LO beam does not work, check there is continuity in the blue/white wire between the relay socket and the LO beam bulb wiring connector.

9 If the relay and its power source are good but the HI beam does not work, check there is continuity in the blue/white wire between the relay socket and the dimmer switch, and in the blue wire from the switch to the HI beam bulb wiring connector.

10 If the relay and its power source are good but both beams do not work, check there is continuity in the black/blue wire between the relay socket and the instrument panel connector.

11 Next check for continuity to earth in the green wire from each bulb connector.

12 If no fault can be found it is likely the instrument panel is faulty.

Tail light

13 If the tail light fails to work, refer to Section 9 and disconnect the wiring connector, and check for battery voltage at the brown/white wire terminal on the loom side of the connector with the ignition switch ON. If voltage is present, check for continuity to earth (ground) in the green wire from the wiring connector. If no voltage is indicated, check the wiring and connectors between the connector and the

6.3a Headlight relay (arrowed)

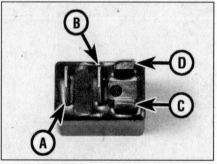

6.3b Relay test terminal identification

fusebox. Refer to the wiring diagrams at the end of this Chapter.

14 If the power, wiring and connectors are good, or if only one or some of the tail light LEDs have failed leaving others working, then the brake/tail light unit is faulty and must be replaced with a new one – individual LEDs are not available.

Brake light

15 If the brake light fails to work, refer to Section 9 and disconnect the tail light wiring connector, and check for battery voltage at the green/yellow wire terminal on the loom side of the connector, first with the front brake lever on, then with the rear brake pedal on. If voltage is present with one brake on but not the other, then the switch or its wiring is faulty. If voltage is present in both cases, check for continuity to earth (ground) in the green wire from the wiring connector. If no voltage is indicated, check the wiring and connectors between the brake light and the brake switches, and the fusebox, then check the switches themselves (Section 14).

16 If the power, wiring and connectors are good, or if only one or some of the brake light LEDs have failed leaving others working, then the brake/tail light unit is faulty and must be replaced with a new one – individual LEDs are not available.

Licence plate light

17 If the licence plate light fails to work, refer to Section 10 and check the bulb. If that is good disconnect the wiring connector, and check for battery voltage at the brown/white wire terminal on the loom side of the connector with the ignition switch ON. If voltage is present, check for continuity to earth (ground) in the green wire from the wiring connector. If no voltage is indicated, check the wiring and connectors between the connector and the fusebox. Refer to the wiring diagrams at the end of this Chapter.

Sidelight

18 If a sidelight fails to work, refer to Section 7 and check there is battery voltage at the brown/white wire terminal on the loom side of the connector in the boot behind the relevant side of the instrument panel with the ignition switch ON. If voltage is present, check there is continuity to earth (ground) in the green wire from the wiring connector. If no voltage is indicated, check the wiring and connectors between the sidelight connector and the fusebox. Also check the wiring from the connector up to the LED in the mirror. If all the wiring is good the LED is faulty – replace the sub-loom in the mirror/front turn signal with a new one (see Section 7).

Turn signals

19 See Section 11.

Instrument and warning lights

20 See Section 16.

7 Headlight bulbs and sidelights

Note: *The headlight bulbs are of the quartz-halogen type. Do not touch the bulb glass as skin acids will shorten the bulb's service life. If the bulb is accidentally touched, it should be wiped carefully when cold with a rag soaked in methylated spirit and dried before fitting.*

Headlight bulbs

1 Turn the relevant cover anti-clockwise to release it **(see illustration)**.
2 Disconnect the wiring connector from the bulb **(see illustration)**.

7.1 Remove the cover...

3 Release the bulb retaining clip, noting how it fits, then remove the bulb, bearing in mind the information in the Note above **(see illustrations)**.
4 Fit the new bulb into the headlight, making sure it locates correctly, and secure it with the retaining clip **(see illustrations 7.3b and a)**.

> **HAYNES HINT** *Always use a paper towel or dry cloth when handling new bulbs to prevent injury if the bulb should break and to increase bulb life.*

5 Connect the wiring connector **(see illustrations 7.2)**.
6 Make sure the cover seal is in good condition. Fit the cover, aligning the marks and locating the tabs in the cut-out, and turn it clockwise **(see illustration 7.1)**.
7 Check the operation of the headlight.

Sidelights

8 The side lights are LEDs rather than conventional bulbs – if the LED fails the wiring sub-loom within the mirror/front turn signal must be replaced with a new one.
9 Pull the rubber boot out from between the fairing and the instrument panel and disconnect the wiring connectors **(see illustration)**.
10 Remove the turn signal bulb (see Section 12).

7.2 ...then disconnect the wiring connector

7.3a Release the clip...

7.3b ...and remove the bulb

7.9 Disconnect the connectors

8•8 Electrical system

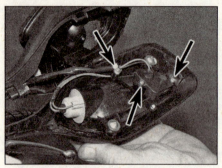
7.11 Undo the screws (arrowed)

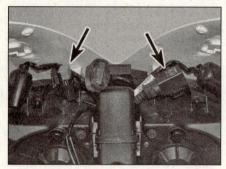
8.4 Displace the two relays (arrowed)

8.6a Undo the two screws (arrowed)...

8.6b ...and the screw (arrowed) on the underside...

8.6c ...then release the tabs on the bottom...

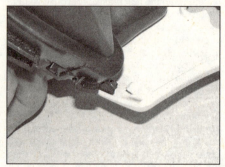
8.6d ...and on each side...

11 Undo the LED unit and wiring clamp screws and draw the wiring out of the mirror stem **(see illustration)**.
12 Fit the new sub-loom into the turn signal in reverse order. Check the operation of the sidelight and turn signal.

8 Headlights

1 Remove the fairing (see Chapter 7).
2 Remove the air intake system vacuum chamber and its holder (see Chapter 4, Section 3).
3 On 2008 to 2011 models undo the screws and remove the lean angle sensor.

4 Displace the two relays (headlight and turn signal) and release the wiring clamp **(see illustration)**.
5 On 2008 to 2011 models undo the five screws and remove the headlight from the fairing. Disconnect the headlight sub-loom wiring connector **(see illustration 8.6e)**.
6 On 2012-on models undo the three screws, then release the tabs and remove the headlight from the fairing **(see illustrations)**. Disconnect the headlight sub-loom wiring connector **(see illustration)**. Undo the nuts and remove the lean angle sensor **(see illustration)**.
7 If required remove the bulbs (see Section 7).
8 Installation is the reverse of removal. Check the operation of the headlights. Check the headlight aim (see Chapter 1).

9 Brake/tail light

1 The brake/tail light contains LEDs rather than a conventional bulb.
2 If one or more of the LEDs within the brake/tail light unit has failed, replace the unit with a new one – individual LEDs are not available.

Removal and installation

3 Remove the seat cowling (see Chapter 7).
4 On RR models disconnect the tail light wiring connector **(see illustration)**.

8.6e ...then disconnect the wiring connector (arrowed)

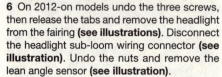
8.6f Lean angle sensor nuts (arrowed)

9.4 Tail light wiring connector (arrowed) – RR models

Electrical system 8•9

9.5a On RA models displace the fuse/relay box...

9.5b ...and disconnect the tail light (white 3-pin) connector (arrowed)

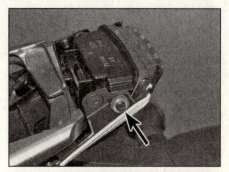

9.7a Undo the screw (arrowed) on each side...

5 On RA models displace the fuse/relay box, then disconnect the tail light wiring connector **(see illustrations)**.
6 Feed the wiring and connector back to the tail light, noting its routing.
7 Undo the screw on each side and remove the tail light **(see illustrations)**.
8 Installation is the reverse of removal. Check the operation of the tail and brake lights.

10 Licence plate light

9.7b ...and draw the tail light out

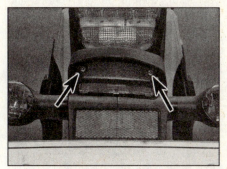

10.1a Undo the screws (arrowed)...

Bulb change

1 Undo the two screws and remove the cover **(see illustrations)**.
2 Carefully pull the bulb out and replace with a new one **(see illustration)**.
3 Make sure the rubber seal is in good condition and correctly in place before fitting the cover. Do not overtighten the screws. Check the operation of the licence plate light.

Removal and installation

4 Remove the rear reflector **(see illustration)**.
5 Undo the screw on each side and remove the licence plate holder **(see illustrations)**.
6 Disconnect the licence plate light wiring

10.1b ...and remove the cover

10.2 Pull the bulb out of the socket

10.4 Undo the nut and remove the reflector

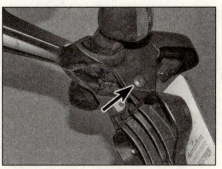

10.5a Undo the screw (arrowed) on each side...

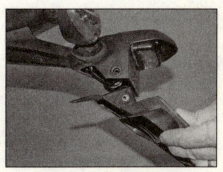

10.5b ...and remove the holder

8•10 Electrical system

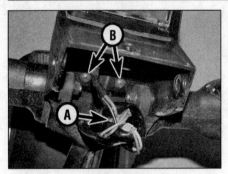

10.6 Disconnect the wiring connector (A), then undo the screws (B) and remove the holder

10.7 Undo the nuts (arrowed) and remove the light

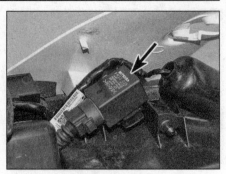

11.3 Turn signal relay (arrowed)

connector, then undo the screws and remove the licence plate light holder **(see illustration)**.

7 Undo the nuts and remove the licence plate light from the holder **(see illustration)**.

8 Installation is the reverse of removal. Check the operation of the light.

11 Turn signal circuit check

Note: *Refer to electrical system fault finding in Section 2 and to the wiring diagram for your model at the end of this Chapter.*

1 Most turn signal problems are the result of a burned out bulb or corroded socket. This is especially true when the turn signals function properly in one direction (although possibly too quickly), but fail to flash in the other direction. If this is the case, first check the bulbs, the sockets and the wiring connectors (see Sections 12 and 13). If all the turn signals fail to work, check the STO/HORN/WINK RLY fuse (see Section 5), and then the relay itself (see Steps 2 to 4). If they are good, the problem lies in the wiring or connectors, or the switch. Refer to Section 19 for the switch testing procedures, and also to the wiring diagrams at the end of this Chapter.

2 To check the relay, displace and support the fairing, leaving the front loom wiring connected (see Chapter 7).

3 Displace the relay and disconnect the wiring connector **(see illustration)**. Short between the white/green and grey wire terminals on the loom side of the connector using a jumper wire. Turn the ignition ON and operate the turn signal switch. If the lights come on (they won't flash), the relay is faulty and must be replaced with a new one.

4 If the lights do not come on, check the grey wire for continuity to the left-hand switch housing and the white/green wire for continuity to the fusebox, and repair or renew the wiring or connectors as required. On 2012-on models also check the green wire for continuity to earth.

5 If all is good so far, or if the lights came on one side but not the other, check the wiring between the left-hand switch housing and the turn signals themselves. Repair or renew the wiring or connectors as necessary.

12 Turn signal bulbs

Note: *It is a good idea to use a paper towel or dry cloth when handling bulbs to prevent injury if the bulb should break and to increase bulb life.*

Front turn signals

1 Undo the screw on the underside **(see illustration)**. Carefully release the tab at the stem, then the tab on the outer end, and finally the two along the top, and detach the turn signal holder from the mirror, noting how it fits **(see illustrations)**.

2 Turn the bulbholder anti-clockwise and draw it out **(see illustration)**.

3 Push the bulb in and twist it anti-clockwise to release it **(see illustration)**. Check the socket terminals for corrosion and clean them if necessary.

12.1a Undo the screw...

12.1b ...then release the stem tab first...

12.1c ...then the others as described

12.2 Release the bulbholder...

12.3 ...then push the bulb in and turn it anti-clockwise

Electrical system 8•11

12.7 Undo the screw and remove the lens

12.8 Push the bulb in and turn it anti-clockwise to release it

12.10 Make sure the tab (arrowed) locates correctly

4 Line up the pins of the new bulb with the slots in the socket, then push the bulb in and turn it clockwise until it locks into place.
5 Fit the bulbholder and turn it clockwise until it locks into place.
6 Fit the turn signal holder onto the mirror, locating the tabs in the reverse order, and fit the screw. Do not overtighten the screw as it is easy to strip the threads or crack the lens.

 Note that the pins on amber bulbs are offset, thus preventing the use of clear lens bulbs.

Rear turn signals

7 Undo the screw and detach the lens from the housing, noting how it fits (see illustration). Remove the rubber seal if it is loose, and discard it if it is damaged, deformed or deteriorated.
8 Push the bulb in and twist it anti-clockwise to release it (see illustration). Check the socket terminals for corrosion and clean them if necessary.
9 Line up the pins of the new bulb with the slots in the socket, then push the bulb in and turn it clockwise until it locks into place.
10 Fit a new rubber seal if required, and make sure it is properly seated and does not get pinched. Fit the lens onto the housing, locating the tab in the cutout, and fit the screw (see

illustration). Do not overtighten the screw as it is easy to strip the threads or crack the lens.

13 Turn signal assemblies

Front turn signals

1 Remove the turn signal bulb (Section 12).
2 Displace the sidelight and wiring from the turn signal – there is no need to disconnect the wiring connectors (see illustration 7.11).
3 Undo two screws and remove the turn signal (see illustration).
4 Installation is the reverse of removal. Check the operation of the turn signals.

Rear turn signals

5 Remove the rear reflector (see illustration 10.4).
6 Undo the screw on each side and remove the licence plate holder (see illustrations 10.5a and b).
7 Disconnect the turn signal wiring connector (see illustration).
8 Unscrew the nut and remove the collar plate, the rubber mount and the turn signal, taking care as you draw the wire through (see illustration 13.7).
9 Installation is the reverse of removal. Check the operation of the turn signals.

14 Brake light switches

Circuit check

Note: *Refer to electrical system fault finding in Section 2 and to the wiring diagram for your model at the end of this Chapter.*

1 Before checking the switches, and if not already done, check the brake light circuit (see Section 6).
2 The front brake light switch is mounted on the underside of the brake master cylinder. Disconnect the wiring connectors from the switch (see illustration). Using a continuity tester, connect the probes to the terminals of

13.3 Front turn signal screws (arrowed)

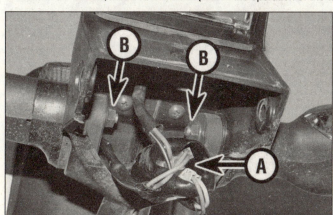

13.7 Turn signal wiring connectors (A) and mounting nuts (B)

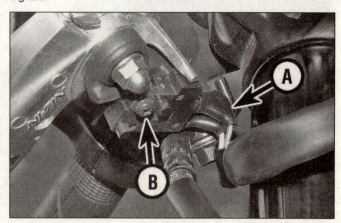

14.2 Front brake switch wiring connectors (A) and mounting screw (B)

14.3a Rear brake switch wiring connector (arrowed) – RR models

14.3b On RA models the black 2-pin switch connector is under the back of the fuel tank

the switch. With the brake lever at rest, there should be no continuity. With the brake lever applied, there should be continuity. If the switch does not behave as described, replace it with a new one.

3 The rear brake light switch is mounted on the inside of the rider's right-hand footrest bracket **(see illustration 14.8)**. To access the wiring connector, on RR models remove the seat (see Chapter 7), and on RA models remove the fuel tank (see Chapter 5). Disconnect the wiring connector **(see illustrations)**. Using a continuity tester, connect the probes to the terminals on the switch side of the wiring connector. With the brake pedal at rest, there should be no continuity. With the brake pedal applied, there should be continuity. If the switch does not behave as described, replace it with a new one, although check first that the spring has not become detached or broken, and the switch is adjusted correctly (see Chapter 1).

4 If the switches are good, check for voltage at the white/green wire, on the loom side of the connector for the rear switch, in each case with the ignition switch ON – there should be battery voltage. If there's no voltage present, check the wiring between the connector and the fusebox (see the wiring diagrams at the end of this Chapter). If voltage is present, check the green/yellow wire for continuity to the brake light, referring to the relevant wiring diagram. Repair or renew the wiring as necessary.

Switch replacement

Front brake lever switch

5 The switch is mounted on the underside of the brake master cylinder. Disconnect the wiring connectors from the switch **(see illustration 14.2)**.

6 Undo the single screw and remove the switch.

7 Installation is the reverse of removal. Make sure the peg on the switch is correctly located in its hole before tightening the screw. The switch isn't adjustable.

Rear brake pedal switch

8 The rear brake light switch is mounted on the inside of the rider's right-hand footrest bracket **(see illustration)**. To access the wiring connector, on RR models remove the seat (see Chapter 7), and on RA models remove the fuel tank (see Chapter 5). Disconnect the wiring connector **(see illustration 14.3a or b)**. Feed the wiring down to the switch, noting its routing and releasing it from any ties.

9 Detach the end of the switch spring from the brake pedal **(see illustration)**. Lift the switch out of its bracket.

10 Installation is the reverse of removal. Make sure the brake light is activated just before the rear brake pedal takes effect. If adjustment is necessary, refer to Chapter 1, Section 2.

14.8 Rear brake light switch (arrowed)

14.9 Unhook the spring (arrowed) from the pedal

Electrical system 8•13

15.2a Undo the screws (arrowed)...

15.2b ...and remove the instrument cluster

15 Instrument removal and installation

1 Remove the fairing (see Chapter 7).
2 Undo the screws, noting the washers, and remove the instrument cluster **(see illustrations)**.
3 Installation is the reverse of removal. Check the rubber grommets in the bracket and replace them with new ones if necessary **(see illustration 15.2b)**.

16 Instrument check and replacement

Check

Note: *Refer to electrical system fault finding in Section 2 and to the wiring diagram for your model at the end of this Chapter.*

Instrument cluster power check

1 If none of the instruments or displays are working, first check the METER ILLUMI fuse (see Section 5).
2 If the fuse is good, displace and support the fairing – disconnect the instrument wiring connector but leave the front loom wiring connected (see Chapter 7). Check the instrument wiring connector for loose or broken connections.
3 To check the power input wire, check for battery voltage between the brown/white wire terminal and a good earth (ground) with the ignition switch ON. There should be battery voltage. If there is no voltage, refer to the wiring diagrams and check the wire between the instrument cluster and the fusebox for loose or broken connections or a damaged wire.
4 To check the back-up power wire, check for battery voltage between the red/green wire terminal on the wiring loom side of the connector and a good earth (ground) with the ignition switch OFF. There should be battery voltage. If there is no voltage, refer to the wiring diagrams and check the wire between the instrument cluster and the fusebox for loose or broken connections or a damaged wire.
5 If there is voltage, and to check the earth (ground) wire, check for continuity between the green/black wire terminal and earth (ground). If there is no continuity, check the circuit for loose or broken connections or a damaged wire and repair as necessary.
6 If all power input and earth wires are good, but there is no display or instrument function, then the printed circuit board (PCB) is faulty. Disassemble the instrument cluster and replace the PCB with a new one (Steps 18 to 20).

Speedometer and speed sensor

7 Displace and support the fairing, leaving the instrument and front loom wiring connected (see Chapter 7). Pull back the rubber boot and check the instrument wiring connector for loose or broken connections **(see illustration)**.
8 If the wiring is good, place the bike on an auxiliary stand so the rear wheel is off the ground and the transmission in neutral. Connect a voltmeter between the pink/green (+) and green/black (-) wire terminals in the connector – make sure the probes make good contact when inserted into the connector. With the ignition switch ON, have an assistant turn the rear wheel by hand and check that a fluctuating voltage reading between 0 and 5 volts is obtained. If the correct reading is obtained the printed circuit board (PCB) is faulty. Disassemble the instrument cluster and replace the PCB with a new one (see below). If no reading is obtained, check for continuity in the pink/green wire to the speed sensor wiring connector (see Steps 21 and 22 for access), and in the green/black wire to earth.

9 If the wiring is good check for battery voltage between the violet (+) and green/black (-) wire terminals on the loom side of the connector. If there is no voltage refer to the wiring diagrams and check the wires for continuity to the fuse box and earth respectively and repair any loose or broken connection or damaged wire.
10 If all is good so far, the speed sensor is faulty and must be replaced with a new one (Steps 21 to 24).

Tachometer

11 When the ignition is switched on the tachometer needle should swing from zero to maximum, then return to zero. If it doesn't check the power input (Steps 1 to 6).
12 If the tachometer does not work, displace and support the fairing, leaving the instrument and front loom wiring connected (see Chapter 7). Pull back the rubber boot and check the instrument wiring connector for loose or broken connections **(see illustration 16.7)**.
13 If the wiring is good, check the tachometer input peak voltage using the peak voltage adapter (Pt. No. MTP07-0286 in the US, and 07HGJ-0020100 elsewhere) with an aftermarket digital multimeter having an impedance of 10 M-ohm/DCV minimum, for this test. Connect the positive (+) lead of the voltmeter and peak voltage adapter arrangement to the yellow/green wire terminal

16.7 Check the connector

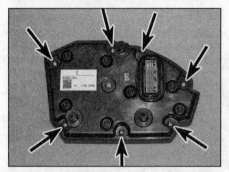

16.19a Undo the screws (arrowed – 2012 model shown)...

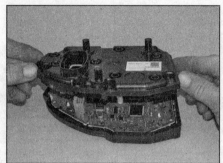

16.19b ...remove the cover...

16.19c ...and lift the PCB out

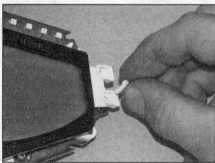

16.19d Take care not to lose the push rods

in the instrument wiring connector and the negative (–) lead to a good earth (ground). Start the engine and measure the tachometer input peak voltage, which should be at least 10.5 volts. If the peak voltage is normal, check the instrument cluster earth wire (see Step 5). If the wire is good then the tachometer is faulty. Disassemble the instrument cluster and replace the PCB with a new one (Steps 18 to 20).

14 If there is no reading, raise the fuel tank (see Chapter 4). Remove the jacket from the air filter housing. Check there is continuity in the yellow/green wire to the ECM grey wiring connector. If there is no continuity there is a break in the wire or faulty connector. Refer to the wiring diagrams and trace and rectify the fault. If the wiring is good, or if there was a voltage recorded in Step 13 but it was lower than specified, the ECM could be faulty (see Chapter 4).

All other functions

15 If none of the functions are working, check the instrument cluster power input and earth wires (Steps 1 to 6). If all is good, disassemble the instrument cluster (see below) and check for any obvious internal fault. If none is apparent replace the PCB with a new one.

16 If an individual function is not working, refer to Chapter 3 for the coolant temperature and warning display, Chapter 4 for the low fuel warning, FI and HISS lights, Chapter 5 for the HESD light, Chapter 6 for the C-ABS light, Section 6 for the HI beam light, Section 17 for the oil pressure switch, and Section 20 for the neutral switch/gear position switch. If the particular component and its circuit are good replace the PCB with a new one (Steps 18 to 20).

Instrument and warning lights

17 All instrument and warning lights are LEDs, which are part of the instrument cluster printed circuit board and are not available individually. If one of the LEDs fails disassemble the instrument cluster and replace the PCB with a new one (Steps 18 to 20).

Instrument disassembly and replacement

18 Remove the instrument cluster (see Section 15).
19 Undo the screws on the back and remove the rear cover, then remove the PCB from the front cover **(see illustrations)**. Note the button pushrods and take care not to lose them.
20 Installation is the reverse of removal. Do not over-tighten the screws.

16.22 Disconnect the wiring connector

Speed sensor removal and installation

21 The speed sensor is mounted behind the starter motor. To access it raise the fuel tank (see Chapter 4). On US models remove the EVAP system purge control valve (see Chapter 4).
22 Disconnect the wiring connector from the sensor **(see illustration)**.
23 Unscrew the bolt and remove the sensor **(see illustration)**. Check the condition of its O-ring and replace it with a new one if it is damaged or there is evidence of leakage around it, but note that Honda do not list it as being available separately. While the sensor is removed plug the orifice with clean rag.
24 Installation is the reverse of removal, using a new O-ring if necessary.

Lap timer – 2012-on models

25 The lap timer is operated by the starter button and functions as described in the owner's handbook supplied with the machine. A lap timer relay in the starter circuit switches the power supply between the starter circuit and lap timer.
26 If the lap timer function fails, check the switching function at the instruments. Remove the fairing to access the instrument connector (see Chapter 7) but leave all wiring connected and support the fairing to prevent strain on the wiring. Using a multimeter set to the 0 to 20 volts dc function, connect the meter's positive probe to the yellow/pink wire terminal of the connector and its negative probe to earth. Turn the ignition ON. With the instruments set to lap timer mode (press SEL and SET at the same time) press the starter/lap button and note the voltage reading. With the button pressed 10 to 16 volts should be shown, and with it released 6 volts should be shown. Switch the ignition OFF after completing the test. If these readings are not obtained refer to the wiring diagram at the end of this chapter and check the yellow/pink wire from the instruments to the handlebar switch for continuity.
27 If there's a problem with the lap timer relay switching between starter and lap timer function (i.e. the starter operates instead of the lap timer when the engine is running), remove the relay and test its operation on the bench as follows.

16.23 Unscrew the bolt (arrowed) and remove the sensor

Electrical system 8•15

28 To access the lap timer relay raise the fuel tank (see Chapter 4). Remove the air filter housing jacket, noting how it fits (see illustration 18.2a). Unplug the relay from its wire connector on the right-hand side of the air filter housing (see illustration) and test it as follows.

29 Using a fully-charged 12 volt battery and two insulated jumper wires, connect the positive (+) terminal of the battery to the E terminal on the relay, and the negative (–) terminal to the C terminal (see illustration). Using either a continuity tester or a multimeter set to the ohms x 1 scale, connect it across the A and B terminals and then across the A and D terminals. If the relay is working correctly there should be continuity across A and B, but no continuity across A and D. Now disconnect the battery and repeat the test across terminals A and B, then A and D; no continuity should be shown across A and B, but continuity across A and D. If the relay does not function as described it is faulty.

30 If the relay's switching function is working correctly, check for battery voltage at the relay connector's white/yellow wire terminal with the ignition ON. No voltage indicates a break in the white/yellow wire between the connector and fusebox. If battery voltage was shown, turn the ignition OFF and plug the relay back into its connector. Now start the engine and check for battery voltage at the black/orange wire terminal whilst operating the lap timer (press SEL and SET at the same time). In lap timer mode 10 to 16 volts should be shown, otherwise 2 volts should be shown. Switch the ignition OFF after completing the test. If these readings are not obtained refer to the wiring diagram at the end of this chapter and check the black/orange wire from the instruments to the relay for continuity.

17 Oil pressure switch

Check

Note: *Refer to electrical system fault finding in Section 2 and to the wiring diagram for your model at the end of this Chapter.*

1 The oil pressure warning light should come on when the ignition switch is turned ON and go out a few seconds after the engine is started. If the oil pressure warning light does not go out or comes on whilst the engine is running, stop the engine immediately and carry out an oil level check (see *Pre-ride checks*), and if the level is correct, an oil pressure check (see Chapter 2).

2 If the oil pressure warning light does not come on when the ignition is turned ON, but all other instrument functions work, remove the lower fairing (see Chapter 7). Pull the rubber cover off the oil pressure switch and undo the screw securing the wiring connector (see illustration). With the ignition switched

16.28 Lap timer relay location

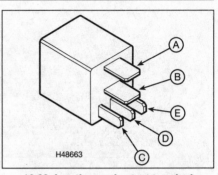

16.29 Lap timer relay test terminal identification

17.2 Pull back the rubber cover, undo the terminal screw (arrowed) and detach the wire

17.9 Make sure the wire is in its guide (arrowed)

ON, earth (ground) the wire on the crankcase and check that the warning light comes on. If the light comes on, the switch is defective and must be replaced with a new one.

3 If the light still does not come on, check for voltage at the wire terminal with the ignition ON. If there is no voltage present, displace and support the fairing, leaving the front loom wiring connected (see Chapter 7). Check for loose or broken connections in the instrument wiring connector (see illustration 16.7). Check there is continuity in the wire between the switch and the connector. Repair the wiring if necessary. If the wiring is all good and the switch is good the instrument PCB could be faulty (see Section 16).

4 If the warning light does not go out when the engine is started or comes on whilst the engine is running, yet the oil pressure is satisfactory, detach the wire from the oil pressure switch (see above). With the wire detached and the ignition switched ON the light should be out. If it is illuminated, the wire between the switch and instrument cluster is earthed (grounded) at some point. If the wiring is good, the switch must be assumed faulty and replaced with a new one.

Removal

5 The oil pressure switch is screwed into the right-hand side of the crankcase. Remove the lower fairing (see Chapter 7).

6 Pull the rubber cover off the switch, then undo the screw securing the wiring connector (see illustration 17.2).

7 Counter-hold the base hex and unscrew and remove the switch – be prepared to catch any residual oil with a rag.

Installation

8 Apply a suitable sealant to the upper portion of the switch threads near the switch body, leaving the bottom 3 to 4 mm of thread clean. Thread the switch into the crankcase, then counter-hold the base hex and tighten the switch to the torque setting specified at the beginning of the Chapter.

9 Attach the wiring connector and secure it with the screw, then fit the rubber cover (see illustration).

10 Run the engine and check that the switch operates correctly and without leakage. Install the lower fairing (see Chapter 7).

18 Ignition switch

 Warning: *To prevent the risk of short circuits, disconnect the battery negative (–) lead before making any ignition switch checks.*

Check

Note: *Refer to electrical system fault finding in Section 2 and to the wiring diagram for your model at the end of this Chapter.*

1 The switch can be checked for continuity using an ohmmeter or a continuity test light. Disconnect the battery negative (–) lead, which

8•16 Electrical system

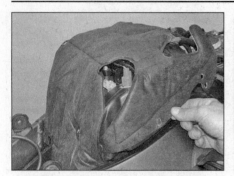
18.2a Unclip and remove the jacket

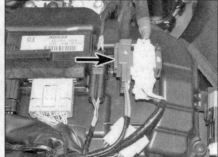
18.2b Ignition switch wiring connector (arrowed)

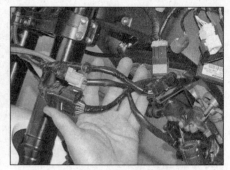
18.6a Disconnect the wiring...

will prevent the possibility of a short circuit, before making the checks (see Section 3).

2 Raise the fuel tank (see Chapter 7). Remove the air filter housing jacket, noting how it fits **(see illustration)**. Disconnect the switch wiring connector **(see illustration)**.

3 Using an ohmmeter or a continuity tester, check the continuity of the connector terminal pairs (see the wiring diagrams at the end of this Chapter). Continuity should exist between the terminals connected by a solid line on the diagram when the switch is in the indicated position.

4 If the switch fails any of the tests, replace it with a new one.

Removal

5 Disconnect the battery negative (–) lead (see Section 3).

6 Remove the fairing side panels (see Chapter 7).

Disconnect the front loom wiring connectors on the left-hand side **(see illustration)**. Detach the vacuum hose to the vacuum chamber from the one-way valve **(see illustration)**. Unscrew the two bolts securing the fairing stay to the steering head and remove the complete fairing assembly **(see illustrations)**.

7 If required separate the contact plate from the bottom of the switch **(see illustration)** – it is available separately from the main body of the switch. Otherwise raise the fuel tank (see Chapter 4), then remove the jacket from the air filter housing and disconnect the switch wiring connector **(see illustrations 18.2a and b)**. Feed the wiring back to the switch, noting its routing and releasing it from any guides.

8 Where fitted remove the HISS receiver wiring cover **(see illustration)**.

9 One-way security bolts (which can be done up but not undone using conventional tools)

are fitted **(see illustration 18.7)** – drive the heads around using a small cold chisel. If necessary remove the top yoke and place it in a vice with some protective card or rag to do this (refer to Chapter 1, Section 12, following the relevant Steps).

Installation

10 Installation is the reverse of removal. Either use new ignition switch bolts or clean the threads of the original ones and apply some fresh threadlock. Tighten them to the torque setting specified at the beginning of the Chapter. Refer to Chapter 1 to install the top yoke. Make sure the wiring connector is correctly routed and securely connected.

19 Handlebar switches

Check

Note: *Refer to electrical system fault finding in Section 2 and to the wiring diagram for your model at the end of this Chapter.*

1 Generally speaking, the switches are reliable and trouble-free. Most troubles, when they do occur, are caused by dirty or corroded contacts, but wear and breakage of internal parts is a possibility that should not be overlooked. If breakage does occur, the entire switch and related wiring harness will have to be replaced with a new one, as individual parts are not available.

2 The switches can be checked for continuity

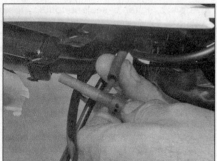
18.6b ...and the vacuum hose

18.6c Unscrew the bolts (arrowed)...

18.6d ...and remove the fairing

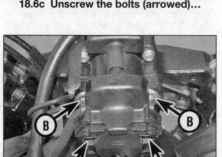
18.7 Ignition switch contact plate screws (A) and one-way security bolts (B)

18.8 Unclip the cover if fitted

Electrical system 8•17

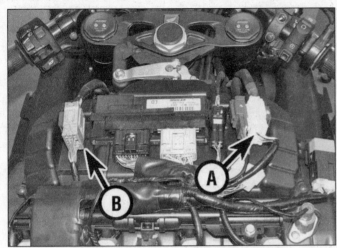

19.3 Right-hand switch wiring connector (A), left-hand switch wiring connector (B)

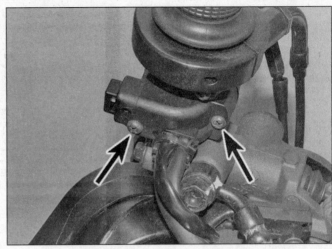

19.8a Right-hand switch housing screws (arrowed)

using an ohmmeter or a continuity test light. Disconnect the battery negative (–) lead, which will prevent the possibility of a short circuit, before making the checks (see Section 3).

3 To access the connectors raise the fuel tank (see Chapter 4). Remove the air filter housing jacket, noting how it fits **(see illustration 18.2a)**. Disconnect the relevant switch wiring connector **(see illustration)**.

4 Check for continuity between the terminals of the switch connector with the switch in the various positions (i.e. switch off – no continuity, switch on – continuity) – see the wiring diagram for your model at the end of this Chapter. Continuity should exist between the terminals connected by a solid line on the diagram when the switch is in the indicated position.

5 If the continuity check indicates a problem exists, displace the switch housing (Step 8), and spray the switch contacts with electrical contact cleaner (there is no need to remove the switch completely). If they are accessible, the contacts can be scraped clean with a knife or polished with crocus cloth. If switch components are damaged or broken, it will be obvious when the switch is disassembled.

Removal and installation

6 To access the connectors raise the fuel tank (see Chapter 4). Remove the air filter housing jacket, noting how it fits **(see illustration 18.2a)**. Disconnect the relevant switch wiring connector **(see illustration 19.3)**. Feed the wiring back to the switch, freeing it from any clips and ties and noting its routing.

7 If removing the right-hand switch disconnect the wires from the brake light switch **(see illustration 14.2)**. If removing the left-hand switch disconnect the wires from the clutch switch **(see illustration 22.2)**.

8 Undo the screws on the underside of the switch housing and separate the halves from the handlebar **(see illustrations)**.

9 Installation is the reverse of removal. Make sure the locating pin in the housing locates in the hole in the handlebar. Tighten the front screw first, then the rear, and do not overtighten them.

20 Neutral switch/gear position switch

Note: *Refer to electrical system fault finding in Section 2 and to the wiring diagram for your model at the end of this Chapter.*

1 The neutral switch or gear position switch (according to model) is located in the left-hand side of the engine above the front sprocket. The neutral light should come whenever the ignition switch is ON and the transmission is in neutral. The switch is part of the starter interlock safety circuit that prevents or stops the engine running if the transmission is in gear whilst the sidestand is down, and prevents the engine from starting if the transmission is in gear unless the sidestand is up and the clutch is pulled in.

Neutral switch – 2008 to 2011 models

Check

2 On RA models remove the left-hand fairing side panel and the engine trim cover (see Chapter 7).

3 Pull the wiring connector off the switch **(see illustration)**. Check for continuity between the switch terminal and the crankcase. With the transmission in neutral, there should be continuity. With the transmission in gear, there should be no continuity. If not, remove the switch (Step 7) and check whether the plunger is bent or damaged, or just stuck **(see illustration)**. Replace the switch with a new one if necessary.

4 If the switch is good check for continuity in the light green wire from the connector to the diode block in the fusebox. Next check the

19.8b Left-hand switch housing screws (arrowed)

20.3a Pull the connector off the switch

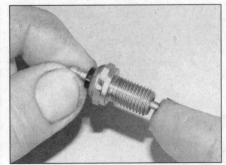

20.3b Make sure the plunger moves in and out smoothly and freely

8•18 Electrical system

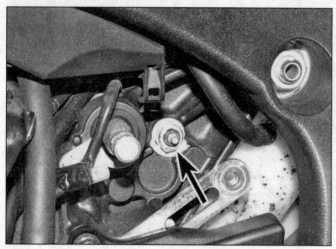

20.7 Unscrew and remove the switch (arrowed)

20.10a Remove the connector from the boot (arrowed)...

other components (clutch switch, sidestand switch, diode block) in the starter safety circuit, and check the wiring between them for continuity, and the connectors for loose or broken connections.

Removal and installation

5 On RA models remove the left-hand fairing side panel and the engine trim cover (see Chapter 7).
6 Pull the wiring connector off the switch **(see illustration 20.3a)**.
7 Clean the area around the switch, then unscrew it from the crankcase **(see illustration)**. Remove the sealing washer – a new one should be used.
8 Fit the switch using a new washer and tighten it to the torque setting specified at the beginning of the Chapter.
9 Connect the wiring connector and check the operation of the neutral light.

Gear position switch – 2012-on models

Check

10 If there is a fault in the switch or its circuit the gear position indicator in the instrument panel blinks '–'. Remove the fuel tank (see Chapter 4). Pull the wiring connector out of the boot and disconnect it **(see illustrations)**.
11 Refer to the table and check there is continuity between the relevant wire and the crankcase with the transmission in the position indicated. If not, replace the switch with a new one.

GEAR POSITION	CONNECTION
1st	Brown
Neutral	Light green
2nd	Red
3rd	Black/yellow
4th	Yellow
5th	Black
6th	Blue

12 If the switch is good check for continuity in each wire from the switch connector to the instrument connector (remove the fairing for access to it – see Chapter 7).

Removal and installation

13 On RR models note the alignment of the punch mark on the gearchange shaft with the slit in the linkage arm clamp **(see illustration)**. Unscrew the linkage arm bolt and slide the arm off the shaft **(see illustration)**.
14 On RA models remove the left-hand fairing side panel and the engine trim cover (see Chapter 7).
15 Remove the fuel tank (see Chapter 4). Pull the wiring connector out of the boot and disconnect it **(see illustrations 20.10a and b)**. Feed the wiring to the switch, noting its routing.
16 Make sure the transmission is in neutral. Clean the area around the switch, then unscrew the bolt and remove the switch **(see illustration)**. Remove the O-ring – a new one should be used.
17 Make sure the switch engagement pin is positioned with the longer section pointing

20.10b ...and disconnect it

20.13a Note the alignment...

20.13b ...then unscrew the bolt and slide the arm off

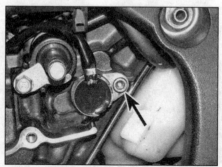

20.16 Unscrew the bolt (arrowed) and remove the switch

Electrical system 8•19

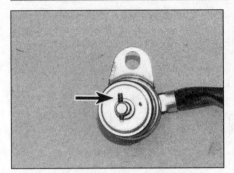

20.17a Align the engagement pin (arrowed) as shown

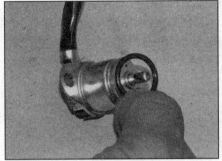

20.17b Fit a new O-ring into the groove

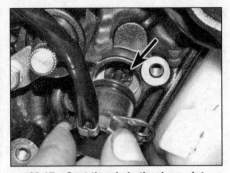

20.17c Seat the pin in the drum slot (arrowed)

just to the left of the mounting bolt hole as shown **(see illustration)**. Fit the switch using a new O-ring smeared with oil, locating the pin in the slot in the end of the selector drum **(see illustrations)**. Align the bolt hole by turning the switch body if required and fit the bolt.

18 Connect the wiring connector and check the operation of the switch. On RR models fit the gearchange linkage arm onto the shaft, aligning it as before **(see illustrations 20.13b and a)**.

21 Sidestand switch

1 The sidestand switch is mounted on the stand pivot. The switch is part of the starter interlock safety circuit that prevents or stops the engine running if the transmission is in gear whilst the sidestand is down, and prevents the engine from starting if the transmission is in gear unless the sidestand is up and the clutch is pulled in.

Check

Note: *Refer to electrical system fault finding in Section 2 and to the wiring diagram for your model at the end of this Chapter.*

2 On RR models remove the left-hand fairing side panel (see Chapter 7). On RA models raise the fuel tank (see Chapter 4). Release and disconnect the sidestand switch 2-pin connector **(see illustration)**.

3 Check the operation of the switch using an ohmmeter or continuity tester. Connect the meter between the terminals on the switch side of the connector. With the sidestand up there should be continuity (zero resistance) between the terminals, and with the stand down there should be no continuity (infinite resistance).

4 If the switch does not perform as expected, it is faulty and must be replaced with a new one.

5 If the switch is good, check the other components (clutch switch, neutral/gear position switch, diode block) in the starter safety circuit, and check the wiring between them for continuity, and the connectors for loose or broken connections.

Removal

6 On RR models remove the left-hand fairing side panel (see Chapter 7). On RA models raise the fuel tank (see Chapter 4).

7 Release and disconnect the sidestand switch 2-pin connector **(see illustration 21.2)**. Feed the wiring back to the switch, noting its routing **(see illustration)**.

8 Unscrew the switch bolt and remove the switch from the stand, noting how it fits **(see illustration)**. Honda specify that the switch bolt be replaced with a new one every time it is disturbed – the new bolt has a locking compound already applied to its threads. However there is nothing to stop you cleaning up the threads on the old bolt and applying a suitable non-permanent thread locking compound on installation.

Installation

9 Fit the new switch onto the sidestand, making sure the pin locates in the hole, and the lug on the stand bracket locates into the cut-out in the switch body **(see illustration 21.8)**. Secure the switch with a new or cleaned and threadlocked bolt and tighten it to the torque setting specified at the beginning of the Chapter.

10 Feed the wiring up to its connector, making sure it is correctly routed and secured **(see illustration 21.7)**.

11 Connect the wiring connector and fit it onto the bracket **(see illustration 21.2)**. Check the operation of the sidestand switch. Install the fairing panel or lower the fuel tank, as applicable.

22 Clutch switch

1 The clutch switch is mounted on the underside of the clutch lever bracket. The switch is part of the starter interlock safety circuit that prevents or stops the engine running if the transmission is in gear whilst the sidestand is down, and prevents the engine from starting if the transmission is in gear unless the sidestand is up and the clutch lever is pulled in. The switch isn't adjustable.

Check

Note: *Refer to electrical system fault finding in Section 2 and to the wiring diagram for your model at the end of this Chapter.*

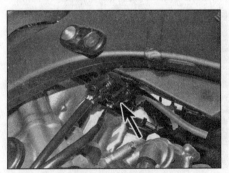

21.2 Sidestand switch wiring connector (arrowed) – RR models

21.7 Note the routing of the wire (arrowed)

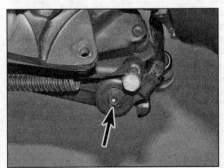

21.8 Sidestand switch bolt (arrowed)

8•20 Electrical system

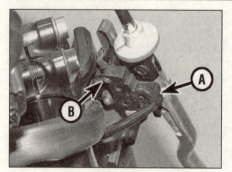

22.2 Clutch switch wiring connectors (A) and mounting screw (B)

23.2 Diode block (arrowed)

23.3 Test the diode as described

2 To check the switch, disconnect the wiring connectors from it **(see illustration)**. Connect the probes of an ohmmeter or a continuity tester to the two switch terminals. With the clutch lever pulled in, there should be continuity. With the clutch lever out, there should be no continuity (infinite resistance).

3 If the switch is good, check the other components (sidestand switch, neutral/gear position switch, diode block) in the starter safety circuit, and check the wiring between them for continuity, and the connectors for loose or broken connections.

Removal and installation

4 Disconnect the wiring connectors from the switch **(see illustration 22.2)**.

5 Undo the single screw securing the switch and remove it, noting how it fits.

6 Installation is the reverse of removal. Clean the threads of the screw and apply some threadlock. Make sure the switch is correctly located before tightening the screw.

23 Diode block
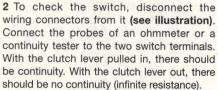

Note: *Refer to electrical system fault finding in Section 2 and to the wiring diagram for your model at the end of this Chapter.*

1 The diode block plugs into a connector in the fuse/relay box, which is located under the rider's seat **(see illustration 5.4a)**. The block contains two diodes, which are part of the starter interlock safety circuit that prevents or stops the engine running if the transmission is in gear whilst the sidestand is down, and prevents the engine from starting if the transmission is in gear unless the sidestand is up and the clutch lever is pulled in.

2 Remove the rider's seat (see Chapter 7). Open the fusebox lid and pull the diode block out of its socket **(see illustration)**.

3 Using an ohmmeter or continuity tester, connect the positive (+) probe to one of the outer terminals of the diode block and the negative (–) probe to the middle terminal of the block **(see illustration)**. The diode being tested should show continuity (with a small resistance). Now reverse the probes. The diode should show no continuity. Repeat the tests between the other outer terminal and the middle terminal. The same results should be achieved. If it doesn't behave as stated, replace the diode block with a new one.

4 If the diode block is good, push it back into its socket, then check the other components (sidestand switch, neutral/gear position switch, clutch switch) in the starter safety circuit, and check the wiring between them for continuity, and the connectors for loose or broken connections.

24 Horn

Check

1 The horn is mounted on the fairing stay above the bottom yoke. If it doesn't work first check the STOP/HORN/WINK RLY fuse (see Section 5).

2 If the fuse is good, remove the fairing (see Chapter 7).

3 Check the wiring connectors for loose wires. Using two jumper wires, apply voltage from a fully-charged 12V battery directly to the terminals on the horn. If the horn doesn't sound, replace it with a new one.

4 If the horn sounds, support the fairing and reconnect the front loom wiring connectors. Check for voltage at the black wire connector with the ignition ON and the horn button pressed. If voltage is present, check the green wire for continuity to earth. Refer to electrical system fault finding in Section 2 and to the wiring diagrams at the end of this Chapter.

5 If no voltage was present, check the black wire for continuity between the horn and the button in the left-hand switch gear. Next, with the ignition switch ON, check that there is voltage at the white/green wire to the horn button. If there is, check the button contacts in the switch housing (see Section 19).

6 If there isn't voltage at the white/green wire, check the wire from the switch to the fusebox.

Replacement

7 The horn is mounted on the fairing stay above the bottom yoke. Remove the fairing (see Chapter 7).

8 Unscrew the bolt and remove the horn **(see illustration)**.

9 Fit the horn and tighten the bolt. Install the fairing. Check that the horn works.

25 Starter relay
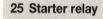

Check

1 If the starter circuit is faulty, first check the fuses (see Section 5).

2 To access the relay, on RR models remove the rider's seat (see Chapter 7), and on RA models remove the fuel tank (see Chapter 4).

3 Make sure the transmission is in neutral. Remove the cover from the relay **(see illustration)**. Unscrew the bolt securing the starter motor lead (the front lead on RR models and the left-hand lead on RA models – the other

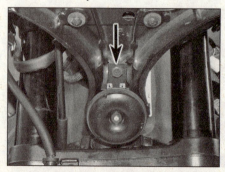

24.8 Horn mounting bolt (arrowed)

25.3a Remove the cover

Electrical system 8•21

25.3b Starter motor lead terminal (A) and battery lead terminal (B)

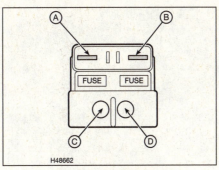

25.6 Starter relay test
- A Yellow/red wire terminal
- B Green/red wire terminal
- C Battery lead terminal
- D Starter motor lead terminal

25.14 Disconnect the wiring connector

lead is the battery lead) **(see illustration)** – be careful not to touch the battery lead with the tool while unscrewing the starter motor lead, and then position the lead away from the relay.
4 With the ignition switch ON, the engine kill switch in the RUN position, and the transmission in neutral, press the starter switch. The relay should be heard to click.
5 If the relay doesn't click, switch off the ignition, remove the relay as described below, and test it as follows:
6 Set a multimeter to the ohms x 1 scale and connect it across the relay's starter motor and battery lead terminals. There should be no continuity. Using a fully-charged 12 volt battery and two insulated jumper wires, connect the positive (+) terminal of the battery to the yellow/red wire terminal of the relay, and the negative (–) terminal to the green/red wire terminal of the relay **(see illustration)**. At this point the relay should be heard to click and the multimeter read 0 ohms (continuity). If this is the case the relay is proved good. If the relay does not click when battery voltage is applied and indicates no continuity (infinite resistance) across its terminals, it is faulty and must be replaced with a new one.
7 If the relay is good, check for continuity in the main power lead from the battery to the relay. Also check that the terminals and connectors at each end of the lead are tight and corrosion-free.
8 Next check for battery voltage at the yellow/red wire terminal in the relay wiring connector with the transmission in neutral, the kill switch in the RUN position, the ignition ON, and the

starter button pressed. If there is no voltage, check the wiring between the relay wiring connector and the starter button.
9 If voltage is present, check that there is continuity to earth in the green/red wire with the transmission in neutral (note that there will be a very slight resistance due to the diodes in the starter interlock circuit). If not check the wiring and connectors between the relay, the fusebox and the neutral/gear position switch, then if that is good check the switch itself and the diode block.
10 Now shift the transmission into gear, raise the sidestand and pull the clutch lever in and check for continuity to earth again. If there is no continuity, check the clutch switch and sidestand switch as described in the relevant sections of this Chapter. If all components are good, check the wiring between the various components (see the wiring diagrams at the end of this Chapter).
11 Failure of the starter circuit could also be caused by the lap timer relay not switching correctly. A test of the relay is given in Section 16.

Replacement

12 To access the relay, on RR models remove the rider's seat (see Chapter 7), and on RA models remove the fuel tank (see Chapter 4).
13 Disconnect the battery (see Section 3).
14 Remove the cover from the relay **(see illustration 25.3a)**. Disconnect the relay wiring

connector **(see illustration)**. Unscrew the bolts securing the starter motor and battery leads to the relay and detach the leads **(see illustration 25.3b)**. If the relay is being replaced with a new one, remove the fuses and fit them into the same position in the new relay **(see illustration 5.2)**.
15 Installation is the reverse of removal. Connect the lead from the battery to the terminal marked B and the lead from the starter motor to the terminal marked M, and make sure the terminal bolts are securely tightened **(see illustration 25.3b)**. Do not forget to fit the fuses into the relay, if removed **(see illustration 5.2)**. Connect the negative (–) lead last when reconnecting the battery.

26 Starter motor removal and installation

Note: *On RA models this procedure will require removal of the C-ABS unit.*

Removal

1 The starter motor is mounted on the crankcase. Disconnect the battery negative (–) lead. Remove the left-hand fairing side panel (see Chapter 7). On RA models remove the C-ABS front valve unit (see Chapter 6).
2 Peel back the rubber terminal cover on the starter motor **(see illustration)**. Unscrew the nut and detach the lead.
3 Unscrew the two bolts securing the starter motor to the crankcase, noting the earth lead **(see illustration)**. Slide the starter motor out **(see illustration)**. If it is tight use a screwdriver

26.2 Pull back the terminal cover then unscrew the nut (arrowed) and detach the lead

26.3a Unscrew the two bolts (arrowed), noting the earth lead...

26.3b ...and remove the motor

8•22 Electrical system

26.5 Fit a new O-ring and lubricate it

27.4 Note the alignment marks (highlighted) between the housing and the covers

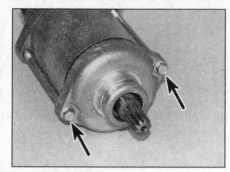

27.5a Unscrew the bolts (arrowed)...

to lever it out – on RR models first raise the fuel tank (see Chapter 4).

4 Remove the O-ring on the end of the starter motor and discard it as a new one must be used **(see illustration 26.5)**.

Installation

5 Fit a new O-ring onto the end of the starter motor, making sure it is seated in its groove **(see illustration)**. Apply a smear of engine oil to the O-ring.

6 Manoeuvre the motor into position and slide it into the crankcase, meshing the starter motor teeth with those of the starter idle/reduction gear **(see illustration 26.3b)**. Fit the mounting bolts, securing the earth lead with the rear bolt, and tighten them **(see illustration 26.3a)**.

7 Connect the starter lead to the motor and secure it with the nut **(see illustration 26.2)**. Fit the rubber cover over the terminal.

27 Starter motor overhaul

Check

1 Remove the starter motor (see Section 26).
2 Using a fully-charged 12 volt battery and two

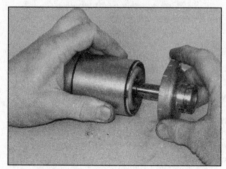

27.5b ...and remove the front cover...

insulated jumper wires, connect the lead from the positive (+) terminal of the battery to the protruding terminal on the starter motor, then hold the motor down on a bench, keeping your fingers clear of the shaft, and touch the lead from the negative (–) jumper terminal to one of the motor's mounting lugs. At this point the starter motor should spin. If this is the case the motor is proved good, though it is worth disassembling it and checking it if you suspect it of not working properly under load. If the motor does not spin, disassemble it for inspection.

Disassembly

3 Remove the starter motor (see Section 26).

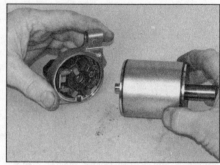

27.6 ...and the rear cover

4 Note any alignment marks between the main housing and the front and rear covers, or make your own if they aren't clear **(see illustration)**.
5 Unscrew the two long bolts and remove the front cover from the motor **(see illustrations)**.
6 Remove the rear cover **(see illustration)**.
7 Withdraw the armature from the main housing **(see illustration)** – it is held in by the attraction of the magnets, so take care not to lose your grip on the armature before the magnets lose theirs.
8 At this stage check for continuity between the terminal bolt and the positive brushes **(see illustration)** – there should be continuity (zero

27.7 Withdraw the armature

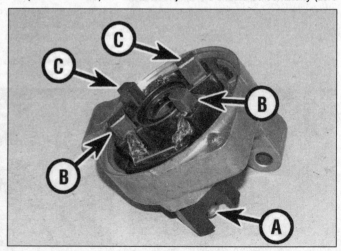

27.8 Terminal bolt (A), positive brushes (B), negative brushes (C)

Electrical system 8•23

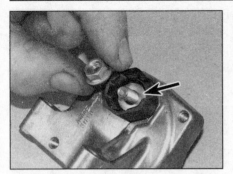
27.9a Undo the nut and remove the plain washer (arrowed)...

27.9b ...the insulator...

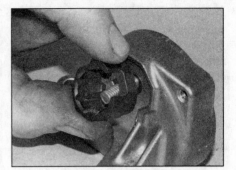
27.9c ...the shield...

27.9d ...and the O-ring

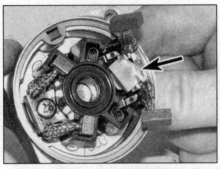
27.9e Withdraw the terminal bolt and brush assembly (arrowed)...

27.9f ...and remove the brush springs

resistance). Check for continuity between the terminal bolt and the cover – there should be no continuity (infinite resistance). Also check for continuity between the negative and positive brushes – there should be no continuity (infinite resistance). If there is no continuity when there should be or *vice versa*, identify the faulty component and replace it with a new one.

9 Noting the correct fitted location of each component, unscrew the nut from the terminal bolt and remove the plain washer, the insulator, the terminal shield and the O-ring **(see illustrations)**. Remove the positive brush and terminal bolt assembly, then remove the positive brush springs **(see illustrations)**.

10 Undo the screw and remove the negative brush assembly **(see illustration)**. Remove the brush springs, then remove the holder **(see illustrations)**.

Inspection

11 The parts of the starter motor that are most likely to require attention are the brushes. Measure the length of each brush and compare the results to the length listed in this Chapter's Specifications **(see illustration)**. If worn replace the brushes with new ones. If the brushes are not worn excessively, nor cracked, chipped, or otherwise damaged, they can be re-used.

12 Inspect the commutator bars on the armature for scoring, scratches and discoloration. The commutator can be cleaned and polished with crocus cloth, but do not use sandpaper or emery paper. After cleaning, wipe away any residue with a cloth soaked in electrical system cleaner or denatured alcohol.

13 Using an ohmmeter or a continuity

27.10a Undo the screw and remove the negative brush assembly...

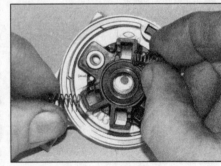
27.10b ...and springs...

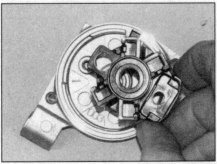
27.10c ...then remove the brushholder

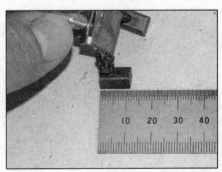
27.11 Measure the length of each brush

8•24 Electrical system

27.13a There should be continuity between the bars...

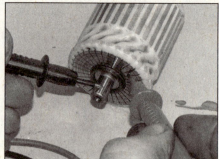

27.13b ...and no continuity between the bars and the shaft

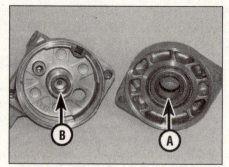

27.15 Check the bearing and seal (A) and the bush (B)

test light, check for continuity between the commutator bars **(see illustration)**. Continuity should exist between each bar and all of the others. Also, check for continuity between the commutator bars and the armature shaft **(see illustration)**. There should be no continuity (infinite resistance) between the commutator and the shaft. If the checks indicate otherwise, the armature is defective and a new starter motor must be obtained – the armature is not available separately.

14 Check the front end of the armature shaft for worn, cracked, chipped and broken teeth. If the shaft is damaged or worn, a new starter motor must be obtained – the armature is not available separately.

15 Inspect the front and rear covers for signs of cracks or wear. Check the oil seal and the needle bearing in the front cover and the bush in the rear cover for wear and damage **(see illustration)** – the seal, bearing, bush and covers are not listed as being available separately so if necessary a new starter motor must be fitted.

16 Inspect the magnets in the main housing and the housing itself for cracks.

17 Inspect the terminal bolt shield, insulator, and O-ring, and the sealing rings on the housing, for signs of damage, deformation and deterioration and replace them with new ones if necessary.

Reassembly

18 Locate the brushholder on the rear cover **(see illustration 27.10c)**. Fit the negative brush springs and brush assembly and secure it and the holder with the screw **(see illustrations 27.10b and a)**.

19 Fit the positive brush springs into their housings **(see illustration 27.9f)**. Fit the terminal bolt through the holder and rear cover **(see illustration 27.9e)**. Roll the O-ring down the bolt and press it into the gap between the bolt and the cover **(see illustration)**. Fit the shield, aligning it as shown **(see illustration 27.9c)**. Fit the insulator and the washer, then tighten the nut **(see illustrations 27.9b and a)**. Locate the brushes in their housings against the springs, with the wires in the slots **(see illustration 27.8)**.

20 To check for correct installation do the continuity checks described in Step 8.

21 If removed fit the sealing rings onto the main housing **(see illustration)**.

22 Grasp the housing and carefully allow the armature to be drawn in, making sure the cut-out in the housing is at the same end as the commutator bars **(see illustration 27.7)**.

23 Apply a smear of grease to the short end of the shaft. Fit the rear cover, aligning the marks, and making sure the brushes remain square and seat against the commutator **(see illustration)**.

24 Apply a smear of grease to the front cover oil seal lip. Slide the front cover on, aligning the marks **(see illustration 27.5b)**.

25 Check the marks made on removal are correctly aligned then fit the long bolts and tighten them **(see illustration 27.5a)**.

26 Install the starter motor (see Section 26).

28 Charging system testing

1 If the performance of the charging system is suspect, the system as a whole should be checked first, followed by testing of the individual components. **Note:** *Before beginning the checks, make sure the battery is in good condition and fully charged, and that all system connections are clean and tight.*

2 Checking the output of the charging system and the performance of the various components within the charging system requires the use of a multimeter (with voltage, current and resistance checking facilities). If a multimeter is not available, the job of checking the charging system should be left to a Honda dealer.

3 When making the checks, follow the procedures carefully to prevent incorrect connections or short circuits resulting in irreparable damage to electrical system components.

Output test

4 Remove the rider's seat (see Chapter 7). Start the engine and warm it up.

5 To check the regulated (DC) voltage output, allow the engine to idle with the headlight main beam (HI) turned ON. Connect a multimeter set to the 0-20 volts DC scale across the terminals of the battery with the positive (+) meter probe to battery positive (+) terminal

27.19 Fit the O-ring between the bolt and the cover

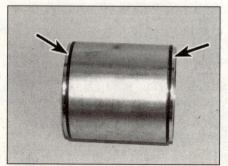

27.21 Main housing sealing rings (arrowed)

27.23 Align the marks when fitting the cover

Electrical system 8•25

and the negative (-) meter probe to battery negative (-) terminal (see Section 3) **(see illustration)**.
6 Slowly increase the engine speed to 5000 rpm and note the reading obtained. Compare the result with the Specification at the beginning of this Chapter. If the regulated voltage output is outside the specification, check the alternator and the regulator/rectifier (Sections 29 and 30).

 Clues to a faulty regulator are constantly blowing bulbs, with brightness varying considerably with engine speed, and battery overheating.

Leakage test

Caution: *Always connect an ammeter in series, never in parallel with the battery, otherwise it will be damaged. Do not turn the ignition ON or operate the starter motor when the ammeter is connected – a sudden surge in current will blow the meter's fuse.*

7 Make sure the ignition is OFF. Remove the rider's seat (see Chapter 7). Disconnect the battery negative (-) lead (see Section 3).
8 Set the multimeter to the Amps function and connect its negative (-) probe to the battery negative (-) terminal, and positive (+) probe to the disconnected negative (-) lead **(see illustration)**. Always set the meter to a high amps range initially and then bring it down to the mA (milli Amps) range; if there is a high current flow in the circuit it may blow the meter's fuse.
9 Battery current leakage should not exceed the maximum limit (see Specifications). If a higher leakage rate is shown there is a short circuit in the wiring, although if an after-market immobiliser or alarm is fitted, its current draw should be taken into account. Disconnect the meter and reconnect the battery negative (-) lead.
10 If leakage is indicated, refer to the Wiring Diagrams at the end of this Chapter to systematically disconnect individual electrical components and repeat the test until the source is identified.

29 Alternator

Check

1 Remove the fuel tank (see Chapter 4).
2 Disconnect the 3-pin alternator wiring connector with the three yellow wires **(see illustrations)**. Check the connector terminals for corrosion and security.
3 Using a multimeter set to the ohms x 1 (ohmmeter) scale measure the resistance between each of the yellow wires on the alternator side of the connector, taking a total

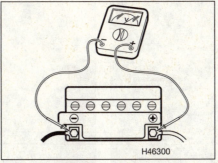

28.5 Checking the charging rate – connect the meter as shown

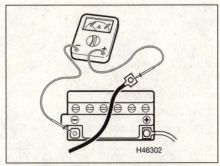

28.8 Checking the charging system leakage rate – connect the meter as shown

of three readings, then check for continuity between each terminal and ground (earth). If the stator coil windings are in good condition the three readings should be within the range shown in the Specifications at the start of this Chapter, and there should be no continuity (infinite resistance) between any of the terminals and ground (earth). If not, the alternator stator coil assembly is at fault and should be replaced with a new one. **Note:** *Before condemning the stator coils, check the fault is not due to damaged wiring between the connector and the coils.*

Removal

Special tools: *A rotor holding strap and rotor puller are needed (see Steps 9 and 10).*
4 Remove the left-hand fairing side panel (see Chapter 7). Remove the fuel tank (see

Chapter 4). Remove the front sprocket cover (see Chapter 6).
5 If you have an auxiliary stand place the bike on it so that it is level – this minimises oil loss. If you do not have an auxiliary stand it is best to drain the oil. Alternatively place a container under the engine to catch the oil that will come out when the alternator cover is removed.
6 Disconnect the 3-pin alternator wiring connector with the three yellow wires **(see illustration 29.2a or b)**. Disconnect the CKP sensor (red 2-pin) wiring connector **(see illustration)**. Feed the wiring down to the alternator cover, releasing it from any ties and noting its routing.
7 On RA models unscrew the C-ABS front valve unit and bracket bolts and remove the bracket **(see illustration)**. Unscrew the bolt securing the brake pipe joint to the bracket

29.2a Alternator wiring connector (arrowed) – RR models

29.2b Alternator wiring connector (arrowed) – RA models

29.6 CKP sensor wiring connector (arrowed)

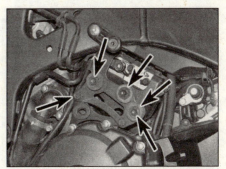

29.7 Unscrew the bolts (arrowed) and remove the bracket

8•26 Electrical system

29.8 Alternator cover bolts (arrowed)

29.9 Using a rotor strap to hold the rotor while unscrewing the bolt

29.10a Thread the puller into the rotor...

29.10b ...then hold the rotor and turn the puller, using a bar for leverage...

at the front of the alternator cover – do not loosen the brake pipe nuts.

8 Working in a criss-cross pattern, evenly slacken then remove the alternator cover bolts, and on RA models remove the three brackets, noting their positions **(see illustration)**. Draw the cover off the engine, noting that it will be restrained by the force of the rotor magnets, and be prepared to catch the residual oil. Remove the dowels from either the cover or the crankcase if they are loose.

9 To remove the rotor bolt it is necessary to stop the rotor from turning using a commercially available rotor strap **(see illustration)**. Unscrew the bolt, noting the washer.

10 To remove the rotor from the shaft it is necessary to use a rotor puller – use either the Honda tool (on 2008 and 2009 models Pt No. 07933-4250000 in the US and 07933-0040001 in Europe, on all later models Pt No. 07933-3950000 in the US and 07933-0020001 in Europe) or a commercially available equivalent designed for this bike. Thread the rotor puller into the centre of the rotor and turn it until the rotor is displaced from the shaft, holding the rotor to prevent the engine turning **(see illustrations)**. If the rotor doesn't come off easily use some extra leverage on the tool, and/or tap the end of the tool when it is tight, and if necessary heat the rotor hub using a hot air gun **(see illustration)**.

11 Remove the Woodruff key from its slot in the crankshaft for safekeeping if loose **(see illustration)**.

12 To remove the stator from the cover, unscrew its bolts, the CKP sensor bolts,

29.10c ...and apply some heat and tap the puller if necessary

29.11 Remove the key (arrowed) if required

Electrical system 8•27

and the wiring clamp bolt, then remove the assembly, noting how the rubber wiring grommet fits **(see illustration)**.

Installation

13 Fit the stator and CKP sensor into the cover, aligning the rubber wiring grommet with the groove **(see illustration 29.12)**. Fit the bolts and tighten them to the torque setting specified at the beginning of the Chapter. Apply a suitable sealant to the wiring grommet, then press it into the cut-out in the cover. Secure the wiring with its clamp and tighten the bolt.

14 Clean all old sealant off the cover and crankcase mating surfaces and wipe them with a suitable solvent. Clean the tapered end of the crankshaft and the corresponding mating surface on the inside of the rotor with the solvent.

15 Fit the Woodruff key into its slot in the crankshaft if removed **(see illustration 29.11)**.

16 Make sure that no metal objects have attached themselves to the magnet on the

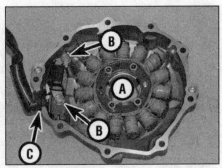

29.12 Stator bolts (A), CKP sensor bolts (B), grommet (C)

29.16 Slide the rotor onto the shaft

inside of the rotor. Slide the rotor onto the shaft, locating the slot in its centre over the key **(see illustration)**.

17 Apply some clean oil to the rotor bolt threads, the underside of the head, and the washer **(see illustration)**. Fit the bolt with its washer and tighten it to the torque setting specified at the beginning of the Chapter, holding the rotor as on removal **(see illustration)**.

18 Apply a smear of suitable sealant to the mating surface of the alternator cover and 10 to 15 mm either side of the crankcase joints **(see illustration)**. Fit the dowels into the cover or crankcase if removed. Fit the alternator cover, noting that the rotor magnets will forcibly draw the cover/stator on, making sure the dowels locate **(see illustration)**. Fit the cover bolts, along with the three brackets

29.17a Lubricate the bolt then install it with its washer...

29.17b ...and tighten it to the specified torque

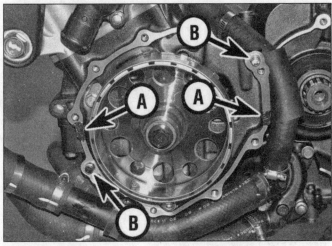

29.18a Apply sealant to the cover and crankcase joints (A). Make sure the dowels (B) are in place...

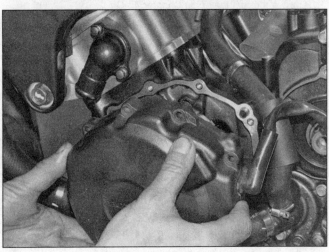

29.18b ...then fit the cover

30.2a Regulator/rectifier wiring connectors (A) and mounting bolts (B) – RR models

30.2b Regulator/rectifier wiring connector – RA models

on RA models, and tighten them evenly in a criss-cross sequence.
19 On RA models fit the brake pipe joint to the bracket at the front of the alternator cover, and fit the C-ABS front valve unit bracket **(see illustration 29.7)**.
20 Route and secure the wiring and connect connectors **(see illustration 29.2a or b)**.
21 Fill the engine with the correct quantity of oil, or top it up to the correct level, as required according to your removal method (see Chapter 1). Install the sprocket cover, fuel tank and fairing side panel.

30 Regulator/rectifier

Check

1 Remove the fuel tank (see Chapter 4). On RA models displace the fuse/relay box **(see illustration 9.5a)**.
2 Disconnect the regulator/rectifier wiring connectors **(see illustration 30.2a or 29.2b and 30.2b)**. Check the connector terminals for corrosion and security.
3 Set the multimeter to the 0 to 20 dc volts setting. Connect the meter positive (+) probe to the red wire terminal on the loom side of the 2-pin connector and the negative (–) probe to a suitable ground (earth) and check for voltage. Full battery voltage should be present at all times.
4 Switch the multimeter to the resistance (ohms) scale. Check for continuity between the green wire terminal on the loom side of the 2-pin connector and ground (earth). There should be continuity to earth.
5 Set the multimeter to the ohms x 1 (ohmmeter) scale and measure the resistance between each of the yellow wires on the alternator side of the 3-pin connector, taking a total of three readings, then check for continuity between each terminal and ground (earth). The three readings should be within the range shown in the Specifications for the alternator stator coil at the start of this Chapter, and there should be no continuity (infinite resistance) between any of the terminals and ground (earth).
6 If the above checks do not provide the expected results check the wiring and connectors between the battery, regulator/rectifier and alternator for shorts, breaks, and loose or corroded terminals (see the wiring diagrams at the end of this chapter).
7 If the wiring checks out, the regulator/rectifier unit is probably faulty. Honda provide no test data for the unit itself. Take it to a Honda dealer for confirmation of its condition before replacing it with a new one.

HAYNES HiNT *Clues to a faulty regulator are constantly blowing bulbs, with brightness varying considerably with engine speed, and battery overheating.*

Removal and installation

8 Remove the fuel tank (see Chapter 4). On RA models displace the fuse/relay box **(see illustration 9.5a)**
9 Disconnect the regulator/rectifier wiring connectors **(see illustration 30.2a or 29.2b and 30.2b)**.
10 On RR models unscrew the two bolts and remove the regulator/rectifier **(see illustration 30.2a)**.
11 On 2009 to 2011 RA models remove the seat cowling (see Chapter 7). Disconnect the rear wiring sub-loom connectors **(see illustration 30.12a)**. Undo the two screws on the top and the four bolts on the underside, noting the washers, and remove the rear light/turn signal/licence plate assembly, noting the routing of the wiring **(see illustration 30.12d)**. Remove the collars for the bolts fitted on the top of the tray for safekeeping if loose. Unscrew the two bolts, noting the wiring clamp, and remove the regulator/rectifier **(see illustration 30.12e)**.
12 On 2012-on RA models remove the seat cowling (see Chapter 7). Disconnect the rear sub-loom wiring connectors **(see illustration)**. Move the wiring aside and undo the screw on the top **(see illustration)** – remove the battery for extra clearance if required (Section 3). Release the trim clip and unscrew the four bolts on the underside, noting the washers, and remove the rear light/turn signal/licence plate assembly, noting the routing of the wiring. Remove the collars for the bolts fitted on the top of the tray for safekeeping if loose. Unscrew the two bolts, noting the wiring clamp, and remove the regulator/rectifier **(see illustration)**.
13 Installation is the reverse of removal.

30.12a Disconnect the wiring

Electrical system 8•29

30.12b Undo the screw (arrowed)

30.12c Release the trim clip (arrowed) and unscrew the four bolts...

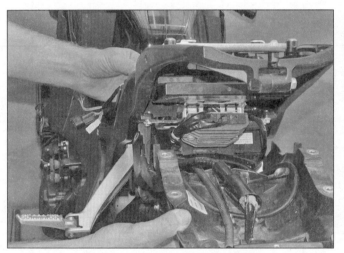
30.12d ...and remove the assembly

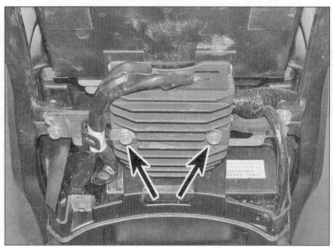
30.12e Regulator/rectifier mounting bolts (arrowed) – RA models

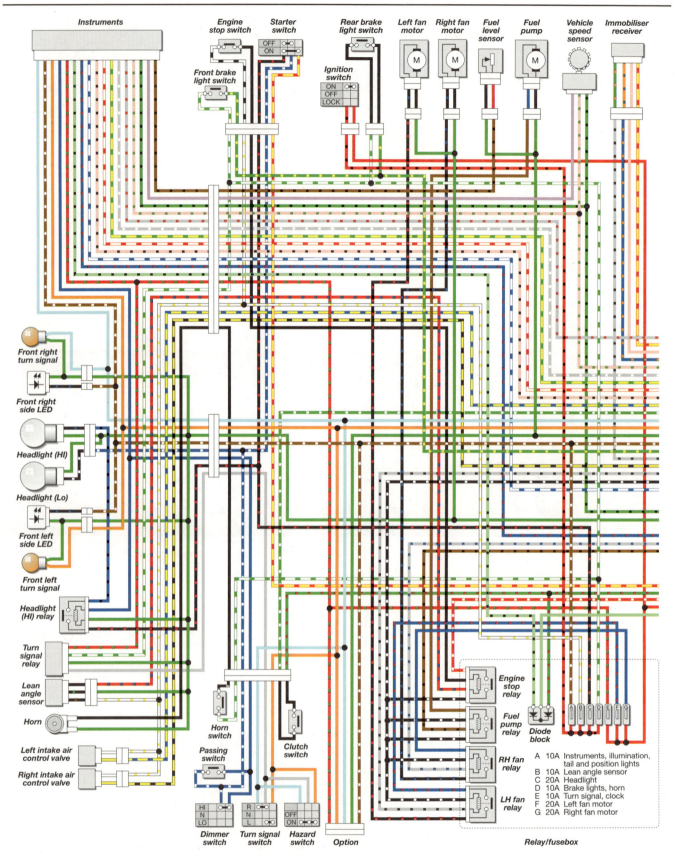

Wiring diagrams 8•31

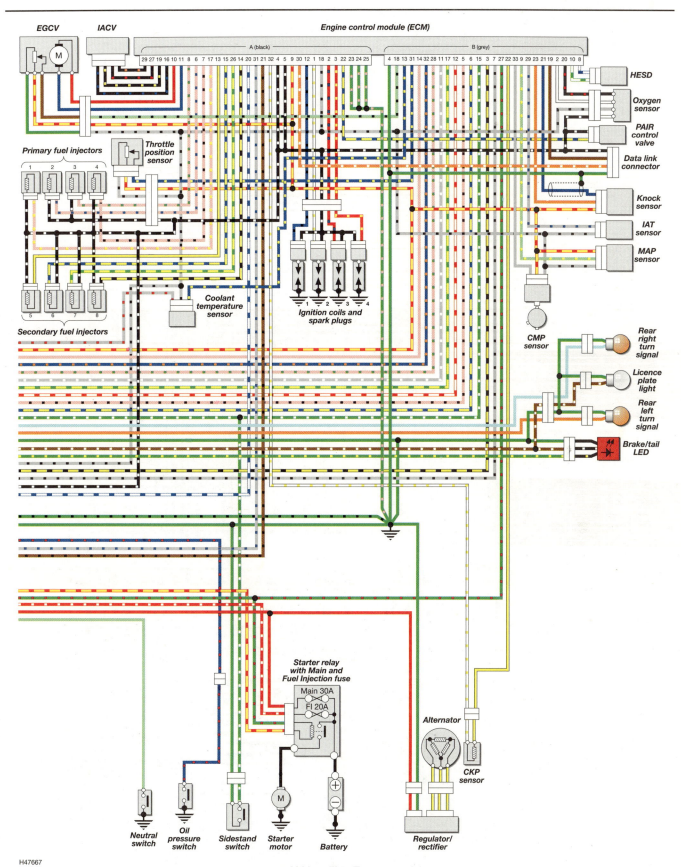

2008 to 2011 Europe models

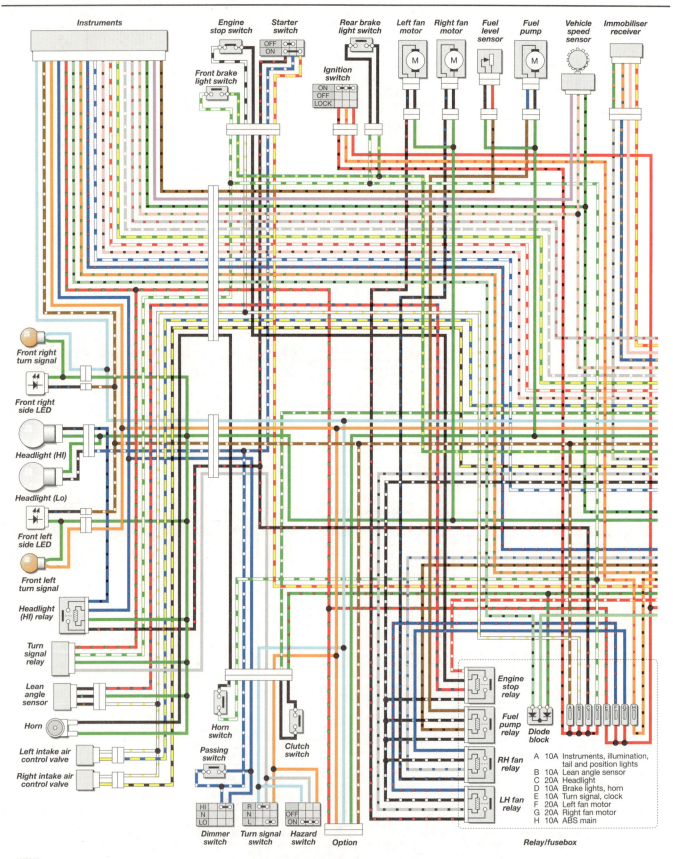

Wiring diagrams 8•33

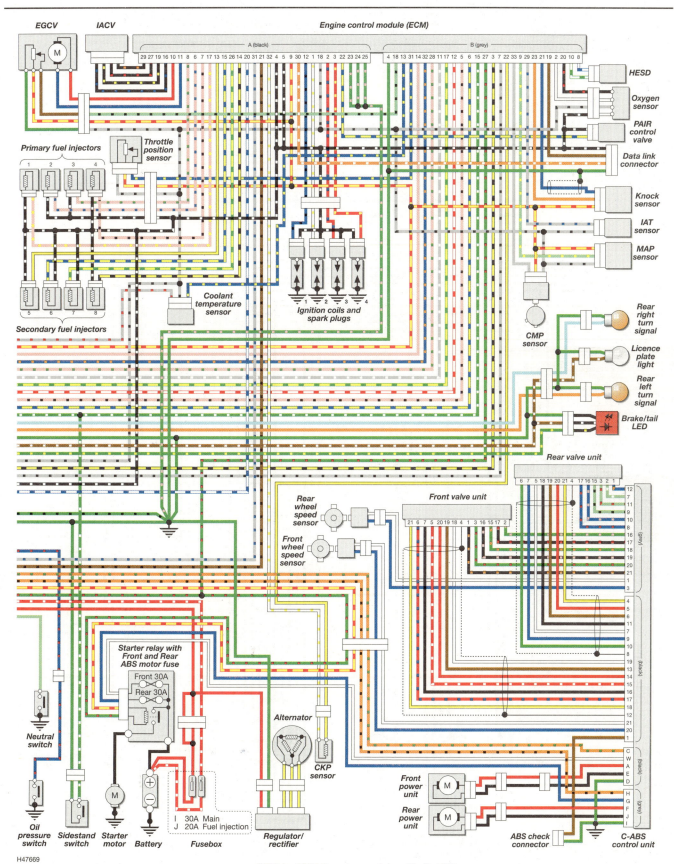

2009 to 2011 Europe models with C-ABS

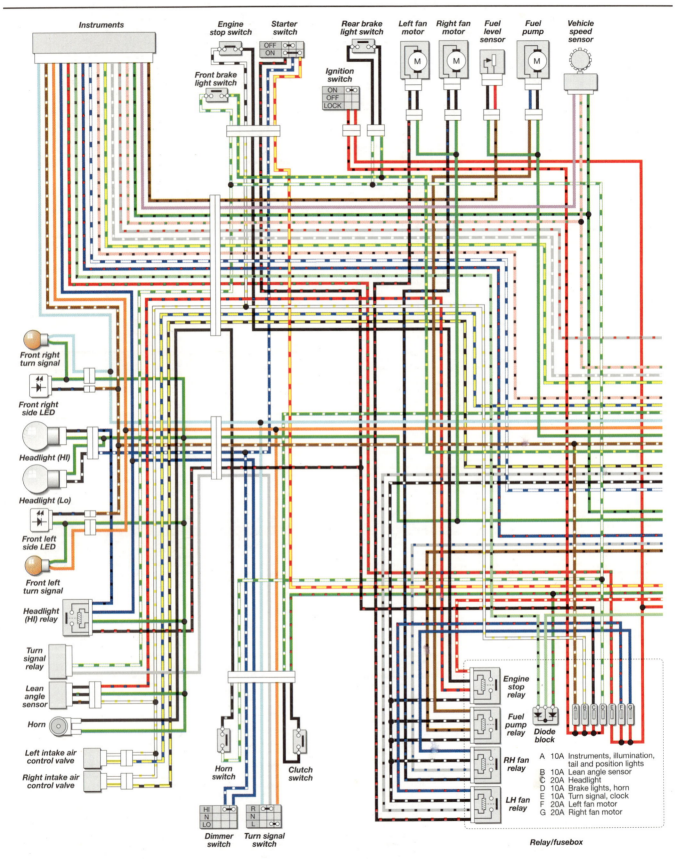

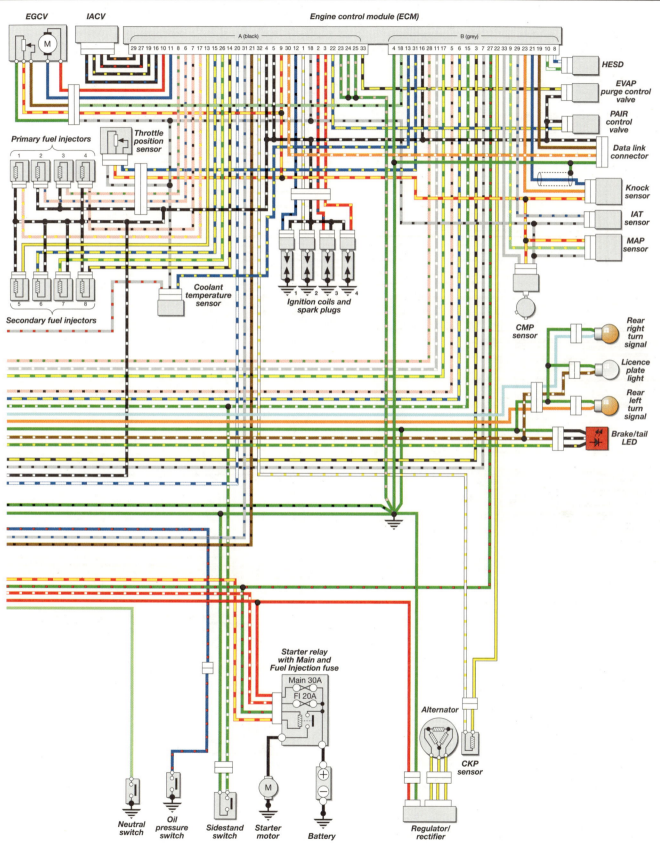

2008 to 2011 US models

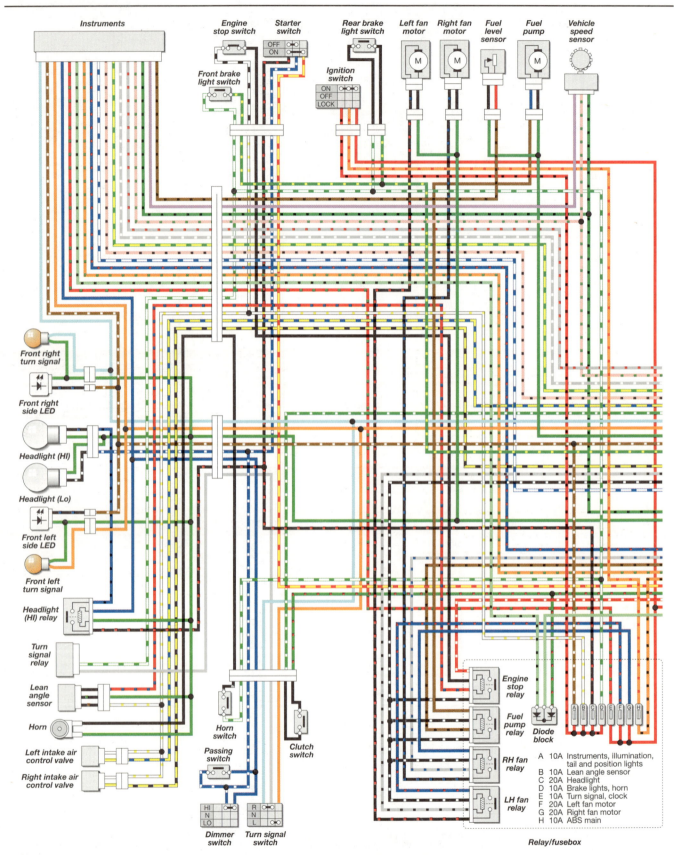

2009 to 2011 US models with C-ABS

Wiring diagrams 8•37

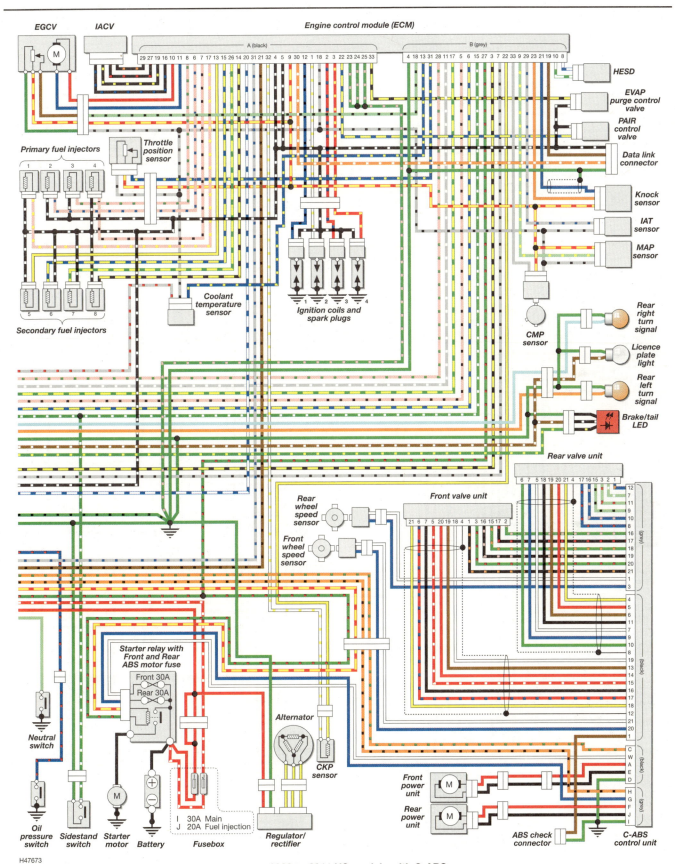

2009 to 2011 US models with C-ABS

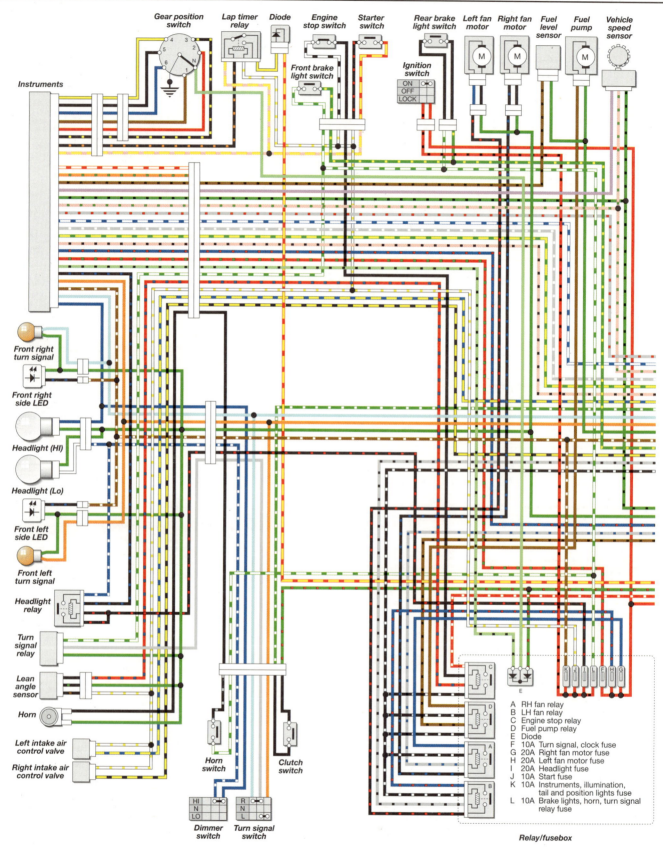

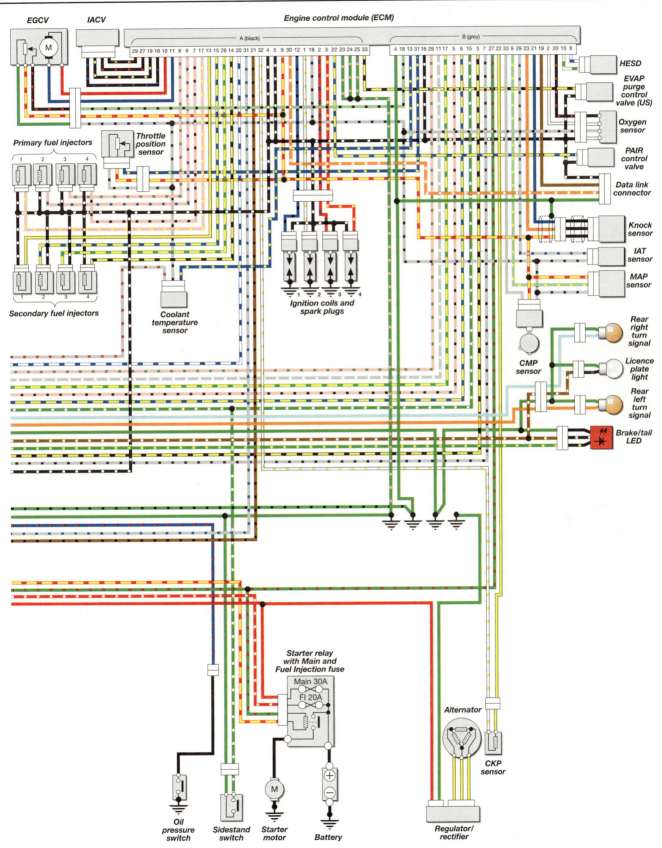

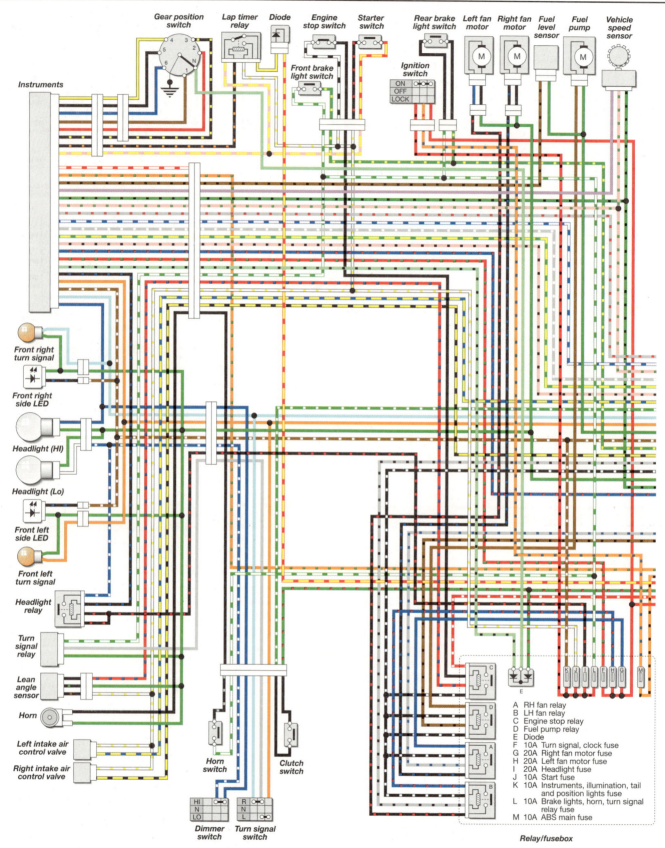

Wiring diagrams 8•41

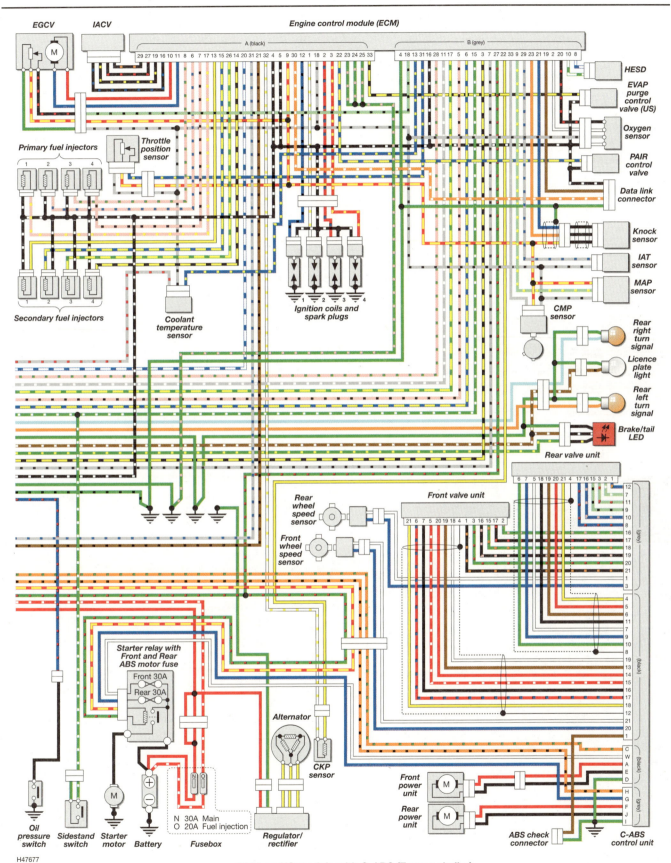

2012-on US models with C-ABS (Europe similar)

Notes

Reference REF•1

Reference

Security — REF•2

- Locks and chains
- U-locks ● Disc locks
- Alarms and immobilisers
- Security marking systems ● Tips on how to prevent bike theft

Lubricants and fluids — REF•5

- Engine oils
- Transmission (gear) oils
- Coolant/anti-freeze
- Fork oils and suspension fluids ● Brake/clutch fluids
- Spray lubes, degreasers and solvents

MOT Test Checks — REF•8

- A guide to the UK MOT test ● Which items are tested ● How to prepare your motorcycle for the test and perform a pre-test check

Storage — REF•13

- How to prepare your motorcycle for going into storage and protect essential systems ● How to get the motorcycle back on the road

Tools and Workshop Tips — REF•16

- Building up a tool kit and equipping your workshop ● Using tools
- Understanding bearing, seal, fastener and chain sizes and markings
- Repair techniques

Conversion Factors — REF•34

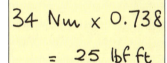

- Formulae for conversion of the metric (SI) units used throughout the manual into Imperial measures

Fault Finding — REF•35

- Common faults and their likely causes ● Links to main chapters for testing and repair procedures

Index — REF•46

REF•2 Security

Introduction

In less time than it takes to read this introduction, a thief could steal your motorcycle. Returning only to find your bike has gone is one of the worst feelings in the world. Even if the motorcycle is insured against theft, once you've got over the initial shock, you will have the inconvenience of dealing with the police and your insurance company.

The motorcycle is an easy target for the professional thief and the joyrider alike and the official figures on motorcycle theft make for depressing reading; on average a motor-cycle is stolen every 16 minutes in the UK!

Motorcycle thefts fall into two categories, those stolen 'to order' and those taken by opportunists. The thief stealing to order will be on the look out for a specific make and model and will go to extraordinary lengths to obtain that motorcycle. The opportunist thief on the other hand will look for easy targets which can be stolen with the minimum of effort and risk.

Whilst it is never going to be possible to make your machine 100% secure, it is estimated that around half of all stolen motorcycles are taken by opportunist thieves. Remember that the opportunist thief is always on the look out for the easy option: if there are two similar motorcycles parked side-by-side, they will target the one with the lowest level of security. By taking a few precautions, you can reduce the chances of your motorcycle being stolen.

Security equipment

There are many specialised motorcycle security devices available and the following text summarises their applications and their good and bad points.

Once you have decided on the type of security equipment which best suits your needs, we recommended that you read one of the many equipment tests regularly carried out by the motorcycle press. These tests compare the products from all the major manufacturers and give impartial ratings on their effectiveness, value-for-money and ease of use.

No one item of security equipment can provide complete protection. It is highly recommended that two or more of the items described below are combined to increase the security of your motorcycle (a lock and chain plus an alarm system is just about ideal). The more security measures fitted to the bike, the less likely it is to be stolen.

Ensure the lock and chain you buy is of good quality and long enough to shackle your bike to a solid object

Lock and chain

Pros: *Very flexible to use; can be used to secure the motorcycle to almost any immovable object. On some locks and chains, the lock can be used on its own as a disc lock (see below).*

Cons: *Can be very heavy and awkward to carry on the motorcycle, although some types will be supplied with a carry bag which can be strapped to the pillion seat.*

● Heavy-duty chains and locks are an excellent security measure **(see illustration 1)**. Whenever the motorcycle is parked, use the lock and chain to secure the machine to a solid, immovable object such as a post or railings. This will prevent the machine from being ridden away or being lifted into the back of a van.

● When fitting the chain, always ensure the chain is routed around the motorcycle frame or swingarm **(see illustrations 2 and 3)**. Never merely pass the chain around one of the wheel rims; a thief may unbolt the wheel and lift the rest of the machine into a van, leaving you with just the wheel! Try to avoid having excess chain free, thus making it difficult to use cutting tools, and keep the chain and lock off the ground to prevent thieves attacking it with a cold chisel. Position the lock so that its lock barrel is facing downwards; this will make it harder for the thief to attack the lock mechanism.

Pass the chain through the bike's frame, rather than just through a wheel . . .

. . . and loop it around a solid object

Security REF•3

U-locks

Pros: *Highly effective deterrent which can be used to secure the bike to a post or railings. Most U-locks come with a carrier which allows the lock to be easily carried on the bike.*

Cons: *Not as flexible to use as a lock and chain.*

● These are solid locks which are similar in use to a lock and chain. U-locks are lighter than a lock and chain but not so flexible to use. The length and shape of the lock shackle limit the objects to which the bike can be secured **(see illustration 4)**.

Disc locks

Pros: *Small, light and very easy to carry; most can be stored underneath the seat.*

Cons: *Does not prevent the motorcycle being lifted into a van. Can be very embarrassing if*

U-locks can be used to secure the bike to a solid object – ensure you purchase one which is long enough

you forget to remove the lock before attempting to ride off!

● Disc locks are designed to be attached to the front brake disc. The lock passes through one of the holes in the disc and prevents the wheel rotating by jamming against the fork/brake caliper **(see illustration 5)**. Some are equipped with an alarm siren which sounds if the disc lock is moved; this not only acts as a theft deterrent but also as a handy reminder if you try to move the bike with the lock still fitted.

● Combining the disc lock with a length of cable which can be looped around a post or railings provides an additional measure of security **(see illustration 6)**.

Alarms and immobilisers

Pros: *Once installed it is completely hassle-free to use. If the system is 'Thatcham' or 'Sold Secure-approved', insurance companies may give you a discount.*

Cons: *Can be expensive to buy and complex to install. No system will prevent the motorcycle from being lifted into a van and taken away.*

● Electronic alarms and immobilisers are available to suit a variety of budgets. There are three different types of system available: pure alarms, pure immobilisers, and the more expensive systems which are combined alarm/immobilisers **(see illustration 7)**.

● An alarm system is designed to emit an audible warning if the motorcycle is being tampered with.

● An immobiliser prevents the motorcycle being started and ridden away by disabling its electrical systems.

● When purchasing an alarm/immobiliser system, check the cost of installing the system unless you are able to do it yourself. If the motorcycle is not used regularly, another consideration is the current drain of the system. All alarm/immobiliser systems are powered by the motorcycle's battery; purchasing a system with a very low current drain could prevent the battery losing its charge whilst the motorcycle is not being used.

A typical disc lock attached through one of the holes in the disc

A disc lock combined with a security cable provides additional protection

A typical alarm/immobiliser system

REF•4 Security

Indelible markings can be applied to most areas of the bike – always apply the manufacturer's sticker to warn off thieves

Chemically-etched code numbers can be applied to main body panels . . .

. . . again, always ensure that the kit manufacturer's sticker is applied in a prominent position

Security marking kits

Pros: Very cheap and effective deterrent. Many insurance companies will give you a discount on your insurance premium if a recognised security marking kit is used on your motorcycle.

Cons: Does not prevent the motorcycle being stolen by joyriders.

● There are many different types of security marking kits available. The idea is to mark as many parts of the motorcycle as possible with a unique security number **(see illustrations 8, 9 and 10)**. A form will be included with the kit to register your personal details and those of the motorcycle with the kit manufacturer. This register is made available to the police to help them trace the rightful owner of any motorcycle or components which they recover should all other forms of identification have been removed. Always apply the warning stickers provided with the kit to deter thieves.

Ground anchors, wheel clamps and security posts

Pros: An excellent form of security which will deter all but the most determined of thieves.

Cons: Awkward to install and can be expensive.

● Whilst the motorcycle is at home, it is a good idea to attach it securely to the floor or a solid wall, even if it is kept in a securely locked garage. Various types of ground anchors, security posts and wheel clamps are available for this purpose **(see illustration 11)**. These security devices are either bolted to a solid concrete or brick structure or can be cemented into the ground.

Permanent ground anchors provide an excellent level of security when the bike is at home

Security at home

A high percentage of motorcycle thefts are from the owner's home. Here are some things to consider whenever your motorcycle is at home:

● Where possible, always keep the motorcycle in a securely locked garage. Never rely solely on the standard lock on the garage door, these are usual hopelessly inadequate. Fit an additional locking mechanism to the door and consider having the garage alarmed. A security light, activated by a movement sensor, is also a good investment.

● Always secure the motorcycle to the ground or a wall, even if it is inside a securely locked garage.

● Do not regularly leave the motorcycle outside your home, try to keep it out of sight wherever possible. If a garage is not available, fit a motorcycle cover over the bike to disguise its true identity.

● It is not uncommon for thieves to follow a motorcyclist home to find out where the bike is kept. They will then return at a later date. Be aware of this whenever you are returning home on your motorcycle. If you suspect you are being followed, do not return home, instead ride to a garage or shop and stop as a precaution.

● When selling a motorcycle, do not provide your home address or the location where the bike is normally kept. Arrange to meet the buyer at a location away from your home. Thieves have been known to pose as potential buyers to find out where motorcycles are kept and then return later to steal them.

Security away from the home

As well as fitting security equipment to your motorcycle here are a few general rules to follow whenever you park your motorcycle.

● Park in a busy, public place.
● Use car parks which incorporate security features, such as CCTV.
● At night, park in a well-lit area, preferably directly underneath a street light.
● Engage the steering lock.
● Secure the motorcycle to a solid, immovable object such as a post or railings with an additional lock. If this is not possible, secure the bike to a friend's motorcycle. Some public parking places provide security loops for motorcycles.
● Never leave your helmet or luggage attached to the motorcycle. Take them with you at all times.

Lubricants and fluids

Lubricants and fluids

A wide range of lubricants, fluids and cleaning agents is available for motor-cycles. This is a guide as to what is available, its applications and properties.

Four-stroke engine oil

● Engine oil is without doubt the most important component of any four-stroke engine. Modern motorcycle engines place a lot of demands on their oil and choosing the right type is essential. Using an unsuitable oil will lead to an increased rate of engine wear and could result in serious engine damage. Before purchasing oil, always check the recommended oil specification given by the manufacturer. The manufacturer will state a recommended 'type or classification' and also a specific 'viscosity' range for engine oil.

● The oil 'type or classification' is identified by its API (American Petroleum Institute) rating. The API rating will be in the form of two letters, e.g. SG. The S identifies the oil as being suitable for use in a petrol (gasoline) engine (S stands for spark ignition) and the second letter, ranging from A to J, identifies the oil's performance rating. The later this letter, the higher the specification of the oil; for example API SG oil exceeds the requirements of API SF oil. **Note:** *On some oils there may also be a second rating consisting of another two letters, the first letter being C, e.g. API SF/CD. This rating indicates the oil is also suitable for use in a diesel engines (the C stands for compression ignition) and is thus of no relevance for motorcycle use.*

● The 'viscosity' of the oil is identified by its SAE (Society of Automotive Engineers) rating. All modern engines require multigrade oils and the SAE rating will consist of two numbers, the first followed by a W, e.g. 10W/40. The first number indicates the viscosity rating of the oil at low temperatures (W stands for winter – tested at –20°C) and the second number represents the viscosity of the oil at high temperatures (tested at 100°C). The lower the number, the thinner the oil. For example an oil with an SAE 10W/40 rating will give better cold starting and running than an SAE 15W/40 oil.

● As well as ensuring the 'type' and 'viscosity' of the oil match the recommendations, another consideration to make when buying engine oil is whether to purchase a standard mineral-based oil, a semi-synthetic oil (also known as a synthetic blend or synthetic-based oil) or a fully-synthetic oil. Although all oils will have a similar rating and viscosity, their cost will vary considerably; mineral-based oils are the cheapest, the fully-synthetic oils the most expensive with the semi-synthetic oils falling somewhere in-between. This decision is very much up to the owner, but it should be noted that modern synthetic oils have far better lubricating and cleaning qualities than traditional mineral-based oils and tend to retain these properties for far longer. Bearing in mind the operating conditions inside a modern, high-revving motorcycle engine it is highly recommended that a fully synthetic oil is used. The extra expense at each service could save you money in the long term by preventing premature engine wear.

● As a final note always ensure that the oil is specifically designed for use in motorcycle engines. Engine oils designed primarily for use in car engines sometimes contain additives or friction modifiers which could cause clutch slip on a motorcycle fitted with a wet-clutch.

Two-stroke engine oil

● Modern two-stroke engines, with their high power outputs, place high demands on their oil. If engine seizure is to be avoided it is essential that a high-quality oil is used. Two-stroke oils differ hugely from four-stroke oils. The oil lubricates only the crankshaft and piston(s) (the transmission has its own lubricating oil) and is used on a total-loss basis where it is burnt completely during the combustion process.

● The Japanese have recently introduced a classification system for two-stroke oils, the JASO rating. This rating is in the form of two letters, either FA, FB or FC – FA is the lowest classification and FC the highest. Ensure the oil being used meets or exceeds the recommended rating specified by the manufacturer.

● As well as ensuring the oil rating matches the recommendation, another consideration to make when buying engine oil is whether to purchase a standard mineral-based oil, a semi-synthetic oil (also known as a synthetic blend or synthetic-based oil) or a fully-synthetic oil. The cost of each type of oil varies considerably; mineral-based oils are the cheapest, the fully-synthetic oils the most expensive with the semi-synthetic oils falling somewhere in-between. This decision is very much up to the owner, but it should be noted that modern synthetic oils have far better lubricating properties and burn cleaner than traditional mineral-based oils. It is therefore recommended that a fully synthetic oil is used. The extra expense could save you money in the long term by preventing premature engine wear, engine performance will be improved, carbon deposits and exhaust smoke will be reduced.

REF•6 Lubricants and fluids

● Always ensure that the oil is specifically designed for use in an injector system. Many high quality two-stroke oils are designed for competition use and need to be pre-mixed with fuel. These oils are of a much higher viscosity and are not designed to flow through the injector pumps used on road-going two-stroke motorcycles.

Transmission (gear) oil

● On a two-stroke engine, the transmission and clutch are lubricated by their own separate oil bath which must be changed in accordance with the Maintenance Schedule.
● Although the engine and transmission units of most four-strokes use a common lubrication supply, there are some exceptions where the engine and gearbox have separate oil reservoirs and a dry clutch is used.
● Motorcycle manufacturers will either recommend a monograde transmission oil or a four-stroke multigrade engine oil to lubricate the transmission.
● Transmission oils, or gear oils as they are often called, are designed specifically for use in transmission systems. The viscosity of these oils is represented by an SAE number, but the scale of measurement applied is different to that used to grade engine oils. As a rough guide a SAE90 gear oil will be of the same viscosity as an SAE50 engine oil.

Shaft drive oil

● On models equipped with shaft final drive, the shaft drive gears are will have their own oil supply. The manufacturer will state a recommended 'type or classification' and also a specific 'viscosity' range in the same manner as for four-stroke engine oil.
● Gear oil classification is given by the number which follows the API GL (GL standing for gear lubricant) rating, the higher the number, the higher the specification of the oil, e.g. API GL5 oil is a higher specification than API GL4 oil. Ensure the oil meets or exceeds the classification specified and is of the correct viscosity. The viscosity of gear oils is also represented by an SAE number but the scale of measurement used is different to that used to grade engine oils. As a rough guide an SAE90 gear oil will be of the same viscosity as an SAE50 engine oil.
● If the use of an EP (Extreme Pressure) gear oil is specified, ensure the oil purchased is suitable.

Fork oil and suspension fluid

● Conventional telescopic front forks are hydraulic and require fork oil to work. To ensure the forks function correctly, the fork oil must be changed in accordance with the Maintenance Schedule.
● Fork oil is available in a variety of viscosities, identified by their SAE rating; fork oil ratings vary from light (SAE 5) to heavy (SAE 30). When purchasing fork oil, ensure the viscosity rating matches that specified by the manufacturer.
● Some lubricant manufacturers also produce a range of high-quality suspension fluids which are very similar to fork oil but are designed mainly for competition use. These fluids may have a different viscosity rating system which is not to be confused with the SAE rating of normal fork oil. Refer to the manufacturer's instructions if in any doubt.

Brake and clutch fluid

● All disc brake systems and some clutch systems are hydraulically operated. To ensure correct operation, the hydraulic fluid must be changed in accordance with the Maintenance Schedule.
● Brake and clutch fluid is classified by its DOT rating with most motorcycle manufacturers specifying DOT 3 or 4 fluid. Both fluid types are glycol-based and can be mixed together without adverse effect; DOT 4 fluid exceeds the requirements of DOT 3 fluid. Although it is safe to use DOT 4 fluid in a system designed for use with DOT 3 fluid, never use DOT 3 fluid in a system which specifies the use of DOT 4 as this will adversely affect the system's performance. The type required for the system will be marked on the fluid reservoir cap.
● Some manufacturers also produce a DOT 5 hydraulic fluid. DOT 5 hydraulic fluid is silicone-based and is not compatible with the glycol-based DOT 3 and 4 fluids. Never mix DOT 5 fluid with DOT 3 or 4 fluid as this will seriously affect the performance of the hydraulic system.

Coolant/antifreeze

● When purchasing coolant/antifreeze, always ensure it is suitable for use in an aluminium engine and contains corrosion inhibitors to prevent possible blockages of the internal coolant passages of the system. As a general rule, most coolants are designed to be used neat and should not be diluted whereas antifreeze can be mixed with distilled water to provide a coolant solution of the required strength. Refer to the manufacturer's instructions on the bottle.
● Ensure the coolant is changed in accordance with the Maintenance Schedule.

Chain lube

● Chain lube is an aerosol-type spray lubricant specifically designed for use on motorcycle final drive chains. Chain lube has two functions, to minimise friction between the final drive chain and sprockets and to prevent corrosion of the chain. Regular use of a good-quality chain lube will extend the life of the drive chain and sprockets and thus maximise the power being transmitted from the transmission to the rear wheel.
● When using chain lube, always allow some time for the solvents in the lube to evaporate before riding the motorcycle. This will minimise the amount of lube which will

Lubricants and fluids REF•7

'fling' off from the chain when the motorcycle is used. If the motorcycle is equipped with an 'O-ring' chain, ensure the chain lube is labelled as being suitable for use on 'O-ring' chains.

Degreasers and solvents

● There are many different types of solvents and degreasers available to remove the grime and grease which accumulate around the motorcycle during normal use. Degreasers and solvents are usually available as an aerosol-type spray or as a liquid which you apply with a brush. Always closely follow the manufacturer's instructions and wear eye protection during use. Be aware that many solvents are flammable and may give off noxious fumes; take adequate precautions when using them (see Safety First!).

● For general cleaning, use one of the many solvents or degreasers available from most motorcycle accessory shops. These solvents are usually applied then left for a certain time before being washed off with water.

Brake cleaner is a solvent specifically designed to remove all traces of oil, grease and dust from braking system components. Brake cleaner is designed to evaporate quickly and leaves behind no residue.

Carburettor cleaner is an aerosol-type solvent specifically designed to clear carburettor blockages and break down the hard deposits and gum often found inside carburettors during overhaul.

Contact cleaner is an aerosol-type solvent designed for cleaning electrical components. The cleaner will remove all traces of oil and dirt from components such as switch contacts or fouled spark plugs and then dry, leaving behind no residue.

Gasket remover is an aerosol-type solvent designed for removing stubborn gaskets from engine components during overhaul. Gasket remover will minimise the amount of scraping required to remove the gasket and therefore reduce the risk of damage to the mating surface.

Spray lubricants

● Aerosol-based spray lubricants are widely available and are excellent for lubricating lever pivots and exposed cables and switches. Try to use a lubricant which is of the dry-film type as the fluid evaporates, leaving behind a dry-film of lubricant. Lubricants which leave behind an oily residue will attract dust and dirt which will increase the rate of wear of the cable/lever.

● Most lubricants also act as a moisture dispersant and a penetrating fluid. This means they can also be used to 'dry out' electrical components such as wiring connectors or switches as well as helping to free seized fasteners.

Greases

● Grease is used to lubricate many of the pivot-points. A good-quality multi-purpose grease is suitable for most applications but some manufacturers will specify the use of specialist greases for use on components such as swingarm and suspension linkage bushes. These specialist greases can be purchased from most motorcycle (or car) accessory shops; commonly specified types include molybdenum disulphide grease, lithium-based grease, graphite-based grease, silicone-based grease and high-temperature copper-based grease.

Gasket sealing compounds

● Gasket sealing compounds can be used in conjunction with gaskets, to improve their sealing capabilities, or on their own to seal metal-to-metal joints. Depending on their type, sealing compounds either set hard or stay relatively soft and pliable.

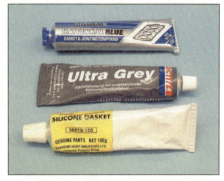

● When purchasing a gasket sealing compound, ensure that it is designed specifically for use on an internal combustion engine. General multi-purpose sealants available from DIY stores may appear visibly similar but they are not designed to withstand the extreme heat or contact with fuel and oil encountered when used on an engine (see 'Tools and Workshop Tips' for further information).

Thread locking compound

● Thread locking compounds are used to secure certain threaded fasteners in position to prevent them from loosening due to vibration. Thread locking compounds can be purchased from most motorcycle (and car) accessory shops. Ensure the threads of the both components are completely clean and dry before sparingly applying the locking compound (see 'Tools and Workshop Tips' for further information).

Fuel additives

● Fuel additives which protect and clean the fuel system components are widely available. These additives are designed to remove all traces of deposits that build up on the carburettors/injectors and prevent wear, helping the fuel system to operate more efficiently. If a fuel additive is being used, check that it is suitable for use with your motorcycle, especially if your motorcycle is equipped with a catalytic converter.

● Octane boosters are also available. These additives are designed to improve the performance of highly-tuned engines being run on normal pump-fuel and are of no real use on standard motorcycles.

REF•8 MOT Test Checks

About the MOT Test

In the UK, all vehicles more than three years old are subject to an annual test to ensure that they meet minimum safety requirements. A current test certificate must be issued before a machine can be used on public roads, and is required before a road fund licence can be issued. Riding without a current test certificate will also invalidate your insurance.

For most owners, the MOT test is an annual cause for anxiety, and this is largely due to owners not being sure what needs to be checked prior to submitting the motorcycle for testing. The simple answer is that a fully roadworthy motorcycle will have no difficulty in passing the test.

This is a guide to getting your motorcycle through the MOT test. Obviously it will not be possible to examine the motorcycle to the same standard as the professional MOT tester, particularly in view of the equipment required for some of the checks. However, working through the following procedures will enable you to identify any problem areas before submitting the motorcycle for the test.

It has only been possible to summarise the test requirements here, based on the regulations in force at the time of printing. Test standards are becoming increasingly stringent, although there are some exemptions for older vehicles. More information about the MOT test can be obtained from the TSO publications, *How Safe is your Motorcycle* and *The MOT Inspection Manual for Motorcycle Testing*.

Many of the checks require that one of the wheels is raised off the ground. If the motorcycle doesn't have a centre stand, note that an auxiliary stand will be required. Additionally, the help of an assistant may prove useful.

Certain exceptions apply to machines under 50 cc, machines without a lighting system, and Classic bikes - if in doubt about any of the requirements listed below seek confirmation from an MOT tester prior to submitting the motorcycle for the test.

Check that the frame number is clearly visible.

Electrical System

Lights, turn signals, horn and reflector

● With the ignition on, check the operation of the following electrical components. **Note:** *The electrical components on certain small-capacity machines are powered by the generator, requiring that the engine is run for this check.*

a) Headlight and tail light. Check that both illuminate in the low and high beam switch positions.
b) Position lights. Check that the front position (or sidelight) and tail light illuminate in this switch position.
c) Turn signals. Check that all flash at the correct rate, and that the warning light(s) function correctly. Check that the turn signal switch works correctly.
d) Hazard warning system (where fitted). Check that all four turn signals flash in this switch position.
e) Brake stop light. Check that the light comes on when the front and rear brakes are independently applied. Models first used on or after 1st April 1986 must have a brake light switch on each brake.
f) Horn. Check that the sound is continuous and of reasonable volume.

● Check that there is a red reflector on the rear of the machine, either mounted separately or as part of the tail light lens.
● Check the condition of the headlight, tail light and turn signal lenses.

Headlight beam height

● The MOT tester will perform a headlight beam height check using specialised beam setting equipment **(see illustration 1)**. This equipment will not be available to the home mechanic, but if you suspect that the headlight is incorrectly set or may have been maladjusted in the past, you can perform a rough test as follows.
● Position the bike in a straight line facing a brick wall. The bike must be off its stand, upright and with a rider seated. Measure the height from the ground to the centre of the headlight and mark a horizontal line on the wall at this height. Position the motorcycle 3.8 metres from the wall and draw a vertical line up the wall central to the centreline of the motorcycle. Switch to dipped beam and check that the beam pattern falls slightly lower than the horizontal line and to the left of the vertical line **(see illustration 2)**.

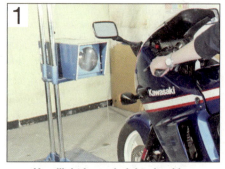

Headlight beam height checking equipment

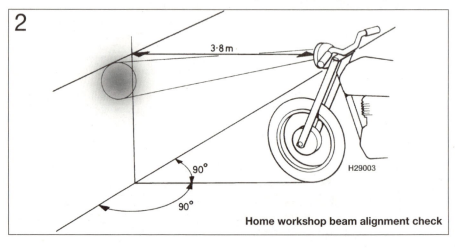

Home workshop beam alignment check

MOT Test Checks

Exhaust System and Final Drive

Exhaust

- Check that the exhaust mountings are secure and that the system does not foul any of the rear suspension components.
- Start the motorcycle. When the revs are increased, check that the exhaust is neither holed nor leaking from any of its joints. On a linked system, check that the collector box is not leaking due to corrosion.
- Note that the exhaust decibel level ("loudness" of the exhaust) is assessed at the discretion of the tester. If the motorcycle was first used on or after 1st January 1985 the silencer must carry the BSAU 193 stamp, or a marking relating to its make and model, or be of OE (original equipment) manufacture. If the silencer is marked NOT FOR ROAD USE, RACING USE ONLY or similar, it will fail the MOT.

Final drive

- On chain or belt drive machines, check that the chain/belt is in good condition and does not have excessive slack. Also check that the sprocket is securely mounted on the rear wheel hub. Check that the chain/belt guard is in place.
- On shaft drive bikes, check for oil leaking from the drive unit and fouling the rear tyre.

Steering and Suspension

Steering

- With the front wheel raised off the ground, rotate the steering from lock to lock. The handlebar or switches must not contact the fuel tank or be close enough to trap the rider's hand. Problems can be caused by damaged lock stops on the lower yoke and frame, or by the fitting of non-standard handlebars.
- When performing the lock to lock check, also ensure that the steering moves freely without drag or notchiness. Steering movement can be impaired by poorly routed cables, or by overtight head bearings or worn bvearings. The tester will perform a check of the steering head bearing lower race by mounting the front wheel on a surface plate, then performing a lock to lock check with the weight of the machine on the lower bearing (see illustration 3).
- Grasp the fork sliders (lower legs) and attempt to push and pull on the forks

Front wheel mounted on a surface plate for steering head bearing lower race check

(see illustration 4). Any play in the steering head bearings will be felt. Note that in extreme cases, wear of the front fork bushes can be misinterpreted for head bearing play.
- Check that the handlebars are securely mounted.
- Check that the handlebar grip rubbers are secure. They should by bonded to the bar left end and to the throttle cable pulley on the right end.

Front suspension

- With the motorcycle off the stand, hold the front brake on and pump the front forks up and down (see illustration 5). Check that they are adequately damped.

Checking the steering head bearings for freeplay

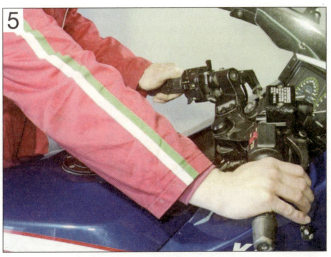

Hold the front brake on and pump the front forks up and down to check operation

REF•10 MOT Test Checks

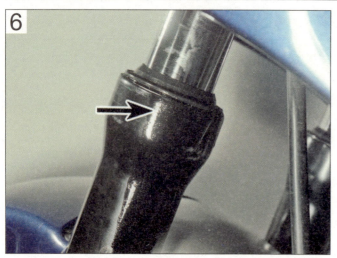

Inspect the area around the fork dust seal for oil leakage (arrow)

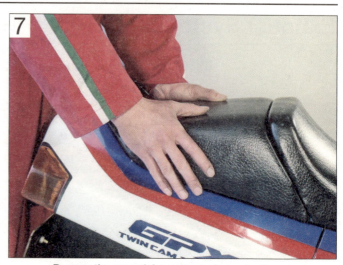

Bounce the rear of the motorcycle to check rear suspension operation

Checking for rear suspension linkage play

- Inspect the area above and around the front fork oil seals **(see illustration 6)**. There should be no sign of oil on the fork tube (stanchion) nor leaking down the slider (lower leg). On models so equipped, check that there is no oil leaking from the anti-dive units.
- On models with swingarm front suspension, check that there is no freeplay in the linkage when moved from side to side.

Rear suspension

- With the motorcycle off the stand and an assistant supporting the motorcycle by its handlebars, bounce the rear suspension **(see illustration 7)**. Check that the suspension components do not foul on any of the cycle parts and check that the shock absorber(s) provide adequate damping.
- Visually inspect the shock absorber(s) and check that there is no sign of oil leakage from its damper. This is somewhat restricted on certain single shock models due to the location of the shock absorber.
- With the rear wheel raised off the ground, grasp the wheel at the highest point and attempt to pull it up **(see illustration 8)**. Any play in the swingarm pivot or suspension linkage bearings will be felt as movement. **Note:** *Do not confuse play with actual suspension movement. Failure to lubricate suspension linkage bearings can lead to bearing failure* **(see illustration 9)**.
- With the rear wheel raised off the ground, grasp the swingarm ends and attempt to move the swingarm from side to side and forwards and backwards - any play indicates wear of the swingarm pivot bearings **(see illustration 10)**.

Worn suspension linkage pivots (arrows) are usually the cause of play in the rear suspension

Grasp the swingarm at the ends to check for play in its pivot bearings

MOT Test Checks REF•11

Brake pad wear can usually be viewed without removing the caliper. Most pads have wear indicator grooves (arrowed) and some also have indicator tangs or cut-outs.

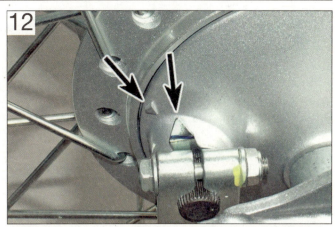

On drum brakes, check the angle of the operating lever with the brake fully applied. Most drum brakes have a wear indicator pointer or scale.

Brakes, Wheels and Tyres

Brakes

● With the wheel raised off the ground, apply the brake then free it off, and check that the wheel is about to revolve freely without brake drag.
● On disc brakes, examine the disc itself. Check that it is securely mounted and not cracked.
● On disc brakes, view the pad material through the caliper mouth and check that the pads are not worn down beyond the limit **(see illustration 11)**.
● On drum brakes, check that when the brake is applied the angle between the operating lever and cable or rod is not too great **(see illustration 12)**. Check also that the operating lever doesn't foul any other components.
● On disc brakes, examine the flexible hoses from top to bottom. Have an assistant hold the brake on so that the fluid in the hose is under pressure, and check that there is no sign of fluid leakage, bulges or cracking. If there are any metal brake pipes or unions, check that these are free from corrosion and damage. Where a brake-linked anti-dive system is fitted, check the hoses to the anti-dive in a similar manner.
● Check that the rear brake torque arm is secure and that its fasteners are secured by self-locking nuts or castellated nuts with split-pins or R-pins **(see illustration 13)**.
● On models with ABS, check that the self-check warning light in the instrument panel works.
● The MOT tester will perform a test of the motorcycle's braking efficiency based on a calculation of rider and motorcycle weight. Although this cannot be carried out at home, you can at least ensure that the braking systems are properly maintained. For hydraulic disc brakes, check the fluid level, lever/pedal feel (bleed of air if its spongy) and pad material. For drum brakes, check adjustment, cable or rod operation and shoe lining thickness.

Wheels and tyres

● Check the wheel condition. Cast wheels should be free from cracks and if of the built-up design, all fasteners should be secure. Spoked wheels should be checked for broken, corroded, loose or bent spokes.
● With the wheel raised off the ground, spin the wheel and visually check that the tyre and wheel run true. Check that the tyre does not foul the suspension or mudguards.
● With the wheel raised off the ground, grasp the wheel and attempt to move it about the axle (spindle) **(see illustration 14)**. Any play felt here indicates wheel bearing failure.

Brake torque arm must be properly secured at both ends

Check for wheel bearing play by trying to move the wheel about the axle (spindle)

REF•12 MOT Test Checks

Checking the tyre tread depth

Tyre direction of rotation arrow can be found on tyre sidewall

Castellated type wheel axle (spindle) nut must be secured by a split pin or R-pin

Two straightedges are used to check wheel alignment

- Check the tyre tread depth, tread condition and sidewall condition **(see illustration 15)**.
- Check the tyre type. Front and rear tyre types must be compatible and be suitable for road use. Tyres marked NOT FOR ROAD USE, COMPETITION USE ONLY or similar, will fail the MOT.
- If the tyre sidewall carries a direction of rotation arrow, this must be pointing in the direction of normal wheel rotation **(see illustration 16)**.
- Check that the wheel axle (spindle) nuts (where applicable) are properly secured. A self-locking nut or castellated nut with a split-pin or R-pin can be used **(see illustration 17)**.
- Wheel alignment is checked with the motorcycle off the stand and a rider seated. With the front wheel pointing straight ahead, two perfectly straight lengths of metal or wood and placed against the sidewalls of both tyres **(see illustration 18)**. The gap each side of the front tyre must be equidistant on both sides. Incorrect wheel alignment may be due to a cocked rear wheel (often as the result of poor chain adjustment) or in extreme cases, a bent frame.

General checks and condition

- Check the security of all major fasteners, bodypanels, seat, fairings (where fitted) and mudguards.
- Check that the rider and pillion footrests, handlebar levers and brake pedal are securely mounted.
- Check for corrosion on the frame or any load-bearing components. If severe, this may affect the structure, particularly under stress.

Sidecars

A motorcycle fitted with a sidecar requires additional checks relating to the stability of the machine and security of attachment and swivel joints, plus specific wheel alignment (toe-in) requirements. Additionally, tyre and lighting requirements differ from conventional motorcycle use. Owners are advised to check MOT test requirements with an official test centre.

Storage REF•13

Preparing for storage

Before you start

If repairs or an overhaul is needed, see that this is carried out now rather than left until you want to ride the bike again.

Give the bike a good wash and scrub all dirt from its underside. Make sure the bike dries completely before preparing for storage.

Engine

● Remove the spark plug(s) and lubricate the cylinder bores with approximately a teaspoon of motor oil using a spout-type oil can **(see illustration 1)**. Reinstall the spark plug(s). Crank the engine over a couple of times to coat the piston rings and bores with oil. If the bike has a kickstart, use this to turn the engine over. If not, flick the kill switch to the OFF position and crank the engine over on the starter **(see illustration 2)**. If the nature on the ignition system prevents the starter operating with the kill switch in the OFF position, remove the spark plugs and fit them back in their caps; ensure that the plugs are earthed (grounded) against the cylinder head when the starter is operated **(see illustration 3)**.

⚠️ **Warning: It is important that the plugs are earthed (grounded) away from the spark plug holes otherwise there is a risk of atomised fuel from the cylinders igniting.**

HAYNES HiNT *On a single cylinder four-stroke engine, you can seal the combustion chamber completely by positioning the piston at TDC on the compression stroke.*

● Drain the carburettor(s) otherwise there is a risk of jets becoming blocked by gum deposits from the fuel **(see illustration 4)**.

● If the bike is going into long-term storage, consider adding a fuel stabiliser to the fuel in the tank. If the tank is drained completely, corrosion of its internal surfaces may occur if left unprotected for a long period. The tank can be treated with a rust preventative especially for this purpose. Alternatively, remove the tank and pour half a litre of motor oil into it, install the filler cap and shake the tank to coat its internals with oil before draining off the excess. The same effect can also be achieved by spraying WD40 or a similar water-dispersant around the inside of the tank via its flexible nozzle.

● Make sure the cooling system contains the correct mix of antifreeze. Antifreeze also contains important corrosion inhibitors.

● The air intakes and exhaust can be sealed off by covering or plugging the openings. Ensure that you do not seal in any condensation; run the engine until it is hot,

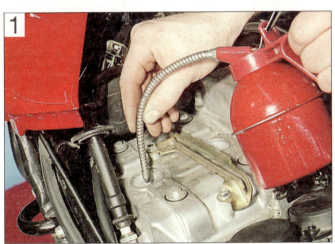
Squirt a drop of motor oil into each cylinder

Flick the kill switch to OFF . . .

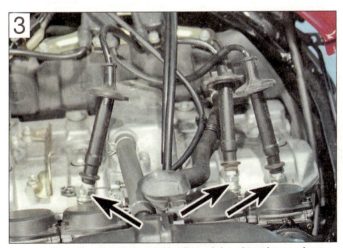
. . . and ensure that the metal bodies of the plugs (arrows) are earthed against the cylinder head

Connect a hose to the carburettor float chamber drain stub (arrow) and unscrew the drain screw

REF•14 Storage

Exhausts can be sealed off with a plastic bag

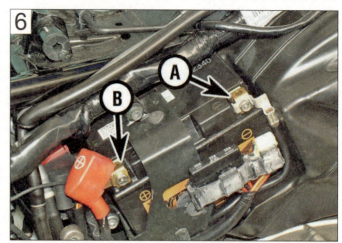
Disconnect the negative lead (A) first, followed by the positive lead (B)

Use a suitable battery charger - this kit also assess battery condition

then switch off and allow to cool. Tape a piece of thick plastic over the silencer end(s) **(see illustration 5)**. Note that some advocate pouring a tablespoon of motor oil into the silencer(s) before sealing them off.

Battery

● Remove it from the bike - in extreme cases of cold the battery may freeze and crack its case **(see illustration 6)**.

● Check the electrolyte level and top up if necessary (conventional refillable batteries). Clean the terminals.
● Store the battery off the motorcycle and away from any sources of fire. Position a wooden block under the battery if it is to sit on the ground.
● Give the battery a trickle charge for a few hours every month **(see illustration 7)**.

Tyres

● Place the bike on its centrestand or an auxiliary stand which will support the motorcycle in an upright position. Position wood blocks under the tyres to keep them off the ground and to provide insulation from damp. If the bike is being put into long-term storage, ideally both tyres should be off the ground; not only will this protect the tyres, but will also ensure that no load is placed on the steering head or wheel bearings.
● Deflate each tyre by 5 to 10 psi, no more or the beads may unseat from the rim, making subsequent inflation difficult on tubeless tyres.

Pivots and controls

● Lubricate all lever, pedal, stand and footrest pivot points. If grease nipples are fitted to the rear suspension components, apply lubricant to the pivots.
● Lubricate all control cables.

Cycle components

● Apply a wax protectant to all painted and plastic components. Wipe off any excess, but don't polish to a shine. Where fitted, clean the screen with soap and water.
● Coat metal parts with Vaseline (petroleum jelly). When applying this to the fork tubes, do not compress the forks otherwise the seals will rot from contact with the Vaseline.
● Apply a vinyl cleaner to the seat.

Storage conditions

● Aim to store the bike in a shed or garage which does not leak and is free from damp.
● Drape an old blanket or bedspread over the bike to protect it from dust and direct contact with sunlight (which will fade paint). This also hides the bike from prying eyes. Beware of tight-fitting plastic covers which may allow condensation to form and settle on the bike.

Getting back on the road

Engine and transmission

● Change the oil and replace the oil filter. If this was done prior to storage, check that the oil hasn't emulsified - a thick whitish substance which occurs through condensation.
● Remove the spark plugs. Using a spout-type oil can, squirt a few drops of oil into the cylinder(s). This will provide initial lubrication as the piston rings and bores comes back into contact. Service the spark plugs, or fit new ones, and install them in the engine.

● Check that the clutch isn't stuck on. The plates can stick together if left standing for some time, preventing clutch operation. Engage a gear and try rocking the bike back and forth with the clutch lever held against the handlebar. If this doesn't work on cable-operated clutches, hold the clutch lever back against the handlebar with a strong elastic band or cable tie for a couple of hours **(see illustration 8)**.
● If the air intakes or silencer end(s) were blocked off, remove the bung or cover used.
● If the fuel tank was coated with a rust

Hold clutch lever back against the handlebar with elastic bands or a cable tie

preventative, oil or a stabiliser added to the fuel, drain and flush the tank and dispose of the fuel sensibly. If no action was taken with the fuel tank prior to storage, it is advised that the old fuel is disposed of since it will go off over a period of time. Refill the fuel tank with fresh fuel.

Frame and running gear

- Oil all pivot points and cables.
- Check the tyre pressures. They will definitely need inflating if pressures were reduced for storage.
- Lubricate the final drive chain (where applicable).
- Remove any protective coating applied to the fork tubes (stanchions) since this may well destroy the fork seals. If the fork tubes weren't protected and have picked up rust spots, remove them with very fine abrasive paper and refinish with metal polish.
- Check that both brakes operate correctly. Apply each brake hard and check that it's not possible to move the motorcycle forwards, then check that the brake frees off again once released. Brake caliper pistons can stick due to corrosion around the piston head, or on the sliding caliper types, due to corrosion of the slider pins. If the brake doesn't free after repeated operation, take the caliper off for examination. Similarly drum brakes can stick due to a seized operating cam, cable or rod linkage.
- If the motorcycle has been in long-term storage, renew the brake fluid and clutch fluid (where applicable).
- Depending on where the bike has been stored, the wiring, cables and hoses may have been nibbled by rodents. Make a visual check and investigate disturbed wiring loom tape.

Battery

- If the battery has been previously removal and given top up charges it can simply be reconnected. Remember to connect the positive cable first and the negative cable last.
- On conventional refillable batteries, if the battery has not received any attention, remove it from the motorcycle and check its electrolyte level. Top up if necessary then charge the battery. If the battery fails to hold a charge and a visual checks show heavy white sulphation of the plates, the battery is probably defective and must be renewed. This is particularly likely if the battery is old. Confirm battery condition with a specific gravity check.
- On sealed (MF) batteries, if the battery has not received any attention, remove it from the motorcycle and charge it according to the information on the battery case - if the battery fails to hold a charge it must be renewed.

Starting procedure

- If a kickstart is fitted, turn the engine over a couple of times with the ignition OFF to distribute oil around the engine. If no kickstart is fitted, flick the engine kill switch OFF and the ignition ON and crank the engine over a couple of times to work oil around the upper cylinder components. If the nature of the ignition system is such that the starter won't work with the kill switch OFF, remove the spark plugs, fit them back into their caps and earth (ground) their bodies on the cylinder head. Reinstall the spark plugs afterwards.
- Switch the kill switch to RUN, operate the choke and start the engine. If the engine won't start don't continue cranking the engine - not only will this flatten the battery, but the starter motor will overheat. Switch the ignition off and try again later. If the engine refuses to start, go through the fault finding procedures in this manual. **Note:** *If the bike has been in storage for a long time, old fuel or a carburettor blockage may be the problem. Gum deposits in carburettors can block jets - if a carburettor cleaner doesn't prove successful the carburettors must be dismantled for cleaning.*
- Once the engine has started, check that the lights, turn signals and horn work properly.
- Treat the bike gently for the first ride and check all fluid levels on completion. Settle the bike back into the maintenance schedule.

REF•16 Tools and Workshop Tips

Buying tools

A toolkit is a fundamental requirement for servicing and repairing a motorcycle. Although there will be an initial expense in building up enough tools for servicing, this will soon be offset by the savings made by doing the job yourself. As experience and confidence grow, additional tools can be added to enable the repair and overhaul of the motorcycle. Many of the specialist tools are expensive and not often used so it may be preferable to hire them, or for a group of friends or motorcycle club to join in the purchase.

As a rule, it is better to buy more expensive, good quality tools. Cheaper tools are likely to wear out faster and need to be renewed more often, nullifying the original saving.

> **Warning:** To avoid the risk of a poor quality tool breaking in use, causing injury or damage to the component being worked on, always aim to purchase tools which meet the relevant national safety standards.

The following lists of tools do not represent the manufacturer's service tools, but serve as a guide to help the owner decide which tools are needed for this level of work. In addition, items such as an electric drill, hacksaw, files, soldering iron and a workbench equipped with a vice, may be needed. Although not classed as tools, a selection of bolts, screws, nuts, washers and pieces of tubing always come in useful.

For more information about tools, refer to the Haynes *Motorcycle Workshop Practice Techbook* (Bk. No. 3470).

Manufacturer's service tools

Inevitably certain tasks require the use of a service tool. Where possible an alternative tool or method of approach is recommended, but sometimes there is no option if personal injury or damage to the component is to be avoided. Where required, service tools are referred to in the relevant procedure.

Service tools can usually only be purchased from a motorcycle dealer and are identified by a part number. Some of the commonly-used tools, such as rotor pullers, are available in aftermarket form from mail-order motorcycle tool and accessory suppliers.

Maintenance and minor repair tools

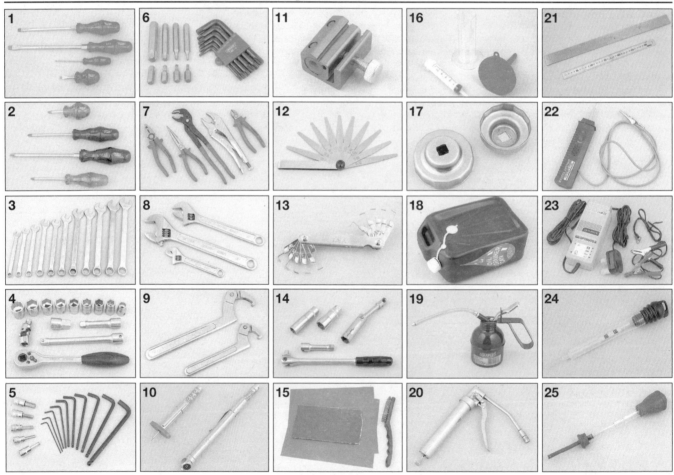

1. Set of flat-bladed screwdrivers
2. Set of Phillips head screwdrivers
3. Combination open-end and ring spanners
4. Socket set (3/8 inch or 1/2 inch drive)
5. Set of Allen keys or bits
6. Set of Torx keys or bits
7. Pliers, cutters and self-locking grips (Mole grips)
8. Adjustable spanners
9. C-spanners
10. Tread depth gauge and tyre pressure gauge
11. Cable oiler clamp
12. Feeler gauges
13. Spark plug gap measuring tool
14. Spark plug spanner or deep plug sockets
15. Wire brush and emery paper
16. Calibrated syringe, measuring vessel and funnel
17. Oil filter adapters
18. Oil drainer can or tray
19. Pump type oil can
20. Grease gun
21. Straight-edge and steel rule
22. Continuity tester
23. Battery charger
24. Hydrometer (for battery specific gravity check)
25. Anti-freeze tester (for liquid-cooled engines)

Tools and Workshop Tips

Repair and overhaul tools

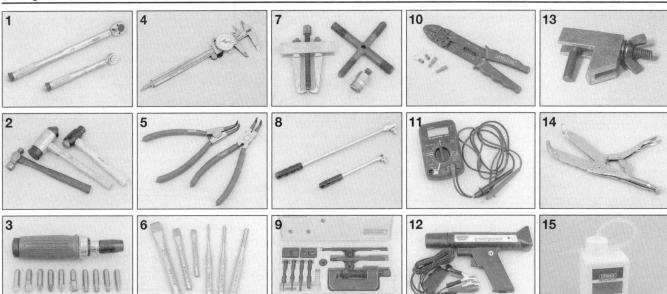

1 Torque wrench (small and mid-ranges)
2 Conventional, plastic or soft-faced hammers
3 Impact driver set
4 Vernier gauge
5 Circlip pliers (internal and external, or combination)
6 Set of cold chisels and punches
7 Selection of pullers
8 Breaker bars
9 Chain breaking/riveting tool set
10 Wire stripper and crimper tool
11 Multimeter (measures amps, volts and ohms)
12 Stroboscope (for dynamic timing checks)
13 Hose clamp (wingnut type shown)
14 Clutch holding tool
15 One-man brake/clutch bleeder kit

Specialist tools

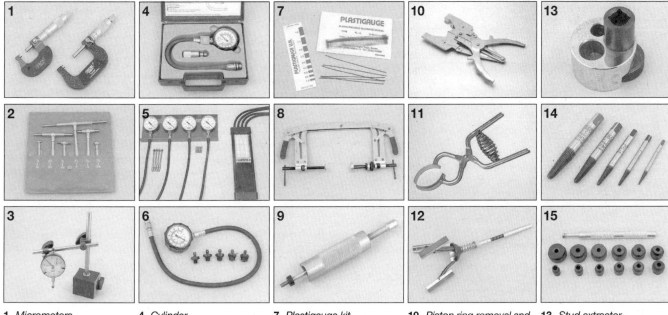

1 Micrometers (external type)
2 Telescoping gauges
3 Dial gauge
4 Cylinder compression gauge
5 Vacuum gauges (left) or manometer (right)
6 Oil pressure gauge
7 Plastigauge kit
8 Valve spring compressor (4-stroke engines)
9 Piston pin drawbolt tool
10 Piston ring removal and installation tool
11 Piston ring clamp
12 Cylinder bore hone (stone type shown)
13 Stud extractor
14 Screw extractor set
15 Bearing driver set

REF•18 Tools and Workshop Tips

1 Workshop equipment and facilities

The workbench

● Work is made much easier by raising the bike up on a ramp - components are much more accessible if raised to waist level. The hydraulic or pneumatic types seen in the dealer's workshop are a sound investment if you undertake a lot of repairs or overhauls **(see illustration 1.1)**.

1.1 Hydraulic motorcycle ramp

● If raised off ground level, the bike must be supported on the ramp to avoid it falling. Most ramps incorporate a front wheel locating clamp which can be adjusted to suit different diameter wheels. When tightening the clamp, take care not to mark the wheel rim or damage the tyre - use wood blocks on each side to prevent this.
● Secure the bike to the ramp using tie-downs **(see illustration 1.2)**. If the bike has only a sidestand, and hence leans at a dangerous angle when raised, support the bike on an auxiliary stand.

1.2 Tie-downs are used around the passenger footrests to secure the bike

● Auxiliary (paddock) stands are widely available from mail order companies or motorcycle dealers and attach either to the wheel axle or swingarm pivot **(see illustration 1.3)**. If the motorcycle has a centrestand, you can support it under the crankcase to prevent it toppling whilst either wheel is removed **(see illustration 1.4)**.

1.3 This auxiliary stand attaches to the swingarm pivot

1.4 Always use a block of wood between the engine and jack head when supporting the engine in this way

Fumes and fire

● Refer to the Safety first! page at the beginning of the manual for full details. Make sure your workshop is equipped with a fire extinguisher suitable for fuel-related fires (Class B fire - flammable liquids) - it is not sufficient to have a water-filled extinguisher.
● Always ensure adequate ventilation is available. Unless an exhaust gas extraction system is available for use, ensure that the engine is run outside of the workshop.
● If working on the fuel system, make sure the workshop is ventilated to avoid a build-up of fumes. This applies equally to fume build-up when charging a battery. Do not smoke or allow anyone else to smoke in the workshop.

Fluids

● If you need to drain fuel from the tank, store it in an approved container marked as suitable for the storage of petrol (gasoline) **(see illustration 1.5)**. Do not store fuel in glass jars or bottles.

1.5 Use an approved can only for storing petrol (gasoline)

● Use proprietary engine degreasers or solvents which have a high flash-point, such as paraffin (kerosene), for cleaning off oil, grease and dirt - never use petrol (gasoline) for cleaning. Wear rubber gloves when handling solvent and engine degreaser. The fumes from certain solvents can be dangerous - always work in a well-ventilated area.

Dust, eye and hand protection

● Protect your lungs from inhalation of dust particles by wearing a filtering mask over the nose and mouth. Many frictional materials still contain asbestos which is dangerous to your health. Protect your eyes from spouts of liquid and sprung components by wearing a pair of protective goggles **(see illustration 1.6)**.

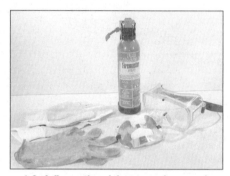

1.6 A fire extinguisher, goggles, mask and protective gloves should be at hand in the workshop

● Protect your hands from contact with solvents, fuel and oils by wearing rubber gloves. Alternatively apply a barrier cream to your hands before starting work. If handling hot components or fluids, wear suitable gloves to protect your hands from scalding and burns.

What to do with old fluids

● Old cleaning solvent, fuel, coolant and oils should not be poured down domestic drains or onto the ground. Package the fluid up in old oil containers, label it accordingly, and take it to a garage or disposal facility. Contact your local authority for location of such sites or ring the oil care hotline.

Note: It is antisocial and illegal to dump oil down the drain. To find the location of your local oil recycling bank in the UK, call 08708 506 506 or visit www.oilbankline.org.uk

In the USA, note that any oil supplier must accept used oil for recycling.

Tools and Workshop Tips

2 Fasteners - screws, bolts and nuts

Fastener types and applications

Bolts and screws

● Fastener head types are either of hexagonal, Torx or splined design, with internal and external versions of each type **(see illustrations 2.1 and 2.2)**; splined head fasteners are not in common use on motorcycles. The conventional slotted or Phillips head design is used for certain screws. Bolt or screw length is always measured from the underside of the head to the end of the item **(see illustration 2.11)**.

2.1 Internal hexagon/Allen (A), Torx (B) and splined (C) fasteners, with corresponding bits

2.2 External Torx (A), splined (B) and hexagon (C) fasteners, with corresponding sockets

● Certain fasteners on the motorcycle have a tensile marking on their heads, the higher the marking the stronger the fastener. High tensile fasteners generally carry a 10 or higher marking. Never replace a high tensile fastener with one of a lower tensile strength.

Washers (see illustration 2.3)

● Plain washers are used between a fastener head and a component to prevent damage to the component or to spread the load when torque is applied. Plain washers can also be used as spacers or shims in certain assemblies. Copper or aluminium plain washers are often used as sealing washers on drain plugs.

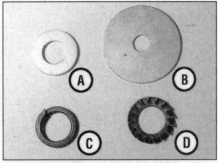

2.3 Plain washer (A), penny washer (B), spring washer (C) and serrated washer (D)

● The split-ring spring washer works by applying axial tension between the fastener head and component. If flattened, it is fatigued and must be renewed. If a plain (flat) washer is used on the fastener, position the spring washer between the fastener and the plain washer.

● Serrated star type washers dig into the fastener and component faces, preventing loosening. They are often used on electrical earth (ground) connections to the frame.

● Cone type washers (sometimes called Belleville) are conical and when tightened apply axial tension between the fastener head and component. They must be installed with the dished side against the component and often carry an OUTSIDE marking on their outer face. If flattened, they are fatigued and must be renewed.

● Tab washers are used to lock plain nuts or bolts on a shaft. A portion of the tab washer is bent up hard against one flat of the nut or bolt to prevent it loosening. Due to the tab washer being deformed in use, a new tab washer should be used every time it is disturbed.

● Wave washers are used to take up endfloat on a shaft. They provide light springing and prevent excessive side-to-side play of a component. Can be found on rocker arm shafts.

Nuts and split pins

● Conventional plain nuts are usually six-sided **(see illustration 2.4)**. They are sized by thread diameter and pitch. High tensile nuts carry a number on one end to denote their tensile strength.

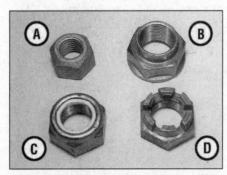

2.4 Plain nut (A), shouldered locknut (B), nylon insert nut (C) and castellated nut (D)

● Self-locking nuts either have a nylon insert, or two spring metal tabs, or a shoulder which is staked into a groove in the shaft - their advantage over conventional plain nuts is a resistance to loosening due to vibration. The nylon insert type can be used a number of times, but must be renewed when the friction of the nylon insert is reduced, ie when the nut spins freely on the shaft. The spring tab type can be reused unless the tabs are damaged. The shouldered type must be renewed every time it is disturbed.

● Split pins (cotter pins) are used to lock a castellated nut to a shaft or to prevent slackening of a plain nut. Common applications are wheel axles and brake torque arms. Because the split pin arms are deformed to lock around the nut a new split pin must always be used on installation - always fit the correct size split pin which will fit snugly in the shaft hole. Make sure the split pin arms are correctly located around the nut **(see illustrations 2.5 and 2.6)**.

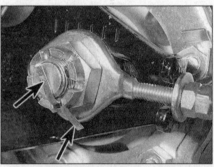

2.5 Bend split pin (cotter pin) arms as shown (arrows) to secure a castellated nut

2.6 Bend split pin (cotter pin) arms as shown to secure a plain nut

Caution: If the castellated nut slots do not align with the shaft hole after tightening to the torque setting, tighten the nut until the next slot aligns with the hole - never slacken the nut to align its slot.

● R-pins (shaped like the letter R), or slip pins as they are sometimes called, are sprung and can be reused if they are otherwise in good condition. Always install R-pins with their closed end facing forwards **(see illustration 2.7)**.

REF•20 Tools and Workshop Tips

2.7 Correct fitting of R-pin. Arrow indicates forward direction

Circlips (see illustration 2.8)

● Circlips (sometimes called snap-rings) are used to retain components on a shaft or in a housing and have corresponding external or internal ears to permit removal. Parallel-sided (machined) circlips can be installed either way round in their groove, whereas stamped circlips (which have a chamfered edge on one face) must be installed with the chamfer facing away from the direction of thrust load **(see illustration 2.9)**.

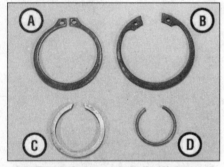

2.8 External stamped circlip (A), internal stamped circlip (B), machined circlip (C) and wire circlip (D)

● Always use circlip pliers to remove and install circlips; expand or compress them just enough to remove them. After installation, rotate the circlip in its groove to ensure it is securely seated. If installing a circlip on a splined shaft, always align its opening with a shaft channel to ensure the circlip ends are well supported and unlikely to catch **(see illustration 2.10)**.

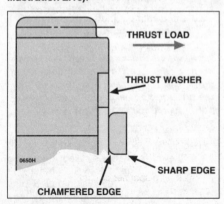

2.9 Correct fitting of a stamped circlip

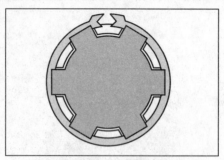

2.10 Align circlip opening with shaft channel

● Circlips can wear due to the thrust of components and become loose in their grooves, with the subsequent danger of becoming dislodged in operation. For this reason, renewal is advised every time a circlip is disturbed.

● Wire circlips are commonly used as piston pin retaining clips. If a removal tang is provided, long-nosed pliers can be used to dislodge them, otherwise careful use of a small flat-bladed screwdriver is necessary. Wire circlips should be renewed every time they are disturbed.

Thread diameter and pitch

● Diameter of a male thread (screw, bolt or stud) is the outside diameter of the threaded portion **(see illustration 2.11)**. Most motorcycle manufacturers use the ISO (International Standards Organisation) metric system expressed in millimetres, eg M6 refers to a 6 mm diameter thread. Sizing is the same for nuts, except that the thread diameter is measured across the valleys of the nut.

● Pitch is the distance between the peaks of the thread **(see illustration 2.11)**. It is expressed in millimetres, thus a common bolt size may be expressed as 6.0 x 1.0 mm (6 mm thread diameter and 1 mm pitch). Generally pitch increases in proportion to thread diameter, although there are always exceptions.

● Thread diameter and pitch are related for conventional fastener applications and the accompanying table can be used as a guide. Additionally, the AF (Across Flats), spanner or socket size dimension of the bolt or nut **(see illustration 2.11)** is linked to thread and pitch specification. Thread pitch can be measured with a thread gauge **(see illustration 2.12)**.

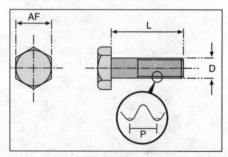

2.11 Fastener length (L), thread diameter (D), thread pitch (P) and head size (AF)

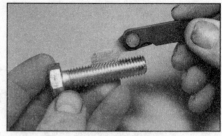

2.12 Using a thread gauge to measure pitch

AF size	Thread diameter x pitch (mm)
8 mm	M5 x 0.8
8 mm	M6 x 1.0
10 mm	M6 x 1.0
12 mm	M8 x 1.25
14 mm	M10 x 1.25
17 mm	M12 x 1.25

● The threads of most fasteners are of the right-hand type, ie they are turned clockwise to tighten and anti-clockwise to loosen. The reverse situation applies to left-hand thread fasteners, which are turned anti-clockwise to tighten and clockwise to loosen. Left-hand threads are used where rotation of a component might loosen a conventional right-hand thread fastener.

Seized fasteners

● Corrosion of external fasteners due to water or reaction between two dissimilar metals can occur over a period of time. It will build up sooner in wet conditions or in countries where salt is used on the roads during the winter. If a fastener is severely corroded it is likely that normal methods of removal will fail and result in its head being ruined. When you attempt removal, the fastener thread should be heard to crack free and unscrew easily - if it doesn't, stop there before damaging something.

● A smart tap on the head of the fastener will often succeed in breaking free corrosion which has occurred in the threads **(see illustration 2.13)**.

● An aerosol penetrating fluid (such as WD-40) applied the night beforehand may work its way down into the thread and ease removal. Depending on the location, you may be able to make up a Plasticine well around the fastener head and fill it with penetrating fluid.

2.13 A sharp tap on the head of a fastener will often break free a corroded thread

Tools and Workshop Tips

- If you are working on an engine internal component, corrosion will most likely not be a problem due to the well lubricated environment. However, components can be very tight and an impact driver is a useful tool in freeing them **(see illustration 2.14)**.

2.14 Using an impact driver to free a fastener

- Where corrosion has occurred between dissimilar metals (eg steel and aluminium alloy), the application of heat to the fastener head will create a disproportionate expansion rate between the two metals and break the seizure caused by the corrosion. Whether heat can be applied depends on the location of the fastener - any surrounding components likely to be damaged must first be removed **(see illustration 2.15)**. Heat can be applied using a paint stripper heat gun or clothes iron, or by immersing the component in boiling water - wear protective gloves to prevent scalding or burns to the hands.

2.15 Using heat to free a seized fastener

- As a last resort, it is possible to use a hammer and cold chisel to work the fastener head unscrewed **(see illustration 2.16)**. This will damage the fastener, but more importantly extreme care must be taken not to damage the surrounding component.

Caution: Remember that the component being secured is generally of more value than the bolt, nut or screw - when the fastener is freed, do not unscrew it with force, instead work the fastener back and forth when resistance is felt to prevent thread damage.

2.16 Using a hammer and chisel to free a seized fastener

Broken fasteners and damaged heads

- If the shank of a broken bolt or screw is accessible you can grip it with self-locking grips. The knurled wheel type stud extractor tool or self-gripping stud puller tool is particularly useful for removing the long studs which screw into the cylinder mouth surface of the crankcase or bolts and screws from which the head has broken off **(see illustration 2.17)**. Studs can also be removed by locking two nuts together on the threaded end of the stud and using a spanner on the lower nut **(see illustration 2.18)**.

2.17 Using a stud extractor tool to remove a broken crankcase stud

2.18 Two nuts can be locked together to unscrew a stud from a component

- A bolt or screw which has broken off below or level with the casing must be extracted using a screw extractor set. Centre punch the fastener to centralise the drill bit, then drill a hole in the fastener **(see illustration 2.19)**. Select a drill bit which is approximately half to three-quarters the diameter of the fastener

2.19 When using a screw extractor, first drill a hole in the fastener . . .

and drill to a depth which will accommodate the extractor. Use the largest size extractor possible, but avoid leaving too small a wall thickness otherwise the extractor will merely force the fastener walls outwards wedging it in the casing thread.

- If a spiral type extractor is used, thread it anti-clockwise into the fastener. As it is screwed in, it will grip the fastener and unscrew it from the casing **(see illustration 2.20)**.

2.20 . . . then thread the extractor anti-clockwise into the fastener

- If a taper type extractor is used, tap it into the fastener so that it is firmly wedged in place. Unscrew the extractor (anti-clockwise) to draw the fastener out.

 Warning: Stud extractors are very hard and may break off in the fastener if care is not taken - ask an engineer about spark erosion if this happens.

- Alternatively, the broken bolt/screw can be drilled out and the hole retapped for an oversize bolt/screw or a diamond-section thread insert. It is essential that the drilling is carried out squarely and to the correct depth, otherwise the casing may be ruined - if in doubt, entrust the work to an engineer.
- Bolts and nuts with rounded corners cause the correct size spanner or socket to slip when force is applied. Of the types of spanner/socket available always use a six-point type rather than an eight or twelve-point type - better grip

REF•22 Tools and Workshop Tips

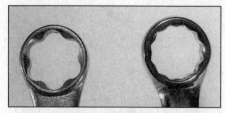

2.21 Comparison of surface drive ring spanner (left) with 12-point type (right)

is obtained. Surface drive spanners grip the middle of the hex flats, rather than the corners, and are thus good in cases of damaged heads **(see illustration 2.21)**.

● Slotted-head or Phillips-head screws are often damaged by the use of the wrong size screwdriver. Allen-head and Torx-head screws are much less likely to sustain damage. If enough of the screw head is exposed you can use a hacksaw to cut a slot in its head and then use a conventional flat-bladed screwdriver to remove it. Alternatively use a hammer and cold chisel to tap the head of the fastener around to slacken it. Always replace damaged fasteners with new ones, preferably Torx or Allen-head type.

HAYNES HiNT

A dab of valve grinding compound between the screw head and screwdriver tip will often give a good grip.

Thread repair

● Threads (particularly those in aluminium alloy components) can be damaged by overtightening, being assembled with dirt in the threads, or from a component working loose and vibrating. Eventually the thread will fail completely, and it will be impossible to tighten the fastener.

● If a thread is damaged or clogged with old locking compound it can be renovated with a thread repair tool (thread chaser) **(see illustrations 2.22 and 2.23)**; special thread

2.22 A thread repair tool being used to correct an internal thread

2.23 A thread repair tool being used to correct an external thread

chasers are available for spark plug hole threads. The tool will not cut a new thread, but clean and true the original thread. Make sure that you use the correct diameter and pitch tool. Similarly, external threads can be cleaned up with a die or a thread restorer file **(see illustration 2.24)**.

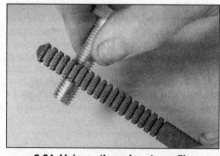

2.24 Using a thread restorer file

● It is possible to drill out the old thread and retap the component to the next thread size. This will work where there is enough surrounding material and a new bolt or screw can be obtained. Sometimes, however, this is not possible - such as where the bolt/screw passes through another component which must also be suitably modified, also in cases where a spark plug or oil drain plug cannot be obtained in a larger diameter thread size.

● The diamond-section thread insert (often known by its popular trade name of Heli-Coil) is a simple and effective method of renewing the thread and retaining the original size. A kit can be purchased which contains the tap, insert and installing tool **(see illustration 2.25)**. Drill out the damaged thread with the size drill specified **(see illustration 2.26)**. Carefully retap the thread **(see illustration 2.27)**. Install the

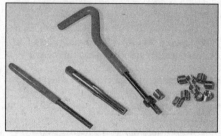

2.25 Obtain a thread insert kit to suit the thread diameter and pitch required

2.26 To install a thread insert, first drill out the original thread . . .

2.27 . . . tap a new thread . . .

2.28 . . . fit insert on the installing tool . . .

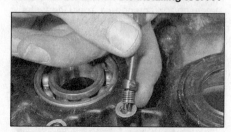

2.29 . . . and thread into the component . . .

2.30 . . . break off the tang when complete

insert on the installing tool and thread it slowly into place using a light downward pressure **(see illustrations 2.28 and 2.29)**. When positioned between a 1/4 and 1/2 turn below the surface withdraw the installing tool and use the break-off tool to press down on the tang, breaking it off **(see illustration 2.30)**.

● There are epoxy thread repair kits on the market which can rebuild stripped internal threads, although this repair should not be used on high load-bearing components.

Tools and Workshop Tips

Thread locking and sealing compounds

● Locking compounds are used in locations where the fastener is prone to loosening due to vibration or on important safety-related items which might cause loss of control of the motorcycle if they fail. It is also used where important fasteners cannot be secured by other means such as lockwashers or split pins.

● Before applying locking compound, make sure that the threads (internal and external) are clean and dry with all old compound removed. Select a compound to suit the component being secured - a non-permanent general locking and sealing type is suitable for most applications, but a high strength type is needed for permanent fixing of studs in castings. Apply a drop or two of the compound to the first few threads of the fastener, then thread it into place and tighten to the specified torque. Do not apply excessive thread locking compound otherwise the thread may be damaged on subsequent removal.

● Certain fasteners are impregnated with a dry film type coating of locking compound on their threads. Always renew this type of fastener if disturbed.

● Anti-seize compounds, such as copper-based greases, can be applied to protect threads from seizure due to extreme heat and corrosion. A common instance is spark plug threads and exhaust system fasteners.

3 Measuring tools and gauges

Feeler gauges

● Feeler gauges (or blades) are used for measuring small gaps and clearances **(see illustration 3.1)**. They can also be used to measure endfloat (sideplay) of a component on a shaft where access is not possible with a dial gauge.

● Feeler gauge sets should be treated with care and not bent or damaged. They are etched with their size on one face. Keep them clean and very lightly oiled to prevent corrosion build-up.

3.1 Feeler gauges are used for measuring small gaps and clearances - thickness is marked on one face of gauge

● When measuring a clearance, select a gauge which is a light sliding fit between the two components. You may need to use two gauges together to measure the clearance accurately.

Micrometers

● A micrometer is a precision tool capable of measuring to 0.01 or 0.001 of a millimetre. It should always be stored in its case and not in the general toolbox. It must be kept clean and never dropped, otherwise its frame or measuring anvils could be distorted resulting in inaccurate readings.

● External micrometers are used for measuring outside diameters of components and have many more applications than internal micrometers. Micrometers are available in different size ranges, eg 0 to 25 mm, 25 to 50 mm, and upwards in 25 mm steps; some large micrometers have interchangeable anvils to allow a range of measurements to be taken. Generally the largest precision measurement you are likely to take on a motorcycle is the piston diameter.

● Internal micrometers (or bore micrometers) are used for measuring inside diameters, such as valve guides and cylinder bores. Telescoping gauges and small hole gauges are used in conjunction with an external micrometer, whereas the more expensive internal micrometers have their own measuring device.

External micrometer

Note: *The conventional analogue type instrument is described. Although much easier to read, digital micrometers are considerably more expensive.*

● Always check the calibration of the micrometer before use. With the anvils closed (0 to 25 mm type) or set over a test gauge

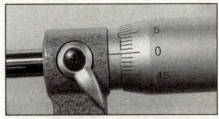

3.2 Check micrometer calibration before use

(for the larger types) the scale should read zero **(see illustration 3.2)**; make sure that the anvils (and test piece) are clean first. Any discrepancy can be adjusted by referring to the instructions supplied with the tool. Remember that the micrometer is a precision measuring tool - don't force the anvils closed, use the ratchet (4) on the end of the micrometer to close it. In this way, a measured force is always applied.

● To use, first make sure that the item being measured is clean. Place the anvil of the micrometer (1) against the item and use the thimble (2) to bring the spindle (3) lightly into contact with the other side of the item **(see illustration 3.3)**. Don't tighten the thimble down because this will damage the micrometer - instead use the ratchet (4) on the end of the micrometer. The ratchet mechanism applies a measured force preventing damage to the instrument.

● The micrometer is read by referring to the linear scale on the sleeve and the annular scale on the thimble. Read off the sleeve first to obtain the base measurement, then add the fine measurement from the thimble to obtain the overall reading. The linear scale on the sleeve represents the measuring range of the micrometer (eg 0 to 25 mm). The annular scale

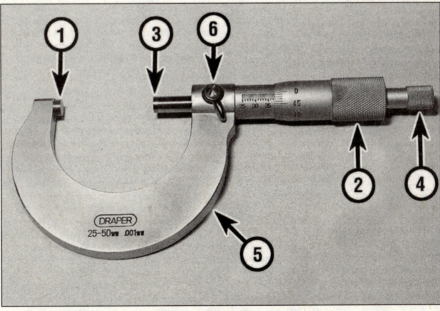

3.3 Micrometer component parts

1 Anvil
2 Thimble
3 Spindle
4 Ratchet
5 Frame
6 Locking lever

REF•24 Tools and Workshop Tips

on the thimble will be in graduations of 0.01 mm (or as marked on the frame) - one full revolution of the thimble will move 0.5 mm on the linear scale. Take the reading where the datum line on the sleeve intersects the thimble's scale. Always position the eye directly above the scale otherwise an inaccurate reading will result.

In the example shown the item measures 2.95 mm (see illustration 3.4):

Linear scale	2.00 mm
Linear scale	0.50 mm
Annular scale	0.45 mm
Total figure	2.95 mm

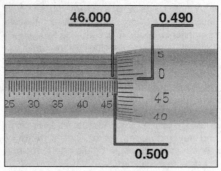

3.5 Micrometer reading of 46.99 mm on linear and annular scales . . .

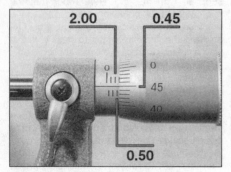

3.4 Micrometer reading of 2.95 mm

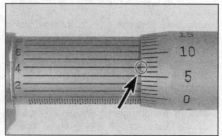

3.6 . . . and 0.004 mm on vernier scale

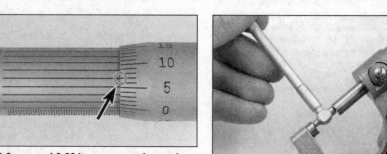

3.7 Expand the telescoping gauge in the bore, lock its position . . .

3.8 . . . then measure the gauge with a micrometer

Most micrometers have a locking lever (6) on the frame to hold the setting in place, allowing the item to be removed from the micrometer.
● Some micrometers have a vernier scale on their sleeve, providing an even finer measurement to be taken, in 0.001 increments of a millimetre. Take the sleeve and thimble measurement as described above, then check which graduation on the vernier scale aligns with that of the annular scale on the thimble
Note: *The eye must be perpendicular to the scale when taking the vernier reading - if necessary rotate the body of the micrometer to ensure this.* Multiply the vernier scale figure by 0.001 and add it to the base and fine measurement figures.

In the example shown the item measures 46.994 mm (see illustrations 3.5 and 3.6):

Linear scale (base)	46.000 mm
Linear scale (base)	00.500 mm
Annular scale (fine)	00.490 mm
Vernier scale	00.004 mm
Total figure	46.994 mm

Internal micrometer

● Internal micrometers are available for measuring bore diameters, but are expensive and unlikely to be available for home use. It is suggested that a set of telescoping gauges and small hole gauges, both of which must be used with an external micrometer, will suffice for taking internal measurements on a motorcycle.
● Telescoping gauges can be used to measure internal diameters of components. Select a gauge with the correct size range, make sure its ends are clean and insert it into the bore. Expand the gauge, then lock its position and withdraw it from the bore (see illustration 3.7). Measure across the gauge ends with a micrometer (see illustration 3.8).
● Very small diameter bores (such as valve guides) are measured with a small hole gauge. Once adjusted to a slip-fit inside the component, its position is locked and the gauge withdrawn for measurement with a micrometer (see illustrations 3.9 and 3.10).

Vernier caliper

Note: *The conventional linear and dial gauge type instruments are described. Digital types are easier to read, but are far more expensive.*
● The vernier caliper does not provide the precision of a micrometer, but is versatile in being able to measure internal and external diameters. Some types also incorporate a depth gauge. It is ideal for measuring clutch plate friction material and spring free lengths.
● To use the conventional linear scale vernier, slacken off the vernier clamp screws (1) and set its jaws over (2), or inside (3), the item to be measured (see illustration 3.11). Slide the jaw into contact, using the thumb-wheel (4) for fine movement of the sliding scale (5) then tighten the clamp screws (1). Read off the main scale (6) where the zero on the sliding scale (5) intersects it, taking the whole number to the left of the zero; this provides the base measurement. View along the sliding scale and select the division which

3.9 Expand the small hole gauge in the bore, lock its position . . .

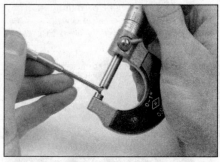

3.10 . . . then measure the gauge with a micrometer

lines up exactly with any of the divisions on the main scale, noting that the divisions usually represents 0.02 of a millimetre. Add this fine measurement to the base measurement to obtain the total reading.

Tools and Workshop Tips

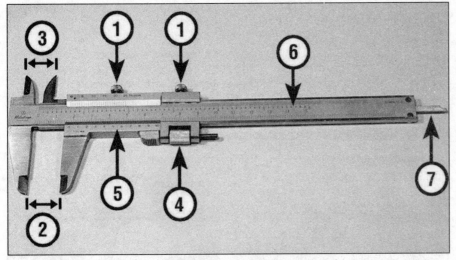

3.11 Vernier component parts (linear gauge)

1 Clamp screws
2 External jaws
3 Internal jaws
4 Thumbwheel
5 Sliding scale
6 Main scale
7 Depth gauge

In the example shown the item measures 55.92 mm (see illustration 3.12):

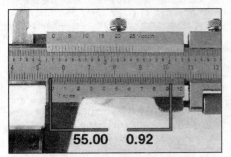

3.12 Vernier gauge reading of 55.92 mm

Base measurement	55.00 mm
Fine measurement	00.92 mm
Total figure	55.92 mm

● Some vernier calipers are equipped with a dial gauge for fine measurement. Before use, check that the jaws are clean, then close them fully and check that the dial gauge reads zero. If necessary adjust the gauge ring accordingly. Slacken the vernier clamp screw (1) and set its jaws over (2), or inside (3), the item to be measured (see illustration 3.13). Slide the jaws into contact, using the thumbwheel (4) for fine movement. Read off the main scale (5) where the edge of the sliding scale (6) intersects it, taking the whole number to the left of the zero; this provides the base measurement. Read off the needle position on the dial gauge (7) scale to provide the fine measurement; each division represents 0.05 of a millimetre. Add this fine measurement to the base measurement to obtain the total reading.

In the example shown the item measures 55.95 mm (see illustration 3.14):

Base measurement	55.00 mm
Fine measurement	00.95 mm
Total figure	55.95 mm

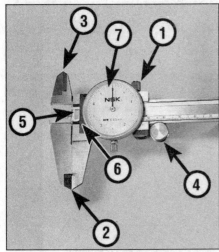

3.13 Vernier component parts (dial gauge)

1 Clamp screw
2 External jaws
3 Internal jaws
4 Thumbwheel
5 Main scale
6 Sliding scale
7 Dial gauge

3.14 Vernier gauge reading of 55.95 mm

Plastigauge

● Plastigauge is a plastic material which can be compressed between two surfaces to measure the oil clearance between them. The width of the compressed Plastigauge is measured against a calibrated scale to determine the clearance.

● Common uses of Plastigauge are for measuring the clearance between crankshaft journal and main bearing inserts, between crankshaft journal and big-end bearing inserts, and between camshaft and bearing surfaces. The following example describes big-end oil clearance measurement.

● Handle the Plastigauge material carefully to prevent distortion. Using a sharp knife, cut a length which corresponds with the width of the bearing being measured and place it carefully across the journal so that it is parallel with the shaft (see illustration 3.15). Carefully install both bearing shells and the connecting rod. Without rotating the rod on the journal tighten its bolts or nuts (as applicable) to the specified torque. The connecting rod and bearings are then disassembled and the crushed Plastigauge examined.

3.15 Plastigauge placed across shaft journal

● Using the scale provided in the Plastigauge kit, measure the width of the material to determine the oil clearance (see illustration 3.16). Always remove all traces of Plastigauge after use using your fingernails.

Caution: Arriving at the correct clearance demands that the assembly is torqued correctly, according to the settings and sequence (where applicable) provided by the motorcycle manufacturer.

3.16 Measuring the width of the crushed Plastigauge

Tools and Workshop Tips

Dial gauge or DTI (Dial Test Indicator)

● A dial gauge can be used to accurately measure small amounts of movement. Typical uses are measuring shaft runout or shaft endfloat (sideplay) and setting piston position for ignition timing on two-strokes. A dial gauge set usually comes with a range of different probes and adapters and mounting equipment.

● The gauge needle must point to zero when at rest. Rotate the ring around its periphery to zero the gauge.

● Check that the gauge is capable of reading the extent of movement in the work. Most gauges have a small dial set in the face which records whole millimetres of movement as well as the fine scale around the face periphery which is calibrated in 0.01 mm divisions. Read off the small dial first to obtain the base measurement, then add the measurement from the fine scale to obtain the total reading.

In the example shown the gauge reads 1.48 mm (see illustration 3.17):

Base measurement	1.00 mm
Fine measurement	0.48 mm
Total figure	1.48 mm

3.17 Dial gauge reading of 1.48 mm

● If measuring shaft runout, the shaft must be supported in vee-blocks and the gauge mounted on a stand perpendicular to the shaft. Rest the tip of the gauge against the centre of the shaft and rotate the shaft slowly whilst watching the gauge reading (see illustration 3.18). Take several measurements along the length of the shaft and record the maximum gauge reading as the amount of runout in the shaft. Note: *The reading obtained will be total runout at that point - some manufacturers specify that the runout figure is halved to compare with their specified runout limit.*

● Endfloat (sideplay) measurement requires that the gauge is mounted securely to the surrounding component with its probe touching the end of the shaft. Using hand pressure, push and pull on the shaft noting the maximum endfloat recorded on the gauge (see illustration 3.19).

3.19 Using a dial gauge to measure shaft endfloat

● A dial gauge with suitable adapters can be used to determine piston position BTDC on two-stroke engines for the purposes of ignition timing. The gauge, adapter and suitable length probe are installed in the place of the spark plug and the gauge zeroed at TDC. If the piston position is specified as 1.14 mm BTDC, rotate the engine back to 2.00 mm BTDC, then slowly forwards to 1.14 mm BTDC.

Cylinder compression gauges

● A compression gauge is used for measuring cylinder compression. Either the rubber-cone type or the threaded adapter type can be used. The latter is preferred to ensure a perfect seal against the cylinder head. A 0 to 300 psi (0 to 20 Bar) type gauge (for petrol/gasoline engines) will be suitable for motorcycles.

● The spark plug is removed and the gauge either held hard against the cylinder head (cone type) or the gauge adapter screwed into the cylinder head (threaded type) (see illustration 3.20). Cylinder compression is measured with the engine turning over, but not running. The gauge will hold the reading until manually released.

Oil pressure gauge

● An oil pressure gauge is used for measuring engine oil pressure. Most gauges come with a set of adapters to fit the thread of the take-off point (see illustration 3.21). If the take-off point specified by the motorcycle manufacturer is an external oil pipe union, make sure that the specified replacement union is used to prevent oil starvation.

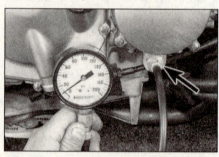

3.21 Oil pressure gauge and take-off point adapter (arrow)

● Oil pressure is measured with the engine running (at a specific rpm) and often the manufacturer will specify pressure limits for a cold and hot engine.

Straight-edge and surface plate

● If checking the gasket face of a component for warpage, place a steel rule or precision straight-edge across the gasket face and measure any gap between the straight-edge and component with feeler gauges (see illustration 3.22). Check diagonally across the component and between mounting holes (see illustration 3.23).

3.22 Use a straight-edge and feeler gauges to check for warpage

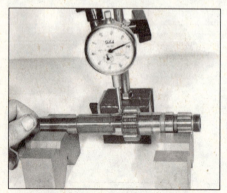

3.18 Using a dial gauge to measure shaft runout

3.20 Using a rubber-cone type cylinder compression gauge

3.23 Check for warpage in these directions

Tools and Workshop Tips

- Checking individual components for warpage, such as clutch plain (metal) plates, requires a perfectly flat plate or piece or plate glass and feeler gauges.

4 Torque and leverage

What is torque?

- Torque describes the twisting force about a shaft. The amount of torque applied is determined by the distance from the centre of the shaft to the end of the lever and the amount of force being applied to the end of the lever; distance multiplied by force equals torque.
- The manufacturer applies a measured torque to a bolt or nut to ensure that it will not slacken in use and to hold two components securely together without movement in the joint. The actual torque setting depends on the thread size, bolt or nut material and the composition of the components being held.
- Too little torque may cause the fastener to loosen due to vibration, whereas too much torque will distort the joint faces of the component or cause the fastener to shear off. Always stick to the specified torque setting.

Using a torque wrench

- Check the calibration of the torque wrench and make sure it has a suitable range for the job. Torque wrenches are available in Nm (Newton-metres), kgf m (kilograms-force metre), lbf ft (pounds-feet), lbf in (inch-pounds). Do not confuse lbf ft with lbf in.
- Adjust the tool to the desired torque on the scale (see illustration 4.1). If your torque wrench is not calibrated in the units specified, carefully convert the figure (see Conversion Factors). A manufacturer sometimes gives a torque setting as a range (8 to 10 Nm) rather than a single figure - in this case set the tool midway between the two settings. The same torque may be expressed as 9 Nm ± 1 Nm. Some torque wrenches have a method of locking the setting so that it isn't inadvertently altered during use.

- Install the bolts/nuts in their correct location and secure them lightly. Their threads must be clean and free of any old locking compound. Unless specified the threads and flange should be dry - oiled threads are necessary in certain circumstances and the manufacturer will take this into account in the specified torque figure. Similarly, the manufacturer may also specify the application of thread-locking compound.
- Tighten the fasteners in the specified sequence until the torque wrench clicks, indicating that the torque setting has been reached. Apply the torque again to double-check the setting. Where different thread diameter fasteners secure the component, as a rule tighten the larger diameter ones first.
- When the torque wrench has been finished with, release the lock (where applicable) and fully back off its setting to zero - do not leave the torque wrench tensioned. Also, do not use a torque wrench for slackening a fastener.

Angle-tightening

- Manufacturers often specify a figure in degrees for final tightening of a fastener. This usually follows tightening to a specific torque setting.
- A degree disc can be set and attached to the socket (see illustration 4.2) or a protractor can be used to mark the angle of movement on the bolt/nut head and the surrounding casting (see illustration 4.3).

4.2 Angle tightening can be accomplished with a torque-angle gauge . . .

4.3 . . . or by marking the angle on the surrounding component

Loosening sequences

- Where more than one bolt/nut secures a component, loosen each fastener evenly a little at a time. In this way, not all the stress of the joint is held by one fastener and the components are not likely to distort.
- If a tightening sequence is provided, work in the REVERSE of this, but if not, work from the outside in, in a criss-cross sequence (see illustration 4.4).

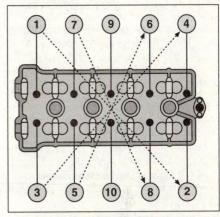

4.4 When slackening, work from the outside inwards

Tightening sequences

- If a component is held by more than one fastener it is important that the retaining bolts/nuts are tightened evenly to prevent uneven stress build-up and distortion of sealing faces. This is especially important on high-compression joints such as the cylinder head.
- A sequence is usually provided by the manufacturer, either in a diagram or actually marked in the casting. If not, always start in the centre and work outwards in a criss-cross pattern (see illustration 4.5). Start off by securing all bolts/nuts finger-tight, then set the torque wrench and tighten each fastener by a small amount in sequence until the final torque is reached. By following this practice,

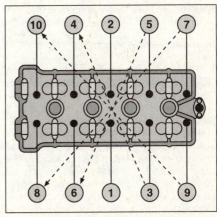

4.5 When tightening, work from the inside outwards

4.1 Set the torque wrench index mark to the setting required, in this case 12 Nm

Tools and Workshop Tips

the joint will be held evenly and will not be distorted. Important joints, such as the cylinder head and big-end fasteners often have two- or three-stage torque settings.

Applying leverage

● Use tools at the correct angle. Position a socket wrench or spanner on the bolt/nut so that you pull it towards you when loosening. If this can't be done, push the spanner without curling your fingers around it **(see illustration 4.6)** - the spanner may slip or the fastener loosen suddenly, resulting in your fingers being crushed against a component.

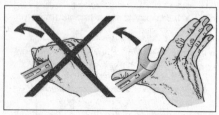

4.6 If you can't pull on the spanner to loosen a fastener, push with your hand open

● Additional leverage is gained by extending the length of the lever. The best way to do this is to use a breaker bar instead of the regular length tool, or to slip a length of tubing over the end of the spanner or socket wrench.

● If additional leverage will not work, the fastener head is either damaged or firmly corroded in place (see Fasteners).

5 Bearings

Bearing removal and installation

Drivers and sockets

● Before removing a bearing, always inspect the casing to see which way it must be driven out - some casings will have retaining plates or a cast step. Also check for any identifying markings on the bearing and if installed to a certain depth, measure this at this stage. Some roller bearings are sealed on one side - take note of the original fitted position.

● Bearings can be driven out of a casing using a bearing driver tool (with the correct size head) or a socket of the correct diameter. Select the driver head or socket so that it contacts the outer race of the bearing, not the balls/rollers or inner race. Always support the casing around the bearing housing with wood blocks, otherwise there is a risk of fracture. The bearing is driven out with a few blows on the driver or socket from a heavy mallet. Unless access is severely restricted (as with wheel bearings), a pin-punch is not recommended unless it is moved around the bearing to keep it square in its housing.

● The same equipment can be used to install bearings. Make sure the bearing housing is supported on wood blocks and line up the bearing in its housing. Fit the bearing as noted on removal - generally they are installed with their marked side facing outwards. Tap the bearing squarely into its housing using a driver or socket which bears only on the bearing's outer race - contact with the bearing balls/rollers or inner race will destroy it **(see illustrations 5.1 and 5.2)**.

● Check that the bearing inner race and balls/rollers rotate freely.

5.1 Using a bearing driver against the bearing's outer race

5.2 Using a large socket against the bearing's outer race

Pullers and slide-hammers

● Where a bearing is pressed on a shaft a puller will be required to extract it **(see illustration 5.3)**. Make sure that the puller clamp or legs fit securely behind the bearing and are unlikely to slip out. If pulling a bearing

5.3 This bearing puller clamps behind the bearing and pressure is applied to the shaft end to draw the bearing off

off a gear shaft for example, you may have to locate the puller behind a gear pinion if there is no access to the race and draw the gear pinion off the shaft as well **(see illustration 5.4)**.

Caution: Ensure that the puller's centre bolt locates securely against the end of the shaft and will not slip when pressure is applied. Also ensure that puller does not damage the shaft end.

5.4 Where no access is available to the rear of the bearing, it is sometimes possible to draw off the adjacent component

● Operate the puller so that its centre bolt exerts pressure on the shaft end and draws the bearing off the shaft.

● When installing the bearing on the shaft, tap only on the bearing's inner race - contact with the balls/rollers or outer race with destroy the bearing. Use a socket or length of tubing as a drift which fits over the shaft end **(see illustration 5.5)**.

5.5 When installing a bearing on a shaft use a piece of tubing which bears only on the bearing's inner race

● Where a bearing locates in a blind hole in a casing, it cannot be driven or pulled out as described above. A slide-hammer with knife-edged bearing puller attachment will be required. The puller attachment passes through the bearing and when tightened expands to fit firmly behind the bearing **(see illustration 5.6)**. By operating the slide-hammer part of the tool the bearing is jarred out of its housing **(see illustration 5.7)**.

● It is possible, if the bearing is of reasonable weight, for it to drop out of its housing if the casing is heated as described opposite.

Tools and Workshop Tips REF•29

5.6 Expand the bearing puller so that it locks behind the bearing . . .

5.7 . . . attach the slide hammer to the bearing puller

If this method is attempted, first prepare a work surface which will enable the casing to be tapped face down to help dislodge the bearing - a wood surface is ideal since it will not damage the casing's gasket surface. Wearing protective gloves, tap the heated casing several times against the work surface to dislodge the bearing under its own weight (see illustration 5.8).

5.8 Tapping a casing face down on wood blocks can often dislodge a bearing

● Bearings can be installed in blind holes using the driver or socket method described above.

Drawbolts

● Where a bearing or bush is set in the eye of a component, such as a suspension linkage arm or connecting rod small-end, removal by drift may damage the component. Furthermore, a rubber bushing in a shock absorber eye cannot successfully be driven out of position. If access is available to a engineering press, the task is straightforward. If not, a drawbolt can be fabricated to extract the bearing or bush.

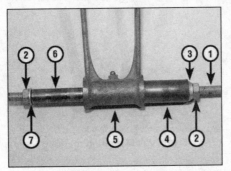

5.9 Drawbolt component parts assembled on a suspension arm

1. Bolt or length of threaded bar
2. Nuts
3. Washer (external diameter greater than tubing internal diameter)
4. Tubing (internal diameter sufficient to accommodate bearing)
5. Suspension arm with bearing
6. Tubing (external diameter slightly smaller than bearing)
7. Washer (external diameter slightly smaller than bearing)

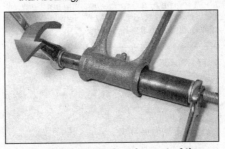

5.10 Drawing the bearing out of the suspension arm

● To extract the bearing/bush you will need a long bolt with nut (or piece of threaded bar with two nuts), a piece of tubing which has an internal diameter larger than the bearing/bush, another piece of tubing which has an external diameter slightly smaller than the bearing/bush, and a selection of washers (see illustrations 5.9 and 5.10). Note that the pieces of tubing must be of the same length, or longer, than the bearing/bush.

● The same kit (without the pieces of tubing) can be used to draw the new bearing/bush back into place (see illustration 5.11).

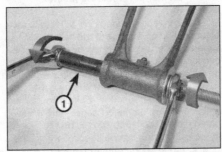

5.11 Installing a new bearing (1) in the suspension arm

Temperature change

● If the bearing's outer race is a tight fit in the casing, the aluminium casing can be heated to release its grip on the bearing. Aluminium will expand at a greater rate than the steel bearing outer race. There are several ways to do this, but avoid any localised extreme heat (such as a blow torch) - aluminium alloy has a low melting point.

● Approved methods of heating a casing are using a domestic oven (heated to 100°C) or immersing the casing in boiling water (see illustration 5.12). Low temperature range localised heat sources such as a paint stripper heat gun or clothes iron can also be used (see illustration 5.13). Alternatively, soak a rag in boiling water, wring it out and wrap it around the bearing housing.

> ⚠ **Warning:** *All of these methods require care in use to prevent scalding and burns to the hands. Wear protective gloves when handling hot components.*

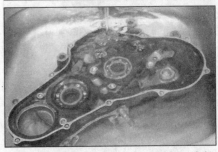

5.12 A casing can be immersed in a sink of boiling water to aid bearing removal

5.13 Using a localised heat source to aid bearing removal

● If heating the whole casing note that plastic components, such as the neutral switch, may suffer - remove them beforehand.

● After heating, remove the bearing as described above. You may find that the expansion is sufficient for the bearing to fall out of the casing under its own weight or with a light tap on the driver or socket.

● If necessary, the casing can be heated to aid bearing installation, and this is sometimes the recommended procedure if the motorcycle manufacturer has designed the housing and bearing fit with this intention.

REF•30 Tools and Workshop Tips

- Installation of bearings can be eased by placing them in a freezer the night before installation. The steel bearing will contract slightly, allowing easy insertion in its housing. This is often useful when installing steering head outer races in the frame.

Bearing types and markings

- Plain shell bearings, ball bearings, needle roller bearings and tapered roller bearings will all be found on motorcycles (see illustrations 5.14 and 5.15). The ball and roller types are usually caged between an inner and outer race, but uncaged variations may be found.

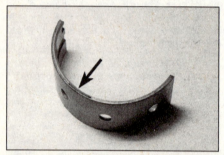

5.14 Shell bearings are either plain or grooved. They are usually identified by colour code (arrow)

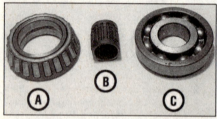

5.15 Tapered roller bearing (A), needle roller bearing (B) and ball journal bearing (C)

- Shell bearings (often called inserts) are usually found at the crankshaft main and connecting rod big-end where they are good at coping with high loads. They are made of a phosphor-bronze material and are impregnated with self-lubricating properties.
- Ball bearings and needle roller bearings consist of a steel inner and outer race with the balls or rollers between the races. They require constant lubrication by oil or grease and are good at coping with axial loads. Taper roller bearings consist of rollers set in a tapered cage set on the inner race; the outer race is separate. They are good at coping with axial loads and prevent movement along the shaft - a typical application is in the steering head.
- Bearing manufacturers produce bearings to ISO size standards and stamp one face of the bearing to indicate its internal and external diameter, load capacity and type (see illustration 5.16).
- Metal bushes are usually of phosphor-bronze material. Rubber bushes are used in suspension mounting eyes. Fibre bushes have also been used in suspension pivots.

5.16 Typical bearing marking

Bearing fault finding

- If a bearing outer race has spun in its housing, the housing material will be damaged. You can use a bearing locking compound to bond the outer race in place if damage is not too severe.
- Shell bearings will fail due to damage of their working surface, as a result of lack of lubrication, corrosion or abrasive particles in the oil (see illustration 5.17). Small particles of dirt in the oil may embed in the bearing material whereas larger particles will score the bearing and shaft journal. If a number of short journeys are made, insufficient heat will be generated to drive off condensation which has built up on the bearings.

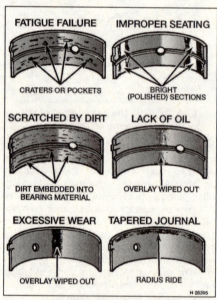

5.17 Typical bearing failures

- Ball and roller bearings will fail due to lack of lubrication or damage to the balls or rollers. Tapered-roller bearings can be damaged by overloading them. Unless the bearing is sealed on both sides, wash it in paraffin (kerosene) to remove all old grease then allow it to dry. Make a visual inspection looking to dented balls or rollers, damaged cages and worn or pitted races (see illustration 5.18).
- A ball bearing can be checked for wear by listening to it when spun. Apply a film of light oil to the bearing and hold it close to the ear - hold the outer race with one hand and spin the inner race with the other hand (see illustration 5.19). The bearing should be almost silent when spun; if it grates or rattles it is worn.

5.18 Example of ball journal bearing with damaged balls and cages

5.19 Hold outer race and listen to inner race when spun

6 Oil seals

Oil seal removal and installation

- Oil seals should be renewed every time a component is dismantled. This is because the seal lips will become set to the sealing surface and will not necessarily reseal.
- Oil seals can be prised out of position using a large flat-bladed screwdriver (see illustration 6.1). In the case of crankcase seals, check first that the seal is not lipped on the inside, preventing its removal with the crankcases joined.

6.1 Prise out oil seals with a large flat-bladed screwdriver

- New seals are usually installed with their marked face (containing the seal reference code) outwards and the spring side towards the fluid being retained. In certain cases, such as a two-stroke engine crankshaft seal, a double lipped seal may be used due to there being fluid or gas on each side of the joint.

Tools and Workshop Tips

- Use a bearing driver or socket which bears only on the outer hard edge of the seal to install it in the casing - tapping on the inner edge will damage the sealing lip.

Oil seal types and markings

- Oil seals are usually of the single-lipped type. Double-lipped seals are found where a liquid or gas is on both sides of the joint.
- Oil seals can harden and lose their sealing ability if the motorcycle has been in storage for a long period - renewal is the only solution.
- Oil seal manufacturers also conform to the ISO markings for seal size - these are moulded into the outer face of the seal (see illustration 6.2).

6.2 These oil seal markings indicate inside diameter, outside diameter and seal thickness

7 Gaskets and sealants

Types of gasket and sealant

- Gaskets are used to seal the mating surfaces between components and keep lubricants, fluids, vacuum or pressure contained within the assembly. Aluminium gaskets are sometimes found at the cylinder joints, but most gaskets are paper-based. If the mating surfaces of the components being joined are undamaged the gasket can be installed dry, although a dab of sealant or grease will be useful to hold it in place during assembly.
- RTV (Room Temperature Vulcanising) silicone rubber sealants cure when exposed to moisture in the atmosphere. These sealants are good at filling pits or irregular gasket faces, but will tend to be forced out of the joint under very high torque. They can be used to replace a paper gasket, but first make sure that the width of the paper gasket is not essential to the shimming of internal components. RTV sealants should not be used on components containing petrol (gasoline).
- Non-hardening, semi-hardening and hard setting liquid gasket compounds can be used with a gasket or between a metal-to-metal joint. Select the sealant to suit the application: universal non-hardening sealant can be used on virtually all joints; semi-hardening on joint faces which are rough or damaged; hard setting sealant on joints which require a permanent bond and are subjected to high temperature and pressure. **Note:** *Check first if the paper gasket has a bead of sealant impregnated in its surface before applying additional sealant.*
- When choosing a sealant, make sure it is suitable for the application, particularly if being applied in a high-temperature area or in the vicinity of fuel. Certain manufacturers produce sealants in either clear, silver or black colours to match the finish of the engine. This has a particular application on motorcycles where much of the engine is exposed.
- Do not over-apply sealant. That which is squeezed out on the outside of the joint can be wiped off, whereas an excess of sealant on the inside can break off and clog oilways.

Breaking a sealed joint

- Age, heat, pressure and the use of hard setting sealant can cause two components to stick together so tightly that they are difficult to separate using finger pressure alone. Do not resort to using levers unless there is a pry point provided for this purpose (see illustration 7.1) or else the gasket surfaces will be damaged.
- Use a soft-faced hammer (see illustration 7.2) or a wood block and conventional hammer to strike the component near the mating surface. Avoid hammering against cast extremities since they may break off. If this method fails, try using a wood wedge between the two components.

Caution: *If the joint will not separate, double-check that you have removed all the fasteners.*

7.1 If a pry point is provided, apply gently pressure with a flat-bladed screwdriver

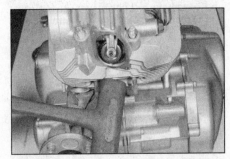

7.2 Tap around the joint with a soft-faced mallet if necessary - don't strike cooling fins

Removal of old gasket and sealant

- Paper gaskets will most likely come away complete, leaving only a few traces stuck

HAYNES HiNT

Most components have one or two hollow locating dowels between the two gasket faces. If a dowel cannot be removed, do not resort to gripping it with pliers - it will almost certainly be distorted. Install a close-fitting socket or Phillips screwdriver into the dowel and then grip the outer edge of the dowel to free it.

on the sealing faces of the components. It is imperative that all traces are removed to ensure correct sealing of the new gasket.
- Very carefully scrape all traces of gasket away making sure that the sealing surfaces are not gouged or scored by the scraper (see illustrations 7.3, 7.4 and 7.5). Stubborn deposits can be removed by spraying with an aerosol gasket remover. Final preparation of

7.3 Paper gaskets can be scraped off with a gasket scraper tool . . .

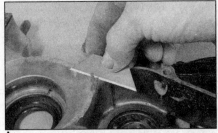

7.4 . . . a knife blade . . .

7.5 . . . or a household scraper

REF•32 Tools and Workshop Tips

7.6 Fine abrasive paper is wrapped around a flat file to clean up the gasket face

7.7 A kitchen scourer can be used on stubborn deposits

the gasket surface can be made with very fine abrasive paper or a plastic kitchen scourer **(see illustrations 7.6 and 7.7)**.

● Old sealant can be scraped or peeled off components, depending on the type originally used. Note that gasket removal compounds are available to avoid scraping the components clean; make sure the gasket remover suits the type of sealant used.

8 Chains

Breaking and joining final drive chains

● Drive chains for all but small bikes are continuous and do not have a clip-type connecting link. The chain must be broken using a chain breaker tool and the new chain securely riveted together using a new soft rivet-type link. Never use a clip-type connecting link instead of a rivet-type link, except in an emergency. Various chain breaking and riveting tools are available, either as separate tools or combined as illustrated in the accompanying photographs - read the instructions supplied with the tool carefully.

> **Warning:** The need to rivet the new link pins correctly cannot be overstressed - loss of control of the motorcycle is very likely to result if the chain breaks in use.

● Rotate the chain and look for the soft link. The soft link pins look like they have been

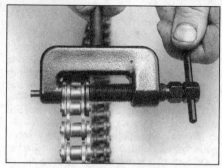

8.1 Tighten the chain breaker to push the pin out of the link . . .

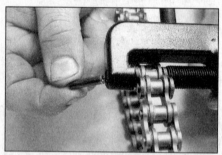

8.2 . . . withdraw the pin, remove the tool . . .

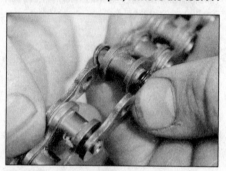

8.3 . . . and separate the chain link

deeply centre-punched instead of peened over like all the other pins **(see illustration 8.9)** and its sideplate may be a different colour. Position the soft link midway between the sprockets and assemble the chain breaker tool over one of the soft link pins **(see illustration 8.1)**. Operate the tool to push the pin out through the chain **(see illustration 8.2)**. On an O-ring chain, remove the O-rings **(see illustration 8.3)**. Carry out the same procedure on the other soft link pin.

> **Caution:** Certain soft link pins (particularly on the larger chains) may require their ends to be filed or ground off before they can be pressed out using the tool.

● Check that you have the correct size and strength (standard or heavy duty) new soft link - do not reuse the old link. Look for the size marking on the chain sideplates **(see illustration 8.10)**.

● Position the chain ends so that they are engaged over the rear sprocket. On an O-ring

8.4 Insert the new soft link, with O-rings, through the chain ends . . .

8.5 . . . install the O-rings over the pin ends . . .

8.6 . . . followed by the sideplate

chain, install a new O-ring over each pin of the link and insert the link through the two chain ends **(see illustration 8.4)**. Install a new O-ring over the end of each pin, followed by the sideplate (with the chain manufacturer's marking facing outwards) **(see illustrations 8.5 and 8.6)**. On an unsealed chain, insert the link through the two chain ends, then install the sideplate with the chain manufacturer's marking facing outwards.

● Note that it may not be possible to install the sideplate using finger pressure alone. If using a joining tool, assemble it so that the plates of the tool clamp the link and press the sideplate over the pins **(see illustration 8.7)**. Otherwise, use two small sockets placed over

8.7 Push the sideplate into position using a clamp

Tools and Workshop Tips

8.8 Assemble the chain riveting tool over one pin at a time and tighten it fully

8.9 Pin end correctly riveted (A), pin end unriveted (B)

the rivet ends and two pieces of the wood between a G-clamp. Operate the clamp to press the sideplate over the pins.
● Assemble the joining tool over one pin (following the maker's instructions) and tighten the tool down to spread the pin end securely **(see illustrations 8.8 and 8.9)**. Do the same on the other pin.

 Warning: Check that the pin ends are secure and that there is no danger of the sideplate coming loose. If the pin ends are cracked the soft link must be renewed.

Final drive chain sizing

● Chains are sized using a three digit number, followed by a suffix to denote the chain type **(see illustration 8.10)**. Chain type is either standard or heavy duty (thicker sideplates), and also unsealed or O-ring/X-ring type.
● The first digit of the number relates to the pitch of the chain, ie the distance from the centre of one pin to the centre of the next pin **(see illustration 8.11)**. Pitch is expressed in eighths of an inch, as follows:

8.10 Typical chain size and type marking

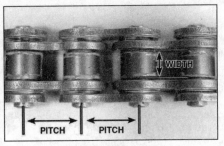

8.11 Chain dimensions

Sizes commencing with a 4 (eg 428) have a pitch of 1/2 inch (12.7 mm)

Sizes commencing with a 5 (eg 520) have a pitch of 5/8 inch (15.9 mm)

Sizes commencing with a 6 (eg 630) have a pitch of 3/4 inch (19.1 mm)

● The second and third digits of the chain size relate to the width of the rollers, again in imperial units, eg the 525 shown has 5/16 inch (7.94 mm) rollers **(see illustration 8.11)**.

9 Hoses

Clamping to prevent flow

● Small-bore flexible hoses can be clamped to prevent fluid flow whilst a component is worked on. Whichever method is used, ensure that the hose material is not permanently distorted or damaged by the clamp.
a) A brake hose clamp available from auto accessory shops **(see illustration 9.1)**.
b) A wingnut type hose clamp **(see illustration 9.2)**.

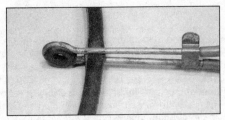

9.1 Hoses can be clamped with an automotive brake hose clamp . . .

9.2 . . . a wingnut type hose clamp . . .

c) Two sockets placed each side of the hose and held with straight-jawed self-locking grips **(see illustration 9.3)**.
d) Thick card each side of the hose held between straight-jawed self-locking grips **(see illustration 9.4)**.

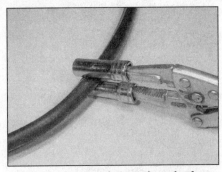

9.3 . . . two sockets and a pair of self-locking grips . . .

9.4 . . . or thick card and self-locking grips

Freeing and fitting hoses

● Always make sure the hose clamp is moved well clear of the hose end. Grip the hose with your hand and rotate it whilst pulling it off the union. If the hose has hardened due to age and will not move, slit it with a sharp knife and peel its ends off the union **(see illustration 9.5)**.
● Resist the temptation to use grease or soap on the unions to aid installation; although it helps the hose slip over the union it will equally aid the escape of fluid from the joint. It is preferable to soften the hose ends in hot water and wet the inside surface of the hose with water or a fluid which will evaporate.

9.5 Cutting a coolant hose free with a sharp knife

Conversion factors

Length (distance)
Inches (in)	x 25.4	= Millimetres (mm)	x 0.0394	=	Inches (in)
Feet (ft)	x 0.305	= Metres (m)	x 3.281	=	Feet (ft)
Miles	x 1.609	= Kilometres (km)	x 0.621	=	Miles

Volume (capacity)
Cubic inches (cu in; in^3)	x 16.387	= Cubic centimetres (cc; cm^3)	x 0.061		Cubic inches (cu in; in^3)
Imperial pints (Imp pt)	x 0.568	= Litres (l)	x 1.76	=	Imperial pints (Imp pt)
Imperial quarts (Imp qt)	x 1.137	= Litres (l)	x 0.88	=	Imperial quarts (Imp qt)
Imperial quarts (Imp qt)	x 1.201	= US quarts (US qt)	x 0.833	=	Imperial quarts (Imp qt)
US quarts (US qt)	x 0.946	= Litres (l)	x 1.057	=	US quarts (US qt)
Imperial gallons (Imp gal)	x 4.546	= Litres (l)	x 0.22	=	Imperial gallons (Imp gal)
Imperial gallons (Imp gal)	x 1.201	= US gallons (US gal)	x 0.833	=	Imperial gallons (Imp gal)
US gallons (US gal)	x 3.785	= Litres (l)	x 0.264	=	US gallons (US gal)

Mass (weight)
Ounces (oz)	x 28.35	= Grams (g)	x 0.035	=	Ounces (oz)
Pounds (lb)	x 0.454	= Kilograms (kg)	x 2.205	=	Pounds (lb)

Force
Ounces-force (ozf; oz)	x 0.278	= Newtons (N)	x 3.6	=	Ounces-force (ozf; oz)
Pounds-force (lbf; lb)	x 4.448	= Newtons (N)	x 0.225	=	Pounds-force (lbf; lb)
Newtons (N)	x 0.1	= Kilograms-force (kgf; kg)	x 9.81	=	Newtons (N)

Pressure
Pounds-force per square inch (psi; lbf/in^2; lb/in^2)	x 0.070	= Kilograms-force per square centimetre (kgf/cm^2; kg/cm^2)	x 14.223	=	Pounds-force per square inch (psi; lbf/in^2; lb/in^2)
Pounds-force per square inch (psi; lbf/in^2; lb/in^2)	x 0.068	= Atmospheres (atm)	x 14.696	=	Pounds-force per square inch (psi; lbf/in^2; lb/in^2)
Pounds-force per square inch (psi; lbf/in^2; lb/in^2)	x 0.069	= Bars	x 14.5	=	Pounds-force per square inch (psi; lbf/in^2; lb/in^2)
Pounds-force per square inch (psi; lbf/in^2; lb/in^2)	x 6.895	= Kilopascals (kPa)	x 0.145	=	Pounds-force per square inch (psi; lbf/in^2; lb/in^2)
Kilopascals (kPa)	x 0.01	= Kilograms-force per square centimetre (kgf/cm^2; kg/cm^2)	x 98.1	=	Kilopascals (kPa)
Millibar (mbar)	x 100	= Pascals (Pa)	x 0.01	=	Millibar (mbar)
Millibar (mbar)	x 0.0145	= Pounds-force per square inch (psi; lbf/in^2; lb/in^2)	x 68.947	=	Millibar (mbar)
Millibar (mbar)	x 0.75	= Millimetres of mercury (mmHg)	x 1.333	=	Millibar (mbar)
Millibar (mbar)	x 0.401	= Inches of water (inH$_2$O)	x 2.491	=	Millibar (mbar)
Millimetres of mercury (mmHg)	x 0.535	= Inches of water (inH$_2$O)	x 1.868	=	Millimetres of mercury (mmHg)
Inches of water (inH$_2$O)	x 0.036	= Pounds-force per square inch (psi; lbf/in^2; lb/in^2)	x 27.68	=	Inches of water (inH$_2$O)

Torque (moment of force)
Pounds-force inches (lbf in; lb in)	x 1.152	= Kilograms-force centimetre (kgf cm; kg cm)	x 0.868	=	Pounds-force inches (lbf in; lb in)
Pounds-force inches (lbf in; lb in)	x 0.113	= Newton metres (Nm)	x 8.85	=	Pounds-force inches (lbf in; lb in)
Pounds-force inches (lbf in; lb in)	x 0.083	= Pounds-force feet (lbf ft; lb ft)	x 12	=	Pounds-force inches (lbf in; lb in)
Pounds-force feet (lbf ft; lb ft)	x 0.138	= Kilograms-force metres (kgf m; kg m)	x 7.233	=	Pounds-force feet (lbf ft; lb ft)
Pounds-force feet (lbf ft; lb ft)	x 1.356	= Newton metres (Nm)	x 0.738	=	Pounds-force feet (lbf ft; lb ft)
Newton metres (Nm)	x 0.102	= Kilograms-force metres (kgf m; kg m)	x 9.804	=	Newton metres (Nm)

Power
Horsepower (hp)	x 745.7	= Watts (W)	x 0.0013	=	Horsepower (hp)

Velocity (speed)
Miles per hour (miles/hr; mph)	x 1.609	= Kilometres per hour (km/hr; kph)	x 0.621	=	Miles per hour (miles/hr; mph)

Fuel consumption*
Miles per gallon, Imperial (mpg)	x 0.354	= Kilometres per litre (km/l)	x 2.825	=	Miles per gallon, Imperial (mpg)
Miles per gallon, US (mpg)	x 0.425	= Kilometres per litre (km/l)	x 2.352	=	Miles per gallon, US (mpg)

Temperature
Degrees Fahrenheit = (°C x 1.8) + 32   Degrees Celsius (Degrees Centigrade; °C) = (°F - 32) x 0.56

It is common practice to convert from miles per gallon (mpg) to litres/100 kilometres (l/100km), where mpg x l/100 km = 282

Fault Finding REF•35

This Section provides an easy reference-guide to the more common faults that are likely to afflict your machine. Obviously, the opportunities are almost limitless for faults to occur as a result of obscure failures, and to try and cover all eventualities would require a book. Indeed, a number have been written on the subject.

Successful troubleshooting is not a mysterious 'black art' but the application of a bit of knowledge combined with a systematic and logical approach to the problem. Approach any troubleshooting by first accurately identifying the symptom and then checking through the list of possible causes, starting with the simplest or most obvious and progressing in stages to the most complex.

Take nothing for granted, but above all apply liberal quantities of common sense.

The main symptom of a fault is given in the text as a major heading below which are listed the various systems or areas which may contain the fault. Details of each possible cause for a fault and the remedial action to be taken are given, in brief, in the paragraphs below each heading. Further information should be sought in the relevant Chapter.

1 Engine doesn't start or is difficult to start
- [ ] Starter motor doesn't rotate
- [ ] Starter motor rotates but engine does not turn over
- [ ] Starter works but engine won't turn over (seized)
- [ ] No fuel flow
- [ ] Engine flooded
- [ ] No spark or weak spark
- [ ] Compression low
- [ ] Stalls after starting
- [ ] Rough idle

2 Poor running at low speed
- [ ] Spark weak
- [ ] Fuel/air mixture incorrect
- [ ] Compression low
- [ ] Poor acceleration

3 Poor running or no power at high speed
- [ ] Firing incorrect
- [ ] Fuel/air mixture incorrect
- [ ] Compression low
- [ ] Knocking or pinking
- [ ] Miscellaneous causes

4 Overheating
- [ ] Engine overheats
- [ ] Firing incorrect
- [ ] Fuel/air mixture incorrect
- [ ] Compression too high
- [ ] Engine load excessive
- [ ] Lubrication inadequate
- [ ] Miscellaneous causes

5 Clutch problems
- [ ] Clutch slipping
- [ ] Clutch not disengaging completely

6 Gearchange problems
- [ ] Doesn't go into gear, or lever doesn't return
- [ ] Jumps out of gear
- [ ] Overselects

7 Abnormal engine noise
- [ ] Knocking or pinking
- [ ] Piston slap or rattling
- [ ] Valve noise
- [ ] Other noise

8 Abnormal driveline noise
- [ ] Clutch noise
- [ ] Transmission noise
- [ ] Final drive noise

9 Abnormal frame and suspension noise
- [ ] Front end noise
- [ ] Shock absorber noise
- [ ] Brake noise

10 Oil pressure low
- [ ] Engine lubrication system

11 Excessive exhaust smoke
- [ ] White smoke
- [ ] Black smoke
- [ ] Brown smoke

12 Poor handling or stability
- [ ] Handlebar hard to turn
- [ ] Handlebar shakes or vibrates excessively
- [ ] Handlebar pulls to one side
- [ ] Poor shock absorbing qualities

13 Braking problems
- [ ] Brakes are spongy, don't hold
- [ ] Brake lever or pedal pulsates
- [ ] Brakes drag

14 Electrical problems
- [ ] Battery dead or weak
- [ ] Battery overcharged

Fault Finding

1 Engine doesn't start or is difficult to start

Starter motor doesn't rotate
- [ ] Engine kill switch OFF.
- [ ] Fuse blown. Check main fuse, starter fuse and FI fuse (Chapter 8).
- [ ] Battery voltage low. Check battery condition and recharge or replace battery (Chapter 8).
- [ ] Loose or corroded battery connections/terminals. Tighten or clean connections.
- [ ] Starter motor defective. Make sure the wiring to the starter is secure and free of corrosion. Replace or repair the motor if defective (Chapter 8).
- [ ] Starter relay defective. Make sure the wiring to relay is secure and free of corrosion. Test the operation of the relay, internal corrosion or arcing can cause the relay to not pass sufficient current to the starter motor even if it clicks when the start button is operated (Chapter 8).
- [ ] Starter switch not contacting. The contacts could be wet, corroded or dirty. Disassemble and clean the switch (Chapter 8).
- [ ] Wiring open or shorted. Check all wiring connections and harnesses to make sure that they are dry, tight and not corroded. Also check for broken or frayed wires that can cause a short to ground (earth) (see *Wiring diagrams*, Chapter 8).
- [ ] Ignition or kill switch defective. This is usually caused by water, corrosion, damage or excessive wear. The switches can be disassembled and cleaned with electrical contact cleaner. If cleaning does not help, replace the switches (Chapter 8).
- [ ] Faulty neutral/gear position switch, sidestand switch, clutch switch or diode. Check the wiring to each switch and the switch itself (Chapter 8).
- [ ] Faulty lap timer relay (Chapter 8).
- [ ] Fuel injection system shutdown due to system fault (Chapter 4).

Starter motor rotates but engine does not turn over
- [ ] Starter clutch defective. Inspect and repair or replace with a new one (Chapter 2).
- [ ] Damaged idler or starter gears. Inspect and replace the damaged parts (Chapter 2).

Starter works but engine won't turn over (seized)
- [ ] Seized engine caused by one or more internally damaged components. Failure due to wear, abuse or lack of lubrication. Damage can include seized valves, followers, camshafts, pistons, crankshaft, connecting rod bearings, or transmission gears or bearings. Refer to Chapter 2 for engine disassembly.

No fuel flow
- [ ] No fuel in tank.
- [ ] Fuel tank breather hose obstructed.
- [ ] Faulty fuel pump relay. Check the relay (Chapter 4).
- [ ] Fuel pump faulty or blocked fuel filter. Replace faulty pump – the filter is not available separately (Chapter 4).
- [ ] Engine control model (ECM) defective (Chapter 4).
- [ ] Ignition key not recognised by immobiliser system.
- [ ] Fuel hose kinked. Replace the fuel hose.
- [ ] Fuel injector clogged. For all the injectors to be clogged, either a very bad batch of fuel with an unusual additive has been used, or some other foreign material has entered the tank. In some cases, if a machine has been unused for several months, the fuel turns to a varnish-like liquid which can cause an injector needle to stick to its seat. Drain the tank and fuel system, ultrasonically clean or replace fuel injectors (Chapter 4).

Engine flooded
- [ ] Injector needle valve worn or stuck open causing excess fuel to be admitted to the throttle body. In this case, the injectors should be renewed.
- [ ] Starting technique incorrect. Under normal circumstances (i.e. if all the components of the fuel injection system are good) the machine should start with the throttle closed.

No spark or weak spark
- [ ] Perform a spark test as described in Chapter 4.
- [ ] Ignition switch OFF.
- [ ] Engine kill switch turned to the OFF position.
- [ ] Ignition or kill switch shorted. This is usually caused by water, corrosion, damage or excessive wear. The switches can be disassembled and cleaned with electrical contact cleaner. If cleaning does not help, replace the switches (Chapter 8).
- [ ] Battery voltage low. Check battery condition and recharge or replace battery (Chapter 8).
- [ ] Spark plugs dirty, defective or worn out. Locate reason for fouled plugs using spark plug condition chart on the inside back cover and follow the plug maintenance procedures (Chapter 1).
- [ ] Incorrect spark plugs. Wrong type or heat range. Check and install correct plugs (Chapter 1).
- [ ] Ignition coil defective or not making good contact with spark plug. Test and replace if necessary (Chapter 4).
- [ ] Fuel injection system shutdown due to system fault (Chapter 4).
- [ ] Crankshaft position (CKP) sensor or camshaft position (CMP) sensor defective (Chapter 4).
- [ ] Faulty engine stop relay (Chapter 4).
- [ ] Faulty lean angle sensor (Chapter 4).
- [ ] Engine control module (ECM) defective (Chapter 4).
- [ ] Faulty sidestand switch (Chapter 8).
- [ ] Ignition key not recognised by immobiliser system.
- [ ] Wiring shorted or broken between:
    a) Ignition switch and engine kill switch (or blown fuse)
    b) Engine kill switch and engine stop relay
    c) engine stop relay and ECM
    d) ECM and ignition coils
    e) ECM and CKP sensor
    f) ECM and CMP sensor
- [ ] Make sure that all wiring connections are clean, dry and tight. Look for chafed and broken wires (Chapters 4 and 8).

Fault Finding

1 Engine doesn't start or is difficult to start (continued)

Compression low

- [ ] Perform a compression test as described in Chapter 2.
- [ ] Spark plug loose. Remove the plugs and inspect their threads. Reinstall and tighten securely (Chapter 1).
- [ ] Improper valve clearance. This means that the valve is not closing completely and compression pressure is leaking past the valve. Check and adjust the valve clearances (Chapter 1).
- [ ] Cylinder and/or piston worn. Excessive wear will cause compression pressure to leak past the rings. This is usually accompanied by worn rings as well. A top-end overhaul is necessary (Chapter 2).
- [ ] Piston rings worn, weak, broken, or sticking. Broken or sticking piston rings usually indicate a lubrication or fuelling problem that causes excess carbon deposits to form on the pistons and rings. Top-end overhaul is necessary (Chapter 2).
- [ ] Piston ring-to-groove clearance excessive. This is caused by excessive wear of the piston ring lands. Piston renewal is necessary (Chapter 2).
- [ ] Cylinder head gasket damaged. If a head is allowed to become loose, or if excessive carbon build-up on the piston crown and combustion chamber causes extremely high compression, the head gasket may leak. Retorquing the head is not always sufficient to restore the seal, so a new gasket is necessary (Chapter 2).
- [ ] Cylinder head warped. This is caused by overheating or improperly tightened head nuts. Machine shop resurfacing or head renewal is necessary (Chapter 2).
- [ ] Valve spring broken or weak. Caused by component failure or wear; the springs must be renewed (Chapter 2).
- [ ] Valve not seating properly. This is caused by a bent valve (from over-revving or improper valve adjustment), burned valve or seat (improper fuelling) or an accumulation of carbon deposits on the seat.

Stalls after starting

- [ ] Engine idle speed incorrect. Faulty idle speed control system (Chapter 4).
- [ ] Ignition malfunction (Chapter 4).
- [ ] Fuel injection system malfunction (Chapter 4).
- [ ] Fuel contaminated. The fuel can be contaminated with either dirt or water, or can change chemically if the machine has been unused for several months. Drain the tank and fuel system (Chapter 4).
- [ ] Intake air leak. Check for loose throttle body-to-intake duct connections or a loose or damaged vacuum hose (Chapter 4).

Rough idle

- [ ] Idle speed incorrect (Chapter 4).
- [ ] Vacuum hose detached or split.
- [ ] Ignition fault (Chapter 4).
- [ ] Fuel injection system malfunction (Chapter 4).
- [ ] Fuel contaminated. The fuel can be contaminated with either dirt or water, or can change chemically if the machine has been unused for several months. Drain the tank and the fuel system (Chapter 4).
- [ ] Intake air leak. Check for loose throttle body-to-intake duct connections (Chapter 4).
- [ ] Air filter clogged. Clean the air filter element or replace it with a new one (Chapter 1).

2 Poor running at low speeds

Spark weak

- [ ] Perform a spark test as described in Chapter 4.
- [ ] Battery voltage low. Check battery condition and recharge or replace battery (Chapter 8).
- [ ] Ignition coils not making good contact with spark plugs. Make sure that the coils are pushed fully onto the spark plugs.
- [ ] Spark plugs dirty, defective or worn out. Locate reason for fouled plugs using spark plug condition chart on the inside back cover and follow the plug maintenance procedures (Chapter 1).
- [ ] Incorrect spark plugs. Wrong type or heat range. Check and install correct plugs (Chapter 1).
- [ ] Ignition coil defective. Test and renew if necessary (Chapter 4).
- [ ] Loose or corroded connections in coil wiring connector. Check security and clean connections.

Fuel/air mixture incorrect

- [ ] Fuel tank breather hose obstructed.
- [ ] Fuel pump faulty or blocked fuel filter. Replace faulty pump – the filter is not available separately (Chapter 4).
- [ ] Fuel hose kinked. Replace the fuel hose.
- [ ] Fuel injector clogged. For all the injectors to be clogged, either a very bad batch of fuel with an unusual additive has been used, or some other foreign material has entered the tank. In some cases, if a machine has been unused for several months, the fuel turns to a varnish-like liquid which can cause an injector needle to stick to its seat. Drain the tank and fuel system, ultrasonically clean or replace fuel injectors (Chapter 4).
- [ ] Intake air leak. Check for loose throttle body-to-intake duct connections and loose or damaged vacuum hoses (Chapter 4).
- [ ] Air filter clogged. Clean the air filter element or replace it with a new one (Chapter 1).

Compression low

- [ ] Perform a compression test as described in Chapter 2.
- [ ] Spark plug loose. Remove the plugs and inspect their threads. Reinstall and tighten securely (Chapter 1).
- [ ] Improper valve clearance. This means that the valve is not closing completely and compression pressure is leaking past the valve. Check and adjust the valve clearances (Chapter 1).
- [ ] Cylinder and/or piston worn. Excessive wear will cause compression pressure to leak past the rings. This is usually accompanied by worn rings as well. A top-end overhaul is necessary (Chapter 2).
- [ ] Piston rings worn, weak, broken, or sticking. Broken or sticking piston rings usually indicate a lubrication or fuelling problem that causes excess carbon deposits to form on the pistons and rings. Top-end overhaul is necessary (Chapter 2).
- [ ] Piston ring-to-groove clearance excessive. This is caused by excessive wear of the piston ring lands. Piston renewal is necessary (Chapter 2).
- [ ] Cylinder head gasket damaged. If the head is allowed to become loose, or if excessive carbon build-up on the piston crown and combustion chamber causes extremely high compression, the head gasket may leak. Retorquing the head is not always sufficient to restore the seal, so a new gasket is necessary (Chapter 2).
- [ ] Cylinder head warped. This is caused by overheating or improperly tightened head nuts. Machine shop resurfacing or head renewal is necessary (Chapter 2).
- [ ] Valve spring broken or weak. Caused by component failure or wear; the springs must be renewed (Chapter 2).
- [ ] Valve not seating properly. This is caused by a bent valve (from over-revving or improper valve adjustment), burned valve or seat (improper fuelling) or an accumulation of carbon deposits on the seat (from fuelling or lubrication problems). The valves must be cleaned and/or renewed and the seats serviced (Chapter 2).

Poor acceleration

- [ ] Timing not advancing. The engine control module (ECM), or CKP sensor, CMP sensor, knock sensor, or vehicle speed sensor may be defective (Chapter 4).
- [ ] Engine oil viscosity too high. Using a heavier oil than that recommended in Chapter 1 can damage the oil pump or lubrication system and cause drag on the engine.
- [ ] Brakes dragging. Usually caused by corrosion behind dust seals, ingress of dirt past a deteriorated seal or from a warped disc or bent axle (Chapter 6).
- [ ] Exhaust gas control valve (EGCV) seized or incorrectly adjusted, or faulty servo. Adjust cables. If they are good check the servo motor (see Chapter 4). Note that the valves are an integral part of the silencer.

Fault Finding   REF•39

3 Poor running or no power at high speed

Firing incorrect
- [ ] Spark plug socket in ignition coil not making good contact. Make sure that the coils are pushed fully onto the spark plugs.
- [ ] Spark plugs dirty, defective or worn out. Locate reason for fouled plugs using spark plug condition chart on the inside back cover and follow the plug maintenance procedures (Chapter 1).
- [ ] Wrongly connected ignition coil wiring.
- [ ] Incorrect spark plugs. Wrong type or heat range. Check and install correct plugs (Chapter 1).
- [ ] Ignition coil defective. Test and renew if necessary (Chapter 4).
- [ ] Faulty engine control module (ECM) (Chapter 4).

Fuel/air mixture incorrect
- [ ] Fuel tank breather hose obstructed.
- [ ] Fuel pump faulty or blocked fuel filter. Replace faulty pump – the filter is not available separately (Chapter 4).
- [ ] Fuel hose kinked. Replace the fuel hose.
- [ ] Fuel pressure low. Perform a fuel pressure test (Chapter 4).
- [ ] Fuel injector clogged. For all the injectors to be clogged, either a very bad batch of fuel with an unusual additive has been used, or some other foreign material has entered the tank. In some cases, if a machine has been unused for several months, the fuel turns to a varnish-like liquid which can cause an injector needle to stick to its seat. Drain the tank and fuel system, ultrasonically clean or replace fuel injectors (Chapter 4).
- [ ] Intake air leak. Check for loose throttle body-to-intake duct connections and loose or damaged vacuum hoses (Chapter 4).
- [ ] Air filter clogged. Clean the air filter element or replace it with a new one (Chapter 1).

Compression low
- [ ] Perform a compression test as described in Chapter 2.
- [ ] Spark plug loose. Remove the plugs and inspect their threads. Reinstall and tighten securely (Chapter 1).
- [ ] Improper valve clearance. This means that the valve is not closing completely and compression pressure is leaking past the valve. Check and adjust the valve clearances (Chapter 1).
- [ ] Cylinder and/or piston worn. Excessive wear will cause compression pressure to leak past the rings. This is usually accompanied by worn rings as well. A top-end overhaul is necessary (Chapter 2).
- [ ] Piston rings worn, weak, broken, or sticking. Broken or sticking piston rings usually indicate a lubrication or fuelling problem that causes excess carbon deposits to form on the pistons and rings. Top-end overhaul is necessary (Chapter 2).
- [ ] Piston ring-to-groove clearance excessive. This is caused by excessive wear of the piston ring lands. Piston renewal is necessary (Chapter 2).
- [ ] Cylinder head gasket damaged. If a head is allowed to become loose, or if excessive carbon build-up on the piston crown and combustion chamber causes extremely high compression, the head gasket may leak. Retorquing the head is not always sufficient to restore the seal, so a new gasket is necessary (Chapter 2).
- [ ] Cylinder head warped. This is caused by overheating or improperly tightened head nuts. Machine shop resurfacing or head renewal is necessary (Chapter 2).
- [ ] Valve spring broken or weak. Caused by component failure or wear; the springs must be replaced with new ones (Chapter 2).
- [ ] Valve not seating properly. This is caused by a bent valve (from over-revving or improper valve adjustment), burned valve or seat (improper fuelling) or an accumulation of carbon deposits on the seat (from fuelling or lubrication problems).

Knocking or pinking
- [ ] Carbon build-up in combustion chamber. Use of a fuel additive that will dissolve the adhesive bonding the carbon particles to the piston crown and chamber is the easiest way to remove the build-up. Otherwise, the cylinder head will have to be removed and decarbonised (Chapter 2).
- [ ] Incorrect or poor quality fuel. Old or improper grades of fuel can cause detonation. This causes the piston to rattle, thus the knocking or pinking sound. Drain old fuel and always use the recommended fuel grade.
- [ ] Spark plug heat range incorrect. Uncontrolled detonation indicates the plug heat range is too hot. The plug in effect becomes a glow plug, raising cylinder temperatures. Install the proper heat range plug (Chapter 1).
- [ ] Improper air/fuel mixture. This will cause the cylinders to run hot, which leads to detonation. A blockage in the fuel system or an air leak can cause this imbalance (Chapter 4).
- [ ] Faulty knock sensor. Check the sensor (Chapter 4).

Miscellaneous causes
- [ ] Throttle valve doesn't open fully. Adjust the throttle twistgrip freeplay (Chapter 1).
- [ ] Clutch slipping due loose or worn clutch components (Chapter 2).
- [ ] Timing not advancing. The engine control module (ECM), or CKP sensor, CMP sensor, knock sensor, or vehicle speed sensor may be defective (Chapter 4).
- [ ] Engine oil viscosity too high. Using a heavier oil than the one recommended in Chapter 1 can damage the oil pump or lubrication system and cause drag on the engine.
- [ ] Brakes dragging. Usually caused by corrosion behind dust seals, ingress of dirt past a deteriorated seal or from a warped disc or bent axle (Chapter 6).
- [ ] Exhaust gas control valve (EGCV) seized or incorrectly adjusted, or faulty servo. Adjust cables. If they are good check the servo motor (see Chapter 4). The valves are an integral part of the silencer.

4 Overheating

Engine overheats

- [ ] Coolant level low. Check the level and add coolant (see *Pre-ride checks*).
- [ ] Leak in cooling system. Check cooling system hoses and radiator for leaks and other damage. Repair or renew parts as necessary (Chapter 3).
- [ ] Faulty thermostat. Check and renew as described in Chapter 3.
- [ ] Faulty pressure cap. Remove the cap and have it pressure tested.
- [ ] Coolant passages clogged. Drain and flush the system, then refill with fresh coolant (Chapter 1).
- [ ] Water pump defective. Remove the pump and check the components (Chapter 3).
- [ ] Clogged or damaged radiator fins (Chapter 3).
- [ ] Faulty cooling fan, relay or ECT sensor (Chapter 3).

Firing incorrect

- [ ] Wrongly connected ignition coil wiring.
- [ ] Spark plugs dirty, defective or worn out. Locate reason for fouled plugs using spark plug condition chart on the inside back cover and follow the plug maintenance procedures (Chapter 1).
- [ ] Incorrect spark plugs. Wrong type or heat range. Check and install correct plugs (Chapter 1).
- [ ] Ignition coil defective. Test and replace with a new one if necessary (Chapter 4).
- [ ] Faulty engine control module (ECM) or CKP sensor (Chapter 4).

Fuel/air mixture incorrect

- [ ] Fuel tank breather hose obstructed.
- [ ] Fuel pump faulty or blocked fuel filter. Replace faulty pump – the filter is not available separately (Chapter 4).
- [ ] Fuel hose kinked. Replace the fuel hose.
- [ ] Fuel injector clogged. For all the injectors to be clogged, either a very bad batch of fuel with an unusual additive has been used, or some other foreign material has entered the tank. In some cases, if a machine has been unused for several months, the fuel turns to a varnish-like liquid which can cause an injector needle to stick to its seat. Drain the tank and fuel system, ultrasonically clean or replace fuel injectors (Chapter 4).
- [ ] Intake air leak. Check for loose throttle body-to-intake duct connections and loose or damaged vacuum hoses (Chapter 4).
- [ ] Air filter clogged. Clean the air filter element or replace it with a new one (Chapter 1).

Compression too high

- [ ] Carbon build-up in combustion chamber. Use of a fuel additive that will dissolve the adhesive bonding the carbon particles to the piston crown and chamber is the easiest way to remove the build-up. Otherwise, the cylinder head will have to be removed and decarbonised (Chapter 2).
- [ ] Improperly machined head surface or installation of incorrect gasket during engine assembly.

Engine load excessive

- [ ] Clutch slipping due to loose or worn clutch components (Chapter 2).
- [ ] Engine oil level too high. Too much oil will cause pressurisation of the crankcase and inefficient engine operation. Check Specifications and drain to proper level (Chapter 1 and *Pre-ride checks*).
- [ ] Engine oil viscosity too high. Using a heavier oil than the one recommended in Chapter 1 can damage the oil pump or lubrication system as well as cause drag on the engine.
- [ ] Brakes dragging. Usually caused by corrosion behind dust seals, ingestion of dirt past deteriorated seal or from a warped disc or bent axle (Chapter 6).

Lubrication inadequate

- [ ] Engine oil level too low. Friction caused by intermittent lack of lubrication or from oil that is overworked can cause overheating. The oil provides a definite cooling function in the engine. Check the oil level (see *Pre-ride checks*).
- [ ] Low engine oil pressure. Check the pressure (Chapter 2).
- [ ] Blocked oil filter or oil cooler (Chapters 1 and 2).
- [ ] Poor quality engine oil or incorrect viscosity or type. Oil is rated not only according to viscosity but also according to type. Some oils are not rated high enough for use in this engine. Check the Specifications section and change to the correct oil (Chapter 1).

Miscellaneous causes

- [ ] Modification to exhaust system. Most aftermarket exhaust systems cause the engine to run leaner, which make them run hotter. When installing an accessory exhaust system, always check with the manufacturer/supplier as to whether the ECM requires re-mapping.

Fault Finding REF•41

5 Clutch problems

Clutch slipping

- ☐ Clutch plates worn or warped. Overhaul the clutch assembly (see Chapter 2).
- ☐ Clutch centre or housing unevenly worn. This causes improper engagement of the plates. Replace the damaged or worn parts (see Chapter 2).
- ☐ Clutch release mechanism fault or clutch cable wrongly adjusted (see Chapter 2).
- ☐ Incorrect type of oil. Use of oils designed for car engines which include friction modifiers can cause clutch slip in a wet clutch application.

Clutch not disengaging completely

- ☐ Clutch release mechanism fault or clutch cable wrongly adjusted (see Chapter 2).
- ☐ Clutch plates warped or damaged. This will cause clutch drag, which in turn will cause the machine to creep. Overhaul the clutch assembly (see Chapter 2).
- ☐ Clutch spring fatigued or sagged. Check the height of both diaphragm springs (see Chapter 2).
- ☐ Engine oil deteriorated. Old, thin oil will not provide proper lubrication for the plates, causing the clutch to drag. Renew the oil and filter (see Chapter 1).
- ☐ Engine oil viscosity too high. Using a heavier oil than recommended in Chapter 1 can cause the plates to stick together. Change to the correct weight oil.

6 Gearchange problems

Doesn't go into gear or lever doesn't return

- ☐ Clutch not disengaging (above).
- ☐ Gearchange mechanism stopper arm spring weak or broken, or arm roller broken or worn. Replace the spring or arm with a new one (Chapter 2).
- ☐ Selector fork(s) bent, worn or seized. Overhaul the transmission (Chapter 2).
- ☐ Selector drum binding. Caused by lubrication failure or excessive wear. Replace the drum and/or its bearing with a new one (Chapter 2).
- ☐ Gearchange mechanism return spring weak or broken (Chapter 2).
- ☐ Gearchange lever or linkage broken. Splines stripped out of arm or shaft, caused by a loose linkage arm pinch bolt or from dropping the machine (Chapter 2).

Jumps out of gear

- ☐ Selector fork(s) worn (Chapter 2).
- ☐ Selector fork groove(s) in selector drum worn (Chapter 2).
- ☐ Gear pinion dogs or dog slots worn or damaged. The gear pinions should be inspected and renewed. No attempt should be made to repair the worn parts.

Overselects

- ☐ Gearchange mechanism stopper arm spring weak or broken, or arm roller broken or worn. Renew the spring or arm (Chapter 2).
- ☐ Gearchange mechanism return spring weak or broken (Chapter 2).

Fault Finding

7 Abnormal engine noise

Knocking or pinking

- ☐ Carbon build-up in combustion chamber. Use of a fuel additive that will dissolve the adhesive bonding the carbon particles to the piston crown and chamber is the easiest way to remove the build-up. Otherwise, the cylinder head will have to be removed and decarbonised (Chapter 2).
- ☐ Incorrect or poor quality fuel. Old or improper grades of fuel can cause detonation. This causes the pistons to rattle, thus the knocking or pinking sound. Drain old fuel and always use the recommended fuel grade.
- ☐ Spark plug heat range incorrect. Uncontrolled detonation indicates the plug heat range is too hot. The plug in effect becomes a glow plug, raising cylinder temperatures. Install the proper heat range plug (Chapter 1).
- ☐ Improper air/fuel mixture. This will cause the cylinders to run hot, which leads to detonation. A blockage in the fuel system or an air leak can cause this imbalance (Chapter 4).
- ☐ Faulty knock sensor. Check the sensor (Chapter 4).

Piston slap or rattling

- ☐ Cylinder-to-piston clearance excessive. Cylinder and/or piston worn, usually accompanied by worn rings as well. A top-end overhaul is necessary (Chapter 2).
- ☐ Piston ring(s) worn, broken or sticking. Overhaul the top-end (Chapter 2).
- ☐ Piston pin, piston pin bore or connecting rod small-end worn from high mileage or seized due to lack of lubrication (Chapter 2).
- ☐ Piston seizure damage. Usually from lack of lubrication or overheating. Replace the pistons and cylinder block, as necessary (Chapter 2).
- ☐ Connecting rod big-end clearance excessive. Caused by excessive wear or lack of lubrication. Replace worn parts.
- ☐ Connecting rod bent. Caused by over-revving, trying to start a badly flooded engine or from ingesting a foreign object into the combustion chamber. Replace the damaged parts (Chapter 2).

Valve noise

- ☐ Incorrect valve clearances – check and adjust (Chapter 1).
- ☐ Valve spring broken or weak. Check and replace weak valve springs with new ones (Chapter 2).
- ☐ Camshaft or camshaft journals in the cylinder head worn or damaged. Lubrication failure at high rpm is usually the cause of damage due to insufficient oil or failure to change the oil at the recommended intervals. Since there are no replaceable bearings in the head, the head itself will have to be replaced with a new one (Chapter 2).

Other noise

- ☐ Cylinder head gasket leaking. Check around the joint for blowing with the engine running.
- ☐ Exhaust pipe leaking at cylinder head connection. Caused by incorrect fit of pipe(s), loose exhaust flange or damaged gasket. All exhaust system fasteners should be tightened evenly and carefully to avoid leaks (Chapter 4).
- ☐ Crankshaft runout excessive. Caused by a bent crankshaft (from over-revving) or damage from an upper cylinder component failure. Can also be attributed to dropping the machine on either of the crankshaft ends.
- ☐ Engine mounting bolts loose – ensure all the bolts are tightened to the specified torque settings (Chapter 2).
- ☐ Crankshaft bearings worn (Chapter 2).
- ☐ Cam chain rattle, due to worn chain or defective tensioner. Also worn chain tensioner/guide blades (Chapter 2).

8 Abnormal driveline noise

Clutch noise

- ☐ Clutch housing/friction plate clearance excessive (Chapter 2).
- ☐ Wear between the clutch housing splines and input shaft splines (Chapter 2).
- ☐ Broken or incorrectly installed anti-judder spring (Chapter 2).
- ☐ Worn release bearing (Chapter 2).

Transmission noise

- ☐ Bearings worn. Also includes the possibility that the shafts are worn. Overhaul the transmission (Chapter 2).
- ☐ Gears worn or chipped (Chapter 2).
- ☐ Engine oil level too low. Causes a howl from transmission. Also affects engine power and clutch operation (see *Pre-ride checks*).

Final drive noise

- ☐ Drive chain excessively loose/worn or drive sprockets excessively worn. Adjust chain or replace chain and sprockets as a set (Chapters 1 and 6).
- ☐ Rear wheel coupling worn or damaged (Chapter 6).
- ☐ Sprocket coupling dampers or bearing worn (Chapter 6).
- ☐ Front or rear sprocket loose. Tighten fasteners (see Chapter 6).

Fault Finding REF•43

9 Abnormal frame and suspension noise

Front end noise

- [ ] Low fluid level or improper viscosity oil in forks. This can sound like spurting and is usually accompanied by irregular fork action (Chapter 5).
- [ ] Spring weak or broken. Makes a clicking or scraping sound. Fork oil, when drained, will have a lot of metal particles in it (Chapter 5).
- [ ] Steering head bearings loose or damaged. Clicks when braking. Check and adjust or replace with new ones as necessary (Chapters 1 and 5).
- [ ] Fork yoke clamp bolts loose – ensure all the bolts are tightened to the specified torque (Chapter 6).
- [ ] Forks bent. Good possibility if machine has been dropped. Replace the inner and outer tubes with new ones as required (Chapter 5).
- [ ] Front axle or axle pinch bolts loose. Tighten them to the specified torque (Chapter 6).
- [ ] Loose or worn wheel bearings. Check and replace with new ones as needed (Chapters 1 and 6).
- [ ] Faulty steering damper (see Chapter 5).

Rear end noise

- [ ] Shock absorber fluid level incorrect. Indicates a leak caused by defective seal. Shock will be covered with oil. Replace shock with a new one or seek advice on repair from a suspension specialist (Chapter 5).
- [ ] Defective shock absorber with internal damage. This is in the body of the shock and can't be remedied. The shock must be replaced with a new one or rebuilt (Chapter 5).
- [ ] Bent or damaged shock body. Replace the shock with a new one (Chapter 5).
- [ ] Loose or worn swingarm bearings. Check and replace with new ones as necessary (Chapter 5).
- [ ] Loose or worn suspension linkage bearings. Check and replace with new ones as necessary (Chapter 5).
- [ ] Loose or worn wheel bearings/sprocket bearing. Check and replace with new ones as needed (Chapters 1 and 6).

Brake noise

- [ ] Squeal caused by pad shim not installed or positioned incorrectly (where fitted) (Chapter 6).
- [ ] Squeal caused by dust on brake pads. Usually found in combination with glazed pads. Clean using brake cleaning solvent (Chapter 6).
- [ ] Pads glazed. Caused by excessive heat from prolonged hard use or from contamination. DO NOT use sandpaper, emery cloth, carborundum cloth or any other abrasive to roughen the pad surfaces as abrasives will stay in the pad material and damage the disc. A very fine flat file can be used, but new pads is the best remedy (Chapter 6).
- [ ] Contamination of brake pads. Oil or brake fluid can cause the brake pads to chatter or squeal. Fit new pads. Identify the cause of the contamination, especially check the caliper piston seals for leaking fluid. Clean disc thoroughly with brake system cleaner (Chapter 6).
- [ ] Disc warped. Can cause a chattering, clicking or intermittent squeal. Usually accompanied by a pulsating lever and uneven braking. Replace the disc with new one (Chapter 6).
- [ ] Loose or worn wheel bearings. Check and replace with new ones as needed (Chapters 1 and 6).
- [ ] Forks incorrectly aligned on front wheel axle causing caliper or mounting to contact disc. Loosen front axle pinch bolts and re-align.

10 Oil pressure low

Engine lubrication system

- [ ] Perform an oil pressure test as described in Chapter 2.
- [ ] Engine oil level low. Inspect for leak or other problem causing low oil level and add recommended oil (see *Pre-ride checks*).
- [ ] Engine oil pump defective, blocked oil strainer gauze or failed pressure relief valve. Carry out an oil pressure check, then remove the components for inspection (Chapter 2).
- [ ] Engine oil viscosity too low. Very old, thin oil or an improper weight of oil used in the engine. Change to correct oil (Chapter 1).
- [ ] Camshaft or crankshaft journals worn. Excessive wear causing drop in oil pressure. Abnormal wear could be caused by oil starvation at high rpm from low oil level or improper weight or type of oil.

Fault Finding

11 Excessive exhaust smoke

White smoke

- [ ] Piston rings worn or broken, causing oil from the crankcase to be pulled past the piston into the combustion chamber. Replace the rings with new ones (Chapter 2).
- [ ] Plating on cylinders worn or scored. Caused by overheating or oil starvation. Renew the cylinder block and pistons (Chapter 2).
- [ ] Valve stem oil seal damaged or worn. Replace the oil seals with new ones (Chapter 2).
- [ ] Valve guide worn. Perform a complete valve job (Chapter 2).
- [ ] Engine oil level too high, which causes the oil to be forced past the rings. Drain oil to the proper level (see *Pre-ride checks*).
- [ ] Head gasket broken between oil return and cylinder. Causes oil to be pulled into the combustion chamber. Replace the head gasket with a new one and check the head for warpage (Chapter 2).
- [ ] Abnormal crankcase pressurisation which forces oil past the rings, usually caused by a clogged breather.

Black smoke

- [ ] Air filter clogged. Clean the air filter element or replace it with a new one (Chapter 1).
- [ ] Fuel injection system malfunction (Chapter 4).

Brown smoke

- [ ] Air filter poorly sealed or not installed (Chapter 1).
- [ ] Fuel injection system malfunction (Chapter 4).

12 Poor handling or stability

Handlebar hard to turn

- [ ] Steering head bearing adjuster nut too tight. Check adjustment as described in Chapter 1.
- [ ] Bearings damaged. Roughness can be felt as the bars are turned from side-to-side. Replace the bearings with new ones (Chapter 5).
- [ ] Races dented or worn. Denting results from wear in only one position (e.g., straight ahead), from a collision or hitting a pothole. Replace the bearings with new ones (Chapter 5).
- [ ] Steering stem lubrication inadequate. Causes are grease getting hard from age or being washed out by high pressure car washes. Disassemble steering head and repack bearings (Chapter 5).
- [ ] Steering stem bent. Caused by a collision, hitting a pothole. Replace damaged part. Don't try to straighten the steering stem (Chapter 5).
- [ ] Front tyre air pressure too low (see *Pre-ride checks*).

Handlebar shakes or vibrates excessively

- [ ] Tyres worn or out of balance (Chapter 6).
- [ ] Swingarm bearings worn. Replace the bearings with new ones (Chapter 5).
- [ ] Wheel rim(s) warped or damaged. Inspect wheels for runout (Chapter 6).
- [ ] Wheel bearings worn. Worn front or rear wheel bearings can cause poor tracking. Worn front bearings will cause wobble (Chapters 1 and 6).
- [ ] Fork yoke clamp bolts or handlebar clamp bolts loose. Tighten them to the specified torque (Chapter 5).
- [ ] Engine mounting bolts loose. Will cause excessive vibration with increased engine rpm – ensure all the bolts are tightened to the specified torque settings (Chapter 2).

Machine pulls to one side

- [ ] Frame bent. Definitely suspect this if the machine has been dropped. May or may not be accompanied by cracking near the steering head, swingarm mountings or engine mountings. Replace the frame with a new one (Chapter 5).
- [ ] Wheels out of alignment. Caused by poor chain adjustment, improper location of axle spacers or from bent steering stem or frame (Chapters 1 and 5).
- [ ] Forks bent. Disassemble the forks and replace the damaged parts (Chapter 5).
- [ ] Swingarm bent or twisted. Replace the arm with a new one (Chapter 5).
- [ ] Fork oil level uneven. Check and add or drain as necessary (Chapter 5).
- [ ] Fork pre-load adjusters set unevenly (Chapter 5).

Poor shock absorbing qualities

- [ ] Too hard:
    a) Suspension adjustment incorrect.
    b) Fork oil level excessive (Chapter 5).
    c) Fork oil viscosity too high. Use a lighter oil (see the Specifications in Chapter 5).
    d) Fork tube bent. Causes a harsh, sticking feeling (Chapter 5).
    e) Fork internal damage (Chapter 5).
    f) Shock shaft or body bent or damaged (Chapter 5).
    g) Shock internal damage.
    h) Swingarm bearings or suspension linkage bearings seized (Chapter 5).
    i) Tyre pressure too high (see *Pre-ride checks*).
- [ ] Too soft:
    a) Suspension adjustment incorrect.
    b) Fork oil level too low (Chapter 5).
    c) Fork oil viscosity too light (Chapter 5).
    d) Fork springs weak or broken (Chapter 5).
    e) Fork or shock oil leaking (Chapter 5).
    f) Shock internal damage (Chapter 5).

Fault Finding REF•45

13 Braking problems

Brakes are spongy, don't hold
- [ ] Low brake fluid level (see *Pre-ride checks*).
- [ ] Air in hydraulic system. Caused by inattention to master cylinder fluid level or by leakage. Locate problem and bleed brakes (Chapter 6).
- [ ] Pad or disc worn (Chapters 1 and 6).
- [ ] Contaminated pads. Caused by contamination with oil, grease, brake fluid, etc. Fit new pads. Identify the cause of the contamination, especially check the caliper piston seals for leaking fluid. Clean disc thoroughly with brake system cleaner (Chapter 6).
- [ ] Brake fluid deteriorated. Fluid is old or contaminated. Drain system, replenish with new fluid and bleed the system (Chapter 6).
- [ ] Master cylinder internal seals worn or damaged causing fluid to bypass (Chapter 6).
- [ ] Master cylinder bore scratched by foreign material or broken spring. Fit a new master cylinder (Chapter 6).
- [ ] Disc warped. Replace disc with new one (Chapter 6)
- [ ] C-ABS system faulty (where fitted, Chapter 6).

Brake lever or pedal pulsates
- [ ] Disc warped. Replace disc with new one (Chapter 6).
- [ ] Axle bent. Replace axle with new one (Chapter 6).
- [ ] Brake caliper bolts loose – tighten the bolts to the specified torque (Chapter 6).
- [ ] Wheel warped or otherwise damaged (Chapter 6).
- [ ] Wheel bearings damaged or worn (Chapters 1 and 6).
- [ ] C-ABS system faulty (where fitted, Chapter 6).

Brakes drag
- [ ] Master cylinder piston seized. Caused by wear or damage to piston or cylinder bore (Chapter 6).
- [ ] Lever balky or stuck. Check pivot and lubricate (Chapter 6).
- [ ] Brake caliper piston seized in bore. Caused by corrosion behind dust seals or ingress of dirt past deteriorated seal (Chapter 6).
- [ ] Rear brake caliper slider pins sticking or corroded, preventing full movement of caliper (Chapter 6).
- [ ] Brake pad damaged. Pad material separated from backing plate. Usually caused by faulty manufacturing process or from contact with chemicals. Fit new pads (Chapter 6).
- [ ] Pads improperly installed (Chapter 6).
- [ ] Brake caliper incorrectly installed (Chapter 6).
- [ ] Forks incorrectly aligned on front wheel axle. Loosen front axle pinch bolts and re-align.
- [ ] ABS system faulty (where fitted, Chapter 6).

14 Electrical problems

Battery dead or weak
- [ ] Battery faulty. Caused by sulphated plates which are shorted through sedimentation. Confirm with battery condition check (Chapter 8).
- [ ] Broken battery terminal making only occasional contact.
- [ ] Battery leads making poor contact (Chapter 8).
- [ ] Load excessive. Caused by addition of high wattage lights or other electrical accessories.
- [ ] Ignition switch defective. Switch either grounds (earths) internally or fails to shut off system. Renew the switch (Chapter 8).
- [ ] Regulator/rectifier defective (Chapter 8).
- [ ] Alternator stator coil open or shorted (Chapter 8).
- [ ] Charging system fault. Check for excessive current leakage (Chapter 8).
- [ ] Wiring faulty. Wiring grounded (earthed) or connections loose in ignition, charging or lighting circuits (Chapter 8).

Battery overcharged
- [ ] Regulator/rectifier defective. Overcharging is noticed when battery gets excessively warm (Chapter 8).
- [ ] Battery faulty. Confirm with battery condition check (Chapter 8).
- [ ] Battery amperage too low, wrong type or size of battery. Install manufacturer's specified amp-hour battery to handle charging load (Chapter 8).

Index

Note: References throughout this index are in the form - "Chapter number" • "Page number"

A

Air filter – 1•24
Air filter housing – 4•5
Air intake system – 4•7
Alternator – 8•25
Anti-lock Braking System (ABS) – 6•2, 6•18, 6•19, 6•23

B

Balancer shaft – 2•66
Bank angle sensor – 4•15
Battery – 1•30, 8•1, 8•4, 8•5
Bodywork – 7•1 et seq
Brake
  bleeding (RA models) – 6•18
  bleeding (RR models) – 6•15
  calipers – 6•5, 6•11
  discs – 6•7, 6•12
  fault finding – REF•45
  fluid – 1•2, 6•1
  fluid change – 1•9
  RA models – 6•18
  RR models – 6•17
  fluid levels – 0•14
  hoses and fittings – 6•15
  master cylinder – 6•8, 6•13
  pads – 1•7, 6•3, 6•10
  specifications – 6•1
  system check – 1•8
Brake light – 8•8
  check – 8•7
  switches – 1•8, 8•11
Brake pedal – 5•3
Bulbs
  headlight – 8•7
  licence plate light – 8•9
  turn signal – 8•10
  wattage – 8•2

C

Cables
  clutch – 1•9, 2•37
  EGCV – 4•28
  lubrication – 1•23
  throttle – 1•11, 4•24
Caliper (brake) – 6•2, 6•5, 6•11
Cam chain tensioner – 2•14
Cam chain, tensioner blades and front guide – 2•22
Camshaft Position (CMP) sensor – 4•13
Camshafts and followers – 2•2, 2•15
Catalytic converter – 4•30

Chain (final drive) – 6•32
  check and adjustment – 1•6
  cleaning and lubrication – 1•7, 6•32
  specification – 1•2, 6•2
Charging system – 8•1, 8•24
Clutch – 2•29
  cable adjustment – 1•9
  cable renewal – 2•37
  fault finding – REF•41
  specifications – 2•3
Clutch lever – 5•7
Clutch switch – 8•19
Coils – 4•31
Combined Anti-lock Braking System (C-ABS) – 6•2, 6•18, 6•19, 6•23
Compression test – 2•7
Coolant – 1•2
  change – 1•16
  level – 0•15
  reservoir – 3•7
Cooling system – 3•1 et seq
  ECT sensor – 3•3
  fan and fan relay – 3•2
  hoses, pipes and unions – 3•7
  radiator – 3•5
  specifications – 3•1
  system check – 1•15
  temperature and warning display – 3•3
  thermostat – 3•4
  water pump – 3•6
Connecting rods – 2•5, 2•50
Conversion factors – REF•34
Crankcases – 2•43, 2•47
Crankshaft – 2•4, 2•48
Crankshaft Position (CKP) sensor – 4•13
Cylinder head – 2•2, 2•23, 2•24
Cylinders – 2•4, 2•55

D

Dimensions – 0•11
Diode block – 8•20
Disc (brake)
  front – 6•2, 6•7
  rear – 6•2, 6•12
Drive chain – 6•32
  check and adjustment – 1•6
  cleaning and lubrication – 1•7, 6•32
  specification – 1•2, 6•2

E

Electrical system – 8•1 et seq
  alternator – 8•25
  battery – 1•30, 8•4, 8•5

brake light switches – 8•11
brake/tail light – 8•8
clutch switch – 8•19
diode block – 8•20
fault finding – 8•2, REF•45
fuses – 8•5
handlebar switches – 8•16
headlight – 8•7, 8•8
horn – 8•20
ignition switch – 8•15
instrument cluster – 8•13
licence plate light – 8•9
lighting system – 8•6
neutral/gear position switch – 8•17
oil pressure switch – 8•15
regulator/rectifier – 8•28
sidelight – 8•7
sidestand switch – 8•19
specifications – 8•1
starter motor – 8•21, 8•22
starter relay 8•20
turn signals – 8•10, 8•11
wiring diagrams – 8•30
Engine – 2•1 et seq
  balancer shaft – 2•66
  cam chain tensioner – 2•14
  cam chain, tensioner blades and front guide – 2•22
  camshafts and followers – 2•15
  compression check – 2•7
  connecting rods – 2•50
  crankcases – 2•43, 2•47
  crankshaft and main bearings – 2•48
  cylinder block – 2•55
  cylinder head – 2•23
  fault finding – REF•36
  oil and filter change – 1•12
  oil cooler – 1•16, 2•12
  oil level – 0•13
  oil pressure check – 2•8
  oil pump and pressure relief valve – 2•41
  oil sump and strainer – 2•40
  overhaul information – 2•12
  piston rings – 2•54
  pistons – 2•53
  removal from frame – 2•8
  running-in – 2•67
  specifications – 0•11, 1•2, 2•1
  starter clutch – 2•27
  valve clearance check – 1•25
  valve cover – 2•13
  wear assessment – 2•7
Engine Control Module (ECM) – 4•16
Engine Coolant Temperature (ECT) sensor – 3•1, 3•3, 4•12
Engine management system – 4•1 et seq
Engine number – 0•9

Index REF•47

Note: References throughout this index are in the form - "Chapter number" • "Page number"

Engine stop relay – 4•16
Engine trim panel – 7•7
EVAP system – 1•25, 4•2, 4•30
Exhaust Gas Control Valve (EGCV) –
  1•29, 4•2, 4•26
Exhaust system – 4•25

F

Fairing – 7•8
Fairing side panels – 7•5
Fan – 3•2
Fan relay – 3•3
Fault finding and codes – REF•35 *et seq*
  C-ABS – 6•19
  electrical system – 8•2
  fuel injection system and codes – 4•10
  immobiliser and codes – 4•33
Filter
  air – 1•24
  oil – 1•12
Footrests – 5•2
Frame – 5•2
Frame number – 0•9
Front brake
  caliper – 6•5
  disc – 6•7
  fluid level – 0•14
  master cylinder – 6•8
  pads – 6•3
Front brake lever – 5•7
  span adjuster – 1•9
Front forks
  adjustment – 5•25
  check – 1•19
  oil change – 5•9
  overhaul – 5•14
  removal and installation – 5•8
  specifications – 5•1
Front mudguard – 7•9
Front power unit – 6•25
Front sprocket – 6•33
Front valve unit – 6•24
Front wheel – 6•27
Front wheel bearings – 6•29
Front wheel sensor and pulse ring – 6•23
Fuel – 4•1
Fuel gauge and sensor – 4•24
Fuel injection system – 4•9
  fault diagnosis and codes – 4•10
  idle air control valve – 4•21
  sensors – 4•12
  specifications – 4•1
Fuel pump relay – 4•16
Fuel supply system
  check – 1•10
  fuel rails and injectors – 4•18
  hoses – 4•28
  pressure check – 4•22
  pump – 4•23
  pump strainer – 1•11
  tank – 4•3
  tank cover – 7•3
  throttle bodies – 4•17
Fuses – 8•2, 8•5

G

Gear position switch – 8•17
Gear ratios – 2•5
Gearbox – 2•56, 2•57
Gearchange lever – 5•3
Gearchange mechanism – 2•38
Gearchange problems – REF•41

H

Handlebar end-weights – 5•6
Handlebar levers – 5•7
Handlebar switches – 8•16
Handlebars – 5•4
Handling and stability problems – REF•44
Headlight – 8•8
  aim – 1•18
  bulbs – 8•7
  relay – 8•6
**Honda Electronic Steering Damper
  (HESD)** – 5•22
**Honda Ignition Security System
  (HISS)** – 4•32
Horn – 8•20

I

Idle air control valve – 4•21
Ignition switch – 8•15
Ignition system
  check – 4•30
  coils – 4•31
  ECM – 4•16
  spark plugs – 1•28
  specifications – 4•2
  timing – 4•32
Immobiliser – 4•32
Injectors (fuel) – 4•18
Instrument cluster – 8•13
**Intake Air Temperature (IAT)
  sensor** – 4•13

K

Knock sensor – 4•15

L

Lap timer – 8•14
Lean angle sensor – 4•15
Legal checks – 0•16
Licence plate light
  bulb – 8•9
  check – 8•7
Lighting system – 8•6
Lower fairing – 7•4

Lubricants and fluids – 1•2, REF•5
Lubrication
  engine
    oil and filter – 0•13, 1•12
    oil pump – 2•41
    oil pressure check – 2•8
    oil pressure relief valve – 2•41
    oil pressure switch – 8•15
  drive chain – 1•7
  pivot points and cables – 1•23
  rear suspension pivots – 1•20, 5•24,
    5•25, 5•28
  steering head bearings – 1•23, 5•21

M

Main bearings – 2•49
Maintenance schedule – 1•3
**Manifold Absolute Pressure (MAP)
  sensor** – 4•12
Master cylinder
  front brake – 6•1, 6•8
  rear brake – 6•2, 6•13
Mirrors – 7•3
Model development – 0•10
MOT test checks – REF•8
Mudguard (front) – 7•9

N

Neutral switch – 8•17

O

Oil (engine)
  oil level – 0•13
  oil and filter change – 1•12
Oil (forks) – 5•1, 5•9
Oil cooler – 1•16, 2•12
Oil pump – 2•3, 2•41
Oil pressure check – 2•8, REF•43
Oil pressure relief valve – 2•41
Oil pressure switch – 8•15
Oil sump and strainer – 2•40
Oxygen sensor – 4•14

P

Pads (brake) – 1•7, 6•3, 6•10
PAIR system – 1•17, 4•2, 4•28
Piston rings – 2•4, 2•54
Pistons – 2•4, 2•53
Pre-ride checks – 0•13 *et seq*
Pump
  fuel – 4•23
  oil – 2•3, 2•41
  water – 3•6

REF•48 Index

Note: *References throughout this index are in the form - "Chapter number" • "Page number"*

R

Radiator – 3•5
Radiator cap – 1•16, 3•1, 3•6
Rear brake
  caliper – 6•11
  disc – 6•12
  fluid level – 0•15
  master cylinder – 6•13
  pads – 6•10
  pedal – 5•3
Rear shock absorber – 5•23, 5•26
Rear sprocket, coupling and dampers – 6•34
Rear suspension
  checks – 1•19
  linkage – 5•25
  shock absorber – 5•23, 5•26
  swingarm – 5•27
Rear valve unit and power unit – 6•25
Rear wheel – 6•28
Rear wheel bearings – 6•30
Rear wheel sensor and pulse ring – 6•23
Regulator/rectifier – 8•28
Relay
  engine stop – 4•16
  fan – 3•3
  fuel pump – 4•16
  headlight – 8•6
  lap timer – 8•15
  starter – 8•20
  turn signal – 8•10
Routine maintenance – 1•1 *et seq*

S

Safety information – 0•12, 0•16, 4•2
Seats – 7•2
Seat cowling – 7•2
Security – REF•2
Selector drum and forks – 2•6, 2•64
Servicing – 1•1 *et seq*
Side covers – 7•2
Sidelight – 8•7
Sidestand – 1•19, 5•4
Sidestand switch – 8•19
Spare parts – 0•9
Spark plugs – 1•2, 1•28
Speedometer and speed sensor – 8•13
Sprockets – 6•33
  check – 1•7
  coupling bearing – 6•30
  coupling dampers – 6•34
  sizes – 6•2
Starter clutch – 2•2, 2•27
Starter interlock circuit – 1•19
Starter motor – 8•1, 8•21, 8•22
Starter relay – 8•20
Steering damper – 5•2, 5•22
Steering head bearings – 1•20, 5•2, 5•21
Steering stem – 5•18
Storage – REF•13
Swingarm – 5•27

T

Tachometer – 8•13
Tail light – 8•8
  check – 8•6
Tank (fuel) – 4•3
Tank cover (fuel) – 7•3
Temperature display – 3•3
Thermostat – 3•1, 3•4
Throttle bodies – 4•17
Throttle cables – 1•11, 4•24
Throttle Position (TP) sensor – 4•12
Throttle twistgrip – 1•12
Tools – REF•16 *et seq*
Torque settings – 1•2, 2•6, 3•1, 4•2, 5•2, 6•3, 8•2
Transmission – 2•5, 2•56, 2•57
Trim clips – 7•3
Turn signals – 8•10, 8•11
Tyres – 6•31
  pressures and tread depth – 0•16
  size – 0•11, 6•2
  valves – 1•23

V

Valve clearances – 1•2, 1•25
Valve cover – 2•13
Valves (cylinder head) – 2•2, 2•24
Vehicle Identification Number (VIN) – 0•9

W

Warning lights – 8•14
Water pump – 3•6
Weight – 0•11
Wheel bearings – 1•23, 6•29
Wheels – 6•27, 6•28
  alignment check – 6•26
  check – 1•23
  inspection and repair – 6•26
  size – 0•11
  specifications – 6•2
Windshield – 7•8
Wiring diagrams – 8•30

Motorcycle Listings page REF•49

Preserving Our Motoring Heritage

The Model J Duesenberg Derham Tourster. Only eight of these magnificent cars were ever built – this is the only example to be found outside the United States of America

Almost every car you've ever loved, loathed or desired is gathered under one roof at the Haynes Motor Museum. Over 300 immaculately presented cars and motorbikes represent every aspect of our motoring heritage, from elegant reminders of bygone days, such as the superb Model J Duesenberg to curiosities like the bug-eyed BMW Isetta. There are also many old friends and flames. Perhaps you remember the 1959 Ford Popular that you did your courting in? The magnificent 'Red Collection' is a spectacle of classic sports cars including AC, Alfa Romeo, Austin Healey, Ferrari, Lamborghini, Maserati, MG, Riley, Porsche and Triumph.

A Perfect Day Out

Each and every vehicle at the Haynes Motor Museum has played its part in the history and culture of Motoring. Today, they make a wonderful spectacle and a great day out for all the family. Bring the kids, bring Mum and Dad, but above all bring your camera to capture those golden memories for ever. You will also find an impressive array of motoring memorabilia, a comfortable 70 seat video cinema and one of the most extensive transport book shops in Britain. The Pit Stop Cafe serves everything from a cup of tea to wholesome, home-made meals or, if you prefer, you can enjoy the large picnic area nestled in the beautiful rural surroundings of Somerset.

John Haynes O.B.E., Founder and Chairman of the museum at the wheel of a Haynes Light 12.

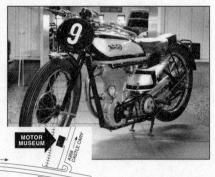

The 1936 490cc sohc-engined International Norton – well known for its racing success

The Museum is situated on the A359 Yeovil to Frome road at Sparkford, just off the A303 in Somerset. It is about 40 miles south of Bristol, and 25 minutes drive from the M5 intersection at Taunton.
Open 9.30am - 5.30pm (10.00am - 4.00pm Winter) 7 days a week, *except Christmas Day, Boxing Day and New Years Day*
Special rates available for schools, coach parties and outings Charitable Trust No. 292048